Frontiers in Belief Revision

APPLIED LOGIC SERIES

VOLUME 22

SCOPE OF THE SERIES

Logic is applied in an increasingly wide variety of disciplines, from the traditional subjects of philosophy and mathematics to the more recent disciplines of cognitive science, computer science, artificial intelligence, and linguistics, leading to new vigor in this ancient subject. Kluwer, through its Applied Logic Series, seeks to provide a home for outstanding books and research monographs in applied logic, and in doing so demonstrates the underlying unity and applicability of logic.

The titles published in this series are listed at the end of this volume.

Frontiers in Belief Revision

Edited by

MARY-ANNE WILLIAMS
University of Newcastle, Australia

and

HANS ROTT
University of Regensburg, Germany

KLUWER ACADEMIC PUBLISHERS
DORDRECHT / BOSTON / LONDON

A C.I.P. Catalogue record for this book is available from the Library of Congress.

ISBN 0-7923-7021-X

Published by Kluwer Academic Publishers,
P.O. Box 17, 3300 AA Dordrecht, The Netherlands.

Sold and distributed in North, Central and South America
by Kluwer Academic Publishers,
101 Philip Drive, Norwell, MA 02061, U.S.A.

In all other countries, sold and distributed
by Kluwer Academic Publishers,
P.O. Box 322, 3300 AH Dordrecht, The Netherlands.

Printed on acid-free paper

Printed in the Netherlands.

CONTENTS

Probability and Multiplicity

HANS ROTT AND MARY-ANNE WILLIAMS

INTRODUCTION

Belief revision studies the impact of acquiring new information. It is an exciting and significant research area because belief revision is a fundamental activity of intelligence. One of the hallmarks of intelligence is adaptability, and belief revision provides sound mechanisms for modelling changes to beliefs. The ability to perform belief revision is imperative for intelligent systems and intelligent agents. The advent of the world wide web and electronic commerce has highlighted the need for sophisticated information management systems.

Belief revision theory first came into focus in the work of the philosophers William Harper [1976; 1977] and Isaac Levi [1977; 1980; 1991] in the 1970s. It was established as a well-defined research programme by the seminal work of Alchourrón, Gärdenfors and Makinson [1985; 1988] in the 1980s, whereupon it is common to read of *the AGM approach* to belief change and *the AGM paradigm*.

After about two decades of intensive research, done mostly by philosophers, logicians and computer scientists, belief revision theory has established itself as a mature field of study. In recent years there has been a number of surveys and thorough presentations of the results achieved so far [Fuhrmann, 1997; Gabbay and Smets, 1998; Gärdenfors and Rott, 1995; Hansson, 1999; Rott, 1996; Williams, 1998]. Belief revision has also been the topic of a number of special issues of logico-philosophical journals [Fuhrmann, 1995; Halbach and Olsson, 1999; Hansson, 1997; Hansson, 1998]. The two collections currently available [Fuhrmann and Morreau, 1991; Gärdenfors, 1992], do not include many of the recent developments. So we feel that it is time to reflect the state of the art of belief revision in a single comprehensive volume. It seems particularly important to us to document that the time has come to build the bridge between theory and practice – a bridge that has its foundations in AGM but that spans a much wider field than the researchers who started the field might have expected.

This volume consists of four invited papers from leading researchers in the area of belief revision, together with 19 contributed papers most of which were presented at the 1998 International Nonmonotonic Reasoning Workshop in Trento, Italy. All of the papers were fully refereed, and we would like to thank the following reviewers for helping us to improve the quality of this volume and ensuring its success: Chris Albert, Horacio Arló-Costa, Carlos Areces, Salem Benferhat, John Cantwell, Gabriella Crocco, Jim Delgrande, Aldo Franco Dragoni, Didier Dubois, Sven Ove Hansson, Matthias Hild, Nikos Massios, Ingrid Neumann, Erik Olsson, Maurice Pagnucco, Henri Prade, Wlodek Rabinowicz, Karl Schlechta, Allard Tamminga and Emil Weydert. We would also like to thank Jane Spurr for technical support in producing the manuscript.

Isaac *Levi* was the Invited Speaker at the workshop and in his contribution he provides an extensive treatise on inductive expansion and nonmonotonic reasoning. He takes us on a fascinating philosophical journey during which the salient

M.-A. Williams and H. Rott (eds.), Frontiers in Belief Revision, 1–6.

features of abduction, induction, doaxastic committment, possibility and probability are compared and contrasted, and their role in the process of decision making by deliberative agents explored. He argues strongly that the conditions under which an inquirer is justified in changing his or her mind are important and need to be part of any decision making model.

In his contribution Krister *Segerberg* demonstrates how the AGM paradigm for belief revision can be rendered within dynamic doxastic logic (DDL) by providing a complete axiomatisation of revision in that framework. Segerberg uses a topological semantics to characterise the one-shot interpretation of belief revision that is perhaps the most faithful to the spirit of the classical approach of AGM. A completeness proof for the iterative interpretation is outlined as well.

The most controversial AGM postulates have been *recovery* for contraction and *success* for revision. In their paper Eduardo *Fermé* and Sven Ove *Hansson* develop the notion of shielded contraction which need not satisfy recovery or success. They provide constructions for shielded contraction based on an epistemic entrenchment and a systems of spheres, together with axiomatisations of these. They also show that shielded contraction satisfies generalised versions of the Harper and Levi identities.

Salem *Benferhat*, Didier *Dubois* and Henri *Prade* present a computational model for belief change and the fusion of prioritised knowledge bases. They describe several syntactic approaches to revision and fusion within the possibility framework. A prioritised knowledge base can be used to induce a complete preorder on interpretations which can be encoded using possibility distributions. The authors reveal the close underlying relationship between revision and fusion, and they examine cases when the input is certain and when it is uncertain.

It is widely accepted that the process of belief revision is driven by the principle of Minimal Change and the related concept of similarity between epistemic states. The idea being that when new information is accepted, changes to the initial epistemic state should be minimal. In other words, the resulting new epistemic state should contain the new information and should be the most similar state to the old state. Unfortunately, formalising this intuition has proved illusive and a definition of minimal change, or indeed similarity, has not been developed. Several papers attempt to tease out some of the issues raised by the notion of minimality. In the first of these *Williams* describes a simple measure of change based on an atomic transformation and the physical concept of *work done*. An epistemic state A is then defined to be more similar to B than to C, if less work, i.e. fewer atomic transformations, is required to change it into B than is required to change it into C. It is shown that such a measure could be implemented and that if one possessed such a measure it could be used to assess belief revision strategies, to provide a method for developing goal-directed belief revision, and to quantify the surprisingness new information is. The minimal change is related to the notion of elaboration tolerance. The more elaboration tolerant a representation is, the more robust it is to change. For example, modular design is often adopted in software engineering because the impact of changes can be limited to certain modules averting the need to trace ramifications of change throughout the whole system. The ability to measure the elaboration tolerance of a logical theory is important from a systems design perspective. All else being equal, a systems designer could rank potential designs according to their elaboration tolerance and use that ranking as the basis of his design choice. In his paper *Amir* proposes a formal definition of elaboration tolerance in a logical setting that is similar in spirit to Williams' measure of change. *Sims* and *Sims* take a novel approach to the problem of defining minimal change. They do so by introducing the idea of a capacity. Intuitively, capacities encapsulate information content so that in determining a revision, the sets of sentences which have the lowest capacity are discarded. In this way Sims and Sims articulate a formal foundation for minimal change. They show how a certain capacity gives rise to an AGM revision by demonstrating that it achieves the same revised belief set as a epistemic entrenchment ordering. They illustrate how new capacities can be constructed from old ones, and they explore several formal properties of capacities, e.g. complementarity and additivity. *Delgrande* uses a generalised system of spheres to define a notion of similarity. In particular, he uses a partial preorder on knowledge bases which is taken to represent similarity. Not surprisingly, the resulting belief revision operators do not satisfy all the AGM postulates. For example, revising with consistent information can lead to an inconsistent knowledge base, and revising with consistent knowledge is not equivalent to simple expansion. Delgrande establishes a representation theorem using a weaker set of postulates.

Several papers address theoretical issues concerning belief revision many of which are yet to be resolved, whilst others – like recovery – may remain controversial forever. Delgrande extends known semantic representations of epistemic states by providing an ordering of knowledge bases rather than possible worlds. *Bochman*'s abstract model, on the other hand, represents multiple belief states within a single epistemic state. Based on this generalisation of the AGM model, Bochman introduces a generalised notion of contraction which can be iterated, and shows how it is related to both the standard "coherentist" theory revision and "foundationalist" base revision operations. *Cantwell* establishes a close relationship between two different kinds of modelling for belief change that do not presume a full comparability of epistemic items in terms of preferential structures: the generalised epistemic entrenchment relations introduced by Rott and the hypertheory semantics in the tradition of Lindström/Rabinowicz and Segerberg. Cantwell gives a completeness theorem for a DDL style axiomatisation of "skeptical" belief change. *Fermé* provides a unified discussion of recovery from the point of view of five different approaches to belief contraction, viz. axiomatics, and constructions using partial meets of maximal non-implying subsets, relations of epistemic entrenchment, the identification of safe beliefs by cutting into kernel sets, and spheres of possible worlds. Fermé concludes that rather surprisingly, the plausiblity of the recovery postulate varies across the different, but formally equivalent modellings. The study of iterated changes of belief states has long been neglected in the literature. Since the publication of Darwiche and Pearl [1997], however, the situation has changed and this challenging problem is being attacked from many different angles. *Areces* and *Becher* show that iterated revision can be achieved using stable, belief-independent extralogical information. They demonstrate how iterated revision can be construed by any of the four standard AGM constructions discussed by Fermé. In contrast to Fermé conclusion, the situation turns out to be formally exactly the same under each of the constructions considered. Finally, *Papini* proposes an efficient method for iterating belief revision. Not only does her revision process satisfy all the AGM postulates, but it also possesses the interesting feature that it takes account of the history of an agents observations. Preference can be given to new observations or to old observations depending on the application. Intuitively, the revision results in as many formulae as possible in a sequence of observations being accepted. Like Spohn's conditionalisation [1988] this process preserves the relative ordering between interpretations which are not models of the preferred formula. A glimpse of how the algorithm works can be found by inspecting the first figure in the paper.

Two of the main strengths of belief revision theory are its simplicity and its wide applicability. In recent years there has been a push to develop implementations and scalable applications. The remaining papers in this volume touch implicitly or focus explicitly on implementation issues. It is well known that belief revision is computationally intractible. Implementations need to take advantage of a rich structuring of knowledge bases, and applications need to use modularised knowledge bases.

In the first group of papers, we encounter layers, compartments and inheritance networks that serve as guidance for changes of beliefs. It is well known that full meet revision, i.e. the method of taking the intersection of all maximally consistent subsets, on theories leads to uninteresting behaviour. *Freund* investigates full meet revision on theory bases. Using the notion of stratification, he explores the conditions under which bases that have been revised in this apparently insensitive way can be re-used for further belief representation and revision. He thereby manages to satisfy the categorial matching principle formulated in [Gärdenfors and Rott, 1995]. In the second paper of this group, *Bezzazi* describes how stratified forward chaining can be used to efficiently implement consistency-preserving revision and update. He highlights the connection his techniques have with preferential logics and, in particular, skeptical inferences based on inheritance systems. *Audibert* and *Schlechta* formalise the use of a reference class to augment the information of a base class in a defeasible propositional setting. They prove by purely algebraic means that two different semantics are equivalent. In addition they demonstrate that there is an important interplay between the concept of reference class and valid paths in defeasible inheritance formalisms. In her paper *Wassermann* explores the notion of relatedness as a means to compartmentalise and restrict the size of the belief base over which revision is conducted. Her local-change approach is based on Hansson's idea of kernels, i.e minimal sets that imply a certain sentence α, and compartments, i.e. the union of α-kernels and $\neg\alpha$-kernels. Although computing a relevance function may be computationally intensive, once computed, Wassermann argues it can be compiled and used to improve the performance of revision. *Bessant*, *Gregoire*, *Marquis* and *Sais* provide an algorithm for base revision. A feature of this algorithm is that it weakens each formula in every minimally inconsistent subbase so that consistency is regained after a revision, instead of removing beliefs from a belief base. The algorithm is based on a number of well behaved heuristics and local search. Both experimental and worst case complexity analysis is provided.

The last group of papers aims at making belief change mechanisms more realistic and powerful by coping with a probabilistic representation of beliefs and a potential multiplicity of agents or sources. *Kern-Isberner* shows how revising and updating can be realised within a generalised probabilistic framework. Using a distinction between belief states and belief bases together with a probabilistic inference, she is able to distinguish implicit and explicit beliefs. She defines belief revision as a change in contextual knowledge, and belief update as modifying a prior distribution to a new context. Both revision and update are implemented using a single non-monotonic, probabilistic inference relation which is applied in different ways. The recent advances in intelligent agent technologies has meant that multiagent belief revision and revision involving information from multiple sources are two of the most exciting areas in belief revision research today. In their paper *de Rosis*, *Covino*, *Falcone* and *Castelfranchi* consider belief revision in a multiagent environment. They investigate how stereotyped belief ascription and revision can be performed in multiagent systems using Bayesian methods. In essence, probabilities are attached to behaviour schemas and belief updating is nonmonotonic. The resulting agents are then able to perform cognitive diagnosis, e.g. they can reason about the intensions of other agents. On other hand, the *Dragoni* and *Giorgini* paper focuses on the belief revision process of a single agent when they receive information from multiple sources. They provide a survey of various approaches and then describe a hybrid architecture that uses techniques from AGM, ATMS, and the probabilistic camps. They raise interesting issues concerning the multiple source scenario throughout their discussion. For example, a system dealing with multiple sources may sometimes need to recover discarded beliefs, and there is a need to cater for the reinforcement of information from more than one source.

REFERENCES

[Alchourrón, Gärdenfors and Makinson, 1985] C. Alchourrón, P. Gärdenfors and D. Makinson. On the logic of theory change: partial meet contraction and revision functions, *The Journal of Symbolic Logic*, **50**, 510–530, 1985.

[Darwiche and Pearl, 1997] A. Darwiche and J. Pearl. On the logic of iterated belief revision, *Artificial Intelligence*, **89**, 1–29, 1997.

[Fuhrmann, 1997] A. Fuhrmann. *An Esssay on Contraction*, CSLI Publications, Stanford University 1997.

[Fuhrmann, 1995] A. Fuhrmann, ed. *Belief Revision*, special issue of *Notre Dame Journal of Formal logic*, **36**, 1995.

[Fuhrmann and Morreau, 1991] A. Fuhrmann and M. Michael, eds. *The Logic of Theory Change*, Lecture Notes in Artificial Intelligence, Vol. 465, Springer-Verlag Berlin, 1991.

[Gabbay and Smets, 1998] D. M. Gabbay and P. Smets, eds. *Belief Change*, Vol. III of the *Handbook of Defeasible Reasoning and Uncertainty Management Systems*, Vol. III, Kluwer, Dordrecht 1998.

[Gärdenfors, 1988] P. Gärdenfors. *Knowledge in flux: Modeling the Dynamics of Epistemic States*, MIT Press, Cambridge, Mass., 1988.

[Gärdenfors, 1992] P. Gärdenfors, ed. *Belief Revision*, Cambridge University Press, Cambridge 1992.

[Gärdenfors and Rott, 1995] P. Gärdenfors and H. Rott. Belief revision. In *Handbook of Logic in Artificial Intelligence and Logic Programming*, Dov M. Gabbay, C. J. Hogger, J. A. Robinson, (eds.), Vol. 4, pp. 35–132. Clarendon Press, Oxford 1995.

[Halbach and Olsson, 1999] V. Halbach and E. Olsson, eds. *Coherence and Dynamics of Belief*, special issue of *Erkenntnis*, **50**, 1999.

[Hansson, 1999] S. O. Hansson. *A Textbook of Belief Dynamics: Theory Change and Database Updating*, Kluwer Academic Publishers, Dordrecht 1999. (With a booklet *Solutions to Exercises*).

[Hansson, 1997] S. O. Hansson. *Non-Prioritized Belief Revision*, special issue of *Theoria*, **63**, 1997.

[Hansson, 1998] S. O. Hansson, ed. *Belief Revision*, special issue of the *Journal of Logic, Language and Information*, **7**, 1998.

[Harper, 1976] W. L. Harper. Ramsey test conditionals and iterated belief change. In Harper, W.L. and Hooker, C.A., eds. *Foundations of Probability Theory, Statistical Inference, and Statistical Theories of Sciences*, Norwell, MA: D. Reidel, 1976, vol. 1, pp. 117–135.

[Harper, 1977] W. L. Harper. Rational conceptual change. In *PSA 1976*, Vol. 2, East Lansing, Mich. 1977, pp. 462–494;

[Levi, 1977] I. Levi. Subjunctives, dispositions and chances, *Synthese*, **34**, 423–455, 1977.

[Levi, 1980] I. Levi. *The Enterprise of Knowledge*, MIT Press, Cambridge, MA, 1980.

[Levi, 1991] I. Levi. *The Fixation of Belief and Its Undoing*, Cambridge University Press, Cambridge 1991;

[Rott, 1996] H. Rott. *Making Up One's Mind: Coherence, Foundations, Non-monotonicity*, Habilitationsschrift University of Constance, 1996. (To appear with Oxford University Press, as *Choice, Change and Inference: A Study in Belief Revision and Nonmonotonic Reasoning*.)

[Spohn, 1988] W. Spohn. Ordinal conditional functions: a dynamic theory of epistemic states. In Harper, W.L. and Skyrms, B. (eds), *Causation in Decision, Belief Change and Statistics II*, Kluwer Academic Publishers, pp. 105–134, 1988.

[Williams, 1998] M.-A. Williams. Applications of belief revision. In *Transactions and Change in Logic Databases*, LNAI 1472, pp. 285–314, Springer Verlag, 1998.

ISAAC LEVI

INDUCTIVE EXPANSION AND NONMONOTONIC REASONING

1 INDUCTION

1.1 What is induction?

In his early writings (e.g. Harvard Lectures of 1865, Peirce [1982]), Peirce followed Aristotle in defining inductive argument formally as the apogogic inversion of valid syllogistic argument where the major premise of the syllogism becomes the conclusion of the induction and the erstwhile conclusion becomes a premise of the induction. Peirce contrasted this kind of argument with hypothetic argument where the conclusion is the minor premise of the categorical syllogism and the premise is the erstwhile conclusion. He then pointed out that both hypothetic and inductive reasoning are ampliative in contrast to deductive reasoning that is explicative.

In his later years, Peirce seems to have altered the distinction between induction and hypothesis as two different types of inference. Hypothetic arguments—which he began to call 'abductions'—have conclusions 'in the interrogative'. That is to say, hypothetic or abductive arguments are designed to justify proposing conjectures as potential answers to the question under investigation rather than to warrant believing them to be true. To be sure, if the arguments are presented linguistically as a set of premises and a conclusion, the formal structure of the argument, such as it is, will fail to be deductive. But that will also be true of genuine inductive arguments which are designed to justify adding new information to the inquirer's stock of full beliefs. In the setting of a given problem, conjecturing that h might be the case is recognizing that h is possibly true relative to the body of background assumptions that constitute the inquirer's current state of full belief. It is, in addition, acknowledging that the possibly true h is a potential answer to the question under consideration that is worth investigating.

In induction, by way of contrast, such a conjecture is converted into a settled conviction or full belief. The already settled assumptions that constitute premises of an inductive argument whose conclusion is the proposition that inquirer comes to fully believe do not logically imply that conclusion. In this sense, the induction is ampliative. But so is the argument from background assumptions to the conjecture in an abduction. Insofar as ampliative argument is *formally* defined as non-deductive argument, we cannot distinguish between abduction and induction on that basis.

In order to differentiate abductions and inductions, appeal may be made to the difference between arguments justifying the adoption of a conjecture and arguments justifying ruling out all rivals to a given conjecture so that it can be added to

M.-A. Williams and H. Rott (eds.), Frontiers in Belief Revision, 7–56.

the inquirer's body of full beliefs. This distinction cannot be made in purely syntactic and semantic terms. Appeal to the distinction between the attitudes represented by the conclusions of abductive and inductive arguments needs to be made. In induction, the inquirer comes to full belief that the conclusion is true. In abduction, the inquirer concludes that the conjecture is worth investigating as a potential answer to the question under study.

I suggest, therefore, that we understand ampliative arguments not only to be non deductive arguments but to be arguments whose conclusions are full beliefs derived from premises already fully believed. The ampliativity of induction will then mark it as distinct from abduction (i.e., hypothesis).

1.2 Anti inductivism

A considerable body of contemporary thought has argued that the philosophical importance of ampliative inference is overrated.

Popperians deny that inductive inference is ever legitimate. We may form conjectures as in Peircean abduction but never rule them out.

The epigones of Quine delegitimize inductive inference by reducing induction to a limiting case of abductive conjecturing acceptable to Popperian anti inductivists.

Probabilists agree with the Popperians that induction understood as ampliative reasoning is never legitimate. Ampliative inference involves the addition of new information to an inquirer's state of certainty or full belief where 'new information' is not entailed by the information already available to the inquirer. Probabilists deny that such inference is legitimate. According to Carnap [1960], ampliative inference is replaced by assignments of degrees of belief to hypotheses on the basis of the total information already fully believed by the inquirer. Such judgment is not ampliative inference; for no new information is added to the body of full beliefs beyond what is already implicit in the inquirer's initial state of full belief.

Probabilists like Carnap acknowledge that inquiring agents do sometimes come to full belief legitimately in response to sensory stimulation. Such responses are not, however, inferences from premisses. A fortiori such responses are not inductive inferences. Probabilists offer a prescription (conditionalizing via Bayes theorem) for adjusting other probability judgments given such changes in full belief.

Radical Probabilists such as Jeffrey (1991, ch. 1) go one step further than Carnap. Carnap restricted attention to changes in probability judgment that are grounded in the acquisition of new full belief in response to sensory stimulation. Jeffrey argued for the possibility of changes in credal probabilities in response to sensory stimulation that fail to yield any new full belief. These responses too are not inductive inferences. All probabilists deny the legitimacy of ampliative inference justifying addition of new information to a body of full belief just as emphatically as the Popperians do. Unlike the Popperians, however, they suggest that assignment of probabilities to extralogical propositions is legitimate.

I do not know how to persuade anti inductivists of the Popperian, Quinean, Carnapian and Jeffrey varieties that their opposition to induction is misguided any more than I know how to persuade those who dismiss the law of the excluded middle that they are confused. The best I can do for the open minded reader is to explain what I take ampliative reasoning to be in a manner that displays why it is obvious that it is sometimes legitimate and why it is important to have some understanding of when it is and when it is not legitimate.

1.3 Serious possibility and Parmenadean epistemology

Inquiring and deliberating agents need to make a distinction between those 'propositions' they judge to be possibly true and those they judge to be impossible. Such a distinction is vital to any deliberation regardless of how it may be expressed in language.

Judgments of serious possibility constitute the framework within which deliberating agents make comparisons regarding the value of having one condition satisfied rather than another. There is no point in judging it better that Dole won the 1996 Presidential election than that Clinton won since all of us agree that Clinton certainly did win. Dole's winning is not a serious possibility for anyone. To be sure, a devotee of Dole's might judge that it would have been better had Dole won rather than Clinton. The Dole follower in such a mood of wishful thinking has, for the sake of the argument, transformed his current assessments of serious possibility so that the issue of the 1996 election has become unsettled. Relative to the suppositional standard of serious possibility, the comparison can be made. Relative to the standard to which the inquirer is currently committed, it cannot. The agent's non suppositional evaluations are framed by the agent's judgments of serious possibility.

In a similar vein, believing propositions to a certain positive degree presupposes that these propositions are serious possibilities. This is so whether or not these degrees of belief are taken to be subjective, credal probabilities or to be degrees of belief in the sense of [Shackle, 1961], [Cohen, 1977], or [Spohn, 1988].

Take the case of credal or subjective probability. If a proposition is judged to be positively probable, it should be judged seriously possible. Of course, a proposition judged impossible might be assigned positive probability suppositionally. We might be convinced that a coin was tossed and landed heads so that according to our current credal probability judgment, the probability that the coin landed tails is 0. Still we might withdraw in fantasy to a point of view where we are in doubt as to whether the coin is tossed or not and then, from that perspective, ask what the credal probability of tails is conditional on the coin being tossed.[1] We might

[1]The conditional probability in question may be understood as the betting rate for called off bets relative to the suppositional belief state where the inquirer is in doubt as to whether the coin is tossed or not. The conditional probability is not relative to the current state where the agent is convinced that the coin has been tossed and landed heads. Relative to that state, the unconditional probability that the coin landed tails is 0 as stated in the text.

reasonably think it is close to 0. 5.

Our current judgment of credal probability is based on our current judgment of serious possibility. This does not preclude our considering probabilities relative to alternative standards for serious possibility. The fact that we can engage in such suppositional fantasizing should alert us to the dangers to our sanity threatened by confusing fantasy with reality. Judgments of serious possibility and impossibility made for the sake of the argument ought to be clearly distinguished from judgments of serious possibility and impossibility endorsed by the inquirer relative to the state of belief he or she earnestly embraces as his or her own. The distinction between the possible and the impossible ought to be grounded in the inquirer's state of full belief—that is to say, in the agent's judgments as to what is true for sure and what is false for sure. The agent may contemplate what would be true were some proposition false that he or she currently judges to be true. But his or her judgment as to what would be true on the supposition ought to be kept clearly distinguished from his or her judgment as to what is true. To confuse the two is a form of madness.

Nonetheless, what X can suppose to be true for the sake of the argument even though X does not believe it, X can come to believe. The question arises as to whether and when X ought to actually change X's standard for serious possibility by actually coming to believe the proposition in earnest.

The same question may be broached from a different direction. The standard for serious possibility embraced by X at t may differ from the standard embraced by Y. Judgments of serious possibility are, in this sense, subjective. But X can come to adopt Y's standard for serious possibility. Under what conditions ought X come to do so?

These questions concern the conditions under which an inquirer is justified in changing his or her standard for serious possibility. That is to say, they concern conditions under which the inquirer is justified in changing his or her state of full belief; for the propositions that inquirer X rules out as not seriously possible are precisely those that X judges to be false for certain and whose negations X fully believes to be true. Changing the standard for serious possibility is changing the state of full belief.

It is entertainable, of course, that inquirers should never change their states of full belief. Partisans of Parmenidean epistemology seek to identify some standard of serious possibility to which every one ought to adhere. For example, one might insist that all and only logical or logical and mathematical possibilities are seriously possible. Or a fixed inter subjective standard based on some ideal of conceptual necessity might be proposed. Advocates of Parmenidean epistemology might concede that agents often do change their standards for serious possibility. Still, they might insist, such changes are illegitimate. There is a single standard to which all rational agents should adhere.

Parmenidean epistemology is not a straw man. Popperian falsificationists and radical probabilists either flirt with this view or endorse it outright.[2]

In part, the animus against full belief or acceptance is a prejudice against certainty. Dogmatism and opinionation is falsely associated with absolute certainty. We are not entitled to be certain about anything substantive—not even death and taxes. Many philosophers find it difficult to understand how one can legitimately cease being certain once one is certain. Certainty breeds rigidity, so the objection goes.

I agree that a systematic examination of the conditions under which one should cease being certain is of paramount philosophical interest. The initiation of systematic discussion of how to choose between rival contraction strategies once it is settled that contraction is to take place is perhaps the most important contribution that the work of Alchourrón, Gärdenfors and Makinson [1985] has made to epistemological studies. I do not think that the prospects for systematic accounts of contraction are any dimmer than the prospects for systematic accounts of induction and would insist on the importance of both. In any event, the question about how to cease being certain appears to be no more daunting than the question about how to cease assigning probability 0. 2 (or whatever).

Sometimes the objection to certainty takes the following form: If X fully believes that h, X should be prepared to accept a bet on the truth of h at any odds. But countless examples suggest that one should not be prepared to accept such bets. It would be tedious to rehearse examples here; but two quick points may be made:

[2]There continues to be a tendency to understand Bayesianism to be hostile to talk of acceptance. I confess I am not a Bayesian or, at any rate, not a strict Bayesian who thinks that being committed to assigning numerical determinate probabilities to propositions is a necessary condition for being ideally rational. But Bayesians do not disavow talk of acceptance. One of the characteristic features of Bayesian statistics as it is understood in the statistics profession is that a Bayesian updates probabilities by conditionalization via Bayes' theorem. Doing so presupposes that inquirers 'accept' or admit into evidence data concerning the outcomes of observations or experiments. The overwhelming majority of Bayesians seem tacitly or explicitly to regard some notion of acceptance as evidence as clear enough for them to use without betraying their Bayesian credentials. To be sure, radical probabilists like R. C. Jeffrey [1965] who find the notion of acceptance obscure have sought to avoid updating according to conditionalization and Bayes theorem. Such radical probabilists break quite clearly with the prevailing Bayesian tradition, just as surely as R. A. Fisher [1959] and H. E. Kyburg [1974] do when they abandon updating according to conditionalization and Bayes theorem for motives different from Jeffrey's. Fisher and Kyburg do not think of themselves as Bayesians. Jeffrey and his epigones are most anxious to retain the Bayesian affiliation. Whether they do or don't is of small importance. But it is surely wrong to allege that talk of acceptance is 'decidedly un-Bayesian' (Charles Chihara, [1994]) or 'sloppy' (p. 167). The shoe is on the other foot. It is 'sloppy' to understand conditionalization on e as applying when 'the agent's degree of belief changes to 1' ([Chihara, 1994], p.167). X's degree of belief that h can change to 1 without X coming to fully believe, becoming certain or accepting as evidence that h. The point was well known to De Finetti [1972] and H. Jeffreys [1961]. The only serious objection to it from the subjectivist version of Bayesianism derives from the argument of Shimony [1955]. One response to this objection is offered in Levi, [1978] and [1980], ch. 5. 5 5. 6. For further elaboration, see Levi, [1989]. In any case, conditioning on e requires coming to accept e as evidence and not merely assigning probability 1 to e. This point is acknowledged in the paper by Van McGee immediately following Chihara's (McGee, [1994]) although McGee thinks that using nonstandard analysis or Popper functions are the best ways to respond to the point rather than relying as De Finetti had done on appeal to called off bets.

(a) We may agree that X fully believes that h as long as X is prepared to accept a bet on the truth of h at any odds. But X can, so I have been suggesting, cease fully believing that h. And this can happen because X is offered a bet on h in circumstances that create suspicions (perhaps legitimately) where there were none.

(b) Sometimes in reporting what X fully believes we specify a content with greater precision than what actually matches X's belief. We may say that X believes that his brother is six feet tall when we should say that X believes that his brother is six feet tall give or take a quarter of an inch. X is not certain that his brother is exactly six feet tall but somewhere very close. Or X may be certain that Y will repay the money he borrowed. His full belief may, nonetheless, be circumscribed by the clause 'barring unforeseen eventualities'. X may or may not be convinced that unforeseen eventualities will not occur. If X is not convinced, X is not certain that Y will repay the money he borrowed. But, of course, X might be convinced and retain his coherence.

A skeptic may challenge X and if he were to take the skeptic's challenge seriously, he might be at a loss for a reply and cease being convinced. But there is no automatic requirement that X should accept the skeptic's challenge. He needs a good reason for doing so. If I open my mind to the logical possibility that I am dreaming or that I am a brain in a vat, I may have serious difficulty in regaining my conviction that I am not. But, as Peirce rightly insisted, I am under no obligation to take paper doubts seriously. Of course, to deal with this matter, we should look at the topic of good reasons for contraction, which is one aspect of the problem of rational change in full belief.

Inductive inference, as I understand it, is a species of change in the state of full belief or standard for serious possibility. Of course, induction is not merely a change in state of full belief. It is a change in full belief via ampliative inference. We need to consider somewhat more explicitly what this means.

1.4 Changes in doxastic commitment and fulfillment of doxastic commitment

A change in full belief is, of course, a change in state of full belief. This may be understood to be a change in an inquirer's standard for serious possibility. But what does such a change amount to?

Philosophers tend to think of propositional attitudes in one of two ways: (1) As dispositions to linguistic and nonlinguistic behaviors of various kinds and (2) as manifestations of such dispositions. X may be convinced that Albany is north of New York even though he rarely has occasion to think about it. The common view is that he has a disposition to answer positively a question about the location of Albany even when he is not thinking about the matter. But as long as X is not thinking about it, he does not consciously or explicitly believe it. When X does think about it, he does not change his doxastic disposition. Hence, in one respect, he does not change his beliefs. But in another sense he does.

Suppose that X acquires the doxastic disposition to assent to and to bet on the truth of the proposition that Montreal is north of Albany (having already acquired the doxastic disposition to assent to and bet on the proposition that Albany is north of New York). Whether X activates these dispositions or not, he may still fail to have the disposition to assent to or bet on the proposition that Montreal is north of New York.

If X subsequently acquires these dispositions by making the requisite deductions and calculations, X will have added to his full beliefs in the dispositional sense and, perhaps, will have manifested these dispositions as well. So both kinds of belief change cited previously could well take place. Yet, there is a respect in which X has not changed his state of full belief at all. Full belief that Montreal is north of New York is a consequence of X's other full beliefs. It is implicit in them. All X has done has been to clarify and explicate beliefs X already has. X has no doubt drawn an inference from what he initially believed to another belief. This is a belief change in the sense that it involves a change in X's doxastic dispositions. But X was already committed by his convictions that Albany is north of New York, Montreal north of Albany and 'is north of' is transitive, to full belief that Montreal is north of New York.

I suggest that we distinguish between three and not just two kinds of belief change:[3] (1) changes in doxastic disposition, (2) changes due to activations of such dispositions and (3) changes in commitments to doxastic dispositions. In our toy example, changes in doxastic disposition of type (1) and, perhaps, in manifestation of type (2) take place although no change in doxastic commitment of type (3) does. X improves his doxastic performance without altering his doxastic commitment. The change in doxastic performance is an improvement and, hence, warranted to the extent that the agent does fulfill his doxastic commitments.

Changes in doxastic commitment cannot be justified by showing that they improve performance in fulfilling the doxastic commitments endorsed prior to change. Changes in doxastic commitments are justified by showing that the changes improve the standards for serious possibility. No matter what constitutes an the improvement in such standards, an improvement in doxastic commitments is a different matter than an improvement in performance relative to standards already adopted.

Principles of logic or rational coherence may, perhaps, be identified that every standard for serious possibility should satisfy. Even though standards for serious possibility differ and, hence, what constitutes an improvement in doxastic performance does depend on which standard is endorsed, there are certain features that may be shared by all coherent standards. Appealing to these generic features, we may hope to engage in systematic efforts to devise technologies to furnish us with prosthetic devices for enhancing our capacity to fulfill our doxastic commitments

[3]My impression is that students of dynamic logic are included among the many who neglect or refuse to recognize the distinctions I advocate.

and develop therapeutic techniques to overcome the psychological difficulties that often stand in the way of good doxastic performance.

Efforts undertaken to improve doxastic commitments require more than new technologies and therapies. They call for inquiry including a general account of the conditions under which changes in doxastic commitments are justified.

1.5 Linguistic representations

Potential standards for serious possibility (i.e., potential states of full belief) **K** are attitudinal states or states of doxastic commitment. We may represent aspects of such states linguistically; but it would be a mistake to confuse a potential state of full belief **K** with a linguistic representation of it. A conceptual framework or space of potential states of full belief K ought to be partially ordered by a relation specifying which states are consequences of which. Such a consequence relation ought to yield a partial ordering satisfying the requirements of an atomless Boolean algebra that is closed under meets and joins of arbitrary cardinality. (See Levi, [1991, Ch. 2].)

Given a sentential or first order regimented language $\underline{L}$, we may represent some potential belief states by sentences in $\underline{L}$ such that if sentence h in $\underline{L}$ represents **K** and h' represents **K**', h' is deducible from h in L if and only if **K**' is a consequence of **K** according to the consequence relation for **K**.

Given such a representation, consider a belief state **K** that is the meet of a countably infinite set A of belief states each of which is representable by a sentence in $\underline{L}$. **K** may not be representable by a sentence in $\underline{L}$. However, consider the set of sentences $\underline{K}$ that consists of all sentences in $\underline{L}$ representing potential belief states representable by sentences in $\underline{L}$ that are consequences of **K**. $\underline{K}$ must represent **K** because **K** is the only potential state of full belief that is the meet of the potential belief states in A and, hence, is the weakest potential belief state having the potential belief states in A as consequences.

Thus, we can represent more potential states of full belief in $\underline{L}$ by sets of sentences in the set K of potential corpora expressible in $\underline{L}$. Such potential corpora consist of deductively closed sets of sentences in $\underline{L}$.

The potential corpora in $\underline{L}$ still cannot adequately represent all potential belief states in K.

In the first place, K is an atomless boolean algebra. No matter how specific a consistent potential state of full belief is, it can be conceptually 'split' into more specific possibilities. By way of contrast, the elements of the set of potential corpora in $\underline{L}$ constitute an atomic Boolean algebra. It is, of course, true that the expressive powers of $\underline{L}$ can be enriched indefinitely. But no enrichment will secure the full richness of the space of potential states of full belief. This means, of course, that there are no maximally complete and consistent potential states of full belief and, hence, no possible worlds except in the sense of maximally consistent descriptions in $\underline{L}$.

In the second place, K is closed under meets and joins of arbitrary cardinality. For example, X is seeking to estimate the value of a real valued parameter whose range is restricted initially to values between 0 and 1. X judges that the true value is between $\frac{1}{8}$ and $\frac{1}{4}$ but is otherwise in doubt as to what the true value is. If the range of alternative point estimates were countable, X's state of full belief could be represented by the logical consequences of all negations of point estimates outside of the range between between $\frac{1}{8}$ and $\frac{1}{4}$. (Whether the end points are in or not makes no difference to the example.) Both the interval from $\frac{1}{8}$ to $\frac{1}{4}$ and the set of values outside are non-countable. Neither the point estimates nor their negations are all representable linguistically. The corpus cannot represent the belief state completely.

While it is important to keep these points firmly in mind, their significance should not be exaggerated. We can reason quite successfully regarding the real numbers and sets of greater cardinality even though we lack linguistic resources to name every item in the given domain. Most of the resources I shall need for characterizing changes in states of doxastic commitment or states of full belief can be developed utilizing the representation in terms of changes in corpora representing such states. And when it cannot, I shall rely on the algebraic structure of the conceptual framework of potential states of full belief K and informal model theoretic ideas.

Thus, a standard for serious possibility or state of full belief $\mathbf{K}$ is at least partially representable linguistically by a deductively closed set of sentences $\underline{K}$ in a suitably regimented language $\underline{L}$. Alternatively such a state may be represented by the set of sentences in $\underline{L}$ that are consistent with $\underline{K}$ (i.e., the sentences representing serious possibilities relative to $\underline{K}$). That is to say, a rational agent is committed to fully believing (in the dispositional sense) all the logical consequences of his full beliefs and to judging seriously possible all propositions consistent with his full beliefs.

A change in doxastic commitment, therefore, can be represented by a transformation of the initial corpus $\underline{K}$ into another deductively closed set $\underline{K}$'. Changes in full belief that emerge from deriving logical consequences of full beliefs incur no change in commitment. Deductive inferences are, in this sense 'explicative'. The new beliefs formed add no new information to the agent's doxastic commitments.

Inductive inference is ampliative. It involves changing doxastic commitments. But not all such changes are ampliative. The change in commitment must add new information and be inferential. To explain this, we need to survey the types of change in doxastic commitment that can occur.

Stated as a change in doxastic commitments or states of full belief, a coarse grained classification of such transformations divides them into the following four categories:

$\mathbf{K_2}$ is an *expansion* of $\mathbf{K_1}$ if and only if $\mathbf{K_1}$ is a consequence of $\mathbf{K_2}$.

$\mathbf{K_2}$ is a *contraction* of $\mathbf{K_1}$ if and only if $\mathbf{K_2}$ is a consequence of $\mathbf{K_1}$.

$\mathbf{K_2}$ is a *replacement* of $\mathbf{K_1}$ if and only if $\mathbf{K_1} \wedge \mathbf{K_2} = \mathbf{0}$.

$\mathbf{K_2}$ is a *residual shift* of $\mathbf{K_1}$ if and only if it is neither an *expansion*, *contraction* nor a *replacement* of $\mathbf{K_1}$.

Stated as a transformation of corpus as in [Levi, 1980], the classification may be reformulated as follows:

$\underline{K}_2$ is an *expansion* of $\underline{K}_1$ if and only if $\underline{K}_1 \subseteq \underline{K}_2$.

$\underline{K}_2$ is a *contraction* of $\underline{K}_1$ if and only if $\underline{K}_2 \subseteq \underline{K}_1$.

$\underline{K}_2$ is a *replacement* of $\underline{K}_1$ if and only if the deductive closure of $\underline{K}_1 \cup \underline{K}_2$ is inconsistent.

$\underline{K}_2$ is a *residual shift* of $\underline{K}_1$ if and only if $\underline{K}_2$ is neither an *expansion*, a *contraction* or a *replacement* of $\underline{K}_1$.

When $\mathbf{K_2}$ is an expansion of $\mathbf{K_1}$, $\mathbf{K_2} = \mathbf{K_1} \wedge \mathbf{J}$ where $\mathbf{J}$ is some potential state of full belief. If $\mathbf{K_1}$ is representable in $\underline{L}$ by $\underline{K}_1$ and $\mathbf{J}$ is representable in $\underline{L}$ by a sentence h, $\mathbf{K_2}$ is representable by the set of deductive consequences in $\underline{L}$ of $\underline{K}_1$ and h and may be written as ${\underline{K}_1}^+{}_h$. $\underline{L}$ may not have the resources to represent the expansion in this manner. The set of sentences $\underline{J}$ in $\underline{L}$ representing consequences of $\underline{J}$ representable by sentences in $\underline{L}$ need not be finitely axiomatisable in $\underline{L}$. It may still be possible to represent the expansion as the set of deductive consequences in $\underline{L}$ of $\underline{K}_1$ and a countably infinite set $\underline{S}$ of sentences (or of the corpus that is the set of consequences of $\underline{S}$.) In the following we shall restrict ourselves, as does AGM, to expansions of $\underline{K}$ by single sentences.

Ampliative or inductive inferences are expansions of states of full belief or the potential corpora that represent such states. Any such expansion adds information not contained in the initial belief state or corpus. Nonetheless, not all such expansions are ampliative inferences. The reason is that some expansions are not the result of inferring the sentence h (sentences in the set $\underline{S}$) from the total information $\underline{K}$.

Suppose that h asserts that the traffic light has turned red on the corner of Grange Road and the Barton Road. The agent who acquires this information often does so without inferring it from his initial corpus $\underline{K}$. The agent is often not in a position to justify the expansion by showing that such expansion was the best answer to the question under investigation relative to the information available to him. There is no ampliative inference even though new information is obtained. The agent did not choose the answer from those proposed via abduction. Rather he let the answer be chosen for him by his responses to sensory stimulation or by the testimony of others. To be sure, if called upon to defend the legitimacy of the expansion, the agent might claim that he followed a highly reliable program whose output was the expansion adding h to $\underline{K}$. There was no inference because the information in $\underline{K}$ (including the assumption that the program is reliable) does not warrant the conclusion that h is true. After all, the program could have been implemented and yielded the result that the traffic light was green. That it did not do so is not information in $\underline{K}$ prior to coming to belief that the light was red. I have discussed such 'routine expansion' via the testimony of the senses or of witnesses elsewhere [Levi, 1980; Levi, 1991]. My focus now is on expansion where the new information h (or $\underline{S}$) added is not the result of the inquirer's pre commitment to a procedure for allowing external signals to dictate what new beliefs are to be added. Rather the addition of h is the conclusion of a deliberation that is justified on the basis of the total information in $\underline{K}$. This kind of expansion is inferential and ampliative.

To sum up, the claim that induction is ampliative inference differentiates such inference from deductive inference (in the standard sense) because deductive inferences yield conclusions that fail to alter doxastic commitments in general and fail to do so by adding new information via expansion in particular. And induction is differentiated from expansion via the testimony of the senses and the consulting of other oracles because the latter is the product of implementing a program for expansion using data as inputs in a manner judged prior to expansion to be highly reliable.

1.6 Induction as non-monotonic inference

Emphasis on the ampliativity of induction is of special importance in contemporary debate. The ampliativity of inductive reasoning requires that such reasoning exhibits a certain non-monotonic character as many logicians and computer scientists might say. And, indeed, students of default reasoning and non-monotonic reasoning often appear to be addressing aspects of inductive inference. Unfortunately, there are many other types of reasoning that also exhibit a non-monotonic character and this circumstance has led to some tendency to conflate inductive reasoning with other forms of reasoning such as belief contravening suppositional or hypothetical reasoning that, in my judgment, ought to be kept distinct from it. I have argued this point at length elsewhere [Levi, 1996] My aim here is to summarize some of the general features of inductive reasoning that reveal the forms of non-monotonicity it can have.

2 INDUCTION AS COGNITIVE DECISION MAKING

2.1 Justifying inductions

Ampliative inferences reflect the choice of one potential answer to a given question over others on the grounds that it promotes the aims of efforts to answer the question under consideration better than the alternative potential answers.

Inductive inference is, according to this view, a species of deliberate decision making. The inquirer decides among available options for changing his doxastic commitment by expanding his state of full belief. The rationality of the decision depends on the principles of rational decision making that apply to any sort of deliberate decision making regardless of the kinds of options from which a choice is to be made, the aims to be promoted and information on the basis of which options are to be evaluated with respect to their efficiency in realizing the given goals.

Consider the issue of controls in the design of experiments. If the inquiring agent has the options of adding h and also of adding $\sim h$ to $\underline{K}$, suspending judgment and thereby remaining with K is also an option. Relative to the goal of acquiring new information relevant to the question under consideration, suspension of judgment will seem less satisfactory than the other two alternatives. This will be so whether the inquirer has controlled for appropriate variables or not. But unless experiments have adequate controls, the risk of error incurred by adding h or by adding $\sim h$ may be too great. If the inquirer cares at all about avoiding error, suspension of judgment may seem the best option. The implementation of an experiment without adequate controls for the purpose of relieving doubt may prove fruitless. The use of controls improves the utility of experiments in promoting the aims of the given inquiry by reducing risk of error.

This kind of argument presupposes a view of the options that should be available in efforts to expand a given corpus, the common features of the goals of problem solving inquiry and a theory of rational choice.

2.2 *The ultimate partition*

Inquiring agent X is in a state of full belief or doxastic commitment $\mathbf{K}$. According to a widely held view, whether X is justified in expanding $\mathbf{K}$ inductively is determined entirely by X's total information or 'evidence' $\mathbf{K}$ supplemented, according to many, by X's judgments of probability relative to $\mathbf{K}$.[4]

This assumption is mistaken. In order for X to be justified in expanding $\mathbf{K}$ in some way or another, X needs to take into account the problem or question X means to be answering or attempting to answer by means of the expansion as well as X's evidence and X's judgments of probability.. From X's point of view prior to expansion, any nontrivial expansion of $\mathbf{K}$ incurs a risk of error. If X cares to avoid error, X needs an incentive to incur such a risk. And such an incentive appeals to the desirability of answering some question. Without a question associated with a range of potential answers, the inquirer X cannot make a sensible judgment as to whether the incentive associated with one potential answer compensates for the risk of error incurred better than would be the case in adopting an alternative potential answer.

Of course, there have been philosophers who do not regard risk of error as a matter to take into account in inductive expansion. Those thinkers surely cannot think that the information already available uniquely determines the correct induc-

[4]By X's evidence at time t, I mean any consequence of X's state of full belief. Insofar as we are speaking of what is representable in language $\underline{L}$, e is evidence for X at t if and only if e is in $\underline{K}$ where $\underline{K}$ is X's corpus at t. Evidence is not restricted to sentences in $\underline{L}$ carrying certain kinds of content. It is not restricted to items in $\underline{K}$ that are acquired in some special way (such as being the testimony of the senses). X's evidence at t is simply whatever X fully believes at t.

tive expansion. They must also take into account some goals or values that are to be promoted in expanding one way or another. Once more alternative expansion strategies need to be compared with respect to a given goal.

I shall suppose that X is investigating some question while initially in state of full belief **K**. Among the many tasks X faces is the task of abduction. The aim of abduction is to identify a list of potential answers or solutions. These will be potential expansions of **K** relevant to the question. I am not focusing on abduction in this discussion. Nonetheless, I need to have some way of characterizing the general structure of the result of completing the abductive task. X is concerned to answer the question under investigation. To do so, X chooses from among the expansion strategies judged relevant to the question via abduction. Induction is the task of justifying a choice among potential answers provided by abduction.

Looking at the matter decision theoretically, a way is required of identifying the doxastic options open to X in seeking to answer the question under study.

> An *ultimate* partition U_K relative to **K** is a set of potential expansions of **K** meeting the following conditions:
>
> No element of U_K. is identical with **0** (the inconsistent belief state). No consistent, potential expansion of **K** that counts as a potential answer to the question under investigation is stronger than any element of U_K according to the partial ordering associated with **K**.
>
> The elements of U_K must be pairwise inconsistent. That is to say,their meets must be identical to **0**.
>
> The join of the elements of U_K must be a consequence of **K**. That is to say, the inquirer must be certain that exactly one element of the ultimate partition is true.

A potential answer relative to **K** and U_K is a subset R of elements of U_K that are rejected. Given this rejection set R, the associated potential answer is the meet of **K** with the meet of the complements of the members of R. Informally, we look to the consequences of rejecting all members of the rejection set and the initial belief state. All elements of the power set of U_K qualify as potential rejection sets or potential answers relative to U_K.

When R is empty, the potential answer is to remain with **K** and completely suspend judgment concerning the range of strongest potential answers to the question under study. In case $R = U_K$, the potential answer is contradicting oneself.

The elements of U_K are strongest consistent potential answers or expansion strategies relative to **K** and the problem under study. They are not and cannot be maximally consistent potential expansions of **K** because there are no such 'possible worlds'. We must tailor the set of alternatives to the demands for information occasioned by the question under study. Three reasons support this view:

(1) The space of potential states of full belief should be an atomless boolean algebra. That is to say, every potential state of full belief can be seen as the join or disjunction of more specific alternatives. Consequently, there can be no possible worlds in the sense of maximally consistent potential states of full belief. ([Levi, 1991], ch. 2.)

(2) Inquiries are directed at answering specific questions. Information that is not relevant to the goals of the inquiry under study does not count as part of an answer.

(3) The range of alternatives given in U_K depends on the inquirer's success in identifying potential alternatives at the abductive phase. Identifying new potential answers can often alter the way conclusions are reached on the basis of given information.

Many though not all problems deal with ultimate partitions that have one of the following properties:

- Case 1: The set of elements of U_K is finite.
- Case 2: The set of elements of U_K consists of point estimates of a real valued parameter to **K**.
- Case 3: The set of elements of U_K is countably infinite.

There are many other cases. For example, the ultimate partition can be represented by the values of an n-dimensional vector or real numbers. I shall focus on these three cases here.

When U_K is either finite (case 1) or countably infinite (case 3), the elements of the ultimate partition can be represented by a set $\underline{U}_K$ of single sentences in some regimented language $\underline{L}$ where $\underline{K}$ is a corpus used to represent $\underline{K}$. In such cases, I shall call $\underline{U}_K$ the ultimate partititon.

Relative to U_K, each potential answer is characterized by a rejection set R. R can also be represented by a subset $\underline{R}$ of elements of $\underline{U}_K$. In case 1, the set $\underline{R}$ is finite so that $\underline{L}$ will contain a sentence h that is the conjunction of the negations of the elements of $\underline{R}$. The potential answer is an expansion $\underline{K}^+{}_h$ of $\underline{K}$ by adding h. In case 1, then we can consider the strongest consistent potential answers relevant to the question under study as the expansions of $\underline{K}$ by adding elements of $\underline{U}_K$ and all other potential answers as expansions of $\underline{K}$ by adding disjunctions of subsets of $\underline{U}_K$ or conjunctions of their negations.

When U_K is countably infinite as in case 3, the strongest consistent potential answers can be represented linguistically as in case 1 as expansions of $\underline{K}$ by adding the sentences in $\underline{U}_K$. When $\underline{R}$ is finite or cofinite in $\underline{U}_K$, the potential answer can be represented as the expansion of $\underline{K}$ by adding a sentence in $\underline{L}$ (the disjunction of the negations of members of $\underline{R}$ if $\underline{R}$ is finite or the disjunction of the elements of $\{\underline{U}_K/\underline{R}\}$ otherwise.) However, when both $\underline{\mathrm{R}}$ and $\{\underline{U}_K/\underline{R}\}$ are countably infinite, there is no way to represent the potential answer as an expansion of $\underline{K}$ by adding a single sentence. The expansion is the deductive closure of $\underline{K}$ and the set $\underline{S}$ of negations of the sentences in $\underline{R}$.

When U_K is the set of point estimates in some subset of the reals, potential answers can be represented by rejection sets belonging to the power set of all point estimates in the interval. But not all members of U_K can be represented by sentences in $\underline{L}$. Consequently, not all potential answers can be represented by sentences in $\underline{L}$ although no specific potential answer associated with a rejection set in U_K is precluded from carrying a linguistic representation.

In formulating criteria for choosing potential answers relative to U_K, I shall focus on cases where U_K is finite. In those cases, we can use the representations of potential expansion strategies in $\underline{L}$ I have indicated. I shall subsequently explain how to extend the procedures proposed for the finite case (1) to the other cases as well.

Let $\underline{L}$ be a regimented language with a truth functional or first order logic. K (which I have also used to represent potential states of full belief) is the set of potential corpora in $\underline{L}$. These are the deductively closed sets of sentences in $\underline{L}$. Such sets represent potential states of full belief insofar as these are representable in $\underline{L}$.

W = set of maximally consistent sets of sentences in $\underline{L}$. $W \subseteq K$. Moreover, the intersection of every subset of W is in K and every potential corpus in K is the intersection of a subset of W.

The inquiring agent X is committed at time t to a potential corpus $\underline{K}$ as X's standard for serious possibility (X's corpus in $\underline{L}$ at t partially representing X's state of full belief at t).

Suppose that at time t, X is concerned with some question. Suppose further that at time t, X has identified via abduction a set of potential answers to that question.

The strongest set of potential answers expressible in $\underline{L}$ consistent with X's full beliefs identified by X as gratifying the demands for information occasioned by X's question is representable by expansions of $\underline{K}$ by adding a member of the ultimate partition $\underline{U}_K$ relative to $\underline{K}$.

Why not equate $\underline{U}_K$ with the subset of members of W consistent with K?

Part of the answer is that $\underline{L}$ regimented though it may be is supposed to be capable of representing information that is not demanded as part of the solution to the problem under investigation as well as information that is. Information pertaining to the DNA found in tissue belonging to a suspect in some criminal investigation will not in general figure in a potential answer to the question: What will be the Fed's policy on interest rates at its next meeting? It is useful to be in a position to use the resources of $\underline{L}$ to plot variations in demands for information as well as changes in states of full belief. Equating elements of W consistent with $\underline{K}$ with the ultimate partition requires us to tailor the language $\underline{L}$ to the demands for information occasioned by the question under investigation more than is necessary.

Closely related to that issue is the question of how fine grained the strongest consistent potential answers to a given question might be. In predicting the outcome of a lottery, shall we count 'ticket 1 will win' and 'ticket 1 will not win' to be the strongest consistent potential answers? Or shall we take all answers of the form 'ticket i will win' for i between 1 and n to be such strongest consistent potential answers? Decisions on these matters could have a bearing on the conclusion to be reached by induction. And both alternatives are sometimes usefully represented in the same linguistic framework.

It would be unwise to legislate a standard for selecting an ultimate partition in cases such as this. The choice of an ultimate partition is in part bound by the imagination of the inquirer and in part by the demands for information that occasion the inquiry. When two or more inquirers engaged in a joint inquiry differ regarding what shall constitute a set of strongest consistent potential answers, it will then be necessary for them to reach some consensus concerning how to proceed. In general, the best recommendation would be to adopt the coarsest common refinement of their respective ultimate partitions. (See [Levi, 1984] Levi, 1984, ch. 7.)

We have already indicated how potential answers may be generated from ultimate partitions with the aid of rejection sets.

Sometimes it is helpful to be able to trace alterations in the ultimate partition due to changes in the inquirer's corpus alone.

Given $\underline{L}$, the basic partition $\underline{V}$ of W is a partition of W. Consider any cell of $\underline{V}$. The intersection of that cell is a potential corpus representing a strongest logically consistent answer among those an inquirer takes to be relevant to the inquirer's demands for information in the context of the inquiry or series of inquiries he is undertaking. The basic partition could be understood as what the inquirer's ultimate partition would be under the 'veil of ignorance' when his or her corpus is the weakest potential corpus in L. (In Levi [1980], I called it the 'urcorpus $\underline{UK}$'.) In some contexts, it is useful to consider something stronger than the set of logical and mathematical truths and so I allowed for beginning with a minimal corpus $\underline{LK}$ and considering the ultimate partition relative to $\underline{U}_{LK}$ as the basic partition.

Attention will be restricted to situations where the number of cells of $\underline{V}$ is finite so that the cells are representable as the logical consequences of single sentences in $\underline{L}$.

Given a consistent potential expansion $\underline{K}$ of $\underline{LK}$, the ultimate partition $\underline{U}_K$ relative to $\underline{K}$ and $\underline{V}$ = the subset of elements of $\underline{V}$ that are consistent extensions of $\underline{K}$.

If an inquirer's current state of full belief is representable in $\underline{L}$ by potential corpus $\underline{K}$ and $\underline{V}$ is the inquirer's current basic partition, the ultimate partition is the set of strongest potential answers to the inquirer's problem consistent with the inquirer's full beliefs.

$\underline{U}_K$ consists of hypotheses or conjectures obtained during the abductive phase of inquiry as explained previously. The conjectures in $\underline{U}_K$ ought not to be confused with the certainties in $\underline{K}$.

Inductive or ampliative reasoning relative to $\underline{K}$ and $\underline{V}$ justifies choosing a potential answer relative to relative to $\underline{K}$ and $\underline{U}_K$.

2.3 *Duality between acceptance and rejection*

The partition sensitivity of inductive inference implies a duality between inductive rejection and inductive acceptance. A potential answer to a given question is representable either by the subset of elements of the ultimate partition that are rejected or the 'acceptance set' which is the set of negations of the elements of this rejection set.

For Peirce as for Braithwaite [1953], induction is an eliminativist procedure as much as it is a method of acceptance. Rejecting h is accepting $\sim h$. Rejecting h by ampliative reasoning is accepting $\sim h$ by ampliative reasoning. This obvious observation does not seem to have been well understood by Popper.

Treating acceptance and rejection as two sides of the same coin is an attitude that prevails to a considerable extent in the traditions of statistical thinking deriving from R. A. Fisher and the rather different approach advanced by J. Neyman and E. S. Pearson. (See T. Seidenfeld, [1979]). Each of the 'points' in an interval estimate is an unrejected element of $\underline{U}_K$. Partition sensitivity is widely acknowledged in statistical methodology. So is its corollary: the duality of acceptance and rejection.

2.4 *Seek information, shun error!*

Peirce [1982, V. 3, Ch. 60] claimed that the sole object of inquiry is to relieve doubt—i.e., obtain information or acquire full belief that is valuable enough to gratify the demands for information occasioning the inquiry. He explicitly denied that we are concerned to obtain true (i.e., error free) information. He dismissed the demands of truth here by noting that, of course, everything we fully believe, we judge to be true. That observation should not to be gainsaid; but it applies to those full beliefs the inquirer has prior to forming new beliefs. At that point, he judges true or is committed to judging true all those assumptions he takes for granted when initiating the inquiry. On the other hand, hypotheses consistent with but not entailed by X's full beliefs are, from X's point of view, possibly false as well as possibly true. These hypotheses include items that belong in expansions of X's initial corpus K that are potential answers to X's question.

Consequently those potential answers or expansion strategies that the inquirer is considering incur a risk of being false at least from the inquirer's point of view prior to expansion. Is Peirce recommending that this risk be ignored in choosing between rival potential answers to the question under investigation?

I do not think he was recommending this. However, even if my understanding of his view is wrong, he should not have made such a recommendation. My conjecture is that Peirce was arguing against those who might wish to dismiss avoidance of error as a desideratum in inquiry. He was considering the methods of tenacity, authority and a priori reasons as rivals to the scientific method and did not wish to beg the question in evaluating the methods. So he evaluated them in terms of their efficiency in producing stability in the inquirer's views. He argued that they could not do so because these methods are not self correcting. The scientific method, by way of contrast, is self correcting, so Peirce maintained, and that was closely related to the circumstance that scientific inquiry seeks to take into account the question of whether its claims are true or not. Peirce was trying to argue that the plain man who does not care a fig about truth would be better off from his point of view if he conducted his deliberations and inquiries as if he did care. As I understand him, he did not wish to beg the question at the onset of his argument. Hence, the appeal to the concern to remove doubt as the sole end of inquiry. By the 'sole' end of inquiry, he meant the sole undisputed end of inquiry.

I am far from convinced that Peirce's arguments in favor of recognizing a concern for truth (i.e., avoidance of error) as a feature of the goals of inquiry are compelling even though I very much endorse his emphasis on truth as a cognitive value worthy of our admiration. I concede to those who do not take avoidance of error seriously as a value when fixing belief that I cannot show their view to be incoherent although I have very little respect for it. As in so many other contexts where there may be disputes regarding the aims of human and social activity, the best arguments for a point of view are provided by elaborating it so that its results may be compared with the results of embracing rival perspectives.

Recently, however, some distinguished authors have attributed a certain thesis to pragmatists that not only is not a feature of classical pragmatism but is deeply confused. Donald Davidson writes:

> We come here to a far more powerful consideration in favor of a somewhat tamer, but clearly recognizable, version of the pragmatic theory of truth. Rorty brings it to the fore when he credits Dewey with the thought that the correspondence theory adds nothing to 'ordinary, workaday, fallible ways of telling...the true from the false". What is clearly right is a point made long ago by Plato in the Theaetetus: truths do not come with a 'mark', like the date in the corner of some photographs, which distinguishes them from falsehoods. The best we can do is test, experiment, compare, and keep an open mind. But no matter how long and well we and coming generations keep at it, we and they will be left with fallible beliefs. We know many things, and will learn more, what we will never know for certain is which of the things we believe are true. Since it is neither visible as a target, nor recognizable when achieved, there is no point in calling truth a goal. Truth is not a value, so the 'pursuit of truth' is an empty enterprise unless it means only that it is often worthwhile to increase our confidence in our beliefs, by collecting further evidence or checking our calculations.
>
> From the fact that we will never be able to tell which of our beliefs are true, pragmatists conclude that we may as well identify our best researched, most successful, beliefs with the true ones, and give up the idea of objectivity. (Truth is objective if the truth of a belief or sentence is independent of whether it is justified by all our evidence, believed by our neighbors, or is good to steer by.) But here we have a choice. Instead of giving up the traditional view that truth is objective, we can give up the equally traditional view (to which the pragmatists adhere) that truth is a norm, something for which to strive. I agree with the pragmatists that we can't consistently take truth to be both objective and something to be pursued. But I think they would have done better to cleave to a view that counts truth as objective, but point-

less as a goal. (Davidson, [1998, pp. 2–3].)

Peirce was a classical pragmatist. He thought truth is objective. And yet, he thought truth was something to strive for. If his view is coherent, as I think it is, Davidson is mistaken both about pragmatism and about truth as a value. The issue of concern to us is not pragmatism (although I do want to correct a certain contemporary distortion of that view). It is whether one can regard truth as something that is objective and something to strive for.

X is in belief state **K** represented by corpus $\underline{K}$. X is committed to judging true every sentence in $\underline{K}$. X is also committed to judging true that X is so committed. Notice that X is not committed to judging that every sentence in $\underline{K}$ is justified by 'all our evidence'.) X is not even committed to judging that every sentence in $\underline{K}$ is justified by the evidence available to X—i.e., the members of $\underline{K}$. For X, no sentence in $\underline{K}$ stands in need of justification. Yet, X judges every sentence in $\underline{K}$ to be true. X may not care one wit about the opinions of X's neighbors. Or X may. That matters little to X's current judgment of truth. And X may or may not be convinced that what X believes is good to steer by. What X judges true may depress and debilitate X.

Thus, if X judges it true that h, X judges h true in Davidson's objective sense. Moreover, X is convinced that X has 'found out' that h is true. X will or should vigorously deny Davidson's claim that 'we never know for certain which of the things we believe are true". X should be certain that everything he fully believes is true.

Perhaps it will be denied that X judges that h is true in an objective sense because X equates truth with what X fully believes. But this is a mistake. X makes no claim to a full belief concerning every issue. X is in doubt about most issues even those where he thinks there is a true answer. So X does not equate truth with what X fully believes.

Now insofar as X strives after truth, X does not do so concerning what X currently judges to be true. X's striving focuses on what is yet in doubt. As I understand it, in removing doubt by expansion, X should be concerned to avoid error in the result.

Before having expanded by adding h, X cannot have an 'infallible guarantee' that h is true. X's 'evidence'—i.e., X's current corpus $\underline{K}$—does not entail h. But X may invoke the information in $\underline{K}$ together with X's probability judgments and goals to argue that the risk of error incurred by coming to fully believe that h is worth incurring for the sake of information acquired.

Will X ever 'know for certain' whether h is true or false? If X is justified in incurring the risk by adding h to K and coming to fully believe the consequences, then upon actually expanding, X will judge that h is true and will be certain that h is true. The upshot is that X can be justified in coming to judge that h is true without equating truth with the justification or with any other condition that Davidson rules out as appropriate for an objective notion of truth.

Of course, true beliefs do not come labeled like the date in the corner of a photograph. But even if the photograph does not come with its date inscribed, inquiry may uncover the date of the photograph. And in so doing, true beliefs will be recognized as such.[5]

In sum, there is no conceptual obstacle to seeking true information in fixing our beliefs where truth is as objective as Davidson requires it to be. To be sure, there is no conceptual obstacle prohibiting anyone from fixing beliefs without caring about avoidance of error. Nonetheless, the account of efforts to change states of full belief by ampliative expansion I am proposing here presupposes that in contemplating rival inductive expansion strategies, one should seek to relieve doubt (obtain worthwhile information) while also attempting to avoid error. The common feature of all goals directing specific inquiries should be to obtain new error free information. I do not claim that inquirers who expand in a way that promotes a political, religious, moral or personal agenda are incoherent. But I do regard promoting such goals in fixing belief as wrong in most situations. I shall not defend this value judgment here. Instead, I shall review and summarize how I understand this claim and how promoting it bears on inductive expansion.

2.5 *Shunning error*

Given $\underline{K}$ and $\underline{V}$, an ultimate partition $\underline{U}_K$ is defined together with the class of rejection subsets determined by $\underline{U}_K$. Each rejection subset represents a potential expansion strategy that may be evaluated with respect to whether it imports error or not and with respect to the value of the new information it adds to $\underline{K}$.

The evaluation of truth and error as well as the assessment of risk of error is carried out from the point of view of the inquirer who takes for granted or is committed to taking for granted that all items in $\underline{K}$ are true. As a consequence, the inquirer is committed to judging that exactly one element of $\underline{U}_K$ is true. Consequently, from the inquirer's point of view an expansion strategy represented by a rejection set $\underline{R}$ imports error if and only if the true element of $\underline{U}_K$ is a member of $\underline{R}$ and avoids error otherwise. Assuming that $\underline{U}_K$ is finite, let h^R be a sentence that is true if and only if the true sentence is in $\underline{R}$ so that the inductive expansion adding $\sim h^R$ to $\underline{K}$ imports error. The inductive expansion represented by the rejection set $\underline{R}$ is also representable as the expansion of $\underline{K}$ by adding $\sim h^R$. The probability of this expansion avoiding error relative to $\underline{K}$ is $P(\sim h^R)$ and the probability of its importing error is $P(h^R)$.

An inquirer concerned to avoid error to the exclusion of anything else, will maximize his chances of avoiding error by adopting the empty rejection set—i.e., by refusing to expand and remaining in suspense concerning the issue under consideration. Since the inquirer is certain that everything in the current corpus $\underline{K}$ is true, the probability of the inquirer's importing error according to that strategy is 0. If the inquirer adopts a rejection set that is nonempty, from his perspective

[5] For a critique of Davidson and of Rorty on this issue along lines I find congenial that is, nonetheless, more sympathetic with the preoccupations of these authors than I have been, see Bilgrami [1998].

there is a positive probability that expansion will lead to false belief. If $\underline{R}' \subseteq \underline{R}$, the probability of importing error using $\underline{R}'$ cannot be greater than the probability of importing error using $\underline{R}$. If $\underline{R} = \underline{U}_K$, the probability of importing error is at a maximum of 1.

The probability of importing error from adopting $\underline{R}$ can be converted into an expected utility by adopting a utility function $T(\sim h^R, x)$ where x takes the values t(rue) and f(alse) and $T(\sim h^R, t) = a\}$ and $T(\sim h^R, f) = b$. $a > b$. It does not matter what values a and b take as long as $a > b$ and the values are finite. If we take T to be a utility function, the expected utility of adopting rejection set $\underline{R}$ is equal to the probability $P(\sim h^R)a + P(h^R)b$. The ranking of the rejection sets with respect to expected utility is the same as long as $a > b$. So we might as well let $a = 1$ and $b = 0$. Then the expected utility is $P(\sim h^R)$ = the probability that the true element of $\underline{U}_K$ is not in $\underline{R}$.

Hence, if the sole concern of the inquirer were to avoid error, the inquirer should choose a rejection set that maximizes expected T-value and rejects no element of $\underline{U}_K$. We can, therefore, think of one source of anti inductivism as deriving from a concern to avoid error to the exclusion of everything else—including the concern to relieve doubt or acquire valuable new information. Indeed, we can argue that an agent whose sole concern is to avoid error would cease being an inquirer at all; for such an agent would not risk error.

Thus, there is at least one respect in which Peirce's observation that relief from doubt is the sole object of inquiry is correct. Unless an inquirer who cares to avoid error has a concern to obtain new information, he will not have any incentive to risk error. And agents who are not concerned to avoid error will be indifferent between stronger and weaker expansions if they do not care about new information. Relief from doubt is a necessary ingredient of any incentive for inductive expansion.

2.6 *Relieving doubt*

Is it sufficient? One could, indeed, seek to identify potential answers to a given question via abduction and then choose between them as if the sole aim were to gratify one's curiosity. An inquirer who proceeded in this fashion would, however, have no incentive to avoid error and should, so I submit, find it optimal to contradict himself.

The set of potential answers generated by an ultimate partition $\underline{U}_K$ may be partially ordered with respect to strength. The potential answer represented by rejection set $\underline{R}'$ is stronger than the potential answer represented by $\underline{R}$ if and only if $\underline{R} \subset \underline{R}'$. Stronger answers remove more doubt than weaker ones because they eliminate more of the strongest consistent potential answers belonging to $\underline{U}_K$.

It follows from this consideration alone that the agent who is concerned exclusively with relieving doubt should contradict himself. Anyone who does not think that contradicting oneself is good thing cannot rationally be focused exclusively on relieving doubt when engaged in inquiry.

One way to remove the difficulty is to stipulate in advance that expanding into inconsistency is not an available option in efforts at inductive expansion. It may, perhaps, not be a coherent option. It may lead to certain importation of error. But what precludes lapsing into incoherence or importing error? Anyone concerned with providing a decision theoretic rationale for principles of ampliative inference should seek to show that expanding into inconsistency serves the aims of inquiry poorly rather than ruling out such expansion as an option in advance.

One might argue against expanding into inconsistency by saying that the concern to remove doubt is best promoted by rejecting more elements of $\underline{U}_K$ rather than less short of rejecting all of them. Rejecting all of them (i.e. contradicting oneself) is judged worse than all others with respect to the goal of relieving doubt because such a change is expansion into incoherence.

Keep in mind, however, that we are considering a point of view where the aim is to remove doubt to the exclusion of every other value. This excludes a concern to avoid incoherence.

We might also seek to avoid inconsistency by saying that expanding into inconsistency is expanding into error the inquirer is certain will ensue. This too brings in another value—to wit, the concern to avoid error and concedes that the interest in removing doubt is not the sole concern of inquiry.

We are no doubt concerned to relieve doubt. But that is not the only value of interest in inquiry. Let us consider the concern with coherent removal of doubt and then removal of doubt with avoidance of error in turn.

2.7 *Coherent removal of doubt*

No matter how one might think of the aim of avoiding incoherence, it does seem to set up a preference among expansion strategies that preserves the preference ordering satisfying the partial ordering with respect to strength except that expansion into contradiction is considered the worst expansion strategy. The idea is to remove doubt coherently. Avoidance of error, however, is not a concern.

Presumably the best potential answers from this point of view are strongest consistent potential answers constituting the ultimate partition $\underline{U}_K$ provided there are any best potential answers. Keep in mind, however, that thus far the evaluation of potential expansion strategies with respect to strength is only a partial ordering of the class of rejection sets with respect to set inclusion. When modified so as to shift expansion into inconsistency to the bottom, there are no best potential expansion strategies. To obtain optimal expansion strategies, the partial ordering may be extended to a complete ordering where every expansion strategy is comparable to every other one. Such a complete ordering includes a complete ordering of the elements of $\underline{U}_K$. If the elements of $\underline{U}_K$ are rival theories (together with a residual hypothesis asserting that the others are all false), the elements of $\underline{U}_K$ may be compared with respect to the explanatory virtues of these hypotheses as seen in the light of the inquirer's research program—whatever these might be. In contexts of parameter estimation or inductive prediction, comparisons may be based on some assessment of specificity.

Given these comparisons, we may obtain a total ordering of the elements of $\underline{U}_K$ with respect to informational value. This total ordering can then be extended somehow to the class of all potential expansion strategies in a manner preserving the partial ordering with respect to strength and relief from doubt. The potential answer that maximizes informational value remains expansion into contradiction.

However, if the goal of maximizing informational value is modified by the constraint that all coherent expansions be preferred to incoherent ones, we get a total ordering with respect to coherent informational value. The best expansion strategies are those elements of $\underline{U}_K$ that maximize informational value among elements of $\underline{U}_K$.

There may be more than one such optimal expansion strategy. But we cannot recommend the strategy of rejecting all and only suboptimal elements of $\underline{U}_K$; for that strategy yields a weaker result than rejecting all but one element of $\underline{U}_K$ and must, for that reason be suboptimal.

Indeed, under no circumstances can we conclude that the best conclusion to reach via ampliative inference is to suspend judgment between two or more elements of $\underline{U}_K$.

From these considerations, we may conclude that an inquirer concerned to relieve doubts while preserving coherence will be driven to reject all but one element of $\underline{U}_K$ even when more than one such expansion strategy is best among elements of $\underline{U}_K$ because no rejection set that is larger than a unit set can be optimal.

But sometimes in our efforts to remove our doubts, the evidence accords its support more or less evenly among rival alternatives. We cannot, however, suspend judgment. Consider, for example, the question of predicting the outcome of the lottery. Each prediction of the form 'ticket i will win' is as specific as any other. So all are optimal and no form of suspense between any subset of them can be optimal. The advocate of coherent relief from doubt as the aim of inquiry may avoid inconsistency. But the prohibition of suspension of belief between elements of $\underline{U}_K$ under all circumstances is unattractive in its own right. Let us then consider the view that the common feature of all well conducted inquiries is to relieve doubt while avoiding error or seeking new error free and important information.

2.8 Seeking new error free information

In discussing concern to relieve doubt coherently, we already considered extending the partial ordering with respect to strength to a total ordering with respect to informational value. This total ordering recommended self contradiction as optimal. For that reason, we considered maximizing informational value coherently as a goal and found it wanting.

The proposal currently to be considered understands the common feature of the goals to be recommended for inquiry to be two - dimensional at least. The inquiring agent is concerned to maximize a utility index that aggregates two other utility functions into a single one. The two utility functions representing two rival goals being 'compromised' in the aggregating utility function are: The utility of truth function $T(\sim h^R, x)$ discussed previously and a utility of information function $C(\sim h^R)$ that preserves the partial ordering with respect to strength and the total ordering with respect to informational value. The method of aggregation is weighted averaging. The epistemic utility function, $V(\sim h^R, x)$ equals $\alpha(T(\sim h^R, x) + (1-\alpha)C(\sim h^R).(0 \leq \alpha \leq 1.)$ (See Levi, [1984, ch. 5] for a brief, technical development of the ideas to be summarized here.)

The chief advantage of weighted averaging here is that it guarantees that whenever there is an agreement between two evaluations concerning how a pair of options are to be rated, the weighted average will preserve it. This unanimity condition, together with the requirement that both the V-function, T-function and the C-function all behave like utility functions for the purpose of assessing expected utility secures the weighted averaging prescription as a sensible way to represent a compromise between the concern to avoid error that leads to total suspense and the concern to obtain new valuable information that recommends contradiction.

In order for this approach to be useful, we need to introduce not only a total order with respect to the relief from doubt afforded by the potential expansion strategies generated by $\underline{U}_K$ but a utility function that preserves that ordering. This cardinal measure of informational value should have the properties of a utility function. Among other things this means that the C-function should be restricted to the range of real values in a finite interval and that any positive affine transformation $aC + b$ of the utility of information function represents the same such function. Since C is unique up to a positive affine transformation, it is possible to stipulate that interval be the unit interval from 0 to 1. Rejecting all elements of $\underline{U}_K$ gets C-value 1 and rejecting none of them C-value 0. An inquirer whose goal was to maximize informational value would have a goal representable by such a utility function. As before, such an inquirer should expand into inconsistency.

But the common feature of the goals of inquirers should not be to maximize informational value as represented by the C function. It should be to maximize the value of obtaining new error free information as represented by a utility function V representing a resolution of the conflict between seeking information and shunning error:

The Seek Information, Shun Error Principle: The quest for new error free information is represented by an epistemic utility function V satisfying the following condition:

$$V(\sim h^R, t) = \alpha + (1-\alpha)C(\sim h^R)$$

$$V(\sim h^R, f) = (1-\alpha)C(\sim h^R).$$

The inquirer concerned to obtain new error free information may seek to obtain as high a value of the V-utility as possible. But the inquirer will not be certain whether or not the strategy will import or avoid error. The only exceptions are expansion into contradiction and refusing to expand at all. Hence, the inquirer should be maximizing the expected epistemic utilities of the cognitive options:

$$EV(\sim h^R) = \alpha P(\sim h^R) + (1-\alpha)C(\sim h^R).$$

We need to look still more closely at the C-function. Let x be any element of $\underline{U}_K$. Rejecting x along with elements of some subset $\underline{A}$ of $\underline{U}_K$ should increase the informational value of the expansion strategy as long as x is not already in $\underline{A}$. But should the increment in informational value be the same no matter what subset not containing x is considered or should it be allowed to vary? The constant returns in informational value principle asserts that the increment should remain the same no matter what other elements of $\underline{U}_K$ are rejected as well. This principle has the following implication.

$$C(\sim h^R) = Cont(\sim h^R) = 1 - N(\sim h^R)$$

Here $1 - N(x)$ is the increment in informational value accruing from rejecting x (a member of $\underline{U}_K$). $N(\sim h^R) = \sum_x N(x)$ where the sum is taken over all x in $\{\underline{U}_K/\underline{R}\}$. Clearly the N-function is a normalized probability function defined for the Boolean algebra generated from $\underline{U}_K$.

In effect, the utility of information is represented by a content measure derived from a probability measure. The basis for this is the substantive constant returns in informational value principle.

Let $q = (1-\alpha)/\alpha$. q varies from 0 to infinity as (varies from 1 to 0. The expected utility function now looks like this:

$$EV(\sim h^R) = [P(\sim h^R) + (1-\alpha)(1 - N(\sim h^R)]/\alpha.$$

Divide EV by (and subtract q from the result. This is a positive affine transformation of EV and, hence, orders cognitive options in the same fashion. This transformation looks like this:

$$EF(\sim h^R) = P(\sim h^R) - qN(\sim h^R)$$
$$= \sum[P(x) - qN(x)]\text{where the sum is taken over all } x \text{ in } \{\underline{U}_K/\underline{R}\}.$$

This sum reaches a maximum when every x in $\{\underline{U}_K/\underline{R}\}$ carries a nonnegative value for $P(x) - qN(x)$ and no element x in $\underline{R}$ carries a positive value for this function.

Notice that there can be several optimal expansion strategies; but there must be a uniquely weakest one that rejects all and only those elements of $\underline{U}_K$ for which the EF- value is negative.

> *Rule for Ties:* When two or more expansion strategies are optimal, choose the weakest one if it exists.

When the aim of expansion is to seek new error free informational value as represented by the V-function, maximizing expected epistemic utility and using the rule for ties yields the following:

> *Inductive Rejection Rule:* x in $\underline{U}_K$ is rejected if and only if $P(x) < qN(x)$ if and only if $P(x)/N(x) < q$.

Strictly speaking, a family of inductive rejection rules is specified here: Given a specific goal that is an instance of seeking error free information, a specific rule stating what inductive expansion to adopt for any given (finite) $\underline{U}_K$ and credal probability distribution P over $\underline{U}_K$ is given. A specific goal is described as a weighted average of the T-function and some C- function or the informational value determining probability that defines it. The index q states what the weighted average must be.

2.9 *Boldness*

Those concerned to obtain new error free information are obviously concerned to avoid expanding into inconsistency. To guarantee that this cannot happen no matter what the credal probability distribution might be, restrictions must be placed on the values q may take in seeking information and shunning error.

The index q represents the relative importance attached to informational value and to avoidance of error. It is an index of boldness. The higher q is, the more relative importance is attached to informational value as compared to avoidance of error. The inquirer who attaches more importance to settling unsettled issues is bold. The inquirer setting great store on avoiding error is cautious. q is, therefore, an index of degree of boldness.

If q is no greater than 1, potential expansion into inconsistency is never recommended.

Clearly if $q = \infty$, contradiction must be optimal. But that is because $\alpha = 0$ and no weight is assigned the desideratum of avoiding error.

However, if q is finite but greater than 1, we cannot guarantee that inductive expansion avoids self contradiction. If $\alpha < 0.5, q > 1$. Given the epistemic utility function representing the aim of obtaining new error free information at the given level q, there may be some credal probability distributions of $\underline{U}_K$ relative to which consistent expansions will be recommended. However, relative to other credal probability distributions inconsistent expansion will be recommended. And this circumstance suggests that the goal embodied in such a utility function does not exhibit a sufficient concern to shun error to guarantee against expansion into inconsistency.

Consider, for example, the thousand ticket lottery. Assume $\underline{U}_K$ consists of all sentences of the form 'ticket i will win' and that each such hypothesis x carries an informational value determining probability $N(x)$ of $.001$. An element of $\underline{U}_K$ will be rejected if and only if its credal probability $P(x) < .001q$. If $1{,}000 > q > 1$, there will be credal probability distributions relative to which some element of $\underline{U}_K$ goes unrejected (e.g. where some element receives a credal probability sufficiently close to 1 to be greater than or equal to . 001q. But there will be others relative to which, all elements of $\underline{U}_K$ should be rejected and contradiction recommended.

Hence, seeking new error free informational value will not preclude rationally expanding into inconsistency as it should unless inquirers do not assign q a value larger than 1. That is to say α must be at least as great as $1 - \alpha$.

This constraint on boldness can be derived from the following requirement:

> *Truth over Error Condition:* No potential expansion that imports error can then be ranked better than any potential expansion that avoids error.

An inquirer concerned to obtain new error free information, as I understand it, is not only promoting a weighted average of the utility of truth with a utility of informational value but is doing so in a manner that satisfies the Truth over Error Condition. This requires that q be no greater than 1.

Maximizing expected epistemic utility so understood and using the rule for ties implies that expansion into inconsistency will be precluded no matter what credal probability over $\underline{U}_K$ is adopted.

2.10 Ratio rejection

It may be tempting to suggest another way to supplement maximizing an expected utility representing a trade off between shunning error and seeking new information that also avoids inductive expansion into inconsistency.

> *Avoidance of Incoherence Constraint:* Given the credal distribution over P, restrict values of q to those that avoid inconsistency when P is used to compute expected utility.

Return to the thousand ticket lottery. When P assigns all elements of the ultimate partition equal credal probability of 0. 001 and assigns all such elements the same N-values as well, assigning q a value greater than 1 leads to contradiction. But suppose that all elements but one received a P-value of 0.0005 and one element received a P-value of 0.501. As long as q is less than 501, no contradiction will ensue. So relative to that credal probability distribution and the equal N-distribution, q is allowed to take values up to 501.

The idea can be reformulated as follows. Consider any element x of $\underline{U}_K$ for which $P(x)/N(x)$ is a maximum and call it x^*. Let $b = q[P(x^*)/N(x^*)]$ where q is restricted to values between 0 and 1 but b is allowed to take all nonnegative finite values. Then using the inductive rejection rule cannot lead to expansion into inconsistency.

Notice that now we appear to have two indices that increase with increasing boldness or willingness to risk error in rejecting elements of $\underline{U}_K$. The index of boldness q used previously had two properties that are not separated. The index had values confined to a finite interval (stipulated to be the interval between 0 and 1). It also was set equal to $(1 - \alpha)/\alpha$. The index $b = (1 - \alpha)/\alpha[P(x^*)/N(x^*)]$ reflects the relative weight α attached to avoiding error as compared to obtaining new information. But b itself is now made to depend on two other factors: A second index of boldness q and a factor $P(x^*)/N(x^*)$ itself partially determined by the agent's state of credal probability judgment. q, therefore, reflects that aspect of the degree of boldness exercised that is independent of X's credal probability judgment..

In effect, when supplemented by the avoidance of incoherence constraint and the rule for ties, maximizing the expected V-function leads to the adoption of the following rule:

Ratio inductive rejection rule:

An element x of $\underline{U}_K$ is to be rejected if and only if

$$P(x)/N(x) < q[P(x*)/N(x*)].$$

That is to say, x is to be rejected if and only if

$$[P(x)/N(x)]/[P(x*)/N(x*)] < q.$$

The avoidance of incoherence constraint implies that the inquirer's trade off between avoidance of error and informational value depends on the inquirer's credal probability judgment. But the goals and, hence, epistemic utility function of the inquirer ought to be specifiable independent of his or her current credal probability function. For this reason, the constraint seems unacceptable.

Of course, the inquirer can sometimes have good reason to alter his values. Inquirer X might modify the demands for explanation associated with X's research program and, hence, modify the N-function. But how bold X is should not depend on X's credal state.

2.11 Stability

The ratio rejection rule does appear to have one benefit. It allows for obtaining stronger potential answers to given questions given q and the credal probability P than the inductive rejection rule does.

The benefits are not as grand as they seem. If one adopts the truth over error constraint on the inductive expansion rule, the result of applying the rule will be an inductive expansion $\underline{K}^i$ of K. $\underline{U}_{ki}$ is a subset of $\underline{U}_K$. The inductive expansion rule can be reapplied relative to the updated probability $P(x/\underline{K}^i)$ and the same index q. Either no new elements of $\underline{U}_K$ will be rejected or some will. If the latter happens, repeat again. Because $\underline{U}_K$ is finite, so we are supposing, the process has to eventually stop with a definite conclusion. Relative to the initial $\underline{K}$ and $\underline{U}_K$, this conclusion is the stable inductive expansion.

Given that inductive expansion involves changing from one state of full belief to another which may then be used as the 'evidence' for further inquiries, there can be no objection to iterating inductive rejection rules in the manner indicated if single stage induction is legitimate as I have assumed.

> Moreover, the net effect of such iterated inductive expansion can also be formulated:
>
> $\sum_A P/\sum_A N$ is the ratio of the sum of the P-values and the sum of the N-values of all elements of the subset $\underline{A}$ of $\underline{U}_K$.
>
> $\underline{A}$ is a stable subset of $\underline{U}_K$ at level of boldness $q(0 < q \leq 1)$ if and only if $\underline{A}$ a subset of $\underline{U}_K$ such that every element x of A satisfies the following conditions:
>
> **(a)** $P(x)/N(x) \geq q$
>
> **(b)** $\{P(x)/N(x)\}/\{\sum_A P/\sum_A N)\} \geq q$.

Given that $\underline{U}_K$ is finite, there will be at most finitely many stable subsets of $\underline{U}_K$ at level q. The union of all of them is itself such a set and is the largest such set.

> *Stable inductive rejection rule*: Let $\underline{S}$ be the largest stable subset of $\underline{U}_K$ at level q. Reject an element x of $\underline{U}_K$ if and only if the following condition is satisfied:

$$\{P(x)/N(x)\}/\{\sum_S P/\sum_S N\} < q$$

When $q = 1$, the stable inductive rejection rule and the ratio inductive rejection rule are equivalent. They both recommend rejecting all elements of $\underline{U}_K$ except those carrying maximum value for which $P(x)/N(x)$ is a maximum.

When $q < 1, \sum_S P/\sum_S N \leq P(x^*)/N(x^*)$. As a consequence, the stable inductive rejection rule tends to reject fewer elements of $\underline{U}_K$ than the ratio inductive rejection rule does for a given q. But the conjectures it does eliminate are rejected according to principled decision theoretic procedures. When the inquirer is very bold, the two procedures tend to resemble one another so that whatever advantage the ratio rejection rule may allegedly possess seems negligible. And when more caution is exercised, the stable rule is less bold than the ratio rule.

The stable inductive rejection rule, like the ratio inductive rejection rule, can be represented as a weighted average of the T and the C functions where the weight depends on the agent's credal state. The ratio inductive rejection rule is found wanting because because the weighting procedure depends on the probabilities assigned the highest probabilities assigned elements of $\underline{U}_K$. Why is this a defect in the ratio inductive rejection rule but not in the stable inductive rejection rule?

Inquirers concerned to obtain new error free information may quite legitimately iterate application of the inductive rejection rule to a fixed point so that they are, in effect, using the stable inductive rejection rule. This rule does not yield as strong conclusions as the ratio rejection rule except in the case of the maximally bold inquirer.

But the stronger conclusions yielded by the ratio rejection rules are derived using a step that is suspect from a decision theoretic point of view. The inquirer is obliged to alter his epistemic utility function by changing the relative importance attached to the concern to avoid error and the informational value to be obtained depending on the credal probability distribution over the hypotheses in $\underline{U}_K$. This alteration is reflected in the presence of two boldness parameters: the parameter q specified independently of the credal probability distribution and the parameter b that is a function of q and $P(x^*)/N(x^*)$ and represents the relative importance assigned to avoidance of error and the demand for new informational value. Since x^* is the element of $\underline{U}_K$ carrying the highest P/N - ratio, the value of b is partially determined by the credal probability distribution..

Defenders of the ratio rejection rule may deny that it must be rationalized in the manner to which I object. It can also be rationalized by iteration of the inductive rejection rule.

This claim is, indeed, true. For example, one may use the stable inductive rejection rule at given level q. If it does not yield the result favored by the ratio rejection rule, iterate again but with an increased degree of boldness q' sufficient to obtain the desired result. There are other ways to proceed as well. But no matter what sequence of iterations is used, at least one iteration step will require appeal to a different value for the index q than the others. Moreover, the index of boldness will have to be varied in ways depending on the credal probability distribution initially adopted over $\underline{U}_K$.

The rationale for introducing the stable inductive rejection rule depended on the notion that all iterations of the inductive rejection rule were relative to the same goal—i.e., the same weighting of the concern to avoid error and to promote informational value. If the inquirer adjusts his cognitive goals in order to obtain a rule (like the ratio rejection rule), we may reasonably say that the cognitive goals are subordinated to the specific rule rather than the other way around. Rationalizations of the ratio rejection rule derived from iterated applications of the inductive rejection rule using diverse values of q are no more acceptable than is the rationalization of the ratio rejection rule initially considered.

By way of contrast, the stable inductive rejection rule can be rationalized as the product of iterating the inductive rejection rule with fixed index of boldness q. The inquirer who uses the stable inductive rule can be seen to aim at the same cognitive goal throughout the process of iteration.

3 CAUTION DEPENDENT FAMILIES OF DEDUCTIVELY COGENT AND PARTITION SENSITIVE INDUCTIVE EXPANSION RULES

3.1 Scoring procedures and inductive expansion rules

From the pragmatist perspective to which I gestured previously, the inductive rejection rule appears to be well suited for use in giving an account of inductive expansion. One of its virtues is that it provides a clear link between probability and inductive expansion or ampliative inference. There is a substantial literature focused on discussing the relation between probability and acceptance; but most of it fails to provide an account of expansion from one state of full belief to another or from one deductively closed theory to another.

The proposal is far from perfect. In particular, it presupposes the use of cardinal epistemic utility functions and numerically determinate credal probability functions. This presupposition should be removed. Attention to this issue, however, will be postponed until later in this discussion.

Inductive or ampliative inference seems to exhibit some formal features of deductive inference but to lack others. Deduction is monotonic, for example, in the sense that adding a premiss to the premisses of a valid deductive argument does not undermine the argument. Induction is notoriously nonmonotonic. But then again so is suppositional or hypothetical reasoning. The question arises as to precisely what are the respects in which ampliative reasoning resembles deductive reasoning, the respects in which it resembles suppositional reasoning and the respects in which it resembles neither.

In what follows I wish to explore the extent to which conclusions about important structural features of induction can be sustained on weak assumptions about ampliative reasoning and to what extent appeal to the inductive rejection rule is essential.

Inductive expansion yields a rejection set $\underline{R}$ relative to $\underline{K}$ and $\underline{V}$ or $\underline{K}$ and $\underline{U}_K$ from a menu of potential expansions. In the previous discussion, we have constructed a method of evaluating rejection sets in terms of an index to be maximized—expected epistemic utility. This yielded an inductive rejection rule (or the stable inductive rejection rule) that specified a way of identifying the recommended rejection set by specifying a necessary and sufficient condition for being in the recommended rejection set $\underline{R}$.

The necessary and sufficient condition stated that the elements of $\underline{U}_K$ are to be rejected if and only if they fail to make passing a grade.with respect to a scoring measure. Elements of $\underline{U}_K$ are thus compared to examinations. Those that receive a failing grade go into $\underline{R}$. The recommended expansion advises adding the disjunction of the passing elements (or conjunction of the negations of the failing elements) to $\underline{K}$ and taking the deductive consequences. I wish, for the present, to focus on this aspect of our inductive rejection rules.

> A *scoring function* relative to $\underline{K}$ and $\underline{V}$ is a real valued function $S_{K,V}(u)$ of elements of $\underline{U}_K$ determined by $\underline{K}$ and $\underline{V}$.

A *scoring procedure* $S(u/K, V) = S_{K,V}(u)$ is a function from potential corpora or belief sets and basic partitions to scoring functions such that when $u, u' \in \underline{U}_K \subseteq \underline{U}_{K'}$, $S(u/K, V) \leq S(u'/K, V)$ iff $S(u/K', V) \leq S(u'/K', V)$.

A *score based inductive expansion rule* $R_q(\underline{K}, \underline{V}, S)$ is a function from triples $< \underline{K}, \underline{V}, S >$ to rejection subsets of $\underline{U}_K$. The rejection subset $\underline{R}$ is the set of elements of u in $\underline{U}_K$ such that $S(u/K, V) < q$.

By definition, a score based inductive expansion rule results in a deductively closed theory or corpus in $\underline{L}$. If in addition, if the rule never yields an inconsistent expansion when $\underline{K}$ is consistent and $\underline{V}$ is nonempty, the rule is *deductively cogent.*

$R_q(\underline{K}, \underline{V}, S)$ is *deductively cogent* if and only if for every consistent $\underline{K}$ and nonempty $\underline{V}$, $R_q(\underline{K}, \underline{V}, S) \subset \underline{U}_K$ where $\underline{U}_K$ is the subset of $\underline{V}$ consistent with $\underline{K}$.

Inductive rejection rules, stable inductive rejection rules and ratio rejection rules are score based inductive expansion rules.

Inductive rejection rule:

$$u \in R_q(\underline{K}, \underline{V}, S) \textit{ iff } S(u/\underline{K}, \underline{V}) = P(u)/N(u) < q.$$

Stable inductive rejection rule:

$$u \in R_q(\underline{K}, \underline{V}, S) \textit{ iff } S(u/K, V) = [P(u)/N(u)]/[\sum_S P/\sum_S N] < q$$

Ratio rejection rule:

$$u \in R_q(\underline{K}, \underline{V}, S) \textit{ iff } S(u/\underline{K}, \underline{V}) = [P(u)/N(u)]/[P(x^*)/N(x^*)] < q.$$

Expansion rules of these three kinds do not exhaust the possibilities. But some other types of inductive expansion rules can be understood as special instances of these. For example, when $\underline{U}_K$ is a set of simple statistical hypotheses, an expansion rule might recommend rejecting an element of the set if its likelihood on the data divided by the maximum likelihood in the set is below some threshold. Such a likelihood ratio rule can be rationalized under certain assumptions as a special case of the ratio rejection rule. An alternative proposal is to recommend rejection of a simple statistical hypothesis if the probability of the data conditional on the hypothesis is low enough. This could be made to look like an inductive rejection rule under suitable assumptions.

I have chosen to consider inductive rejection rules and the stable inductive rejection rules because they have acceptable decision theoretic rationales. The ratio rejection rule lacks an adequate rationale. But it is simple and simulates the stable inductive rejection rule under some circumstances. Because it is desirable to have some viable alternatives to the approaches I favor for purposes of comparison, the ratio rejection rules have been and will continue to be discussed.

3.2 *Partition sensitive inductive expansion rules*

Let $\underline{U}_K$ be the truncation of $\underline{V}$ relative to $\underline{K}$ and let $\underline{U}_{K+e}$ be the truncation of $\underline{V}$ relative to $\underline{K}^+{}_e$. Finally let e entail some nonempty subset of the rejection set $\underline{R}$ according to the score S assigned to elements of $\underline{U}_K$ relative to $\underline{K}$. Thus, the scores assigned elements of $\underline{U}_{K+e}$ according to $S(u/\underline{K}, \underline{V})$ are less than q. Clearly if the elements of $\underline{U}_{K+e}$ relative to $\underline{K}^+{}_e$ receive the same scores relative to $\underline{K}^+{}_e$ as they do relative to $\underline{K}$, the rejection rule R_q will lead to the rejection of all elements of $\underline{U}_{K+e}$ in violation of deductive cogency.

To prevent this possibility, we must modify the scoring function when shifting from $\underline{U}_K$ to U_{K+e}. Deductive cogency requires that the scores assigned by a scoring procedure with a fixed passing score should satisfy the requirement that at least one element of the ultimate partition should have a passing grade at least as great as q. This should be so for every consistent $\underline{K}$ and basic partition $\underline{V}$—i.e., for every ultimate partition $\underline{U}_K$.

In the example given, the change in the value of the scoring function could be attributed to a change in state of full belief. However, there are cases where a change in $\underline{V}$ could be responsible unattended by a change in $\underline{K}$.

The infamous lottery paradox illustrates the point. If $\underline{V}$ consists of the two hypotheses that ticket 1 will win and ticket 1 will not 1, one might reject ‘ticket 1 will not win". If $\underline{V}$ consists of the 1000 hypotheses of the form ‘ticket i will win", a failure to change the score of ‘ticket 1 will win’ will continue to lead to its rejection. But then the same is true for ‘ticket 2 will win’, etc. To avoid inconsistency, the scoring procedure will need to be altered.

Inductive inference is, in this respect, partition sensitive.

3.3 *Caution dependent families of partition sensitive inductive expansion rules*

A family $R(\underline{K}, \underline{V}, S, q)$ of partition sensitive inductive expansion rules is caution (boldness) dependent if and only if

(1) for every rule $R_q(\underline{K}, \underline{V}, \underline{S})$ in the family, $R_q(\underline{K}, \underline{V}, S) = R(\underline{K}, \underline{V}, S, q)$.

(2) there is a degree of boldness q_0 such that for every q such that $q_0 \geq q$ and every coherent $< \underline{K}, \underline{V}, S >$, $R(\underline{K}, \underline{V}, S, q) = \emptyset$.

(3) For every coherent $< \underline{K}, \underline{V}, S >$ and every sentence u representing a cell in $\underline{U}_K$ determined by $\underline{K}$ and $\underline{V}$, there is a threshold level of boldness $q(u)$ such that u fails to be rejected for levels of boldness no greater than $q(u)$ and is rejected for any levels of boldness that are greater if there are such levels.

(4) The scoring procedures that belong to the range of values for the argument S satisfy the following requirement. There is a value q_1 such that for every $\underline{K}$ and $\underline{V}$. either (1) all elements of $\underline{U}_K$ determined by

$\underline{K}$ and $\underline{V}$ have an equal score and $S(u/\underline{K}, \underline{V}) = q_1$ for every u in $\underline{U}_K$ or (2) the elements of $\underline{U}_K$ do not all have an equal score and there is at least one element u of $\underline{U}_K$ such that $S(u/\underline{K}, \underline{V}) < q_1$ and another element u' such that $S(u'/\underline{K}, \underline{V}) \geq q_1$.

In arguing for partition sensitivity, it was noted that deductive cogency requires that if q_1 is set as a passing score, there must be at least one element of $\underline{U}_K$ such that S(u/K,V) is at least as great as q_1.

Observe, however, that if the passing score is set at levels greater than q_1, in cases where the elements of $\underline{U}_K$ carry equal score, deductive cogency will fail. So q_1 is the maximum level of boldness that is guaranteed not to fail deductive cogency. In this sense condition (4) guarantees the existence of a maximum level of boldness.

A caution dependent family of partition sensitive and deductively cogent inductive expansion rules is a *caution dependent family of partition sensitive inductive expansion rules* from which all rules that are so bold as to allow inconsistency for some $\underline{K}$ and $\underline{V}$ are removed. q_1 is the maximum level of boldness allowed in such a family and q_0 is the minimum level.

3.4 Potential surprise and degrees of belief

DEFINITION 1. *of potential surprise* (Levi, [1966; 1967], and [1984, Ch. 14]):

The degree of disbelief (potential surprise, degree of confidence of rejection) that h relative to a deductively cogent, partition sensitive and caution dependent family of inductive expansion rules given $\underline{K}$ and $\underline{V}$ is equal to $d(h) = 1 - q(h)$.

$q(h)$ is the threshold level of boldness for h relative to $\underline{K}$ and $\underline{V}$ as given by (3) of section 3.3.

The degree of belief (degree of confidence of acceptance or degree of belief that (h) is equal to $b(h) = d(\sim h)$.

These definitions guarantee that degrees of disbelief and degrees of belief satisfy the formal requirements laid out by G. L. S. Shackle as early as 1949 in Expectations in Economics and more explicitly in the second edition of 1952.

For sentences in $\underline{L}$ equivalent given $\underline{K}$ to disjunctions of sentences in $\underline{U}_K$ the following are postulates for degrees of disbelief or surprise and for degrees of belief:

POSTULATE 2. *for degree of disbelief:*

$d(h(f) = min[d(h), d(f)]$

If $\underline{K} \vdash \sim h, d(h) = 1$ (maximum in set of values of the d-function.)

Either $d(h) = 0$ (minimum in set of values of d-function) or $d(\sim h) = 0$.

COROLLARY 3. *If* $K \vdash \sim h, d(\sim h) = 0$.

POSTULATE 4. *for degree of belief:*

$b(h(f) = min[b(h), b(f)]$

If $K \vdash \sim h, b(\sim h) = 1$

Either $b(h) = 0$ or $b(\sim h) = 0$.

COROLLARY 5. *If* $K \vdash \sim h, b(h) = 0$.

Neither Shackle nor any of the reinventors of Shackle's idea (these include, L. Zadeh, L. J. Cohen, W. Spohn, D. Dubois and H. Prade, P. Gärdenfors and D. Makinson among others) with the exception of Cohen and myself attempted to supply an interpretation in terms of other ideas. It is all very well to speak of degrees of belief and disbelief, expectations, grades of possibility and impossibility and the like; but since probabilists can do the same and can offer an account of how their notions connect with other ideas (utility, preference, choice), it is strongly desirable to offer more than rhetorical flourishes in the way of an explanation of the intended applications of these ideas.

Appeal to caution dependent families of deductively cogent and partition sensitive inductive expansion rules contribute to explaining the intended applications. It becomes relevant to ask which kinds of families of rules should be adopted.

We can derive a caution dependent families of deductively cogent and partition sensitive expansion rules from a given potential corpus $\underline{K}$, ultimate partition $\underline{U}_K$, and degree of belief function. The rules have the following form:

> Surprise based inductive rejection rule: Reject an element u of $\underline{U}_K$ if and only if $d(u) > c$. $(0 \leq c < 1)$.

This rule is a satisficing criterion. c is the degree of caution and equals $1 - q$ where $q =$ the degree of boldness. So the rule says that u is to be rejected if $q(u) < q$ where $q(u)$ is the threshold level boldness as defined in clause (3) of the definition of a caution dependent family of expansion rules in section 3.3. And it infallibly delivers a caution dependent family of deductively cogent and partition sensitive expansion rules.

Unfortunately surprise based inductive rejection rules are of little use unless the d-function representing potential surprise can be derived from rejection rules where surprise is not taken as a primitive notion. To be sure, it is important to appreciate that potential surprise retains its salient structural features independently of the particular caution dependent family of deductively cogent and partition sensitive rules used to derive the measure of surprise. But surprise based rules are no substitute for rules that link rejection with informational value and risk of error or subjective probability.

On the other hand, which caution dependent family of deductively cogent and partition sensitive rules ought to be used to derive assessment of potential surprise may remain a matter of controversy. It is important to appreciate that no matter whether we adopt inductive rejection rules, stable inductive rejection rules, ratio rejection rules or some other caution dependent family of deductively cogent and partition sensitive expansion rules, the structure of measures of potential surprise and degree of belief remain as just specified.

Caution dependent family of deductively cogent and partition sensitive inductive expansion rules do more than define degrees of belief and potential surprise. They can be used to define certain transformations of potential belief states into other potential belief states or transformations of potential corpora into other potential corpora. We may explore the merits of different families by exploring the properties of the transformations they characterize. In this way, the study of such families can be brought into relation with the work done by Alchourrón, Gärdenfors and Makinson [1985].

4 INDUCTIVELY EXTENDED EXPANSION

4.1 *Inductively extended expansion and revision*

$R_q(\underline{B}, \underline{V}, S)$ is a function from a consistent potential corpus $\underline{B}$ and ultimate partition $\underline{U}_B$ relative to fixed $\underline{V}, S, q$ to a rejection set. The closure of $\underline{B}$ and the negations of the elements of this rejection set is another corpus $\underline{B}^i$ @ $R_q < \underline{B}\ \underline{V}, S >$ abbreviated as $\underline{B}^i$ when the context is clear. So inductive expansion rules define transformations of potential corpora into other corpora.

The justly celebrated paper of Alchourrón, Gärdenfors and Makinson [1985] has opened up the study of various kinds of transformations of belief states relevant to giving accounts of belief change and suppositional reasoning. Transformations of the kind just described are worth investigating.

DEFINITION 6. $\underline{B}^i$@ $R_q < \underline{B}, \underline{V}, S >$ is the *inductive expansion of* $\underline{B}$ *relative to* $R_q < \underline{B}, \underline{V}, S >$ by rejecting those elements of $\underline{U}_B$ that are recommended for rejection according to $R_q < \underline{B}, \underline{V}, S >$.

This definition is equivalent to stipulating that x is in $\underline{B}^i$ if and only if $b(h)$ (the degree of belief of x relative to $\underline{B}$) is greater than $1 - q$.

DEFINITION 7. The *inductively extended expansion* $\underline{B}^{+i}{}_h$ of $\underline{B}$ by adding h (relative to $\underline{B}\ \underline{V}, S$ *and* q) is the inductive expansion $[\underline{B}^+{}_h]^i$ of $\underline{B}^+{}_h$ (relative to $R_q < \underline{B}^+{}_h, \underline{V}, S >$).

DEFINITION 8. The *inductively extended AGM revision* $\underline{B}^{*i}{}_h$ of $\underline{B}$ by adding h (relative to $\underline{B}\ \underline{V}, S$ *and* q) is the inductive expansion $[\underline{B}^*{}_h]^i$ of $\underline{B}^*{}_h$ (relative to $R_q < \underline{B}^*{}_h, \underline{V}, S >$).

In Fuhrmann and Levi attention to inductively extended revisions with a special focus on the 'open' case where neither h nor $\sim h$ is in $\underline{B}$. In those special cases, of course, inductively extended revision is equivalent to inductively extended expansion because in those cases AGM revision is identical with AGM expansion. We did not make explicit use of inductive expansion rules or of caution dependent families of such rules. But we did introduce the idea of an inductively extended Ramsey test for the acceptability of inductively extended conditionals and a corresponding interpretation of inductively extended nonmonotonic implication in terms of inductively extended revision. Here is a sketch of the approach making explicit mention of caution dependent families of inductive expansion rules.

Positive Inductively Extended AGM Revision based Ramsey Test:

$$h \rhd f \ @ < \underline{B}\, \underline{V}, S, q > \text{ iff } f \text{ is in } B_h^{*i} \ @ \ R_q < \underline{B}_h^*\, \underline{V}, S >$$

Inductively Extended implication:

$$h \mid\!\sim f \ @ < \underline{B}\, \underline{V}, S, q > \text{ iff } f \text{ is in } B_h^{*i} \ @ < R_q < \underline{B}_h^*, \underline{V}, S >.$$

Fuhrmann and Levi [1994] showed by appeal to counterinstances that inductively extended implications fail restricted weakening or rational monotony as well as a no undercutting principle. Inductively extended implication is clearly nonmonotonic. In this discussion, attention will be focused on inductively extended revisions of $\underline{B}$ where h is consistent with $\underline{B}$. These are, of course, inductively extended expansions.

Makinson and Gärdenfors [1993] had already approached similar issues in the following manner. They took the view that beliefs can be represented by an ordering of hypotheses with respect to 'expectation'. It is clear from their work that degrees of expectation can be represented by Shackle degree of belief measures. Items that are fully believed get maximum b-value. Let us say they belong to $\underline{B}$ although Gärdenfors and Makinson offer no explicit characterization of this set of (linguistically expressed) beliefs. Instead, they consider the set $\underline{K}$ of all sentences that are expected or believd to some positive degree.

The set $\underline{K}$ is an expansion of $\underline{B}$ and, indeed, an inductive expansion utilizing the surprise based rejection rule when $c = 1 - q = 0$. In effect this is urging inductive expansion with maximum boldness. $\underline{K} = \underline{B}^i$ where the transformation is defined with reference to a maximally bold inductive expansion rule in a caution dependent family.

Let h be a sentence consistent with $\underline{B}$. Gärdenfors and Makinson take the view that if datum h is added to the store of information, $\underline{K}$ should be transformed to $\underline{K}^*{}_h$ where * is the AGM revision transformation. This recommendation holds so it seems whether h is added to $\underline{B}$ first and then an inductive expansion is done so that the result is $[\underline{B}^+{}_h]^i$ or the inductive expansion is performed on $\underline{B}$ first to form $\underline{B}^i = \underline{K}$ and the result is then AGM-revised by adding h. Presumably the two procedures are supposed to be equivalent: $[\underline{B}^+{}_h]^i = [\underline{B}^i]^*{}_h = \underline{K}^*{}_h$.

Assuming maximum boldness is deployed, the inductive rejection rule does not yield this identity; but both the stable inductive rejection rule and the ratio rejection rule do.

When $q < 1$, neither the stable inductive rejection rule nor the ratio rejection rule yields the identity tacitly assumed by Gärdenfors and Makinson.

I shall argue that adopting $q = 1$ with either the stable inductive rejection rule or the ratio rejection rule leads to dubious recommendations from a presystematic point of view. One should not be maximally bold.

This means the Gärdenfors - Makinson approach should be reconsidered and the properties of inductively extended expansion and revision examined when $q < 1$.

4.2 *Ampliativity, nonmonotonicity and permutability*

All deductively cogent and partition sensitive inductive expansion rules satisfy the following condition whether they are embedded in a caution dependent family or not:

Ampliativity: For all $\underline{K}$, $\underline{K} \subseteq \underline{K}^i$ and for some consistent $\underline{K}$, $\underline{K} \subset \underline{K}^i$.

Let specific values be assigned to $\underline{V}$, q and S so that $R_q < \underline{B}\ \underline{V}, S >$ is a single deductively cogent inductive expansion rule. Given $\underline{B}$ and h, ${\underline{B}^{+i}}_h$ is defined by that rule. Replace ${\underline{K}^*}_h$ in the AGM postulates for revision by ${\underline{B}^{+i}}_h$.. Call the resulting version of (K^*x), $(K + ix)$ where x is the number of the AGM postulate in the standard listing.

OBSERVATION 9. $(K + i1)$, $(K + i2)$, $(K + i4)$, $(K + i5)$ and $(K + i6)$ hold for any consistent $\underline{B}$, and h consistent with $\underline{B}$.[6]

OBSERVATION 10. $(K + i3)$ asserting that ${\underline{K}^{+i}}_h \subseteq {\underline{K}^+}_h$ in general fails.[7]

OBSERVATION 11. $+i$ is nonmonotonic.[8]

COROLLARY 12. *$+i$ is conjunctively nonmonotonic. That is to say. ${\underline{B}^{+i}}_h$ need not be a subset of ${\underline{B}^{+i}}_{h\&f}$.*

We have obtained the nonmonotonicity of any inductive expansion from its ampliativity. In particular, if we look at the inductively extended implication relation specified in 4. 1, it is a nonmonotonic implication or consequence relation.

It is well known, of course, that the AGM revision of a corpus which satisfies the postulates $(K^*1) - (K^*8)$ can also be used to define a nonmonotonic implication. The question arises concerning the relation between the nonmonotonic implication determined by AGM revision * and inductively extended expansion $+i$.

[6] For any h and consistent $\underline{K}$, $(K + i1){\underline{K}^{+i}}_h$ is a corpus. $(K + i2)$: $h \in {\underline{K}^{+i}}_h$. $(K + i4)$ If $\sim h \notin \underline{K}$, ${\underline{K}^+}_h \subseteq {\underline{K}^{+i}}_h$. $(K + i5){\underline{K}^{+i}}_h$ is inconsistent iff $\vdash\sim h$. $(K + i6)$: If $\vdash h \equiv h$', then ${\underline{K}^{+i}}_h = {\underline{K}^{+i}}_h$.

Proof for $(K + i4)$. We have restricted h in ${\underline{B}^{+i}}_h$ to sentences consistent with $\underline{B}$. The inductive expansion operator is ampliative so that ${B^+}_h \subseteq {\underline{B}^{+i}}_h$.

[7] Proof: Obvious from ampliativity.

[8] That is to say, even though $\underline{H} \subseteq \underline{J}$, ${\underline{H}^{+i}}_h$ may not be a subset of ${\underline{J}^{+i}}_h$.

Proof: By ampliativity for some $\underline{B}$, $\underline{B} \subset \underline{B}^i$. There is an h in $\underline{B}^i$ such that neither h nor $\sim h$ is in $\underline{B}$. ${\underline{B}^+}_{\sim h}$ is consistent and, hence, ${\underline{B}^{+i}}_{\sim h}$ is well defined and consistent. Let $\underline{H} = \underline{B}$ and $\underline{J} = {\underline{B}^+}_{\sim h}$. $\underline{B}^i$ is not a subset of ${\underline{B}^{+i}}_{\sim h}$ in violation of monotonicity.

The next set of questions concerns the status of the substitution instances of $(K^*7), (K^*8)$.

DEFINITION 13. $R_q < \underline{B}\ \underline{V}, S >$ satisfies the importability property iff for every consistent $\underline{B}$ and consistent h, $\underline{B}^{+i}{}_h \subseteq [\underline{B}^i]^+{}_h$.

DEFINITION 14. $R_q < \underline{B}\ \underline{V}, S >$ satisfies the exportability property iff for every consistent $\underline{B}$ and h consistent with $\underline{B}^i$, $[\underline{B}^i]^+{}_h \subseteq \underline{B}^{+i}{}_h$.

DEFINITION 15. $R_q < \underline{B}\ \underline{V}, S >$ is permutable iff it is both importable and exportable that is to say, if and only if for every consistent $\underline{B}$ and h consistent with $\underline{B}$, $[\underline{B}^i]^+{}_h = \underline{B}^{+i}{}_h$.

OBSERVATION 16. $R_q < \underline{B}\ \underline{V}, S >$ is importable iff $\underline{B}^{*i}{}_h \subseteq [\underline{B}^i]^+{}_h$.[9]

OBSERVATION 17. $R_q < \underline{B}\ \underline{V}, S >$ is importable iff $(K + i7)$ asserting that $\underline{B}^{+i}{}_{h\wedge f} \subseteq [\underline{B}^{+i}{}_h]^+{}_f$ holds.[10]

OBSERVATION 18. $R_q < \underline{B}\ \underline{V}, S >$ is exportable iff $(K + i8)$ holds.[11]

OBSERVATION 19. $R_q < \underline{B}\ \underline{V}, S >$ is permutable iff both $(K+i7)$ and $(K+i8)$ hold.

If $+i$ is, indeed, permutable, it is easily seen that $[\underline{B}^{+i}{}_h] = [\underline{B}^i]^+{}_h$ if h is consistent with $\underline{B}^i$. If it is not so consistent, we can still say $[\underline{B}^{+i}{}_h] = [\underline{B}^i]^*{}_h$ as Gärdenfors and Makinson seem to require provided that the 'entrenchment' relation relevant to contraction removing $\sim h$ from $\underline{B}^i$ is the same as the expectation ordering that enabled derivation of $\underline{B}^i$ in the first place. If these conditions hold, $(K + i3)$ which fails because of the ampliativity of inductive expansion may be replaced by the following inductively extended version of $(K + i3)$.

$$(K + i3m) \quad \underline{B}^{+i}{}_h \subseteq (\underline{B}^i)^+{}_h.$$

Thus, given the two conditions just mentioned, inductive extended expansion of $\underline{B}$ by h can always be equated with AGM revision of $\underline{B}^i$ by h. Inductively extended expansion is, in this sense reducible to AGM revision.

Neither permutability nor the equivalence of entrenchment and expectation orderings should hold in general. It is not my concern now to explore the relations between expectation (Shackle degrees of belief) and entrenchment. But I do want to question the requirement of permutability.

[9] *Proof:* By AGM's version of (K^*3) and (K^*4), if h is consistent with $\underline{B}$, $\underline{B}^{*i}{}_h = \underline{B}^{+i}{}_h$. $\underline{B}^{+i}{}_h \subseteq [\underline{B}^i]^+{}_h$ (importability) holds iff $\underline{B}^{*i}{}_h \subseteq [\underline{B}^i]^+{}_h$. The thesis holds trivially when h is inconsistent with $\underline{B}$ and, hence, $\underline{B}^i$.

[10] $(K + i7)$: $\underline{B}^{+i}{}_{h\wedge f} \subseteq [\underline{B}^{+i}{}_h]^+{}_f$

Proof: $\underline{B}^{+i}{}_{h\wedge f} = [\underline{B}^+{}_h]^{+i}{}_f$ which by importability is a subset of $[\underline{B}^{+i}{}_h]^+{}_f$. Conversely, if $(K + i7)$ holds, then by substituting a logical truth for h, we obtain importability.

[11] $(K + i8)$: If $\sim g$ is not in $\underline{B}^{+i}{}_h$, $[\underline{B}^{+i}{}_h] \subseteq \underline{B}^{+i}{}_{h\wedge g}$.

Proof: If f is consistent with $\underline{B}^{+i}{}_h$, exportability implies that $[\underline{B}^{+i}{}_h]^+{}_f$ is a subset of $\{[\underline{B}^+{}_h]^+{}_f\}^i$ as $(K + i8)$ requires. The converse is obtainable by substituting a tautology for h.

None of the caution dependent families of deductively cogent and partition sensitive families of inductive expansion rules underwrite permutability except under very special circumstances. And these special circumstances ought not to be mandated as conditions that inquirers should satisfy. If so, one of the requirements tacitly taken for granted by Gärdenfors and Makinson is seriously undermined and with it their effort to assimilate the sort of nonmonotonicity associated with ampliative inference into the nonmonotonicity supported by AGM revision.

4.3 *Inductive expansion via the inductive rejection rule*

Let $\underline{U}_B = \{f \wedge g, f\wedge \sim g, \sim f \wedge g, \sim f\wedge \sim g\}$. Each element of $\underline{U}_B$ carries equal N-value 0.25. The credal probability assignments to these hypotheses are 0.2, 0.65, 0.1 and 0.05 respectively. Let $0.4 < q \leq 0.8$. For all values of q in this range, $f \wedge g$ and $f\wedge\sim g$ survive rejection. The inductive rejection rule recommends that $\underline{B}^i = \underline{B}^+{}_f$. So $[\underline{B}^i]^+{}_f = \underline{B}^i$.

Consider, however, $\underline{B}^+{}_f$. The truncated ultimate partition contains $f \wedge g$ and $f\wedge\sim g$ with probabilities of $\frac{4}{17}$ and $\frac{13}{17}$ respectively. $f \wedge g$ is rejected if and only if $q > \frac{8}{17}$. Hence, for all values of q in the range $\frac{8}{17} < q \leq \frac{8}{10}$, $\underline{B}^{+i}{}_f = [\underline{B}^+{}_f]^i = \underline{B}^+{}_{f\wedge\sim g}$. Hence, $[\underline{B}^i]^+{}_f \subset \underline{B}^{+i}{}_f$. Thus, if one follows the inductive rejection rule for values of q in the stipulated range, importability fails and with it, $(K+i7)$ fails. It is easily possible to adjust the initial distribution over $\underline{U}_B$ so that importability fails even when $q = 1$. For example, the distribution 0.25, 0.65, 0.09, 0.01 will do.

OBSERVATION 20. If the inductive rejection rule determines $R_q < \underline{B}, \underline{V}, S >$, inductively extended expansion fails to be importable.

Suppose that $\underline{B} = \underline{B}'^+{}_h$ so that $\underline{U}_{B'}$ has the four elements of $\underline{U}_B$ each conjoined with h and then with $\sim h$ and with probabilities arranged so that the probability distribution over $\underline{U}_B$ remains as it was relative to $\underline{B}$ in the original example. We may then say that $\sim g$ is in $\underline{B}^{+i}{}_{h\wedge f}$ so that $h \wedge f \mid\!\sim g$. Observe, however, that f is in $\underline{B}^{+i}{}_h$. Hence, we also have, $h \mid\!\sim f$. However, we do not have $h \mid\!\sim g$. In this sense, inductive expansion defined by the inductive rejection rule violates a Cut Condition.

> *Cut:* If f is a member of $\underline{K}^{+i}{}_h$ and g is a member of $\underline{K}^{+i}{}_{h\wedge f}$, then g is in $\underline{K}^{+i}{}_h$.

OBSERVATION 21. If the inductive rejection rule determines $R_q < \underline{K}, \underline{V}, S >$, inductively extended expansion permits violations of *Cut*.

Keeping to our initial example with $0.4 < q \leq 0.67$, $f \wedge g$ and $f\wedge\sim g$ survive rejection relative to $\underline{U}_B$ so that $B^i = \underline{B}^+{}_f$. Hence, $[\underline{B}^i]^+{}_g = \underline{B}^+{}_{f\wedge g}$. Consider the inductive expansion of $\underline{B}^+{}_g$. The truncated ultimate partition contains $f \wedge g$ and $\sim f \wedge g$ with probabilities $\frac{2}{3}$ and $\frac{1}{3}$. For q values no greater than 0.67 (i.e., $\frac{2}{3}$), neither alternative is rejected according to the inductive rejection rule. Hence,

$\underline{B}^{+i}{}_g \subset [\underline{B}^i]^+{}_g$. Since g is consistent with $\underline{B}^i$, the result is in violation of exportability. By suitable adjustments of the figures, examples such as this can be made to show failure of exportability when $q = 1$.

OBSERVATION 22. If the inductive rejection rule determines $R_q < \underline{B}, \underline{V}, S >$, inductively extended expansion fails to be exportable. $(K + i8)$ is violated.

Thus, the inductive rejection rule licenses forms of ampliative and, hence, nonmonotonic reasoning that violate the requirements on inductively extended expansion (and revision) that Gärdenfors and Makinson in effect imposed within the framework of their theory of expectations.

The caution dependent family of deductively cogent and partition sensitive rules characterized as inductive rejection rules have a clear decision theoretic rationalization—something that Gärdenfors and Makinson fail to provide for their rules. Whether, as I think, Gärdenfors and Makinson should provide such a rationalization for their rules or not, they should not impose constraints on nonmonotonic princples that rule out of court a host of rules that do have such a rationalization without further argument.

As I have already indicated, rules belonging to the inductive rejection family ought to be used in inductive reasoning; but because these rules do not yield stable results, we are entitled to reiterate the rules until stable conclusions are reached. The stable inductive rejection rules that are the product of such iteration with constant q seem to have acceptable decision theoretic credentials. So we may reasonably ask whether the proposal of Gärdenfors and Makinson that presupposes permutability can be rationalized by appealing to rules in the families of stable inductive rejection rules.

The answer is that when $q = 1$, they can. Otherwise they cannot. We shall now explore this issue in closer detail.

4.4 *Inductive expansion via stable inductive expansion rules*

DEFINITION 23. A score based inductive expansion rule $R_q < \underline{B}, \underline{V}, S >$ is *stable* if and only if the inductively extended expansion transformation satisfies the condition $[\underline{B}^i]^i = \underline{B}^i$ for every consistent $\underline{B}$

OBSERVATION 24. If $R_q < \underline{B}, \underline{V}, S >$ is stable and u is a member both of $\underline{U}_B$ and $\underline{U}_B i$, $S_{q,B,V}(u) = S_{q,\underline{B}^i,\underline{V}}(u)$.

OBSERVATION 25. $+i$ defined by a stable score based inductive expansion rule satisfies Cut.

Proof: Suppose f is in $\underline{B}^{+i}{}_h$ and g is in $\underline{B}^{+i}{}_{h\wedge f}$. The critical case is where $f \wedge \sim g$ is consistent with $\underline{B}^+{}_h$ and $\underline{B}^+{}_{h\wedge f}$. The scores of the elements common to the ultimate partitions relative to both of these corpora must be the same in virtue of Observation 23. Hence, such cells rejected in the inductive expansion $\underline{B}^{+i}{}_h$ of $\underline{B}^+{}_h$ will also be rejected in the inductive expansion $\underline{B}^{+i}{}_{h\wedge f}$ of $\underline{B}^+{}_{h\wedge f}$ and vice versa. The cells entailed by $f\wedge\sim g$ relative to $\underline{B}^{+}{}_{h\wedge f}$ have failing scores and are rejected in the inductive expansion $\underline{B}^{+i}{}_{h\wedge f}$ by hypothesis. Hence, they are rejected in the inductive expansion $\underline{B}^{i}{}_{h}$ so that g is in that expansion. Cut is satisfied.

For the converse, let Cut be satisfied. Let $\underline{B}_{h}^{+i} = \underline{B}_{h\wedge x}^{+}$. Satisfaction of Cut clearly then implies that $\underline{B}_{h\wedge x}^{+i} \subseteq \underline{B}_{h}^{+i}. = \underline{B}_{h\wedge x}^{+}$. Hence, $\underline{B}_{h\wedge x}^{+i} = \underline{B}_{h\wedge x}^{+} = \underline{B}_{h}^{+i}$. So $[\underline{B}_{h\wedge x}^{+i}]^{i} = \underline{B}_{h\wedge x}^{+i}$ and $[\underline{B}^{+i}{}_{h}]^{i} = [\underline{B}_{n}^{+}]^{ii}$. Stability is satisfied..

Observations 23 and 24 are based on properties of stable inductive expansion rules that do not presuppose the more specialized features of stable inductive rejection rules or ratio inductive rejection rules. Observation 25 states that these two latter kinds of rules, indeed, contain specializations of stable score based inductive expansion rules.

OBSERVATION 26. Both stable inductive rejection rules and ratio rejection rules at any positive level of boldness are stable inductive expansion rules and satisfy Cut..

OBSERVATION 27. Let $+i$ be defined by an inductive expansion rule belonging to a caution dependent family of deductively cogent and partition sensitive stable inductive expansion rules. The maximally bold rule in the family has the permutability property.[12]

4.5 *Inductive expansion via stable inductive rejection rules*

According to Observation 26 of Section 4.4, stable inductive rejection rules derived from inductive rejection rules by iteration with constant q are stable inductive expansion rules. When $q = 1$, therefore, stable inductive rejection defines a permutable inductively extended expansion transformation $+i$. This much is established by Observation 27.

In this particular case, we can go somewhat further. If $q = 1$, the largest stable subset $\underline{S}$ of $\underline{U}_B$ (Section 2.10) is such that u is in $\underline{S}$ if and only if for every u' in $\underline{U}_B$, $P(u)/N(u) \geq (P(u')/N(u')$. (See the definition of the scoring procedure

[12]*Proof:* Given $q = q_1$ (that is, 1) and a stable inductive expansion rule, let $\underline{U}_B i$ be the set of unrejected elements of $\underline{U}_B$ when $\underline{B}$ is inductively expanded stably to $\underline{B}^i$. In virtue of stability, $\underline{B}^i = [\underline{B}^i]^i$. Hence, no u in $\underline{U}_B i$ has a score relative to $\underline{B}^i$ less than q_1. By condition (4) on caution dependent rules, the elements of $\underline{U}_B i$ must have the same score relative to $\underline{V}$ and $\underline{B}^i$ and it must be q_1. Let d be any disjunction of elements of a subset of $\underline{U}_B{}^i$. By the definition of a scoring procedure given in 3.1, the elements of $\underline{U}_B{}^i$ that are disjuncts in d must have equal scores relative to $\underline{V}$ and $\underline{B}^{+}{}_d = [\underline{B}^i]^{+}{}_d$. Relative to $\underline{B}^{+}{}_d$, that score must be q_1 because of condition (4) on caution dependent rules. So $[\underline{B}^{+}{}_d]^i = \underline{B}^{+}{}_d = [\underline{B}^i]^{+}{}_d$ and permutability is satisfied.

Let f be a disjunction of d with e where e is a disjunction of elements of $\{\underline{U}_B/\underline{U}_B i\}$. By condition (4), the elements of e must carry scores less than q_1 relative to $\underline{B}^{+}{}_f$ and, hence must be rejected whereas the disjunctions in d by the previous argument carry scores equal to q_0 and q_1 unrejected. Hence, $[\underline{B}^{+}f]^i = \underline{B}^{+}{}_d$. But $\underline{B}^{+}{}_d = [\underline{B}^i]^{+}{}_f$ and permutability is once more satisfied. All cases of inductively extended expansion by adding a sentence compatible with $\underline{B}^i$ are of one of these two varieties. Stable inductive expansion rules with maximum boldness yield permutable transformations of corpus.

for a stable inductive rejection rule in Section 3.1.) All elements of $\underline{U}_B$ are rejected except those carrying maximum P/N ratios. All unrejected elements carry a common score of 1. So must the elements of $\underline{U}_B i$ that survive rejection via stable inductive expansion. So the conditions for carrying through the argument of observation 4 of section 4.4 are satisfied.

Consider the case where $q < 1$. I will show that stable inductive rejection rules fail to be permutable in such cases by producing examples of such failure.

EXAMPLE 28. Let $r(x) = x$ is a radical, $f(x) = x$ is a feminist and $b(x) = x$ is a bank teller. Suppose the percentages of individuals in a given population that belong in the eight categories derivable from these predicates are given in the following table:

Table 1.

rfb	$rf\neg b$	$r\neg fb$	$r\neg f\neg b$	$\neg rfb$	$\neg rf\neg b$	$\neg r\neg fb$	$\neg r\neg f\neg b$
2	15	1	2	5	10	10	55

Linda is selected at random from the population so that probabilities of her belonging to these categories equal the given percentages. $\underline{U}_B$ relative to initial $\underline{B}$ consists of the eight hypotheses as to which category Linda belongs. The value of N is $\frac{1}{8}$ for each so that the expected epistemic rule is to reject an element of $\underline{U}_B$ if its probability is less than $\frac{q}{8}$. If one seeks to reiterate rejection, having k unrejected elements relative to an expansion $\underline{K}$ of B, the rule becomes, reject an erstwhile unrejected element if its probability relative to $\underline{K}$ is less than $\frac{q}{k}$.

Given an element x of $\underline{U}_B$, the value of $q(x)$—the maximum value of q at which x goes unrejected—is given in Table 2:

Table 2.

rfb	$rf\neg b$	$r\neg fb$	$r\neg f\neg b$	$\neg rfb$	$\neg rf\neg b$	$\neg r\neg fb$	$\neg r\neg f\neg b$
0.16	1.00	0.08	0.16	0.40	0.80	0.80	1.00

One application of the inductive rejection rule recommends suspense between $rf\neg b$ and $\neg r\neg f\neg b$. The probabilities of these two hypotheses relative to this information are $\frac{3}{14}$ and $\frac{11}{14}$ respectively. Clearly, bookkeeping to stability recommends accepting $\neg r\neg f\neg b$ when $q = 1$ and the rejection level is $\frac{1}{2}$. Hence, if we use the rule for stable expansion derived from bookkeeping, the value of $q(rf\neg b)$ is not equal to 1 as given in Table 2.

One might think the proper value of $q(rf\neg b)$ relative to the stable inductive rejection rules is $\frac{6}{14}$; for then the rejection level when the choice is between this and $\neg r\neg f\neg b$ is $\frac{3}{14}$ where $rf\neg b$ escapes rejection. But this is not so if we start with $\underline{B}$. For at $q = \frac{6}{14}$, the rejection level for the eight element partition is $\frac{3}{56}$ and only $r\neg fb$ is rejected. The rejection level is then $\frac{3}{49}$ and rfb and $r\neg f\neg b$ are added

Table 3.

rfb	$rf\neg b$	$r\neg fb$	$r\neg f\neg b$	$\neg rfb$	$\neg rf\neg b$	$\neg r\neg fb$	$\neg r\neg f\neg b$
0.16	0.44	0.08	0.16	0.26	0.44	0.44	1.00

Table 4.

0.04	0.27	0.02	0.04	0.09	0.18	0.18	1.00

to the heap of the rejected. Now the rejection level is $\frac{6}{70}$ and $\neg rfb$ is rejected. 4 elements of $\underline{U}_B$ remain. Further iteration yields no new rejections at $q = \frac{6}{14}$. Indeed, one can increase q to $\frac{4}{9}$ and still no new elements of $\underline{U}_B$ are rejected. And when q increases beyond that all but $\neg r\neg f\neg b$ get rejected.

The upshot is that $q(rf\neg b)$ relative to the stable expansion rule is $\frac{4}{9}$ as it is for $\neg rf\neg b$ and $\neg r\neg fb$. The full table of $q(x)$ for stable rejection in our example is given in Table 3. For future reference, Table 4 specifies the values of $q(x)$ according to the probability ratio family

Appealing to Tables 2 and 3, use bookkeeping with expected epistemic utility from $\underline{B}$ with $q = .44^+$ to form $\underline{B}^i$ and then expand by adding $h = \neg rf\neg b \vee \neg r\neg f\neg b$. Contrast this with first expanding B by adding h and then making an induction. The result in this case will be $\neg r\neg f\neg b$. The rejection level is $\frac{q}{2} = \frac{.44^+}{2} = .22^+$ whereas the probability of $\neg rf\neg b$ conditional on the disjunction is .15. Exportability is satisfied. Importability is not.

Using the same rules and level of boldness $q = .44$, let the item h' to be added by expansion be $rf\neg b \vee (\neg rfb.\ [\underline{B}^i]^+{}_h$' will be $\underline{B}^+{}_{rf\neg b}$). However, if we perform an inductive expansion on this corpus at the same level of boldness, the rejection level is 0.22 but the conditional probability of $\neg rfb$ is $\frac{1}{4}$. It will not be rejected. Importability is satisfied. Exportability is not.

So iteration to a stable conclusion from $\underline{B}$ at a given level of caution and with the same probability distribution can lead both to violations of importation and of exportation.

OBSERVATION 29. Stable inductive rejection at level of boldness $q < 1$ can lead to violations of importability, exportability and, hence, permutability of $+i$.

We have already established that stable inductive expansion rules satisfy Cut and that when $q = 1$, they must be permutable. When $q < 1$, they fail to be permutable, importable or exportable—provided the stable inductive expansion rules are stable inductive rejection rules.

Let us now turn to ratio rejection rules.

4.6 *Ratio rejection rules*

Like stable inductive rejection rules, ratio rejection rules are stable inductive expansion rules. Moreover, when $q = 1$, as we have noted, the ratio rejection rule and the stable inductive rejection rule are the same and define the same permutable inductively extended expansion transformation $+i$.

Turning to Table 4 in Section 4.5 and using the ratio rejection rules, set q at .27. $\underline{B}^i$ is the expansion of $\underline{B}$ by adding $\neg r\neg f\neg b \vee rf\neg b$. Let h be, as before, the disjunction of $rf\neg b$ and $\neg r\neg f\neg b$. Again let h' be the disjunction of $rf\neg b$ with $\neg rfb$..

$[\underline{B}^+{}_h]^i = \underline{B}^+{}_h$. $[\underline{B}^i]^+{}_h =$ expansion of $\underline{B}$ by adding $\neg r\neg f\neg b$. Importability is satisfied but not exportability.

$[\underline{B}^i]^+{}_{h'} = \underline{B}^+{}_{rf\neg b}$. Now take the inductive expansion of $\underline{B}^+{}_h$' Thus the ratio of the probabilities of the disjuncts are 1 to 3 so that $\neg rf\neg b$ fails to be rejected at $q = .27$ and the inductive expansion is weaker than $\underline{B}^+{}_{rf\neg b}$. Importation is satisfied but exportation fails.

The ratio rejection principle must always satisfy importability. This is obvious when h is inconsistent with $\underline{B}^i$. But it holds when h is consistent as well. Let h be consistent with $\underline{B}^i$. Consider any u in the set of elements of $\underline{U}_K$ consistent both with $\underline{B}^i$ and h.

According to the ratio rejection rule, if u is unrejected relative to $\underline{B}$, it is unrejected relative to $\underline{B}^+{}_h$. The elements of $\underline{U}_B$ carrying maximum P/N-value bear at least as great a P/N-value as the maximum among the elements of $\underline{U}_B$ consistent with h. (Notice that this need not be true for the stable inductive rejection rule for $q < 1$ as our previous examples based on Table 3 illustrate.)

OBSERVATION 30. The inductive expansion transformations $+i$ defined by ratio rejection rules are importable at any level of boldness.

OBSERVATION 31. When $q < 1$, $+i$ defined by ratio rejection rules fails to be exportable and, hence, permutable.

4.7 *Boldness*

Should inquirers be maximally bold? Not if one uses either the inductive rejection rule or the ratio rejection rule with $q = 1$. To see this, consider any case where $\underline{U}_B$ consists of elements all or which are regarded as carrying equal informational value so that $N(u) = \frac{1}{n}$ when $\underline{U}_B$ has n elements. Stable inductive rejection rules and ratio rejection rules agree that when $q = 1$, the inquirer should reject all elements of $\underline{U}_B$ except those carrying maximum probability. This idea seems absurd.

Consider the example of predicting the outcome of a thousand tosses of a coin known to be fair. The agent X is typically interested in what the relative frequency of heads will be so that the ultimate partition consists of 1,001 alternatives each of which specifies a precise relative frequency of heads. Moreover, X will not, in many cases, regard any one of these hypotheses as more informative than any other. They all carry N-value of $\frac{1}{1001}$. The most probable element of the ultimate partition is the hypothesis that the relative frequency is 0.5. Presystematically, however, anyone who predicted that outcome would be regarded as excessively rash. To be sure, a relative frequency of $\frac{1}{2}$ would not be surprising. But relative frequencies close to $\frac{1}{2}$ would not be very surprising either. An appropriately cautious inquirer would not reject these hypotheses but would predict that the coin will land heads with a relative frequency approximately equal to 0.5.

Both the stable inductive rejection rule and the ratio rejection rule used with maximum boldness lead to the dubious prediction that the coin will land heads exactly 50% of the time. Use of stable inductive rejection rules ought not to be blamed for the result. The stable inductive rejection rule has a clear and sensible decision theoretic rationale. It is far better to single out maximum boldness as the culprit..

If this is right, the view advanced by Gärdenfors and Makinson [1993] should be rejected. As I have argued, their view requires that inductively extended expansion, $\underline{B}^{+i}{}_h$ should be equated with AGM revision $[\underline{B}^i]^*{}_h$ by adding h of the inductive expansion of $\underline{B}$. As noted previously, this thesis presupposes (1) the permutability of inductively extended expansion and (2) that the entrenchment used in revision of an inductive expansion should be equated with the Shackle belief measure used in inductive expansion of B. Both of these theses are extremely questionable. In this discussion, I have been arguing against the first. Inductively extended expansion should conform to the stable inductive rejection rule and this rule should be used with less than maximum boldness.

Fuhrmann and Levi [1994] offer counterinstances to conditions that inductively extended expansion ought to satisfy if the approach of Gärdenfors and Makinson [1985] to nonmonotonic reasoning is sound. Intuition mongering, however, is a dangerous practice. I have indulged in it here only when the appeal to presystematic judgment is fairly noncontroversial. I hope that it is so in the case of the prediction of relative frequency of heads in a thousand tosses. But what is noncontroversial is the dubiety of predicting that the coin will land heads exactly 500 times rather than approximately 500 times. Theoretical reflection has been invoked to establish that this judgment conflicts with the Gärdenfors-Makinson view.

Not only has it been shown that using the stable inductive rejection rule with $q = 1$ is unreasonably rash, it has also been shown that using the stable inductive rejection rule with $q < 1$ allows for the violation of importability and exportability as well as principles like so called 'cautious monotony'.

The Cut condition does survive when stable inductive rejection rules are used although it too fails for the one shot application of the inductive rejection rule per se.[13]

[13]Risto Hilpinen [Hilpinen, 1988] took note of the violation of Cut. Hilpinen took this to be an objection to the proposal. I do not think so; a stable family may be obtained by iteration. The rejection levels for elements of the ultimate partition according to the stable family will depend on the probability distribution P over $\underline{U}_B$. But those rejection levels will themselves be derivable via bookkeeping according to a family of rules that is not so dependent and can be given a compelling decision theoretic rational (as in [Levi, 1967], [Levi, 1984], ch. 5).

4.8 *Finale*

Counter to the view I took in ch. 9. 3 of [Levi, 1996], final paragraph, p. 288, importability is satisfied by ratio rejection rules even when $q < 1$. But such rules lack a satisfactory decision theoretic rationale. The stable inductive rejection rules are to be favored over these and such rules violate importability as well as exportability. And for $q < 1$, exportability fails for ratio rejection rules.

So the main conclusions of [Levi, 1996], hold. Given adherence to the decision theoretically grounded inductive rejection rules, without bookkeeping, at no positive level of boldness less than or equal to 1 is any condition on $+i$ satisfied except $(K + i1)$, $(K + i2)$, $(K + i4)$, $(K + i5)$ and $(K + i6)$.

With bookkeeping to stability, Cut may be added. As noted in [Levi, 1996], this forms the basis for a vindication of the properties of default reasoning found in Reiter [1980]. I am grateful to Michael Morreau for having corrected a misinterpretation of Reiter's paper that appeared in [Levi, 1996]. What I had taken to be an improvement on Reiter's proposal was actually implied by Reiter as Morreau [Morreau, 1998] correctly noted.

With stable inductive rejection at $q = 1$, $(K + i7)$ and $(K + i8)$ also hold.

Inductive inference is nonmonotonic because it is ampliative.

Suppositional reasoning is nonmonotonic due to its being belief contravening.

Only if $q = 1$, do these two forms of nonmonotonic reasoning exhibit the same structure.

Two large questions need to be addressed:

(1) How to deal with infinite basic partitions.

(2) When credal probability or epistemic utility (i.e., the informational value determining probability) go indeterminate, how should one proceed?

Both problems are considered in [Levi, 1980] and the first is addressed again in [Levi, 1996]. In the appendix, I shall examine the second issue briefly.

APPENDIX

In the previous discussion, I presupposed that decision makers aiming at seeking information and avoiding error were committed to making numerically determinate credal probability and utility judgments relative to the initial state of full belief B. Not only is this assumption unrealistic in practice it should be so; for rational agents should be entitled to be in doubt concerning their credal probability judgments and their utility judgments. In [Levi, 1974], [Levi, 1980] and [Levi, 1996], I have given an account of credal probability and utility judgment according to which credal probability judgment is represented by a nonempty convex set of probability functions and utility judgment by a convex set of utility functions. Given each 'permissible' probability function in the credal state and each permissible utility function in the set of utility functions, we can determine a permissible expected utility function for the options. An option is E- admissible if and only if it maximizes expected utility according to some permissible expected utility function. Secondary criteria of admissibility can then be invoked to choose among E- admissible options, tertiary criteria can then be introduced etc. Initially I had tended to recommend certain kind of criteria as rational; but soon recognized that the choice of secondary criteria is a substantive value judgment that should not be legislated by principles of rationality.

In [Levi, 1980], I brought this scheme to bear on the question of inductive expansion where the aim is to obtain new error free informational value. Here I had wanted to use as the secondary criterion, the rule for ties that recommends suspension of judgment between E-admissible 'options.

In the special case, where the set of expected epistemic utility functions contains a single member, the rule for ties works very well. It recommends the weakest of the optimal (which will be the E-admissible) options. There is a uniquely weakest such optimal option. When there are several permissible expected epistemic utility functions, matters are somewhat messier. There are indeed many well behaved situations where there is a uniquely weakest E-admissible inductive expansion strategy. But there are situations where this condition fails. An example from Levi [1980] may serve to illustrate the nature of the problem.

EXAMPLE 32. $\underline{U}_K$ contains for elements h_1, h_2, h_3 and h_4. Let the credal state be the convex hull (the set of all weighted averages) of the following pair of probabilities. p_1 assigns probabilities 0.7, 0.2, 0.01 and 0.09 to the four members of $\underline{U}_K$ respectively. p_2 assigns 0.7, 0.01, 0.2 and 0.09 to the same hypotheses. Each element of $\underline{U}_K$ carries an N-value of $\frac{1}{4}$ and $q = 0.5$. The rejection level is therefore, 0.125. h_3 and h_4 are rejected when p_1 is used with the inductive rejection rule. That result maximizes expected epistemic utility according to the corresponding expected utility function. h_2 and h_4 are rejected when p_2 is used. There are weighted averages of these functions that reject all hypotheses in $\underline{U}_K$ but $h1$. So we have identified three E-admissible options. The rule for ties recommends adopting the weakest E-admissible option. But there is no uniquely weakest such option. If the strategy of rejecting h_4 alone were E-admissible, it would qualify. But it is not E-admissible. The best we can say is that there are two weakest E-admissible options and the agent is allowed according to the Rule for Ties to choose either one.

In [Levi, 1980] p.26, I was dissatisfied with this result and thought one should reject only h_4. I bent the general shape of the decision theory I was proposing in order to secure this result. I was convinced by T. Seidenfeld that this approach was not a good idea and have abandoned it.

I now think that the best way to proceed is to look at the result of iterating the inductive rejection rule until stability is reached for each permissible expected epistemic utility and then apply the rule for ties. In our example, this will lead in two iterations to rejecting all elements of $\underline{U}_K$ but h_1 so that there is no need for a rule for ties. In other cases where q is less than 0.5, we will find cases where rejecting h_4 alone is E-admissible as are the options of rejecting h_2 and h_4 and of rejecting h_3 and h_4. Here the rule for ties will recommend rejecting h_4 alone at the first cut. Depending on the level of boldness, this result will be stable or will give way to a stronger result without any need to modify the prescription.

Columbia University

REFERENCES

[Alchourrón *et al.*, 1985] C. Alchourrón, P. Gärdenfors and D. Makinson. On the logic of theory change: partial meet functions for contraction and revision. *Journal of Symbolic Logic*, **50**, 510–530, 1985.

[Bilgrami, 1998] A. Bilgrami. Is Truth a Goal of Inquiry?: Rorty and Davidson on Truth," to be published, 1998.

[Braithwaite, 1953] R. B. Braithwaite. *Scientific Explanation*, Cambridge University Press, Cambridge, 1953.

[Carnap, 1962] R. Carnap. *The Logical Foundations of Probability*, 2nd ed. University of Chicago, Chicago, 1962. (First edition, 1950.)

[Carnap, 1960] R. Carnap. The aim of inductive logic. In *Logic, Methodology and Philosophy of Science*, E. Nagel, P. Suppes and A. Tarski, eds. pp. 302–318. Stanford University Press, 1960.

[Chihara, 1994] C. Chihara. The Howson–Urbach proofs of Bayesian principles. In *Probability and Conditionals*, E. Eells and B. Skyrms, eds. Cambridge University Press, 1994.

[Cohen, 1977] L. J. Cohen. *The Probable and the Provable*, Clarendon Press, Oxford, 1977.

[Cohen and Nagel, 1934] M. R. Cohen and E. Nagel. *Introduction to Logic and Scientific Method*, Harcourt Brace, New York, 1934.

[Davidson, 1998] D. Davidson. *Truth Rehabilitated*, to be published, 1998.

[De Finetti, 1972] B. De Finetti. *On the Axiomatization of Probability Theory, Probability, Induction and Statistics*, Wiley, New York, 1972.

[Fisher, 1959] R. A. Fisher. (1959), *Statistical Methods and Scientific Inference*, 2nd ed. Hafner, New York, 1959.

[Fuhrmann and Levi, 1994] A. Fuhrmann and I. Levi. Undercutting and the Ramsey test for conditionals. *Synthese*, **101**, 157–169, 1994.

[Gärdenfors and Makinson, 1993] P. Gärdenfors and D. Makinson. Nonmontonic inference based on expectations. *Artificial Intelligence*, **65**, 197–246, 1993.

[Hilpinen, 1988] R. Hilpinen. *Rules of Acceptance and Inductive Logic*, North Holland, 1988.

[Harper, 1975] W. Harper. Rational belief change, Popper functions and counterfactuals. *Synthese*, **30**, pt. 2, 1975.

[Jeffrey, 1965] R. C. Jeffrey. *The Logic of Decision*, McGraw Hill, New York, 1965.

[Jeffrey, 1970] R. C. Jeffrey. Dracula meets Wolfman: acceptance vs. partial belief. In *Acceptance, Induction and Partial Belief*, M. Swain, ed. pp. 157–185. Reidel, Dordrecht, 1970.

[Jeffreys, 1961] H. Jeffreys. *Theory of Probability*, 3rd ed. Oxford Univeristy Press. Oxford, 1961.

[Keynes, 1921] J. M. Keynes. *A Treatise on Probability*, MacMillan, London, 1921.

[Kyburg, 1974] H. E. Kyburg. *The Logical Foundations of Statistical Inference*, Reidel, Dordrecht, 1974.

[Levi, 1965] I. Levi. Hacking Salmon on induction. *Journal of Philosophy*, **63**, 481–487, 1965.

[Levi, 1966] I. Levi. On potential surprise. *Ratio*, 107–129, 1966.

[Levi, 1967] I. Levi. , I. (1967), *Gambling with Truth*, Knopf, New York. 1967. (Paperback edition, 1973, MIT Press.)

[Levi, 1974] I. Levi. On indeterminate probabilities. *Journal of Philosophy*, **71**, 391–418, 1974.

[Levi, 1978] I. Levi. Coherence, regularity and conditional probability. *Theory and Decision*, **9**, 1–15, 1978.

[Levi, 1980] I. Levi. *The Enterprise of Knowledge*, The MIT Press, Cambridge, MA, 1980.

[Levi, 1984] I. Levi. *Decisions and Revisions*, Cambridge University Press, Cambridge, 1984.

[Levi, 1989] I. Levi. Possibility and probability. *Erkenntnis*, **31**, 365–386, 1989.

[Levi, 1991] I. Levi. *The Fixation of Belief and Its Undoing*, Cambridge University Press, Cambridge, 1991.

[Levi, 1996] I. Levi. *For The Sake of The Argument*, Cambridge University Press, Cambridge, 1996.

[McGee, 1994] V. McGee. Learning the impossible. In *Probability and Conditionals*, E.Eells and B. Skyrms, eds. Cambridge University Press, Cambridge, 1994.

[Makinson and Gärdenfors, 1991] D. Makinson and P. Gärdenfors. Relations between the logic of theory change and nonmonotonic logic. In *The Logic of Theory Change*, A. Fuhrmann and M. Morreau, eds. pp. 185–205. Springer Verlag, Berlin, 1991.

[Morreau, 1998] M. Morreau. Review of [Levi, 1996], *Journal of Philosophy*, **95**, 540–546, 1998.

[Peirce, 1982] C. S. Peirce. *Writings of C. S. Peirce*, M. Fish *et al.*, eds. Vols. 1–5, Indiana University Press, 1982.

[Popper, 1959] K. Popper. *The Logic of Scientific Discovery*, Hutchinson, London, 1959.

[Ramsey, 1990] F. P. Ramsey. *Philosophical Papers*, D.H. Mellor, ed. Cambridge University Press, Cambridge, 1990.

[Reiter, 1980] R. Reiter. A logic for default reasoning. *Artificial Intelligence*, **13**, 81–132, 1980.

[Rorty, 1998] R. Rorty. Is truth a goal of enquiry? Davidson vs. Wright. *The Philosophical Quarterly*, **45**, 281–300, 1998.

[Seidenfeld, 1979] T. Seidenfeld. *Philosophical Problems of Statistical Inference*, Reidel, Dordrecht, 1979.

[Shackle, 1961] G. L. S. Shackle. *Decision, Order and Time in Human Affairs*, Cambridge University Press, Cambridge, 1961.

[Shimony, 1955] A. Shimony. Coherence and the axioms of confirmation. *Journal of Symbolic Logic*, **20**, 8–20, 1955.

[Spohn, 1988] W. Spohn. A general non-probabilistic theory of inductive reasoning. In *Causation in Decision, Belief Change and Statistics*, W. Harper and B. Skyrms, eds. pp. 105–134. Reidel, Dordrecht, 1988.

KRISTER SEGERBERG

THE BASIC DYNAMIC DOXASTIC LOGIC OF AGM

1 INTRODUCTION

As pointed out by Hans Rott and others, there are two ways of reading AGM, the theory of Alchourrón, Gärdenfors and Makinson presented in a classic paper that has come to be regarded as the *fons et origo* of today's formal study of belief revision [Alchourrón *et al.*, 1985]. Under the "iterative" reading there is room for multiple sequential belief change, but under the "one-shot" reading the perspective is limited to one change. Roughly and informally, the "one-shot" reading recognizes doxastic situations of two kinds. First, there is *status quo*, the (generic but unique) anterior situation. Then a belief change takes place, landing the agent in a posterior situation. And this is the entire scenario! There is no inkling that there could be further belief changes and corresponding post-posterior situations. Iterative theories are richer and more interesting. But as they are more difficult to devise, one might begin by studying one-shot theories (to which from now on we will refer without scare quotes). In this paper, we suggest how one-shot AGM can be rendered within dynamic doxastic logic (DDL). This author's first effort in this area was [Segerberg, 1994a], but only with van Linder, van der Hoek and Meyer [1995] did we get a faithful interpretation of AGM in a DDL language (that is, a model theoretical analysis of Gärdenfors's characterization in [1988] of the three main doxastic operations: expansion, contraction, and revision of belief sets). However, in neither paper was the question of a complete axiomatization of the set of valid formulæ addressed; here, it is.

The paper may be described as an exercise in modal logic. Once again is demonstrated the great versatility of the old canonical model technique that originated with Lemmon and Scott's adaption to modal logic of Henkin's well-known construction (cf. [Segerberg, 1995; Segerberg, to appear]). We begin by going over and slightly extending, in Section 2, work done by David Lewis and Adam Grove, in particular notions of 'sphere system' and 'selection' function [Grove, 1988; Lewis, 1973]. This we do in terms borrowed from topology, an expedient that has been used before in modal logic; see, for example, Hansson [1969] and, more recently, Surendonk [1998]. Section 3 is devoted to syntax and Section 4 to semantics. In Section 5 the completeness proof for our one-shot interpretation of AGM is given in detail, and in Section 6 we outline a completeness proof for an iterative interpretation. (In order to avoid unnecessary technical complication we have limited our study to what might be called the positive fragment of AGM, that is, the part of AGM that deals with expansion and revision; contraction is not considered. Thus when we speak of AGM here, then we are actually speaking of only half of

M.-A. Williams and H. Rott (eds.), Frontiers in Belief Revision, 57–84.

AGM. However, readers who desire an analysis of the entire theory of AGM will not find it difficult to extend the analysis given here.)

2 SOME SET THEORETICAL CONCEPTS

2.1 Topologies

Let U be any nonempty set (referred to as a *universe*). A *topology* in U is a family T of subsets of U satisfying three conditions:

(i) $U \in T$ and $\emptyset \in T$, and

(ii) $\bigcup S \in T$, for all families $S \subseteq T$, and

(iii) $\bigcap S \in T$, for all nonempty finite families $S \subseteq T$.

The structure (U, T) is a *topological space*, but when it is clear what the intended topology is one may refer to U itself as a topological space. The subsets of U that are elements of T are said to be *open* sets; a *closed* set is one that is the complement of an open set. In general, a set need not be either open or closed, but on the other hand some sets are both; we will use the term *clopen* (adjective or noun) for the latter. Notice that the complement of a clopen set is clopen and that U and $\emptyset$ are clopen in any topology. A *base* is a family B of elements of T such that, for every $X \in T$, there is some family $C \subseteq B$ such that $X = \bigcup C$. In other words, B is a base if every open set is the union of elements of B. We shall be particularly interested in topologies in which the set of clopens is a base.

The *closure* of a set $X \subseteq U$, in our symbolism $\mathbf{C}X$, is defined by the condition

$$\mathbf{C}X = \bigcap\{Y \subseteq U : X \subseteq Y \& Y \text{ is closed}\}.$$

It is clear that $\mathbf{C}X$ is the smallest closed set that includes X. Note the following formal properties of $\mathbf{C}$: $\mathbf{C}\emptyset = \emptyset$ and $\mathbf{C}U = U$; for all subsets $X, Y \subseteq U$, $X \subseteq \mathbf{C}X$ and $\mathbf{CC}X = \mathbf{C}X$ and $\mathbf{C}(X \cup Y) = \mathbf{C}X \cup \mathbf{C}Y$; and if $X \subseteq Y$ then $\mathbf{C}X \subseteq \mathbf{C}Y$.

A *cover* of a set $X \subseteq U$ is a nonempty family C of subsets of U such that $X \subseteq \bigcup C$. A cover, every element of which is an open set, is an *open cover*. If C is a cover of X and a family $D \subseteq C$ is also a cover of X, then D is a *subcover* of C of X. A topology T is *compact* if every open cover of the whole space has a finite subcover; a logically equivalent condition is that every family of closed subsets of U whose intersection is empty has a finite subfamily whose intersection is empty. A topology T is *totally separated* if, for any pair of distinct elements of U, one is an element of a clopen set of which the other is not. A *Stone topology* is a topology that is compact and totally separated. (Classical logicians will find it helpful to think of clopen sets in a Stone topology as *propositions*. By Proposition

3 below, closed sets—*theory sets* (Bengt Hanssons's term [1969]) or *theories in the semantic sense*—may be regarded as intersections of propositions.)

LEMMA 1. *In a Stone topology, if X is a closed set and w is a point not in X, then there is a clopen set that includes X but does not contain w.*

Proof. Suppose that X is closed and $w \notin X$. Define

$$S = \{P : P \text{ is clopen } \& \ w \notin P\}.$$

Suppose that $u \in X$. Clearly, $u \neq w$. By the condition of total separation, there is some clopen set containing u but not w; hence $u \in \bigcup S$. This argument shows that

$$X \subseteq \bigcup S.$$

That X is closed implies that $U - X$ is open. Hence $S \cup \{U - X\}$ is an open cover of U. By compactness there is then a finite set $S_0 = \{P_0, \ldots, P_{n\text{-}1}\}$, for some number $n \geq 0$ and some clopen sets $P_0, \ldots, P_{n\text{-}1}$, such that $S_0 \bigcup \{U - X\}$ is a cover of U and, therefore, S_0 a cover of X. Note that $Q = P_0 \bigcup \ldots \bigcup P_{n\text{-}1}$ is clopen. Evidently, $X \subseteq Q$ and $w \notin Q$. ■

LEMMA 2. *Suppose that (U, T) is a Stone topology and that Y is a closed set. Then, for all sets X and Y, $X \subseteq Y$ if and only if, for all clopen sets P, $Y \subseteq P$ only if $X \subseteq P$.*

Proof. We claim that, for any set $X \subseteq U$ and any closed set $Y \subseteq U$,

$$X \subseteq Y \text{iff} \, \forall P(P \text{ is clopen} \Rightarrow (Y \subseteq P \Rightarrow X \subseteq P)).$$

One half of the claim is obviously true. For the other, assume that

$$(*) \qquad \forall P \, (P \text{ is clopen} \Rightarrow (Y \subseteq P \Rightarrow X \subseteq P)).$$

Suppose that $w \notin Y$. By the preceding lemma, there exists a clopen set P such that $Y \subseteq P$ and $w \notin P$. Hence by $(*)$, $X \subseteq P$. Therefore, $w \notin X$. This argument shows that $X \subseteq Y$. ■

PROPOSITION 3. *In a Stone topology, the family of clopen sets is a base.*

Proof. Let (U, T) be a Stone space. The family of clopen sets is of course a family of open sets. Suppose that X is an open set. Then $U - X$ is closed. By Lemma 1, for each point $w \in X$ there is a clopen set Y_w such that $(U - X) \subseteq Y_w$ and $w \notin Y_w$. Hence $(U - X) \subseteq \bigcap\{Y_w : w \in X\}$ and $X \cap \bigcap\{Y_w : w \in X\} = \emptyset$. From this it follows that $(U - X) = \bigcap \{Y_w : w \in X\}$. In other words, $X = \bigcup\{U - Y_w : w \in X\}$. And $U - Y_w$ is open (since it is clopen), for every $w \in X$. ■

For the remainder of this section, let (U, T) be a fixed topological space. If X and Y are subsets of U, we shall refer to the ordered pair (X, Y) as a *complex*.

2.2 *Onions*

An *onion* in (U, T) is a nonempty family O of subsets of U satisfying two conditions:

(i) if $X, Y \in O$ then $X \subseteq Y$ or $Y \subseteq X$,

(ii) for any clopen set P, if $P \cap \bigcup O \neq \emptyset$, then there is a least element $X \in O$ such that $P \cap X \neq \emptyset$ (meaning that, for all $Y \in O$, if $P \cap Y \neq \emptyset$ then $X \subseteq Y$).

We name these conditions, respectively, NESTEDNESS and LIMIT (for 'Limit Assumption'). If all elements of O are closed we say that O is a *closed* onion. By a *Lewis* onion we mean an onion satisfying closure under arbitrary nonempty intersection (AINT) and closure under arbitrary nonempty union (AUNI); that is,

(iii) if $\emptyset \neq C \subseteq O$ then $\bigcap C \in O$,

(iv) if $\emptyset \neq C \subseteq O$ then $\bigcup C \in O$.

An onion is *replete* if

(v) $U \in O$

Note that Lewis onions need not be either closed or replete.

Associated with each onion O is the *belief set* B_O of O and the (*doxastic*) *commitment set* C_O of O defined by the conditions

$$B_O = \bigcap O, \qquad C_O = \bigcup O.$$

The belief set is always an element of O:

LEMMA 4. *For every onion* $O, \bigcap O \in O$.

Proof. First suppose that $\emptyset \in O$. Then $\bigcap O = \emptyset$, so we get the desired result for free. Next suppose that $\emptyset \notin O$. Since O is nonempty by definition, there exists some $X \in O$. Evidently, $X \neq \emptyset$. Hence X intersects U, which of course is clopen. By LIMIT therefore there is a least element $X_0 \in O$. By NESTEDNESS, $X_0 = \bigcap O$, so again the desired result follows. ∎

It is clear that $\bigcap O$ is the smallest element of O. This is often expressed by saying that O is *centred* on $\bigcap O$. The following proposition was pointed out (in conversation) by John Cantwell:

PROPOSITION 5. *Suppose that* (U, T) *is a Stone topology and that* O *is a family of closed subsets of* U *satisfying* NESTEDNESS *and* AINT. *Then* O *also satisfies* LIMIT.

Proof. Suppose that P is a clopen set such that $P \cap \bigcup O \neq \emptyset$. Consider the collection $C = \{S \in O : P \cap S \neq \emptyset\}$; evidently, C is nonempty. Suppose that $P \cap \bigcap C = \emptyset$. Then by compactness there is some $n \geq 0$ and some $S_0, \ldots, S_{n\text{-}1} \in C$ such that $P \cap S_0 \cap \ldots \cap S_{n\text{-}1} = \emptyset$. By NESTEDNESS there is some $k < n$ such that $S_k = S_0 \cap \ldots \cap S_{n\text{-}1}$, whence the absurdity that $P \cap S_k = \emptyset$. Consequently, $P \cap \bigcap C \neq \emptyset$. Moreover, $\bigcap C \in O$ by AINT. ■

There are logical reasons for preferring to work with Stone spaces and philosophical reasons for regarding closed onions as central. In that light, the last result suggests that closed onions are more simply defined as nested families of closed subsets that are closed under arbitrary nonempty intersection. Such a definition has the virtue of avoiding explicit mention of the cumbersome limit condition.

2.3 *Selectors*

We say that a function f from the set of clopen sets into the set $\mathcal{P}U$ of subsets of U is a *selector for* (U, T) if, for all clopen sets P and Q,

(i) $fP \subseteq P$

(ii) $P \subseteq Q \Rightarrow (fP \neq \emptyset \Rightarrow fQ \neq \emptyset)$

(iii) $P \subseteq Q \Rightarrow (P \cap fQ \neq \emptyset \Rightarrow fP = P \cap fQ)$.

We say that f is *trivial* if, for all clopens P, $fP = \emptyset$, otherwise *nontrivial*.

We need mnemonic aids to talk about these things. Call fP the *segment of* P *under* f. For condition (i) INCLUSION is a natural name. Condition (ii) may be said to guarantee a kind of MOnotonicity for NonEmptY Segments; let us use the artificial abbreviation MONEYS for this condition. Condition (iii), finally, is a condition of a kind introduced into the theory of social choice by Kenneth Arrow; so let us refer to it as Arrow's Condition or just ARROW.

Associated with each selector is the *belief set* B_f of f and the *(doxastic) commitment set* C_f of f, defined by the conditions

$$B_f = fU, \qquad C_f = \bigcup\{fP : P \text{ is clopen}\}.$$

2.4 *From selectors to onions*

Let f be a nontrivial selector. Define a subset S of U as a *sphere under* f if

(i) $\forall w \in S\ \exists P(w \in fP)$,

(ii) $\forall P(S \cap P \neq \emptyset \Rightarrow fP \subseteq S)$,

(iii) $S \neq \emptyset$

By (i) and (ii), S has a certain 'all-or-nothing' property: if $S \cap fP \neq \emptyset$, then $fP \subseteq S$. (Notice the strength of (ii): whenever S overlaps any clopen set whatsoever, then the corresponding segment—nonempty!—is completely included in S. Thus S is a nonempty union of segments.)

Define $O_f = \{S \subseteq U : S$ is a sphere under $f\} \cup \{\emptyset$: $fP = \emptyset$, for all $P\}$. (Thus $\emptyset \in O_f$ if and only if, for all P, $fP = \emptyset$. Consequently, $O_f = \{\emptyset\}$ if and only if f is trivial.) Although there are many tedious details to check, the proof of the following result is easy to find with the help of [Lewis, 1973, Section 2.7].

LEMMA 6. *Suppose that f is a selector.*

(i) O_f is a Lewis onion.

(ii) B_f is the smallest sphere under f (and hence $B_{O_f} = B_f$).

(iii) C_f is the largest sphere under f (and hence $C_{O_f} = C_f$).

3 SYNTAX

3.1 Language

The languages of DDL studied in this paper have a denumerable supply of *propositional letters*. Other primitive symbols used here are (a truth-functionally complete set of) *Boolean connectives*, the *doxastic propositional operators* **B** (for 'belief') and **K** (for 'knowledge'), the *doxastic action operators* + ('expansion') and $*$ ('revision'), and the *dynamic operator* [ ] ('after'). It is a virtue of DDL languages that they can easily accommodate further resources in order to express other philosophically important concepts, not only doxastic but also agentive and deontic. Here, however, we have a very limited purpose in mind—the formalization of AGM—and for this a simplified presentation will suffice. We begin with a (too) general definition of 'formula':

1. Propositional letters are *formulæ*.
2. If **o** is an n-ary Boolean connective and $\varphi_0, \ldots, \varphi_{n\text{-}1}$ are *formulæ*, then $\mathbf{o}(\varphi_0, \ldots, \varphi_{n\text{-}1})$ is a *formula*.
3. If φ is a *formula*, then $\mathbf{B}\varphi$ and $\mathbf{K}\varphi$ are *formulæ*.
4. If φ and χ are *formulæ*, then $[+\varphi]\chi$ and $[*\varphi]\chi$ are *formulæ*.
5. Nothing is a *formula* except by virtue of clauses 1-4.

Call expressions of type $[+\varphi]$ and $[*\varphi]$, where φ is a formula, *change operators*. We say that a formula is

- *purely Boolean*, if it consists exclusively of propositional letters and Boolean operators;
- *basic*, if the doxastic operators **B**, **K**, $+$, $*$ operate only on purely Boolean formulæ;
- *static*, if there are no change operators;
- *one-shot*, if there is no nesting of change operators.

The unrestricted language is that of *full* DDL. The fragment of basic (or static, or one-shot) formulæ is called the language of *basic* (or *static*, or *one-shot*) DDL. These conventions extend to combinations. Notice that static DDL is simply ordinary doxastic propositional logic with two primitive doxastic operators (cf. [Segerberg, 1999]). (Purely Boolean DDL would of course be nothing but ordinary classical propositional logic.)

Some examples will illustrate the last few definitions. If P is a propositional letter and therefore a purely Boolean formula (and so *a fortiori* basic, static and one-shot as well), then $\mathrm{P} \wedge \mathbf{B}\mathrm{P}$ is a static formula that is not purely Boolean (even though it is a Boolean combination of two formulæ). $[*\mathrm{P}][*\mathrm{P}]\mathbf{B}\mathrm{P}$ is basic but not one-shot, and $[*\mathbf{B}\mathrm{P}]\mathbf{B}\mathrm{P}$ and $[*\mathrm{P}]\mathbf{B}\mathbf{B}\mathrm{P}$ are one-shot but not basic, while $[*\mathrm{P}]\mathbf{B}\mathrm{P}$ is both basic and one-shot.

A language that permits nesting of change operators is called *iterative*. The distinction one-shot/iterative deserves a comment. What it is for a theory to be one-shot was explained in Section 1. According to such a theory, the agent is initially in an anterior doxastic position; after the belief change, if there is one, he finds himself in a new, posterior position. The question of further change does not arise. Consequently, in a posterior position only static formulæ make sense. It is clear that for a language to be suitable for this kind of theory, formulæ should contain at most one layer of change operators. It is equally clear that for iterative theories such a restriction would be malapropos.

The distinction basic/full also deserves a comment. The difference between basic and full DDL has to do with the distinction between matter and mind or, better, between world and belief. Think of the world as that about which the agent is able to hold beliefs! It is the job of purely Boolean formulæ to describe the world. In basic DDL the agent's beliefs are not part of the world, which explains why our doxastic operators can only operate on purely Boolean formulæ. By contrast, in full DDL the object language has none of these restrictions, and the agent is able to hold beliefs about anything. In this more expressive language one allows not only formulæ of type $\mathbf{K}\varphi \supset \mathbf{K}\mathbf{K}\varphi$ ("if the agent knows that φ, then he knows that he knows that φ"—Hintikka's famous KK-thesis) but also $\mathbf{B}([*\varphi]\psi)$ ("the agent believes that if he were to revise his beliefs by φ, then ψ") and even monsters like $[*([*\varphi]\mathbf{B}\psi)]\mathbf{B}\theta$ ("if the agent were to revise his beliefs in such a way as to believe that coming to believe that φ would lead to belief in ψ as well, then he would believe that θ"). (Between basic and full DDL there are several intermediate possibilities according to the range of the agent's doxastic faculties and the information by which he is supposed to be able to modify his beliefs; see, for example, [Lindström and Rabinowicz, 1997].)

We assume that the usual Boolean operators, if not primitive, have been introduced by definition. Other definitions: $\mathbf{b} =_{df} \neg\mathbf{B}\neg$, $\mathbf{k} =_{df} \neg\mathbf{K}\neg$, $\langle\ \rangle =_{df} \neg[\ ]\neg$. Suggested readings:

$\mathbf{B}\chi$	'the agent believes that χ',
$\mathbf{b}\chi$	'it is consistent with what the agent believes that χ',
$\mathbf{K}\chi$	'the agent is doxastically committed to belief in χ' or 'the agent considers that he knows that χ' or (for example, in AGM) 'it is implied by the agent's background theory that χ',
$\mathbf{k}\chi$	'it is consistent with the agent's doxastic commitments that χ' or 'it is consistent with what the agent considers that he knows that χ' or (for example, in AGM) 'it is consistent with the agent's background theory that χ',
$[+\varphi]\chi$	'(necessarily) after the agent has expanded his beliefs by φ it is the case that χ',
$\langle *\varphi\rangle\chi$	'(possibly) after the agent has expanded his beliefs by φ it is the case that χ',
$[*\varphi]\chi$	'(necessarily) after the agent has revised his beliefs by φ it is the case that χ',
$\langle *\varphi\rangle\chi$	'(possibly) after the agent has revised his beliefs by φ it is the case that χ'.

CONVENTION. In this paper we are dealing with basic DDL; in fact, except in the last section, with basic one-shot DDL. Thus throughout the paper we shall assume that, when expressions of type $\mathbf{B}\varphi$ or $\mathbf{K}\varphi$ are discussed, φ is a purely Boolean formula, even if this assumption has not been made explicit. Furthermore, when expressions of type $[+\varphi]\chi$ or $[*\varphi]\chi$ are discussed, the assumption, tacit if not voiced, is that φ is a purely Boolean formula and, except in the last section, that χ is a basic static formula (in the last section, χ may be any basic formula).

3.2 An axiom system for minimal normal basic one-shot DDL

We will define a system of one-shot DDL that is minimal in the same sense that the system K is minimal in the family of normal modal logics. We do so by a modular technique, listing our postulates in blocks. All expressions are assumed to be well-formed in the sense of basic one-shot DDL.

FIRST BLOCK. All (well-formed!) tautologies are axioms, and modus ponens is an inference rule:

(τ) τ, if τ is basic one-shot and a tautology.

(MP) If φ and $\varphi \supset \psi$ are theorems, then ψ is a theorem.

As usual, formula sets satisfying (τ) and (MP) are called *theories*; theories closed under uniform substitution of formulæ for propositional letters are called *logics*.

SECOND BLOCK. All (well-formed!) instances of four K-schemata are axioms, and there are four necessitation rules plus a rule of congruence:

(**B**K) $\mathbf{B}(\varphi \supset \psi) \supset (\mathbf{B}\varphi \supset \mathbf{B}\psi)$,

(**K**K) $\mathbf{K}(\varphi \supset \psi) \supset (\mathbf{K}\varphi \supset \mathbf{K}\psi)$,

(+K) $[+\theta](\varphi \supset \psi) \supset ([+\theta]\varphi \supset [+\theta]\psi)$,

($*$K) $[*\theta](\varphi \supset \psi) \supset ([*\theta]\varphi \supset [*\theta]\psi)$.

(**B**N) If φ is purely Boolean and a theorem, then $\mathbf{B}\varphi$ is a theorem.

(**K**N) If φ is purely Boolean and a theorem, then $\mathbf{K}\varphi$ is a theorem.

(+N) If φ is static and a theorem and θ is purely Boolean, then $[+\theta]\varphi$ is a theorem.

($*$N) If φ is static and a theorem and θ is purely Boolean, then $[*\theta]\varphi$ is a theorem.

(RC) If $\varphi \equiv \psi$ is purely Boolean and a theorem, then $[+\varphi]\chi \equiv [+\psi]\chi$ and $[*\varphi]\chi \equiv [*\psi]\chi$ are theorems, for all static χ.

Theories or logics providing all these postulates are said to be *normal*. Notice that the Rule of Replacement of Tautological Equivalents holds in all normal theories and logics:

(RTE) Suppose γ and γ^* are formulæ that are identical except that γ contains an occurrence of a formula φ in a place where γ^* contains an occurrence of a formula ψ. Then if $\varphi \equiv \psi$ is a purely Boolean tautology, γ is a theorem only if γ^* is a theorem.

3.3 *Additional axioms for one-shot AGM*

Next we wish to translate into DDL the AGM postulates as presented by Gärdenfors in [1988, pp. 49–50, 54–56]. The latter concern belief sets K (in the syntactical sense of the term, not to be confused with with the semantical notion defined in the preceding section) and what you can do with them. With our convention of using lower case Greek letters for formulæ and writing $\mathrm{K} + \varphi$ and $\mathrm{K} * \varphi$ for Gärdenfors's K^{+}_{φ} and K^{*}_{φ}, respectively, we employ the following dictionary:

$\chi \in \mathrm{K}$	$\mathbf{B}\chi$,
$\chi \in \mathrm{K} + \varphi$	$[+\varphi]\mathbf{B}\chi$,
$\chi \in \mathrm{K} * \varphi$	$[*\varphi]\mathbf{B}\chi$,
$\vdash \varphi$	$\mathbf{K}\varphi$.

We keep Gärdenfors's numbering (cf. [van Linder *et al.*, 1995, Propositions 5.3.6 and 5.3.34]):

(+2) $[+\varphi]\mathbf{B}\chi$,

(+3) $\mathbf{B}\chi \supset [+\varphi]\mathbf{B}\chi$,

(+4) $\mathbf{B}\varphi \supset (\mathbf{B}\chi \equiv [+\varphi]\mathbf{B}\chi)$,

(∗2) $[*\varphi]\mathbf{B}\varphi$,

(∗3) $[*\varphi]\mathbf{B}\chi \supset [+\varphi]\mathbf{B}\chi$,

(∗4) $\mathbf{b}\varphi \supset ([+\varphi]\mathbf{B}\chi \supset [*\varphi]\mathbf{B}\chi)$,

(∗5) $[*\varphi]\mathbf{B}\bot \equiv \mathbf{K}\neg\varphi$,

(∗6) $\mathbf{K}(\varphi \equiv \psi) \supset ([*\varphi]\mathbf{B}\chi \equiv [*\psi]\mathbf{B}\chi)$,

(∗7) $[*(\varphi \wedge \psi)]\mathbf{B}\chi \supset [*\varphi]\mathbf{B}(\psi \supset \chi)$,

(∗8) $\langle *\varphi \rangle \mathbf{b}\psi \supset ([*\varphi]\mathbf{B}(\psi \supset \chi) \supset [*(\varphi \wedge \psi)]\mathbf{B}\chi)$.

As a THIRD BLOCK we adopt all (well-formed!) instances of the preceding schemata as axioms of our system along with all (well-formed!) instances of the following:

(+0) $\chi \equiv [+\varphi]\chi$, if χ is purely Boolean,

(∗0) $\chi \equiv [*\varphi]\chi$, if χ is purely Boolean,

(+D) $[+\varphi]\chi \supset \langle +\varphi \rangle \chi$,

(+F) $\langle +\varphi \rangle \chi \supset [+\varphi]\chi$,

(∗D) $[*\varphi]\chi \supset \langle *\varphi\rangle\chi$,

(∗F) $\langle *\varphi\rangle\chi \supset [*\varphi]\chi$,

(KB) $\mathbf{K}\varphi \supset \mathbf{B}\varphi$,

(K+) $\mathbf{K}\chi \equiv [+\varphi]\mathbf{K}\chi$,

(K∗) $\mathbf{K}\chi \equiv [*\varphi]\mathbf{K}\chi$.

The logic defined by this axiom system, the smallest normal logic containing all instances of these axiom schemata, we call the (*basic normal*) *one-shot DDL of AGM* or DDL①AGM for short—not an elegant name but descriptive. It is this logic that is the central object of study in this paper. However, from a historical point of view, the name is not quite accurate. The original AGM involves what we call a background theory, a theory that, intuitively, represents fundamental assumptions of the agent that are not open to change by the doxastic operations considered by Alchourrón, Gärdenfors and Makinson. Let T_0 be such a background theory. In our paper, we treat T_0 as formulated in purely Boolean terms. Evidently, in order to be true to AGM, we should regard also the following as axioms:

$$(\mathbf{K}T_0) \qquad \mathbf{K}\varphi, \text{ for all } \varphi \in T_0.$$

It should be noted that T_0 need not be well-behaved. In particular, T_0 need not be closed under uniform substitution, nor need T_0 be finitely axiomatizable. This proposition is of course important for the analysis of the DDT defined by the above axiom system including the new schema ($\mathbf{K}T_0$); call it DDT①AGM. It is that theory, rather than the logic DDL①AGM, that has a claim to be the DDL counterpart of the classical AGM theory under the one-shot reading.

LEMMA 7. *The following theorem schemata and rules are derivable in all normal logics:*

(a) $[*\top]\mathbf{B}\chi \supset \mathbf{B}\chi$,

(b) $\mathbf{b}\top \supset (\mathbf{B}\chi \supset [*\top]\mathbf{B}\chi)$,

(c) If $\varphi \supset \psi$ *is a purely Boolean formula and a tautology, then* $\langle *\varphi\rangle\mathbf{b}\top \supset \langle *\psi\rangle\mathbf{b}\top$ *is a theorem.*

(d) If $\varphi \supset \psi$ *is a purely Boolean formula and a tautology, then* $\langle *\psi\rangle\mathbf{b}\varphi \supset ([*\varphi]\mathbf{B}\chi \equiv [*\psi]\mathbf{B}(\varphi \supset \chi))$ *is a theorem.*

Postulates (+4) and (∗3) are needed for the proof of 7.a: similarly, (+4) and (∗4) are needed for 7.b, (∗5) for 7.c, and $(**7-8\}$ for 7.d.

A comment on the dynamic operators ⟨ ⟩ and [ ]: In the presence of postulates (+D)-(+F) and (∗D)-(∗F), one of these operators is in a sense superfluous—if one is primitive, the other can be introduced by definition. Accordingly, it might be considered a simpliflication to omit one, for example, $\langle\,\rangle$. However, there are interesting DDLs in which the postulates (+F) and (∗F) are not valid, and in those systems the two operators are not equivalent (see [Cantwell, 1999; Segerberg, 1997; Segerberg, 1999]). It is with an eye to such systems that we maintain the distinction between these operators that just happen to be equivalent in our system.

4 SEMANTICS

4.1 The topological connection

The languages discussed in the preceding section are formal languages—what might their interpretations be like? We shall build ours in three stages of increasing scope: first (in this subsection) for the purely Boolean fragment, then (in the next subsection) for the basic static one, and finally (in the last two subsections) for the class of all basic one-shot formulæ. Fundamental to all our model building are Stone spaces. If (U, T) is a Stone space and V a valuation in (U, T) (that is, a function assigning to each propositional letter a clopen set), then, for every purely Boolean formula φ, there is an associated proposition $||\varphi||$ (if it is desirable to indicate V, then put it as a subscript: $||\varphi||_V$):

(i) $||\mathrm{P}|| = V(\mathrm{P})$, if P is a propositional letter,

(ii) $||\varphi \wedge \psi|| = ||\varphi|| \cap ||\psi||$,

(iii) $||\varphi \vee \psi|| = ||\varphi|| \cup ||\psi||$,

(iv) $||\neg\varphi|| = U - ||\varphi||$,

and similarly for other Boolean connectives. The structure $\mathcal{S} = (U, T, V)$ might be called a topological model. If u is a point in U, we may say that φ is *true at u in $\mathcal{S} = (U, T, V)$*, in symbols $\models^{\mathcal{S}}_u \varphi$, if and only if $u \in ||\varphi||_V$. (If the reference to $\mathcal{S}$ is clear, we usually write just $\models_u \varphi$.) A purely Boolean formula is *valid in* (U, T) if and only if true at all points under all valuations in (U, T). It is easy to see that the class of formulæ valid in all Stone spaces is exactly the class of purely Boolean truth-functional tautologies.

4.2 Static semantics

In order to extend the semantics of the preceding subsection to all (basic) static formulæ we must add complexes: suppose that (X, Y) is a complex (meaning that X and Y are subsets of U), while u is still a point of U. We define the notion of a static formula φ being *true in* the structure $\mathcal{S} = (U, T, V)$ *at u with respect to* (X, Y), in symbolic notation $(X, Y) \models^{\mathcal{S}}_u \varphi$ (or just $(X, Y) \models_u \varphi$, if the reference to $\mathcal{S}$ is clear):

1. $(X, Y) \models_u \chi$ iff $u \in ||\chi||_V$, if χ is purely Boolean,

2. (X, Y) $\models_u \psi \wedge \theta$ iff $(X, Y) \models_u \psi$ and $(X, Y) \models_u \theta$,

3. $(X, Y) \models_u \neg\psi$ iff not $(X, Y) \models_u \psi$,

and similarly for other Boolean operators;

4. $(X, Y) \models_u \mathbf{B}\chi$ iff $X \subseteq ||\chi||_V$,

5. $(X, Y) \models_u \mathbf{K}\chi$ iff $Y \subseteq ||\chi||_V$.

(Here ψ and θ are static in 2–3 and χ is purely Boolean in 4–5.) The following result is in part a corollary of Lemma 2. (The fact that will be needed later is the equivalence of conditions (i) and (iii) of the lemma.)

LEMMA 8. *For all static formulæ φ the following conditions are equivalent:*

(i) $(X, Y) \models_u \varphi$,

(ii) $(\mathbf{C}X, Y) \models_u \varphi$,

(iii) $(X, \mathbf{C}Y) \models_u \varphi$,

(iv) $(\mathbf{C}X, \mathbf{C}Y) \models_u \varphi$.

In the next two subsections we will extend, in two different ways, our semantics to all (basic) one-shot formulæ.

4.3 Onion semantics

Suppose O is an onion in (U, T). We give an inductive definition of a formula φ being true in the structure $\mathcal{S} = (U, T, V)$ at a point u in U with respect to O, in symbols $O \models_u^{\mathcal{S}} \varphi$ (or just $O \models_u \varphi$ when the reference to $\mathcal{S}$ is clear). In the three clauses of the basic step of the definition we assume that φ is a purely Boolean and χ a static formula:

1. $O \models_u \chi$ iff $(B_O, C_O) \models_u \chi$,

2. $O \models_u [+\varphi]\chi$ iff $(X, Y) \models_u \chi$, where $X = B_O \cap ||\varphi||$ and $Y = C_O$,

3. $O \models_u [*\varphi]\chi$ iff $(X, Y) \models_u \chi$, where either $\{S \in O : S \cap ||\varphi|| \neq \emptyset\}$ has no smallest element and $X = \theta$, or else $X = Z \cap ||\varphi||$, where Z is least in $\{S \in O : S \cap ||\varphi|| \neq \emptyset\}$, but in any case $Y = C_O$.

In the two clauses of the inductive step, ψ and θ are any one-shot formulæ:

4. $O \models_u \psi \wedge \theta$ iff $O \models_u \psi$ and $O \models_u \theta$,

5. $\models_u \neg\psi$ iff not $O \models_u \psi$,

and similarly for other Boolean operators. (In clause 1, B_O is the belief set and C_O the commitment set of O, as defined in Section 2.2.)

Suppose that (U, T) is a Stone space and V a valuation in (U, T). We call (U, T, O) *a one-shot onion space* if O is an onion in (U, T), and we call (U, T, O, V) *a one-shot onion model* (in the space (U, T, O)). A formula φ is *true at* a point u in a one-shot onion model (U, T, O, V) if $O \models_u \varphi$. A formula φ is *valid in* a one-shot onion space if true at all points in all models in the space. A set Σ of formulæ is *one-shot onion satisfiable* if there is a one-shot onion model such that all formulæ of Σ are true in the model at one and the same point.

Let us say that a one-shot onion model (U', T', O', V') is the *replete reduct* of a one-shot onion model (U, T, O, V) if $U' = \bigcup O$ and $T' = \{X \cap \bigcup O : X \in T\}$ and $O' = O$ and, for every propositional letter P, $V'(\mathrm{P}) = V(\mathrm{P}) \cap \bigcup O$. (Notice that T' is also a topology—Stone if $\bigcup O$ is closed in T.) The following result shows that, in the present context, repleteness makes no difference to validity.

PROPOSITION 9. *Suppose that (U', T', O', V') is the replete reduct of (U, T, O, V). Then, for all u in U' and formulæ φ, $O \models_u \varphi$ if and only if $O' \models_u \varphi$.*

In one-shot onion semantics, the *raison d'être* of the onion is to define the truth-value of nonstatic formulæ. Notice that onions are nonreusable—they are indispensable in the anterior position but useless in the posterior one.

4.4 Selector semantics

Suppose f is a selector for (U, T). We define the notion of a formula φ being *true in* the structure $\mathcal{S} = (U, T, V)$ at a point u in U *with respect to f*, in symbols $f \models_u^{\mathcal{S}} \varphi$ (or just $f \models_u \varphi$ when the implicit reference to $\mathcal{S}$ is clear). Basic step (three clauses): if φ is purely Boolean and χ is static, then

1. $f \models_u \chi$ iff $(B_f, C_f) \models_u \chi$,

2. $f \models_u [+\varphi]\chi$ iff $(X, Y) \models_u \chi$, where $X = B_f \cap ||\varphi||$ and $Y = C_f$,

3. $f \models_u [*\varphi]\chi$ iff $(X, Y) \models_u \chi$, where $X = f||\varphi||$ and $Y = C_f$.

In the inductive step (two clauses), ψ and θ are one-shot formulæ:

4. $f \models_u \psi \wedge \theta$ iff $f \models_u \psi$ and $f \models_u \theta$,

5. $f \models_u \neg\psi$ iff not $f \models_u \psi$,

and similarly for other Boolean operators. (In clause 1, B_f is the belief set of f and C_f is the commitment set of f as defined in Section 2.3.)

Let (U, T) be a Stone space and V a valuation in (U, T). We say that (U, T, f) is a *one-shot selector space* if f is a selector in (U, T) and that (U, T, f, V) *is a one-shot selector model* (in the space (U, T, f)). A formula φ is *true at* a point u *in* a one-shot selector model (U, T, f, V) if $f \models_u \varphi$. A formula φ is *valid* in a one-shot selector space if it is true at all points in all models in that space. A set Σ of formulæ is *one-shot selector satisfiable* if the formulæ of Σ are simultaneously true at some point in some selector model.

THEOREM 10. *Suppose that (U, T, f, V) is a one-shot selector model and (U, T, O_f, V) a one-shot onion model, and that the onion O_f has been derived from the selector f as described in Section 2.4. Then, for all u in U and formulæ φ,*

$$f \models_u \varphi \text{ if and only if } O_f \models_u \varphi$$

Similar remarks about nonreusability as were made about onions apply to selectors as well.

5 COMPLETENESS OF ONE-SHOT AGM

DDL①AGM, the normal logic determined by the axiom system in Section 3 (without the axiom schema ($\mathbf{KT}_0$)), is sound with respect to the class of all onion spaces (as well as the class of all selector spaces). In this section we will prove that it is also complete.

By U_ω denote the set of all maximal PC-consistent sets of purely Boolean formulæ. ('PC' for (the classical) propositional calculus, 'ω' for the number of propositional letters.) For purely Boolean φ, define

$$|\varphi| = \{u \in U_\omega : \varphi \in u\}.$$

The family $\{|\varphi| : \varphi \text{ is a purely Boolean formula}\}$ is a base for a topology T_ω on U_ω. This topology is totally separated, for if $u, v \in U_\omega$ and $u \neq v$, then there is some purely Boolean φ such that $\varphi \in u$ but $\varphi \notin v$; hence u but not v belongs to the set $|\varphi|$, which is open by definition but also closed since it is the complement of the open set $|\neg\varphi|$. That the topology is compact follows from the fact that tautological implication is finitary. Hence (U_ω, T_ω) is a Stone space. The clopen sets of this space we sometimes refer to as "propositions". Notice that every proposition is of the form $|\psi|$, for some purely Boolean ψ. (For suppose that X is a clopen subset of U_ω. Since X is open, there is a nonempty index set I and a set $\{|\varphi_i| : i \in I\}$ of base elements such that $X = \bigcup\{|\varphi_i| : i \in I\}$. Since X is also closed, $U_\omega - X$ is open and so $(U_\omega - x) \cap \bigcup\{|\varphi_i| : i \in I\}$ is an open cover of U_ω. By compactness, there is some $n \geq 0$ and indices $i_0, \ldots, i_{n-1} \in I$ such that $(U_\omega - X) \cup |\varphi_{i_0}| \cup \ldots \cup |\varphi_{i_{n-1}}|$ is a cover of U_ω. Hence $X = |\varphi_{i_0} \vee \ldots \vee \varphi_{i_{n-1}}|$. (Thus $X = |\bot|$ in the special case that $n = 0$.))

The completeness proof is carried out in a general form. Let L be a fixed normal logic. Let Σ be a maximal L-consistent set of one-shot DDL-formulæ. We define three concepts that will be crucial in what follows: *wst* Σ (the *world state induced by* Σ), *bst* Σ (the *belief set induced by* Σ) and *cst* Σ (the *commitment set induced by* Σ):

$$\begin{aligned} wst\,\Sigma &= \Sigma \cap \{\chi : \chi \text{ is purely Boolean}\}, \\ bst\,\Sigma &= \{u \in U_\omega : \forall\chi\,(\mathbf{B}\chi \in \Sigma \Rightarrow \chi \in u)\}, \\ cst\,\Sigma &= \{u \in U_\omega : \forall\chi\,(\mathbf{K}\chi \in \Sigma \Rightarrow \chi \in u)\}. \end{aligned}$$

Thus it is a consequence of the lemma to follow that

$$\begin{aligned} bst\,\Sigma &= \bigcap\{|\chi| : \mathbf{B}\chi \in \Sigma\}, \\ cst\,\Sigma &= \bigcap\{|\chi| : \mathbf{K}\chi \in \Sigma\}. \end{aligned}$$

LEMMA 11.

(i) $wst\,\Sigma$ is an element of U_ω.

(ii) $bst\,\Sigma \subseteq |\varphi|$ if and only if $\mathbf{B}\varphi \in \Sigma$, for all purely Boolean φ.

(iii) $cst\,\Sigma \subseteq |\varphi|$ if and only if $\mathbf{K}\varphi \in \Sigma$, for all purely Boolean φ.

Proof. We give the proof of (ii). The claim from right to left is obviously correct. For the converse, assume that $\mathbf{B}\varphi \notin \Sigma$. By an argument familiar from modal logic, the set

$$(*) \quad \{\chi : \mathbf{B}\chi \in \Sigma\} \cup \{\neg\varphi\}$$

must be L-consistent (here we use the fact that L is normal). All the formulæ of $(*)$ are purely Boolean, and L-consistency implies PC-consistency. Hence $(*)$ can be extended by a Lindenbaum construction to a maximal PC-consistent set of purely Boolean formulæ, say v. By definition, $v \in U_\omega$. And by construction, $v \in bst\,\Sigma$ but $v \notin |\varphi|$. ■

We define a function f_ω^Σ on the set of propositions by the condition

$$f_\omega^\Sigma|\varphi| = \{u \in U_\omega : \forall\chi\,([*\varphi]\mathbf{B}\chi \in \Sigma \Rightarrow \chi \in u)\}.$$

For greater ease of notation we shall usually write f^Σ in lieu of the official f_ω^Σ. Note that $f^\Sigma|\varphi| = \bigcap\{|\chi| : [*\varphi]\mathbf{B}\chi \in \Sigma\}$; hence $f^\Sigma|\varphi|$ is a closed set.

LEMMA 12. *$f^\Sigma|\varphi| = \emptyset$ if and only if $\mathbf{K}\neg\varphi \in \Sigma$.*

Proof. First suppose that $f^\Sigma|\varphi| = \emptyset$. Then $\bigcap\{|\chi| : [*\varphi]\,\mathbf{B}\chi \in \Sigma\} = \emptyset$. Using compactness we conclude that there is some number $n > 0$ and formulæ $\chi_0, \ldots, \chi_{n-1}$ such that

(1) $[*\varphi]\mathbf{B}\chi_0, \ldots, [*\varphi]\mathbf{B}\chi_{n-1} \in \Sigma$,

(2) $|\chi_0| \cap \ldots \cap |\chi_{n-1}| = \emptyset$.

By (2), $|\chi_0| \wedge \ldots \wedge \chi_{n\text{-}1}| = \emptyset$, and consequently, $\chi_0 \wedge \ldots \wedge \chi_{n\text{-}1}$ is a contradiction. In other words, $\neg(\chi_0 \wedge \ldots \wedge \chi_{n\text{-}1})$ is a tautology. Therefore, since $\mathbf{B}$ and $[*\varphi]$ are normal operators, $[*\varphi]\mathbf{B}\neg(\chi_0 \wedge \ldots \wedge \chi_{n\text{-}1})$ is a theorem of L and hence

(3) $[*\varphi]\mathbf{B}\neg(\chi_0 \wedge \ldots \wedge \chi_{n\text{-}1}) \in \Sigma$

But by (1) we have, by modal logic,

(4) $[*\varphi]\mathbf{B}(\chi_0 \wedge \ldots \wedge \chi_{n\text{-}1}) \in \Sigma$

From (3) and (4) it follows, by modal logic, that $[*\varphi]\mathbf{B}\bot \in \Sigma$. Hence $\mathbf{K}\neg\varphi \in \Sigma$ by postulate (∗5).

Conversely, suppose that $\mathbf{K}\neg\varphi \in \Sigma$. Then $[*\varphi]\mathbf{B}\bot \in \Sigma$, by postulate (∗5) and modal logical reasoning. Suppose there exists some element $u \in U_\omega$ such that $u \in f^\Sigma|\varphi|$. Then, by the definition of $f^\Sigma|\varphi|$, we have to conclude that $\bot \in u$, which is absurd. Hence $f^\Sigma|\varphi|$ is empty. ■

LEMMA 13. *f^Σ is a selector for U_ω.*

Proof. We have to check the three conditions.

INCLUSION. Suppose that $w \in f^\Sigma|\varphi|$. By (∗2), $[*\varphi]\mathbf{B}\varphi \in \Sigma$. Hence $w \in |\varphi|$.

MONEYS. Assume that φ and ψ are purely Boolean formulæ such that $|\varphi| \subseteq |\psi|$; hence $\varphi \supset \psi$ is a tautology. Suppose that $f^\Sigma|\psi| = \emptyset$. Then $[*\psi]\mathbf{B}\bot \in \Sigma$, by the same argument as was used in the proof of Lemma 12. Hence, by Lemma 7.(c), $[*\varphi]\mathbf{B}\bot \in \Sigma$. Consequently, $f^\Sigma|\varphi| = \emptyset$.

ARROW. Assume that φ and ψ are purely Boolean formulæ such that

(1) $|\varphi| \subseteq |\psi|$.

Again $\varphi \supset \psi$ is a tautology. Suppose that

(2) $|\varphi| \cap f^\Sigma|\psi| \neq \emptyset$

By (2) there exists some element $u \in |\varphi| \cap f^\Sigma|\psi|$. If it were the case that $[*\psi]\mathbf{B}\neg\varphi \in \Sigma$, then $\varphi \in u$ (since $u \in |\varphi|$) but also $\neg\varphi \in u$ (since $u \in f^\Sigma|\psi|$), which is absurd. Hence $[*\psi]\mathbf{B}\neg\varphi \notin \Sigma$, whence $\langle *\psi\rangle\mathbf{b}\varphi \in \Sigma$ by the maximality of Σ. Therefore, by Lemma 7.(d),

(3) $[*\varphi]\mathbf{B}\chi \equiv [*\psi]\mathbf{B}(\varphi \supset \chi) \in \Sigma$.

We divide the task of proving that $f^\Sigma|\varphi| = |\varphi| \cap f^\Sigma|\varphi|$ into two natural halves. First suppose that $w \in f^\Sigma|\varphi|$. By postulate (∗2), $[*\varphi]\mathbf{B}\varphi \in \Sigma$, hence $w \in |\varphi|$. Furthermore, take any χ such that $[*\psi]\mathbf{B}\chi \in \Sigma$. By modal logic, $[*\psi]\mathbf{B}(\varphi \supset \psi) \in \Sigma$. Hence, by (3), $[*\varphi]\mathbf{B}\chi \in \Sigma$ and so $w \in |\chi|$. This proves that $w \in f^\Sigma|\psi|$ and ends the first half of our task. For the other half, suppose that $w \in |\varphi| \cap f^\Sigma|\psi|$. Take any χ such that $[*\varphi]\mathbf{B}\chi \in \Sigma$. By (3), $[*\psi]\mathbf{B}(\varphi \supset \chi) \in \Sigma$. Hence $f^\Sigma|\varphi| \subseteq |\varphi \supset \chi|$. Thus $w \in |\varphi \supset \chi|$ and $w \in |\varphi|$, whence $w \in |\chi|$. This argument proves that $w \in f^\Sigma|\varphi|$, as we wanted to show. ■

LEMMA 14.

(i) $bst\,\Sigma = f^{\Sigma}|\top|$.

(ii) $cst\,\Sigma \supseteq \bigcup\{f^{\Sigma}|\varphi| : \varphi$ *is purely Boolean*$\}$.

(iii) $cst\,\Sigma = \mathbf{C}(\bigcup\{f^{\Sigma}|\varphi| : \varphi$ *is purely Boolean*$\})$.

Proof. Proof of (i). Assume that $u \in bst\,\Sigma$. Suppose that χ is any purely Boolean formula such that $[*\top]\mathbf{B}\chi \in \Sigma$. By Lemma 7(a), $[*\top]\mathbf{B}\chi \supset \mathbf{B}\chi \in \Sigma$, hence $\mathbf{B}\chi \in \Sigma$. By the assumption, then, $u \in |\chi|$. This argument shows that $bst\,\Sigma \subseteq f^{\Sigma}|\top|$. Conversely, suppose that $u \in f^{\Sigma}|\top|$. Then $\mathbf{b}\top \in \Sigma$ (for otherwise $\mathbf{B}\bot \in \Sigma$ by the maximality of Σ and hence $\bot \in u$, which is absurd). Let χ be any purely Boolean formula such that $\mathbf{B}\chi \in \Sigma$. By Lemma 7(b) $\mathbf{b}\top \supset (\mathbf{B}\chi \supset [*\top]\mathbf{B}\chi) \in \Sigma$. Hence $[*\top]\mathbf{B}\chi \in \Sigma$. By the definition of f^{Σ} therefore $\chi \in u$. This argument shows that $u \in bst\,\Sigma$. Hence $f^{\Sigma}|\top| \subseteq bst\,\Sigma$.

Proof of (ii). Suppose that $v \notin cst\,\Sigma$. Then there is some φ such that $\mathbf{K}\varphi \in \Sigma$ and $\varphi \notin v$. Take any purely Boolean ψ. By ($\mathbf{K}*$), ($\mathbf{KB}$) and modal logic, $[*\psi]\mathbf{B}\varphi \in \Sigma$. Since $\varphi \notin v$, it follows that $v \notin f^{\Sigma}\,|\psi|$. Since this argument holds for every choice of ψ, we conclude that $v \notin \bigcup\{f^{\Sigma}|\psi| : \psi$ is purely Boolean$\}$.

Proof of (iii). Suppose that $w \notin \mathbf{C}(\bigcup\{f^{\Sigma}|\varphi| : \varphi$ is purely Boolean$\})$. Then by Lemma 1 there must be some purely Boolean formula $\theta \notin w$ such that $\mathbf{C}(\bigcup\{f^{\Sigma}|\varphi|$ $: \varphi$ is purely Boolean$\}) \subseteq |\theta|$. Thus in particular $f^{\Sigma}|\neg\theta| \subseteq |\theta|$, whence $f^{\Sigma}|\neg\theta| = \emptyset$. By Lemma 12 (and modal logic), $\mathbf{K}\theta \in \Sigma$. Hence $w \notin cst\,\Sigma$. This proves that $cst\,\Sigma \subseteq \mathbf{C}(\bigcup\{f^{\Sigma}|\varphi| : \varphi$ is purely Boolean$\})$. The converse follows from (ii) and the fact that $cst\,\Sigma$ is closed. ■

Define, for any purely Boolean formula φ, two relations $R^{+\varphi}$ and $R^{*\varphi}$ in the set of maximal L-consistent sets of (basic one-shot) formulæ:

$$R^{+\varphi}(\Sigma,\Theta) \text{ iff } \forall\chi([+\varphi]\chi \in \Sigma \Rightarrow \chi \in \Theta),$$
$$R^{*\varphi}(\Sigma,\Theta) \text{ iff } \forall\chi([*\varphi]\chi \in \Sigma \Rightarrow \chi \in \Theta).$$

LEMMA 15. *Let Σ, Θ and Θ' be a maximal L-consistent sets.*

(i) There is a maximal L-consistent set Ω such that $R^{+\varphi}(\Sigma,\Omega)$.

(ii) There is a maximal L-consistent set Ω such that $R^{*\varphi}(\Sigma,\Omega)$.

(iii) If $R^{+\varphi}(\Sigma,\Theta)$ and $R^{+\varphi}(\Sigma,\Theta')$ then $\Theta = \Theta'$.

(iv) If $R^{*\varphi}(\Sigma,\Theta)$ and $R^{*\varphi}(\Sigma,\Theta')$, then $\Theta = \Theta'$.

(v) If $R^{+\varphi}(\Sigma,\Theta)$, then $wst\,\Theta = wst\,\Sigma$ and $bst\,\Theta = bst\,\Sigma \cap |\varphi|$ and $cst\,\Theta = cst\,\Sigma$.

(vi) If $R^{*\varphi}(\Sigma,\Theta)$, then $wst\,\Theta = wst\,\Sigma$ and $bst\,\Theta = f^{\Sigma}|\varphi|$ and $cst\,\Theta = cst\,\Sigma$.

(vii) $[+\varphi]\chi \in \Sigma$ *iff* $\forall\Theta\,(R^{+\varphi}(\Sigma,\Theta) \Rightarrow \chi \in \Theta)$.

(viii) $[*\varphi]\chi \in \Sigma$ *iff* $\forall\Theta\,(R^{*\varphi}(\Sigma,\Theta) \Rightarrow \chi \in \Theta)$.

Proof. Many of our postulates are needed here: (+D) and (∗D) for (i)–(ii), (+F) and (∗F) for (iii)-(iv), (+0), (+2)-(+4) and (**K**+) for (v), (∗0) and (**K**∗) for (vi). Conditions (vii) and (viii) depend on the normality of L. ■

We define a valuation V_ω in (U_ω, T_ω) by the condition:

$$V_\omega(\mathrm{P}) = |\mathrm{P}|, \text{ if P is a propositional letter.}$$

In the remainder of this section we shall write $||\varphi||$ for $||\varphi||_{V_\omega}$.

LEMMA 16. *For all purely Boolean* φ, $||\varphi|| = |\varphi|$.

All static formulæ have a truth-value in the structure $(U_\omega, T_\omega, V_\omega)$ with respect to the point *wst* Σ and the complex (*bst* Σ, *cst* Σ):

LEMMA 17. *For all static formulæ* φ,

$$(\mathit{bst}\,\Sigma,\ \mathit{cst}\,\Sigma) \models_{\mathit{wst}\Sigma} \varphi \textit{ if and only if } \varphi \in \Sigma.$$

Proof. By induction on the complexity of the static formula φ. First the basic step, where P is a propositional letter:

$$(\mathit{bst}\,\Sigma, \mathit{cst}\,\Sigma) \models_{\mathit{wst}\Sigma} \mathrm{P} \text{ iff } \mathit{wst}\,\Sigma \in V_\omega(\mathrm{P}) \text{ iff } \mathrm{P} \in \mathit{wst}\,\Sigma \text{ iff } \mathrm{P} \in \Sigma.$$

The inductive step consists of three cases: (i) $\varphi = \mathbf{B}\psi$, for some purely Boolean ψ; (ii) $\varphi = \mathbf{K}\psi$, for some purely Boolean ψ; or (iii) φ is a Boolean combination of formulæ that are purely Boolean or of type (i) or of type (ii). The last case is trivial. The other two follow by the truth-conditions for **B** and **K**, respectively, plus Lemmata 11 and 16:

$$\begin{aligned}&(\mathit{bst}\,\Sigma, \mathit{cst}\,\Sigma) \models_{\mathit{wst}\Sigma} \mathbf{B}\psi \text{ iff } \mathit{bst}\,\Sigma \subseteq ||\psi|| \text{ iff } \mathit{bst}\,\Sigma \subseteq |\psi|\\ &\quad \text{iff } \mathbf{B}\psi \in \Sigma,\\ &(\mathit{bst}\,\Sigma, \mathit{cst}\,\Sigma) \models_{\mathit{wst}\Sigma} \mathbf{K}\psi \text{ iff } \mathit{cst}\,\Sigma \subseteq ||\psi|| \text{ iff } \mathit{cst}\,\Sigma \subseteq |\psi|\\ &\quad \text{iff } \mathbf{K}\psi \in \Sigma.\end{aligned}$$

■

By *the canonical one-shot selector model of* L *induced by* Σ we mean the structure $\mathcal{M}^\Sigma_\omega = (U_\omega, T_\omega, f^\Sigma_\omega, V_\omega)$; usually we denote it by just $\mathcal{M}^\Sigma$. Note that, by Lemma 14, *bst* Σ is the belief set of $\mathcal{M}^\Sigma$ and *cst* Σ is the closure of the commitment set of $\mathcal{M}^\Sigma$:

$$\mathit{bst}\,\Sigma = B_{f^\Sigma}, \qquad \mathit{cst}\,\Sigma = \mathbf{C}C_{f^\Sigma}.$$

THEOREM 18. *For all one-shot formulæ* φ,

$$f^{\Sigma} \models_{wst\Sigma} \varphi \text{ if and only if } \varphi \in \Sigma.$$

Proof. By induction on the complexity of φ. The basic step consists of three parts: (i) φ is a static formula, (ii) $\varphi = [*\psi]\chi$, for some purely Boolean ψ and static χ, (iii) $\varphi = [*\psi]\chi$, for some purely Boolean ψ and static χ. The inductive step deals with the case (iv) when φ is a Boolean combination of one-shot formulæ for which the theorem is supposed to hold. Obviously, the inductive step is trivial. The three parts of the basic step we give.

Part (i). $f^{\Sigma} \models_{wst\Sigma} \varphi$ iff $(B_{f^{\Sigma}}, C_{f^{\Sigma}}) \models_{wst\Sigma} \varphi$

iff (by Lemma 8) $(B_{f^{\Sigma}}, \mathbf{C}C_{f^{\Sigma}}) \models_{wst\Sigma} \varphi$

iff (by Lemma 14) $(bst\ \Sigma, cst\ \Sigma) \models_{wst\Sigma} \varphi$

iff (by Lemma 17) $\varphi \in \Sigma$.

Part (ii). $f^{\Sigma} \models_{wst\Sigma} [+\psi]\chi$ iff $(B_{f^{\Sigma}} \cap ||\psi||, C_{f^{\Sigma}}) \models_{wst\Sigma} \chi$

iff (by Lemma 16) $(B_{f^{\Sigma}} \cap |\psi|, C_{f^{\Sigma}}) \models_{wst\Sigma} \chi$

iff (by Lemma 8) $(B_{f^{\Sigma}} \cap |\psi|, \mathbf{C}C_{f^{\Sigma}}) \models_{wst\Sigma} \chi$

iff (by Lemma 14) $(bst\ \Sigma \cap |\psi|, cst\ \Sigma) \models_{wst\Sigma} \chi$

iff (by Lemma 15(i) & (v)) $(bst\ \Theta, cst\ \Theta) \models_{wst\Theta} \chi$,
for all Θ such that $R^{+\psi}(\Sigma,\Theta)$

iff (by Lemma 17) $\chi \in \Theta$, for all Θ such that $R^{+\psi}(\Sigma,\Theta)$

iff (by Lemma 15(vii)) $[+\psi]\chi \in \Sigma$.

Part (iii). $f^{\Sigma} \models_{wst\Sigma} [*\psi]\chi$ iff $(f^{\Sigma}||\psi||, C_{f^{\Sigma}}) \models_{wst\Sigma} \chi$

iff (by Lemma 16) $(f^{\Sigma}|\psi|, C_{f^{\Sigma}}) \models_{wst\Sigma} \chi$

iff (by Lemma 8) $(f^{\Sigma}|\psi|, \mathbf{C}C_{f^{\Sigma}}) \models_{wst\Sigma} \chi$

iff (by Lemma 14) $(f^{\Sigma}|\psi|, cst\ \Sigma) \models_{wst\Sigma} \chi$

iff (by Lemma 15(ii) & (vi)) $(bst\ \Theta, cst\ \Theta) \models_{wst\Theta} \chi$,
for all Θ such that $R^{*\psi}(\Sigma,\Theta)$

iff (by Lemma 17) $\chi \in \Theta$, for all Θ such that $R^{*\psi}(\Sigma,\Theta)$

iff (by Lemma 15(viii)) $[*\psi]\chi \in \Sigma$. ∎

We are now at the end of our journey to completeness of the normal logic with the ugly name, DDL①AGM. The argument is obvious: If a set is consistent, then it can be extended to a maximal consistent set Σ, and our argument shows that it will be satisfied at some point in the model determined by Σ. Therefore we have established strong completeness with respect to the class of selector spaces. Furthermore, by Theorem 10, we also have strong completeness with respect to the class of all onion spaces. In fact, thanks to Proposition 9, we have strong completeness with respect to the class of replete onion spaces and, thanks to Lemma 6, to the class of (replete) (closed) Lewis onion spaces.

One consequence of this result is that if the theory DDT①AGM—the closure under modus ponens of the set DDL①AGM $\cup$ $\{\mathbf{K}\varphi : \varphi \in \mathrm{T}_0\}$—is consistent, then it is one-shot (onion or selector) satisfiable.

A final remark on decidability. Suppose that U_ω is replaced by the set U_n of all maximal L-consistent sets of formulæ whose propositional letters are in a certain set $\{\mathrm{P}_0, \ldots, \mathrm{P}_{n\text{-}1}\}$, where $n \geq 0$. Then the entire argument goes through as before. A corollary is that DDL①AGM is decidable.

6 COMPLETENESS OF ITERATIVE AGM

When we go to the iterative reading of AGM, our analysis will be guided by two conditions that—in the author's view, not shared by all—may reasonably be seen as implicit in AGM. One is that the commitment set remain constant over any sequence of doxastic changes, the other that, in every doxastic position, the belief set determine the onion. For many applications, the former condition may be reasonable; for almost all, the latter—called the condition of 'unique methodology' in [Segerberg, 1996]—is questionable if not outright absurd. Nevertheless, because of the historical interest of the system, we outline, in this concluding section, how the analysis of one-shot AGM can be extended to iterative AGM. Before doing so, let us review the evidence for the claim that these conditions might be thought to be implicit in the AGM theory.

That the commitment set remain constant: The syntactical counterpart of the commitment set is what we have called the background theory. This corresponds to $Cn\ \emptyset$, where Cn is the 'consequence operation' described in [Alchourrón *et al.*, 1985, pp. 511f.], and to the 'logic that is identified with its consequence relation $\vdash$' in [Gärdenfors, 1988, p. 24]. Nowhere is there any suggestion that the kind of belief change that is discussed by AGM will affect that notion. (Notice that postulates (**K**+) and (**K**$*$) above would not be valid even in the one-shot semantics without the constancy of the commitment set.)

That the belief set determine the onion: The Gärdenfors axioms govern theories in the syntactical sense of the word. In [Alchourrón *et al.*, 1985, p. 512f.] it is explained how, given a theory K (in fact, any formula set) and what is called a selection function for K, a certain revision function is determined that yields, for every formula φ, the revision $\mathrm{K} * \varphi$ of K (our notation differs from that in [Alchourrón *et al.*, 1985]). In order for a second change to be possible, yielding the revision $(K * \varphi) * \psi$ of $K * \varphi$ by a formula ψ, a selection function for $K * \varphi$ would be needed. It is true that the AGM analysis does not provide such a function. This proposition is presumably the argument for holding that it is the one-shot interpretation that is implicit in [Alchourrón *et al.*, 1985]. One might ask why we may not assume the existence of a second selection function, just as we assumed the existence of the first one. One possible answer is that, if we do, we go beyond what the fathers of the AGM theory envisaged in [Alchourrón *et al.*, 1985]. Since they say little about where selection functions come from, it is difficult to pursue this question further.

By contrast, the following quotes from [Gärdenfors, 1988, pp. 48f. and 53f.]. are unambiguous. (Note that they concern belief sets in the syntactical sense and that we have modified Gärdenfors's notation.)

> Where K is the initial belief set, the expansion of K by φ is denoted $K + \varphi$. Formally it is assumed that $+$ is a function from pairs of belief sets and sentences, that is, from $\mathcal{K} \times \mathcal{L}$, to belief sets, that is, $\mathcal{K}$.
>
> It is assumed that, for any belief set K and any sentence φ, there is a *unique* revision representing a selected minimal change. In more mathematical terms this amounts to the assumption that there is a *revision function* $*$ from $\mathcal{K} \times \mathcal{L}$ to $\mathcal{K}$ that takes a belief set K and a sentence φ into a new belief set, which is denoted $K * \varphi$.

Under the AGM conception, belief change consists in going from one belief set (in the syntactical sense) to another as guided by the Gärdenfors axioms. But if those axioms hold generally, they will guide any subsequent change in the same way; in that sense, belief change is iterative. Translated into terms of our onion semantics: belief change consists in going from one belief set (now in the semantical sense) to another as guided by an onion. Or, since the belief set in the semantical sense is the intersection of the onion, one-shot change consists in going from an onion to a belief set. If iterated change is to be possible, we must be able to go from an onion to an onion. But if all that a change actually yields is a belief set, while an onion is what is needed, and if a method of constructing an onion from the belief set is not available, then obviously a Postulate of Unique Methodology is a minimal requirement. How else will we get our onions?

6.1 Iterative semantics

Let (U, T) be a Stone space. An *onion frame* is a triple (U, T, D) where (U, T) is a topological space and D is a function (the *onion determiner*) defined on a set of subsets of U and satisfying four conditions (we write *dom* D for the domain of D):

(i) for every $X \in dom\ D$, DX is an onion,

(ii) $\emptyset \in dom\ D$,

(iii) there is a subset $C \subseteq U$ such that, for all $X \in dom\ D$, $C = \bigcup(DX)$,

(iv) if $X \in dom\ D$, then, for every clopen set P, if $C \cap P \neq \emptyset$, then $S \cap P \in dom\ D$, where S is the smallest element in DX to overlap with P.

The elements in the range of D are called *D-possible belief sets*. Note that (U, T, DX) is a one-shot onion space, for each $X \in dom\ D$. An onion frame, therefore, is just a certain kind of conglomeration of one-shot onion spaces with a common, constant commitment set. An *iterative onion model* is a structure (U, T, D, V) such that (U, T, D) is an onion frame and V is a valuation in (U, T). The truth-conditions are simplified by the fact that complexes can now be dispensed with. Let $\mathcal{M} = (U, T, D, V)$ be an iterative onion model, O an onion in the domain of D, and u a point in U. We write $O \models_u^{\mathcal{M}} \chi$ or just $O \models_u \chi$ to indicate that a formula φ is *true in* $\mathcal{M}$ *with respect to O and u.*

1. $O \models_u \chi$ iff $u \in ||\chi||$, if χ is purely Boolean,
2. $O \models_u \psi \wedge \theta$ iff $O \models_u \psi$ and $O \models_u \theta$,
3. $O \models_u \neg\psi$ iff not $O \models_u \psi$,

and similarly for other Boolean operators;

4. $O \models_u \mathbf{B}\chi$ iff $\bigcap O \subseteq ||\chi||$,
5. $O \models_u \mathbf{K}\chi$ iff $\bigcup O \subseteq ||\chi||$,
6. $O \models_u [+\varphi]\chi$ iff $O' \models_u \chi$, where $O' = D(\bigcap O \cap ||\varphi||)$,
7. $O \models_u [*\varphi]\chi$ iff $O' \models_u \chi$, where either $\{S \in O : S \cap ||\varphi|| \neq \emptyset\}$ has no smallest element and $O' = D\emptyset$, or else Z is its smallest element and $O' = D(Z \cap ||\varphi||)$.

Validity of a formula in a frame is truth with respect to all onions and all points in all models on the frame. We say that a set is *iterative onion satisfiable* if there is a model on an onion frame and a point such that all the formulæ are true at that point in that model.

A *selector frame* is a triple (U, T, F), where (U, T) is a Stone topology and F (the *superselector*) is a function defined on a set of subsets of U and satisfying four conditions (we write *dom F* for the domain of F):

(i) for every $X \in dom\ F, FX$ is a selector,

(ii) $\emptyset, U \in dom\ F$,

(iii) there is a set $C \subseteq U$ such that, for every $X \in dom\ F, C = \bigcup\{(FX)P : P$ is clopen$\}$,

(iv) if $X \in dom\ F$, then for every clopen set P, $(FX)P \in dom\ F$.

The elements in the range of F are called *F-possible belief sets.* Evidently, for each $X \in dom\, F$, (U, T, FX) is a one-shot selector space. A selector frame is thus a kind of conglomeration of one-shot selector spaces with a common, constant commitment set. An *iterative selector model* is a structure (U, T, F, V) such that (U, T, F) is a selector frame and V is a valuation in (U, T). As with onion frames, the definition of truth no longer requires complexes. Let $\mathcal{M} = (U, T, D, V)$ be an iterative selector model, f a selector in the domain of F, and u a point in U. We write $f \models_u^{\mathcal{M}} \chi$ or just $f \models_u \chi$ to indicate that a formula φ is *true in $\mathcal{M}$ with respect to f and u.*

1. $f \models_u \chi$ iff $u \in ||\chi||$, if χ is purely Boolean,
2. $f \models_u \psi \wedge \theta$ iff $f \models_u \psi$ and $f \models_u \theta$,
3. $f \models_u \neg\psi$ iff not $f \models_u \psi$,

and similarly for other Boolean operators;

1. $f \models_u \mathbf{B}\chi$ iff $fU \subseteq ||\chi||$,
2. $f \models_u \mathbf{K}\chi$ iff $\bigcup\{fP : P \text{ is clopen}\} \subseteq ||\chi||$,
3. $f \models_u [+\varphi]\chi$ iff $f' \models_u \chi$, where $f' = F(fU \cap ||\varphi||)$,
4. $f \models_u [*\varphi]\chi$ iff $f' \models_u \chi$, where $f' = F(f||\varphi||)$.

Validity of a formula in a frame is truth with respect to all selectors and all points in all models on the frame. We say that a set is *iterative selector satisfiable* if all of its formulæ are simultaneously true with respect to some selector and some point in some model on some selector frame.

6.2 *Iterative syntax*

Formulæ of (basic) iterative DDL are still required to be basic (that is, operators **B**, **K**, + and $*$ apply only to purely Boolean formulæ), but nestings of change operators are now allowed. For example, if P and Q are propositional letters, the expression $[+\varphi]([*\psi]\neg[*\theta]P \wedge [*\theta]\neg[*\psi]Q)$ is a well-formed formula of iterative DDL if φ, ψ and θ are purely Boolean.

Say that a sequence $\alpha = \alpha_0; \ldots; \alpha_{n\text{-}1}$ is a *term sequence* if, for every $i < n$ there is some formula φ_i such that $\alpha_i = +\varphi_i$ or $\alpha_i = *\varphi_i$; we shall use $[\alpha]\chi$ and $\langle\alpha\rangle\chi$ as abbreviations for $[\alpha_0]\ldots[\alpha_{n\text{-}1}]\chi$ and $\langle\alpha_0\rangle\ldots\langle\alpha_{n\text{-}1}\rangle\chi$, respectively. This convention is (in this paper) merely a typographical convenience, but it is handy if one wants to formulate succinctly a syntactical condition corresponding to the semantical condition of unique methodology: instead of writing,

for all $m, n = 0$ and all terms $\alpha_0, \ldots, \alpha_{m\text{-}1}$ and $\beta_0, \ldots, \beta_{n\text{-}1}$,
from $\{[\alpha_0]\ldots[\alpha_{m\text{-}1}]\mathbf{B}\chi \equiv [\beta_0]\ldots[\beta_{n\text{-}1}]\mathbf{B}\chi : \chi \text{ is purely Boolean}\}$
to deduce $[\alpha_0]\ldots[\alpha_{m-1}]\theta \equiv [\beta_0]\ldots[\beta_{n-1}]\theta$

we may write more perspicuously,

for all term sequences α and β,
from $\{[\alpha]\mathbf{B}\chi \equiv [\beta]\mathbf{B}\chi : \chi$ is purely Boolean$\}$
to deduce $[\alpha]\theta \equiv [\beta]\theta$.

(The claim that such a condition is needed was first made in [14].) The trouble here is of course that the set mentioned in this rule is infinite. Thus for this analysis to be carried out we have to go beyond the confines of finitary logic. Actually to carry out the analysis would require more space than is available for this paper, but we shall offer some comments.

Instead of concentrating on theoremhood, as we have done in most of this paper, we will now consider deducibility. Let us write $\Gamma \vdash \varphi$ if φ is *deducible from* Γ (or Γ *proves* φ, a phrase often used today). As usual, we write $\vdash \varphi$ for $\emptyset \vdash \varphi$. In finitary logic, $\Gamma \vdash \varphi$ only if there is a finite subset Γ_0 of Γ such that $\Gamma_0 \vdash \varphi$. But the logic of this section is not going to be finitary!

An axiom system for iterative AGM can be constructed by drawing on the work in [9] (readers are referred to that paper for notation, concepts and ideas not explained here). Also here can we build our system block by block. A FIRST BLOCK consists of the structural rules (RX), (MN) and (CT), a SECOND BLOCK of (TF). A THIRD BLOCK consists of the rule (SR) for both + and $*$,

if $\Gamma \vdash \chi$ then $\{[+\varphi]\chi : \chi \in \Gamma\} \vdash [+\varphi]\chi$,
if $\Gamma \vdash \chi$ then $\{[*\varphi]\chi : \chi \in \Gamma\} \vdash [*\varphi]\chi$,

plus the rule (RC) of congruence:

if $\varphi \equiv \psi$ is purely Boolean and a tautology, then $\vdash [+\varphi]\chi \equiv [+\psi]\chi$
and $\vdash [*\varphi]\chi \equiv [*\psi]\chi$.

A FOURTH BLOCK consists of so-called categorical postulates of type $\vdash \theta$, where θ is an instance of one of the axiom schemata in Section 3 except ($\mathbf{KT}_0$). As a FIFTH BLOCK we have a new infinitary rule all by itself (the formal counterpart of the rule mentioned above): for all term sequences α and β,

$$(\infty)\ \{[\alpha]\mathbf{B}\chi \equiv [\beta]\mathbf{B}\chi : \chi \text{ is purely Boolean }\} \vdash [\alpha]\theta \equiv [\beta]\theta.$$

The logic (deducibility relation) defined by this axiom system we call the (*basic normal*) *iterated DDL of AGM* or $\mathrm{DDL}^i\mathrm{AGM}$ for short. As in the one-shot case we might go on to add a SIXTH BLOCK, consisting of the categorical axioms

$$\vdash \mathbf{K}\varphi, \text{ if } \varphi \in \mathrm{T}_0.$$

The resulting theory we call $\mathrm{DDT}^i\mathrm{AGM}$. The remarks made in Section 3.3 about DDL①AGM and DDT①AGM apply, mutatis mutandis, to $\mathrm{DDL}^i\mathrm{AGM}$ and $\mathrm{DDT}^i\mathrm{AGM}$.

LEMMA 19. *For all term sequences* α, $\vdash \langle\alpha\rangle\chi \supset [\alpha]\chi$.

Proof. By induction on the length of α. The proof uses the fact that ingredient operators $[+\varphi]$ and $[*\varphi]$ are normal and that the logic provides (+F) and (∗F). ■

6.3 The completeness proof

The fact that our logic is not finitary makes for complication. Notably, Lindenbaum's Lemma is no longer applicable. Nevertheless, we can carry out a modified construction along the lines of Section 5. For simplicity we refrain from giving a general exposition and concentrate instead on the logic defined by the new, infinitary axiom system. A set Σ is *finitely consistent* if, for all $n \geq 0$ and formulæ $\varphi_0, \ldots, \varphi_{n\text{-}1}$ it is not the case that $\{\varphi_0, \ldots, \varphi_{n\text{-}1}\} \vdash \bot$ and *maximal finitely consistent* if maximal with respect to finite consistency. We say that Σ has the *witness property* if, for all term sequences α and β, for every θ such that $[\alpha]\theta \not\equiv [\beta]\theta \in \Sigma$, there is some χ such that $[\alpha]\mathbf{B}\chi \not\equiv [\beta]\mathbf{B}\chi \in \Sigma$ (where $\not\equiv$ stands for material nonequivalence). A *saturated* set of formulæ is one that is maximal finitely consistent and has the witness property. By a result in [Segerberg, 1994]—a kind of modified Lindenbaum Lemma—is that every DDL^{i}AGM-consistent set has a saturated extension. (This is because, in the terminology of [Segerberg, 1994], (∞) is a categorical postulate with only denumerably many instances.) The relations $R^{+\varphi}$ and $R^{*\varphi}$ are defined as before except now they hold between saturated sets. By R^α let us understand the relation $R^{\alpha_0} \circ \ldots \circ R^{\alpha_{n\text{-}1}}$, where $\alpha = \alpha_0;\ldots;\alpha_{n\text{-}1}$ and $\circ$ is the operation of relative product. We note the following obvious but vital fact:

LEMMA 20. *Suppose that* Γ *and* Δ *are saturated sets. For all term sequences* α *and formulæ* χ, *if* $(\Gamma, \Delta) \in R^\alpha$ *then* $[\alpha]\chi \in \Gamma$ *only if* $\chi \in \Delta$ *(equivalently,* $\langle\alpha\rangle\chi \in \Gamma$ *if* $\chi \in \Delta$*).*

Now, given a saturated set Σ, define the required superselector F^Σ as follows. First, *dom* F^Σ is the set of subsets X of U such that, for some saturated set Θ and some term sequence α, $(\Sigma, \Theta) \in R^\alpha$ and $X = bst\,\Theta$. Second, for $X \in dom\, F^\Sigma$,

$$F^\Sigma X = f^\Theta,$$

where $X = bst\,\Theta$ and, for some term sequence α, $(\Sigma, \Theta) \in R^\alpha$. With this definition and a little help from [Segerberg, 1994], the completeness proof in Section 5 can be adapted. One nontrivial task is to prove that the definition of superselector is correct; to show this is particularly germane as it is here that the new, infinitary rule (∞) is needed. The following lemma does the job:

LEMMA 21. *Suppose that* Σ, Θ *and* Ξ *are saturated sets such that* $(\Sigma, \Theta) \in R^\alpha$ *and* $(\Sigma, \Xi) \in R^\beta$, *for some term sequences* α *and* β. *If* $bst\,\Theta = bst\,\Xi$, *then* $\Theta = \Xi$.

Proof. Let $\Sigma, \Theta, \Xi, \alpha$ and β be as in the hypothesis of the lemma. Suppose that $bst\,\Theta = bst\,\Xi$. Now,

$$bst\,\Theta = \bigcap\{|x| : \mathbf{B}\chi \in \Theta\},$$
$$bst\,\Xi = \bigcap\{|x| : \mathbf{B}\chi \in \Xi\}.$$

Hence it holds that, for all $\chi, \mathbf{B}\chi \in \Theta$ if and only if $\mathbf{B}\chi \in \Xi$. Suppose that $[\alpha]\mathbf{B}\chi \in \Sigma$. Then $\mathbf{B}\chi \in \Theta$ and hence $\mathbf{B}\chi \in \Xi$. By Lemma 20, $\langle\beta\rangle\mathbf{B}\chi \in \Sigma$. Hence $[\beta]\mathbf{B}\chi \in \Sigma$, by Lemma 19. This argument shows that $[\alpha]\mathbf{B}\chi \equiv [\beta]\mathbf{B}\chi \in \Sigma$, for all χ. Suppose that ψ in Θ. Then $\langle\alpha\rangle\psi \in \Sigma$ by Lemma 20. Hence $[\alpha]\psi \in \Sigma$ by Lemma 19. But by the new rule ∞, $[\alpha]\psi \equiv [\beta]\psi \in \Sigma$. Hence $[\beta]\psi \in \Sigma$. Therefore, $\psi \in \Xi$. We conclude that $\Theta = \Xi$. ■

THEOREM 22. *A formula set is consistent in DDL^{i}AGM if and only if it is selector satisfiable if and only if it is onion satisfiable.*

ACKNOWLEDGEMENTS

This paper is dedicated to Rob Goldblatt who celebrated his fiftieth anniversary on 21 April 1999. It grew out of notes prepared for a graduate course on belief revision in Stockholm 16–27 March 1998 as part of the peripatetic Nordic Graduate Programme in Philosophy. The author is grateful to Sten Lindström, who taught that course jointly with him, and to John Cantwell for many fruitful discussions. He would also like to thank an anonymous referee for a close reading and many useful remarks.

Department of Philosophy, Uppsala University, Sweden.

REFERENCES

[Alchourrón *et al.*, 1985] C. Alchourrón, P. Gärdenfors and D. Makinson. On the logic of theory change. *The Journal of Symbolic Logic*, **50**, 510–530, 1985.

[Cantwell, 1999] J. Cantwell. Some logics of iterated belief change. *Studia Logica*, **63**, 49–84, 1999.

[Gärdenfors, 1988] P. Gärdenfors. *Knowledge in Flux: Modeling the Dynamic of Epistemic States*. The MIT Press, Cambridge, MA, 1988.

[Grove, 1988] A. Grove. Two modellings for theory change. *Journal of Philosophical Logic*, **17**, 157–170, 1988.

[Hansson, 1969] B. Hansson. An analysis of some deontic logics. *Noûs*, **3**, 373–398, 1969.

[Lewis, 1973] D. Lewis. *Counterfactuals*. Blackwell, Oxford, 1973.

[van Linder *et al.*, 1995] B. van Linder, W. van der Hoek and J.-J. Meyer. Actions that make you change your mind. In *Knowledge and Belief in Philosophy and Artificial Intelligence*, A. Laux and H. Wansing, eds. pp. 103–146. Akademie Verlag GmbH, Berlin, 1995.

[Lindström and Rabinowicz, 1997] S. Lindström and W. Rabinowicz. Extending dynamic doxastic logic: accommodating iterated beliefs and Ramsey conditionals with DDL. In *For Good Measure*, L. Lindahl, P. Needham and R. Sliwinski, eds. pp. 126–153. Uppsala Philosophical Studies, vol. 46, 1997.

[Segerberg, 1994] K. Segerberg. A model existence theorem in infinitary propositional modal logic. *Journal of Philosophical Logic*, **23**, 337–367, 1994.

[Segerberg, 1994a] K. Segerberg. Trying to understand the logic of theory change in terms of modal logic. Extended abstract. In *Record of the Workshop on Logic and Action*, December 13–14, 1993, Norman Y. Foo, *et al.*, eds. pp. 1–12. University of Sydney, 1994.

[Segerberg, 1995] K. Segerberg. Belief revision from the point of view of doxastic logic. *Bulletin of the IGPL*, **3**, 534–553, 1995.

[Segerberg, 1996] K. Segerberg. A general framework for the logic of theory change. *Bulletin of the Section of Logic*, (Polish Academy of Sciences), **25**, 2–8, 1996.

[Segerberg, 1997] K. Segerberg. Belief revision along the lines of Lindström and Rabinowicz. *Fundamenta Informaticæ*, **32**, 183–191, 1997.

[Segerberg, 1999] K. Segerberg. Two traditions in the logic of belief: bringing them together. In *Logic, Language and Reasoning: Essays in Honour of Dov Gabbay*, U. Reyle and H. J. Ohlbach, eds. pp. 135–147. Kluwer, Dordrecht, 1999.

[Segerberg, to appear] K. Segerberg. Irrevocable belief revision in dynamic doxastic logic. To appear in *Notre Dame Journal for Formal Logic*.

[Surendonk, 1998] T. Surendonk. *Canonicity for Intensional Logics*. PhD dissertation, Australian National University. Canberra, 1998.

EDUARDO L. FERMÉ AND SVEN OVE HANSSON

SHIELDED CONTRACTION

1 INTRODUCTION

One of the major recent developments in the theory of belief change is the construction of models of belief change in which one or more of the postulates of the original AGM model [Alchourrón *et al.*, 1985] are not satisfied. In studies of belief *revision* (consistency-preserving incorporation of new beliefs), the most controversial postulate seems to be that of *success* ($\alpha \in \mathbf{K}{*}\alpha$), according to which the input sentence is always accepted, and incorporated into the new belief set. Several non-prioritized revision operators have been proposed, for which the success postulate does not hold. (See [Cantwell, 1997; Fermé and Hansson, 1999; Hansson, 1991a; Hansson, 1997; Hansson *et al.*, 1999; Makinson, 1997; Olsson, 1997], and, for an overview, [Hansson, 1999b].)

In studies of belief *contraction*, by far the most controversial AGM postulate is that of *recovery* ($\mathbf{K} \subseteq (\mathbf{K}{-}\alpha) + \alpha$), where $+$ denotes set-theoretical expansion). The (im)plausibility of this postulate is probably the most debated issue in the belief change literature [Fermé, 2000; Hansson, 1999a; Lindström and Rabinowicz, 1991; Makinson, 1987; Makinson, 1997; Nayak, 1994]. Several contraction operators that violate the recovery postulate have also been proposed [Fermé, 1998; Hansson, 1991b; Levi, 1991; Levi, 1997; Niederée, 1991; Rott and Pagnucco, 1999].

In this paper, we venture to question another of the basic Gärdenfors postulates for contraction, namely *success* (If $\nvdash \alpha$, then $\mathbf{K}{-}\alpha \nvdash \alpha$). The success postulate can be interpreted as requiring that all non-tautological beliefs are retractible. As was observed by Rott [1992, p.54], this is not a fully realistic requirement, since actual doxastic agents are known to have beliefs (of a non-logical nature) that nothing can bring them to give up. It should be of interest, therefore, to develop models of contraction in which some non-tautological beliefs may be shielded from contraction; in short: models of shielded contraction.

We will follow the AGM approach in representing belief states by belief sets, i.e. sets of sentences that are closed under a consequence operator Cn. This operator is assumed to satisfy the traditional properties, $\mathbf{A} \subseteq Cn(\mathbf{A})$, $Cn(Cn(\mathbf{A})) \subseteq Cn(\mathbf{A})$, and $Cn(\mathbf{A}) \subseteq Cn(\mathbf{B})$ if $\mathbf{A} \subseteq \mathbf{B}$. We also assume that Cn includes classical logical consequence, satisfies the rule of introduction of disjunction into premises and is compact. $\vdash \alpha$ is an alternative notation for $\alpha \in \mathrm{Cn}(\emptyset)$, and $\perp$ is the falsity constant. Lower-case Greek letters denote sentences, and capital letters denote sets of sentences. $\mathbf{K}$ denotes a belief set and $\mathbf{K}_\perp$ the inconsistent belief set. AGM-style contraction will be denoted by $-$, and shielded contraction by $\ominus$.

In Section 2, postulates for shielded contraction are proposed. In Section 3, three types of constructions are proposed, and in Section 4 they are axiomatically

M.-A. Williams and H. Rott (eds.), Frontiers in Belief Revision, 85–107.

characterized. In Section 5, connections with non-prioritized belief revision are explored. Proofs are deferred to an Appendix.

2 POSTULATES FOR SHIELDED CONTRACTION

The following are the Gärdenfors postulates for belief contraction,

Closure: $\mathbf{K}-\alpha$ is a belief set whenever $\mathbf{K}$ is a belief set.

Success: If $\nvdash \alpha$, then $\mathbf{K}-\alpha \nvdash \alpha$.

Inclusion: $\mathbf{K}-\alpha \subseteq \mathbf{K}$.

Vacuity: If $\mathbf{K} \nvdash \alpha$, then $\mathbf{K} \subseteq \mathbf{K}-\alpha$.

Extensionality: If $\vdash \alpha \leftrightarrow \beta$ then $\mathbf{K}-\alpha = \mathbf{K}-\beta$.

Recovery: $\mathbf{K} \subseteq (\mathbf{K}-\alpha) + \alpha$.

Conjunctive overlap: $\mathbf{K}-\alpha \cap \mathbf{K}-\beta \subseteq \mathbf{K}-(\alpha \wedge \beta)$.

Conjunctive inclusion: If $\mathbf{K}-(\alpha \wedge \beta) \nvdash \alpha$, then $\mathbf{K}-(\alpha \wedge \beta) \subseteq \mathbf{K}-\alpha$.

The first six of these postulates characterize partial meet contraction, the basic contraction operator of AGM [Alchourrón *et al.*, 1985]. All eight postulates characterize a whole series of equivalent constructions, that include sphere-based contraction [Grove, 1988] and entrenchment-based contraction [Gärdenfors, 1988; Gärdenfors and Makinson, 1988].

We are going to focus on the effects of giving up the success postulate, and will therefore not question any of the other postulates here.

The following weakened version of success is a plausible property for shielded contraction:

Persistence: If $\mathbf{K} \ominus \beta \vdash \beta$, then $\mathbf{K} \ominus \alpha \vdash \beta$.

According to persistence, if a sentence β is at all removable from the belief set, then it is removed in contraction by itself.

If an input sentence cannot be removed, then the original belief set should be retained:

Relative Success: [Rott, 1992] $\mathbf{K} \ominus \alpha = \mathbf{K}$ or $\mathbf{K} \ominus \alpha \nvdash \alpha$.

A sentence α such that $\mathbf{K} \ominus \alpha \vdash \alpha$ can be called an *irretractible* sentence. Given relative success, a sentence $\alpha \in \mathbf{K}$ is irretractible if and only if $\mathbf{K} \ominus \alpha = \mathbf{K}$. Shielded contraction differs from classical contraction in that non-tautological sentences may be irretractible.

If two sentences α and β are both irretractible, then we should expect their conjunction to also be irretractible:

Conjunctive Constancy: If $\mathbf{K} \ominus \alpha = \mathbf{K} \ominus \beta = \mathbf{K}$ then $\mathbf{K} \ominus (\alpha \wedge \beta) = \mathbf{K}$.

It can also be reasonably expected that the logical consequence of an irretractible belief should itself be irretractible:

Success Propagation: If $\mathbf{K} \ominus \beta \vdash \beta$ and $\vdash \beta \rightarrow \alpha$ then $\mathbf{K} \ominus \alpha \vdash \alpha$.

Success propagation can be shown to follow from *persistence*:

OBSERVATION 1. If an operator $\ominus$ on the belief set $\mathbf{K}$ satisfies *persistence*, then it satisfies *success propagation*.

The new postulates introduced in this section can all be shown to follow from the AGM contraction postulates (including *success*):

OBSERVATION 2. Let $\mathbf{K}$ be a belief set and $-$ an operator on $\mathbf{K}$ that satisfies *closure, inclusion, vacuity, success* and *recovery*. Then $-$ satisfies *relative success, persistence* and *conjunctive constancy*.

OBSERVATION 3. Let $\mathbf{K}$ be a belief set and $-$ an operator on $\mathbf{K}$ that satisfies *inclusion* and *conjunctive overlap*. Then it satisfies *conjunctive constancy*.

3 THREE CONSTRUCTIONS OF SHIELDED CONTRACTION

In this section, we are going to introduce three alternative constructions of shielded contraction. They are all derived through minor adjustments of well-known constructions of conventional contraction.

A fairly obvious method to construct shielded contraction is to divide the language into two parts, the retractible and the irretractible sentences, and apply a conventional contraction operator to the retractible sentences. This can be done as follows:

DEFINITION 4. Let $\mathbf{K}$ be a belief set, $-$ an AGM contraction operator on $\mathbf{K}$ and $\mathcal{R}$ a subset of $\mathcal{L}$ (the set of retractible sentences). Then $\ominus$ is the *shielded AGM contraction* induced by $-$ and $\mathcal{R}$ if and only if:

$$\mathbf{K} \ominus \alpha = \begin{cases} \mathbf{K} - \alpha & \text{if } \alpha \in \mathcal{R} \\ \mathbf{K} & \text{otherwise} \end{cases}$$

This construction can be further specified by adding requirements on the structure of $\mathcal{R}$.

Since a conjunctive sentence $\alpha \wedge \beta$ can be removed from a belief set only if at least one of its conjuncts α and β is removed, we should expect that $\alpha \wedge \beta$ cannot be retractible without either α or β being so.

Conjunctive Completeness: If $\alpha \wedge \beta \in \mathcal{R}$ then $\alpha \in \mathcal{R}$ or $\beta \in \mathcal{R}$.

The irretractible sentences are such that they cannot be removed from $\mathbf{K}$, no matter what contraction we perform, hence:

Non-Retractability Preservation: $\mathcal{L} \setminus \mathcal{R} \subseteq \mathbf{K} \dot{-} \alpha$.

Next, suppose that α is irretractible, $\vdash \alpha \rightarrow \beta$ and β is retractible. Then $\beta \notin \mathbf{K} \dot{-} \beta$, hence $\alpha \notin \mathbf{K} \dot{-} \beta$, so that α can be retracted after all. This implausible combination is precluded by the following condition:

Non-Retractability Propagation: If $\alpha \notin \mathcal{R}$, then $Cn(\{\alpha\}) \cap \mathcal{R} = \emptyset$.

A quite different approach to the construction of shielded contraction is to base it on an entrenchment relation. The standard set of postulates for entrenchment is as follows:

(EE1) Transitivity: If $\alpha \leq_{\mathbf{K}} \beta$ and $\beta \leq_{\mathbf{K}} \delta$, then $\alpha \leq_{\mathbf{K}} \delta$.

(EE2) Dominance: If $\alpha \vdash \beta$, then $\alpha \leq_{\mathbf{K}} \beta$.

(EE3) Conjunctiveness: $\alpha \leq_{\mathbf{K}} (\alpha \wedge \beta)$ or $\beta \leq_{\mathbf{K}} (\alpha \wedge \beta)$.

(EE4) Minimality: If $\mathbf{K} \nvdash \bot$, then $\alpha \notin \mathbf{K}$ if and only if $\alpha \leq_{\mathbf{K}} \beta$ for all β.

(EE5) Maximality: If $\beta \leq_{\mathbf{K}} \alpha$ for all β, then $\vdash \alpha$.

Note that *intersubstitutivity* follows from (**EE1**) and (**EE2**), i.e., if $\vdash \alpha \leftrightarrow \alpha'$ and $\vdash \beta \leftrightarrow \beta'$, then $\alpha \leq_{\mathbf{K}} \beta$ iff $\alpha' \leq_{\mathbf{K}} \beta'$. Furthermore, *completeness* ($\alpha \leq_{\mathbf{K}} \beta$ or $\beta \leq_{\mathbf{K}} \alpha$) follows from (**EE1**), (**EE2**), and (**EE3**).

Peter Gärdenfors, who proposed these postulates [Gärdenfors, 1988], also showed how they can be used to construct a constraction operator:

$$(-_G) \qquad \beta \in \mathbf{K}-\alpha \text{ if and only if } \beta \in \mathbf{K} \text{ and either } \vdash \alpha \text{ or } \alpha <_{\mathbf{K}} (\alpha \vee \beta).$$

Gärdenfors's maximality property (**EE5**) says that only tautologies can be maximally entrenched. This is exactly the condition that we want to relax: in shielded contraction non-tautologies may be maximally entrenched. Therefore, as was noted by Rott [1992, p.54], an obvious way to modify entrenchment-based contraction for our purposes is to just withdraw this property (**EE5**) from the definition. In addition, however, a minor modification of the $(-_G)$ condition is necessary: The clause "either $\vdash \alpha$ or" has the purpose of ensuring that $\mathbf{K} \dot{-} \alpha = \mathbf{K}$ whenever α is maximally entrenched, i.e., a tautology. It would make no difference to replace $\vdash \alpha$ here by "$\beta \leq_{\mathbf{K}} \alpha$ for all β" or, equivalenty "$\alpha \not<_{\mathbf{K}} \top$". However, when (**EE5**) has been removed, this replacement is mandatory, since tautologies and maximally entrenched sentences no longer coincide. We therefore arrive at the following definition:

DEFINITION 5. Let $\mathbf{K}$ be a belief set and $\leq_{\mathbf{K}}$ a relation satisfying (**EE1**)–(**EE4**) with respect to $\mathbf{K}$. Then $\mathbin{-\!\!\ominus\!\!-}$ is the *shielded entrenchment-based contraction* based on $\leq_{\mathbf{K}}$ if and only if:

$$\mathbf{K}\mathbin{-\!\!\ominus\!\!-}\alpha = \begin{cases} \{\beta \in \mathbf{K} \colon \alpha <_{\mathbf{K}} (\alpha \vee \beta)\} & \text{if } \alpha <_{\mathbf{K}} \top \\ \mathbf{K} & \text{otherwise} \end{cases}$$

This definition gives rise to the following simple "backwards" connection between $\mathbin{-\!\!\ominus\!\!-}$ and $\leq_{\mathbf{K}}$.

OBSERVATION 6. Let $\mathbf{K}$ be a consistent belief set and $\leq_{\mathbf{K}}$ a relation satisfying (**EE1**)–(**EE4**) with respect to $\mathbf{K}$. Let $\mathbin{-\!\!\ominus\!\!-}$ be the shielded entrenchment-based contraction induced by $\leq_{\mathbf{K}}$. Then:

$(C \leq)$ $\alpha \leq_{\mathbf{K}} \beta$ if and only if: If $\alpha \in \mathbf{K}\mathbin{-\!\!\ominus\!\!-}(\alpha \wedge \beta)$ then $\beta \in \mathbf{K}\mathbin{-\!\!\ominus\!\!-}(\alpha \wedge \beta)$.

Our third construction is based on possible world models of belief change. A proposition (set of possible worlds) can represent either a belief set or an input sentence. The belief set $\mathbf{K}$ can be replaced, as a belief state representation, by the following proposition:

$$||\mathbf{K}|| = \{X \mid \mathbf{K} \subseteq X \in \mathcal{L} \perp\!\perp\},$$

which is the set of worlds that contain $\mathbf{K}$. ($\alpha \perp\!\perp$ is the set of maximal consistent subsets of α.) Similarly, each sentence α can be represented by the set $||\alpha|| = ||Cn(\{\alpha\})||$. Contraction by α takes the form of adding new possible worlds in which $\neg\alpha$ holds, i.e.:

DEFINITION 7. [Hansson, 1999c] Let X be a proposition. A *propositional selection function* for X is a function f such that for all sentences α:

(I) $f(||\alpha||) \subseteq ||\alpha||$

(II) If $||\alpha|| \neq \emptyset$ then $f(||\alpha||) \neq \emptyset$.

(III) If $X \cap ||\alpha|| \neq \emptyset$, then $f(||\alpha||) = X \cap ||\alpha||$.

DEFINITION 8. Let X be a proposition. An operator $\ominus$ is a *propositional contraction operator* for X if and only if there is a propositional selection function f for X such that for all α:

$$X \ominus ||\alpha|| = X \cup f(||\neg\alpha||)$$

The propositional contraction operators on $||\mathbf{K}||$ coincide with the partial meet contractions on $\mathbf{K}$. For each $\ominus$ on $||\mathbf{K}||$ there is some partial meet contraction $-$ on $\mathbf{K}$ such that $\mathbf{K}-\alpha = \bigcap(||\mathbf{K}|| \ominus ||\alpha||)$, and vice versa [Grove, 1988; Hansson, 1999c].

This construction can be adopted to shielded contraction by shielding off a set $\Im$ of inaccessible worlds:

DEFINITION 9. Let X be a proposition. A *shielded propositional selection function* for X is a function f such that, for some set $\Im \subseteq \mathcal{L}\perp\perp$ (the set of inaccessible worlds), it holds for all sentences α that:

(I) $f(||\alpha||) \subseteq ||\alpha|| \setminus \Im$

(II) If $||\alpha|| \setminus \Im \neq \emptyset$ then $f(||\alpha||) \neq \emptyset$.

(III) If $(X \cap ||\alpha||) \setminus \Im \neq \emptyset$, then $f(||\alpha||) = (X \cap ||\alpha||) \setminus \Im$.

DEFINITION 10. Let X be a proposition. An operator $\ominus$ is a *shielded propositional contraction operator* for X if and only if there is a shielded propositional selection function f for X such that for all α:

$$X \ominus ||\alpha|| = X \cup f(||\neg\alpha||)$$

The most well-known propositional models of belief change make use of a system of concentric spheres around the proposition that represents the present belief state [Grove, 1988]. Intuitively, each sphere represents a degree of closeness or similarity to $||\mathbf{K}||$. In contraction by α, the closest $\neg\alpha$-worlds are added to $||\mathbf{K}||$.

DEFINITION 11. [Grove, 1988] \$ is a *system of spheres* if and only if it satisfies:

\$1 $\emptyset \neq \$ \subseteq \mathcal{P}(\mathcal{L}\perp\perp)$,

\$2 $\cap\$ \in \$$,

\$3 If $\mathbf{G}, \mathbf{G}' \in \$$, then $\mathbf{G} \subseteq \mathbf{G}'$ or $\mathbf{G}' \subseteq \mathbf{G}$,

\$4 $\cup\$ \in \$$,

\$5 If $||\alpha|| \cap (\cup\$) \neq \emptyset$, then $\mathbf{S}_\alpha \in \$$ and $\mathbf{S}_\alpha \cap ||\alpha|| \neq \emptyset$, and

\$6 $\mathcal{L}\perp\perp \in \$$,

where $\mathbf{S}_\alpha = \bigcap\{\mathbf{G} \in \$ \mid \mathbf{G} \cap ||\alpha|| \neq \emptyset\}$.

DEFINITION 12. Let \$ be a system of spheres. Then:

$$\mathbf{K}_\$ = \bigcap\cap\$.$$

$\mathbf{S}_\alpha$ is the closest sphere that is compatible with α. $\mathbf{K}_\$$ is the belief set corresponding to \$.

DEFINITION 13. [Grove, 1988] A propositional selection function f for a proposition X is *sphere-based* if and only if there is a system of spheres \$ such that for all α: If $||\alpha|| \neq \emptyset$, then $f(||\alpha||) = \mathbf{S}_\alpha \cap ||\alpha||$.

A propositional contraction operator is sphere-based if and only if it is based on a sphere-based propositional selection function.

We can adopt these definitions to shielded contraction simply by making the outermost sphere inaccessible, i.e., by relaxing condition $\$6$ of Definition 11.

DEFINITION 14. $\$$ is a *shielded system of spheres* if and only if it satisfies conditions $\$1 - \$5$ of Definition 11.

DEFINITION 15. A shielded propositional function f for a proposition X, with the associated set $\Im$ of inaccessible worlds, is *sphere-based* if and only if there is a shielded system of spheres $\$$ such that:

1. $\Im = (\mathcal{L} \perp\perp) \setminus (\cup\$)$ and
2. for all α, if $||\alpha|| \setminus \Im \neq \emptyset$, then $f(||\alpha||) = \mathbf{S}_\alpha \cap ||\alpha||$.

A shielded propositional contraction-operator is sphere-based if and only it is based on a sphere-based propositional selection function.

4 REPRESENTATION THEOREMS

The following two representation theorems characterize the major constructions introduced in the previous section.

THEOREM 16. *Let* $\mathbf{K}$ *be a consistent belief set and* $\ominus$ *an operation on* $\mathbf{K}$*. Then the following conditions are equivalent:*

1. $\ominus$ *satisfies* closure, inclusion, vacuity, extensionality, recovery, relative success, success propagation, *and* conjunctive constancy.

2. $\ominus$ *is the operator of shielded partial meet contraction induced by a partial meet contraction operator for* $\mathbf{K}$ *and a set* $\mathcal{R} \subseteq \mathcal{L}$ *that satisfies* non-retractability propagation *and* conjunctive completeness.

3. $\ominus$ *is the operator of shielded partial meet contraction induced by a partial meet contraction operator for* $\mathbf{K}$ *and a set* $\mathcal{R} \subseteq \mathcal{L}$ *such that* $\mathcal{L} \setminus \mathbf{K} \subseteq \mathcal{R}$ *and that* $\mathcal{R}$ *satisfies* non-retractability propagation *and* conjunctive completeness.

THEOREM 17. *Let* $\mathbf{K}$ *be a consistent belief set and* $\ominus$ *an operation on* $\mathbf{K}$*. Then the following three conditions are equivalent:*

1. $\ominus$ *satisfies* closure, inclusion, vacuity, extensionality, recovery, relative success, persistence, conjunctive inclusion, *and* conjuntive overlap.

2. $\ominus$ *is the operator of shielded partial meet contraction induced by a transitively relational partial meet contraction operator for* $\mathbf{K}$ *and a set* $\mathcal{R} \subseteq \mathcal{L}$ *that satisfies* non-retractability propagation, conjunctive completeness, *and* non-retractability preservation.

3. *$\mathbin{-\!\!\!\ominus}$ is the operator of shielded partial meet contraction induced by a transitively relational partial meet contraction operator for* $\mathbf{K}$ *and a set* $\mathcal{R} \subseteq \mathcal{L}$ *such that* $\mathcal{L} \setminus \mathbf{K} \subseteq \mathcal{R}$ *and that* $\mathcal{R}$ *satisfies* non-retractability propagation, conjunctive completeness, *and* non-retractability preservation.

4. *$\mathbin{-\!\!\!\ominus}$ is a shielded entrenchment-based contraction.*

5. *There exists a shielded sphere-based contraction* $\ominus$ *on* $||\mathbf{K}||$ *such that* $\mathbf{K} \mathbin{-\!\!\!\ominus} \alpha = \bigcap ||\mathbf{K} \ominus \alpha||$ *for all* α.

(Note that due to Observations 1 and 3, *success propagation* and *conjunctive constancy* could redundantly be added the above list of postulates).

5 GENERALIZED LEVI AND HARPER IDENTITIES

One of the hallmarks of the AGM theory is the interdefinability of its contraction and revision operators. In this section we are going to search for similar relationships between shielded contraction and non-prioritized revision, i.e., revision that does not satisfy the *success* postulate for revision ($\alpha \in \mathbf{K} * \alpha$). The symbol $\circ$ will be used to denote non-prioritized revision.

In AGM theory, revision is defined in terms of contraction as follows:

$$\mathbf{K} \circ \alpha = (\mathbf{K} \mathbin{-\!\!\!\ominus} \neg\alpha) + \alpha \qquad \text{(Levi identity)}$$

A revision operator obtained through the Levi identity always satisfies the *success* postulate for revision. We should expect a revision operator that corresponds to shielded contraction not to satisfy that postulate. One way to achieve this is to modify the definition so that it satisfies *consistency preservation* (If $\mathbf{K} \not\vdash \bot$, then $\mathbf{K} \circ \alpha \not\vdash \bot$), which is a fairly plausible condition that contradicts *success*:

DEFINITION 18. Consistency-preserving Levi identity:

$$\mathbf{K} \circ \alpha = \begin{cases} (\mathbf{K} \mathbin{-\!\!\!\ominus} \neg\alpha) + \alpha & \text{if } \mathbf{K} \mathbin{-\!\!\!\ominus} \neg\alpha \not\vdash \neg\alpha \\ \mathbf{K} & \text{otherwise} \end{cases}$$

For our present purposes, the consistency-preserving version of the Levi identity turned out to be the more useful one. With this definition, the postulates of shielded contraction studied above give rise, in the corresponding revision operator, to properties that have been used to characterize operators of non-prioritized revision. (The reader will have to forbear with the use of the same name both for a property of contraction and for a property of revision; this is traditional terminology in belief revision theory.) Among the revision postulates mentioned in the literature, the following can be used to relate revision with shielded contraction:

Closure: [Alchourrón *et al.*, 1985] $\mathbf{K} \circ \alpha$ is a belief set.

Relative success: [Hansson *et al.*, 1999] $\mathbf{K} \circ \alpha \vdash \alpha$ or $\mathbf{K} \circ \alpha = \mathbf{K}$.

Inclusion: [Alchourrón *et al.*, 1985] $\mathbf{K} \circ \alpha \subseteq \mathbf{K} + \alpha$.

Vacuity: [Alchourrón *et al.*, 1985] If $\mathbf{K} \nvdash \neg\alpha$, then $\mathbf{K} + \alpha \subseteq \mathbf{K} \circ \alpha$.

Consistency preservation: [Hansson, 1996] If $\mathbf{K} \nvdash \bot$ then $\mathbf{K} \circ \alpha \nvdash \bot$.

Extensionality: [Alchourrón *et al.*, 1985] If $\vdash \alpha \leftrightarrow \beta$, then $\mathbf{K} \circ \alpha = \mathbf{K} \circ \beta$.

Superexpansion: [Alchourrón *et al.*, 1985] $\mathbf{K} \circ (\alpha \wedge \beta) \subseteq (\mathbf{K} \circ \alpha) + \beta$.

Guarded subexpansion: [Hansson *et al.*, 1999] If $\mathbf{K} \circ \alpha \vdash \alpha$ and $\mathbf{K} \circ \alpha \nvdash \neg\beta$, then $(\mathbf{K} \circ \alpha) + \beta \subseteq \mathbf{K} \circ (\alpha \wedge \beta)$.

Strict improvement: [Fermé and Hansson, 1999] If $\mathbf{K} \circ \alpha \vdash \alpha$ and $\vdash \alpha \rightarrow \beta$, then $\mathbf{K} \circ \beta \vdash \beta$.

Disjunctive constancy: [Hansson *et al.*, 1999] If $\mathbf{K} \circ \alpha = \mathbf{K} \circ \beta = \mathbf{K}$ then $\mathbf{K} \circ (\alpha \vee \beta) = \mathbf{K}$.

Strong Regularity: [Hansson *et al.*, 1999] If $\mathbf{K} \circ \alpha \nvdash \neg\beta$ then $\mathbf{K} \circ \beta \vdash \beta$.

OBSERVATION 19. Let $\mathbf{K}$ be a belief set. Let $\circ$ be defined via the consistency-preserving Levi identity from $\mathbf{K}$ and $\div$. Then:

1. $\circ$ satisfies *closure, consistency preservation* and *relative success*.
2. If $\div$ satisfies *inclusion*, then $\circ$ satisfies *inclusion*.
3. If $\div$ satisfies *inclusion* and *vacuity*, then $\circ$ satisfies *vacuity*.
4. If $\div$ satisfies *extensionality*, then $\circ$ satisfies *extensionality*.
5. If $\div$ satisfies *inclusion* and *persistence*, then $\circ$ satisfies *strong regularity*.
6. If $\div$ satisfies *relative success, vacuity, extensionality*, and *conjunctive constancy*, then $\circ$ satisfies *disjunctive constancy*.
7. If $\div$ satisfies *inclusion* and *success propagation*, then $\circ$ satisfies *strict improvement*.
8. If $\div$ satisfies *extensionality, relative success*, and *conjunctive inclusion*, then $\circ$ satisfies *guarded subexpansion*.

9. If $\div$ satisfies *closure, inclusion, extensionality, recovery, persistence, relative success*, and *conjunctive overlap*, then $\circ$ satisfies *superexpansion*.

In AGM theory, contraction is definable from revision via the Harper identity. This identity can be used in its original form for shielded contraction:

DEFINITION 20. Harper Identity:

$$\mathbf{K} \div \alpha = \mathbf{K} \cap \mathbf{K} \circ \neg \alpha$$

The postulates used for non-prioritized revision give rise, via the Harper identity, to postulates that were shown above to hold for shielded contraction:

OBSERVATION 21. Let $\mathbf{K}$ be a belief set. Let $\div$ be defined via the Harper identity from $\mathbf{K}$ and $\circ$. Then:

1. $\div$ satisfies *inclusion*.
2. If $\circ$ satisfies *closure*, then $\div$ satisfies *closure*.
3. If $\circ$ satisfies *vacuity*, then $\div$ satisfies *vacuity*.
4. If $\circ$ satisfies *extensionality*, then $\div$ satisfies *extensionality*.
5. If $\circ$ satisfies *closure* and *relative suceess*, then $\div$ satisfies *recovery*.
6. If $\mathbf{K} \nvdash \perp$ and $\circ$ satisfies *closure, consistency preservation*, and *strong regularity*, then $\div$ satisfies *persistence*.
7. If $\circ$ satisfies *closure, consistency preservation*, and *relative success*, then $\div$ satisfies *relative success*.
8. If $\circ$ satisfies *vacuity, consistency preservation, extensionality, relative success*, and *disjunctive constancy*, then $\circ$ satisfies *conjunctive constancy*.
9. If $\mathbf{K} \nvdash \perp$ and $\circ$ satisfies *strict improvement, relative success*, and *consistency preservation*, then $\div$ satisfies *success propagation*.
10. If $\circ$ satisfies *closure, extensionality, relative success*, and *superexpansion*, then $\div$ satisfies *conjunctive overlap*.
11. If $\circ$ satisfies *vacuity, strong regularity, strict improvement*, and *guarded subexpansion*, then $\div$ satisfies *conjunctive inclusion*.

Through the Harper identity and the consistency-preserving Levi identity, operators of (non-prioritized) revision and (shielded) contraction are interdefinable. To express this more precisely, it is convenient to introduce functions that take us from contractions to revisions and vice versa [Makinson, 1987]. This can be done as follows:

DEFINITION 22. [Makinson, 1987] For every operator $\mathrel{-\!\!\!\ominus}$, $\mathbb{R}(\mathrel{-\!\!\!\ominus})$ is the operator generated from $\mathrel{-\!\!\!\ominus}$ through the consistency-preserving Levi identity (Definition 18). Furthermore, for every operator $\circ$, $\mathbb{C}(\circ)$ is the operator generated from $\circ$ by the Harper identity (Definition 20).

THEOREM 23. *Let* $\mathbf{K}$ *be a belief set and* $\mathrel{-\!\!\!\ominus}$ *an operator for* $\mathbf{K}$ *that satisfies the contraction postulates closure, inclusion, recovery, and relative success. Then* $\mathbb{C}(\mathbb{R}(\mathrel{-\!\!\!\ominus})) = \mathrel{-\!\!\!\ominus}$.

THEOREM 24. *Let* $\mathbf{K}$ *be a belief set and* $\circ$ *an operator for* $\mathbf{K}$ *that satisfies the revision postulates closure, vacuity, relative success, and consistency preservation. Then* $\mathbb{R}(\mathbb{C}(\circ)) = \circ$.

In summary, we have managed to relax the success postulate for contraction while at the same time retaining two central features of the AGM model: (1) Our constructions are axiomatically characterized, which means that they can be tested against both semantical and syntactical intuitions. (2) The interdefinability of revision and contraction via the Levi and Harper identities has been retained.

APPENDIX: PROOFS

LEMMA 25. *[Rott, 1992] Let* $\mathbf{K}$ *be a belief set and* $-$ *an operator on* $\mathbf{K}$ *that satisfies* closure, inclusion, success, vacuity *and* recovery. *Then:* $\mathbf{K}-\alpha = \mathbf{K}$ *if and only if either* $\mathbf{K} \nvdash \alpha$ *or* $\vdash \alpha$.

LEMMA 26. *[Foo, 1990] Let* $\mathbf{K}$ *be a belief set and* $\leq_{\mathbf{K}}$ *a relation satisfying* $(\mathbf{EE1})$ *and* $(\mathbf{EE4})$ *with respect to* $\mathbf{K}$. *If* $\alpha \notin \mathbf{K}$ *and* $\beta \in \mathbf{K}$, *then* $\alpha <_{\mathbf{K}} \beta$.

LEMMA 27. *[Hansson* et al., *1999] Let* $\$$ *be a shielded system of spheres as defined in Definition 14 and let* $\leq$ *be the following relation:* $\alpha \leq \beta$ *if and only if for all* $T \in \$$: *If* $T \subseteq \|\alpha\|$ *then* $T \subseteq \|\beta\|$.
Then $\leq$ *satisfies* $(\mathbf{EE1})$–$(\mathbf{EE4})$ *with respect* $\mathbf{K}_{\$}$.

LEMMA 28. *[Hansson* et al., *1999] Let* $\leq_{\mathbf{K}}$ *be a relation on* $\mathcal{L}$ *that satisfies the epistemic entrenchment postulates* $(\mathbf{EE1})$–$(\mathbf{EE4})$ *with respect to a consistent belief set* $\mathbf{K}$. *Let* $\$_{\leq}$ *be the set such that* $X \in \$_{\leq}$ *if and only if it satisfies the following conditions:*

($\$_{\leq}1$*)* $\|\mathbf{K}\| \subseteq X$,

($\$_{\leq}2$*)* $X = \cap\{\|\alpha\| \mid X \subseteq \|\alpha\|\}$,

($\$_{\leq}3$*)* $X \subseteq \mathcal{P}(\mathcal{L} \perp\perp)$,

($\$_{\leq}4$*) For all* $\alpha, \beta \in \mathcal{L}$, *if* $X \subseteq \|\alpha\|$ *and* $\alpha \leq_{\mathbf{K}} \beta$, *then* $X \subseteq \|\beta\|$.

Let $\mathbf{S}_\alpha$ *and* $\mathbf{K}_{\$}$ *be defined as in Definitions 11 and 12. Then:*

(a) $\$_{\leq}$ *is a shielded sphere system defined as in Definition 14.*

(b) $\mathbf{K}_{\$} = \mathbf{K}$.

(c) $\alpha <_{\mathbf{K}} \top$ *if and only if* $\bigcup \$_{\leq} \not\subseteq \|\alpha\|$.

(d) *If* $\alpha <_{\mathbf{K}} \top$ *then* $\mathbf{S}_{\neg\alpha} = \bigcap\{\|\beta\| \mid \alpha <_{\mathbf{K}} \beta\}$.

Proof of Observation 1: Let $\mathbf{K} \mathbin{-\!\!\!\ominus} \beta \vdash \beta$ and $\vdash \beta \rightarrow \alpha$. It follows by *persistence* that $\mathbf{K} \mathbin{-\!\!\!\ominus} \alpha \vdash \beta$, and from this the desired result follows directly. ■

Proof of Observation 2:
Relative success: Let $\mathbf{K} \mathbin{-\!\!\!\ominus} \alpha \neq \mathbf{K}$. Then by Lemma 25, $\not\vdash \alpha$, hence by *success*, $\mathbf{K} \mathbin{-\!\!\!\ominus} \alpha \not\vdash \alpha$.
Persistence: Let $\mathbf{K} \mathbin{-\!\!\!\ominus} \beta \vdash \beta$. Then by *success* $\vdash \beta$. Hence $\mathbf{K} \mathbin{-\!\!\!\ominus} \alpha \vdash \beta$.
Conjunctive constancy: For *reductio ad absurdum* suppose that $\mathbf{K} \mathbin{-\!\!\!\ominus} \alpha = \mathbf{K} \mathbin{-\!\!\!\ominus} \beta = \mathbf{K}$ and $\mathbf{K} \mathbin{-\!\!\!\ominus} (\alpha \wedge \beta) \neq \mathbf{K}$. It follows by Lemma 25 from $\mathbf{K} \mathbin{-\!\!\!\ominus} (\alpha \wedge \beta) \neq \mathbf{K}$ that $\mathbf{K} \vdash \alpha \wedge \beta$ and $\not\vdash \alpha \wedge \beta$. Then $\mathbf{K} \vdash \alpha$ and $\mathbf{K} \vdash \beta$. From this and $\mathbf{K} \mathbin{-\!\!\!\ominus} \alpha = \mathbf{K} \mathbin{-\!\!\!\ominus} \beta = \mathbf{K}$ follows, by Lemma 25, $\vdash \alpha$ and $\vdash \beta$, contrary to $\not\vdash \alpha \wedge \beta$ that was just shown. ■

Proof of Observation 3: Let $\mathbf{K} \mathbin{-\!\!\!\ominus} \alpha = \mathbf{K} \mathbin{-\!\!\!\ominus} \beta$. It follows from *inclusion* that $\mathbf{K} \mathbin{-\!\!\!\ominus} (\alpha \wedge \beta) \subseteq \mathbf{K}$ and from *conjunctive overlap* that $\mathbf{K} \subseteq \mathbf{K} \mathbin{-\!\!\!\ominus} (\alpha \wedge \beta)$. ■

Proof of Observation 6: For the left to right direction, let $\alpha \leq_{\mathbf{K}} \beta$ and $\alpha \in \mathbf{K} \mathbin{-\!\!\!\ominus} (\alpha \wedge \beta)$. It follows by Definition 5 that $\alpha \in \mathbf{K}$. Due to the completeness of $\leq_{\mathbf{K}}$, we have two cases: First case, $\top \leq_{\mathbf{K}} \alpha$: Then (**EE1**) yields $\top \leq_{\mathbf{K}} \beta$. It follows from (**EE1**) and (**EE3**) that $\top \leq_{\mathbf{K}} \alpha \wedge \beta$. According to Definition 5 $\mathbf{K} \mathbin{-\!\!\!\ominus} (\alpha \wedge \beta) = \mathbf{K}$. Since $\mathbf{K}$ is consistent and logically closed, it follows from (**EE1**), (**EE2**) and (**EE4**) that $\bot <_{\mathbf{K}} \top$. Hence by (**EE1**) $\bot <_{\mathbf{K}} \alpha \wedge \beta$. It follows from (**EE4**) that $\alpha \wedge \beta \in \mathbf{K}$, hence $\beta \in \mathbf{K} = \mathbf{K} \mathbin{-\!\!\!\ominus} (\alpha \wedge \beta)$. Second case, $\alpha <_{\mathbf{K}} \top$. Then it follows from Definition 5 that $\alpha \wedge \beta <_{\mathbf{K}} (\alpha \wedge \beta) \vee \alpha$. By intersubstitutivity, $\alpha \wedge \beta <_{\mathbf{K}} \alpha$. Then by (**EE1**), $\alpha \wedge \beta <_{\mathbf{K}} \beta$; and by intersubstitutivity, $\alpha \wedge \beta <_{\mathbf{K}} (\alpha \wedge \beta) \vee \beta$. It follows from Definition 5 that $\beta \in \mathbf{K} \mathbin{-\!\!\!\ominus} (\alpha \wedge \beta)$.

For the other direction assume that *if* $\alpha \in \mathbf{K} \mathbin{-\!\!\!\ominus} (\alpha \wedge \beta)$, *then* $\beta \in \mathbf{K} \mathbin{-\!\!\!\ominus} (\alpha \wedge \beta)$. We have two cases: First case, $\alpha \in \mathbf{K} \mathbin{-\!\!\!\ominus} (\alpha \wedge \beta)$ and $\beta \in \mathbf{K} \mathbin{-\!\!\!\ominus} (\alpha \wedge \beta)$: If $\alpha \wedge \beta <_{\mathbf{K}} \top$, then it follows from Definition 5, since $\alpha, \beta \in \mathbf{K} \mathbin{-\!\!\!\ominus} (\alpha \wedge \beta)$ that $\alpha \in \mathbf{K}$, $\beta \in \mathbf{K}$, $\alpha \wedge \beta <_{\mathbf{K}} (\alpha \wedge \beta) \vee \alpha$ and $\alpha \wedge \beta <_{\mathbf{K}} (\alpha \wedge \beta) \vee \beta$. This contradicts (**EE3**) and we can conclude that $\top \leq_{\mathbf{K}} \alpha \wedge \beta$. Then by (**EE2**) and (**EE1**), $\top \leq_{\mathbf{K}} \beta$; and since by (**EE2**) $\alpha \leq_{\mathbf{K}} \top$, by (**EE1**) we obtain $\alpha \leq_{\mathbf{K}} \beta$. Second case, $\alpha \notin \mathbf{K} \mathbin{-\!\!\!\ominus} (\alpha \wedge \beta)$: If $\alpha \notin \mathbf{K}$, then it follows by (**EE4**) that $\alpha \leq_{\mathbf{K}} \beta$. If $\alpha \in \mathbf{K}$, then Definition 5 yields $(\alpha \wedge \beta) \vee \alpha \leq_{\mathbf{K}} \alpha \wedge \beta$. By intersubstitutivity, $\alpha \leq_{\mathbf{K}} \alpha \wedge \beta$. (**EE2**) yields $\alpha \wedge \beta \leq_{\mathbf{K}} \beta$ and we can use to (**EE1**) conclude that $\alpha \leq_{\mathbf{K}} \beta$. ■

Proof of Theorem 16:
(1) to (3): We first define $\mathcal{R}$ and $-$:

$$\mathcal{R} = \{\alpha : \mathbf{K}\ominus\alpha \nvdash \alpha\}.$$

$$\mathbf{K}-\alpha = \begin{cases} \text{(i) } \mathbf{K}\ominus\alpha & \text{if } \alpha \in \mathcal{R} \\ \text{(ii) } \mathbf{K} \cap Cn(\{\neg\alpha\}) & \text{otherwise} \end{cases}$$

$\mathbf{K}\cap Cn(\{\neg\alpha\})$ is *full meet contraction*, that satisfies the basic (and supplementary) AGM contraction postulates [Alchourrón and Makinson, 1982]. We have to prove: **(a)** that $\mathcal{R}$ has the listed properties, **(b)** that $-$ satisfies the basic AGM contraction postulates, and **(c)** that $\ominus$ is induced by $\mathcal{R}$ and $-$.

(a): $\mathcal{L} \setminus \mathbf{K} \subseteq \mathcal{R}$**:** Directly from *inclusion* and definition of $\mathcal{R}$.

Non-Retractability Propagation: Let $\alpha \notin \mathcal{R}$ and $\beta \in Cn(\{\alpha\})$. Then $\mathbf{K}\ominus\alpha \vdash \alpha$, and by *success propagation* $\mathbf{K}\ominus\beta \vdash \beta$. Hence $\beta \notin \mathcal{R}$.

Conjunctive Completeness: Let $\alpha \notin \mathcal{R}$ and $\beta \notin \mathcal{R}$. Then $\mathbf{K}\ominus\alpha \vdash \alpha$ and $\mathbf{K}\ominus\beta \vdash \beta$. By *relative success*, $\mathbf{K}\ominus\alpha = \mathbf{K}\ominus\beta = \mathbf{K}$. Then $\mathbf{K} \vdash \alpha \wedge \beta$. By *conjunctive constancy* $\mathbf{K}\ominus(\alpha \wedge \beta) = \mathbf{K}$; hence $\mathbf{K}\ominus(\alpha \wedge \beta) \vdash \alpha \wedge \beta$ and $\alpha \wedge \beta \notin \mathcal{R}$.

(b): Closure: Follows in case (i) from $\ominus$ *closure* and in case (ii) since full meet contraction satisfies *closure*.

Inclusion, **success** and **recovery** are proved in the some way as *closure*.

Vacuity: Let $\mathbf{K} \nvdash \alpha$. It follows from $\ominus$ *vacuity* that $\mathbf{K}\ominus\alpha = \mathbf{K}$. Hence $\mathbf{K}\ominus\alpha \nvdash \alpha$, hence $\alpha \in \mathcal{R}$, then by our definition of $-$, $\mathbf{K}-\alpha = \mathbf{K}\ominus\alpha$, hence $\mathbf{K}-\alpha = \mathbf{K}$.

Extensionality: Let $\vdash \alpha \leftrightarrow \beta$. There are two cases: First case, $\mathbf{K}\ominus\alpha \nvdash \alpha$: Then $\alpha \in \mathcal{R}$, so that $\mathbf{K}-\alpha = \mathbf{K}\ominus\alpha$. By $\ominus$ *extensionality*, $\mathbf{K}\ominus\alpha = \mathbf{K}\ominus\beta$, hence $\mathbf{K}-\alpha = \mathbf{K}\ominus\beta$. It follows from $\mathbf{K}\ominus\alpha = \mathbf{K}\ominus\beta$, $\mathbf{K}\ominus\alpha \nvdash \alpha$ and $\vdash \alpha \leftrightarrow \beta$ that $\mathbf{K}\ominus\beta \nvdash \beta$, from which follows $\mathbf{K}-\beta = \mathbf{K}\ominus\beta$, hence $\mathbf{K}-\alpha = \mathbf{K}-\beta$. Second case, $\mathbf{K}\ominus\alpha \vdash \alpha$: Then by *extensionality* $\mathbf{K}\ominus\beta \vdash \beta$. Hence $\mathbf{K}-\alpha = \mathbf{K} \cap Cn(\{\neg\alpha\}) = \mathbf{K} \cap Cn(\{\neg\beta\}) = \mathbf{K}-\beta$.

(c): Let $\ominus'$ be the shielded contraction induced by $\mathcal{R}$ and $-$. We are going to show that for all α, $\mathbf{K}\ominus\alpha = \mathbf{K}\ominus'\alpha$. If $\alpha \in \mathcal{R}$, then $\mathbf{K}\ominus'\alpha = \mathbf{K}-\alpha = \mathbf{K}\ominus\alpha$. If $\alpha \notin \mathcal{R}$, then it follows from the definition of shielded contraction that $\mathbf{K}\ominus'\alpha = \mathbf{K}$. Furthermore, it follows from the definition of $\mathcal{R}$ that $\mathbf{K}\ominus\alpha \vdash \alpha$, and then from $\ominus$ *relative success* that $\mathbf{K}\ominus\alpha = \mathbf{K}$.

(2) to (1): Closure, Inclusion and **Vacuity:** Trivial.

Extensionality: From non-retractability propagation and $-$ *extensionality*.

Recovery: If $\alpha \in \mathcal{R}$, then by $-$ *recovery* $\mathbf{K} \subseteq (\mathbf{K}-\alpha) + \alpha = (\mathbf{K}\ominus\alpha) + \alpha$. If $\alpha \notin \mathcal{R}$, then $\mathbf{K} \subseteq \mathbf{K}+\alpha = (\mathbf{K}\ominus\alpha) + \alpha$.

Relative success: Let $\mathbf{K}\ominus\alpha \neq \mathbf{K}$. It follows from Definition 4 that $\mathbf{K}\ominus\alpha = \mathbf{K}-\alpha$, and from Observation 2 that either $\mathbf{K}-\alpha = \mathbf{K}$ or $\mathbf{K}-\alpha \nvdash \alpha$.

Success Propagation: Let $\vdash \beta \rightarrow \alpha$ and $\mathbf{K}\ominus\alpha \nvdash \alpha$. We have two cases: **(a)** $\alpha \in \mathcal{R}$: Since $\nvdash \alpha$ we have $\nvdash \beta$, hence by *success* $\mathbf{K}-\beta \nvdash \beta$. Hence, since by non-retractability propagation $\beta \in \mathcal{R}$, $\mathbf{K}\ominus\beta \nvdash \beta$. **(b)** $\alpha \notin \mathcal{R}$, then $\mathbf{K}\ominus\alpha = \mathbf{K}$

and $\mathbf{K}\ominus\alpha \nvdash \alpha$. Hence $\mathbf{K} \nvdash \beta$, from which follows that $\nvdash \beta$ and (by *inclusion*) $\mathbf{K}-\beta \nvdash \beta$. Hence $\mathbf{K}\ominus\beta \nvdash \beta$.
Conjunctive constancy: Let $\mathbf{K} = \mathbf{K}\ominus\alpha = \mathbf{K}\ominus\beta$. We have three cases: **(a)** $\alpha \in \mathcal{R}$. Then $\mathbf{K}\ominus\alpha = \mathbf{K}-\alpha$, and it follows from Lemma 25 that either $\vdash \alpha$ or $\mathbf{K} \nvdash \alpha$. If $\vdash \alpha$, then by *extensionality*, that was just proved, $\mathbf{K}\ominus(\alpha \wedge \beta) = \mathbf{K}\ominus\beta = \mathbf{K}$. If $\mathbf{K} \nvdash \alpha$, then $\mathbf{K} \nvdash \alpha \wedge \beta$ and due to *vacuity*, that was just proved, $\mathbf{K}\ominus(\alpha \wedge \beta) = \mathbf{K}$. **(b)** $\beta \in \mathcal{R}$. This is similar to case (a). **(c)** $\alpha \notin \mathcal{R}$ and $\beta \notin \mathcal{R}$. Then by conjunctive completeness, $(\alpha \wedge \beta) \notin \mathcal{R}$, hence $\mathbf{K}\ominus(\alpha \wedge \beta) = \mathbf{K}$.
(3) to (2): Trivial. ∎

Proof of Theorem 17:
(1) to (3): We use the same construction as in the corresponding part of the proof of Theorem 16. Then we need to prove only that $-$ satisfies *conjunctive inclusion* and *conjunctive overlap*, and that $\mathcal{R}$ satisfies non-retractability preservation.
Conjunctive inclusion: Let $\mathbf{K}-(\alpha \wedge \beta) \nvdash \alpha$. We have two cases: **(a)** $\mathbf{K}\ominus\alpha \nvdash \alpha$: Then $\mathbf{K}\ominus\alpha = \mathbf{K}-\alpha$ and, since by *success propagation* $\mathbf{K}\ominus(\alpha \wedge \beta) \nvdash \alpha \wedge \beta$, we also have $\mathbf{K}\ominus(\alpha \wedge \beta) = \mathbf{K}-(\alpha \wedge \beta)$. Then $\mathbf{K}\ominus(\alpha \wedge \beta) \nvdash \alpha$, hence by $\ominus$ *conjunctive inclusion* $\mathbf{K}\ominus(\alpha \wedge \beta) \subseteq \mathbf{K}\ominus\alpha$, from which we obtain $\mathbf{K}-(\alpha \wedge \beta) \subseteq \mathbf{K}-\alpha$. **(b)** $\mathbf{K}\ominus\alpha \vdash \alpha$: Then by *persistence* $\mathbf{K}\ominus(\alpha \wedge \beta) \vdash \alpha$, then $\mathbf{K}-(\alpha \wedge \beta) \neq \mathbf{K}\ominus(\alpha \wedge \beta)$. It follows from the construction of $-$ that $\mathbf{K}-(\alpha \wedge \beta) = \mathbf{K} \cap Cn(\{\neg\alpha \vee \neg\beta\}) \subseteq \mathbf{K} \cap Cn(\{\neg\alpha\}) = \mathbf{K}-\alpha$.
Conjunctive Overlap: There are three cases: **(a)** $\mathbf{K}\ominus\alpha \nvdash \alpha$, $\mathbf{K}\ominus\beta \nvdash \beta$: Then by *success propagation* $\mathbf{K}\ominus(\alpha \wedge \beta) \nvdash \alpha \wedge \beta$. It follows from the definition of $-$ that $\mathbf{K}-\alpha = \mathbf{K}\ominus\alpha$, $\mathbf{K}-\beta = \mathbf{K}\ominus\beta$ and $\mathbf{K}-(\alpha \wedge \beta) = \mathbf{K}\ominus(\alpha \wedge \beta)$. By $\ominus$ *conjunctive overlap* $\mathbf{K}\ominus\alpha \cap \mathbf{K}\ominus\beta \subseteq \mathbf{K}\ominus(\alpha \wedge \beta)$, hence $\mathbf{K}-\alpha \cap \mathbf{K}-\beta = \mathbf{K}-(\alpha \wedge \beta)$. **(b)** $\mathbf{K}\ominus\alpha \vdash \alpha$, $\mathbf{K}\ominus\beta \vdash \beta$: By *relative success*, $\mathbf{K}\ominus\alpha = \mathbf{K}\ominus\beta = \mathbf{K}$. Then by $\ominus$ *conjunctive overlap* $\mathbf{K}\ominus(\alpha \wedge \beta) \vdash \alpha \wedge \beta$. Hence by the definition of $-$, $\mathbf{K}-\alpha \cap \mathbf{K}-\beta = \mathbf{K} \cap Cn(\{\neg\alpha\}) \cap \mathbf{K} \cap Cn(\{\neg\beta\}) = \mathbf{K} \cap Cn(\{\neg(\alpha \wedge \beta)\}) = \mathbf{K}-(\alpha \wedge \beta)$. **(c)** $\mathbf{K}\ominus\alpha \vdash \alpha$, $\mathbf{K}\ominus\beta \nvdash \beta$: Then by *success propagation* $\mathbf{K}\ominus(\alpha \wedge \beta) \nvdash \alpha \wedge \beta$. By the definition of $-$, $\mathbf{K}-\alpha = \mathbf{K} \cap Cn(\{\neg\alpha\})$, $\mathbf{K}-\beta = \mathbf{K}\ominus\beta$ and $\mathbf{K}-(\alpha \wedge \beta) = \mathbf{K}\ominus(\alpha \wedge \beta)$. Due to *relative success*, $\mathbf{K}\ominus\alpha = \mathbf{K}$, so that $\mathbf{K} \cap Cn(\{\neg\alpha\}) \subseteq \mathbf{K}\ominus\alpha$. Hence by $\ominus$ *conjunctive overlap* $\mathbf{K}-\alpha \cap \mathbf{K}-\beta = \mathbf{K} \cap Cn(\{\neg\alpha\}) \cap \mathbf{K}\ominus\beta \subseteq \mathbf{K}\ominus\alpha \cap \mathbf{K}\ominus\beta \subseteq \mathbf{K}\ominus(\alpha \wedge \beta) = \mathbf{K}-(\alpha \wedge \beta)$.
Non-retractability preservation: Let $\beta \notin \mathcal{R}$. Then $\beta \in \mathbf{K}\ominus\beta$; hence by *persistence* $\beta \in \mathbf{K}\ominus\alpha$.
(2) to (1): Let (2) be satisfied. Due to Theorem 16 we only need to prove that $\ominus$ satisfies *persistence, conjunctive inclusion* and *conjunctive overlap*.
Persistence: Let $\mathbf{K}\ominus\beta \vdash \beta$. First case, $\beta \in \mathcal{R}$: Then $\mathbf{K}\ominus\beta = \mathbf{K}-\beta$. It follows from *success* that $\vdash \beta$, hence $\mathbf{K}\ominus\alpha \vdash \beta$. Second case, $\beta \notin \mathcal{R}$: Then by non-retractability preservation, $\mathbf{K}\ominus\alpha \vdash \beta$.
Conjunctive inclusion: Let $\mathbf{K}\ominus(\alpha \wedge \beta) \nvdash \alpha$. We have three cases: **(a)** $\alpha \wedge \beta \in \mathcal{R}$ and $\alpha \in \mathcal{R}$: Then $\mathbf{K}\ominus(\alpha \wedge \beta) = \mathbf{K}-(\alpha \wedge \beta)$ and $\mathbf{K}\ominus\alpha = \mathbf{K}-\alpha$. Hence by

$-$ *conjunctive inclusion* $\mathbf{K}\ominus(\alpha \wedge \beta) = \mathbf{K}-(\alpha \wedge \beta) \subseteq \mathbf{K}-\alpha = \mathbf{K}\ominus\alpha$. **(b)** $\alpha \wedge \beta \in \mathcal{R}$ and $\alpha \notin \mathcal{R}$: Then $\mathbf{K}\ominus(\alpha \wedge \beta) = \mathbf{K}-(\alpha \wedge \beta)$ and $\mathbf{K}\ominus\alpha = \mathbf{K}$. By *inclusion*, $\mathbf{K}\ominus(\alpha \wedge \beta) = \mathbf{K}-(\alpha \wedge \beta) \subseteq \mathbf{K} = \mathbf{K}\ominus\alpha$. **(c)**: $\alpha \wedge \beta \notin \mathcal{R}$: Then $\mathbf{K}\ominus(\alpha \wedge \beta) = \mathbf{K}$. By non-retractability propagation $\alpha \notin \mathcal{R}$, hence $\mathbf{K}\ominus\alpha = \mathbf{K} = \mathbf{K}\ominus(\alpha \wedge \beta)$.
Conjunctive overlap: There are three cases: **(a)** α, $\beta \in \mathcal{R}$: Then by non-retractability propagation, $\alpha \wedge \beta \in \mathcal{R}$. By $-$ *conjunctive overlap* and definition of $\ominus$, $\mathbf{K}\ominus\alpha \cap \mathbf{K}\ominus\beta = \mathbf{K}-\alpha \cap \mathbf{K}-\beta \subseteq \mathbf{K}-(\alpha \wedge \beta) = \mathbf{K}\ominus(\alpha \wedge \beta)$. **(b)** $\alpha \notin \mathcal{R}$, $\beta \notin \mathcal{R}$: Then by conjunctive completeness $\alpha \wedge \beta \notin \mathcal{R}$, and by definition of $\ominus$, $\mathbf{K}\ominus\alpha \cap \mathbf{K}\ominus\beta = \mathbf{K}\ominus(\alpha \wedge \beta) = \mathbf{K}$. **(c)** $\alpha \in \mathcal{R}$, $\beta \notin \mathcal{R}$: Then $\mathbf{K}\ominus\alpha = \mathbf{K}-\alpha$ and $\mathbf{K}\ominus\beta = \mathbf{K}$. By non-retractability propagation, $\alpha \wedge \beta \in \mathcal{R}$, so that $\mathbf{K}\ominus(\alpha \wedge \beta) = \mathbf{K}-(\alpha \wedge \beta)$. According to $-$ *conjunctive factoring* (that follows from the AGM basic and supplementary postulates) we have three subcases: **(c1)** $\mathbf{K}-(\alpha \wedge \beta) = \mathbf{K}-\alpha$: Hence $\mathbf{K}\ominus\alpha \cap \mathbf{K}\ominus\beta = \mathbf{K}-\alpha \cap \mathbf{K} = \mathbf{K}-\alpha = \mathbf{K}-(\alpha \wedge \beta) = \mathbf{K}\ominus(\alpha \wedge \beta)$. **(c2)** $\mathbf{K}-(\alpha \wedge \beta) = \mathbf{K}-\beta$: It follows by non-retractability preservation that $\mathbf{K}\ominus(\alpha \wedge \beta) \vdash \beta$, then since $\mathbf{K}\ominus(\alpha \wedge \beta) = \mathbf{K}-(\alpha \wedge \beta) = \mathbf{K}-\beta$, $\mathbf{K}-\beta \vdash \beta$. Then it follows by $-$ *success* that $\vdash \beta$ and consequently $\mathbf{K}-\beta = \mathbf{K} = \mathbf{K}\ominus\beta$. The rest follows by $-$ *conjunctive overlap*. **(c3)** $\mathbf{K}-(\alpha \wedge \beta) = \mathbf{K}-\alpha \cap \mathbf{K}-\beta$: Due to non-retractability preservation $\mathbf{K}\ominus(\alpha \wedge \beta) \vdash \beta$, which it follows that $\mathbf{K}-(\alpha \wedge \beta) = \mathbf{K}-\alpha \cap \mathbf{K}-\beta \vdash \beta$. Hence $\mathbf{K}-\beta \vdash \beta$ and the rest is similar to case (c2).
(3) to (2): Trivial.
(4) to (1): Let $\leq_{\mathbf{K}}$ be a relation satisfying $(\mathbf{EE1})$–$(\mathbf{EE4})$ with respect to $\mathbf{K}$. Let $\ominus$ the shielded entrenchment-based contraction induced by $\leq_{\mathbf{K}}$. We have to show that $\ominus$ satisfies the listed postulates.
Closure: Let $\varepsilon \in Cn(\mathbf{K}\ominus\alpha)$. We have to show that $\varepsilon \in \mathbf{K}\ominus\alpha$. If $\top \leq_{\mathbf{K}} \alpha$, then $\mathbf{K}\ominus\alpha = \mathbf{K}$, and the desired result follows since $\mathbf{K}$ is a belief set. Hence we may assume that $\alpha <_{\mathbf{K}} \top$. Since the underlying logic is compact, there is a finite subset $\{\beta_1, ..., \beta_n\} \subseteq \mathbf{K}\ominus\alpha$, such that $\{\beta_1, ..., \beta_n\} \vdash \varepsilon$. It follows from $\beta_1 \in \mathbf{K}\ominus\alpha$ and $\beta_2 \in \mathbf{K}\ominus\alpha$ that $\alpha <_{\mathbf{K}} \alpha \vee \beta_1$ and $\alpha <_{\mathbf{K}} \alpha \vee \beta_2$; then by $(\mathbf{EE3})$ and $(\mathbf{EE1})$, $\alpha <_{\mathbf{K}} (\alpha \vee \beta_1) \wedge (\alpha \vee \beta_2)$; and by intersubstitutivity $\alpha <_{\mathbf{K}} \alpha \vee (\beta_1 \wedge \beta_2)$. Hence $\beta_1 \wedge \beta_2 \in \mathbf{K}\ominus\alpha$. By iteration of the some procedure we obtain $\beta_1 \wedge ... \wedge \beta_n \in \mathbf{K}\ominus\alpha$. Next, let $\vdash \beta \leftrightarrow \beta_1 \wedge ... \wedge \beta_n$. Then $\alpha <_{\mathbf{K}} \alpha \vee \beta$. It follows from $\vdash \beta \rightarrow \varepsilon$ that $\vdash (\alpha \vee \beta) \rightarrow (\alpha \vee \varepsilon)$. $(\mathbf{EE2})$ yields $(\alpha \vee \beta) \leq_{\mathbf{K}} (\alpha \vee \varepsilon)$. It follows by $(\mathbf{EE1})$ that $\alpha <_{\mathbf{K}} (\alpha \vee \varepsilon)$. Hence $\varepsilon \in \mathbf{K}\ominus\alpha$.
Inclusion: Follows trivially from Definition 5.
Vacuity: Let $\alpha \notin \mathbf{K}$. It follows by Lemma 26 that $\top \not\leq_{\mathbf{K}} \alpha$. Then by Definition 5, $\beta \in \mathbf{K}\ominus\alpha$ if and only if $\beta \in \mathbf{K}$ and $\alpha <_{\mathbf{K}} \alpha \vee \beta$. By Lemma 26 $\alpha <_{\mathbf{K}} \alpha \vee \beta$ follows for all $\beta \in \mathbf{K}$, since $\mathbf{K}$ is a belief set. Then $\beta \in \mathbf{K}\ominus\alpha$ if and only if $\beta \in \mathbf{K}$; hence $\mathbf{K}\ominus\alpha = \mathbf{K}$.
Extensionality: Let $\vdash \delta \leftrightarrow \alpha$. Then by intersubstitutivity, $\alpha <_{\mathbf{K}} \top$ if and only if $\delta <_{\mathbf{K}} \top$ and $\alpha <_{\mathbf{K}} \alpha \vee \beta$ if and only if $\delta <_{\mathbf{K}} \delta \vee \beta$. Hence, by Definition 5, $\mathbf{K}\ominus\alpha = \mathbf{K}\ominus\delta$.
Recovery: Let $\beta \in \mathbf{K}$. We have to prove that $\alpha \rightarrow \beta \in \mathbf{K}\ominus\alpha$. Assume to the

contrary that $\alpha \to \beta \notin \mathbf{K}\div\alpha$. Then, since $\beta \in \mathbf{K}$ it follows by Definition 5 that $\alpha <_{\mathbf{K}} \top$ and $\alpha \vee (\alpha \to \beta) \leq_{\mathbf{K}} \alpha$. By intersubstitutivity $\top \leq_{\mathbf{K}} \alpha$. From this contradiction we may conclude that $\alpha \to \beta \in \mathbf{K}\div\alpha$.
Relative Success: Let $\mathbf{K}\div\alpha \neq \mathbf{K}$. Then by Definition 5 it follows that $\alpha <_{\mathbf{K}} \top$. By $(\mathbf{EE2})$, $\alpha \not<_{\mathbf{K}} \alpha \vee \alpha$ and then by Definition 5 $\alpha \notin \mathbf{K}\div\alpha$.
Persistence: Let $\mathbf{K}\div\beta \vdash \beta$. Then by *closure*, $\beta \in \mathbf{K}\div\beta$. By *inclusion*, $\beta \in \mathbf{K}$. Suppose that $\beta <_{\mathbf{K}} \top$. Then it follows by Definition 5 that $\beta <_{\mathbf{K}} \beta \vee \beta$, contrary to $(\mathbf{EE2})$. We can conclude from this contradiction that $\top \leq_{\mathbf{K}} \beta$. According to $(\mathbf{EE2})$ it holds for all α that $\beta \leq_{\mathbf{K}} \alpha \vee \beta$. Hence by $(\mathbf{EE1})$,$\top \leq_{\mathbf{K}} \alpha \vee \beta$. Hence by $(\mathbf{EE1})$, it holds for all α that if $\alpha <_{\mathbf{K}} \top$, then $\alpha <_{\mathbf{K}} \alpha \vee \beta$. Since $\beta \in \mathbf{K}$, we can conclude from Definition 5 that $\beta \in \mathbf{K}\div\alpha$.
Conjunctive inclusion: Let $\mathbf{K}\div(\alpha \wedge \beta) \nvdash \alpha$: By *closure* $\alpha \notin \mathbf{K}\div(\alpha \wedge \beta)$. If $\alpha \notin \mathbf{K}$; then by the previous proof of *vacuity*, $\mathbf{K}\div(\alpha \wedge \beta) = \mathbf{K}\div\alpha = \mathbf{K}$. We can therefore assume that $\alpha \in \mathbf{K}$. It follows from Definition 5, $\alpha \in \mathbf{K}$, and $\alpha \notin \mathbf{K}\div(\alpha \wedge \beta)$ that $\alpha \wedge \beta <_{\mathbf{K}} \top$ and $\alpha \vee (\alpha \wedge \beta) \leq_{\mathbf{K}} \alpha \wedge \beta$. By intersubstitutivity, $\alpha \leq_{\mathbf{K}} \alpha \wedge \beta$.

Let $\delta \in \mathbf{K}\div(\alpha \wedge \beta)$: Then, by Definition 5, $\delta \in \mathbf{K}$ and $\alpha \wedge \beta <_{\mathbf{K}} (\alpha \wedge \beta) \vee \delta$. By intersubstitutivity $\alpha \wedge \beta <_{\mathbf{K}} (\alpha \vee \delta) \wedge (\beta \vee \delta)$. By $(\mathbf{EE2})$, $(\alpha \vee \delta) \wedge (\beta \vee \delta) \leq_{\mathbf{K}} \alpha \vee \delta$. Applying $(\mathbf{EE1})$ to $\alpha \leq_{\mathbf{K}} \alpha \wedge \beta$, $\alpha \wedge \beta <_{\mathbf{K}} (\alpha \vee \delta) \wedge (\beta \vee \delta)$ and $(\alpha \vee \delta) \wedge (\beta \vee \delta) \leq_{\mathbf{K}} \alpha \vee \delta$, we obtain $\alpha <_{\mathbf{K}} \alpha \vee \delta$. Furthermore, it follows by $(\mathbf{EE1})$ from $\alpha \leq_{\mathbf{K}} \alpha \wedge \beta$ and $\alpha \wedge \beta <_{\mathbf{K}} \top$ that $\alpha <_{\mathbf{K}} \top$. It follows by Definition 5 from $\alpha <_{\mathbf{K}} \top$, $\delta \in \mathbf{K}$ and $\alpha <_{\mathbf{K}} \alpha \vee \delta$ that $\delta \in \mathbf{K}\div\alpha$. We may conclude that $\mathbf{K}\div(\alpha \wedge \beta) \subseteq \mathbf{K}\div\alpha$.
Conjunctive overlap: Let $\delta \in \mathbf{K}\div\alpha$ and $\delta \in \mathbf{K}\div\beta$: According to Definition 5, there are four cases: **(a)** $\top \leq_{\mathbf{K}} \alpha$ and $\top \leq_{\mathbf{K}} \beta$: Then it follows by $(\mathbf{EE3})$ and $(\mathbf{EE1})$ that $\top \leq_{\mathbf{K}} \alpha \wedge \beta$. It follows from Definition 5 that $\mathbf{K}\div\alpha = \mathbf{K}\div\beta = \mathbf{K}\div(\alpha \wedge \beta) = \mathbf{K}$, hence $\delta \in \mathbf{K}\div(\alpha \wedge \beta)$. **(b)** $\top \not\leq_{\mathbf{K}} \alpha$ and $\top \leq_{\mathbf{K}} \beta$: Then by $(\mathbf{EE2})$ and $(\mathbf{EE1})$, $\top \not\leq_{\mathbf{K}} \alpha \wedge \beta$. It follows by Definition 5 from $\delta \in \mathbf{K}\div\alpha$ and $\alpha <_{\mathbf{K}} \top$ that $\delta \in \mathbf{K}$ and $\alpha <_{\mathbf{K}} \alpha \vee \delta$. Then by $(\mathbf{EE2})$ and $(\mathbf{EE1})$, $\alpha \wedge \beta <_{\mathbf{K}} \alpha \vee \delta$. Due to $(\mathbf{EE2})$, $\beta \leq_{\mathbf{K}} \beta \vee \delta$. It follows by $(\mathbf{EE1})$ from this and $\top \leq_{\mathbf{K}} \beta$ that $\top \leq_{\mathbf{K}} \beta \vee \delta$. Since $\alpha \wedge \beta <_{\mathbf{K}} \top$, it follows by $(\mathbf{EE1})$ that $\alpha \wedge \beta <_{\mathbf{K}} \beta \vee \delta$. From this and $\alpha \wedge \beta <_{\mathbf{K}} \alpha \vee \delta$ it follows by $(\mathbf{EE3})$ and $(\mathbf{EE2})$ that $\alpha \wedge \beta <_{\mathbf{K}} (\alpha \wedge \beta) \vee \delta$. Hence, according to Definition 5, $\delta \in \mathbf{K}\div(\alpha \wedge \beta)$. **(c)** $\top \leq_{\mathbf{K}} \alpha$ and $\top \not\leq_{\mathbf{K}} \beta$: Simmetrical with case (b). **(d)** $\top \not\leq_{\mathbf{K}} \alpha$ and $\top \not\leq_{\mathbf{K}} \beta$: Then by $(\mathbf{EE2})$ and $(\mathbf{EE1})$ it follows that $\top \not\leq_{\mathbf{K}} \alpha \wedge \beta$. It follows from Definition 5 that $\delta \in \mathbf{K}$, $\alpha <_{\mathbf{K}} \alpha \vee \delta$ and $\beta <_{\mathbf{K}} \beta \vee \delta$. Then by $(\mathbf{EE1})$ and $(\mathbf{EE2})$, $\alpha \wedge \beta <_{\mathbf{K}} \alpha \vee \delta$ and $\alpha \wedge \beta <_{\mathbf{K}} \beta \vee \delta$. It follows from $(\mathbf{EE1})$, $(\mathbf{EE2})$, and $(\mathbf{EE3})$ that $\alpha \wedge \beta <_{\mathbf{K}} (\alpha \wedge \beta) \vee \delta$; hence from Definition 5, $\delta \in \mathbf{K}\div(\alpha \wedge \beta)$.
(1) to (4): Let $\div$ be an operator satisfying the postulates listed in (1), and let $\leq_{\mathbf{K}}$ defined as follows:

$$(\text{def} \leq_{\mathbf{K}}) \qquad \alpha \leq_{\mathbf{K}} \beta \text{ iff } \textit{if } \alpha \in \mathbf{K}\div(\alpha \wedge \beta), \textit{ then } \beta \in \mathbf{K}\div(\alpha \wedge \beta).$$

We need to show that $(\mathbf{EE1}) - (\mathbf{EE4})$ are satisfied and that $\div$ is induced by $\leq_{\mathbf{K}}$

in the sense of Definition 5.

(**EE1**) Let $\alpha \leq_{\mathbf{K}} \beta$ and $\beta \leq_{\mathbf{K}} \delta$. In order to prove that $\alpha \leq_{\mathbf{K}} \delta$, let $\alpha \in \mathbf{K}{\div}(\alpha \wedge \delta)$. We have to prove $\delta \in \mathbf{K}{\div}(\alpha \wedge \delta)$. There are two cases: First case, $\alpha \in \mathbf{K}{\div}(\alpha \wedge \beta)$: By (def $\leq_{\mathbf{K}}$), $\beta \in \mathbf{K}{\div}(\alpha \wedge \beta)$. Then by *closure* $\alpha \wedge \beta \in \mathbf{K}{\div}(\alpha \wedge \beta)$, by *success propagation*, $\beta \in \mathbf{K}{\div}\beta$, by *persistence*, $\beta \in \mathbf{K}{\div}(\beta \wedge \delta)$, and by (def $\leq_{\mathbf{K}}$), $\delta \in \mathbf{K}{\div}(\beta \wedge \delta)$. By *closure* $\beta \wedge \delta \in \mathbf{K}{\div}(\beta \wedge \delta)$, by *success propagation* $\delta \in \mathbf{K}{\div}\delta$, and by *persistence* $\delta \in \mathbf{K}{\div}(\alpha \wedge \delta)$.

Second case, $\alpha \notin \mathbf{K}{\div}(\alpha \wedge \beta)$: Let $\delta \notin \mathbf{K}{\div}(\alpha \wedge \delta)$. By *persistence* $\delta \notin \mathbf{K}{\div}\delta$; from which it follows by *success propagation* that $\beta \wedge \delta \notin \mathbf{K}{\div}(\beta \wedge \delta)$. Since $\beta \leq_{\mathbf{K}} \delta$ we can conclude from *closure* and (def $\leq_{\mathbf{K}}$) that $\beta \notin \mathbf{K}{\div}(\beta \wedge \delta)$. We will arrive at a contradiction by proving both that $\alpha \in \mathbf{K}{\div}(\alpha \wedge \beta \wedge \delta)$ and that $\alpha \notin \mathbf{K}{\div}(\alpha \wedge \beta \wedge \delta)$: By *conjunctive overlap* it follows that $\mathbf{K}{\div}(\alpha \wedge \delta) \cap \mathbf{K}{\div}(\neg\alpha \vee \beta) \subseteq \mathbf{K}{\div}(\alpha \wedge \beta \wedge \delta)$. By hypothesis $\alpha \in \mathbf{K}{\div}(\alpha \wedge \delta)$. Furthermore by *inclusion* $\alpha \in \mathbf{K}$ and it follows by *recovery* that $\alpha \in (\mathbf{K}{\div}(\neg\alpha \vee \beta)) + (\neg\alpha \vee \beta)$, so that by *closure* $\alpha \in \mathbf{K}{\div}(\neg\alpha \vee \beta)$. Hence, $\alpha \in \mathbf{K}{\div}(\alpha \wedge \beta \wedge \delta)$.

Due to the hypothesis condition $\alpha \notin \mathbf{K}{\div}(\alpha \wedge \beta)$ it now suffices to prove that $\mathbf{K}{\div}(\alpha \wedge \beta \wedge \delta) \subseteq \mathbf{K}{\div}(\alpha \wedge \beta)$. Due to *conjunctive inclusion* this can be done by showing that $\alpha \wedge \beta \notin \mathbf{K}{\div}(\alpha \wedge \beta \wedge \delta)$. It follows by *persistence* from $\alpha \notin \mathbf{K}{\div}(\alpha \wedge \beta)$ that $\alpha \notin \mathbf{K}{\div}\alpha$. Hence by *success propagation*, $(\alpha \wedge \beta \wedge \delta) \notin \mathbf{K}{\div}(\alpha \wedge \beta \wedge \delta)$. It follows from *closure* that either $\mathbf{K}{\div}(\alpha \wedge \beta \wedge \delta) \nvdash \alpha \wedge \beta$ or $\mathbf{K}{\div}(\alpha \wedge \beta \wedge \delta) \nvdash \delta$. In the second case, it follows by *closure* that $\mathbf{K}{\div}(\alpha \wedge \beta \wedge \delta) \nvdash \beta \wedge \delta$. By *conjunctive inclusion*, $\mathbf{K}{\div}(\alpha \wedge \beta \wedge \delta) \subseteq \mathbf{K}{\div}(\beta \wedge \delta)$ and since $\beta \notin \mathbf{K}{\div}(\beta \wedge \delta)$, $\beta \notin \mathbf{K}{\div}(\alpha \wedge \beta \wedge \delta)$, so that by *closure* $\mathbf{K}{\div}(\alpha \wedge \beta \wedge \delta) \nvdash \alpha \wedge \beta$ in this case as well. It follows by *conjunctive inclusion* from $\mathbf{K}{\div}(\alpha \wedge \beta \wedge \delta) \nvdash \alpha \wedge \beta$ that $\mathbf{K}{\div}(\alpha \wedge \beta \wedge \delta) \subseteq \mathbf{K}{\div}(\alpha \wedge \beta)$. By hypothesis, $\alpha \notin \mathbf{K}{\div}(\alpha \wedge \beta)$, so that $\alpha \notin \mathbf{K}{\div}(\alpha \wedge \beta \wedge \delta)$, contrary to what shown above. This contradiction conclude this part of the proff.

(**EE2**) Let $\vdash \alpha \rightarrow \beta$. Then if $\alpha \in \mathbf{K}{\div}(\alpha \wedge \beta)$ it follows by *closure* that $\beta \in \mathbf{K}{\div}(\alpha \wedge \beta)$; hence by (def $\leq_{\mathbf{K}}$), $\alpha \leq_{\mathbf{K}} \beta$.

(**EE3**) Let $\alpha \not\leq_{\mathbf{K}} \alpha \wedge \beta$. Then by (def $\leq_{\mathbf{K}}$), $\alpha \in \mathbf{K}{\div}((\alpha \wedge \beta) \wedge \alpha)$ and $\alpha \wedge \beta \notin \mathbf{K}{\div}((\alpha \wedge \beta) \wedge \alpha)$. It follows by *closure* that $\beta \notin \mathbf{K}{\div}((\alpha \wedge \beta) \wedge \alpha)$ and by *extensionality* that $\beta \notin \mathbf{K}{\div}((\alpha \wedge \beta) \wedge \beta)$. Hence, by (def $\leq_{\mathbf{K}}$), $\beta \not\leq_{\mathbf{K}} \alpha \wedge \beta$.

(**EE4**) For one direction, let $\beta \notin \mathbf{K}$. Then by *inclusion* for all α, $\beta \notin \mathbf{K}{\div}(\alpha \wedge \beta)$; hence for all α, $\beta \leq_{\mathbf{K}} \alpha$. For the other direction, let $\beta \leq_{\mathbf{K}} \alpha$ for all α. Then, in particular $\beta \leq_{\mathbf{K}} \bot$. It follows from (def $\leq_{\mathbf{K}}$) that *if* $\beta \in \mathbf{K}{\div}(\beta \wedge \bot)$, *then* $\bot \in \mathbf{K}{\div}(\beta \wedge \bot)$. It follows by *inclusion*, that $\bot \notin \mathbf{K}{\div}(\beta \wedge \bot)$, so that $\beta \notin \mathbf{K}{\div}(\beta \wedge \bot)$. By *vacuity*, $\mathbf{K}{\div}(\beta \wedge \bot) = \mathbf{K}$, so that $\beta \notin \mathbf{K}$ as desired.

$\div$ is based on $\leq_{\mathbf{K}}$ in the manner of Definition 5: There are two cases. First case, $\top \leq_{\mathbf{K}} \alpha$: Then it follows from (def $\leq_{\mathbf{K}}$) that *if* $\top \in \mathbf{K}{\div}(\alpha \wedge \top)$, *then* $\alpha \in \mathbf{K}{\div}(\alpha \wedge \top)$. By *extensionality* and *closure*, we obtain $\alpha \in \mathbf{K}{\div}\alpha$. By *relative success*, $\mathbf{K}{\div}\alpha = \mathbf{K}$ as desired.

Second case, $\alpha <_{\mathbf{K}} \top$: We need to show that $\beta \in \mathbf{K}{\div}\alpha$ iff $\beta \in \mathbf{K}$ and $\alpha <_{\mathbf{K}} (\alpha \vee \beta)$. Due to *inclusion*, this is trivial if $\beta \notin \mathbf{K}$. Let $\beta \in \mathbf{K}$. For one direction, let $\beta \in \mathbf{K} \div \alpha$. Suppose for *reductio* that $(\alpha \vee \beta) \leq_{\mathbf{K}} \alpha$, *i.e.*, that *if* $\alpha \vee \beta \in \mathbf{K} \div ((\alpha \vee \beta) \wedge \alpha)$, *then* $\alpha \in \mathbf{K} \div ((\alpha \vee \beta) \wedge \alpha)$. It follows by *closure* and *extensionality* from $\beta \in \mathbf{K} \div \alpha$ that $\alpha \vee \beta \in \mathbf{K} \div ((\alpha \vee \beta) \wedge \alpha)$. Hence $\alpha \in \mathbf{K} \div ((\alpha \vee \beta) \wedge \alpha)$, by *extensionality* $\alpha \in \mathbf{K} \div (\alpha \wedge \top)$. By *closure*, $\top \in \mathbf{K} \div (\alpha \wedge \top)$. It follows by (def $\leq_{\mathbf{K}}$) that $\top \leq_{\mathbf{K}} \alpha$, contrary to the conditions from this case. We can conclude from this contradiction that $\alpha <_{\mathbf{K}} (\alpha \vee \beta)$.

For the other direction, let $\alpha <_{\mathbf{K}} (\alpha \vee \beta)$. It follows from (def $\leq_{\mathbf{K}}$) that $\alpha \vee \beta \in \mathbf{K} \div (\alpha \wedge (\alpha \vee \beta))$ and then from *extensionality* that $\alpha \vee \beta \in \mathbf{K} \div \alpha$. By *recovery*, $\alpha \rightarrow \beta \in \mathbf{K} \div \alpha$. Hence, by *closure*, $\beta \in \mathbf{K} \div \alpha$.

(4) to (5): Due to Lemma 28, we only have to prove that the contraction functions are equivalent. Let $\div_{\leq}$ be the contraction function based on $\leq_{\mathbf{K}}$ and $\div_{\$}$ the shielded sphere-based contraction defined as in Lemma 28.

(a) For the first direction, let $\beta \in \mathbf{K} \div_{\leq} \alpha$. According to Definition 5, $\beta \in \mathbf{K}$ and we have two cases:

(a1) $\alpha <_{\mathbf{K}} \top$: Then $\alpha <_{\mathbf{K}} \alpha \vee \beta$. It follows from $\|\mathbf{K}\| \subseteq \|\beta\|$ and Lemma 28.b that $\|\mathbf{K}_{\$}\| \subseteq \|\beta\|$. Due to $\alpha <_{\mathbf{K}} \top$ it follows by Lemma 28.c that $\cup\$_{\leq} \not\subseteq \|\alpha\|$. Then $\|\neg\alpha\| \cap (\cup\$_{\leq}) \neq \emptyset$. Since $\alpha <_{\mathbf{K}} \alpha \vee \beta$, Lemma 28.d yields that $\mathbf{S}_{\neg\alpha} \subseteq \|\alpha \vee \beta\|$; then $\mathbf{S}_{\neg\alpha} \subseteq \|\alpha\| \cup \|\beta\|$, from which it follows that $\mathbf{S}_{\neg\alpha} \cap \|\neg\alpha\| \subseteq (\|\alpha\| \cup \|\beta\|) \cap \|\neg\alpha\| = \|\beta\| \cap \|\neg\alpha\| \subseteq \|\beta\|$. Then, since $\|\mathbf{K}_{\$}\| \subseteq \|\beta\|$, it follows that $\|\mathbf{K}_{\$}\| \cup (\|\neg\alpha\| \cap \mathbf{S}_{\neg\alpha}) \subseteq \|\beta\|$; hence $\beta \in \bigcap(\|\mathbf{K}_{\$}\| \cup (\|\neg\alpha\| \cap \mathbf{S}_{\neg\alpha}))$ and consequently $\beta \in \mathbf{K} \div_{\$} \alpha$.

(a2) $\alpha \not<_{\mathbf{K}} \top$: Then $\mathbf{K} \div_{\leq} \alpha = \mathbf{K}$. By Lemma 28.c it follows that $\cup\$_{\leq} \subseteq \|\alpha\|$. Then $\|\neg\alpha\| \cap (\cup\$_{\leq}) = \emptyset$, which it follows that $\|\neg\alpha\| \cap \mathbf{S}_{\neg\alpha} = \emptyset$ hence by definition of $\div_{\$}$ and Lemma 28.b that $\mathbf{K} \div_{\$} \alpha = \mathbf{K}_{\$} = \mathbf{K}$.

(b) For the second direction, let $\beta \in \mathbf{K} \div_{\$} \alpha$. We have two cases, according to definition of $\div_{\$}$:

(b1) $\|\neg\alpha\| \cap \mathbf{S}_{\neg\alpha} \neq \emptyset$. Then, since $\mathbf{S}_{\neg\alpha} \subseteq (\cup\$_{\leq})$, $\|\neg\alpha\| \cap (\cup\$_{\leq}) \neq \emptyset$. Then $(\cup\$_{\leq}) \not\subseteq \|\alpha\|$, from which it follows by Lemma 28.c that $\alpha <_{\mathbf{K}} \top$. Since $\beta \in \bigcap(\|\mathbf{K}_{\$}\| \cup (\|\neg\alpha\| \cap \mathbf{S}_{\neg\alpha}))$, we then have $\|\mathbf{K}_{\$}\| \subseteq \|\beta\|$ and $\|\neg\alpha\| \cap \mathbf{S}_{\neg\alpha} \subseteq \|\beta\|$. From the first part we conclude that $\beta \in \mathbf{K}$. From the second part we obtain $\mathbf{S}_{\neg\alpha} \subseteq \|\alpha \vee \beta\|$. Suppose that $\alpha \not<_{\mathbf{K}} \alpha \vee \beta$. Then $\alpha \vee \beta \leq_{\mathbf{K}} \alpha$, and it follows from condition ($\$_{\leq}4$) of Lemma 28, since $\mathbf{S}_{\neg\alpha}$ is a sphere and $\mathbf{S}_{\neg\alpha} \subseteq \|\alpha \vee \beta\|$, that $\mathbf{S}_{\neg\alpha} \subseteq \|\alpha\|$. This contradicts the condition for this case, and we may conclude from this contradiction that $\alpha <_{\mathbf{K}} \alpha \vee \beta$; hence $\beta \in \mathbf{K} \div_{\leq} \alpha$.

(b2) $\mathbf{K} \div_{\$} \alpha = \mathbf{K}_{\$} =$ (by Lemma 28.b) $\mathbf{K}$: Then $\|\neg\alpha\| \cap \mathbf{S}_{\neg\alpha} = \emptyset$, from which it follows that $\|\neg\alpha\| \cap (\cup\$_{\leq}) = \emptyset$. Then $(\cup\$_{\leq}) \subseteq \|\alpha\|$, then by Lemma 28.c $\top \leq_{\mathbf{K}} \alpha$; hence $\mathbf{K} \div_{\leq} \alpha = \mathbf{K}$.

(5) to (4): Let \$ be a sphere system and let $\leq$ be defined as in Lemma 27. Due to Lemma 27, we only have to prove that the contraction functions are equivalent:

(a) For the first direction, let $\beta \in \mathbf{K} \div_{\$} \alpha$. We have two cases:

(a1) $\|\neg\alpha\| \cap \mathbf{S}_{\neg\alpha} \neq \emptyset$. Then, since $\mathbf{S}_{\neg\alpha} \subseteq (\cup\$_{\leq})$, $\|\neg\alpha\| \cap (\cup\$_{\leq}) \neq \emptyset$, from which it follows that $\beta \in \bigcap(\|\mathbf{K}_{\$}\| \cup (\|\neg\alpha\| \cap \mathbf{S}_{\neg\alpha}))$. Then $\|\mathbf{K}_{\$}\| \subseteq \|\beta\|$ and $\|\neg\alpha\| \cap \mathbf{S}_{\neg\alpha} \subseteq \|\beta\|$. From the first part we conclude that $\beta \in \mathbf{K}$. From the second part we obtain that $\mathbf{S}_{\neg\alpha} \subseteq \|\alpha \vee \beta\|$. By definition $\mathbf{S}_{\neg\alpha} \not\subseteq \|\alpha\|$. Let $\mathbf{G} \in \$$

and $\mathbf{G} \subseteq ||\alpha||$: then, since $\mathbf{S}_{\neg\alpha} \not\subseteq ||\alpha||$, it follows that $\mathbf{S}_{\neg\alpha} \not\subseteq \mathbf{G}$. Then by **($3)** $\mathbf{G} \subseteq \mathbf{S}_{\neg\alpha}$. Then $\mathbf{G} \subseteq ||\alpha \vee \beta||$, from which it follows by the definition of $\leq$ that $\alpha \leq \alpha \vee \beta$. From $\mathbf{S}_{\neg\alpha} \subseteq ||\alpha \vee \beta||$ and $\mathbf{S}_{\neg\alpha} \not\subseteq ||\alpha||$ we obtain by the definition of $\leq$ that $\alpha \vee \beta \not\leq \alpha$. Hence $\alpha < \alpha \vee \beta$ and consequently $\beta \in \mathbf{K} \div_{\leq} \alpha$.
(a2) $||\neg\alpha|| \cap \mathbf{S}_{\neg\alpha} = \emptyset$. Then $\cup\$ \subseteq ||\alpha||$. Then $\mathbf{K} \div_{\$} \alpha = \mathbf{K}$, hence $\beta \in \mathbf{K}$. Let $\mathbf{G}$ be a sphere such that $\mathbf{G} \subseteq ||\top||$. Then, since $\mathbf{G} \subseteq \cup\$ \subseteq ||\alpha||$, it follows that $\top \leq \alpha$, hence $\beta \in \mathbf{K} \div_{\leq} \alpha$.
(b) For the other direction, let $\beta \in \mathbf{K} \div_{\leq} \alpha$. Then $\beta \in \mathbf{K}$. We have two cases:
(b1) $\alpha \leq_{\top}$. Then, according to Definition 5, $\alpha < \alpha \vee \beta$. It follows from the definition of $\leq$ that for all $\mathbf{G} \in \$$, if $\mathbf{G} \subseteq ||\alpha||$ then $\mathbf{G} \subseteq ||\alpha \vee \beta||$; and that there is some $\mathbf{G}' \in \$$ such that $\mathbf{G}' \subseteq ||\alpha \vee \beta||$ and $\mathbf{G}' \not\subseteq ||\alpha||$. By $\mathbf{G}' \not\subseteq ||\alpha||$ it follows that $\mathbf{G}' \cap ||\neg\alpha|| \neq \emptyset$. Then by definition of $\mathbf{S}_{\neg\alpha}$, $\mathbf{S}_{\neg\alpha} \subseteq \mathbf{G}'$. Hence $\mathbf{S}_{\neg\alpha} \subseteq ||\alpha \vee \beta||$. Then $\mathbf{S}_{\neg\alpha} \cap ||\neg\alpha|| \subseteq ||\beta||$; and since $\beta \in \mathbf{K}$ it follows that $||\mathbf{K}_{\$}|| \subseteq \beta$ and consequently that $||\mathbf{K}_{\$}|| \cup (\mathbf{S}_{\neg\alpha} \cap ||\neg\alpha||) \subseteq ||\beta||$ which it follows that $\beta \in \bigcap(||\mathbf{K}_{\$}|| \cup (||\neg\alpha|| \cap \mathbf{S}_{\neg\alpha}))$; hence $\beta \in \mathbf{K} \div_{\$} \alpha$.
(b2) $\top \leq \alpha$. Then $\mathbf{K} \div_{\leq} \alpha = \mathbf{K}$. By definition of $\leq$ it follows that if $\mathbf{G} \subseteq ||\top||$, then $\mathbf{G} \subseteq ||\alpha||$. Since $\mathbf{G} \subseteq ||\top||$ for all $\mathbf{G} \in \$$; it follows that $\mathbf{G} \subseteq ||\alpha||$ for all $\mathbf{G} \in \$$. In particular $\mathbf{S}_{\neg\alpha} \subseteq ||\alpha||$, then $\mathbf{S}_{\neg\alpha} \cap ||\neg\alpha|| = \emptyset$, hence by definition of $\div_{\$}$ it follows that $\mathbf{K} \div_{\$} \alpha = \mathbf{K}$. ■

Proof of Observation 19.
1: Directly from the definition of $\circ$.
2: If $\mathbf{K}\circ\alpha \neq \mathbf{K}$, then by $\div$ *inclusion* $\mathbf{K}\div\neg\alpha \subseteq \mathbf{K}$, hence $\mathbf{K}\circ\alpha = (\mathbf{K}\div\neg\alpha) + \alpha \subseteq \mathbf{K} + \alpha$.
3: Let $\mathbf{K} \nvdash \neg\alpha$. Then by $\div$ *inclusion* $\mathbf{K}\div\neg\alpha \nvdash \neg\alpha$. By $\div$ *vacuity* $\mathbf{K}\div\neg\alpha = \mathbf{K}$; hence $\mathbf{K}\circ\alpha = \mathbf{K}+\alpha$.
4: Directly from the definition of $\circ$.
5: Let $\mathbf{K}\circ\alpha \nvdash \neg\beta$. We have two cases: **(a)** $\mathbf{K}\circ\alpha = \mathbf{K}$: Then $\mathbf{K} \nvdash \neg\beta$. By $\div$ *inclusion*, $\mathbf{K}\div\neg\beta \nvdash \neg\beta$, hence $\beta \in \mathbf{K}\circ\beta = (\mathbf{K}\div\neg\beta) + \beta$. **(b)** $\mathbf{K}\circ\alpha \neq \mathbf{K}$: Then by definition $\mathbf{K}\circ\alpha = (\mathbf{K}\div\neg\alpha) + \alpha$. Then $(\mathbf{K}\div\neg\alpha) + \alpha \nvdash \neg\beta$ and consequently $\mathbf{K}\div\neg\alpha \nvdash \neg\beta$. It follows by *persistence* that $\mathbf{K}\div\neg\beta \nvdash \neg\beta$, hence $\mathbf{K}\circ\beta = (\mathbf{K}\div\neg\beta) + \beta$. Then $\beta \in \mathbf{K}\circ\beta$ follows directly.
6: Let $\mathbf{K}\circ\alpha = \mathbf{K}\circ\beta = \mathbf{K}$. There are three cases: First case, $\mathbf{K}\div\neg\alpha \nvdash \neg\alpha$: Then $\mathbf{K}\circ\alpha = (\mathbf{K}\div\neg\alpha)+\alpha = \mathbf{K}$, so that $\mathbf{K} \vdash \alpha\vee\beta$. It also follows from $\mathbf{K}\div\neg\alpha \nvdash \neg\alpha$ that $(\mathbf{K}\div\neg\alpha) + \alpha \nvdash \bot$ so that $\mathbf{K} \nvdash \bot$ and consequently $\mathbf{K} \nvdash \neg(\alpha \vee \beta)$. Then by $\div$ *vacuity*, $\mathbf{K}\div\neg(\alpha \vee \beta) = \mathbf{K}$. Hence $\mathbf{K}\circ(\alpha \vee \beta) = \mathbf{K}\div\neg(\alpha \vee \beta) + (\alpha \vee \beta) = \mathbf{K}+(\alpha \vee \beta) = \mathbf{K}$. Second case, $\mathbf{K}\div\neg\beta \nvdash \neg\beta$: Similar to the first case. Third case, $\mathbf{K}\div\neg\alpha \vdash \neg\alpha$ and $\mathbf{K}\div\neg\beta \vdash \neg\beta$: Then by $\div$ *relative success* $\mathbf{K}\div\neg\alpha = \mathbf{K}\div\neg\beta = \mathbf{K}$. By *conjunctive constancy* $\mathbf{K}\div(\neg\alpha \wedge \neg\beta) = \mathbf{K}$, hence by $\div$ *extensionality* $\mathbf{K}\div\neg(\alpha \vee \beta) = \mathbf{K}$. Since $\mathbf{K} \vdash \neg(\alpha \vee \beta)$, then $\mathbf{K}\div\neg(\alpha \vee \beta) \vdash \neg(\alpha \vee \beta)$. Hence, by definition of $\circ$, $\mathbf{K}\circ(\alpha \vee \beta) = \mathbf{K}$.
7: Let $\vdash \alpha \rightarrow \beta$ and $\alpha \in \mathbf{K}\circ\alpha$. We have two cases: First case $\mathbf{K}\div\neg\alpha \nvdash \neg\alpha$: Then by *success propagation* $\mathbf{K}\div\neg\beta \nvdash \neg\beta$, so that $\mathbf{K}\circ\beta = (\mathbf{K}\div\neg\beta) + \beta$ and hence $\beta \in \mathbf{K}\circ\beta$. Second case, $\mathbf{K}\div\neg\alpha \vdash \neg\alpha$: Then $\mathbf{K}\circ\alpha = \mathbf{K}$. Due to $\div$

inclusion $\neg\alpha \in \mathbf{K}$. Since $\alpha \in \mathbf{K}\circ\alpha = \mathbf{K}$, it follows that $\mathbf{K} \vdash \bot$. Then, since $\mathbf{K}\circ\beta = (\mathbf{K}\div\neg\beta) + \beta$ or $\mathbf{K}\circ\beta = \mathbf{K}$, it follows that in $\beta \in \mathbf{K}\circ\beta$.
8: Let $\mathbf{K}\circ\alpha \vdash \alpha$ and $\mathbf{K}\circ\alpha \nvdash \neg\beta$. First suppose that $\mathbf{K}\div\neg\alpha \vdash \neg\alpha$. Then $\div$ *relative success* yields $\mathbf{K}\div\neg\alpha = \mathbf{K}$; and from the definition of $\circ$ we obtain $\mathbf{K}\circ\alpha = \mathbf{K}$. Then, since $\mathbf{K} \vdash \alpha$ and $\mathbf{K} \vdash \neg\alpha$, it follows that $\mathbf{K} \vdash \bot$, contrary to the assumption that $\mathbf{K}\circ\alpha \nvdash \beta$. It follows from this contradiction that $\mathbf{K}\div\neg\alpha \nvdash \neg\alpha$, hence $\mathbf{K}\circ\alpha = (\mathbf{K}\div\neg\alpha) + \alpha$. Since $\mathbf{K}\circ\alpha \nvdash \neg\beta$, it follows that $\mathbf{K}\div\neg\alpha \nvdash \alpha \rightarrow \neg\beta$. By $\div$ *extensionality* $\mathbf{K}\div\neg\alpha = \mathbf{K}\div(\neg\alpha \wedge (\alpha \rightarrow \neg\beta))$. Then by *conjunctive inclusion* and $\div$ *extensionality*, $\mathbf{K}\div(\neg\alpha \wedge (\alpha \rightarrow \neg\beta)) \subseteq \mathbf{K}\div(\alpha \rightarrow \neg\beta) = \mathbf{K}\div\neg(\alpha \wedge \beta)$.

Since $\mathbf{K}\div\neg(\alpha\wedge\beta) \nvdash \neg(\alpha\wedge\beta)$, $\mathbf{K}\circ(\alpha\wedge\beta) = (\mathbf{K}\div\neg(\alpha\wedge\beta)) + (\alpha\wedge\beta)$. Then $(\mathbf{K}\circ\alpha) + \beta = ((\mathbf{K}\div\neg\alpha) + \alpha) + \beta = (\mathbf{K}\div\neg\alpha) + (\alpha \wedge \beta) \subseteq (\mathbf{K}\div\neg(\alpha\wedge\beta)) + (\alpha\wedge\beta) = \mathbf{K}\circ(\alpha\wedge\beta)$.
9: There are three cases: **(a)** $\mathbf{K}\div\neg(\alpha\wedge\beta) \vdash \neg(\alpha\wedge\beta)$: Then by *persistence* $\mathbf{K}\div\neg\alpha \vdash \neg(\alpha\wedge\beta)$. Then $((\mathbf{K}\div\neg\alpha) + \alpha) + \beta = \mathbf{K}_\bot = (\mathbf{K}\circ\alpha) + \beta$. Hence $\mathbf{K}\circ(\alpha\wedge\beta) \subseteq (\mathbf{K}\circ\alpha) + \beta$. **(b)** $\neg(\alpha\wedge\beta) \notin \mathbf{K}\div\neg(\alpha\wedge\beta)$: Then by *success propagation*, $\neg\alpha \notin \mathbf{K}\div\neg\alpha$. **(b1)** $\neg(\alpha\wedge\neg\beta) \in \mathbf{K}\div\neg(\alpha\wedge\neg\beta)$: Then by *relative success*, $\mathbf{K}\div\neg(\alpha\wedge\neg\beta) = \mathbf{K}$. By *conjunctive overlap* and *extensionality*, $\mathbf{K}\div\neg(\alpha\wedge\beta) \cup \mathbf{K}\div\neg(\alpha\wedge\neg\beta) \subseteq \mathbf{K}\div\neg\alpha$, then by *inclusion* $\mathbf{K}\div\neg(\alpha\wedge\beta) \subseteq \mathbf{K}\div\neg\alpha$. Hence $\mathbf{K}\circ(\alpha\wedge\beta) = (\mathbf{K}\div\neg(\alpha\wedge\beta)) + (\alpha\wedge\beta) \subseteq ((\mathbf{K}\div\neg\alpha) + \alpha) + \beta = (\mathbf{K}\circ\alpha) + \beta$. **(b2)** $\neg(\alpha\wedge\neg\beta) \notin \mathbf{K}\div\neg(\alpha\wedge\neg\beta)$: Let $\delta \in \mathbf{K}\circ(\alpha\wedge\beta)$. Then $(\neg\alpha\vee\neg\beta\vee\delta) \in \mathbf{K}\div\neg(\alpha\wedge\beta)$. Then by *inclusion* $(\neg\alpha\vee\neg\beta\vee\delta) \in \mathbf{K}$. It follows by *recovery* that $(\neg\alpha\vee\neg\beta\vee\delta) \in (\mathbf{K}\div\neg(\alpha\wedge\neg\beta)) + \neg(\alpha\wedge\neg\beta)$ and since $(\mathbf{K}\div\neg(\alpha\wedge\neg\beta)) + \neg(\alpha\wedge\neg\beta) \subseteq (\mathbf{K}\div\neg(\alpha\wedge\neg\beta)) + (\alpha\wedge\beta)$, it follows by *closure* that $(\neg\alpha\vee\neg\beta\vee\delta) \in \mathbf{K}\div\neg(\alpha\wedge\neg\beta)$. Then by *conjunctice overlap* $(\neg\alpha\vee\neg\beta\vee\delta) \in \mathbf{K}\div\neg\alpha$, hence $\delta \in ((\mathbf{K}\div\neg\alpha)+\alpha)+\beta = (\mathbf{K}\circ\alpha)+\beta$.■

Proof of Observation 21.
1: Trivial.
2: Trivial.
3: Let $\mathbf{K} \nvdash \alpha$. Then by $\circ$ *vacuity* $\mathbf{K}+\neg\alpha \subseteq \mathbf{K}\circ\neg\alpha$, hence $\mathbf{K}\cap\mathbf{K}\circ\neg\alpha = \mathbf{K}$.
4: Trivial.
5: Due to $\circ$ *relative success* either $\mathbf{K}\circ\neg\alpha = \mathbf{K}$ or $\mathbf{K}\circ\neg\alpha \vdash \neg\alpha$. If $\mathbf{K}\circ\neg\alpha = \mathbf{K}$, then $\mathbf{K}\div\alpha = \mathbf{K}$, hence $\mathbf{K} \subseteq (\mathbf{K}\div\alpha)+\alpha$. In the other case, when $\mathbf{K}\circ\neg\alpha \vdash \neg\alpha$, let $\beta \in \mathbf{K}$. It follows from the logical closure of $\mathbf{K}$ that $\alpha \rightarrow \beta \in \mathbf{K}$ and from $\mathbf{K}\circ\neg\alpha \vdash \neg\alpha$ that $\mathbf{K}\circ\neg\alpha \vdash \alpha \rightarrow \beta$. Due to $\circ$ *closure*, $\alpha \rightarrow \beta \in \mathbf{K}\circ\neg\alpha$. Hence $\alpha \rightarrow \beta \in (\mathbf{K}\cap(\mathbf{K}\circ\neg\alpha))$, so that $\beta \in (\mathbf{K}\cap(\mathbf{K}\circ\neg\alpha)) + \alpha = (\mathbf{K}\div\alpha)+\alpha$.
6: Let $\beta \notin \mathbf{K}\div\alpha$. Then it follows by Harper identity that either $\beta \notin \mathbf{K}\circ\neg\alpha$ or $\beta \notin \mathbf{K}$. If $\beta \notin \mathbf{K}$, then $\beta \notin \mathbf{K}\cap\mathbf{K}\circ\neg\beta$, hence $\beta \notin \mathbf{K}\div\beta$. If $\beta \notin \mathbf{K}\circ\neg\alpha$, then it follows from *closure* that $\mathbf{K}\circ\neg\alpha \vdash \beta$, and hence by *strong regularity* that $\mathbf{K}\circ\neg\beta \vdash \neg\beta$. Then, since $\mathbf{K} \neq \mathbf{K}_\bot$, it follows by *consistency preservation* that $\beta \notin \mathbf{K}\circ\neg\beta$, hence $\beta \notin \mathbf{K}\div\beta$.

7: If $\mathbf{K}\circ\neg\alpha = \mathbf{K}$, then $\mathbf{K}\div\alpha = \mathbf{K}$ follows directly. If $\mathbf{K}\circ\neg\alpha \neq \mathbf{K}$, then it follows from $\circ$ *relative success* that $\mathbf{K}\circ\neg\alpha \vdash \neg\alpha$. If $\mathbf{K} = \mathbf{K}_{\perp}$, then it follows by $\circ$ *closure* that $\mathbf{K}\circ\neg\alpha \nvdash \perp$. If $\mathbf{K} \neq \mathbf{K}_{\perp}$, then it follows by *consistency preservation* that $\mathbf{K}\circ\neg\alpha \nvdash \perp$. In both cases it follows from $\mathbf{K}\circ\neg\alpha \vdash \alpha$ and the consistency of $\mathbf{K}\circ\neg\alpha$ that $\alpha \notin \mathbf{K}\circ\neg\alpha$, hence $\alpha \notin \mathbf{K}\div\alpha = \mathbf{K} \cap (\mathbf{K}\circ\neg\alpha)$.
8: Let $\mathbf{K}\div\alpha = \mathbf{K}\div\beta = \mathbf{K}$. There are three cases: First case $\alpha \notin \mathbf{K}\circ\neg\alpha$: Then, since $\alpha \notin \mathbf{K} \cap \mathbf{K}\circ\neg\alpha = \div K\alpha = \mathbf{K}$, it follows that $\alpha \notin \mathbf{K}$. Then $\alpha \wedge \beta \notin \mathbf{K}$, and it follows from $\circ$ *vacuity* that $\mathbf{K} \subseteq \mathbf{K}\circ\neg(\alpha \wedge \beta)$, so that $\mathbf{K}\div(\alpha \wedge \beta) = \mathbf{K} \cap \mathbf{K}\circ\neg(\alpha \wedge \beta) = \mathbf{K}$. Second case, $\beta \notin \mathbf{K}\circ\neg\beta$: Symmetrical with the first case. Third case, $\alpha \in \mathbf{K}\circ\neg\alpha$ and $\beta \in \mathbf{K}\circ\neg\beta$: If $\neg\alpha \in \mathbf{K}\circ\neg\alpha$, then $\mathbf{K}\circ\neg\alpha = \mathbf{K}_{\perp}$, then by *consistency preservation*, $\mathbf{K} = \mathbf{K}_{\perp}$; then $\mathbf{K}\circ\neg\alpha = \mathbf{K}$. If $\neg\alpha \notin \mathbf{K}\circ\neg\alpha$, then by $\circ$ *relative success*, $\mathbf{K}\circ\neg\alpha = \mathbf{K}$. By the same reasoning we obtain $\mathbf{K}\circ\neg\beta = \mathbf{K}$. It follows by *disjunctive constancy* that $\mathbf{K}\circ(\neg\alpha \vee \neg\beta) = \mathbf{K}$. Then by $\circ$ *extensionality*, $\mathbf{K}\div(\alpha \wedge \beta) = \mathbf{K} \cap \mathbf{K}\circ(\neg\alpha \vee \neg\beta) = \mathbf{K}$.
9: Let $\mathbf{K}\div\alpha \nvdash \alpha$ and $\vdash \beta \rightarrow \alpha$. If $\alpha \notin \mathbf{K}$, then $\beta \notin \mathbf{K}$, hence $\beta \notin \mathbf{K} \cap (\mathbf{K}\circ\neg\beta)$. If $\alpha \in \mathbf{K}$, then it follows from $\mathbf{K} \cap (\mathbf{K}\circ\neg\alpha) \nvdash \alpha$ that $\mathbf{K}\circ\neg\alpha \nvdash \alpha$. Hence $\mathbf{K}\circ\neg\alpha \neq \mathbf{K}$ and it follows from $\circ$ *relative success* that $\neg\alpha \in \mathbf{K}\circ\neg\alpha$. By *strict improvement*, $\neg\beta \in \mathbf{K}\circ\neg\beta$ and by *consistency preservation*, $\mathbf{K}\circ\neg\beta \nvdash \beta$. Hence $\mathbf{K} \cap \mathbf{K}\circ\neg\beta = \mathbf{K}\div\beta \nvdash \beta$.
10: Let $\delta \in \mathbf{K}\div\alpha$ and $\delta \in \mathbf{K}\div\beta$. Then $\delta \in \mathbf{K} \cap \mathbf{K}\circ\neg\alpha$ and $\delta \in \mathbf{K} \cap \mathbf{K}\circ\neg\beta$. Due to $\vdash \alpha \leftrightarrow \neg(\neg(\alpha \wedge \beta) \wedge \neg\alpha)$, it follows by $\circ$ *extensionality* that $\delta \in \mathbf{K} \cap \mathbf{K}\circ(\neg(\alpha \wedge \beta) \wedge \neg\alpha) \subseteq$ (by *superexpansion*) $\mathbf{K} \cap (\mathbf{K}\circ\neg(\alpha \wedge \beta)) + \neg\alpha$. Then $\neg\alpha \rightarrow \delta \in \mathbf{K}\circ\neg(\alpha \wedge \beta)$. By the same reasoning we obtain $\neg\beta \rightarrow \delta \in \mathbf{K}\circ\neg(\alpha \wedge \beta)$. Then by $\circ$ *closure* $\neg(\alpha \wedge \beta) \rightarrow \delta \in \mathbf{K}\circ\neg(\alpha \wedge \beta)$. If $\mathbf{K}\circ\neg(\alpha \wedge \beta) = \mathbf{K}$, then it follows, since $\delta \in \mathbf{K}$, that $\delta \in \mathbf{K} \cap \mathbf{K}\circ\neg(\alpha \wedge \beta) = \mathbf{K}\div(\alpha \wedge \beta)$. If $\mathbf{K}\circ\neg(\alpha \wedge \beta) \neq \mathbf{K}$, then it follows from $\circ$ *relative success* that $\mathbf{K}\circ\neg(\alpha \wedge \beta) \vdash \neg(\alpha \wedge \beta)$; then by $\circ$ *closure* $\delta \in \mathbf{K}\circ\neg(\alpha \wedge \beta)$, hence $\delta \in \mathbf{K} \cap \mathbf{K}\circ\neg(\alpha \wedge \beta) = \mathbf{K}\div(\alpha \wedge \beta)$.
11: Let $\mathbf{K}\div(\alpha \wedge \beta) \nvdash \alpha$. We have two possible cases according to Harper identity: First case, $\alpha \notin \mathbf{K}$: Then by $\circ$ *vacuity*, $\mathbf{K}\div\alpha = \mathbf{K} \cap \mathbf{K}+\neg\alpha = \mathbf{K}$. Hence $\mathbf{K}\div(\alpha \wedge \beta) = \mathbf{K} \cap \mathbf{K}\circ\neg(\alpha \wedge \beta) \subseteq \mathbf{K} = \mathbf{K}\div\alpha$. Second case, $\mathbf{K}\circ\neg(\alpha \wedge \beta) \nvdash \alpha$: Then by *strong regularity* $\mathbf{K}\circ\neg\alpha \nvdash \neg\alpha$. By *strict improvement* $\mathbf{K}\circ\neg(\alpha \wedge \beta) \nvdash \neg(\alpha \wedge \beta)$. It follows from *guarded subexpansion* and $\circ$ *extensionality* that $(\mathbf{K}\circ\neg(\alpha \wedge \beta)) + \neg\alpha \subseteq \mathbf{K}\circ(\neg(\alpha \wedge \beta) \wedge \neg\alpha) = \mathbf{K}\circ\neg\alpha$. Due to $(\mathbf{K}\circ\neg(\alpha \wedge \beta)) + \neg\alpha \subseteq \mathbf{K}\circ\neg\alpha$ it follows that $\mathbf{K}\circ\neg(\alpha \wedge \beta) \subseteq \mathbf{K}\circ\neg\alpha$. Hence $\mathbf{K}\div(\alpha \wedge \beta) = \mathbf{K} \cap \mathbf{K}\circ\neg(\alpha \wedge \beta) \subseteq \mathbf{K} \cap \mathbf{K}\circ\neg\alpha = \mathbf{K}\div\alpha$. ■

Proof of Theorem 23: Let $\circ = \mathbb{R}(\div)$ and $\div_2 = \mathbb{C}(\mathbb{R}(\div))$. Then:

$$\mathbf{K} \circ \neg\alpha = \begin{cases} (\mathbf{K} \div \alpha) + \neg\alpha & \text{if } \mathbf{K} \div \alpha \nvdash \alpha \\ \mathbf{K} & \text{otherwise} \end{cases}$$

$$\mathbf{K} \div_2 \alpha = \mathbf{K} \cap \mathbf{K} \circ \neg\alpha.$$

There are two cases: First case, $\mathbf{K} \div \alpha \vdash \alpha$: Then $\mathbf{K}\circ\neg\alpha = \mathbf{K}$. By *relative success*, $\mathbf{K} \div \alpha = \mathbf{K}$. Then $\mathbf{K} \div_2 \alpha = \mathbf{K} \cap \mathbf{K}\circ\neg\alpha = \mathbf{K} \cap \mathbf{K} = \mathbf{K} = \mathbf{K} \div \alpha$.

Second case, $\mathbf{K} \div \alpha \nvdash \alpha$: Then $\mathbf{K} \div_2 \alpha = \mathbf{K} \cap ((\mathbf{K} \div \alpha) + \neg\alpha)$. For one direction, let $\delta \in \mathbf{K} \div \alpha$. Then by *inclusion*, $\delta \in \mathbf{K}$ from which it follows that $\delta \in \mathbf{K} \div_2 \alpha$; hence $\mathbf{K} \div \alpha \subseteq \mathbf{K} \div_2 \alpha$. For the other direction, let $\delta \in \mathbf{K} \div_2 \alpha$. Then $\delta \in \mathbf{K}$ and by $\div$ *closure*, $\neg\alpha \to \delta \in \mathbf{K} \div \alpha$. By *recovery*, $\alpha \to \delta \in \mathbf{K} \div \alpha$. Then by *closure* $\delta \in \mathbf{K} \div \alpha$; hence $\mathbf{K} \div_2 \alpha \subseteq \mathbf{K} \div \alpha$. This concludes the proof.■

Proof of Theorem 24: Let $\div = \mathbb{C}(\circ)$ and $\circ_2 = \mathbb{R}(\mathbb{C}(\circ))$. Then:

$$\mathbf{K} \div \neg\alpha = \mathbf{K} \cap \mathbf{K} \circ \alpha$$
$$\mathbf{K} \circ_2 \alpha = \begin{cases} (\mathbf{K} \div \neg\alpha) + \alpha & \text{if } \mathbf{K} \div \neg\alpha \nvdash \neg\alpha \\ \mathbf{K} & \text{otherwise} \end{cases}$$

If $\neg\alpha \notin \mathbf{K}$, then by *vacuity* $\mathbf{K} \circ \alpha = \mathbf{K}+\alpha$, hence $\mathbf{K} \div \neg\alpha = \mathbf{K}$ and $\mathbf{K} \circ_2 \alpha = \mathbf{K}+\alpha$. For the principal case, let $\neg\alpha \in \mathbf{K}$. There are two subcases: **Case (a)**, $\mathbf{K} \circ \alpha \vdash \neg\alpha$: Then $\mathbf{K} \div \neg\alpha \vdash \neg\alpha$, hence $\mathbf{K} \circ_2 \alpha = \mathbf{K}$. If $\mathbf{K} \circ \alpha \vdash \alpha$, then $\mathbf{K} \circ \alpha = \mathbf{K}_\perp$, and by *consistency preservation*, $\mathbf{K} = \mathbf{K}_\perp$, so that $\mathbf{K} \circ \alpha = \mathbf{K} \circ_2 \alpha = \mathbf{K}_\perp$. If $\mathbf{K} \circ \alpha \nvdash \alpha$, then it follows from *relative success* that $\mathbf{K} \circ \alpha = \mathbf{K}$, and consequently $\mathbf{K} \circ \alpha = \mathbf{K} \circ_2 \alpha$ in this case as well. **Case (b)**, $\mathbf{K} \circ \alpha \nvdash \neg\alpha$: Since $\mathbf{K} \vdash \neg\alpha$, we have $\mathbf{K} \circ \alpha \neq \mathbf{K}$, and *relative success* yields $\mathbf{K} \circ \alpha \vdash \alpha$. We also have $\mathbf{K} \div \neg\alpha \nvdash \neg\alpha$, so that $\mathbf{K} \circ_2 \alpha = (\mathbf{K} \div \neg\alpha) + \alpha = (\mathbf{K} \cap \mathbf{K} \circ \alpha) + \alpha$. It follows for all δ that $\delta \in \mathbf{K} \circ_2 \alpha$ iff $\alpha \to \delta \in (\mathbf{K} \cap \mathbf{K} \circ \alpha)$, iff $\alpha \to \delta \in \mathbf{K}$ and $\alpha \to \delta \in \mathbf{K} \circ \alpha$, iff $\alpha \to \delta \in \mathbf{K} \circ \alpha$ (since $\neg\alpha \in \mathbf{K}$), iff $\delta \in \mathbf{K} \circ \alpha$ (by *closure*, since $\mathbf{K} \circ \alpha \vdash \alpha$). Hence $\mathbf{K} \circ \alpha = \mathbf{K} \circ_2 \alpha$. ■

E. Fermé
University of Buenos Aires, Argentina.

Sven Ove Hansson
Royal Institute of Technology, Stockholm, Sweden.

REFERENCES

[Alchourrón and Makinson, 1982] Carlos Alchourrón and David Makinson. On the logic of theory change: Contraction functions and their associated revision functions. *Theoria*, **48**, 14–37, 1982.

[Alchourrón *et al.*, 1985] Carlos Alchourrón, Peter Gärdenfors, and David Makinson. On the logic of theory change: Partial meet contraction and revision functions. *Journal of Symbolic Logic*, **50**, 510–530, 1985.

[Cantwell, 1997] John Cantwell. On the logic of small change in hypertheories. *Theoria*, **63**, 54–89, 1997.

[Fermé, 1998] Eduardo Fermé. On the logic of theory change: Contraction without recovery. *Journal of Logic, Language and Information*, **7**, 127–137, 1998.

[Fermé, 2000] Eduardo Fermé. Five faces of recovery. This volume, 2000.

[Fermé and Hansson, 1999] Eduardo Fermé and Sven Ove Hansson. Selective revision. *Studia Logica*, in press.

[Foo, 1990] Norman Foo. Observation on AGM entrenchment. Computer Science Technical Report 389. University of Sydney, 1990.

[Gärdenfors and Makinson, 1988] Peter Gärdenfors and David Makinson. Revisions of knowledge systems using epistemic entrenchment. In Moshe Y. Vardi, editor, *Proceedings of the Second Conference on Theoretical Aspects of Reasoning About Knowledge*, pages 83–95, Los Altos, 1988. Morgan Kaufmann.

[Gärdenfors, 1988] Peter Gärdenfors. *Knowledge in Flux: Modeling the Dynamics of Epistemic States*. The MIT Press, Cambridge, 1988.

[Grove, 1988] Adam Grove. Two modellings for theory change. *Journal of Philosophical Logic*, **17**, 157–170, 1988.

[Hansson *et al.*, 1999] Sven Ove Hansson, Eduardo Fermé, John Cantwell, and Marcelo Falappa. Credibility-limited revision. (manuscript), 1999.

[Hansson, 1991a] Sven Ove Hansson. *Belief Base Dynamics*. PhD thesis, Uppsala University, 1991.

[Hansson, 1991b] Sven Ove Hansson. Belief contraction without recovery. *Studia Logica*, **50**, 251–260, 1991.

[Hansson, 1996] Sven Ove Hansson. A test battery for rational database updating. *Artificial Intelligence*, **82**, 341–352, 1996.

[Hansson, 1997] Sven Ove Hansson. Semi-revision. *Journal of Applied Non-Classical Logic*, **7**, 151–175, 1997.

[Hansson, 1999a] Sven Ove Hansson. Recovery and epistemic residue. *Journal of Logic, Language and Information*, 1999. (In press).

[Hansson, 1999b] Sven Ove Hansson. A survey of non-prioritized belief revision. *Erkenntnis*, **50**, 413–427, 1999.

[Hansson, 1999c] Sven Ove Hansson. *A Textbook of Belief Dynamics*. Kluwer Academic Publishers, Dordrecht, 1999.

[Levi, 1991] Isaac Levi. *The fixation of belief and its undoing: changing beliefs through inquiry*. Cambridge University Press, Cambridge, 1991.

[Levi, 1997] Isaac Levi. Contraction and informational value. (manuscript), 1997.

[Lindström and Rabinowicz, 1991] Sten Lindström and Wlodek Rabinowicz. Epistemic entrenchment with incomparabilities and relational belief revision. In Fuhrmann and Morreau, editors, *The Logic of Theory Change*, pages 93–126, Berlin, 1991. Springer-Verlag.

[Makinson, 1987] David Makinson. On the status of the postulate of recovery in the logic of theory change. *Journal of Philosophical Logic*, **16**, 383–394, 1987.

[Makinson, 1997] David Makinson. On the force of some apparent counterexamples to recovery. In E. Garzón Valdéz et al., editor, *Normative Systems in Legal and Moral Theory: Festschrift for Carlos Alchourrón and Eugenio Bulygin*, pages 475–481, Berlin, 1997. Duncker & Humblot.

[Makinson, 1997] David Makinson. Screened revision. *Theoria*, **63**, 14–23, 1997.

[Nayak, 1994] Abhaya Nayak. Foundational belief change. *Journal of Philosophical Logic*, **23**, 495–533, 1994.

[Niederée, 1991] Reinhard Niederée. Multiple contraction: A further case against Gärdenfors' principle of recovery. In Fuhrmann and Morreau, editors, *The Logic of Theory Change*, pages 322–334, Berlin, 1991. Springer-Verlag.

[Olsson, 1997] Erik Olsson. *Coherence*. PhD thesis, Uppsala University, 1997.

[Rott and Pagnucco, 1999] Hans Rott and Maurice Pagnucco. Severe withdrawal (and recovery). *Journal of Philosophical Logic*, **28**, 501–547, 1999.

[Rott, 1992] Hans Rott. Preferential belief change using generalized epistemic entrenchment. *Journal of Logic, Language and Information*, **1**, 45–78, 1992.

SALEM BENFERHAT, DIDIER DUBOIS AND HENRI PRADE

A COMPUTATIONAL MODEL FOR BELIEF CHANGE AND FUSING ORDERED BELIEF BASES

1 INTRODUCTION

The problem of belief change has traditionally been a topic of investigation for philosophers of cognition (e.g., [Levi, 1980]). In the last decade, it has become a major issue in Artificial Intelligence and Information Systems for the purpose of managing the flux of information in databases. The revision of a database, due to the insertion of some input of information (often called update) has been considered since the early eighties [Fagin *et al.*, 1983] and solved at the syntactic level often in an *ad hoc* way. On the contrary, revision tools proposed by philosophers are axiomatically justified [Gärdenfors, 1988], but difficult to implement in practice (see e.g., Nebel, [1992; 1998]); moreover the representation of epistemic states (also called cognitive states which gather the available beliefs about the real world) is carried out at the semantic level, sometimes by deductively closed logical theories, sometimes by set of possible worlds [Grove, 1988].

Whether theory- or practice-oriented, all revision tools lay bare the necessity of prioritizing belief bases or their deductive closures, belief sets. An ordered or prioritized belief base can be cast in the framework of possibilistic logic, which induces a complete pre-order on interpretations that can be encoded by means of possibility distributions [Dubois *et al.*, 1994], or kappa rankings [Spohn, 1988; Benferhat, 1998; Williams, 1994]. Possibilistic logic enables the closure of a prioritized belief base to be defined under the form of an epistemic entrenchment, that can be encoded as a necessity measure. At the semantic level, the revision of a possibility distribution can be achieved as a form of conditioning [Spohn, 1988; Dubois and Prade, 1992], or more generally as a transmutation that modifies the ranking of interpretations so as to give priority to the input information [Williams, 1994]. Various forms of ranking revisions have been suggested by [Boutilier, 1993; Williams, 1994; Darwiche and Pearl, 1997; Papini, 1999]. A syntactic counterpart of AGM revision [Gärdenfors, 1988], which corresponds to conditioning possibility distributions can be defined as follows [Dubois and Prade, 1992]: add the input formula to the prioritized belief base so as to give the highest priority to it; compute the level of inconsistency of the resulting possibly inconsistent belief base; drop all formulas with priority less or equal to this level of inconsistency. This process is very drastic and deletes more formulas than necessary. More parsimonious syntactic revision processes have been proposed by [Nebel, 1992; Benferhat *et al.*, 1997a; Williams, 1996; Williams, 1997].

Another issue that slowly comes to the forefront of information systems research is that of databases merging [Baral *et al.*, 1992; Cholvy, 1998; Lin and

M.-A. Williams and H. Rott (eds.), Frontiers in Belief Revision, 109–134.

Mendelzon, 1992; Konieczny and Pino-Pérez, 1998]. At the semantic level, fusing two epistemic states, viewed as plausibility relations over a set of interpretations, can be achieved if the relations are commensurate, that is, represented by mappings from interpretations to the same plausibility scale. In possibility theory, many fusion modes can be defined, especially disjunctive and conjunctive modes, based on fuzzy set-theoretic operations. Syntactic fusion modes should be in accordance with semantic ones in order to be meaningful.

Fusion and revision are closely related because revision can be viewed as a fusion process where the input information has priority over a priori beliefs, while fusion is basically considered as a symmetric operation. Both fusion and revision involve inconsistency handling. The similarity between fusion and revision is even clearer if we envisage the revision by uncertain inputs. At the semantic level such forms of revision operations have been studied by [Spohn, 1988] who has shown their close relationship with Jeffrey's rule of revision in probability theory. Possibilistic counterparts of the revision by uncertain inputs have been discussed by Dubois and Prade [1991; 1992; 1997]. They have laid bare the fact that revision operations with an uncertain input, can be expressed by a combination of conditioning and fusion operations. At the syntactic level such a form of revision comes down to adding a formula to a prioritized belief base at a certain prescribed level (see [Williams, 1994]). The problem is difficult because the belief base must be modified so that the added formula remains exactly with the prescribed priority, that is, it is neither implicitly inhibited by higher priority formulas that contradict it, nor pushed to higher priority levels by formulas that imply it.

This paper is devoted to semantically meaningful syntactic fusion and revision methods. After a brief presentation of the possibilistic setting of prioritized belief bases, a general tool for syntactic fusion which covers a large class of fuzzy set-theoretic operations is proposed. Then extensions of the drastic revision of belief bases to the handling of uncertain inputs are presented in detail, pursuing an investigation started by Dubois and Prade [1997].

2 REPRESENTING EPISTEMIC STATES AND BELIEF SETS IN POSSIBILITY THEORY

This section introduces the representation of epistemic states in the possibility theory framework. A semantic (global) and syntactic (compact) representation of epistemic states have been proposed. The semantic representation is encoded by a so-called possibility distribution which rank-orders all the interpretations with respect to their level of plausibility, while the syntactic representation is represented by a set of weighted propositional formulas, called possibilistic belief bases.

We first introduce the semantic and syntactic representations of epistemic states, then we recall how to jump from a syntactic to a semantic representation, and lastly we briefly describe an efficient machinery for doing inference from a set of weighted formulas.

2.1 Possibility distributions

In this paper, we only consider a finite propositional language denoted by $\mathcal{L}$. We denote by $\models$ the classical consequence relation, Greek letters $\alpha, \beta, \phi, \psi \ldots$ represent formulas. Let Ω be the finite set of interpretations, called also possible worlds, of the propositional logic language $\mathcal{L}$. Only one element of Ω is the real world, but in general the real world is not completely identified. $[\phi]$ denotes the set of classical models of ϕ.

Often epistemic states, i.e., agent's beliefs or simply the available beliefs about the real world, are semantically characterized by the existence of a total pre-order $\leq$ between the set of all interpretations. This ordering encodes agent's current beliefs (whose models are those which are maximal w.r.t. this ordering), and indicates how the agent changes his beliefs in the light of a new information.

In a possibility theory framework, at the semantic level, an epistemic state is represented by a possibility distribution π which is a mapping from Ω to the interval $[0, 1]$. $\pi(\omega)$ represents the degree of compatibility of ω with the available beliefs about the real world. By convention, $\pi(\omega) = 0$ means that the interpretation ω is impossible, and $\pi(\omega) = 1$ means that nothing prevents ω from being the real world. When $\pi(\omega) > \pi(\omega'), \omega$ is a preferred candidate to ω' for being the real state of the world. π is thus a convenient encoding of a preference relation that can embody concepts such as normality, typicality, plausibility, consistency with available beliefs, etc.

A possibility distribution π is said to be normal if $\exists \omega \in \Omega$, such that $\pi(\omega) = 1$, namely there exists at least an interpretation which is completely coherent with the available beliefs.

Given a possibility distribution π, we can define two different ways to rank-order formulas of the language from this possibility distribution. This is obtained using two mappings grading respectively the possibility and the certainty of a formula ϕ:

- the possibility degree $\Pi(\phi) = \max\{\pi(\omega) : \omega \in [\phi]\}$ which evaluates to what extent ϕ is consistent with the available beliefs expressed by π [Zadeh, 1978]. It satisfies the characteristic property:

$$\forall \phi \, \forall \psi, \; \Pi(\phi \vee \psi) = \max(\Pi(\phi), \Pi(\psi));$$

- the necessity (or certainty) degree $N(\phi) = 1 - \Pi(\neg\phi)$ which evaluates to what extent ϕ is entailed by the available beliefs. We have:

$$\forall \phi \, \forall \psi, \; N(\phi \wedge \psi) = \min(N(\phi), N(\psi)).$$

2.2 A possibilistic belief base and its induced possibility distribution

In the previous section, we have seen how to represent an epistemic state at the semantic level. In this section, we propose to represent this epistimic state syntactically by specifying explicitly the certainty degree of some formulas of the language, that we call a possibilistic belief base.

A possibilistic belief base is made of a finite set of weighted formulas

$$\Sigma = \{(\phi_i, a_i), i = 1, n\}$$

where a_i is understood as a lower bound on the degree of necessity $N(\phi_i)$. Formulas with null degree are not put explicitly in the belief base (only beliefs which are somewhat accepted by the agent are explicitly represented).

Given a possibilistic belief base Σ, we can generate a possibility distribution from Σ by associating to each interpretation, the level of compatibility with agent's beliefs, namely with Σ, as explained in the following.

When a possibilistic belief base is only made of one formula $\{(\phi, a)\}$, then each interpretation ω which satisfies ϕ will get the possibility degree $\pi(\omega) = 1$ since it is completely consistent with ϕ and each interpretation ω which falsifies ϕ will get a possibility degree $\pi(\omega)$ such that the higher a is (i.e., the more certain ϕ is), the lower $\pi(\omega)$ is. In particular, if $a = 1$ (i.e., ϕ is completely certain), then $\pi(\omega) = 0$, namely ω is impossible. One way to realize this constraint is to assign to $\pi(\omega)$ the degree $1 - a$ with a numerical encoding. More generally if π takes its value on a linearly ordered scale, $1 - (\cdot)$ is to be understood as an order-reversing map of the scale. Therefore, the possibility distribution associated to $\Sigma = \{(\phi, a)\}$ is:

$$\begin{aligned} \forall \omega \in \Omega, \pi_{\{(\phi,a)\}}(\omega) &= 1 && \text{if } \omega \vDash \phi \\ &= 1 - a && \text{otherwise.} \end{aligned}$$

When $\Sigma = \{(\phi_i, a_i), i = 1, n\}$ is a general possibilistic belief base then all the interpretations satisfying all the beliefs in Σ will have the highest possibility degree, namely 1, and the other interpretations will be ranked w.r.t. the higher belief that they falsify, namely we get [Dubois *et al.*, 1994]:

$$\begin{aligned} \forall \omega \in \Omega, \pi_\Sigma(\omega) &= 1 && \text{if } \omega \vDash \Sigma \\ &= 1 - \max\{a_i : (\phi_i, a_i) \in \Sigma \text{ and } \omega \vDash \neg\phi_i\} && \text{otherwise.} \end{aligned}$$

Thus π_Σ can be viewed as the result of the conjunctive combination of the $\pi_{\{(\phi_i a_i)\}}$'s using the min operator, that is:

$$\pi_\Sigma(\omega) = \min\{\pi_{\{(\phi_i,a_i)\}}(\omega) : (\phi_i, a_i) \in \Sigma\}.$$

The possibility distribution π_Σ is not necessarily normal, and $\text{Inc}(\Sigma) = 1 - \max_{\omega\in\Omega}\pi_\Sigma(\omega)$ is called the degree of inconsistency of the belief base Σ. $\text{Inc}(\Sigma) \neq 0$ means that Σ is classically inconsistent (i.e., without taking the degrees a_i into account).

The following definition and lemma are useful for the proofs of next Propositions.

DEFINITION 1. Let (ϕ, a) be a belief in Σ. Let A be a subbase of Σ containing beliefs having a weight greater or equal to a. Then (ϕ, a) is said to be subsumed by Σ if:

$$\{\psi : (\psi, b) \in A - \{(\phi, a)\}\} \vdash \phi.$$

LEMMA 2. *Let (ϕ, a) be a subsumed belief of Σ. Then Σ and $\Sigma' = \Sigma - \{(\phi, a)\}$ are semantically equivalent, namely,*

$$\pi_\Sigma = \pi_{\Sigma'}.$$

As a corollary of the previous lemma, we can add subsumed beliefs without changing the possibility distribution. This means that several syntactically different possibilistic belief bases may have the same possibility distribution as a semantic counterpart. In such a case, it can be shown that these belief bases are equivalent in the following sense: their a-cuts, which are classical belief bases, are logically equivalent in the usual sense, where the a-cut of a possibilistic belief base Σ is the set of classical formulas whose level of certainty is greater than or equal to a.

Lastly, given a possibility distribution π, the determination of the belief set (corresponding to the agent's current beliefs) denoted by $\mathrm{BS}(\pi)$, is obtained as follows. We denote by $\mathrm{Pref}(\pi)$ the set of interpretations with maximal weights, namely:

$$\mathrm{Pref}(\pi) = \{\omega : \nexists \omega' \text{ such that } \pi(\omega') > \pi(\omega)\}.$$

Then:

$$\mathrm{BS}(\pi) = \{\phi : [\phi] \supseteq \mathrm{Pref}(\pi)\}.$$

We can check that:

$$\mathrm{BS}(\pi) = \{\phi : N(\phi) > N(\neg\phi)\}.$$

2.3 Possibilistic inference and computing belief sets

The possibilistic logic inference can be performed at the syntactic level by means of a weighted version of the resolution principle:

$$\frac{(\phi \vee \psi, a), (\neg\phi \vee \delta, b)}{(\psi \vee \delta,\ \min(a, b))}.$$

It has been shown that $\mathrm{Inc}(\Sigma)$ corresponds to the greatest lower bound that can be obtained for the empty clause by the repeated use of the above resolution rule and using a refutation strategy.

The syntactic computation of the belief set, denoted by $\mathrm{BS}(\Sigma)$, is obtained by considering only the first and most important consistent formulas of Σ having high levels of certainty, namely:

$$\mathrm{BS}(\Sigma) = \{\phi : \mathrm{Cons}(\Sigma) \vdash \phi\},$$

where

$$\mathrm{Cons}(\Sigma) = \{\phi_i : (\phi_i, a_i) \in \Sigma \text{ and } a_i > \mathrm{Inc}(\Sigma)\}.$$

Clearly, possibilistic reasoning copes with partial inconsistency. It yields non-trivial conclusions by using a consistent sub-part of Σ, which corresponds to formulas belonging to the layers having sufficiently high levels of certainty.

It has been shown that the syntactic entailment is sound and complete [Dubois *et al.*, 1994] in the sense that:

$$\mathrm{BS}(\Sigma) = \mathrm{BS}(\pi_\Sigma).$$

This entailment is non-monotonic, and is chracteristic of the so-called "rational inference" of Lehmann and Magidor as shown by Benferhat et al. (1997).

3 SEMANTIC AND SYNTACTIC FUSION OF EPISTEMIC STATES

In this section, we propose syntactic and semantic approaches for fusing pieces of uncertain information provided by different sources. There exists a large panoply of operations which have been studied for aggregating fuzzy sets (They can be used for combining possibility distributions π_i's whose valuation scales are commensurate. This section provides the syntactic counterpart of classical fuzzy set aggregation operations on the possibilistic beliefs bases Σ_{π_i} associated with the π_i's.

In the following, we first describe the syntactic counterpart of the combination of two possibility distributions by an operator $\oplus$ which is very weakly constrained. The extension to more than two possibility distributions is straightforward, see [Benferhat *et al.*, 1997a]. Then, we propose to discuss some particular cases of $\oplus$ which are of special interest.

3.1 Syntactic counterpart of the combination of two possibility distributions

Let Σ_1 and Σ_2 be two possibilistic belief bases. Let π_1 and π_2 be their associated possibility distributions. Let $\oplus$ be a semantic operator which aggregates the two possibility distributions π_1 and π_2 into a new one $\pi_\oplus$. Then from Σ_1 and Σ_2, we are interested in building a new possibilistic belief base $\Sigma_\oplus$ such that $\pi_{\Sigma_\oplus} = \pi_\oplus$.

We first analyse the general case where $\oplus$ is very weakly constrained. Then we discuss some interesting combination modes in next section. The only requirements for $\oplus$ are the following properties:

$1 \oplus 1 = 1$;
if $a \geq c, b \geq d$ then $a \oplus b \geq c \oplus d$ (monotonicity).

The first one acknowledges the fact that if two sources agree for considering that an interpretation ω is fully possible, the result of the combination should confirm it. The second property expresses that a possibility degree resulting from a combination cannot decrease if the combined degrees increase. Let us first consider the syntactic counterpart of $\oplus$ (denoted by the same symbol) when the combination is applied to two one-formula belief bases $\Sigma_1 = \{(\phi, a)\}$ and $\Sigma_2 = \{(\psi, b)\}$. Then we can easily check that it results in three possibilistic formulas:

LEMMA 3. $\Sigma_\oplus = \Sigma_1 \oplus \Sigma_2 = \{(\phi, 1-(1-a)\oplus 1)\} \cup \{(\psi, 1-1\oplus(1-b))\} \cup \{(\phi \vee \psi, 1-(1-a)\oplus(1-b))\}$.

Proof. Let π_i be associated to Σ_i; there are two different cases:

- If $\omega \models \phi$ or $\omega \models \psi$ then this trivially implies that $\omega \models \phi \vee \psi$.
  - If $\omega \models \phi \wedge \psi$ then $\pi_1(\omega) = \pi_2(\omega) = 1$, hence:
  $$\pi_{\Sigma_\oplus}(\omega) = 1 = \pi_1(\omega) \oplus \pi_2(\omega);$$
  - if $\omega \models \phi \wedge \neg\psi$ then $\pi_1(\omega) = 1$ and $\pi_2(\omega) = 1-b$, hence:
  $$\begin{aligned}\pi_{\Sigma_\oplus}(\omega) &= 1-(1-1\oplus(1-b)) = 1\oplus(1-b)\\ &= \pi_1(\omega)\oplus\pi_2(\omega);\end{aligned}$$
  - by symmetry, if $\omega \models \neg\phi \wedge \psi$ then $\pi_1(\omega) = 1-a$ and $\pi_2(\omega) = 1$
  $$\begin{aligned}\pi_{\Sigma_\oplus}(\omega) &= 1-(1-(1-a)\oplus 1)\\ &= (1-a)\oplus 1\\ &= \pi_1(\omega)\oplus\pi_2(\omega).\end{aligned}$$
- If $\omega \not\models \phi$ and $\omega \not\models \psi$ then this implies that $\omega \not\models \phi \vee \psi$. Hence:

$$\begin{aligned}\pi_{\Sigma_\oplus}(\omega) &= 1-\max(1-(1-a)\oplus 1,\\ &\qquad 1-1\oplus(1-b), 1-(1-a)\oplus(1-b))\\ &= \min((1-a)\oplus 1, 1\oplus(1-b), (1-a)\oplus(1-b))\\ &= (1-a)\oplus(1-b) = \pi_1(\omega)\oplus\pi_2(\omega)\\ &\qquad \text{(since } 1 \geq 1-a \text{ and } 1 \geq 1-b\\ &\qquad \text{and due to the monotonicity of } \oplus).\end{aligned}$$

■

The result given in Lemma 3 can be generalized to the case of general possibilistic belief bases. Let $\Sigma_1 = \{(\phi_i, a_i) : i \in I\}$ and $\Sigma_2 = \{(\psi_j, b_j) : j \in J\}$. Namely, we have the following result.

PROPOSITION 4. *Let $\pi_\oplus$ be the result of the combination of π_1 and π_2 based on the operator $\oplus$.*

Then, $\pi_\oplus$ is associated with the following belief base:

$$\begin{aligned}\Sigma_\oplus = \; & \{(\phi_i, 1-(1-a_i)\oplus 1) : (\phi_i, a_i) \in \Sigma_1\} \cup \\ & \{(\psi_j, 1-1\oplus(1-b_j)) : (\psi_j, b_j) \in \Sigma_2\} \cup \\ & \{(\phi_i \vee \psi_j, 1-(1-a_i)\oplus(1-b_j)) : (\phi_i, a_i) \in \Sigma_1 \text{ and } \\ & (\psi_j, b_j) \in \Sigma_2\}.\end{aligned}$$

The proof is given in Appendix. Next sub-sections discuss particular cases of the combination operator $\oplus$ which are meaningful. The first one (idempotent conjunction) is meaningful when the sources are consistent but may be dependent, the second one (idempotent disjunction) is appropriate when the sources are highly conflicting, the third one deals with independent sources, and the last one is the usual weighted average.

3.2 *Idempotent conjunction*

The first combination mode that we consider in this section is the idempotent conjunction (i.e., the minimum) of possibility distributions. Namely define:

$$\forall\omega, \pi_{\text{cm}}(\omega) = \min(\pi_1(\omega), \pi_2(\omega)). \qquad \text{(CM)}$$

In the binary case, (CM) amounts to performing the intersection of subsets models A_1 and A_2 suggested by each formula. Conjunctive aggregation makes sense if all the sources are regarded as equally and fully reliable since any interpretation that is considered as impossible by one source is rejected even if other sources consider it to be possible. This is true for any combination operation $\oplus$ such that $a \oplus b \leq \min(a, b), \forall a, b$. If we insist that $\oplus$ be associative, and $1 \oplus 0 = 0$, then the operation min is the greatest and the only idempotent conjunctive aggregation. Otherwise, one may envisage other idempotent conjunctive aggregations that display a conjunctive behaviour, like $\sqrt{ab}$, for instance. But there are no longer associative.

An important issue with conjunctive combination as defined by (CM) is the fact that the result may be subnormalized, i.e., it may happen that $\nexists\omega, \pi_{\text{cm}}(\omega) = 1$. In that case it expresses a conflict between the sources. Clearly the conjunctive mode makes sense if all the π_i's significantly overlap, i.e., $\exists\omega, \forall i, \pi_i(\omega) = 1$, expressing that there is at least a value of ω that all sources consider as completely possible. If $\forall\omega, \pi_{\text{cm}}(\omega)$ is significantly smaller than 1 this mode of combination is debatable since in that case at least one of the sources (or experts) is likely to be wrong.

Besides, if two sources provide the same information $\pi_1 = \pi_2$, the result of the conjunction is still the same distribution with $\oplus = \min$. There is no reinforcement effect between the sources and they are thus not assumed to be independent. More generally, if the information provided by a source k is more specific[1] than the information given by the other then $\pi_{\text{cm}} = \pi_k$.

Syntactic counterpart

Letting $\oplus$ =min in Proposition 4, the min-based conjunction mode (CM) leads simply to take the union of Σ_1 and Σ_2 at the syntactic level, namely:

PROPOSITION 5. $\Sigma_{\text{cm}} = \Sigma_1 \cup \Sigma_2$.

Proof. Letting $\oplus$ =min in Proposition 4, and noticing that $1-(1-x)\oplus 1 = x$ and $1-(1-x)\oplus(1-y) = max(x,y)$, we get:

$$\begin{aligned}\Sigma_{\text{cm}} &= \Sigma_1 \cup \Sigma_2 \cup \{(\phi_i \vee \psi_j,\ \max(a_i,b_j)) : (\phi_i a_i) \in \Sigma_1 \text{ and} \\ &\quad (\psi_j b_j) \in \Sigma_2\} \equiv \Sigma_1 \cup \Sigma_2\end{aligned}$$

since $(\phi_i \vee \psi_j,\ \max(a_i,b_j))$ is either subsumed by (ϕ_i, a_i) (if $a_i \geq b_j$) or by (ψ_j, b_j) (if $b_j \geq a_i$). ■

3.3 *Idempotent disjunction*

When the pieces of information provided by the sources are conflicting (i.e., if $\forall\omega, \pi_{\text{cm}}(\omega)$ is significantly smaller than 1), then the disjunction (i.e., the maximum) of possibility distributions can be more appropriate. Namely define:

$$\forall\omega, \pi_{\text{dm}}(\omega) = \max(\pi_1(\omega), \pi_2(\omega)). \qquad \text{(DM)}$$

The disjunctive aggregation corresponds to a weaker reliability hypothesis. Namely, in the group of sources there is at least one reliable source for sure, but we do not know which one. In the binary case, it amounts to performing the union of the sets of models A_1 and A_2 suggested as possible by each source.

The disjunction mode (DM) in this case is natural if $A_1 \cap A_2$ is empty. Besides, if two sources provide the same information $\pi_1 = \pi_2$, the result of the disjunctive combination is still the same distribution. And if the information provided by a source k is less specific than the information given by the other(s) then $\pi_{\text{dm}} = \pi_k$.

Syntactic counterpart

Letting $\oplus$ = max in Proposition 4, the max-based conjunction mode (DM) leads to:

PROPOSITION 6.

$$\Sigma_{\text{dm}} = \{(\phi_i \vee \psi_j,\ min(a_i,b_j)) : (\phi_i, a_i) \in \Sigma_1 \ and \ (\psi_j, b_j) \in \Sigma_2\}.$$

[1]A possibility distribution π_1 is said to be more specific (more informative) than another possibility distribution π_2 if $\forall\omega, \pi_1(\omega) \leq \pi_2(\omega)$ and $\exists\omega'$, such that $\pi_1(\omega') < \pi_2(\omega')$.

Proof. Letting $\oplus$ = max in Proposition 4, note that $1 - (1 - x) \oplus 1 = 0$ and $1 - (1 - x) \oplus (1 - y) = min(x, y)$. Then:
$\Sigma_{\text{dm}} = \{(\phi_i \vee \psi_j, \min(a_i, b_j)) : (\phi_i, a_i) \in \Sigma_1 \text{ and } (\psi_j, b_j) \in \Sigma_2\}$
since formulas with certainty zero are not explicitly stated in the belief base. ■

Note that Σ_{dm} is always consistent (provided that one of Σ_1 or Σ_2 is consistent).

3.4 *Reinforcement combination modes*

The min-based conjunctive combination mode has no reinforcement effect. Namely, if source 1 assigns possibility $\pi_1(\omega) < 1$ to an interpretation ω, and source 2 assigns possibility $\pi_2(\omega) < 1$ to this interpretation, then overall, in the conjunctive mode, $\pi_\oplus(\omega) = \pi_1(\omega)$ if $\pi_1(\omega) < \pi_2(\omega)$, regardless of the value of $\pi_2(\omega)$. However since both sources consider ω as rather impossible, and if these opinions are independent, it may sound reasonable to consider ω as less possible than what each of the sources claims. More generally, if a pool of independent sources is divided into two unequal groups that disagree, we may want to favor the opinion of the biggest group. This type of combination cannot be modelled by the minimum operation, nor by any idempotent operation (in particular a similar argumentation holds for the disjunctive combination using maximum). What is needed is a reinforcement effect. A reinforcement effect can be obtained using a conjunctive operation other than the minimum operator. The most usual associative ones are the product and the so-called 'Łukasiewicz t-norm' (since it is directly related to Łukasiewicz many-valued implication) [Boldrin and Sossai, 1995]:

$$\forall \omega, \pi_{\text{Prod}}(\omega) = \pi_1(\omega) \cdot \pi_2(\omega). \qquad \text{(PROD)}$$

$$\forall \omega, \pi_{\text{LUK}}(\omega) = \max(0, \pi_1(\omega) + \pi_2(\omega) - 1). \qquad \text{(LUK)}$$

These combination modes are not idempotent. Their syntactic counterparts are directly derived from Proposition 4:

PROPOSITION 7. $\Sigma_{\text{PROD}} = \Sigma_1 \cup \Sigma_2 \cup \{(\phi_i \vee \psi_j, a_i + b_j - a_i \cdot b_j) : (\phi_i, a_i) \in \Sigma_1$ *and* $(\psi_j, b_j) \in \Sigma_2\}$.
$\Sigma_{\text{LUK}} = \Sigma_1 \cup \Sigma_2 \cup \{(\phi_i \vee \psi_j, \min(1, a_i + b_j)) : (\phi_i, a_i) \in \Sigma_1$ *and* $(\psi_j, b_j) \in \Sigma_2\}$.

Proof. Note that for both aggregations PROD and LUK it holds that $1 - (1 - x) \oplus 1 = x$. Moreover, $1 - (1 - x) \cdot (1 - y) = x + y - x \cdot y$, and $1 - max(0, (1 - x) + (1 - y) - 1) = min(1, x + y)$. The result is then an obvious consequence of Proposition 4. ■

3.5 *Weighted Average*

The last combination mode that we consider is the weighted average (WA). Let x_1 and x_2 be two non-negative real numbers such that $x_1 + x_2 = 1$. Then (WA) is defined by:

$$\forall \omega, \pi_{\text{WA}}(\omega) = x_1 \cdot \pi_1(\omega) + x_2 \cdot \pi_2(\omega). \qquad \text{(WA)}$$

The syntactic counterpart is:

PROPOSITION 8. $\Sigma_{\text{WA}} = \{(\phi_i, x_1 \cdot a_i) : (\phi_i, a_i) \in \Sigma_1\} \cup \{(\psi_j, x_2 \cdot b_j) : (\psi_j, b_j) \in \Sigma_2\} \cup \{(\phi_i \vee \psi_j, x_1 \cdot a_i + x_2 \cdot b_j) : (\phi_i, a_i) \in \Sigma_1$ *and* $(\psi_j, b_j) \in \Sigma_2\}$.

Proof. Note that $1 - 1 \oplus (1 - b) = 1 - x_1 - x_2 \cdot (1 - b) = x_2 b$. Moreover, $1 - x_1 \cdot (1 - a) - x_2 \cdot (1 - b) = x_1 \cdot a + x_2 \cdot b = a \oplus b$. Then the result follows immediately from Proposition 4. ■

Note that if $x_1 = 1$ then:

$$\Sigma_{\text{WA}} = \{(\phi_i, a_i) : (\phi_i, a_i) \in \Sigma_1\} \cup \{(\phi_i \vee \psi_j, a_i) : (\phi_i, a_i) \in \Sigma_1\} \equiv \Sigma_1.$$

The weights x_1 and x_2 in (WA) can account for the reliability of the sources. Conjunctions (and disjunctions) can be weighted as well. For instance, the weighted version of $\min_i a_i$ is $\min_i \max(a_i, 1 - w_i)$ with $\max_i w_i = 1$. The weights can also depend on the amount of conflicts, or the sources can be prioritized in the combination process. See [Benferhat *et al.*, 1997a] for more details.

3.6 *Particular cases: fusing with constants*

This section presents particular cases of combinations with a constant possibility distribution $\pi(\omega) = 1 - a, \forall\omega$. For this aim, we define three parameterized actions which operate on a belief base Σ, which will be useful in the next section for expressing revision:

- *Truncate*(Σ, a), which basically consists in removing formulas from the possibilistic belief base Σ having certainty degrees less or equal than a, and
- *Discount*(Σ, a) which basically consists in decreasing to level a the certainty degree of the formulas of Σ whose certainty is higher than a, and
- *Confirm*(Σ, a) which basically consists in increasing the certainty degree b of the formula in Σ to the degree $a + b - a \cdot b$.

More formally, we have:

$$\begin{aligned} \text{Truncate}(\Sigma, a) &= \{(\phi, b) : (\phi, b) \in \Sigma \text{ and } b > a\} \\ \text{Discount}(\Sigma, a) &= \{(\phi, a) : (\phi, b) \in \Sigma \text{ and } b \geq a\} \cup \{(\phi, b) : (\phi, b) \in \Sigma \\ &\quad \text{and } b < a\} \\ &= \{(\phi \min(a, b)) : (\phi, b) \in \Sigma\} \\ \text{Confirm}\ (\Sigma, a) &= \{(\phi, a + b - a \cdot b) : (\phi, b) \in \Sigma\}, \end{aligned}$$

The following proposition gives the semantic counterparts of these syntactic treatments by means of the combination of a possibility distribution π with a constant possibility distribution $\pi'(\omega) = 1 - a, \forall\omega$.

PROPOSITION 9. *Let Σ be a possibilistic belief base, and π its associated possibility distribution. Then:*

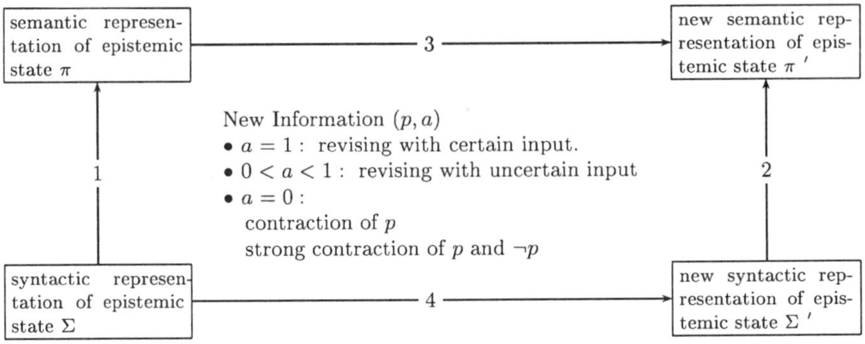

Figure 1.

- $\pi' =$ *min*$(\pi, 1 - a)$ *is associated to Truncate* $(\Sigma, a) \cup \{(\bot, a)\}$, *and*
- $\pi' =$ *max*$(\pi, 1 - a)$ *is associated to Discount* (Σ, a), *and*
- $\pi' = \pi \cdot (1 - a)$ *is associated to Confirm* $(\Sigma, a) \cup \{(\bot, a)\}$.

The proof is given in Appendix.

4 SYNTACTIC REVISION AND CONTRACTION IN ORDINAL FRAMEWORKS

This section addresses the problem of performing revision and contraction at the syntactic level, in agreement with the semantic level (See Figure 1). We assume that Σ is consistent.

The choice of a revision method partially depends on the status of the input information. Here, we first consider revising under a sure input, then we discuss the revision with uncertain inputs and lastly we consider contraction.

In all these cases, we first discuss these operations at the semantic level (Link 3) by providing operators which transform a possibility distribution π and a new information (p, a) into a new possibility distribution π'. Then we give their syntactic counterparts, which transform a possibilistic belief base Σ and a new information (p, a) into Σ' such that $\pi_{\Sigma'} = \pi'$ where π' is the result of revising π_Σ with (p, a) using Link 3.

4.1 Revision with a sure input

In the case of revision with a sure input p, it is assumed that all interpretations that falsify p are declared to be impossible. In possibility theory, this is performed by means of a conditioning device which transforms a possibility distribution π

and a new and sure information p into a new possibility distribution denoted by $\pi' = \pi(. \mid p)$. Natural properties for $\pi' = \pi(. \mid p)$ are:

(A_1) π' should be normalized,

(A_2) $\forall \omega \notin [p]$: $\pi'(\omega) = 0$,

(A_3) $\forall \omega, \omega' \in [p]$: $\pi(\omega) > \pi(\omega') \Leftrightarrow \pi'(\omega) > \pi'(\omega')$,

(A_4) if p is a priori accepted, then $\forall \omega \in [p] : \pi(\omega) = \pi'(\omega)$,

A_1 means that the new epistemic state is consistent. A_2 confirms that p is a sure piece information; it contradicts the axiom (CR2) of Darwiche and Pearl [1997] which stipulates that the ordering on countermodels of p should be preserved. A_3 means that the new possibility distribution should not alter the previous relative order between models of p. A_3 simply corresponds to the axiom (CR1) of Darwiche and Pearl [1997]. A_4 means that when $N(p) > 0$ (p is a priori accepted) then revision does not affect π. Then from A_1–A_4 it can be checked that the revision of the belief set BS(π) by p, namely BS$(\pi)^*p =$ BS$(\pi(. \mid p))$, satisfies all AGM postulates [Gärdenfors, 1988].

The previous properties do not guarantee a unique definition of conditioning. Indeed, the effect of the axiom A_2 may result in a sub-normalized possibility distribution. Restoring the normalisation, so as to satisfy A_1, can be done in two different ways (when $\Pi(p) > 0$):

- In an ordinal setting, we assign maximal possibility to the best models of p, then we get:

$$\begin{aligned}\pi(\omega \mid_m p) &= 1 \text{ if } \pi(\omega) = \Pi(p), \omega \vDash p\\ &= \pi(\omega) \text{ if } \pi(\omega) < \Pi(p), \omega \vDash p\\ &= 0 \text{ if } \omega \notin [p].\end{aligned}$$

- In a numerical setting, we proportionally rescale up all models of p:

$$\begin{aligned}\pi(\omega \mid_. p) &= \pi(\omega)/\Pi(p) \text{ if } \omega \vDash p\\ &= 0 \quad \text{otherwise}\end{aligned}$$

These revision methods satisfy an equation of the form

$$\forall \omega, \pi(\omega) = \pi(\omega \mid p) * \Pi(p)$$

which is similar to Bayesian conditioning, respectively for $*$ are min and the product. See [Dubois and Prade, 1990] for mathematical justifications that parallel Coxean justifications of probabilistic conditioning, and [De Baets *et al.*, 1999] for the unsuitability of the minimum rule in non-finite settings. The rule based on the product is much closer to genuine Bayesian conditioning than the qualitative conditioning based on the minimum which is purely based on comparing levels;

conditioning based on the product requires more of the structure of the unit interval. Besides, when $\Pi(p) = 0, \pi(\omega \mid_m p) = \pi(\omega \mid_\times p) = 1, \forall \omega$, by convention.

Another possible definition of conditioning that might be thought of is the following:

$$\begin{aligned} \pi(\omega \mid_L p) &= \pi(\omega) + (1 - \Pi(p)) \quad \text{if } \pi(\omega) \leq \Pi(p) \text{ and } \omega \vDash p \\ &= 0 \quad \text{if } \omega \vDash \neg p. \end{aligned}$$

Note that if $\pi(\omega) = \Pi(p)$ for $\omega \vDash p$ then $\pi(\omega \mid_L p) = 1$. This last definition is to some extent similar to the Bayesian one based on the product and it simply means that after pushing down all countermodels of p to zero, then if the result of this step is a subnormalized possibility distribution, then the models of p are translated up until normalization. This way of renormalizing may be debatable in practice since we may have $\pi(\omega) = 0$ and $\pi(\omega \mid_L p) > 0$, i.e., interpretations previously considered as impossible are now somewhat possible.

A syntactic counterpart of revising with a sure information consists of constructing from a possibilistic base Σ and the new information p, a new possibilistic base Σ' such that:

$$\forall \omega, \pi_{\Sigma'}(\omega) = \pi_\Sigma(\omega \mid p).$$

The simplest syntactic (and most drastic revision) is defined as follows: add the input p to the belief base with highest possible priority; compute the level of inconsistency $\chi = \mathrm{Inc}(\Sigma \cup \{(p, 1)\})$ of the resulting possibly inconsistent belief base; drop all formulas with priority less than or equal to this level of inconsistency. It guarantees that the remaining beliefs are consistent with p. Concerning the weights of remaining beliefs, $|_m$ leaves them unchanged, however $|.$ leads to discounting them by decreasing their weight (except for the completely certain ones), turning b into $f(b) = (b - \chi)/(1 - \chi)$, and the discounting with $|_L$ is more drastic.

In the rest of the paper, we denote by Σ_a the strict a-cut of Σ, namely:

$$\Sigma_a = \{(\phi, b) : (\phi, b) \in \Sigma \text{ and } b > a\}.$$

Table 1 provides the expression of Σ' for the three considered definitions of conditioning.

4.2 Revision with uncertain input

We shall consider the revision of π by some uncertain input information of the form (p, a) into a new epistemic state denoted by $\pi' = \pi(\omega \mid (p, a))$. The input (p, a) is interpreted as a constraint which forces π' to satisfy:

$$N'(p) = a \ \text{ (i.e., } \Pi'(p) = 1 \text{ and } \Pi'(\neg p) = 1 - a).$$

Clearly, properties defined for revision with a sure input are not all suitable for revising with an uncertain input. A_1 and A_3 are still acceptable. A_2 is no longer appropriate since $\Pi'(\neg p) \neq 0$ for $a < 1$. A_2 is replaced by:

(A'_2) $\Pi'(p) = 1, \Pi'(\neg p) = 1 - a$.

(A_5) $\forall \omega, \omega' \notin [p]$ then: $\pi(\omega) \geq \pi(\omega') \Rightarrow \pi'(\omega) \geq \pi'(\omega')$.

Table 1. Semantic and syntactic counterpart of $\pi(\omega \mid p)$, with $\chi = \text{Inc}(\Sigma \cup \{(p,1)\})$

	Result of revising π by p	Result of revising Σ by p
$\vert_m$ Ordinal	$= 1$ if $\pi(\omega) = \Pi(p), \omega \models p$ $= \pi(\omega)$ if $\pi(\omega) < \Pi(p), \omega \models p$ $= 0$ if $\omega \models \neg p$	$\Sigma_\chi \cup \{(p,1)\}$
$\vert.$	$= \frac{\pi(\omega)}{\Pi(p)}, \forall \omega \models p$ $= 0$ otherwise	$\{(\phi, f(b)) : (\phi, b) \in \Sigma_\chi\} \cup \{(p,1)\}$
$\vert_L$	$= 1$ if $\pi(\omega) = \Pi(p), \omega \models p$ $= \pi(\omega) + (1 - \Pi(p))$ if $\pi(\omega) < \Pi(p), \omega \models p$ $= 0$ if $\omega \models \neg p$.	$\{(\phi, b - \chi) : (\phi, b) \in \Sigma_\chi\} \cup \{(p,1)\}$

Table 2. Definition of $\pi(\omega \mid (p,a))$

*	|	$\omega \models p$		$\omega \models \neg p$	
min	$\vert_m$	1 $\pi(\omega)$	if $\pi(\omega) - \Pi(p)$ otherwise.	$1 - a$ $\pi(\omega)$	if $\pi(\omega = \Pi(\neg p)$ or $\pi(\omega) > 1 - a$ otherwise.
min	$\vert_\times$	$\pi(\omega)/\Pi(p)$		$\min(1 - a,\ pi(\omega)/\Pi(\neg p))$	
$\cdot$	$\vert_m$	1 $\pi(\omega)$	if $\pi(\omega) = \Pi(p)$ otherwise.	1-a $(1 - a) \cdot \pi(\omega)$	if $\pi(\omega) = \Pi(\neg p)$ otherwise.
$\cdot$	$\vert_\times$	$\pi(\omega)/\Pi(p)$		$(1 - a) \cdot \pi(\omega)/\Pi(\neg p)$	

A_5 preserves the relative order between countermodels of p, but in a weaker sense than in axiom A_3. Note that there is no further constraints which relate models of p and countermodels of p in the new epistemic state. Papini [1999], has considered a stronger constraint (also hinted by Spohn [1988]) by imposing that each model of p should be strictly preferred to each countermodels of $\neg p$. Let $\Delta'(p) = \min\{\pi'(\omega) : \omega \models p\}$. Then if $\Delta'(p) > 0$ Papini's constraint can be handled by letting $1 - a < \Delta'(p)$. The condition $\Delta'(p) > 0$ is necessary, since in all the definitions of possibilistic conditioning, impossible worlds remain impossible after conditioning, which is not the case in Papini's approach, since she encodes uncertainty by means of a total pre-order where the notion of impossible worlds does not exist.

A_3 and A_5 suggest that revising with uncertain input can be achieved using two parallel changes with a sure input in parallel: first, separately a conditioning on p and on $\neg p$. Then, in order to satisfy A_2', the distribution $\pi(\cdot \mid \neg p)$ is denormalized, so as to satisfy $\Pi'(\neg p) = 1 - a$. Therefore, revising with uncertain information can be achieved using the following definition:

$$\begin{aligned} \pi(\omega \mid (p,a)) &= \pi(\omega \mid p) && \text{if } \omega \models p \\ &= (1 - a) * \pi(\omega \mid \neg p) && \text{otherwise} \end{aligned}$$

where $*$ is either min or the product, see Table 2. Although it is natural to use the conditioning based on the same operation $*$, it would be possible to compute syntactic counterparts also if it is not the case. See Table 3.

The new ranking of countermodels of p depends on the relative position of the a priori certainty of p, and the prescribed posterior certainty of p:

- If $N(p) \leq a$ and when $*$ =min, all interpretations that were originally more plausible than $1-a$, are forced to level $1-a$, which means that some strict ordering between countermodels of p may be lost. When $*$ =product, all plausibility levels are proportionally shifted down.

- If $N(p) > a$ the best countermodels of p are forced to level $1-a$. Moreover, when $*$ =product, the plausibility levels of other countermodels are proportionally shifted up.

When $*$ =product, the stronger version of A_5 holds whereby the order of countermodels of p is fully preserved, hence it satisfies:
A_6: If $\omega_1 \models \neg$ p and $\omega_2 \models \neg$ p then $\pi(\omega_1) \leq \pi(\omega_2)$ iff $\pi'(\omega_1) \leq \pi'(\omega_2)$.

This postulate is equivalent to the postulate CR_2 defined in [Darwiche and Pearl, 1997]. Moreover if $N(p) \leq a$, we can check that the following two postulates are also satisfied:
A_7: If $\omega_1 \models$ p and $\omega_2 \models \neg$ p then $\pi(\omega_1) < \pi(\omega_2)$ only if $\pi'(\omega_1) < \pi'(\omega_2)$.
A_8: If $\omega_1 \models$ p and $\omega_2 \models \neg$ p then $\pi(\omega_1) \leq \pi(\omega_2)$ only if $\pi'(\omega_1) \leq \pi'(\omega_2)$.

A_7 and A_8 respectively correspond to CR_3 and CR_4 of [Darwiche and Pearl, 1997], and hence in the case when $*$ = product all the postulates for iterated revision [Darwiche and Pearl, 1997] are satisfied. Moreover, these authors always consider the assumption $N(p) \leq a$.

Table 3 gives the syntactic method for efficiently inserting a formula at some prescribed level in a prioritized belief base in accordance with above semantic principles. These results are easily obtained noticing that $\pi(\omega \mid (p, a))$ can be rewritten as $\pi(\omega \mid (p, a)) = \max(\pi(\omega \mid p), (1-a) * \pi(\omega \mid \neg p))$, and using disjunctive syntactic fusion, fusion with a constant, and syntactic conditioning described in the previous sections. In Table 3, the following notation is assumed:

$$\chi = \text{Inc}(\Sigma \cup \{p, 1)\}), \qquad \mathbf{y} = \text{Inc}(\Sigma \cup \{(\neg p, 1)\}),$$
$$f(b) = (b - \chi)/(1 - \chi) \quad \text{and} \quad g(b) = (b - \mathbf{y})/(1 - \mathbf{y}).$$

The proof of the first line of Table 3 is given in the Appendix. The other cases follow in a similar way.

Remarks

1. The size of the revised knowledge base is at most $\mid \Sigma \mid$.

2. In Table 3, if we let $\mathbf{y} = 0$ in column 2 (or $\chi = 0$ in column 3) we recover column 1.

Mary-Anne Williams [1994] has defined a general form of belief change she calls 'transmutations', in the setting of Spohn's [1988] kappa-functions. A κ-ranking $\kappa : \Omega \rightarrow \mathbb{N}$ is a function which assigns to each interpretation a positive

Table 3. Syntactic counterparts of conditioning with uncertain input

$*$	$\mid$	Σ is consistent with p and $\neg p$
min	$\mid_m$	$\Sigma \cup \{(p, a)\}$
min	$\mid_\times$	$\Sigma \cup \{(p, a)\}$
$\cdot$	$\mid_m$	$\Sigma \cup \{(p, a)\} \cup$ $\{(\phi \vee p, a + b - ab) : (\phi, b) \in \Sigma\}$
$\cdot$	$\mid_\times$	$\Sigma \cup \{(p, a)\} \cup$ $\{(\phi \vee p, a + b - ab) : (\phi, b) \in \Sigma\}$

$*$	$\mid$	Σ is inconsistent with $\neg p$
min	$\mid_m$	$\{(p, a)\} \cup \Sigma_{\mathbf{y}} \cup$ $\{(\phi \vee \neg p, b) : (\phi, b) \in \Sigma \text{ and } b \leq \mathbf{y}\}$
min	$\mid_\times$	$\{(\phi, g(b)) : (\phi, b) \in \Sigma_{\mathbf{y}}\} \cup$ $\{(\phi \vee \neg p, b) : (\phi, b) \in \Sigma\} \cup \{(p, a)\}$
$\cdot$	$\mid_m$	$\{(p, a)\} \cup \{(\phi \vee p, a + b - ab) : (\phi, b) \in \Sigma_{\mathbf{y}}\} \cup$ $\{(\phi, b) : (\phi, b) \in \Sigma_{\mathbf{y}}\} \cup \{(\phi \vee \neg p, b) : (\phi, b) \in \Sigma, b \leq \mathbf{y}\}$
$\cdot$	$\mid_\times$	$\{(\phi \vee p, g(b) + a - a.g(b)) : (\phi, b) \in \Sigma_{\mathbf{y}}\} \cup$ $\{(\phi \vee \neg p, b) : (\phi, b) \in \Sigma\} \cup \{(p, a)\}$

$*$	$\mid$	Σ is inconsistent with p
min	$\mid_m$	$\{(p, a)\} \cup \Sigma_\chi$ $\cup \{(\phi \vee p, b) : (\phi, b) \in \Sigma, a < b \leq \chi\}$
min	$\mid_\times$	$\{(\phi, f(b)) : (\phi, b) \in \Sigma_\chi\} \cup \{(p, a)\} \cup \{(\phi \vee p, b) : (\phi, b) \in \Sigma\}$
$\cdot$	$\mid_m$	$\Sigma_\chi \cup \{(p, a)\} \cup$ $\{(\phi \vee p, a + b - ab) : (\phi, b) \in \Sigma\}$
$\cdot$	$\mid_\times$	$\{(\phi, f(b)) : (\phi, b) \in \Sigma_\chi\} \cup \{(p, a)\} \cup$ $\{(\phi \vee p, a + b - ab) : (\phi, b) \in \Sigma\}$

integer such that $\exists \omega \in \Omega$ with $\kappa(\omega) = 0$. The higher $\kappa(\omega)$, the more implausible world ω is. $\kappa(\omega) = 0$ means that nothing forbids ω. Total impossibility corresponds to $+\infty$. A κ-ranking uniquely defines an epistemic entrenchment relation by associating to each formula ϕ a rank $\kappa(\phi)$:

$$\kappa(\phi) = \min\{\kappa(\omega) : \omega \vDash \phi\},$$

with by stipulation $\kappa(\bot) = 0$ and $\kappa(\top) = \infty$.

Given an uncertain input (p, i) taken as a constraint and a Spohn function κ describing the agent's a priori epistemic state, a transmutation of κ by (p, i) produces a Spohn function κ' such that $\kappa'(\neg p) = i$ and $\kappa'(p) = 0$, i.e., the degree of acceptance of p is enforced to level i. Williams [1994] has introduced a more qualitative transmutation called an adjustment. An adjustment of κ by (p, i) is defined as follows:

$$\begin{aligned} \kappa^*_{(p,n)} &= \kappa^-_p \text{ if } i = 0 \\ &= (\kappa^-_p)^x_{(p,i)} \text{ if } 0 < i < \kappa(\neg p) \\ &= \kappa^x_{(p,i)} \text{ otherwise} \end{aligned}$$

where

$$\begin{aligned}
\kappa_p^-(\omega) &= 0 \text{ if } \omega \vDash \neg p \text{ and } \kappa(\omega) = \kappa(\neg p) \\
&= \kappa(\omega) \text{ otherwise} \\
\kappa^x_{(p,i)}(\omega) &= 0 \text{ if } \omega \vDash p \text{ and } \kappa(\omega) = \kappa(p) \\
&= \kappa(\omega) \text{ if either } \omega \vDash p \text{ and } \kappa(\omega) \neq \kappa(p) \text{ or } \omega \vDash \neg p \text{ and } \kappa(\omega) > i \\
&= i \text{ otherwise}
\end{aligned}$$

κ_p^- is a contraction. Dubois and Prade [1997] have shown that for $i > 0$ the expression of Williams' adjustment can be simplified as follows:

$$\kappa^*_{(p,i)}(\omega) = \min(\kappa(\omega \mid p),\ \max(i, \kappa(\omega \mid \neg p)))$$

where

$$\begin{aligned}
\kappa(\omega \mid p) &= +\infty \text{ if } \omega \vDash \neg p \\
&= \kappa(\omega) \text{ if } \kappa(\omega) > \kappa(p) \\
&= 0 \text{ if } \kappa(\omega) = \kappa(p).
\end{aligned}$$

They show, when $i > 0$, that Williams' adjustment can be encoded as a conditioning with uncertain input (line $(|_m, \min)$ of Table 2) by letting:

$$\pi(\omega) = 2^{-\kappa(\omega)}, N(\phi) = 1 - 2^{-\kappa(\phi)}, a = 1 - 2^i, \text{ and } \Pi(p) = 2^{-\kappa(p)}.$$

Natural belief revision [Boutilier, 1993], also hinted by Spohn [1988], can also be viewed as a conditioning with uncertain input. A natural revision by input b only comes down to assigning to the most plausible interpretations in $[p]$ a degree of possibility higher than to other interpretations (this is enough to ensure that $N^*_p(p) > 0$) while retaining the same ordering of interpretations as before revision, including *for interpretations outside* $[p]$. It implies that, after revision, some interpretations where $[p]$ is not true may remain more plausible than interpretations where $[p]$ is true.

Let a be such that $0 < a < \min\{a_i : (\phi_i\ a_i) \in \Sigma\}$. Then the syntactic counterpart of Boutilier's natural belief revision is:

Table 4. Natural belief revision

Σ entails p	Σ is consistent with p and with $\neg p$	Σ is inconsistent with p
Σ	$\Sigma \cup \{(p, a)\}$	$\{(p, a)\} \cup \Sigma_\chi$ $\cup\{(\phi \vee p, b) : (\phi, b) \in \Sigma \text{ and } b \leq \chi\}$

Let us briefly give the proof of Table 4. Let Σ be associated to π_Σ. Denote Σ' the syntactic revision given in Table 4, and π' be the result of natural belief revision of π with p. Our aim is to show that $\pi_{\Sigma'} = \pi'$. When Σ entails p, then $\forall\omega$ such that $\pi(\omega) = 1$ we have $\omega \models p$, hence $\pi' = \pi$, therefore $\pi_{\Sigma'} = \pi'$ since $\Sigma' = \Sigma$.

If Σ is consistent with p and $\neg$p, then we have:

$\pi_{\Sigma'}(\omega) = 1$ if $\omega \models \Sigma$ and $\omega \models p$

$\pi_{\Sigma'}(\omega) = 1$ - a if $\omega \models \Sigma$ and $\omega \models \neg p$
$\pi_{\Sigma'}(\omega) = \pi_{\Sigma}(\omega)$ otherwise.
Recall that $0 < a < \min\{a_i : (\phi_i\ a_i) \in \Sigma\}$. Clearly $\pi_{\Sigma'} = \pi'$.
The last case is when Σ is inconsistent with p. Note that in this case, $\Pi_{\Sigma}(p) = 1 - \chi$, and that for any interpretation ω such that $\omega \models p$ and $\pi_{\Sigma}(\omega) \neq \Pi_{\Sigma}(p)$, we have:
$\pi_{\Sigma}(\omega) = \pi_A(\omega)$, where A $=\{(\phi \vee p, b) : (\phi, b) \in \Sigma$ and $b \leq \chi\}$ (since $\pi_{\Sigma}(\omega) < 1 - \chi$). Hence we have:
$\pi_{\Sigma'}(\omega) = 1$ if $\omega \models \Sigma_{\chi}$ and $\omega \models p$
$\pi_{\Sigma'}(\omega) = 1$- a if $\omega \models \Sigma$ and $\omega \models \neg p$
$\pi_{\Sigma'}(\omega) = \pi_{\Sigma}(\omega)$ otherwise.
Again, we can easily check that $\pi_{\Sigma'} = \pi'$.

4.3 Semantic and syntactic contraction

Contraction is the process of forgetting some old beliefs. Hence, one may define a contraction as a particular case of revising with uncertain input (p, a) with $a = 0$. Clearly, using this interpretation, contracting p also leads to contract $\neg p$. Indeed, when $a = 0$, the definition of $\pi(. \mid (p, a))$ from Section 4.2. yields a result which is symetric with respect to p and ¬p:
$\pi(\omega \mid (p, 0)) = \pi(\omega \mid p)$ if $\omega \models p$
$= \pi(\omega \mid \neg p)$ if $\omega \models \neg p$
such that $\Pi(p) = \Pi(\neg p) = 1$. This is stronger than the definition of contraction used in [Gärdenfors, 1988] since when $\neg p$ is believed, then contracting with p does not modify π. In this section, we propose to see how contraction in the sense of Gärdenfors can be handled in the possibility theory framework.

The contraction of a possibility distribution with respect to p corresponds to forgetting that p is believed if p was previously in the belief set ($N(p) > 0 \Leftrightarrow \Pi(p) = 1 > \Pi(\neg p)$). In such a case, the result π_p^- of the contraction must lead to a possibility measure Π_p^- such that $\Pi_p^-(p) = \Pi_p^-(\neg p) = 1$, i.e. complete ignorance about p. Intuitively if $\Pi(p) = \Pi(\neg p) = 1$ already exists, then we should have $\pi_p^- = \pi$. Besides if $\Pi(p) = 1 > \Pi(\neg p)$ then we should have $\pi_p^-(\omega) = 1$ for some $\omega \models \neg p$, and especially for those ω such that $\Pi(\neg p) = \pi(\omega)$. If $\Pi(\neg p) = 1 > \Pi(p)$, i.e. $\neg p$ represents an accepted belief, π should be unchanged. It leads to [Dubois and Prade, 1992]:

$$\begin{aligned} \pi_p^-(\omega) &= 1 \text{ if } \pi(\omega) = \Pi(\neg p), \omega \models \neg p \\ &= \pi(\omega) \text{ otherwise.} \end{aligned}$$

If $\Pi(\neg p) = 0$, what is obtained is the fullmeet contraction [Gärdenfors, 1988]. By construction, π_p^- again corresponds to the idea of minimally changing π so as to forget p, when there is a unique $\omega \models \neg p$ such that $1 > \Pi(\neg p) = \pi(\omega)$. When there are several elements in $\{\omega \models \neg p, \pi(\omega) = \Pi(\neg p)\}$, minimal change contractions correspond to letting $\pi_p^-(\omega) = 1$ for any selection of such situation, and π_p^- corresponds to considering the envelope of the minimal change solutions. This contraction coincides exactly with a natural contraction in the sense of Boutilier and Goldzsmidt [1993].

In the classical case, Levi and Harper's identities [Gärdenfors, 1988] respectively define the revision by p as first a contraction forgetting $\neg p$ and then an expansion adding p, and the contraction by p as retaining the beliefs accepted both in the epistemic state π and its revision by $\neg p$. These results remain valid in the possibilistic setting, namely [Dubois and Prade, 1992]:

$$\pi_p^- = \max(\pi, \pi(\cdot \mid \neg p)).$$

An alternative contraction rule is:

$$\begin{aligned}\pi_p^-(\omega) &= \frac{\pi(\omega)}{\Pi(\neg p)} \text{ if } \omega \models \neg p \\ &= \pi(\omega) \text{ otherwise,}\end{aligned}$$

that is the companion to the numerical Bayesian-like possibilistic revision rule. again Levi's and Harper's identity hold between the two Bayesian-like rules of conditioning and contraction. The following table gives the syntactic counterpart of contraction

Table 5. Semantic and syntactic contraction

	π^-	Σ'
$\vert_m$	$= 1$ if $\pi(\omega) = \Pi(\neg p), \omega \models \neg p$	$\Sigma_{\mathbf{y}} \cup \{(\phi \vee \neg p, b) : b \leq \mathbf{y}\}$
$\vert_{\dots}$	$= \frac{\pi(\omega)}{\Pi(\neg p)}$ if $\omega \models \neg p$ $= \pi(\omega)$ otherwise	$\{(\phi, g(b)) : b > \mathbf{y}\} \cup \{(\phi \vee \neg pb)\}$

5 CONCLUSION

This paper offers a simple generic tool for merging and modifying prioritized belief bases. The fusion methods are semantically meaningful since they amount to specific combinations of commensurate rankings of interpretations. A larger class of elementary changes in a prioritized belief base can be expressed in terms of conditioning, merging and/or rescaling steps. What is obtained is a basis for a symbolic computation of belief revision and fusion based on elementary standard steps. These operations can be easily implemented in practice, although the computational complexity of fusion operations in the general case remains to be studied. Note that the syntactic revision schemes under uncertain inputs as well as the contraction operation are based on a drastic view of syntactic conditioning. More parsimonious syntactic methods (hence more complex) could be used, so as to retain more information from the original belief base.

In this paper, it has been assumed that the prioritized bases we have considered gather beliefs of various strengths. Combination and revision operations would be also meaningful for preference profiles as well. Then the base would contain goals with different priority levels, which would be the syntactic counterpart of the preference profiles encoded by the possibility distributions (which would now defined over sets of possible choices). See [Moura-Pires *et al.*, 1998] and [Moura-Pires and Prade, 1998] for preliminary works along this line.

APPENDIX

Most of the proofs of this Appendix use particular cases of Proposition 4. In some proofs, we indifferently use the two equivalent belief bases:

Truncate $(\Sigma, a) \cup \{(\bot, a)\}$ and $\Sigma \cup \{(\bot, a)\}$.

PROPOSITION 1. Let $\Sigma_1 = \{(\phi_i, a_i) : i \in I\}$ and $\Sigma_2 = \{(\psi_j, b_j) : j \in J\}$ be two possibilistic bases associated with possibility distributions π_1 and π_2. Let $\pi_\oplus$ be the result of the combination of π_1 and π_2 using $\oplus$. Then, $\pi_\oplus$ is associated with the following belief base:

$$\begin{aligned}\Sigma_\oplus \;=\; & (\phi_i, 1-(1-a_i)\oplus 1) : (\phi_i, a_i) \in \Sigma_1\} \cup \\ & \{(\psi_j, 1-1\oplus(1-b_j)) : (\psi_j, b_j) \in \Sigma_2\} \cup \\ & \{(\phi_i \vee \psi_j, 1-(1-a_i)\oplus(1-b_j)) : (\phi_i, a_i) \in \Sigma_1 \\ & \text{and } (\psi_j, b_j) \in \Sigma_2\}.\end{aligned}$$

Proof. Let π_1^i be the possibility distribution induced by $\{(\phi_i, a_i)\}$ and π_2^j induced by $\{(\psi_j, b_j)\}$. Then, $\pi_1 = min_i \pi_1^i$ and $\pi_2 = min_j \pi_2^j$. Hence:

$\pi_1 \oplus \pi_2 = min_i \pi_1^i \oplus min_j \pi_2^j$
= $\min_{i,j} \pi_1^i \oplus \pi_2^j$ (since $\oplus$ is non-decreasing).
Now from Lemma 3, a syntactic counterpart of $\pi_1^i \oplus \pi_2^j$ is $\Sigma_{ij} = \{(\phi_i, 1-(1-a_i)\oplus 1), (\psi_j, 1-1\oplus(1-b_j)), (\phi_i \vee \psi_j, 1-(1-a_i)\oplus(1-b_j))\}$. It is clear that $\Sigma = \bigcup_{i,j} \Sigma_{ij}$ is a syntactic counterpart of $\pi_1 \oplus \pi_2$ using the semantic account of possibilistic logic. ∎

PROPOSITION 7. Let Σ be a possibilistic belief base, and π its associated possibility distribution. Then:

- $\pi' = \min(\pi, 1-a)$ is associated with Truncate $(\Sigma, a) \cup \{(\bot, a)\}$, and
- $\pi' = \max(\pi, 1-a)$ is associated with Discount (Σ, a), and
- $\pi' = \pi \cdot (1-a)$ is associated with Confirm $(\Sigma, a) \cup \{(\bot, a)\}$.

Proof. The proof can be easily obtained using Propositions 5, 6 and 7, viewing $(1-a)$ as the constant possibility distribution associated to the belief base $\{(\bot, a)\}$.

Hence, using Proposition 5, $\min(\pi, 1-a)$ is associated with the following belief base:

$$\begin{aligned} \Sigma' &= \Sigma \cup \{(\bot, a)\} \\ &\equiv \{(\phi, b) : (\phi, b) \in \Sigma \text{ and } b > a\} \cup \{(\bot, a)\} \end{aligned}$$

(since all formulas having certainty degrees less than a are subsumed by $(\bot, a)$).

Using Proposition 6, $\max(\pi, 1-a)$ is associated with the following belief base:

$$\begin{aligned} \Sigma' &= \{(\phi \vee \bot, \ \min(b, a)) : (\phi, b) \in \Sigma\} \\ &\equiv \{(\phi, a) : (\phi, b) \in \Sigma \text{ and } b \geq a\} \cup \{(\phi, b) : (\phi, b) \in \Sigma \text{ and } b < a\}. \end{aligned}$$

Using Proposition 7, $\pi' = \pi \cdot (1-a)$ is associated with the following belief base:

$$\begin{aligned} \Sigma' &= \Sigma \cup \{(\bot, a)\} \cup \{(\phi \vee \bot, a + b - b \cdot a) : (\phi, b) \in \Sigma\} \\ &\equiv \Sigma \cup \{(\bot, a)\} \cup \{(\phi, a + b - b \cdot a) : (\phi, b) \in \Sigma\} \\ &\equiv \{(\bot, a)\} \cup \{(\phi, a + b - b \cdot a) : (\phi, b) \in \Sigma\} \end{aligned}$$

(since formulas of Σ are subsumed by $\{(\phi, a + b - b \cdot a) : (\phi, b) \in \Sigma\}$). ■

PROOF OF THE SYNTACTIC COUNTERPART OF REVISING WITH UNCERTAIN INPUT WHEN $*$ =MIN AND $\models = \models_H$

Let χ and $\mathbf{y}$ be the inconsistency degrees of $\Sigma \cup \{(p, 1)\}$ and $\Sigma \cup \{(\neg p, 1)\}$ respectively. The syntactic counterpart of:

$$\pi(\omega \mid (p, a)) = \max(\pi(\omega \mid p), \ \min((1-a), \pi(\omega \mid \neg p)), \qquad (£)$$

is given by the following three lemmas.

To obtain the proof first use Table 1 to get the syntactic counterpart of $\pi(\omega \mid \neg p)$ and $\pi(\omega \mid p)$. Then use Proposition 9 for looking to a syntactic counterpart of $\min((1-a), \pi(\omega \mid \neg p))$, viewing $(1-a)$ as the constant possibility distribution associated to the belief base $\{(\bot, a)\}$. Lastly, use Proposition 6 for the syntactic counterpart of (£). In the next proofs, the notation:
$\Sigma_1 \bigvee \Sigma_2 = \{(\phi_i \vee \psi_j, \ \min(a_i, b_j)) : (\phi_i, a_i) \in \Sigma_1 \text{ and } (\psi_j, a_i) \in \Sigma_2\}$
is used to denote the combination with the idempotent disjunction.

LEMMA 3. If Σ is consistent with $\neg p$ and with p, namely $\chi = 0$ and $\mathbf{y} = 0$ then the result of the revision of Σ by (p,a) is:

$$\Sigma \cup \{(p, a)\}.$$

Proof. The proof is immediate from the next lemmas by letting $\chi = 0$ and $\mathbf{y} = 0$. ■

LEMMA 4. If Σ is inconsistent with $\neg p$, namely $\chi = 0$ and $\mathbf{y} > 0$ then the result of the revision of Σ by (p,a) is:

$$\{(p,a)\} \cup \Sigma_{\mathbf{y}} \cup \{(\phi \vee \neg p, b) : (\phi, b) \in \Sigma \text{ and } b \leq \mathbf{y}\}.$$

Proof. A syntactic counterpart of $\pi(\omega \mid p)$ is $\Sigma \cup \{(p,1)\}$ and a syntactic counterpart of $\pi(\omega \mid \neg p)$ is: $\Sigma_{\mathbf{y}} \cup \{(\neg p, 1)\}$, and, a syntactic counterpart of $\min((1-a), \pi(\omega \mid \neg p))$ is (using Proposition 9):

$$\Sigma_{\mathbf{y}} \cup \{(\neg p, 1)\} \cup \{(\bot, a)\}.$$

Hence a syntactic counterpart of (£) is
$[\Sigma_{\mathbf{y}} \cup \{(\neg p, 1)\} \cup \{(\bot, a)\}] \bigvee [\Sigma \cup \{(p,1)\}]$. Note that:

- $\Sigma \bigvee \Sigma_{\mathbf{y}}$ is equivalent to $\Sigma_{\mathbf{y}}$
- $\Sigma \bigvee \{(\neg p, 1)\}$ leads to $\{(\phi \vee \neg p, b) : (\phi, b) \in \Sigma\}$ where formulas with weight greater than $\mathbf{y}$ are subsumed by $\Sigma_{\mathbf{y}}$.
- $\Sigma \bigvee (\bot, a)$ leads to: $\{(\phi, \min(a,b)) : (\phi, b) \in \Sigma\}$, where formulas with weight greater than $\mathbf{y}$ are subsumed by $\Sigma_{\mathbf{y}}$
- $\Sigma_{\mathbf{y}} \bigvee \{(p,1)\}$ leads to $\{(\phi \vee p, b) : (\phi, b) \in \Sigma_{\mathbf{y}}\}$, which is subsumed by $\Sigma_{\mathbf{y}}$.
- $\{(\neg p, 1)\} \bigvee \{(p,1)\}$ leads to a tautology, and
- $\{(p,1)\} \bigvee \{(\bot, a)\}$ leads to $\{(p,a)\}$.

Finally, a syntactic counterpart of (£) is (after removing subsumed formulas) simply given by:

$$\begin{aligned} &\Sigma_{\mathbf{y}} \cup \{(\phi, \min(a,b)) : (\phi, b) \in \Sigma \text{ and } b \leq \mathbf{y}\} \\ &\cup \{(\phi \vee \neg p, b : (\phi, b) \in \Sigma \text{ and } b \leq \mathbf{y}\} \cup \{(p,a)\} \\ \equiv\ & \{(\phi, b) \in \Sigma : b > \mathbf{y}\} \cup \{(\phi \vee \neg p, b) : (\phi, b) \in \Sigma, b \leq \mathbf{y}\} \cup \{(p,a)\}. \end{aligned}$$

Indeed, formulas $\{(\phi, \min(a,b)) : (\phi, b) \in \Sigma \text{ and } b \leq \mathbf{y}\}$ are subsumed by $\{(\phi \vee \neg p, b) : (\phi, b) \in \Sigma, b \leq \mathbf{y}\} \cup \{(p,a)\}$. Indeed, if $a \geq b$, then $(\phi, \min(a,b)) = (\phi, b)$ is subsumed by $(\phi \vee \neg p, b)$ and (p,a). Now, if $a < b$, then $(\phi, \min(a,b)) = (\phi, a)$ is a consequence of $\{(\phi \vee \neg p, b), (p,a)\}$ using possibilistic resolution principle. ■

LEMMA 5. If Σ is inconsistent with p, namely $\chi > 0$ and $\mathbf{y} = 0$ then the result of the revision of Σ by (p,a) is:

$$\{(p,a)\} \cup \Sigma_{\chi} \cup \{(\phi \vee p, b) : \text{ and } a < b \leq \chi\}.$$

Proof. A syntactic counterpart of $\min((1-a), \pi(\omega \mid \neg p))$ is:

$$\Sigma \cup \{(\neg p, 1)\} \cup \{(\bot, a)\}$$

and a syntactic counterpart of $\pi(\omega \mid p)$ is:
$\Sigma_\chi \cup \{(p, 1)\}$.

Hence a syntactic counterpart of (£) is $[\Sigma \cup \{(\neg p, 1)\} \cup \{(\bot, a)\}] \bigvee [\Sigma_\chi \cup \{(p, 1)\}]$. Note that:

- $\Sigma_\chi \bigvee \Sigma$ is equivalent to Σ_χ.
- $\Sigma_\chi \bigvee \{(\neg p, 1)\}$ leads to $\{(\phi \vee \neg p, b) : (\phi, b) \in \Sigma_\chi\}$ (which are subsumed by Σ_χ.
- $\Sigma_\chi \bigvee (\bot, a)$ leads to $\{(\phi, \ \min(a, b)) : (\phi, b) \in \Sigma_\chi\}$ (which is subsumed by Σ_χ.
- $\{(p, 1)\} \bigvee \Sigma$ leads to: $\{(\phi \vee p, b) : (\phi, b) \in \Sigma\}$.
- $\{(\neg p, 1)\} \bigvee \{(p, 1)\}$ leads to a tautology, and
- $\{(p, 1)\} \bigvee \{(\bot, a)\}$ leads to $\{(p, a)\}$.

Finally, a syntactic counterpart of (£) is simply:

$$\Sigma_\chi \cup \{(\phi \vee p, b) : b \leq \chi\} \cup \{(p, a)\} \tag{§}$$

Note that when $b \leq a$ then formulas $(\phi \vee p, b)$ are subsumed by (p, a), therefore (§) becomes:

$$\Sigma_\chi \cup \{(p, a)\} \cup \{(\phi \vee p, b) : a < b \leq \chi\}.$$

Note that when $a \leq \chi$ then we simply get:

$$\Sigma_\chi \cup \{(p, a)\}.$$

■

IRIT, Université Paul Sabatier, Toulouse, France.

REFERENCES

[Baral *et al.*, 1992] C. Baral, S. Kraus, J. Minker and V. S. Subrahmanian. Combining knowledge bases consisting in first-order theories. *Computational Intelligence*, **8**, 45–71, 1992.

[Benferhat, 1998] S. Benferhat. Infinitesimal theories of uncertainty for plausible reasoning. In *Handbook of Defeasible and Uncertainty Management Systems, Volume 1: Quantified Representation of Uncertainty and Imprecision*, P. Smets, ed. pp 303–356. Kluwer Academic Publishers, 1998.

[Benferhat *et al.*, 1997a] S. Benferhat, D. Dubois and H. Prade. From semantic to syntactic approaches to information combination in possibilistic logic. In *Aggregation and Fusion of Imperfect Information*, pp. 141–151, Physica Verlag, 1997.

[Benferhat *et al.*, 1997b] S. Benferhat, D. Dubois and H. Prade. Nonmonotonic reasoning, conditional objects and possibility theory. Artificial Intelligence 92:259-276, 1997.

[Benferhat *et al.*, 1998] S. Benferhat, D. Dubois and H. Prade. Some syntactic approaches to the handling of inconsistent knowledge bases: A comparative study. Part 2: The prioritized case. In *Logic at Work*, E. Orlowska, ed. pp. 473–511. 1998

[Boldrin and Sossai, 1995] L. Boldrin and C. Sossai. An algebraic semantics for possibilistic logic. In *Proceedings of the 11th Conference on Uncertainty in Artificial Intelligence (UAI '95)*, P. Besnard and S. Hank, eds. pp. 27–35. Morgan Kaufmann, CA, 1995.

[Boutilier, 1993] C. Boutilier. Revision sequences and nested conditionals. In *Proceedings of the 13th International Joint Conference on Artificial Intelligence (IJCAI'93)*, Chambéry, pp. 519–525, 1993.

[Boutilier and Goldszmidt, 1993] C. Boutilier and M. Goldszmidt. Revision by conditional beliefs. In *Proceedings of AAAI'93*, pp. 649–654, 1993.

[Cholvy, 1998] L. Cholvy. Reasoning about merging information. In *Handbook of Defeasible Reasoning and Uncertainty Management Systems*, Vol. 3, P. Smets and D. Gabbay, eds. pp. 233–263. Kluwer Academic Publishers, 1998.

[Darwiche and Pearl, 1997] A. Darwiche and J. Pearl. On the logic of iterated belief revision. *Artificial Intelligence*, **89**, 1–29, 1997.

[De Baets *et al.*, 1999] B. De Baets, E. Tsiporkova and R. Mesiar. Conditioning in possibility theory with strict order norms. In *Fuzzy sets and systems*, 106, Number 2, pp.221–229, 1999.

[Dubois *et al.*, 1994] D. Dubois, J. Lang and H. Prade. Possibilistic logic. In *Handbook of Logic in Artificial Intelligence and Logic Programming*, Vol. 3, D. M. Gabbay *et al.*, eds. pp. 439–513. Oxford University Press, 1994.

[Dubois and Prade, 1985] D. Dubois and H. Prade. A review of fuzzy set aggregation connectives. *Information Sciences*, **36**, 85–121, 1985.

[Dubois and Prade, 1990] D. Dubois and H. Prade. The logical view of conditioning and its application to possibility and evidence theories. *International Journal of Approximate Reasoning*, **4**, 24–46, 1990.

[Dubois and Prade, 1991] D. Dubois and H. Prade. Updating with belief functions, ordinal conditional functions and possibility measures. In *Uncertainty in Artificial Intelligence*, Vol. 6 (P. Bonissone *et al.*, eds. pp. 311–329. Elsevier Science Publications, New York, 1991.

[Dubois and Prade, 1992] D. Dubois and H. Prade. Belief change and possibility theory. In *Belief Revision*, P. Gärdenfors, ed. pp. 142–182. Cambridge University Press, Cambridge, 1992.

[Dubois and Prade, 1997] D. Dubois and H. Prade. A Synthetic View of Belief Revision with Uncertain Inputs in the Framework of Possibility Theory. *International Journal of Approximate Reasoning*, **17**, 295–324, 1997.

[Fagin *et al.*, 1983] R. Fagin, J. D. Ullman and M. Y. Vardi. On the semantics of updates in database. In *Proceedings of the 2nd ACM SIGACT-SIGMOD Symposium on the Principles of Databases Systems*, Atlanta, pp. 352–365, 1983.

[Gärdenfors, 1988] P. Gärdenfors. *Knowledge in Flux: Modeling the Dynamics of Epistemic States*. The MIT Press, 1988.

[Grove, 1988] A. Grove. Two modellings for theory change. *Journal of Philosophical Logic*, **15**, 157–170, 1988.

[Hisdal, 1978] E. Hisdal. Conditional possibilities, independence and noninteraction. *Fuzzy Sets and Systems*, **1**, 283–297, 1978.

[Levi, 1980] I. Levi. *The entreprise of Knowledge. An Essay on Knowledge, Credal Probability, and Chance*. The MIT Press, 1980.

[Lin and Mendelzon, 1992] F. Lin and E. Mendelzon. Merging databases under constraints. *International Journal of Cooperative Information Systems*, **7**, 55–76, 1992.

[Moura-Pires and Prade, 1998] J. Moura-Pires and H. Prade. Logical analysis of fuzzy constraint satisfaction problems. In *Proceedings of the 1998 IEEE International Conference on Fuzzy Systems (FUZZ-IEEE'98)*, Anchorage, Alaska, May 4-9, pp. 857–862, 1998.

[Moura-Pires *et al.*, 1998] J. Moura-Pires, D. Dubois and H. Prade. Fuzzy constraint problems with general aggregation operations under possibilistic logic form. In *Proceedings of the 6th European Congress on Intelligent Techniques and Soft Computing*, Aachen, Germany, Sept. 7-10, pp. 535–539, 1998.

[Nebel, 1992] B. Nebel. Syntax-based approaches to belief revision. In *Belief Revision*, P. Gärdenfors, ed. pp. 52–88. Cambridge University Press, Cambridge, 1992.

[Nebel, 1998] B. Nebel. How hard is to revise a belief base? In *Handbook of Defeasible and Uncertainty Management Systems*, Volume 3: Belief change, D. Dubois and H. Prade, eds. pp. 77–145. Kluwer Academic Publishers, 1998.

[Papini, 1999] O. Papini. Iterated revision operations stemming from the history of an agent's observations. Frontiers of belief revision, H. Rott and M. Williams, eds. This volume. 1999.

[Konieczny and Pino-Pérez, 1998] S. Konieczny and R. Pino-Pérez. On the logic of merging. In *Proceedings of the 6th International Conference on Principles of Knowledge Representation and Reasoning (KR'98)*, pp. 488-498, 1998.

[Spohn, 1988] W. Spohn. Ordinal conditional functions: A dynamic theory of epistemic states. In *Causation in Decision, Belief Change, and Statistics*, Vol. 2, W. L. Harper and B. Skyrms, eds. pp. 105–134. D. Reidel, Dordrecht, 1988.

[Williams, 1994] M. A. Williams. Transmutations of knowledge systems. In *Proceedings of the 4th International Conference on Principles of Knowledge Representation and Reasoning (KR'94)*, Bonn. J. Doyle *et al.*, eds. pp. 619–629. Morgan Kaufmann, 1994.

[Williams, 1996] M. A. Williams. Towards a practical approach to belief revision: Reason-based change. In *Proceedings of the 5th International Conference on Principles of Knowledge Representation and Reasoning (KR'96)*, 1996.

[Williams, 1997] M. A. Williams. Anytime belief revision. In *Proceedings of the International Joint Conference on Artificial Intelligence IJCAI'97*, pp. 74–79, 1997.

[Zadeh, 1978] L. A. Zadeh. Fuzzy sets as a basis for a theory of possibility. *Fuzzy Sets and Systems*, **1**, 3–28, 1978.

MARY-ANNE WILLIAMS

AN OPERATIONAL MEASURE OF SIMILARITY BASED ON CHANGE

1 INTRODUCTION

Similarity between information states has always been of central interest in Knowledge Representation. The notion of similarity underlies belief revision, analogical reasoning, hypothetical reasoning, normative reasoning, counterfactuals, causality, and reasoning about action. However it is a concept that has presented numerous philosophical and practical difficulties.

We seek a measure of similarity which will provide the foundation for a framework upon which to assess design decisions for belief revision, to evaluate the plausibility of belief revision strategies as models for human belief change, to model goal-directed belief revision, to compare possible explanations, and to evaluate surprising information. In these endeavours the following questions suggest themselves:

(a) Is information state I more *similar* to state J than it is to state K?

(b) Is state I as *similar* to state J as state N is to state M?

(c) How *best* can state I be achieved from state J?

(d) Is information α more effective than β in achieving state J from state I?

(e) From among a set of explanations which is *best*?

(f) Is α more *surprising* than $\neg\alpha$ for state I?

(g) Is it more *surprising* to obtain state J or state K from state I?

(h) In accepting the information that α is more important than β should the importance of α be increased or the importance of β decreased?

(i) How psychologically plausible is a particular belief revision strategy?

A measure of similarity is necessary for accessing the resultant possible states after new information has been incorporated, and can be used to determine the *best* belief revision procedure for a particular application. The best belief revision procedure might construct the most similar state to the expected outcome, alternatively it might construct the state that includes all the desired changes and resembles the initial information state the most. A means of determining the distance between information states is imperative for evaluating how well belief revision fairs as a model for human belief change. Furthermore, a notion of similarity

M.-A. Williams and H. Rott (eds.), Frontiers in Belief Revision, 135–145.

is necessary for a full treatment of hypothetical reasoning, surprise, explanation, reasoning about action, and planning tasks that involve goal-directed change.

The measure we propose provides a simple, yet powerful, mechanism for measuring the similarity among information states based on the amount of *work* needed to transform one state into another. The epistemic distance from state I to state J is given by the number of primitive belief revision operations it takes to *transmute* I into J.

Not unnaturally the resultant measure of similarity may not be symmetric. For instance, it may be easier to transform state I into state J, than to change J into I in which case we say I is more similar to J than J is to I. If one desires a symmetric measure of similarity, then the maximum of the epistemic distances, I to J and J to I, could be adopted. Lewis [1973, p. 52] argues that *symmetry is not necessarily desirable.* In particular, he asserts it is possible that I is more similar to J from the standpoint of I than J to I from the standpoint of J.

In section 2 we describe a simple graph representation of the problem where the state space comprises the set of all possible information states (defined in section 2.1), and arcs in the graph represent a primitive operation that transforms information states (defined in section 2.2). The shortest path from node I to node J represents the *epistemic distance* from I to J. We interpret this epistemic distance as a measure of similarity; the larger the distance between two states the less similar they are. In section 3 we discuss decision procedures for determining the epistemic distance from state I to state J. In section 4 we illustrate how the proposed framework can be used to answer the list of questions (a)–(i) above. Measures of similarity have been explored in the philosophical and artificial intelligence literature for some time, and in section 5 we compare and contrast some prominent related approaches. We summarise our contribution in section 6.

2 INFORMATION SPACE

2.1 Information States

An information state, or epistemic state, is represented by an entrenchment ranking, formally defined below. It was shown in [Williams, 1994] that entrenchment rankings can be used to support iterated belief revision for theories. Their partial specification can be used to support iterated *base* change revision [Williams, 1994b], and implementations based on this approach is described in [Williams *et al.*, 1995; Williams and Williams, 1997].

Intuitively, an entrenchment ranking maps sentences to ordinals in $\mathcal{O}$ which is an ordinal chosen to be sufficiently large for the purpose of the discussion.

DEFINITION. An *entrenchment ranking* is a function $\mathbf{E}$ from the sentences in a language, $\mathcal{L}$, into $\mathcal{O}$ such that the following conditions are satisfied.

(ER1) For all $\alpha,\ \beta \in \mathcal{L}$, if $\alpha \vdash \beta$, then $\mathbf{E}(\alpha) \leq \mathbf{E}(\beta)$.

(ER2) For all $\alpha,\ \beta \in \mathcal{L}$, $\mathbf{E}(\alpha) \leq \mathbf{E}(\alpha \wedge \beta)$ or $\mathbf{E}(\beta) \leq \mathbf{E}(\alpha \wedge \beta)$.

(ER3) $\vdash \alpha$ if and only if $\mathbf{E}(\alpha) = \mathcal{O}$.

(ER4) If α is inconsistent, then $\mathbf{E}(\alpha) = 0$.

Essentially, an entrenchment ranking is an *epistemic entrenchment ordering* [Gärdenfors and Makinson, 1988]; the higher the ordinal assigned to a sentence the more entrenched it is. We denote the family of all entrenchment rankings by $\mathcal{E}$. We define the *information content* of $\mathbf{E} \in \mathcal{E}$ to be $\{\alpha \in \mathcal{L} : \mathbf{E}(\alpha) > 0\}$, and denoted it by **content**($\mathbf{E}$). The information content of $\mathbf{E}$ is interpreted to be the set of accepted information (or the set of beliefs), and it is always a consistent theory. Gärdenfors and Makinson [1988] have shown that for a finite language an epistemic entrenchment ordering is uniquely determined by its dual atoms (maximal disjunctions). Hence an entrenchment ranking of a finite language can be described by assigning an ordinal to each dual atom. The numerical assignment of all other sentences is then uniquely determined by (ER1) – (ER4), and the set $\mathcal{E}$ consists of all possible orderings of the dual atoms.

EXAMPLE. If the ranking on dual atoms is given by $\mathbf{E}(\alpha \vee \beta) = 3$, $\mathbf{E}(\alpha \vee \neg\beta) = 2$, $\mathbf{E}(\neg\alpha \vee \beta) = 1$, and $\mathbf{E}(\neg\alpha \vee \neg\beta) = 0$, then the properties (ER1)–(ER4) force $\mathbf{E}(\alpha)$ to be 2 and $\mathbf{E}(\beta)$ to be 1.

It will be convenient to restrict the discussion to a finite language; however all the concepts and ideas are easily extended to the infinite case. In the infinite case we use Groves' [1988] system of spheres construction which is an equivalent conjugate construction to one we adopt herein based on an entrenchment ranking. A system of spheres is a total preordering of consistent complete theories,[1] and there is a straightforward translation from well-ranked systems of spheres to epistemic entrenchment rankings such that they generate the *same* revision and contraction function, see [Grove, 1988; Gärdenfors and Makinson, 1988; Peppas and Williams, 1995]. We denote the set of dual atoms in $\mathcal{L}$ by $\mathcal{D}$. If $\mathcal{L}$ is finite then there is a one-to-one correspondence between $\mathcal{D}$ and the set of consistent complete theories (or possible worlds).

2.2 *Transmutations*

A (α, i)-transmutation of an entrenchment ranking $\mathbf{E}$ was defined in [Williams, 1994], and is denoted by $\mathbf{E}^\star(\alpha, i)$. It is a process that modifies $\mathbf{E}$ by assigning i the degree of acceptance of α such that **content**($\mathbf{E}^\star(\alpha, i)$) satisfies the AGM postulates. In particular, **content**($\mathbf{E}^\star(\alpha, i)$) for $i > 0$ is an AGM revision, and **content**($\mathbf{E}^\star(\alpha, 0)$) is an AGM contraction. The main purpose of transmutations is to model iterated belief revision.

[1] The usual interpretation of the set of consistent complete theories is the set of state descriptions or possible worlds.

Several transmutation strategies for iterated belief revision exist, e.g. conditionalisation and adjustment. We define a *unit transmutation* to be a transmutation that moves a sentence up or down a single rank in an entrenchment ranking. Although, unit transmutations serve well as a primitive operation upon which to build a measure of similarity, no restriction is placed on the adopted transmutations in the sequel.

2.3 A Graphical Representation

Given a set of admissible transmutations $\mathcal{T}$ we define a directed *graph of information space* based on $\mathcal{T}$ to be the pair $\langle \mathcal{E}, \mathcal{A}_{\mathcal{T}} \rangle$ where $\mathcal{E}$ is the set of all entrenchment rankings, and $\mathcal{A}_{\mathcal{T}}$ is the set of arcs; where there is an arc from $\mathbf{E}_1 \in \mathcal{E}$ to $\mathbf{E}_2 \in \mathcal{E}$ precisely when $\mathbf{E}_2$ is the image of $\mathbf{E}_1$ under a transmutation in $\mathcal{T}$. The length of a trajectory from $\mathbf{E}_1$ to $\mathbf{E}_2$ is given by the number of arcs that comprise it, we denote the minimum length from $\mathbf{E}_1$ to $\mathbf{E}_2$ by $\mathbf{dist}_{\mathcal{T}}(\mathbf{E}_1, \mathbf{E}_2)$, and refer to it as the *distance* from $\mathbf{E}_1$ to $\mathbf{E}_2$. Whenever $\mathcal{T}$ is clearly understood we write **dist** instead of $\mathbf{dist}_{\mathcal{T}}$.

THEOREM 1. **dist** *is a quasi-metric*[2] *on* $\langle \mathcal{E}, \mathcal{A}_{\mathcal{T}} \rangle$.

Conditionalisation is an invertible transmutation, consequently it produces a symmetric distance measure.

COROLLARY 2. *If* $\mathcal{T}$ *is the set of all conditionalisations, then* **dist** *is a metric on* $\langle \mathcal{E}, \mathcal{A}_{\mathcal{T}} \rangle$.

For other transmutations that lead to an asymmetric **dist**, if symmetry is desired then $\max(\{\mathbf{dist}(\mathbf{E}_1, \mathbf{E}_2), \mathbf{dist}(\mathbf{E}_2, \mathbf{E}_1)\})$ defines a metric on $\langle \mathcal{E}, \mathcal{A}_{\mathcal{T}} \rangle$.

We say that $\mathbf{E}_1$ is *at least as similar* to $\mathbf{E}_2$ as it is to $\mathbf{E}_3$ if and only if $\mathbf{dist}(\mathbf{E}_1, \mathbf{E}_2) \leq \mathbf{dist}(\mathbf{E}_1, \mathbf{E}_3)$, and we also say that $\mathbf{E}_1$ is *at least as similar* to $\mathbf{E}_2$ as $\mathbf{E}_3$ is to $\mathbf{E}_4$ if and only if $\mathbf{dist}(\mathbf{E}_1, \mathbf{E}_2) \leq \mathbf{dist}(\mathbf{E}_3, \mathbf{E}_4)$.

An important property of conditionalizations and adjustments is that all information states are *reachable*. In particular, if the domain of a ranking is finite then any ranking can be achieved from any starting state via a finite number of operations. Consequently the directed graphs of information space based on conditionalization or adjustment are connected. Unfortunately their si˙e grows hyper-exponentially with $|\mathcal{D}|$ (the number of dual atoms).

3 DECISION PROCEDURES

Since dual atoms are logically independent, they can be reassigned a new rank without being constrained by (ER1) and (ER2), in addition conditionalisation preserves the ranking of all dual atoms other than the one being reranked. Consequently, dual atoms can be reranked using conditionalisations independently of

[2] **dist** satisfies the *triangle inequality* and $\mathbf{dist}(\mathbf{E}_1, \mathbf{E}_2) = 0$ only if $\mathbf{E}_1 = \mathbf{E}_2$, but **dist** may not be symmetric.

one another. Reranking arbitrary sentences, on the other hand, can lead to *logical interaction*, and as a result other sentences may need to change position. An interesting feature of the adjustment $\mathbf{E}^{\star}(\alpha, i)$ is that it preserves the ranking of sentences assigned ranks greater than $\max(\{i, \mathbf{E}_1(\neg\alpha), \mathbf{E}_1(\alpha)\})$. We show later how this property can be exploited for the purpose of developing a heuristic for computing **dist**.

Conceptually, the problem of determining the similarity of information states is like assessing the similarity of bookcases using the number of shelves books must be transfered so that books in each bookshelf are on the corresponding shelves (relative order of books along a single bookshelf is irrelevant). The shelves in this analogy represent the ranks in the ranking, books represent dual atoms, transmuting a ranking using arbitrary sentences is like moving several books in a single transfer, and the measure of distance is obtained by attributing a cost to the transfers. One systematic approach would proceed top-down; remove books that do not belong to the top shelf, move books in lower shelves that belong on the top shelf up to it, continue the process downwards to the bottom shelf. Alternatively, one could perform a similar process bottom-up; start at the bottom shelf and work upwards to the top shelf.

If the input of conditionalisation is restricted to dual atoms then **dist** is related to Ulam's distance (a distance for measuring the similarity of permutations based on the length of the longest common increasing subsequence). This is made more precise in the following theorem. First we note, that the largest subranking of dual atoms common to $\mathbf{E}_1$ and $\mathbf{E}_2$ is given by $\mathbf{E}_1 \cap \mathbf{E}_2$, that is, $\{\delta \in \mathcal{D} : \mathbf{E}_1(\delta) = \mathbf{E}_2(\delta)\}$.

THEOREM 3. *If $\mathcal{T}$ be the set of all conditionalisations of $\mathcal{D}$, then* $\mathbf{dist}(\mathbf{E}_1, \mathbf{E}_2) = |\mathcal{D}| - |\mathbf{E}_1 \cap \mathbf{E}_2|$.

This theorem says that the minimum number of conditionalisations required to transmute $\mathbf{E}_1$ to $\mathbf{E}_2$ using dual atoms is equivalent to the number of dual atoms out of place. Using the results of Fredman [1975] who analyses Floyd's algorithm [1964][3] for finding the longest increasing subsequence with respect to two permutations we obtain the following result.

THEOREM 4. *Let $\mathcal{T}$ be the set of all conditionalisations of dual atoms. Let $\langle \mathcal{E}, \mathcal{A}_{\mathcal{T}} \rangle$ be a a graph of information space. If $\mathbf{E}_1, \mathbf{E}_2$ are in $\mathcal{E}$, then the best algorithm for finding* **dist** *has order $|\mathcal{D}|$ log $|\mathcal{D}|$.*

If the conditionalisations are *unit*, then after finding the largest common subranking, we must find the total number of ranks each dual atom is out of place in $\mathbf{E}_1$ with respect to $\mathbf{E}_2$.

If the number of propositions in the language is p then in terms of p the algorithm has order $p\,2^p$. In other words, it is hopelessly intractable in general. At least two approaches can be used to address the problem of intractability in practice. For example one can use a heuristic search of a ranking on a theory base rather than an

[3]This algorithm is similar in principle to the card game *solitaire*.

entrenchment ranking on a theory, or one can use fractional factorial orthogonal arrays instead of $\mathcal{D}$, the set of all dual atoms. In section 4 we illustrate the second approach using a real application in marketing research.

$\mathbf{E}_2$ may be obtained in fewer (unit) transmutations of $\mathbf{E}_1$ if sentences other than dual atoms are taken as input. For example, changing the rank of a particular non dual atom may result in more than one dual atom being moved during a (unit) transmutation. If arbitrary sentences are used as input to a transmutation then the number required to transmute $\mathbf{E}_1$ to $\mathbf{E}_2$ cannot exceed the number required if dual atoms are used. Therefore, Theorem 3 places an upper bound on $\mathbf{dist}(\mathbf{E}_1, \mathbf{E}_2)$.

In practice, entrenchment rankings are not used as the underlying representation for belief revision applications because they are exponential in the number of atomic propositions. Successful implementations of belief revision have been developed using a partial specification of an entrenchment ranking, namely *partial entrenchment rankings of a theory base*. The idea is that a ranking on a finite base is used to generate a entrenchment ranking on a theory. For example, the domain of a partial entrenchment ranking may consist of the 4 sentences in $\{\alpha, \alpha \rightarrow \beta, \gamma, \delta \rightarrow (\lambda \vee \psi)\}$ instead of the 36 dual atoms needed for an entrenchment ranking over a language with 6 propositions. A partial entrenchment ranking can be used to generate a unique entrenchment ranking in which implied sentences, i.e. those not explicitly in the base, are assigned the least rank allowable. An adjustment preserves the ranking of sentences which are strictly higher in the ranking than the sentence to be moved down to a lower rank. Adjustments have also been defined on partial entrenchment rankings [Williams, 1995]. A top down approach would be guaranteed to transmute one ranking into the desired ranking, and an informed searching algorithm based on simple elaborations of the Hamming distance would lead to an A* algorithm; the Hamming distance would always overestimate the cost.

Recall that adjustments preserve sentences assigned ranks greater than $\max(\{i, \mathbf{E}_1(\neg\alpha), \mathbf{E}_1(\alpha)\})$. This property also holds for partial entrenchment rankings, and can be exploited for the purpose of developing a heuristic for **dist**. For example, $\mathbf{E}_1$ can be transmuted so that its highest ranked sentences are identical with the highest ranked sentences in $\mathbf{E}_2$; this process can be continued rank by rank down to the first rank. This top-down procedure will transmute $\mathbf{E}_1$ to $\mathbf{E}_2$, and if it is followed then it is not hard to show that it is guaranteed to always find a trajectory from $\mathbf{E}_1$ to $\mathbf{E}_2$, since $\max(\{i, \mathbf{E}(\neg\alpha), \mathbf{E}(\alpha)\}) = i$ for $\mathbf{E}^\star(\alpha, i)$.

The results above can be extended to partial entrenchment rankings (by slightly abusing the notation) if we make some simplifying assumptions such as the rankings being compared share the same domain, i.e. they rank the same set of sentences.

THEOREM 5. *Let $\mathcal{T}$ be the set of all adjustments on partial entrenchment rankings. Let $\langle \mathcal{E}, \mathcal{A}_\mathcal{T} \rangle$ be a graph of information space where $\mathcal{E}$ is the set of partial entrenchment rankings. If* $\mathrm{dom}(\mathbf{E}_1) = \mathrm{dom}(\mathbf{E}_2)$, *then* $\mathbf{dist}(\mathbf{E}_1, \mathbf{E}_2) \leq |\mathrm{dom}(\mathbf{E}_1)| - |\mathbf{E}_1 \cap \mathbf{E}_2|$.

This theorem says that the minimum number of adjustments required to transmute $\mathbf{E}_1$ to $\mathbf{E}_2$ is always less than or equal to the number of sentences in the domain out of place. Hence the best algorithm for finding **dist** is never worse than $n \, log \, n$ where n is the number of sentences in the domain.

4 APPLICATIONS

In this section we show how the proposed measure of similarity, **dist**, can be used in the assessment of design decisions for modeling belief revision in real world applications, for evaluating the plausibility of belief revision strategies as models for human belief change, for modeling goal-directed belief revision, for the determination of a best explanation, and for the evaluation of surprising information.

The appropriate set of admissible transmutations from which a graph in information space is generated will depend on the application at hand. In particular, the application will suggest the type of similarity of interest. For example, if deeply entrenched beliefs should be protected during changes, and moving a sentence several ranks is a larger change than moving it a single rank, then a unit adjustment would be a reasonable admissible transmutation. This situation occurs in other areas where measures of similarity provide enormous value. For instance, in signal processing numerous measures of similarity are routinely used; measures for a given application are selected on the basis of the features of interest, e.g. similarities of certain frequencies might be ignored in one application, and at focus in another.

Our account of trajectories in information space based on graph search provides a framework for modeling goal-directed belief revision, and can accommodate the use of heuristics which will render the search for successful paths from an initial information state to a desired goal state feasible. An example of such a heuristic was given in the previous section.

A measure of similarity based on the quasi-metric, **dist**, can be used to measure the degree of surprise of information, e.g. if $\mathbf{dist}(\mathbf{E}_1, \mathbf{E}_1^\star(\alpha, i)) < \mathbf{dist}(\mathbf{E}_1, \mathbf{E}_1^\star(\beta, j))$ then α with degree i is less suprising than β with degree j for state $\mathbf{E}_1$. We can also say if $\mathbf{dist}(\mathbf{E}_1, \mathbf{E}_2) < \mathbf{dist}(\mathbf{E}_1, \mathbf{E}_3)$ then state $\mathbf{E}_3$ is more surprising than state $\mathbf{E}_2$ from the standpoint of $\mathbf{E}_1$.

The measure **dist** can also be used to determine the most desirable explanatory state. For instance it might be that the best explanatory state is the most similar state to the original state, e.g. if α and β are explanations for an observation γ and $\mathbf{dist}(\mathbf{E}, \mathbf{E}^\star(\alpha, \mathbf{E}(\gamma))) < \mathbf{dist}(\mathbf{E}, \mathbf{E}^\star(\beta, \mathbf{E}(\gamma)))$ then α changes $\mathbf{E}$ less than β and as a result it might be prefered as an explanation. This approach can also be used to model a preference for a *revolutionary* explanation over an explanation supported by a sequence of smaller changes, because more than a single change can be taken into consideration. In other words, a single large change may be a shorter distance from a starting state than the state resulting from a series of smaller changes. For example, a change incorporating Kepler's *elliptic orbits* may be closer to a state where the planets move in circular orbits than the host of modifications needed to model Ptolemy's elaborate *epicycles* to account for the observed retrograde motion of the planets.[4]

Finally, we briefly describe a specific application in the Marketing Research domain. Consumer preferences influence consumer behaviour. Preferences tend to change as consumer's beliefs and desires change, or as consumers acquire more information about a particular product. Modeling consumer preferences for a particular product class involves the collection of data and culminates in a preference ranking. Conjoint analysis [Green and Srinivasan, 1978] is then used to estimate the willingness of consumers to trade off varying levels of product attributes on the basis of their preferences. This is achieved by determining utility functions for each of the attributes of a product which are then used to design products with the optimum appeal. In practice only a small number of attributes (typically less than 10) are used in conjoint analysis studies. To reduce the combinatorial explosion of possible product combinations, fractional factorial orthogonal arrays [Cochran and Cox, 1966] of full product profiles are used. If consumer preferences change after the time of data collection then the changes are either ignored, or the preference information is recollected from the consumers (a highly demanding and expensive activity) and another conjoint analysis study is carried out. Williams and Polonsky [1997] described an integrated framework for conjoint analysis and belief revision as a means to circumvent the need for data recollection when consumer preferences change.

In order to determine whether belief revision techniques can obviate the need for data recollection experiments must be conducted in which the new ranking obtained via data recollection and the new ranking obtained via belief revision operations are *compared*. This comparison requires a *measure of similarity* for preference rankings. For example, consider the situation where a consumer's initial ranking of the orthogonal array of product profiles is given by I, and as they learn about the product they change their preferences to form the new ranking J. In other words, assume if the data collection procedure was repeated the ranking J would be obtained. We want to compare the state J with the state, say K, that would result from the use of belief revision. We can use techniques described in the previous section to determine the similarity between J and K. The ultimate aim of this exercise is to formulate a belief revision operation that minimises the differences between J and K. Not only will a successful belief revision operation avoid the need for data recollection when consumers change their preferences, but it can be used by marketers to perform hypothetical reasoning and 'what if' scenario analysis which should lead to more effective design decisions. A prototype system that implements a measure of similarity based on unit conditionalisation has been developed in Prolog,[5] and will be used to evaluate how closely belief revison strategies model consumers preference change.

[4]Just as an aside it is interesting to note that the motion of planets is typically calculated using Fourier Series which can be naturally conceptualised as epicycles.

[5]Dual atoms are represented and manipulated as lists, not as clauses.

5 RELATED WORK

Similarity has been of considerable interest in Knowledge Representation over the years, unfortunately it has proved to be a difficult notion to capture formally. For example, Lewis' seminal work [1973] on the subject of counterfactuals relies on a notion of *comparative similarity*, a measure which according to him is either well-understood and vague, or ad hoc and limited in scope.

There are *scads* of measures of similarity based on, for the want of a better foundation, set theoretical measures. This type of measure is used in various forms of nonmontonic reasoning, and some interpretations of the principle of Minimal Change in the area of Belief Revision. The problem with such measures is that they do not take the internal structure of the information state into consideration, and as a consequence they are superficial indicators of similarity. The quasi-metric, **dist**, is able to gauge the difference between losing one important belief and losing several less important beliefs. Set theoretic measures neglect the property that similarity of system laws have a tendency to outweigh similarities in particular facts [Lewis, 1973, p. 75].

Hansson argues convincingly that minimal change is definable in terms of similarity. In particular, he says "to make a change minimal is to make it result in a state that is as similar to the original state as possible". Hansson [1992] analyses two forms of similarity measures on information content: *concurrence* and *difference*. A concurrence measure of similarity is founded on the idea that if I has more *in common* with J than it has with K then I is more similar to J than K. In other words, the larger $I \cap J$ is, the more similar I is to J. A difference measure on the other hand, is determined by how two entities differ. In particular, he studies the following measures: *symmetric set difference* $I \Delta J = (I \backslash J) \cup (J \backslash I)$, and *dyadic difference* $I \pm J = \{I \backslash J, J \backslash I\}$. All of these measures are symmetric.

The semantics of belief revision is based on a distance measure derived from a system of spheres (a total preorder of state descriptions). This measure has been variously interpreted by numerous authors as a similarity measure, a plausibility measure, a measure of importance with respect to change, a measure of importance for problem solving, a possibilistic measure, and a probability measure. Schlechta *et al* [1996] propose a distance semantics for belief revision functions based on a given distance metric which can also be used to analyse iterated operations.

Dalal's measure [1988] of similarity on which he founds his definition of revision is the number of propositional letters on which two interpretations differ; a measure which induces an ordering among interpretations. Winslett [1988], Borgida [1985] and Satoh [1990] among others use a difference measure based on set inclusion: Diff(I, J) is the set of propositional letters whose interpretation is different in I and J.

Hansson [1995] also analyses changes in preference. In particular he allows input of the form $\beta < \alpha$ which means α is preferred to β. If we assume this preference is contravened by the current preference ordering then either the rank of α must be increased, or the rank of β must be decreased. The best choice will be the one that results in a preference ranking that is most similar to the original one. Hansson uses set-inclusion measures to determine which choice should be adopted and studies its relational properties. Our distance measure could also be used to determine the best choice. For example, if $\mathbf{dist}(\mathbf{E}, \mathbf{E}^{\star}(\alpha, \mathbf{E}(\beta) + 1)) < \mathbf{dist}(\mathbf{E}, \mathbf{E}^{\star}(\beta, \mathbf{E}(\alpha) - 1))$, then increasing the rank of α above the rank of β is preferred to decreasing the rank of β below the rank of α because it results in a ranking that is more similar to the original ranking, **E**. On the other hand, if $\mathbf{dist}(\mathbf{E}, \mathbf{E}^{\star}(\alpha, \mathbf{E}(\beta) + 1)) > \mathbf{dist}(\mathbf{E}, \mathbf{E}^{\star}(\beta, \mathbf{E}(\alpha) - 1))$, then decreasing the rank of β below the rank of α would cause the least disturbance, and hence preferable.

6 DISCUSSION

Many belief revision applications require a measure of similarity. We have described a simple, yet powerful, operational measure of similarity based on change. The advantages of this measure are that it: (i) is nonprobabilistical, (ii) is quantitative in character, (iii) not set theoretical, (iv) takes the internal structure of the information state into consideration, (v) is not necessarily symmetric, (vi) can model accumulated effects of change, (vii) is operational, and (viii) is implementable.

We showed that the graphical representation of information space and the similarity measure based on transmutation schemas provides a useful framework for modeling goal-directed belief revision, for evaluating the plausibility of belief revision strategies as models for human belief change, for assessing design decisions for belief revision, for comparing possible explanations, and for evaluating surprising information.

The proposed framework enhances our understanding of the concept of similarity in the present context, and it provides the necessary practical machinery for computing a natural form of epistemic distance. There are vastly too many possible information states to implement the framework in full, and we outlined two approaches that can be used to address the complexity problem: the use of orthogonal arrays, and the use of partial entrenchment rankings together with heuristic search.

University of Newcastle, Australia.

REFERENCES

[Alchourrón *et al.*, 1985] C. Alchourrón, P. Gärdenfors and D. Makinson. On the logic of theory change: partial meet functions for contraction and revision. *Journal of Symbolic Logic*, **50**, 510–530, 1985.

[Borgida, 1985] A. Borgida. *Language features for flexible handling of exceptions in information systems, ACM–Transactions on Database Systems*, **10**, 565–603, 1985.

[Borowski and Borwein, 1989] E. J. Borowski and J. M. Borwein. *Dictionary of Mathematics*, Collins, London, 1989.

[Cochran and Cox, 1966] W. G . Cochran and G. M. Cox. *Experimental Designs*, Second Edition, Wiley, 1966.

[Dalal, 1988] M. Dalal. Investigations into a theory of knowledge base revision, *AAAI*, pp. 475–479, 1988.

[Diaconis, 1988] P. Diaconis. Group representations in probability and statistics. *Institute of Mathematical Statistics, Lecture Notes – Monograph Series*, Shanti S. Gupta, Series Editor, Volume 11, 1988.

[Frednab, 1975] M. Fredman. On computing the length of longest increasing subsequences, *Discrete Mathematics*, **11**, 29–35, 1975.

[Floyd, 1964] R. Floyd. Letter to Don Knuth, 1964.

[Gärdenfors and Makinson, 1988] P. Gärdenfors and D. Makinson. Revisions of knowledge systems using epistemic entrenchment. In *Proceedings of the Second Conference on Theoretical Aspects of Reasoning about Knowledge*, pp. 83–96, 1988.

[Green and Srinivasan, 1978] P. E. Green and V. Srinivasan. Conjoint analysis in consumer research: issues and outlook, *Journal of Consumer Research*, **5**, 103–123, 1978.

[Grove, 1988] A. Grove. Two modellings for theory change, *Journal of Philosophical Logic*, **17**, 157–170, 1988.

[Hansson, 1992] S. O. Hansson. Similarity semantics and minimal changes of belief, *Erkenntis*, **37**, 401–429, 1992.

[Hansson, 1995] S. O. Hansson. Changes in preference, *Theory and Decision*, **38**, 1–28, 1995.

[Lewis, 1973] D. Lewis. *Counterfactuals*, Blackwell, Oxford, 1973.

[Peppas and Williams, 1995] P. Peppas and M. A. Williams. Contructive modelings for theory change, *Notre Dame Journal of Formal Logic*, **36**, 120–133, 1995.

[Satoh, 1990] K. Satoh. *A probabilistic interpretation for lazy nonmonotonic reasoning*, *AAAI*, pp. 959–664, 1990.

[Schlechta *et al.*, 1996] K. Schlechta, D. Lehmann and M. Magidor. Distance semantics for belief revision, *Theoretical Aspects of Reasoning about Knowledge*, 137–145, 1996.

[Spohn, 1988] W. Spohn. Ordinal conditional functions: a dynamic theory of epistemic states. In *Causation in Decision, Belief Change, and Statistics, II*, W. L. Harper and B. Skyrms, eds. pp. 105-134. Kluwer Academic Publishers, 1988.

[Williams, 1994] M. A. Williams. Transmutations of knowledge systems. In *Principles of Knowledge Representation and Reasoning: Proceedings of the Fourth International Conference*, J. Doyle, E. Sandewall and P. Torasso, eds. pp. 619–629. Morgan Kaufmann, San Mateo, CA, 1994.

[Williams, 1994b] M. A. Williams. On the logic of theory base change. In *Logics in Artificial Intelligence*, C. MacNish, D. Pearce and L. M. Pereira, eds. pp. 86–105. LNCS 835, Springer Verlag, 1994.

[Williams, 1995] M. A. Williams. Iterated theory base change: a computational model. In *Proceedings of the Fourteenth International Joint Conference on Artificial Intelligence*, pp. 1541–1550. Morgan Kaufmann, 1995.

[Williams, 1997] M. A. Williams. Anytime belief revision. In *Proceedings of the Fifteenth International Joint Conference on Artificial Intelligence*, Morgan Kaufmann, 1997.

[Williams, 1997b] M. A. Williams. Implementing belief revision. In *Nonmonotonic Reasoning with Incomplete and Changing Information*, G. Antoniou, ed. Chapter 14. The MIT Press, 1997.

[Williams and Polonsky, 1997] M. A. Williams and M. J. Polonsky. Modeling changes in consumer preferences using belief revision. In *Proceedings of the Australiasian Cognitive Science Conference*, in press.

[Williams and Williams, 1997] M. A. Williams and D. Williams. A belief revision system for the World Wide Web. In *Proceedings of the IJCAI Workshop on Artificial Intelligence and the Internet*, 1997. http://infosystems.newcastle.edu.au/webworld/java

[Williams *et al.*, 1995] M. A. Williams, K. Wallace and G. Antoniou. An object-oriented implementation of belief revision. In *Proceedings of the Australian Joint Conference on Artificial Intelligence*, pp. 259–267, 1995.

[Winslett, 1988] M. Winslett. Reasoning about action using possible models approach, *AAAI-88*, pp. 89–93, 1988.

EYAL AMIR

TOWARD A FORMALIZATION OF ELABORATION TOLERANCE: ADDING AND DELETING AXIOMS

1 INTRODUCTION

The notion of *Elaboration Tolerance* was proposed by McCarthy [1988] for the problem of extending a logical theory, with the intuition that a logical system should have the ability to absorb additions the way Natural Language allows. Several intuitions coincide in this description: axiomatizing a theory in a flexible way; not needing to rebuild one's ontology when new features and facts are added; Being able to modify one's axioms relatively easily; and needing only a small amount of recomputation, given new information. Elaboration Tolerance is important for Knowledge Base construction and development, as well as for scaling up results and techniques in Knowledge Representation. Past treatments of the concept referred only to intuitive accounts. In order to investigate Elaboration Tolerance, however, we need formal definitions and comparison tools. The major contribution of this work is supplying such tools.

In this paper, we propose a formal definition for a *syntactic* aspect of the property of Elaboration Tolerance. We refer to Elaborations as sequences of actions as executed on a certain Knowledge Base. In this paper, we restrict our treatment to Knowledge Bases that are formal systems and to actions that add or delete axioms (other possible actions that we ignore here are adding constants to the language, adding preconditions to axioms, etc., depending on what is allowed by the knowledge base). We intuitively say that a Knowledge Base is *elaboration-tolerant* to the extent that elaborations are representable and require "short" sequences of actions for these elaborations. The *Problem of Elaboration* (as examined in this paper) is, given an intended elaboration (e.g., using semantics to specify these intentions), finding a sequence of actions that will give us the intended result.

To keep our discussion simple, we restrict our treatment in this paper in two ways: we allow the addition and deletion of disjunctive clauses only, and we restrict the formal systems to have a propositional language. The reason for the first restriction will become clear in Section 2.3. The second restriction simplifies most of the theorems but most of them follow for the general First-Order case.

Using this framework, we show the following (some intuitive and some surprising) results. On the intuitive side, we show that a propositional knowledge base with a larger set of constant symbols is more elaboration-tolerant than an equivalent one with fewer symbols. On a somewhat less intuitive angle, we show that some nonmonotonic theories are not more elaboration-tolerant than some equivalent monotonic theories. We then show that, despite this fact, from a monotonic

M.-A. Williams and H. Rott (eds.), Frontiers in Belief Revision, 147–162.

theory there is a way to construct an equivalent nonmonotonic theory that is more elaboration-tolerant than the original one. Finally, we show that there is no one most elaboration-tolerant system.

A few authors have informally discussed Elaboration Tolerance in the past. McCarthy [1998] gives some examples and discusses intuitions of Elaboration Tolerance. It attributes the creation of Nonmonotonic Reasoning techniques to Elaboration Tolerance. Shanahan [1996] further discusses Elaboration Tolerance and shows how the desire for Elaboration Tolerance invigorates major portions of the Knowledge Representation endeavor. Costello [1997] and [Amir, 1997] showed how different theories of action relate with respect to certain elaborations. Other relevant material is [Giunchiglia and Walsh, 1992] and the work on abstraction. This work is relevant in supplying both elaborations (reverse abstractions[1]) and translation functions (used in comparing systems).

In contrast to these discussions, we try to define a region on which some formal work can be done. We seek guidelines for choosing a formal machinery and writing the theory so that extensions are simple. The theory that we provide in this paper aids in finding these guidelines by focusing on the number of actions that need to be performed in order to amend the knowledge base. Consequently, we wish to minimize the length of that sequence of actions.

2 THE ELABORATION MODEL

This section is the core of the paper. Here we will first go through an intuitive explanation, then define our notions and eventually explore a detailed example using these notions.

2.1 *Intuitions & Intentions*

We want to compare knowledge base design decisions, preferring those decisions that give us more Elaboration Tolerance. One simple intuitive example is the following. Assume that we are given the logical theory

$$Rain \Longrightarrow Cold \tag{1}$$

$$Wet \Longrightarrow Cold \tag{2}$$

Now, we want to add the fact that in the tropics it is not cold but it may rain and it is wet. One way to do that is to rewrite the theory from scratch:

$$Rain \Longrightarrow (Cold \lor Tropics)$$
$$Wet \Longrightarrow (Cold \lor Tropics)$$

[1]A proposal made by Alon Levy in a personal communication.

Consider the following theory, which is similar to the original theory above.

(3) $$Rain \Longrightarrow Preconditions$$

(4) $$Wet \Longrightarrow Preconditions$$

(5) $$Preconditions \Longrightarrow Cold$$

In this theory we added the observation that being wet and having rain are two properties that share preconditions. In this case, instead of rewriting the entire theory from scratch, we can simply replace the third sentence (5) with

$$Preconditions \Longrightarrow (Cold \vee Tropics)$$

We would like to prefer compact changes, like the last one, over rewriting extended sections of our knowledge base, as seen in the first case.

Coming up with a complete characterization of the set of possible tricks one might pull seems like an open-ended task. These "tricks" may include design decisions like Object-Oriented design (e.g., using Frames (see [Minsky, 1975] and [Brachman and Levesque, 1985])), but may also include simple aggregations such as the one demonstrated in the example just described.

To understand the tradeoffs and to find new ways of enhancing the Elaboration Tolerance of a knowledge base, we now turn to introduce a formal account of the comparisons that we wish to make and the qualifications that we want to measure.

2.2 *A Model of Knowledge-Base Change*

In this section we describe a model for knowledge-base change. We take a syntactic approach to knowledge-base change since, as the example above demonstrated, the actions done by a human knowledge engineer are syntactic (for relations to Belief Revision, see Section 5). This treatment corresponds to the approach taken by researchers working on Theory Revision (see [De Raedt, 1992], [Adé *et al.*, 1994] and [Koppel *et al.*, 1994]). For now, we ignore the decisions that the knowledge engineer may face and their complexity, and focus on the final product of her changes.

We restrict our discussion to knowledge bases that are *Axiomatic Formal Systems*. In later sections we will see the reason we need such a broad definition.

DEFINITION 1 (From [Shoenfield, 1967]). An *Axiomatic Formal System* Σ is a triple $\langle \mathcal{L}, \mid\!\sim, \Gamma \rangle$ where $\mathcal{L}$ is the language, Γ is the set of axioms and $\mid\!\sim$ is the inference relation[2] of Σ.

In this paper, we treat the language as its set of sentences and we use the notation $|\mathcal{L}|$ to represent the set of propositional symbols of the language $\mathcal{L}$. For $\Sigma = \langle \mathcal{L}, \mid\!\sim, \Gamma \rangle$, we take $C(\Sigma)$ to be the theory entailed by the formal system's axioms (C comes for the *completion* of Σ):

$$C(\Sigma) \stackrel{def}{=} \{\varphi \in \mathcal{L} \mid \Gamma \mid\!\sim \varphi\}$$

[2]Possibly nonmonotonic.

We define an equivalence relation between formal systems as follows:

$$\Sigma \equiv \Sigma' \iff C(\Sigma) = C(\Sigma').$$

Notice that $C(\Sigma) = C(\Sigma')$ is determined extensionally (equality of sets). Also, notice that although this definition allows different languages in Σ and Σ', the equality of languages is in fact implied for all logics that entail tautologies.

In what follows we describe actions for changing the knowledge base. Each action transforms a formal system into another formal system. In this paper we restrict our attention to adding and deleting axioms.

If $\varphi \subset \mathcal{L}$ is an *additional axiom*, then we write $add(\varphi)(\Sigma)$ for the result of adding φ to Σ, i.e.,

$$add(\varphi)(\Sigma) \stackrel{def}{=} \langle \mathcal{L}, \mid\!\sim, \Gamma \cup \{\varphi\} \rangle.$$

To *delete an axiom* from the knowledge base, we use the action $delete(\varphi)(\Sigma)$:

$$delete(\varphi)(\Sigma) \stackrel{def}{=} \langle \mathcal{L}, \mid\!\sim, \Gamma \setminus \{\varphi\} \rangle.$$

Notice that because of the syntactic nature of these actions, deleting an axiom that does not exist in the knowledge base (even though it may be entailed by the knowledge base) results in the original knowledge base (we prefer this definition over leaving it undefined).

To represent the result of a sequence of actions performed on the knowledge base, we shall use the convention that applying the sequence of actions $\alpha = \langle a_1, ..., a_n \rangle$ (where each of the actions $\{a_i\}_{i \leq n}$ is of the form $add(\varphi)$ or $delete(\varphi)$ for a sentence φ in the relevant language) is written as

$$\alpha(\Sigma) \stackrel{def}{=} a_n(a_{n-1}(...(a_1(\Sigma))...)).$$

Thus, if $\alpha = \langle delete(\psi), add(\varphi) \rangle$ then $\alpha(\Sigma) = add(\varphi)(delete(\psi)(\Sigma))$. Finally, we write $Actions(\mathcal{L})$ for all the sequences α of actions that can be performed in $\mathcal{L}$.

The reason we chose to focus on the actions of adding and deleting axioms is two-fold: first, these action seem to be the simplest, yet extremely common, operations done during knowledge base construction and expansion, and second, in this stage of inquiry, constraining ourselves to only two, very simple, actions, helps in clarifying and focusing the investigation and explanation.

2.3 Comparing Elaboration Tolerance

Now we turn to define a simplified account of Elaboration Tolerance. Intuitively, we ignore the difficulties encountered in formalizing the process of conceptualization, and focus only on the syntactic work that has to be done (possibly after long deliberation) to change the knowledge base to its target meaning.

To compare two systems, we first have to translate them to some "common ground". Somewhat similar to the approach taken by [Giunchiglia and Walsh,

1992], we first define a translation between two formal systems ([Giunchiglia and Walsh, 1992] call their function an *abstraction function*, but this name is not necessarily appropriate in our context).

DEFINITION 2 (Translation). A *translation* t is a partial function that accepts a formal system and returns a formal system. In other words, $t : S \rightarrow S$ a partial function, where S is a set of axiomatic formal systems.

We can now use the equivalence relation defined by t:

$$Def: \ \Sigma_1 \equiv_t \Sigma_2 \iff C(t(\Sigma_1)) = C(t(\Sigma_2))$$

Notice that this is indeed an equivalence relation. Also, notice that the translation t does not translate Σ_1 to Σ_2 but rather translates both formal system to one (possibly different than both) common ground.

Now we define the problem of elaboration to be the problem of finding a sequence of actions that transforms an original knowledge base to a desired knowledge base (modulo our equivalence relation $\equiv_t$).

DEFINITION 3 (Elaboration Problem). We are given two axiomatic formal systems, Σ, Σ_{target} and a translation t. The *problem of elaboration* is to find an elaboration (i.e., a sequence of actions) α such that $\alpha(\Sigma) \equiv_t \Sigma_{target}$.

Given this definition, we would like to give a criterion for Σ' to be more elaboration-tolerant than Σ with respect to the target Σ_{target}. The following measure tries to capture the difficulty encountered in the syntactic operations performed on the knowledge base.

DEFINITION 4 (Syntactic Distance). Let Σ, Σ_{target} be two axiomatic formal systems. The *Syntactic Distance*[3] of Σ_{target} from Σ is

$$dist_t(\Sigma, \Sigma_{target}) \stackrel{def}{=} \min \left\{ len(\alpha) \;\middle|\; \begin{array}{l} \alpha \in Actions(\mathcal{L}) \\ \wedge\, \alpha(\Sigma) \equiv_t \Sigma_{target} \end{array} \right\}$$

where $len(\alpha)$ is the number of actions in α. We take $dist_t(\Sigma, \Sigma_{target})$ to be ∞ in the case that there is no sequence of actions that will transform Σ to Σ_{target}.

Intuitively, we wish $dist_t(\Sigma, \Sigma_{target})$ to measure the minimal work we need to do in order to change Σ into something equivalent (modulo $\equiv_t$) to Σ_{target}. Syntactic Distance (in the case where there is an elaboration (i.e., $dist_t(\Sigma, \Sigma') < \infty$)) is useful when we want to compare two systems that can both represent the same elaborations. Recalling the intuition that we wish to minimize the work done in changing the knowledge base, the weight function ($len(\alpha)$) that we use here does not seem convincing. Why does this $dist_t$ capture our intuition of *difficulty* of expanding the theory?

First, it is reasonable to say that the less you have to add to your theory, the more robust it was to begin with, so this measure approximates some of our intuitions of Elaboration Tolerance. The real problem in choosing a weight function

[3]This is a quasi-distance measure, i.e., it is not symmetric.

for this case is that many people have different intuitions for it. One would rather have it be either 0 (there *is* an elaboration) or ∞ (there *is no* such elaboration). Another would rather have the weight measure the *difficulty of finding the elaboration* (however that might be formulated). I propose this function as a quick-and-dirty measure that one can do with for some time. Most of the results (e.g., theorems 10 and 11) are independent of which measure we take (given that, if there is no elaboration, we get ∞).

To compare two systems Σ_1 and Σ_2, we use the translation t to give Σ_1 and Σ_2 a common ground. It is important to notice that the comparison is highly dependent on our choice of t (one possible choice of t is demonstrated in Section 4).

DEFINITION 5 (Elaboration Comparison). Let $\Sigma_1 = \langle \mathcal{L}_1, \mid\!\sim_1, \Gamma_1 \rangle$, $\Sigma_2 = \langle \mathcal{L}_2, \mid\!\sim_2, \Gamma_2 \rangle$ be two axiomatic formal systems and t a translation such that $\Sigma_1 \equiv_t \Sigma_2$.

Given t, define Σ_1 to be more *syntactically elaboration-tolerant* (abbr. elaboration tolerant) than Σ_2 on $\alpha \in Actions(\mathcal{L}_1)$, by

$$\Sigma_1 \leq_{t,\alpha} \Sigma_2 \stackrel{def}{=} dist_t(\Sigma_1, \alpha(\Sigma_1)) \leq dist_t(\Sigma_2, \alpha(\Sigma_1)).$$

Given t, define Σ_1 to be more *elaboration-tolerant* than Σ_2, by

$$\begin{aligned} \Sigma_1 \leq_t \Sigma_2 \stackrel{def}{=} \quad & \forall \alpha \in Actions(\mathcal{L}_1)\ \Sigma_1 \leq_{t,\alpha} \Sigma_2 \wedge \\ & \forall \alpha \in Actions(\mathcal{L}_2)\ \exists \alpha' \in Actions(\mathcal{L}_1) (\alpha'(\Sigma_1) \equiv_t \alpha(\Sigma_2)) \end{aligned}$$

For the strict cases, we require that there is $\alpha \in Actions(\mathcal{L}_1)$ such that $dist_t(\Sigma_1, \alpha(\Sigma_1)) < dist_t(\Sigma_2, \alpha(\Sigma_1))$. For that case, we say *strictly more elaboration-tolerant* and write the corresponding strict inequality relation.

We postpone the re-examination of the example covered in beginning of this section to Section 4.2, where we prove a general theorem that captures this example.

2.4 Examples

Let us look at a variant of the example given in Section 2.1. Assume that we have a theory describing some aspects of weather. For simplicity, assume that the theory has the following axioms:

$$Rain \Longrightarrow Preconditions \tag{6}$$

$$Preconditions \Longrightarrow Cold \tag{7}$$

Let $\Sigma = \langle \mathcal{L}, \vdash, \{(6), (7)\} \rangle$ where $\mathcal{L}$ is the propositional language of the propositional symbols $Rain, Preconditions, Cold, Tropics$ and $\vdash$ is the classical propositional entailment relation.

Now we wish to say that it is possible that there will be rain without being cold if we are in the tropics. We will have to perform the sequence of actions $\alpha = \langle delete((7)), add(\text{“}Preconditions \Longrightarrow (Cold \vee Tropics)\text{''}) \rangle$. The resulting formal system $\alpha(\Sigma)$ then has the same language $\mathcal{L}$, the same entailment relation $\vdash$ and the following set of axioms:

$$(8)\quad \begin{array}{l} Rain \Longrightarrow Preconditions \\ Preconditions \Longrightarrow (Cold \vee Tropics) \end{array}$$

Thus, $\alpha(\Sigma) = \Sigma_{target} = \langle \mathcal{L}, \vdash, \{(8)\}\rangle$. Because of the monotonicity of propositional logic, this change cannot be done if we allow only the addition axioms (without deletion), and thus there is no way to perform the change with only one action.

There are other systems that will allow for that elaboration in a shorter manner. Take, for example, the following nonmonotonic system. Assume that, instead of the original set of axioms, we have

$$(9)\quad \begin{array}{l} Rain \Longrightarrow Preconditions \\ Cold \Longrightarrow Preconditions \end{array}$$

The system is $\Sigma' = \langle \mathcal{L}, \mid\!\sim_C, \{(9)\}\rangle$, where

$$\Gamma \mid\!\sim_C \varphi \iff Circ[\Gamma; Preconditions; \mathcal{L}] \vdash \varphi$$

Here, $Circ[A; P; Q]$ is the circumscription formula $A(P, Q) \wedge \forall pq[A(p, q) \Rightarrow \neg(p < P)]$, as defined in [McCarthy, 1980], which intuitively says that P is minimized even at the price of changing Q. In our context, that means (intuitively) that the proposition $Preconditions$ take the truth value FALSE, unless it "must" be TRUE. We can get the result required by Σ_{target} (our target system above) by simply adding sentence

$$(10)\quad Tropics \Longrightarrow Preconditions$$

Basically, what we are saying is that every formula is assumed to be true, given no contradictory information. Without the knowledge (10), a result of minimizing the preconditions would be that $Preconditions \iff Cold$. Given the additional knowledge (10), we conclude that $Preconditions \iff (Cold \vee Tropics)$.

If we take t to be the identity translation $t(\Sigma) = \Sigma$, then we can conclude $\Sigma \equiv_t \Sigma'$ and that

$$\Sigma' \leq_{t,\alpha} \Sigma$$

for $\alpha = \langle add(\text{“}Tropics \Longrightarrow Preconditions\text{''})\rangle$. Notice, that α itself can be applied to Σ, but it will yield a different result than Σ_{target}.

3 SOME INTERMEDIATE RESULTS

We prove a few basic properties of the above relations. Notice that we put no restriction on t.

PROPOSITION 6. *If $\Sigma_1 \leq_{t,\alpha_1} \Sigma_2$ and $\Sigma_2 \leq_{t,\alpha_2} \Sigma_3$ and $\alpha_1(\Sigma_1) \equiv_t \alpha_2(\Sigma_2)$, then $\Sigma_1 \leq_{t,\alpha_1} \Sigma_3$. For the strict case, if any of the two preconditions is a strict inequality, the result is also a strict inequality.*

Proof. By the definition, we get $dist_t(\Sigma_1, \alpha_1(\Sigma_1)) \leq dist_t(\Sigma_2, \alpha_1(\Sigma_1))$ and $dist_t(\Sigma_2, \alpha_2(\Sigma_2)) \leq dist_t(\Sigma_3, \alpha_2(\Sigma_2))$. Since $\alpha_1(\Sigma_1) \equiv_t \alpha_2(\Sigma_2)$, the first inequality implies that $dist_t(\Sigma_1, \alpha_1(\Sigma_1)) \leq dist_t(\Sigma_2, \alpha_2(\Sigma_2))$ and so $dist_t(\Sigma_1, \alpha_1(\Sigma_1)) \leq dist_t(\Sigma_3, \alpha_2(\Sigma_2))$ and finally

$$dist_t(\Sigma_1, \alpha_1(\Sigma_1)) \leq dist_t(\Sigma_3, \alpha_1(\Sigma_1)).$$

For the strict cases, assume first that $\Sigma_1 <_{t,\alpha_1} \Sigma_2$. By the definition, we get $dist_t(\Sigma_1, \alpha_1(\Sigma_1)) < dist_t(\Sigma_2, \alpha_1(\Sigma_1))$ and $dist_t(\Sigma_2, \alpha_2(\Sigma_2)) \leq dist_t(\Sigma_3, \alpha_2(\Sigma_2))$. Since $\alpha_1(\Sigma_1) \equiv_t \alpha_2(\Sigma_2)$, we get that $dist_t(\Sigma_1, \alpha_1(\Sigma_1)) < dist_t(\Sigma_2, \alpha_2(\Sigma_2))$ and so $dist_t(\Sigma_1, \alpha_1(\Sigma_1)) < dist_t(\Sigma_3, \alpha_2(\Sigma_2))$ and finally $dist_t(\Sigma_1, \alpha_1(\Sigma_1)) < dist_t(\Sigma_3, \alpha_1(\Sigma_1))$. The other strict case is treated identically. ■

COROLLARY 7. *If* $\Sigma_1 \leq_t \Sigma_2$ *and* $\Sigma_2 \leq_t \Sigma_3$, *then* $\Sigma_1 \leq_t \Sigma_3$.

Proof. We first prove the first requirement of $\Sigma_1 \leq_t \Sigma_3$. Let $\alpha_1 \in Actions(\mathcal{L}_1)$. We distinguish between two cases: In the first case, there is $\alpha_2 \in Actions(\mathcal{L}_2)$ such that $\alpha_1(\Sigma_1) \equiv_t \alpha_2(\Sigma_2)$. In this case, by proposition 6 and from $\Sigma_1 \leq_{t,\alpha_1} \Sigma_2$ and $\Sigma_2 \leq_{t,\alpha_2} \Sigma_3$, we get that $\Sigma_1 \leq_{t,\alpha_1} \Sigma_3$.

If there is no such α_2 (this is the second case) then we can show that there is no such α_3 either (i.e., $\alpha_3 \in Actions(\mathcal{L}_3)$ such that $\alpha_1(\Sigma_1) \equiv_t \alpha_3(\Sigma_3)$). The reason is that if there is $\alpha_3 \in Actions(\mathcal{L}_3)$ such that $\alpha_3(\Sigma_3) \equiv_t \alpha_1(\Sigma_1)$, then, because of the *second requirement* of $\leq_t$ (definition 5), there is $\alpha_2(\Sigma_2) \equiv_t \alpha_3(\Sigma_3)$. Thus, $\alpha_2(\Sigma_2) \equiv_t \alpha_1(\Sigma_1)$. Contradiction to our assumption that there is no α_2 as above. Therefore, if there is no $\alpha_2 \in Actions(\mathcal{L}_2)$ as above, then there is no $\alpha_3 \in Actions(\mathcal{L}_3)$ as above. Thus, $\Sigma_1 \leq_{t,\alpha_1} \Sigma_3$.

To prove the second requirement of $\Sigma_1 \leq_t \Sigma_3$, notice that if $\alpha_3 \in Actions(\mathcal{L}_3)$, then $\exists \alpha_2 \in Actions(\mathcal{L}_2)$ such that $\alpha_3(\Sigma_3) \equiv_t \alpha_2(\Sigma_2)$ and $\exists \alpha_1 \in Actions(\mathcal{L}_1)$ such that $\alpha_2(\Sigma_2) \equiv_t \alpha_1(\Sigma_1)$. ■

COROLLARY 8. $\leq_t$ *is a pre-order.* $<_t$ *is a strict partial order.*

Proof. The reflexivity for $\leq_t$ is obvious, and thus $\leq_t$ is a pre-order.

For the irreflexivity of $<_t$, assume that $\Sigma <_{t,\alpha} \Sigma$ for $\alpha \in Actions(\mathcal{L})$. Then $dist_t(\Sigma, \alpha(\Sigma)) < dist_t(\Sigma, \alpha(\Sigma))$. Contradiction. Thus, we have irreflexivity.

For transitivity of $<_t$, assume $\Sigma_1 <_t \Sigma_2 <_t \Sigma_3$. Then, $\exists \alpha_1 \Sigma_1 <_{t,\alpha_1} \Sigma_2$. If there is no $\alpha_2 \in Actions(\mathcal{L}_2)$ such that $\alpha_1(\Sigma_1) \equiv_t \alpha_2(\Sigma_2)$, then there is no $\alpha_3 \in Actions(\mathcal{L}_3)$ such that $\alpha_1(\Sigma_1) \equiv_t \alpha_3(\Sigma_3)$ and $\Sigma_1 <_{t,\alpha_1} \Sigma_3$. If there is such α_2, then $\Sigma_2 \leq_{t,\alpha_2} \Sigma_3$ and by proposition 6 (the strict case), $\Sigma_1 <_{t,\alpha_1} \Sigma_3$. ■

The following lemma will become useful in the next section.

LEMMA 9. *Let* Σ_1, Σ_2 *be formal systems such that* $\Sigma_1 \equiv_t \Sigma_2$. *Assume* $\mathcal{L}_2 \subseteq \mathcal{L}_1$ *and* $\forall \alpha \in Actions(\mathcal{L}_2)$ $\alpha(\Sigma_1) \equiv_t \alpha(\Sigma_2)$. *Then,* $\Sigma_1 \leq_t \Sigma_2$.

Proof. Take $\alpha \in Actions(\mathcal{L}_1)$. We need to show $\Sigma_1 \leq_{t,\alpha} \Sigma_2$. Let $\alpha' \in Actions(\mathcal{L}_2)$ such that $\alpha(\Sigma_1) \equiv_t \alpha'(\Sigma_2)$ (if there is no such α' then we are done, since then we showed $\Sigma_1 \leq_{t,\alpha} \Sigma_2$). Since $\alpha' \in Actions(\mathcal{L}_1)$ and $\alpha'(\Sigma_2) \equiv_t \alpha'(\Sigma_1)$ (by the lemma's conditions), $\alpha'(\Sigma_1) \equiv_t \alpha(\Sigma_1)$. Thus, $dist_t(\Sigma_1, \alpha(\Sigma_1)) \leq dist_t(\Sigma_2, \alpha(\Sigma_1))$, and since α was arbitrary, the first condition is proved. The second requirement is supplied by the premises of the lemma. ■

4 COMPARISONS USING *CONSEQUENCE TRANSLATIONS*

In this section, we describe various knowledge bases and compare their elaboration tolerance using translations t that are *consequence translations*. Recall that a translation is used to compare knowledge bases by mapping both to some common-ground on which they agree.

The *consequence translation* to $\mathcal{L}, \mid\!\sim$ is $t(\langle \mathcal{L}_0, \mid\!\sim_0, \Gamma_0 \rangle) = \langle \mathcal{L}, \mid\!\sim, \Gamma \rangle$ for $\Gamma = C(\langle \mathcal{L}_0, \mid\!\sim_0, \Gamma_0 \rangle) \cap \mathcal{L}$ ([Giunchiglia and Walsh, 1992] have somewhat similar mappings they call *Predicate Abstractions* and *ABSTRIPS* abstractions). Intuitively, a consequence translation maps a formal system to a new formal system that has a preset language and a preset entailment relations (both "preset" for that consequence translation). The set of axioms of the new formal system is exactly the set of consequences of the axioms of the original formal system (using the original entailment relation).

Throughout this section we give special treatment to the case that only adding-axioms actions are allowed. This special case turns out to have some nice intuitive properties (some of the theorems proved below are true only for that case) and contrasting these properties with those of the general case is instructive.

4.1 Different Languages

Next, we show that adding a constant symbol to a propositional theory increases the Elaboration Tolerance.

Let us look at the following theory.

(11) $$Rain \Longrightarrow Clouds$$

(12) $$Clouds \Longrightarrow \neg Sun$$

the language includes the propositional symbols $Rain, Clouds, Sun$ and the entailment relation is the propositional entailment relation $\vdash$. Assume now that we added the propositional symbol $Moon$ to our language. Every elaboration that we could do before is still a valid elaboration here. More importantly, it yields the same results that it had in the original system (see the proof of the theorem below). Aside from that, there are some new elaborations that we can include, such as adding the axiom $Moon \iff \neg Sun$.

THEOREM 10. *Let $\vdash$ be the propositional entailment relation. Let $\mathcal{L}_2 \subseteq \mathcal{L}_1$ be two propositional languages and t be the consequence translation to $\mathcal{L}_2, \vdash$. If*

$\Sigma_1 = \langle \mathcal{L}_1, \vdash, \Gamma_1 \rangle$, $\Sigma_2 = \langle \mathcal{L}_2, \vdash, \Gamma_2 \rangle$ such that $\Sigma_2 \equiv_t \Sigma_1$ and only axiom-adding actions are allowed (for both systems), then $\Sigma_1 \leq_t \Sigma_2$ (Σ_1 is more elaboration-tolerant than Σ_2).

Proof. Let $\alpha_2 \in Actions(\mathcal{L}_2)$. We want to prove that $\alpha_2(\Sigma_2) \equiv_t \alpha_2(\Sigma_1)$, which will allow us to use lemma 9 to complete the proof.

$\Sigma_1 \equiv_t \Sigma_2$ implies that $\mathcal{L}_2 \cap C(\Sigma_1) = C(\Sigma_2)$. α_2 adds a sentence (or a conjunction of sentences), $\varphi \in \mathcal{L}_2$. Since $\varphi \in \mathcal{L}_2$, $\mathcal{L}_2 \cap (C(\Sigma_1) \cup \{\varphi\}) \equiv \mathcal{L}_2 \cap C(\Sigma_1 \wedge \varphi)$. This is because we can replace every axiom $\xi \in C(\Sigma_1 \wedge \varphi) \cap \mathcal{L}_2$, in a proof in the system on the right, with the two axioms $\varphi, \varphi \rightarrow \xi$, both in $(C(\Sigma_1) \cup \{\varphi\}) \cap \mathcal{L}_2$. Our ability to do this replacement is a direct result of the deduction theorem.

Since $C(\Sigma_2) \cup \{\varphi\} \equiv C(\Sigma_2 \wedge \varphi)$, we get that $(\mathcal{L}_2 \cap C(\Sigma_1)) \cup \{\varphi\} \equiv C(\Sigma_2) \cup \{\varphi\}$, which implies that $C(\Sigma_2 \wedge \varphi) \equiv C(\Sigma_1 \wedge \varphi) \cap \mathcal{L}_2$. Thus, $\Sigma_2 \wedge \varphi \equiv_t \Sigma_1 \wedge \varphi$ and $\alpha_2(\Sigma_2) \equiv_t \alpha_2(\Sigma_1)$. Now, all that is left is to use lemma 9 and get $\Sigma_1 \leq_t \Sigma_2$. ∎

Notice that, as a result of this theorem, two logically equivalent propositional formal systems have the same elaboration tolerance (given that we allow only axiom additions and no deletions). Of course, this is true under the assumptions that the translation is a consequence translation to $\mathcal{L}, \vdash$.

If we allow actions that delete axioms then the theorem above is not true. If the theorem held in the general case, we would have concluded that equivalent monotonic systems with the same language have the same elaboration tolerance (allowing both adding and removing axioms). An example that this is not the case was seen in Section 2.1.

The proof reveals the pleasant surprise that the last theorem is not in general true for nonmonotonic entailment relations (even if we allow only axiom-adding actions). This is hinted at by the use of the deduction theorem in the proof above and is illustrated by example 12 in Section 4.2.

4.2 *Propositional Monotonic and Nonmonotonic Systems*

Our exposition in this section is stated using the nonmonotonic system of Circumscription that we already used in Section 2.4. The same results can be stated for the nonmonotonic systems of Default Logic [Reiter, 1980], Autoepistemic Logic [Moore, 1987] and possibly others, but for simplicity, we restrict ourselves and discuss only the case of Circumscription.

Let $\Sigma_1 = \langle \mathcal{L}_1, \vdash, \Gamma_1 \rangle$, with $\mathcal{L}_1$ a propositional language, $\vdash$ the propositional entailment and Γ_1 a set of axioms in $\mathcal{L}_1$. The *associated abnormality theory* of Σ_1 is $\Sigma_2 = \langle \mathcal{L}_2, \mid\!\sim_C, \Gamma_2 \rangle$, with $\Gamma_2 = \{ab_\varphi \rightarrow \zeta \mid \varphi \in \Gamma_1\}$, $\mathcal{L}_2$ the propositional language $\mathcal{L}_1 \cup \{ab_\varphi | \varphi \in \Gamma_1\}$ (i.e., $\mathcal{L}_2 = \mathcal{L}_1 \cup \mathcal{L}(\Gamma_2)$) and $\mid\!\sim_C$ an entailment relation that first circumscribes the ab_φ's in parallel (varying the propositions of $\mathcal{L}_1$) and then treats the result propositionally. More precisely,

$$\Gamma \mid\!\sim_C \psi \iff Circ[\Gamma; ab_{\varphi_1}, ..., ab_{\varphi_n}; p_1, ..., p_m] \vdash \psi$$

The following theorem says that the associated abnormality theory of a propositional theory is strictly (under some assumptions) more elaboration-tolerant than the original propositional theory:

THEOREM 11. *Let* $\Sigma_1 = \langle \mathcal{L}_1, \vdash, \Gamma_1 \rangle$ *and* Σ_2 *be the associated abnormality theory of* Σ_1. *Assume that* Σ_1 *is not a contradiction (If it is a contradiction, then* $\Sigma_2 \not\equiv_t \Sigma_1$*) and assume that we are allowed only the addition of axioms (no axiom-deleting actions). Then* $\Sigma_2 \leq_t \Sigma_1$*, for* t *the consequence translation to* $\mathcal{L}_1, \vdash$. *If, in addition,* Σ_1 *is not a tautology, then* $\Sigma_2 <_t \Sigma_1$.

Proof. First, notice that $\Sigma_2 \equiv_t \Sigma_1$. It is also simple to see that for all $\alpha_1 \in Actions(\mathcal{L}_1)$, that does not cause inconsistency (i.e., $\alpha_1(\Sigma_1)$ is consistent), $\alpha_1(\Sigma_2) \equiv_t \alpha_1(\Sigma_1)$. The reason is that, if the axioms are consistent, then the circumscription will simply entail that all the *ab*'s are false, leading to an equivalent theory $\mathcal{L}_1 \cap \alpha_1(\Sigma_2) \equiv \alpha_1(\Sigma_1)$.

In the case of inconsistency in $\alpha_1(\Sigma_1)$, take[4] $\alpha_2 = \{\{\}\}$. α_2 causes inconsistency in Σ_2. Thus, we have shown the second condition of $\Sigma_2 \leq_t \Sigma_1$.

To show the first condition of $\Sigma_2 \leq_t \Sigma_1$, take $\alpha \in Actions(\mathcal{L}_2)$. We need to show that $dist_t(\Sigma_2, \alpha(\Sigma_2)) \leq dist_t(\Sigma_1, \alpha(\Sigma_2))$. Assume that this is not the case. Then there is $\alpha' \in Actions(\mathcal{L}_1)$ such that $\alpha(\Sigma_2) \equiv_t \alpha'(\Sigma_1)$ and for all $\beta \in Actions(\mathcal{L}_2)$ such that $\alpha(\Sigma_2) \equiv_t \beta(\Sigma_2)$, $len(\alpha') < len(\beta)$. If $\alpha'(\Sigma_1)$ is not inconsistent, then $\alpha' \in Actions(\mathcal{L}_2)$ and $\alpha'(\Sigma_2) \equiv_t \alpha'(\Sigma_1)$, contradicting our claim about α'. If $\alpha'(\Sigma_1)$ is inconsistent, then $\alpha(\Sigma_2)$ is inconsistent, thus having $\beta = \{\{\}\}$ with $\alpha(\Sigma_2) \equiv_t \beta(\Sigma_2)$ and again $dist_t(\Sigma_2, \alpha(\Sigma_2)) \leq dist_t(\Sigma_1, t(\alpha(\Sigma_2)))$. So the first condition of $\Sigma_2 \leq_t \Sigma_1$ is proved. Thus, $\Sigma_2 \leq_t \Sigma_1$.

To show that Σ_2 is in fact strictly more elaboration-tolerant than Σ_1, assuming Σ_1 is not a tautology, it is enough to show an elaboration that is expressible in Σ_2 but is not expressible (under the translation t) in Σ_1. Let $\alpha = \{ab_\varphi \mid \varphi \in \Gamma_1\}$. Since Σ_1 is assumed not to be a tautology, there is no addition to Σ_1 that will cause it to accept all the interpretations of $\mathcal{L}_1$ (because of monotonicity). This set of interpretations[5] is yet implied by $t(\alpha(\Sigma_2))$. Thus, in this case, $\Sigma_2 <_t \Sigma_1$. ■

It is important to notice that the above theorem is not in general true for non-monotonic theories and their equivalent monotonic counterparts. The following example demonstrates that.

EXAMPLE 12. Let $\Gamma_2 = \{r \vee (p \leftrightarrow q)\}$, $\mid\!\sim_C$ an entailment relation defined by $A \mid\!\sim_C \varphi \iff Circ[A; p; q] \vdash \varphi$. An equivalent monotonic theory is $\Gamma_1 = \{\neg p \wedge (q \rightarrow r)\}$. With the elaboration $\{q\}$ to Γ_1 we get $r \wedge \neg p \wedge q$. To get the equivalent theory for the nonmonotonic case, we must add both $\neg p$ and q. Adding only q will result in

$$Circ[(r \vee (p \leftrightarrow q)) \wedge q; p; q] \equiv q \wedge (r \vee p)$$

[4] We assume that the empty clause is a possible addition.

[5] Notice that the set of interpretations of $\alpha(\Sigma_2)$ is not the entire set of interpretations of $\mathcal{L}_2$.

and there is no use in trying to add either r or $\neg p$ by themselves.

4.3 Limits

The last two sections describe example applications of our definitions from Section 2.2. We shall now examine some of the limits of our system. The following theorem intuitively says that there is no formal system that is *the most* elaboration-tolerant (Again, given a certain translation t). Notice that here we allow both axiom-adding and axiom-deleting actions.

THEOREM 13. *Let $\mathcal{L}$ be a propositional language and t the consequence translation to $\mathcal{L}, \vdash$. Let $\Sigma = \langle \mathcal{L}, \mid\!\sim, \Gamma \rangle$ be an axiomatic formal system. Then there is another axiomatic formal system $\Sigma' = \langle \mathcal{L}, \mid\!\sim', \Gamma' \rangle$ (same language as Σ) and an elaboration $\alpha \in Actions(\mathcal{L})$ such that $\Sigma' <_{t,\alpha} \Sigma$.*

Proof. We use a combinatorial argument to show that there is a system Σ_{target} such that $dist(\Sigma, \Sigma_{target}) > 1$, and then find $\Sigma' \equiv_t \Sigma$ such that $dist(\Sigma', \Sigma_{target}) = 1$.

Take c to be the cardinality of the set of propositions in $\mathcal{L}$. Since Every proposition may either not show, show positively or show negatively, in every clause, there are 3^c possible clauses in $\mathcal{L}$ (if $\mathcal{L}$ is infinite, take the appropriate cardinals). Also, there are 2^c possible propositional models (each clause may either be true or not in each), and so there are exactly 2^{2^c} non-equivalent (equivalence measured using $\vdash$) propositional theories in $\mathcal{L}$. Thus, we have at most $2 * 3^c$ possible actions at our disposal (either adding or removing one of the clauses) and 2^{2^c} possible Σ_{target}'s. So, there is at least one (in fact there are many) elaboration $\alpha \in Actions(\mathcal{L})$ such that $dist_t(\Sigma, \alpha(\Sigma)) > 1$.

Take φ a clause in α that is not entailed by Σ (i.e., $\varphi \in \alpha \setminus C(\Sigma)$). Define $\mid\!\sim'$ as follows:

$$\begin{aligned} \mid\!\sim' \stackrel{def}{=} \ & \{\langle \Gamma, \psi \rangle \mid \psi \in C(\Sigma)\} \cup \\ & \{\langle \Gamma \cup \{\varphi\}, \psi \rangle \mid \psi \in C(\alpha(\Sigma))\} \end{aligned}$$

Notice that we did not have any problem defining this entailment relation, as we did not put any restrictions on it, and most importantly, it is a *relation* between sets of axioms in $\mathcal{L}$. Now, define $\Sigma' = \langle \mathcal{L}, \mid\!\sim', \Gamma \rangle$ and sure enough, $dist_t(\Sigma', \alpha(\Sigma)) = 1$. ■

The theorem intuitively says that for every formal system Σ there is a target formal system Σ_{target} that is not easy to reach (there is an equivalent formal system to Σ that reaches Σ_{target} easier).

This proof used the fact that we put no restrictions on the entailment relation $\mid\!\sim'$, but it is not too difficult to come up with a "conservative" nonmonotonic example that will give the same proof.

5 RELATION TO BELIEF REVISION AND ILP

A close issue to our presentation of Elaboration Tolerance is *Belief Revision*. Belief Revision is the process that a logical theory T goes through when we wish to incorporate some new information φ (see [Alchourrón *et al.*, 1985], [Katsuno and Mendelzon, 1991], [Lehmann, 1995], [Antoniou, 1997]). The main difference between the work done on Belief Revision and the Elaboration Tolerance treatment we presented here is that the latter is interested in the sequence of actions (e.g., syntactic additions to the knowledge base) necessary to reach a target Knowledge Base, while Belief Revision theory is interested in the change that result from adding or retracting some knowledge from the Knowledge Base.

As a result of the different motivations, there are several practical differences. Our treatment of Elaboration Tolerance is interested in *any* action for the Knowledge Base change, while Belief Revision is restricted to the actions of *add* and *remove* and their variances. Furthermore, Elaboration Tolerance is interested in the difficulty of specifying the set of actions, the length of the specification and the difficulty of executing the given change, only the last of which is interesting from the Belief Revision perspective. Another practical difference is that in Belief Revision, the underlying theory is always taken to be monotonic, and nonmonotonicity is introduced through the semantics of the revision and contraction operators. In our exposition of Elaboration Tolerance we explicitly allowed our base theory to be nonmonotonic. The work on syntactic forms of Belief Revision (e.g., [Nebel, 1991]) has mostly focused on Theory Base Change [Fagin *et al.*, 1983] and the information that can be elicited from the syntactic form of the theory.

Some authors interested in syntactic Belief Revision and Inductive Logic Programming and especially Theory Revision/Refinement (see [Abiteboul, 1988], [Koppel *et al.*, 1994], [De Raedt, 1992]) are more closely related to our treatment. The major differences here come in our measurement of the difficulty of change between specific theories, our ignorance of the algorithm for choosing the modification, our ability to compare theories that are neither similar nor have the same ontological background and our ability to talk about higher-level constructs (such as Object-Oriented designs).

6 CRITICISM AND DISCUSSION

Elaboration Tolerance may be a philosophical notion but its ramifications touch the everyday life of knowledge engineers. How does our treatment here relate to knowledge engineering efforts? In this section we criticize the current work and try to show where it may link to practical considerations.

The main criticism we wish to raise is that the notion of syntactic elaboration tolerance does not correspond to our intuitions of elaboration tolerance. For example, the system presented in Section 4.2 is nonmonotonic. Is it more *readable* than the monotonic equivalent? Is the question of the computational complexity of inference irrelevant to elaboration tolerance? Also, how do propositional results reflect the difficulties of building first-order theories?

What about the knowledge held by the engineer? It should be relevant to our task of KB expansion. Proficiency in the utilized knowledge representation influences the ease with which the KB is expanded and the representation picked by the knowledge engineer. And who picks Σ_{target}? The problem of finding this Σ_{target} is in fact the most important one and is seemingly ignored in our setting. Finally, our intuition says that the difficulty of changing a KB for a human is more than a syntactic one.

Our syntactic elaboration tolerance does not account for these considerations by itself, but there is a context in which it serves as one among several acting forces: If we view the problem of elaboration as one that is posed to a computer agent rather than a human agent.

Briefly, if the computer agent knows what it wants another agent to believe (the other agent is presumably a knowledge base), then the problem it faces is a problem of search: what sequence of actions on the other agent's KB will lead to an "acceptable" KB (i.e., a KB that is "$\equiv_t$" to our first agent's goal)? In such a search problem there are several playing factors: (1) the depth of the search (our syntactic distance); (2) the breadth of the search (our limit to disjunctive clauses rather than arbitrary axioms keeps this breadth manageable); (3) the complexity of checking for the goal (in the general classical propositional case, NP-complete); and (4) heuristic information.

Although we did not create a single comprehensive formula for "measuring" elaboration tolerance, our syntactic elaboration tolerance plays a significant role for such an "elaborating" agent. We will treat the larger problem as a whole in future works.

7 CONCLUSIONS

Restricting our attention to propositional languages and the actions of adding and deleting axioms to/from a knowledge base, we were able to compare systems with respect to their Elaboration Tolerance (with these allowed actions and language restrictions). For the case where only additions of axioms are allowed, we found that propositional systems with more propositional symbols are more Elaboration Tolerant, nonmonotonic systems are sometimes not more Elaboration Tolerant than an equivalent monotonic theory, there are ways to build nonmonotonic theories from monotonic ones such that the former are more Elaboration Tolerant than the latter and that there is no one most elaboration tolerant system (in our restricted scope).

Continuing the work on Elaboration Tolerance, we are currently working in three major directions. First, we wish to extend the model of knowledge-base evolution to include the fact that the knowledge engineer is not aware of the exact properties of the knowledge base when he changes it. Despite this lack of knowledge/awareness on the part of the knowledge engineer, he still manages to change the knowledge base to some degrees of success. It is our hope that this extended model will better approximate the uncertainty and difficulty of changing a knowledge base. Second, we try to make the comparison between knowledge bases more qualitative (possibly without using a distance *measure*). The quantitative model has its virtues but it seems that we can get a different point of view when we have a qualitative model. Third, we work on finding new ways to write theories so that they are more Elaboration Tolerant. This direction benefits directly from the theorems proved in this and similar articles.

A generalization of the above definition to arbitrary languages and to arbitrary actions can become useful in comparing first-order systems or systems with other actions (adding preconditions to axioms, adding constant symbols, generalizing an axiom, specializing an axiom and changing the entailment relation are only a few of the possibilities). These tools promise to give us new insights into the process of knowledge base construction and expansion and this work is just an initial step in that direction.

ACKNOWLEDGMENTS

This work benefited greatly from discussions with Josefina Sierra, Berthe Choueiry, Alon Levy, Sasa Buvac, John McCarthy, Tom Costello, Leora Morgenstern, Ray Reiter, Fausto Giunchiglia and Shlomit Pinter. This work would not be the same without their help in various stages of the work. Leora Morgenstern, Tom Costello, Mary-Anne Williams, Fausto Giunchiglia, Alon Levy, Shlomit Pinter and Erika Henik read drafts of this work, and I am grateful for their remarks. I also wish to thank the anonymous referees whose remarks helped me shape the final form of this work. Last, I wish to thank Josefiña Sierra again for reading many versions, listening to many complaints and difficulties and commenting during various stages of the ongoing work. Without her support I am doubtful this work would have been in the shape it is now.

This research was supported by an ARPA (ONR) grant N00014-94-1-0775 and an Air Force grant F49620-97-1-0207.

Stanford University, USA.

REFERENCES

[Abiteboul, 1988] S. Abiteboul. Updates, a new frontier. In *ICDT'88, 2nd International Conference on Database Theory*, Bruges, Belgium. M. Gyssens, J. Paredaens, and D. Van Gucht, eds. pp. 1–18. Volume 326 of *Lecture Notes in Computer Science*, Springer, 1988.

[Adé *et al.*, 1994] H. Adé, B. Malfait, and L. De Raedt. RUTH: an ILP theory revision system. In *Proceedings of the 8th International Symposium on Methodologies for Intelligent Systems*, Berlin. Z. W. Raś and M. Zemankova, eds. pp. 336–345. Volume 869 of *LNAI*, Springer, 1994.

[Alchourrón *et al.*, 1985] C. E. Alchourrón, P. Gärdenfors and D. Makinson. On the logic of theory change: Partial meet contraction and revision functions. *Journal of Symbolic Logic*, **50**, 510–530, 1985.

[Amir, 1997] E. Amir. Machinery for elaborating action – Preliminary Report http://www-formal.stanford.edu/eyal/nmr/machinery-ea.ps. In NRAC-97' and in http://www-formal.stanford.edu/eyal/nmr/machinery-ea.ps, 1997.

[Antoniou, 1997] G. Antoniou. *Nonmonotonic Reasoning*. MIT Press, Cambridge, Massachusetts, 1997.

[Brachman and Levesque, 1985] R. Brachman and H. Levesque. *Readings in Knowledge Representation*. Morgan Kaufmann, 1985.

[Costello, 1997] T. Costello. Beyond minimizing change. In *Proceedings of AAAI-97*, 1997.

[De Raedt, 1992] L. De Raedt. *Interactive Theory Revision: An Inductive Logic Programming Approach*. Academic Press, New York, 1992. De Raedt, L.

[Fagin *et al.*, 1983] R. Fagin, J. D. Ullman and M. Y. Vardi. On the semantics of updates in databases. In *Proceedings of the Second ACM SIGACT-SIGMOD Symposium on Principles of Database Systems*, Atlanta, Georgia. pp. 352–365, 1983.

[Giunchiglia and Walsh, 1992] F. Giunchiglia and T. Walsh. A theory of abstraction. *Artificial Intelligence*, **57**, 323–389, 1992.

[Katsuno and Mendelzon, 1991] H. Katsuno and A. O. Mendelzon. Propositional knowledge base revision and minimal change. *Artificial Intelligence*, **52**, 263–294, 1991.

[Koppel *et al.*, 1994] M. Koppel, R. Feldman and A. M. Segre. Bias-driven revision of logical domain theories. *Journal of Artificial Intelligence Research*, **1**, 1994.

[Lehmann, 1995] D. Lehmann. Belief revision, revised. In *IJCAI-95*, pp. 1534–1540, 1995.

[McCarthy, 1980] J. McCarthy. Circumscription—A Form of Non-Monotonic Reasoning http://www-formal.stanford.edu/jmc/circumscription.html. *Artificial Intelligence*, **13**, 27–39, 1980.

[McCarthy, 1988] J. McCarthy. Mathematical logic in artificial intelligence. *Daedalus*, **117**, 297–311, 1988.

[McCarthy, 1998] John McCarthy. Elaboration Tolerance In *CommonSense '98* and in http://www-formal.stanford.edu/jmc/elaboration.html, 1998.

[Minsky, 1975] M. Minsky. *A Framework for Representing Knowledge*, Winston, 1975.

[Moore, 1987] R. C. Moore. Possible-world semantics for autoepistemic logic. In *Readings in non-monotonic reasoning*, M. Ginsberg, ed. pp. 137–142. Morgan Kaufmann, San Mateo, CA, 1987.

[Nebel, 1991] B. Nebel. Belief revision and default reasoning: syntax-based approaches. In *KR91*, pp. 417–428. Morgan Kaufmann, San Mateo, 1991.

[Reiter, 1980] Raymond Reiter. A logic for default reasoning. *Artificial Intelligence*, **13**, 81–132, 1980.

[Shanahan, 1996] M. P. Shanahan. Robotics and the common sense informatic situation. In *Proceedings ECAI 96*, pp. 684–688, 1996.

[Shoenfield, 1967] J. R. Shoenfield. *Mathematical Logic*. Addison-Wesley, Duke University, 1967.

AIDAN SIMS AND BRAILEY SIMS

ASSESSING THE MINIMALITY OF CHANGE IN BELIEF REVISION: CAPACITIES

1 INTRODUCTION

The process of belief revision [Alchourrón *et al.*, 1985] was developed to model the effect of accepting incoming information into a knowledge base. It can be based on a total preordering of the set of beliefs held by the system. When this ordering relates in a natural way to the semantics of the underlying knowledge base, it is dubbed an epistemic entrenchment ordering [Gärdenfors and Makinson, 1988]. This ranks beliefs in order of the agent's reluctance to give them up. Thus the belief *the sun will rise tomorrow* would be ranked higher than *the universe started with a big bang*. Such an ordering leads to the construction of a unique AGM transformation on the knowledge base to allow for the acceptance of new information; information which may be inconsistent with the current beliefs. This original work was purely theoretical, concerning itself only with one revision. The outcome was a revised set of beliefs, but the question of how those beliefs could be fitted with a "revised" ranking was not addressed. This question is, however, not only theoretically interesting but also vital for implementation since, in that situation, it is necessary to iterate the procedure and so a new epistemic entrenchment needs to be the outcome of each revision.

Later work extended this system to accomodate iterated belief revision, the process of moving under revision from one entrenchment to another being termed a transmutation. Following the lead of earlier work on Bayesian and Jeffrey conditionalisation, and Spohn's ordinal conditional functions [Spohn, 1988], this was effected by allowing new information to be inserted with a rank allocated prior to insertion [Williams, 1994a]. This provided revision operations for ensconcements [Williams, 1994b], which allowed for an actual computer-based implementation of iterated belief revision [Williams, 1995; Williams, 1997a; Williams, 1997b].

Since then, a number of algorithms for determining the set of beliefs to be discarded in the event of a revision have been proposed and implemented with the focus generally either on speed of execution (for example Linear revision [Nebel, 1994], and Adjustment [Williams, 1995]), or intuitiveness of the output (for example Maxi Adjustment [Williams, 1997a]). Typically, the algorithm moves through the ranking until it determines the largest 'cut' in which no inconsistency exists, and then locates a minimal set of beliefs — either in the next rank, or in the rest of the ensconcement — whose removal eliminates inconsistencies.

In every case, the heart of the algorithm lies in the method for deciding on a set of beliefs to discard. Intuitively, this set should be in some sense minimal, but various algorithms have differed considerably as to how this should be interpreted.

M.-A. Williams and H. Rott (eds.), Frontiers in Belief Revision, 163–177.

Qualitatively, a notion of minimality was captured by imposing heuristically plausible constraints on the transformations to be applied. However, little has been done to provide quantative measures of this minimality in this context.

We introduce the notion of capacity for a belief set. In order that a capacity reflects the underlying desire for minimal change, it is tied monotonically to the set-theoretic structure of the knowledge base, as well as to the preference ordering associated to it. The axioms have, however, been kept to a minimum so as to permit as much freedom as possible in the construction of capacities.

Examples showing how capacities may be constructed are presented. A theory of capacities is then developed; in particular some general properties of capacties are examined, and general techniques for constructing new capacities from given ones are explored. We then go on to demonstrate that there is a capacity associated to each epistemic entrenchment which exposes the sense in which the beliefs removed in the corresponding AGM transformation are minimal.

Our final consideration of capacities relates to the problem of simultaneous revision with respect to multiple beliefs. The behaviours of the existing standard belief revision strategies when used to revise with respect to multiple beliefs depend quite heavily on the order in which the new beliefs are added to the system, and require that a position in the ranking for each new belief be provided. While this can be a beneficial aspect of belief revision, it can also be restrictive in that it requires some external system (either user or calling program) to determine where new beliefs should lie in the ranking. Capacities can be used to provide an alternative to these iterated belief revision strategies; one that does not rely on a rank being preassigned to each new belief, and that is not dependent upon the order in which the beliefs are added.

The aim of capacities, then, is to formalise the concept of minimality by describing a set of axioms that circumscribe a family of functions that can be used naturally to identify minimal sets of beliefs.

2 CAPACITIES

2.1 *Definitions*

Before presenting the definition of capacities, we recall the definitions of a number of well-known concepts.

DEFINITION 1. A *theory* is a set T of beliefs (logical sentences) that is closed under the operation of entailment, that is, $A \subseteq T$ and $A \vdash b$ implies $b \in T$. The *theory closure* of a set X of beliefs, denoted $\text{Th}(X)$, is the closure of X under entailment. That is, $\text{Th}(X) := \{y | X \vdash y\}$.

DEFINITION 2. Following [Gärdenfors and Makinson, 1988], an *epistemic entrenchment* is a pair $(T, \leq)$ where T is a theory, and $\leq$ is a total preordering on T in which tautology is ranked strictly higher than any other belief and which is such that, for any $b \in T$, $\text{Th}(\{a \in T | a \geq b\}) \cap \{c \in T | c < b\} = \emptyset$.

REMARK 3. To avoid techinical distractions, we will restrict our attention to finitely representible epistemic entrenchments [Williams, 1994b]. That is, an epistemic entrenchment $(T, \leq)$ in which there are only a finite number of distinct subtheories ('cuts') of the form $C_a := \{b \in T | a \leq b\}$ where $a \in T$, each of which is finitely axiomatisible. Such entrenchments are of prime importance from the point of view of implementation of AGM belief revision. Thus, throughout what follows, epistemic entrenchment should be understood to mean finitely representible epistemic entrenchment.

REMARK 4. In an epistemic entrenchment $(T, \leq)$, it is not uncommon to associate a number in $[0, 1]$ with the beliefs in each of the ranks, where 1 is reserved for tautologies, whilst 0 is reserved for contradictions, and also assigned to non-beliefs; that is, beliefs not in T.

DEFINITION 5. An *entrenchment basis* for a finitely representible epistemic entrenchment $(T, \leq)$ is a finite subset $B \subseteq T$, together with the restriction of $\leq$ to B (denoted $(B, \leq)$), such that for each $a \in T$, $C_a = \mathrm{Th}(B \cap C_a)$. Such bases always exist, and have elsewhere been referred to as ensconcements [Williams, 1994b].

For our purposes, it will be convenient to introduce a more general concept.

DEFINITION 6. A *belief ranking* is a finite set X of beliefs with a total preordering $\leq$. We will refer to such a ranking by the pair $(X, \leq)$.

REMARK 7. It should be noted that there is no requirement that a belief ranking relate to the underlying logical structure of the set X, and so the concept of a belief ranking is more general than that of an entrenchment basis. Thus every entrenchment basis is a belief ranking, but the converse is not, in general, true.

DEFINITION 8. A function $m : \mathcal{P}(X) \to [0, \infty)$ is called a *capacity* on the belief ranking $(X, \leq)$ if for all $A, B \subseteq X$,

a) $m(\emptyset) = 0$;

b) $A \subseteq B \Rightarrow m(A) \leq m(B)$; and

c) $m(A) \leq m((A \setminus \{x\}) \cup \{y\}) \Leftrightarrow x \leq y$ whenever $x \in A$ and $y \notin A$.

REMARK 9. The requirement that $m(\emptyset) = 0$ is not entirely necessary, but it does lead to nicer behaviour. In particular, as we shall see later, it ensures that the complement of the complement of a capacity is, in fact, equal to the original capacity.

REMARK 10. Although we define capacities as functions from $\mathcal{P}(X)$ to $[0, \infty)$, it should be clear that every capacity m is equivalent in every respect to the capacity m' which maps from $\mathcal{P}(X)$ to $[0, 1]$ defined by $m'(A) := m(A)/m(X)$. For this reason, we shall assume that every capacity maps to $[0, 1]$ rather than to $[0, \infty)$, and that $m(X) = 1$ for every capacity m on a belief ranking $(X, \leq)$.

DEFINITION 11. Suppose $(X, \leq)$ is a belief ranking, and define $m : \mathcal{P}(X) \to [0, 1]$ by $m(A) = |A|/|X|$ for every $A \subseteq X$. This will be referred to as *counting measure*, and is useful in the construction of various capacities.

We now give two illustrative examples of capacities.

EXAMPLE 12. Suppose $(X, \leq)$ is a belief ranking, and define a function $r : X \to \mathbb{N}$ by defining $r(x)$ to be the number of distinct ranks below the one containing x. For example, $r(\perp) = 0$. That is, the function r assigns to each belief its rank counted up from the bottom of the belief ranking. We can then define a capacity m by

$$m(A) := \sum_{x \in A} r(x) \Big/ \sum_{x \in X} r(x)$$

Note that this example reduces to the counting measure when there is only one rank in the belief ranking.

EXAMPLE 13. Again suppose $(X, \leq)$ is a belief ranking, and define $r : X \to \mathbb{N}$ as in 12. Then for each $y \in (0, 1]$ we can define a capacity m_y by

$$m_y(A) := \sum_{x \in A} y^{-r(x)} \Big/ \sum_{x \in X} y^{-r(x)}$$

We refer to this set of capacities as the *geometric capacities*, since they are based on a geometric sequence.

2.2 *Capacity Constructions*

Given the definition of capacities, we now begin to investigate some methods for constructing new capacities from old ones. The first of these is the complement of a capacity.

DEFINITION 14. Let $(X, \leq)$ be a belief ranking, and let m be a capacity on $(X, \leq)$. We define the *complement* of m, denoted m^* by

$$m^*(A) := m(X) - m(X \setminus A)$$

for every $A \subseteq X$.

PROPOSITION 15. *Let $(X, \leq)$ be a belief ranking, and let m be a capacity on $(X, \leq)$. Then m^* is also a capacity on $(X, \leq)$.*

Proof.
a) $m^*(\emptyset) = m(X) - m(X \setminus \emptyset) = 0$
b)

$$\begin{aligned} A \subseteq B &\Rightarrow X \setminus B \subseteq X \setminus A \\ &\Rightarrow m(X \setminus B) \leq m(X \setminus A) \\ &\Rightarrow m^*(A) \leq m^*(B) \end{aligned}$$

c) Let $x \in A$ and $y \notin A$ and let $B := (A \setminus \{x\}) \cup \{y\}$. We need $x \leq y \Leftrightarrow m^*(A) \leq m^*(B)$. For this, first suppose $x \leq y$. Then:

$$\begin{aligned} m^*(A) &= m(X) - m(X \setminus A) \\ &\leq m(X) - m(((X \setminus A) \setminus \{y\}) \cup \{x\}) \qquad (y \notin A, x \in A). \\ &= m(X) - m(X \setminus ((A \setminus \{x\}) \cup \{y\})) \\ &= m^*(B) \end{aligned}$$

Now, suppose $m^*(A) \leq m^*(B)$. Then we have:

$$\begin{aligned} m^*(A) \leq m^*(B) &\Rightarrow m(X \setminus A) \geq m(X \setminus B) \\ &\Rightarrow m(X \setminus A) \geq m(X \setminus ((A \setminus \{x\}) \cup \{y\})) \\ &\Rightarrow m(X \setminus A) \geq m(((X \setminus A) \setminus \{y\}) \cup \{x\}) \\ &\Rightarrow x \leq y \qquad \text{(since } m \text{ is a capacity)} \end{aligned}$$

■

PROPOSITION 16. *Let* $(X, \leq)$ *be a belief ranking, and let* m *be a capacity on* $(X, \leq)$. *Then* $(m^*)^* = m$.

Proof.

$$\begin{aligned} (m^*)^*(A) &= m^*(X) - m^*(X \setminus A) \\ &= (m(X) - m(\emptyset)) - (m(X) - m(X \setminus (X \setminus A))) \\ &= m(A) - m(\emptyset) \\ &= m(A) \text{ for all } A \subseteq X \end{aligned}$$

■

REMARK 17. Philosophically, rather than removing a set A of minimal capacity to acheive minimal change, one might argue for the removal of a set A' whose complement has maximal capacity. 15 and 16 taken in conjunction with 14 show that there is no essential difference; it is really a choice between the use of two well-defined capacities. The latter strategy applied to the capacity m is identical to the first strategy applied to m^* and vice-versa.

In fact, the question of whether the complement of a capacity is necessary at all is not an obvious one. One would like to discover that every capacity m has the property that the ranking of the sets of beliefs given by m^* is the same as that given by m. We call capacities for which this is true *complementary*. It is not, however, the case that all capacities are complementary, though we do get the following result in the case where there is a minimum element.

LEMMA 18. *Let* $(X, \leq)$ *be a belief ranking, and* m *a capacity on* $(X, \leq)$. *If* $\emptyset \subset A \subseteq X$ *is such that* $m(A) < m(B)$ for all $B \in \mathcal{P}(X) \setminus \{A\}$, *then* $m(X \setminus A) \geq m(C)$ for all $C \subset X$.

Proof. Clearly $|A| = 1$ or else every singleton set that is a subset of A is at least as small as A by axiom (a). Hence, $A = \{a\}$ for some $a \in X$. Now suppose that $C \subset X$. If $C \neq X \setminus A$, then clearly there is a set $C' \neq X \setminus A$ with $|C'| = |X| - 1$ and $C \subseteq C'$, so that, in particular, $m(C) \leq m(C')$. But now, $C' = X \setminus \{c\}$ for some $c \in X$ so $a \in C'$, and hence $C' = (X \setminus \{c\}) \cup \{a\}$.

Then,

$$\begin{aligned} m(X \setminus A) &= m(X \setminus \{a\}) \\ &\geq m(((X \setminus \{a\}) \setminus \{c\}) \cup \{a\}), \quad \text{by axiom (b)} \\ &= m(X \setminus \{c\}) \\ &= m(C') \\ &\geq m(C) \end{aligned}$$

as required. But if $C = X \setminus A$ the result is trivially true. ■

COROLLARY 19. *Let* $(X, \leq)$ *be a belief ranking, and* m *a capacity on* $(X, \leq)$. *If* $A \subseteq X$ *is such that* $m(A) > m(B)$ for all $B \in \mathcal{P}(X) \setminus \{A\}$ *then* $m(X \setminus A) \leq m(C)$ for all $C \subseteq X$.

Proof. Since A is the maximum under m we know by the definition of the complement capacity that $X \setminus A$ is the minimum under m^*. Applying 18 to the complement capacity, this tells us that A is maximal under m^*, and again by the definition of m^*, this implies that $X \setminus A$ is minimal under m. ■

However, as the following example demonstrates, m and m^* can behave quite differently when there are no single maximum or minimum beliefs.

EXAMPLE 20. Define m on $\mathcal{P}(\{a, b, c, d\})$ by:

$$\begin{aligned} &m(\emptyset) = 0.0 \\ &m(\{a\}) = m(\{b\}) = m(\{a, b\}) = 0.1 \\ &m(\{c\}) = m(\{d\}) = m(\{a, c\}) \\ &\quad = m(\{a, d\}) = m(\{b, c\}) = m(\{b, d\}) = 0.2 \\ &m(\{c, d\}) = 0.3 \\ &m(\{a, b, c\}) = m(\{a, b, d\}) = 0.4 \\ &m(\{a, c, d\}) = m(\{b, c, d\}) = 0.5 \\ &m(\{a, b, c, d\}) = 1.0 \end{aligned}$$

Note that the example is not without substance: $\{a, b, c, d\}$, with the ordering that arises from the capacities of the singleton sets in 20, is an entrenchment basis.

REMARK 21. We see in 20 that whilst $\{a, b\}$ is minimal, $X \setminus \{a, b\} = \{c, d\}$ is not maximal, and furthermore that m and m^* rank the subsets of X differently in the sense that (for example) $m(\{a, b\}) = 0.1 < m(\{c\}) = 0.2$ but $m^*(\{a, b\}) = 0.7 > m^*(\{c\}) = 0.6$.

It would be rather nice to know precisely when a capacity is complementary. A fairly obvious sufficient condition presents itself:

LEMMA 22. *Let m be a capacity on a belief ranking $(X, \leq)$. If there is a $k \in \mathbb{R}$ so that*

$$m(A) + m(X \setminus A) = k, \text{ for all } A \subseteq X,$$

then m is equivalent to m^* in the sense that $m(A) \leq m(B)$ if and only if $m^*(A) \leq m^*(B)$ for all $A, B \subseteq X$.

Proof. Suppose $m(A) + m(X \setminus A) = k \; \forall A \subseteq X$. Then let $k' = k - m(X)$, and we have

$$\begin{aligned} m(A) \leq m(B) &\Leftrightarrow m(A) - k' \leq m(B) - k' \\ &\Leftrightarrow m(X \setminus A) \geq m(X \setminus B) \\ &\Leftrightarrow m(X) - m(X \setminus A) \leq m(X) - m(X \setminus B) \\ &\Leftrightarrow m^*(A) \leq m^*(B) \end{aligned}$$

■

REMARK 23. It is clear that any additive capacity satisfies the hypotheses of 22, so the existence of non-complementary capacities (20) demonstrates that there exist capacities that are not equivalent to any additive capacity. Consequently the notion of a capacity is more general than that of a measure.

We now consider combinations of two capacities on the same belief ranking that allow us to combine the characteristics of pairs of existing capacities on a set of beliefs, as well as allowing us to construct a complementary capacity from any capacity at all. Before doing this, we first demonstrate that the set of capacities on a given belief ranking is convex.

LEMMA 24. *Let $(X, \leq)$ be a belief ranking, and suppose that m and m' are both capacities on $(X, \leq)$. Then for each $\lambda \in [0, 1]$ the sum $\lambda m + (1 - \lambda)m'$ defined on X by $(\lambda m + (1 - \lambda)m')(A) = \lambda m(A) + (1 - \lambda)m'(A)$ is also a capacity.*

Proof. It is clear that $\lambda m + (1 - \lambda)m'$ is 1 at X, 0 at $\emptyset$, and takes values between these two extremes. Since the remaining axioms, (b) and (c), for a capacity hold if and only if they hold for a positive multiple of the capacity, it is sufficient to show that (b) and (c) hold for the pointwise sum of any two capacities. For this, let m and m' be any two capacities on $(X, \leq)$.

b)

$$\begin{aligned} A \subseteq B &\Rightarrow m(A) \leq m(B) \wedge m'(A) \leq m'(B) \qquad (m, m' \text{ capacities}) \\ &\Rightarrow m(A) + m'(A) \leq m(B) + m'(B) \end{aligned}$$

c) Let $x \in A$ and $y \notin A$ and let $B := (A \setminus \{x\}) \cup \{y\}$. We need $x \leq y \Leftrightarrow m(A) + m'(A) \leq m(B) + m'(B)$. For this, first suppose $x \leq y$. Then $m(A) \leq m(B)$ since m is a capacity, and $m'(A) \leq m'(B)$ since m' is a capacity. Thus $m(A) + m'(A) \leq m(B) + m'(B)$.

Now, suppose $(m + m')(A) \leq (m + m')(B)$. Then $m(A) + m'(A) \leq m(B) + m'(B)$, so either $m(A) \leq m(B)$ or $m'(A) \leq m'(B)$. In either case, it follows that $x \leq y$ since m and m' are capacities. ■

We now move on to the capacity sum we were aiming for.

DEFINITION 25. Let m and m' be capacities on a belief ranking $(X, \leq)$. We define the *sum capacity* of m and m' by

$$(m \oplus m')(A) := \frac{m(A) + m'(A)}{2}, \qquad \text{for all } A \subseteq X.$$

As an immediate consequence of 24, we have

COROLLARY 26. *Let $(X, \leq)$ be a belief ranking, and suppose that m and m' are both capacities on $(X, \leq)$. Then the sum capacity $m \oplus m'$ of m and m' is a capacity.*

REMARK 27. The division by two in the above is not necessary to define the capacity sum sensibly; the simple pointwise sum of the two functions would do equally well. The only reason for dividing by two is to conform to our convention that capacities map $\mathcal{P}(X)$ to $[0, 1]$ and that $m(X) = 1$.

Now, given any capacity m on a belief ranking, we can construct a complementary capacity from it as follows:

LEMMA 28. *Let $(X, \leq)$ be a belief ranking, and m a capacity on $(X, \leq)$. Then the sum capacity $m \oplus m^*$ is a complementary capacity.*

Proof.

$$\begin{aligned} (m \oplus m^*)(A) + (m \oplus m^*)(X \setminus A) &= \frac{1}{2}((m(A) + m^*(A)) \\ &\quad + (m(X \setminus A) + m^*(X \setminus A)) \\ &= \frac{1}{2}((m(A) + m(X) - m(X \setminus A)) \\ &\quad + (m(X \setminus A) + m(X) \\ &\quad - m(X \setminus (X \setminus A)))) \end{aligned}$$

$$
\begin{aligned}
&= \frac{1}{2}(2m(X)) \\
&= m(X) \\
&= 1
\end{aligned}
$$

Hence, by 22 with $k = 1$ we have $(m \oplus m^*)$ a complementary capacity. ■

REMARK 29. Note that the capacity $m \oplus m^*$ may have desirable features in so far as minimising with respect to it would, in some sense, represent a balance between the two strategies discussed in 17.

Next we introduce the *extension capacity* which we use to extend an existing capacity to a slightly larger belief ranking. This capacity will be used in our development of a belief revision strategy based on capacities.

DEFINITION 30. Let m be a capacity on a belief ranking $(X, \leq)$, and suppose $a \notin X$. Suppose that $(X \cup \{a\}, \leq_a)$ is also a belief ranking, with $\leq_a$ extending $\leq$ on X. Then we define the *extension capacity* m_a on $(X \cup \{a\}, \leq_a)$ by

$$
m_a(A) := \begin{cases} \max\limits_{b \leq_a a}(\max\{m(B) | B \subseteq X, (B \setminus \{b\}) \subseteq (A \setminus \{a\})\}) \text{ if } a \in A \\ m(A) \text{ if } a \notin A \end{cases}.
$$

LEMMA 31. *Let m be a capacity on a belief ranking $(X, \leq)$, and suppose $a \notin X$. Suppose that $(X \cup \{a\}, \leq_a)$ is also a belief ranking, with $\leq_a$ extending $\leq$ on X. Then m_a defined above is a capacity on $(X \cup \{a\}, \leq_a)$ extending m.*

Proof. It is clear that m_a agrees with m on X, so that it is, in fact, an extension of m to $X \cup \{a\}$.

a) $m_a(\emptyset) = m(\emptyset) = 0$

b) Suppose $A \subseteq B$. Then $C \subseteq A \Rightarrow C \subseteq B$ (and specifically, $A \setminus \{x\} \subseteq B \setminus \{x\}$ for all $x \in X$), so that

$$
\begin{aligned}
m_a(A) &= max\{m(C) \mid C \subseteq (A \setminus \{a\})\} \\
&\leq max\{m(C) \mid C \subseteq (B \setminus \{a\})\} \\
&= m_a(B)
\end{aligned}
$$

c) Suppose $x \in A$, $y \notin A$, and let $B := (A \setminus \{x\}) \cup \{y\}$. In the case where $x \neq a$ and $y \neq a$ it is clear that the result follows from the definition of m_a and the fact that m is a capacity. Suppose now that $x = a$. Then

$$
\begin{aligned}
x \leq_a y &\Rightarrow m(B) \geq \max\{m((A \setminus \{a\}) \cup \{c\}) \mid c \leq_a a\} \\
&\Rightarrow m_a(B) \geq m_a(A)
\end{aligned}
$$

and

$$\begin{aligned} m_a(B) \le m_a(A) \quad &\Rightarrow \quad m_a(B) \le \max\{m(C) \mid \exists\, c \le_a a \; s.t. \\ &\qquad\qquad A = (C \setminus \{c\}) \cup \{a\}\} \\ &\Rightarrow \quad m((A \setminus \{a\}) \cup \{y\}) \le m((A \setminus \{a\}) \cup \{c\}), \\ &\qquad\qquad \text{(for some } c \le_a a) \\ &\Rightarrow \quad y \le \max\{c \le_a a \mid A = (C \setminus \{c\}) \cup \{a\}\} \end{aligned}$$

Finally, suppose $y = a$ and $x \neq a$. Then $x \le_a y$ implies that A is one of the sets the maximum capacity of which is assigned to B by m_a, so $m_a(B) \ge m_a(A)$. On the other hand, $m_a(A) = m(A)$, so

$$\begin{aligned} m_a(A) \le m_a(B) \quad &\Rightarrow \quad m(A) \le \max\{m((B \setminus \{a\}) \cup \{c\}) \mid c \le_a a\} \\ &\Rightarrow \quad m(A) \le m((B \setminus \{a\}) \cup \{c\}) \text{ for some } c \le_a a \\ &\Rightarrow \quad m((B \setminus \{a\}) \cup \{x\}) \le m((B \setminus \{a\}) \cup \{c\}) \\ &\Rightarrow \quad x \le c \qquad \text{(since } m \text{ is a capacity)} \\ &\Rightarrow \quad x \le_a a \qquad \text{by the definition of } \le_a . \end{aligned}$$

■

Finally, we introduce the *substitution capacity* on a belief ranking X with regard to a subset R of X and a belief $a \notin X$.

DEFINITION 32. Suppose that $(X, \le)$ is a belief ranking, that m is a capacity on X, that $R \subseteq X$ and that $a \notin X$. Then we define the *substitution capacity* $m_{a,R}$ on $(X \setminus R) \cup \{a\}$ via the extension capacity where a is ranked in $(X \setminus R) \cup \{a\}$ in such a way that $a \le b$ if and only if $m(R) \le m(\{b\})$ and $a \ge b$ if and only if $m(R) \ge m(\{b\})$.

LEMMA 33. *For any set $R \subseteq X$ and for any belief $a \in X$ the substitution capacity $m_{a,R}$ is a capacity.*

Proof. The proof is an immediate consequence of the fact that the new ranking is, in fact, a belief ranking, and 31. ■

3 CAPACITY BASED REVISION

3.1

Suppose that we are given an entrenchment basis $(X, \le)$, a belief a, and a position we would like to assign a relative to the elements of X in $X \cup \{a\}$. This gives rise to a total ordering $\le_a$ on $X \cup \{a\}$. Then to perform a capacity belief revision with a on $(X, \le)$ we begin by testing whether $a \in X$. If so, we do nothing.

If not, we must insert a into the belief ranking, and then find the minimal set of beliefs not containing a whose removal will eliminate any contradictions in the new belief ranking. To do this, of course, we require a capacity on the belief ranking $(X \cup \{a\}, \leq_a)$. If such a capacity already exists, we use this. If we do not already have a capacity on $(X \cup \{a\}, \leq_a)$, however, we can easily generate one, namely the extension m_a of m to $(X \cup \{a\}, \leq_a)$ as defined in 30.

We now select the subset $M \subseteq X$ (so $a \notin M$) such that $\bot \notin Th(X \setminus M)$ that is minimal under m_a. This set is removed, giving a new belief ranking $((X \cup \{a\}) \setminus M, \leq_a)$. To convert the belief ranking into an entrenchment, we move any beliefs that are ranked higher than a and which would be removed by a revision with $\neg a$ down to the same rank as a, and move any beliefs ranked below a that can now be proved from higher ranked beliefs up to the highest rank at which they can be proved. This done, we have a new ranking, which is clearly an epistemic entrenchment in which a is ranked as required.

Note that the smallest set may be non-unique — there may be more than one such set. Given that there is no way to distinguish them, a skeptical policy would consider only the union of equally-ranked sets for removal. Another policy is to choose randomly between them. A third is to maintain all equally acceptable adjustments until further information is introduced which allows a distinction to be made. Only the skeptical policy is discussed in this paper.

Under the skeptical policy, when a search reveals that several sets tie for minimal capacity, the removal of any particular one of them is not allowed; the only set derived from them which could, in keeping with the policy, be removed is their union. Their union may, however, have a capacity larger than that of some other set whose removal is allowable under the policy. Thus, the tied minimal sets are removed from consideration, and the search is reiterated on the sets that remain — one of which is obviously the union of the excluded tied sets.

Operation of the algorithm is made more clear by the following example. It should, however, be noted that considerable searching among the elements of the power set of B is required, but has been suppressed.

EXAMPLE 34. Consider the geometric capacity (13) where $y = \frac{1}{2}$ acting on the entrenchment basis B =

$$\begin{gathered}\neg\alpha \\ \epsilon \to \alpha \\ \beta \to \alpha, \gamma \to \beta, \gamma \\ \gamma \to \alpha, \delta \to \alpha \\ \delta \\ \kappa \to \epsilon, \kappa\end{gathered}$$

Where the beliefs on a given line are ranked higher than those on the line below. We begin by determining the sets which generate contradictions:

$$\{\neg\alpha, \beta \to \alpha, \gamma \to \beta, \gamma\}, \{\neg\alpha, \gamma, \gamma \to \alpha\}, \{\neg\alpha, \delta \to \alpha, \delta\},$$

$$\{\neg\alpha, \epsilon \to \alpha\ , \kappa \to \epsilon, \kappa\}.$$

Clearly we need to find a set of beliefs of minimal capacity containing at least one belief from each of the above sets. It is readily checked that there are two sets meeting this requirement ($\{\gamma, \delta, \kappa \rightarrow \epsilon\}, \{\gamma, \delta, \kappa\}$). Each has a capacity of $\frac{22}{178}$, so they are indistinguishable. Hence we can only consider their union, $\{\gamma, \delta, \kappa \rightarrow \epsilon, \kappa\}$ for removal. Comparing it to the next best set (one of $\{\gamma, \delta \rightarrow \alpha, \kappa \rightarrow \epsilon\}, \{\gamma, \delta \rightarrow \alpha, \kappa\}$, each with capacity $\frac{26}{178}$), we note that its capacity $\frac{24}{178}$ is now uniquely minimal amongst those sets left under consideration, so we remove it. The revised entrenchment basis is:

$$\begin{gathered}\neg\alpha \\ \epsilon \rightarrow \alpha \\ \beta \rightarrow \alpha, \gamma \rightarrow \beta \\ \gamma \rightarrow \alpha, \delta \rightarrow \alpha\end{gathered}$$

4 AGM REVISION FROM A CAPACITY

4.1

To simulate the AGM entrenchment construction [Gärdenfors and Makinson, 1988] of a theory via capacities, we show how to construct an appropriate capacity on an entrenchment basis. Revising the basis by minimising with respect to this capacity implements revision of the basis, yeilding a new basis whose theory closure is the AGM revision of the initial basis' theory closure [Williams, 1994b; Williams, 1995]. To acheive this we merely need to construct a capacity which throws away any and all beliefs which are ranked at or below the first point in the belief ranking at which a contradiction will follow from the incoming information. This is shown to be equivalent to base revision in [Williams, 1994b]. The appropriate capacity is the one defined as follows:

DEFINITION 35. Let $(X, \leq)$ be a belief ranking. Define a funtion $f : X \rightarrow \{0, 1\}$ by

$$f(x) := \begin{cases} 0 \text{ if } \{y \in X | x \leq y\} \Rightarrow \bot \\ 1 \text{ otherwise} \end{cases}$$

Then we define the *AGM-capacity* by

$$m_{AGM}(A) := \sum_{y \in A} f(y) / \sum_{y \in X} f(y).$$

LEMMA 36. *m_{AGM} is a capacity on $(X, \leq)$.*

Proof. a)

$$\begin{aligned} m_{AGM}(\emptyset) &= \sum_{y \in \emptyset} f(y) / \sum_{y \in X} f(y) \\ &= 0 \end{aligned}$$

b) is trivial as we are taking a sum over a smaller set, and c) is trivial because the capacity is defined additively. ∎

THEOREM 37. *Let a be a belief and let $(T, \leq)$ be a finitely representible epistemic entrenchment. If $(X, \leq)$ is an entrenchment basis for $(T, \leq)$, then the theory closure of the AGM-capacity belief revision with a of $(X, \leq)$ is the same as the standard AGM revision (with a on T) based on the entrenchment construction.*

Proof. In view of the above discussion, it is sufficient to show that the beliefs removed from X are precisely those that are ranked at or below the first point in the ranking at which a contradiction follows from the inclusion of the belief to be incorporated.

Clearly if all beliefs x such that $m_{AGM}(x) = 0$ are removed, then the belief ranking will become consistent. No less than all of them will be removed because they are indistinguishable. On the other hand, no other beliefs will be selected for removal because doing so would necessarily increase the capacity of the removed set to at least 1. Consequently the set of such beliefs is exactly the set removed, as required. ∎

5 MEASURE BASED TRANSMUTATION

It has been noted that, in some situations, the fact that a rank needs to be provided for each new belief can be a drawback to the methodology of standard belief revision. Another drawback is the fact that only revision with a single belief at a time is well-defined.

Capacities provide a method for avoiding the first of these difficulties using substitution capacities (32) to iterate the transmutation process on a belief ranking. At the nth step, we progress from a belief ranking $(X_n, \leq_n)$ with a capacity m_n to a new belief ranking $(X_{n+1}, \leq_{n+1})$ and a capacity m_{n+1} which are all defined as in definition 32 with $R \subseteq X_n$ the subset that is minimal (in the sense dictated by the skeptical policy) with respect to m_n subject to $\neg a_n \notin Th(X_n \setminus R_n)$. It is clear that at each step we are left with a belief ranking and a capacity, and that we can iterate for as many beliefs as required.

Furthermore, if an entrenchment is to be maintained throughout the iteration, it should be clear that at each step we can use the current capacity to determine the smallest set of beliefs that needs to be moved up to the same ranking as a to maintain the entrenchment property (that is, the analagous procedure to that employed in 3).

Capacities also allow us to deal with the second problem in one of two ways: the first is to take the minimum of $m_n(R_n)$, over all permutations of the finite set A of beliefs to be inserted, as the revision to accept. The second is simply find the set $R \subseteq X$ that is minimal with respect to m subject to $Th(X \setminus R) \cap \{\neg a : a \in A\} = \emptyset$. This second solution, however, does not give a belief ranking on the new set, but it does allow us instead to avoid the iteration by revising with all the required beliefs at once.

6 DISCUSSION

This paper defines capacities, a family of functions that provide a general method for capturing the principle of minimal change. Some preliminary results concerning the behaviour of capacities were presented, and a capacity that can be used to implement a standard AGM revision based on the entrenchment construction [Gärdenfors and Makinson, 1988] was introduced. A capacity-based method of iterating transmutations on a belief ranking, or indeed, an entrenchment basis, to incorporate new beliefs in such a way that a rank for each new belief need not be provided was also outlined, as was a method for revising to accept a set of beliefs rather than an individual belief.

Since we have been concerned with transmutations on entrenchment bases, we have restricted ourselves to finite belief sets. However, it is clear that much of the theory extends to the case of an infinite belief set with an infinite number of distinct ranks provided that convergence of the appropriate sums is accounted for.

Future work will look at capacity transmutations that correspond to other existing strategies for nonmonotonic reasoning [Brewka, 1989] and belief revision [Nebel, 1989; Williams, 1994a; Williams, 1997a], will determine the relationship between the operators defined by capacity transmutations and the AGM rationality postulates [Alchourrón *et al.*, 1985], and will investigate topologies on the set of capacities of a belief ranking $(X, \leq)$ and attempt to identify its extreme points; that is, fundamental generating sets of capacities.

ACKNOWLEDGEMENTS

The authors wish to thank Dr. Williams for a number of very insightful discussions regarding the material, and the subject of Belief Revision in general.

The authors are also grateful to the referees for drawing to our attention a number of points which needed clarification; in particular, and oversight in the construction of 20. As a result of suggestions made, we feel that a considerable improvement in the exposition has been achieved.

Finally, the authors would like to acknowledge the contributions of Steven Kucera in the early genesis of the idea of a capacity.

Aidan Sims
School of Management, Newcastle University, Australia.

Brailey Sims
Department of Mathematics, Newcastle University, Australia.

REFERENCES

[Alchourrón *et al.*, 1985] C. Alchourrón, P. Gärdenfors and D. Makinson, On the logic of theory change: partial meet functions for contraction and revision, *Journal of Symbolic Logic*, **50**, 510–530, 1985.

[Brewka, 1989] G. Brewka. Preferred subtheories: an extended logical framework for default reasoning , In *Proceedings of the International Joint Conference on Artificial Intelligence*, pp. 1043–1048, 1989.

[Gärdenfors and Makinson, 1988] P. Gärdenfors and D. and Makinson. Revisions of knowledge systems using epistemic entrenchment. In *Proceedings of the Second Conference on Theoretical Aspects of Reasoning about Knowledge*, pp. 83–96, 1988.

[Nebel, 1989] B. Nebel. A knowledge level analysis of belief revision. In *Principles of Knowledge Representation and Reasoning: Proceedings of the First International Conference*, R. Brachman, H. Levesque and R. Reiter, eds. pp. 301–311. Morgan Kaufmann, San Mateo, CA, 1989.

[Nebel, 1994] B. Nebel. Base revision operations and schemes: semantics, representation, and complexity. In *Proceedings of the European Conference on Artificial Intelligence*, pp. 341–345. John Wiley and Sons, 1994.

[Spohn, 1988] W. Spohn. Ordinal conditional functions: a dynamic theory of epistemic states. In *Causation in Decision, Belief Change, and Statistics II*, W. L. Harper and B. Skyrms, eds. pp. 105–134. Kluwver Academic Publishers, 1988.

[Williams, 1994a] M. A. Williams. Transmutations of knowledge systems. In *Principles of Knowledge Representation and Reasoning: Proceedings of the Fourth International Conference*, J. Doyle, E. Sandewall and P. Torasso, es. pp. 619–629. Morgan Kaufmann, San Mateo , CA, 1994.

[Williams, 1994b] M. A. Williams. On the logic of theory base change. In *Logics in Artificial Intelligence*, C. MacNish, D. Pearce and L. M. Pereira, eds. pp. 86–105. LNCS No 835, Springer Verlag, 1994.

[Williams, 1995] M. A. Williams. Iterated theory base change: a computational model. In *Proceedings of the Fourteenth International Joint Conference on Artificial Intelligence*, Montréal, pp. 1541–1550, 1995.

[Williams, 1997a] M. A. Williams. Anytime belief revision. In *Proceedings of the International Joint Conference on Artificial Intelligence*, pp. 74–79. Morgan Kaufmann, 1997.

[Williams, 1997b] M. A. Williams. Implementing belief revision. In *Nonmonotonic Reasoning*, G. Antoniou, ed. MIT Press 1997.

JAMES P. DELGRANDE

A MINIMAL MODELLING FOR SUCCESSFUL KNOWLEDGE BASE REVISION

1 INTRODUCTION

A fundamental type of belief change is that of *belief revision* wherein an agent changes its beliefs given new information. The work of Alchourrón, Gärdenfors, and Makinson [1985; 1988] (called the *AGM approach*) has provided a very well-known and successful approach to revision. In this approach, a belief state is represented as a *belief set*, or a set of sentences closed under the consequence operator of some logic. Revision is modelled as a function taking a belief set and a sentence into a belief set such that certain postulates are satisfied. These postulates provide *rationality criteria* bounding the properties of any revision function. There have been various modellings of these postulates, including that of the *epistemic entrenchment* of sentences in a language [Gärdenfors and Makinson, 1988]. In this paper we will be most concerned with a modelling of revision, due to Adam Grove [1988], that is based on Lewis' *system of spheres* semantics for counterfactuals [Lewis, 1973].

In this paper I am concerned with fundamental notions of belief revision. The question addressed is a familiar one: given a knowledge base and sentence by which the knowledge base is to be revised, what can we say about the revised knowledge base? Two assumptions are made. First I assume that revision will be *successful*, so that after a belief set is revised by a sentence, that sentence is believed in the resulting belief set(s). While the AGM postulates (see the next section) require that revision be successful, it may be argued that this need not necessarily be the case. For example, one could envisage revision by a sentence whose credibility is less than any sentence in the belief set; in such a case revision might leave the belief set unchanged. A counter to this argument is that whether or not a sentence is to be accepted in a knowledge base is independent of revision: having decided that a sentence should be accepted, the problem of revision then is concerned with the (successful) incorporation of this sentence. Second, I assume that revision is based on a notion of *similarity* among knowledge bases. Thus if a knowledge base I is revised by sentence α, then the revision should, in some fashion or another, be the knowledge base most similar to I in which α is believed. This essentially reduces the notion of revision, in large part, to that of similarity between knowledge bases.

Clearly, there is not a great deal that can be said in general about similarity between knowledge bases. In the approach presented here, it is assumed that a knowledge base I has associated with it a (binary) metric of relative similarity to

M.-A. Williams and H. Rott (eds.), Frontiers in Belief Revision, 179–194.

I, and that this metric is a partial preorder. That is, if $\preceq$ is the relative similarity metric associated with I then[1]

1. I is the minimum of $\preceq$.
2. $\preceq$ is reflexive. So $I \preceq I$ for every knowledge base I.
3. $\preceq$ is transitive. So if $I_1 \preceq I_2$ and $I_2 \preceq I_3$ then $I_1 \preceq I_3$.

I assume further, for technical convenience, that $\preceq$ satisfies the Limit Assumption [Lewis, 1973]. That is, for every α there is a least knowledge base or set of knowledge bases in which α is believed.

In this framework, the result of revising I by α is the knowledge base or knowledge bases most like I, or most similar to I, in which α is believed. This arguably is the fundamental intuition underlying revision, that I in some sense be changed as little as possible. Given this modelling, we can ask what postulates are validated by this approach. It proves to be the case that the postulates validated are a subset of the AGM postulates. This isn't surprising, since the modelling given here is a generalisation of that given by Grove, for which there is a correspondence result with the AGM postulates.

In the present approach, revising a consistent knowledge base by a sentence that is itself consistent does not necessarily yield a consistent revised knowledge base. This is reasonable in that, given knowledge base I, there is no a priori reason to assert that the inconsistent knowledge base is more or less similar than other knowledge bases to I. In this instance, one could go further and rule that the inconsistent knowledge base is maximally dissimilar to I, but this would be a condition added on to the base semantics. Also, in the AGM approach, if the sentence α is consistent with a knowledge base I then the revision of I by α is the intersection of I and α. Again this doesn't necessarily hold in the approach presented. Again, arguably this is not unreasonable; while such postulates may be desirable under the assumptions of the AGM approach, for revision in general, a case can be made to not have these postulates. As an example, consider where, in a medical diagnosis program, disease D is very strongly indicated by symptom S_1, but in the presence of S_2 disease D is strongly contraindicated. Given S_1, a doctor, for example, will believe that D is the case: drugs will be prescribed and actions taken based on the belief of D being present. However the subsequent observation of S_2, while consistent with what is accepted, leads to the conclusion of $\neg D$ – i.e. one doesn't simply add S_2 to the knowledge base.

Arguably the approach is *minimal* for a notion of revision founded on similarity among knowledge bases, in that for the postulates that do obtain, all should hold for a successful revision operator based on a notion of similarity. A benefit of this approach then is that it allows a very "fine-grained" investigation of proposed principles underlying belief revision. That is, in this approach distinct notions are, in fact, distinguished. For example, the fact that revision by a consistent (with the

[1]For simplicity I don't have $\preceq$ indexed by I, but leave it understood.

knowledge base) formula doesn't necessarily reduce to expansion illustrates that *this* notion is separate from that of similarity. Consequently the semantics illustrates that in the AGM approach there are a number of distinct (albeit very basic, and perhaps beyond debate) principles composing the base approach. Secondly, the approach is arguably intuitive and plausible, in that it is based on commonsense intuitions regarding revision. By imposing constraints on the semantic theory, additional postulates may be verified. Arguably, such constraints will reflect plausible intuitions concerning revision, and so the approach will help provide insight into different revision operators. Section 2 briefly reviews the AGM approach and the Grove construction. Section 3 presents the approach, while Section 4 is a discussion.

2 BACKGROUND

There are two major ways of abstractly characterizing a belief state. On the one hand, a belief state may be represented as a set of sentences closed under the consequence operator of some logic. Such *belief sets* are employed for example in the postulates of the AGM approach. On the other hand, a belief state can be modelled by a set of complete and consistent descriptions of how the world might be, assuming that the system's beliefs are true. I will refer to this latter characterisation, in terms of *possible worlds*, as a *knowledge base*. This second characterisation is used for example in [Grove, 1988]. Given these precedents, I will use both belief sets (in specifying postulates) and knowledge bases (in the modelling) in this paper. These notions are easily interdefinable. Roughly speaking, for belief state K and knowledge base $|K|$ (where the notation will be made clear later) and for associated consequence and entailment operators $\vdash$ and $\models$, we have

$$\alpha \in K \quad \text{iff} \quad K \vdash \alpha \quad \text{iff} \quad |K| \models \alpha.$$

In any case, it is a truism that belief set from time to time must be *revised* with new information. Since this information may be inconsistent with the original belief set, some of the original beliefs may be retracted. On the other hand, one would want to retain some of the original information. For revision there is no purely logical reason for making one choice rather than another among the sentences to be retracted. Hence from a logical view there may be several ways of specifying a revision $K\dot{+}\alpha$. However, general properties of a revision function can be investigated. In the approach of Alchourrón, Gärdenfors, and Makinson, standards for revision functions are given by various *rationality postulates*. The goal is to describe belief revision at the *knowledge level*, that is on an abstract level, independent of how beliefs are represented and manipulated. As mentioned above, belief states are modelled by sets of sentences closed under the logical consequence operator of some logic in some language L, where the logic includes classical propositional logic. Thus K can be seen as a partial theory of the world.

Define $Cn(\Gamma)$ as the set of logical consequences of a set of sentences Γ, i.e. $Cn(\Gamma) = \{\alpha \in L \mid \Gamma \vdash \alpha\}$. $K + \alpha$ abbreviates $Cn(K \cup \{\alpha\})$. $K_\perp$ is used for the inconsistent KB (i.e. $K_\perp = L$). $\mathcal{T}$ is the set of all belief sets. In the AGM approach, a revision function $\dot{+}$ is a function from $\mathcal{T} \times L$ to $\mathcal{T}$ satisfying the following postulates.

($K\dot{+}1$) For any sentence α and belief set K, $K\dot{+}\alpha$ is a belief set.

($K\dot{+}2$) $\alpha \in K\dot{+}\alpha$.

($K\dot{+}3$) $K\dot{+}\alpha \subseteq K + \alpha$.

($K\dot{+}4$) If $\neg\alpha \notin K$, then $K + \alpha \subseteq K\dot{+}\alpha$.

($K\dot{+}5$) $K\dot{+}\alpha = K_\perp$ iff $\vdash \neg\alpha$.

($K\dot{+}6$) If $\alpha \equiv \beta$, then $K\dot{+}\alpha = K\dot{+}\beta$.

($K\dot{+}7$) $K\dot{+}(\alpha \wedge \beta) \subseteq (K\dot{+}\alpha) + \beta$.

($K\dot{+}8$) If $\neg\beta \notin K\dot{+}\alpha$, then $(K\dot{+}\alpha) + \beta \subseteq K\dot{+}(\alpha \wedge \beta)$.

In [Grove, 1988] a modelling of these postulates is given based on a *system of spheres*. A *maximal consistent set of sentences* (cf. [Hughes and Cresswell, 1984] for example) is a set of sentences that is *maximal* (and so α or $\neg\alpha$ is in such a set for every $\alpha \in L$) and *consistent* (in the logic underlying the knowledge base). M_L is the set of all maximal consistent sets of sentences of L. Intuitively M_L can be thought of as corresponding to an interpretation in the language, or to a complete possible state of affairs, or possible world. Define $|\alpha| = \{I \in M_L \mid \alpha \in I\}$ with the obvious extension for sets of sentences.

DEFINITION 1 ([Grove, 1988]). A set of subsets $\mathcal{S}$ of M_L is a system of spheres centred on X where $X \subseteq M_L$ if it satisfies the conditions:

S1 $\mathcal{S}$ is *totally ordered* by $\subseteq$: for every $I, J \in \mathcal{S}$, either $I \subseteq J$ or $J \subseteq I$.

S2 X is the minimum of $\mathcal{S}$ under $\subseteq$: $X \subseteq I$ for every $I \in \mathcal{S}$.

S3 $M_L \in \mathcal{S}$.

S4 If $|\alpha| \neq \emptyset$ then there is a least (wrt $\subseteq$) sphere $c(\alpha)$ such that $c(\alpha) \cap |\alpha| \neq \emptyset$ and $J \cap |\alpha| \neq \emptyset$ implies $c(\alpha) \subseteq J$ for every $J \in \mathcal{S}$.

$f_S(\alpha)$ is defined to pick out the least (if such there be) interpretations containing α; i.e. $f_S(\alpha) = |\alpha| \cap c(\alpha)$.

The principal result is a correspondence between systems of spheres and the AGM postulates:

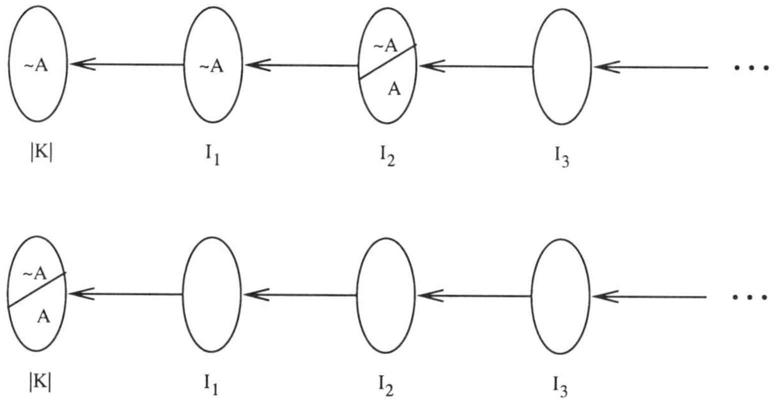

Figure 1. Examples of systems of spheres.

THEOREM 2 ([Grove, 1988]). *Let $\mathcal{S}$ be any system of spheres in M_L centred on $|K|$ for some theory K in $\mathcal{T}$. If one defines for any $\alpha \in L$ that $K\dot{+}\alpha$ is $\cap\{x \in f_S(\alpha)\}$ then the AGM axioms are satisfied.*

THEOREM 3 ([Grove, 1988]). *Let $\dot{+}$ be a function from $\mathcal{T} \times L$ to $\mathcal{T}$ satisfying the AGM postulates. Then for any fixed theory K there is a system of spheres on M_L (call it $\mathcal{S}$) centred on $|K|$ and satisfying $K\dot{+}\alpha = \cap\{x \in f_S(\alpha)\}$ for all $\alpha \in L$.*

For what this means informally, consider where a knowledge base K believes that $\neg A$ is true. A corresponding system of spheres is illustrated in the top part of Figure 1. Each ellipse represents a set of maximal consistent sets of formulas. If we identify I_0 with $|K|$ then for each j, we would have that $\bigcup_{i=0}^{j} I_i$ is a sphere in the set of spheres. A relation $\preceq$ can be defined between maximal consistent sets, such that for $I, J \in \mathcal{S}$ and $i \in I, j \in J$ and $I \subseteq J$ we have $i \preceq j$. So in the figure, for $i, j \in I_k$ we have $i \preceq j$ and $j \preceq i$. The relations $\subseteq$ and $\preceq$ are easily shown to be interdefinable.

The leftmost (or $\preceq$-least) set in the figure represents the original knowledge base, $|K|$. If we revise K by A then informally we look at the nearest set of worlds (or maximal consistent sets) in which there is a world containing A; the revised knowledge base is given by the belief set corresponding to the set of worlds in this set in which A is true. In the top part of the figure, this corresponds to the lower part of I_2, labelled with A. As a special case, if the formula for revision A is consistent with K, then there are maximal consistent sets in $|K|$ containing A. Here we just accept those worlds in $|K|$ containing A; this then corresponds to the expansion of K by A.

3 SIMILARITY ORDERINGS ON KNOWLEDGE BASES

3.1 Similarity and Knowledge Bases

Consider again the first system of spheres in Figure 1. In this approach, worlds are ranked by their closeness to a given knowledge base, or set of worlds, $|K|$. There is a nearest set of worlds, I_1, where in this instance $\neg A$ is true at each world. Each world in this set is a member of the closest set of worlds to $|K|$ that aren't part of $|K|$. However, it is not entirely clear how "close" should be read in this case. In [Grove, 1988] it is suggested that the associated relation $\preceq$ may be interpreted as how "compatible" alternative worlds are with our current beliefs, $|K|$. So in this interpretation, $\preceq$ is a relation between worlds, the specification of which was somehow determined with respect to a set of worlds (viz. $|K|$) and pairs of worlds. In some sense then this notion of "close" rests on that of a "knowledge base" (given as a set of possible worlds).[2]

Consider further the systems of spheres in Figure 1. We have that the $\preceq$-least set of worlds represents the knowledge base under consideration. However, this being the case, the other sets of worlds (labelled I_i) can just as well be interpreted as knowledge bases, in which case a system of spheres model can be interpreted as a linear order on knowledge bases. On this ("unintended") interpretation, revision seems to be a curiously-defined notion. We have a strict order on knowledge bases, and the revision of K by A is given by: we locate the nearest knowledge base that considers A possible, and then restrict that knowledge base so that in the resulting restriction A is believed. This, to be sure, is a weird interpretation of the Grove modelling (and I am not suggesting that it is the appropriate informal interpretation), but it does provide the point of departure for the present approach.

For the present approach, the central semantic intuition is that in revision of K by A, we want to select the *knowledge base* that is the most similar to $|K|$ but in which A is believed. So $\preceq$ will now be a relation among knowledge bases, rather than among worlds. For a knowledge base $|K|$ corresponding to (belief set) K, there is some metric of similarity determining for other knowledge bases their relative similarity to $|K|$. Formal details are given in the next subsection, but essentially I assume that the relation of similarity is reflexive and transitive, and obeys a constraint analogous to the Limit Assumption.

Figure 2 is an example. There is one $\preceq$-least set with just one member, $|K|$. There are other sets of knowledge bases, each set representing knowledge bases that are equally similar to $|K|$. In revising K by A, we look for the knowledge bases most similar to $|K|$ in which A is true. In Figure 2, the set consisting of $|K|$ isn't such a knowledge base, even though A is consistent with $|K|$, since A isn't *believed* in $|K|$. Neither is the next set of knowledge bases, where there are some knowledge bases where $\neg A$ is believed and others where A is consistent. In the next set, there is a subset of the knowledge bases where A is believed and

[2]Note that this point does not hold in Lewis' approach, since in his "official" logic of counterfactuals a system of spheres is centred on a single world.

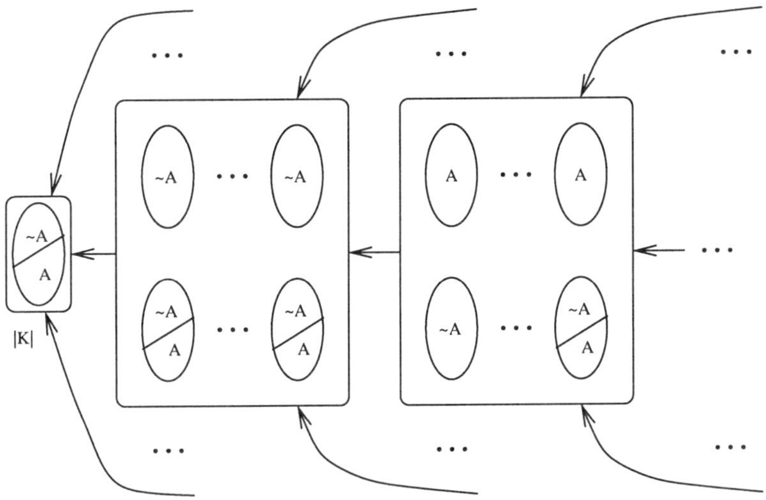

Figure 2. Example of a similarity order on knowledge bases.

a subset where A is possible or where $\neg A$ is believed. As well there are other incommensurable knowledge bases. So the closest knowledge bases where A is believed would constitute the most similar knowledge bases to $|K|$ where A is believed. Since there is nothing to distinguish these knowledge bases, the revision of K by A corresponds to this set of knowledge bases.

This is in contrast with the AGM approach, where a revision function has as value a single knowledge base. However, in the present approach, it seems not unreasonable that a revision function might not return a unique knowledge base. If one wanted a unique knowledge base, then there are several avenues that could be taken. First, one could have some *selection function* that returns a single knowledge base, given a set of equally-similar knowledge bases. For example, this function could select an arbitrary knowledge base, or it might select a knowledge base on the basis of some other criterion, for example, the overall *simplicity* of the knowledge base. Or it might return some canonical representative, for example, the union of the set.

Alternately, one might decide that revision should be defined so that a revision function returns a single knowledge base. Again, there are various alternatives. For example, one could require that the similarity order be antisymmetric, so that if $|K_i| \preceq |K_j|$ then $|K_j| \not\preceq |K_i|$ unless $|K_i| = |K_j|$. Alternately, one could require that the knowledge bases in a set be closed under union, so that if $|K_i|$ and $|K_j|$ were in a set then $|K_i| \cup |K_j|$ would also be in the set; the revision then could return the maximal (in terms of worlds) knowledge base. The point here is that the approach allows such distinctions to be made. In the latter case where one imposes further requirements on the underlying notion of similarity among knowledge bases, presumably one could justify such additional requirements by appeal to intuitions. I return to this topic after the approach has been presented.

3.2 A Minimal Modelling for Revision

Revision is founded on a notion of similarity among knowledge bases, where a knowledge base consists of a set of possible worlds. As is standard in modal logic, truth at a possible world is established via a function from atomic sentences onto sets of possible worlds.

The set of possible worlds is denoted W. The set of knowledge bases $\mathcal{KB}$ is the powerset of W. If $\mathbf{P}$ is the set of atomic sentences, a similarity order model on knowledge bases is given by $M = \langle W, \preceq, P \rangle$ where

1. $P : \mathbf{P} \mapsto 2^W$.

2. $\preceq$ is a function $\preceq: \mathcal{KB} \mapsto 2^{\mathcal{KB} \times \mathcal{KB}}$ with properties specified below.

P is a function that determines what atomic sentences are true at what possible worlds. Truth of the standard propositional connectives at a world is given by the usual recursive definition. We write $w \models \alpha$ is α is true at w in a (understood) similarity order model. For a given similarity order model on knowledge bases, I, I_1, J, ... will denote sets of possible worlds, or knowledge bases, while K, K_1, ... will be used for theories, or (equivalently) belief sets, or deductively closed sets of sentences in some logic.

DEFINITION 4. For belief set K, define $K \vdash \alpha$ iff $\alpha \in K$.

DEFINITION 5.
$|\alpha| = \{w \in W \mid w \models \alpha\}$
$|K| = \{w \in W \mid \text{ for every } \alpha \in K \text{ we have } w \models \alpha\}$

For a knowledge base I the corresponding belief set is defined as follows:

DEFINITION 6. For $I \subseteq W$, define $kb(I) = \{\alpha \in L \mid \text{ for every } w \in I \text{ we have } w \models \alpha\}$

When we come to the revision postulates, it will be convenient to be able to talk about the knowledge bases in which a sentence α is believed:

DEFINITION 7. $KB(\alpha) = \{K \subseteq L \mid \alpha \in K\}$

$\preceq$ is a function that associates a binary relation on sets of knowledge bases with each knowledge base. The intent is that $\preceq$ is a similarity metric on knowledge bases for each knowledge base.[3] Define $I \prec J$ just if $I \preceq J$ but not $J \preceq I$.

DEFINITION 8. M, as given above, is a *similarity order model centred on* $|K|$ for theory K if it satisfies the conditions:

[3]So again $\preceq$ should be indexed by a set of worlds, as should min_M below. For simplicity of notation, and because I do not deal with iterated revision, I leave the index understood.

P1 The relation $\preceq$ is reflexive. That is for every I, we have $I \preceq I$.

P2 The relation $\preceq$ is transitive. That is if $I_i \preceq I_j$ and $I_j \preceq I_k$ then we have $I_i \preceq I_k$.

P3 $|K|$ is the minimum of $\preceq$. That is, for every I, $|K| \preceq I$, and if $I \preceq |K|$ then $I = |K|$.

P4 If $|\alpha| \neq \emptyset$ then there is a knowledge base I such that $I \subseteq |\alpha|$, and for every J where $J \subseteq |\alpha|$, if $J \preceq I$ then $I \preceq J$.

P4 states that if there is a knowledge base where α is believed, then there is a least such knowledge base. This condition is analogous to the condition ($S \leq 3$) of [Grove, 1988] which for that approach expresses the Limit Assumption. Here it also provides a weak connectivity condition: if there is a knowledge base where α is believed, then there is a set of knowledge bases minimal for all knowledge bases in which α is believed. In common with (or: analogous to) Grove, I find this condition troublesome, but am unable to remove it without losing the representation theorem of knowledge base revision given in a similarity order model.

$min_M(\alpha)$ is defined as the least set of knowledge bases in which α is true:

DEFINITION 9. $min_M(\alpha) = \{I \subseteq |\alpha| \mid \text{ for every } J \subseteq |\alpha|, I \preceq J\}$.

Given a system of spheres based on knowledge bases and centred on $|K|$, we can define revision in this framework.

DEFINITION 10. The revision of theory K by α in M is given by: $K \dot{\scriptstyle\square}\, \alpha = kb(min_M(\alpha))$.

Given this semantics we can ask what postulates are validated. For reference I distinguish these postulates in a definition. The numbering is with reference to the corresponding (or most similar) AGM postulates.

DEFINITION 11. The following constitute the set of *KB revision postulates*.

($K \dot{\scriptstyle\square}\, 1$) For any sentence α and belief set K, $K \dot{\scriptstyle\square}\, \alpha$ is a non-empty set of belief sets.

($K \dot{\scriptstyle\square}\, 2$) $K \dot{\scriptstyle\square}\, \alpha \subseteq KB(\alpha)$

($K \dot{\scriptstyle\square}\, 3$) If $K \vdash \alpha$ then $K \dot{\scriptstyle\square}\, \alpha = \{K\}$

($K \dot{\scriptstyle\square}\, 6$) If $\vdash \alpha \equiv \beta$ then $K \dot{\scriptstyle\square}\, \alpha = K \dot{\scriptstyle\square}\, \beta$.

($K \dot{\scriptstyle\square}\, 7$) If $K \dot{\scriptstyle\square}\, \alpha \cap KB(\beta) \neq \emptyset$ then $K \dot{\scriptstyle\square}\, (\alpha \wedge \beta) = K \dot{\scriptstyle\square}\, \alpha \cap KB(\beta)$.

($K \dot{\scriptstyle\square}\, 8$) If $K \dot{\scriptstyle\square}\, \alpha_i \cap KB(\alpha_{i+1}) \neq \emptyset$ for $0 \leq i < n$, and $K \dot{\scriptstyle\square}\, \alpha_n \cap KB(\alpha_0) \neq \emptyset$ then $K \dot{\scriptstyle\square}\, (\alpha_0 \wedge \alpha_n) \subseteq K \dot{\scriptstyle\square}\, \alpha_0$.

The only postulates that are the same as their AGM counterparts are $K \mathbin{\dot{\square}} 2$ and $K \mathbin{\dot{\square}} 6$. In terms of our semantics and knowledge bases, for $K \mathbin{\dot{\square}} 1$, although the result of a revision exists (in that the result isn't the empty set), the revision may result in the inconsistent knowledge base. Moreover, insofar as revision is based on similarity between knowledge bases, and given that there may be equally-similar knowledge bases, revision isn't guaranteed to result in a unique knowledge base.

$K \mathbin{\dot{\square}} 2$ reflects the requirement that the revision be successful. Thus the result of revising a knowledge base K by α is a set of knowledge bases in which α is believed. $K \mathbin{\dot{\square}} 3$ is an obvious weakening of $K \dot{+} 3$; it is difficult to think of a situation where it shouldn't hold. In contrast, it seems feasible that a revision function may not satisfy the AGM postulates $K \dot{+} 3$ and $K \dot{+} 4$, as discussed in the introduction.

$K \dot{+} 5$ is missing here: for $K \mathbin{\dot{\square}} \alpha$ where $\not\vdash \neg\alpha$, there is nothing that forbids the inconsistent knowledge base $K_\perp$ from being the most similar knowledge base to K. Now it may be that one wouldn't want to allow this (and so would wish to adopt a postulate equivalent to $K \dot{+} 5$). Moreover, this would be easy to do; one just needs relegate $K_\perp$ to the most distant set of knowledge bases. However, in so doing, one is obliged to make this assumption explicit, that $K_\perp$ is the most dissimilar knowledge base to K. An advantage of this approach then, as a foundational approach to revision, is that while the semantic basis is intuitive, such additional assumptions must be explicitly made.

$K \mathbin{\dot{\square}} 7$ and $K \mathbin{\dot{\square}} 8$ play (roughly) the same role as the AGM postulates $K \dot{+} 7$ and $K \dot{+} 8$. However, whereas $K \dot{+} 7$ and $K \dot{+} 8$ deal with conjunctions and revision, here $K \mathbin{\dot{\square}} 7$ and $K \mathbin{\dot{\square}} 8$ deal with relations among equally-similar knowledge bases. Some of the results below (notably Theorem 13.2-3) have similarities in form to AGM postulates $K \dot{+} 7$ and $K \dot{+} 8$.

There are a number of reasonable and interesting results following from these postulates. I begin with the following elementary consequences.

THEOREM 12.

1. *If* $\vdash \neg\alpha$ *then* $K \mathbin{\dot{\square}} \alpha = \{K_\perp\}$.
2. $K \mathbin{\dot{\square}} \alpha = K \mathbin{\dot{\square}} \beta$ *iff* $K \mathbin{\dot{\square}} \alpha \subseteq KB(\beta)$ *and* $K \mathbin{\dot{\square}} \beta \subseteq KB(\alpha)$.

The next theorem deals with various possibilities concerning the revision of a knowledge base K by α and the revision of a conjunction with α as conjunct.

THEOREM 13.

1. *If* $K \mathbin{\dot{\square}} \alpha \cap KB(\beta) = \emptyset$ *then* $K \mathbin{\dot{\square}} (\alpha \wedge \beta) \cap K \mathbin{\dot{\square}} \alpha = \emptyset$.
2. *If* $K \mathbin{\dot{\square}} \alpha \cap KB(\beta) \neq \emptyset$ *then* $K \mathbin{\dot{\square}} (\alpha \wedge \beta) \subseteq K \mathbin{\dot{\square}} \alpha$
3. *If* $K \mathbin{\dot{\square}} \alpha \subseteq KB(\beta)$ *then* $K \mathbin{\dot{\square}} (\alpha \wedge \beta) = K \mathbin{\dot{\square}} \alpha$
4. *If* $K \mathbin{\dot{\square}} \alpha \cap K \mathbin{\dot{\square}} \beta \neq \emptyset$ *then* $K \mathbin{\dot{\square}} (\alpha \wedge \beta) = K \mathbin{\dot{\square}} \alpha \cap K \mathbin{\dot{\square}} \beta$

For the first of the following results, if we have $K \dot{\square} \alpha_i \subseteq KB(\alpha_{i+1})$ then the least α_i knowledge bases are no more similar to K than the least α_{i+1} knowledge bases. If we have a chain of such containments that (in the last antecedent condition) eventually forms a "loop", then then revisions are equally similar and, in fact, equal. The remaining three parts of the theorem show that "iterated" conjuncts behave in a reasonable fashion.

THEOREM 14.

1. *If* $K \dot{\square} \alpha_i \subseteq KB(\alpha_{i+1})$ *for* $0 \leq i < n$ *and* $K \dot{\square} \alpha_n \subseteq KB(\alpha_0)$
   then $K \dot{\square} \alpha_i = K \dot{\square} \alpha_{i+1}$ *for* $0 \leq i < n$.
2. *If* $K \dot{\square} \alpha \cap K \dot{\square} (\alpha \wedge \beta) = \emptyset$ *then* $K \dot{\square} \alpha \cap K \dot{\square} (\alpha \wedge \beta \wedge \gamma) = \emptyset$.
3. *If* $K \dot{\square} (\alpha \wedge \beta) \cap K \dot{\square} (\alpha \wedge \beta \wedge \gamma) = \emptyset$ *then* $K \dot{\square} \alpha \cap K \dot{\square} (\alpha \wedge \beta \wedge \gamma) = \emptyset$.
4. *If* $K \dot{\square} (\alpha \wedge \beta \wedge \gamma) \subseteq K \dot{\square} \alpha$ *then* $K \dot{\square} (\alpha \wedge \beta \wedge \gamma) \subseteq K \dot{\square} (\alpha \wedge \beta) \subseteq K \dot{\square} \alpha$.

The next theorem provides weaker versions of the "factoring" result obtained in the AGM postulates (see [Gärdenfors, 1988, p. 57 (3.16)] for example).

THEOREM 15.

1. $K \dot{\square} \alpha \cap K \dot{\square} \beta = \emptyset$ *or*
   $K \dot{\square} (\alpha \wedge \beta) \subseteq K \dot{\square} \alpha$ *or* $K \dot{\square} (\alpha \wedge \beta) \subseteq K \dot{\square} \beta$
2. $K \dot{\square} (\alpha \vee \beta) \cap (K \dot{\square} \alpha \cup K \dot{\square} \beta) = \emptyset$ *or*
   $K \dot{\square} \alpha \subseteq K \dot{\square} (\alpha \vee \beta)$ *or* $K \dot{\square} \beta \subseteq K \dot{\square} (\alpha \vee \beta)$.

We also obtain the following results relating the KB revision postulates to the semantic approach based on similarity among knowledge bases.

THEOREM 16. *Let M be any similarity order model on knowledge bases centred on $|K|$. If one defines $K \dot{\square} \alpha$ to be $kb(min_M(\alpha))$ then the KB revision postulates are satisfied in M.*

THEOREM 17. *Let $\dot{\square}$ be a function from $\mathcal{KB} \times L$ to $2^{\mathcal{KB}}$ satisfying the KB revision postulates. Then for any fixed theory K there is a similarity order model on knowledge bases centred on $|K|$ (call it M) satisfying $K \dot{\square} \alpha = kb(min_M(\alpha))$ for all $\alpha \in L$.*

We can ask what conditions are required to recover other of the AGM postulates. The following results are for the most part straightforward. We define $K \dot{\square} \alpha$ to be $kb(min_M(\alpha))$ throughout.

First, as suggested, we might declare that the inconsistent knowledge base is the most dissimilar of knowledge bases to a consistent knowledge base $|K|$.

THEOREM 18. *Let M be any similarity order model on knowledge bases centred on $|K|$ where $|K| \neq |K_\perp|$ and where we have the condition: For every $|K'| \in \mathcal{KB}$ we have $|K'| \preceq |K_\perp|$. Then the following postulate is satisfied in M:*

($K \dot{\square} 5$) $\vdash \neg\alpha$ *iff* $K_\bot \in K \dot{\square} \alpha$.

We can define a similarity ranking centred on $|K|$ to be $|K|$-*preserving* if those knowledge bases that are subsumed by $|K|$ are more similar to $|K|$ than those that are not. The intuition is that knowledge bases that preserve the information in $|K|$ are more similar to $|K|$ than those that don't.

THEOREM 19. *Let M be any similarity order model on knowledge bases centred on $|K|$ where we have the condition: If for $|K_1|, |K_2| \in \mathcal{KB}$ we have: if $|K_1| \subseteq |K|$ but $|K_2| \not\subseteq |K|$ then $|K_1| \prec |K_2|$, then the following postulate is satisfied in M:*

($K \dot{\square} 4$) *If $K \not\vdash \neg\alpha$ then for every $K' \in K \dot{\square} \alpha$ we have $K + \alpha \subseteq K'$.*

Moreover, we can define a similarity ranking centred on $|K|$ to be *strongly* $|K|$-*preserving* if it is $|K|$-preserving and we also rank knowledge bases by their closeness to $|K|$:

THEOREM 20. *Let M be any similarity order model on knowledge bases centred on $|K|$ that is $|K|$-preserving and where we have the condition: For $|K_1| \subset |K_2| \subseteq |K|$ we have $|K_2| \prec |K_1|$. Then the following postulate is satisfied in M:*

($K \dot{\square} 3b$) $K \dot{\square} \alpha = \{K'\}$ *where* $K' = K + \alpha$.

So to this point we have essentially recovered the basic set of AGM postulates (with the exception of the first postulate). Presumably the same thing can be done for postulates corresponding to $K\dot{+}7$ and $K\dot{+}8$, although we don't do so here. For the first postulate, as discussed earlier, there are two general strategies that can be adopted to obtain a unique knowledge base.

First, one can take the position that revision may result in a set of equally-similar (or equally plausible) knowledge bases. Given such a set, a single knowledge base can be selected. *How* such a knowledge base would be selected would be a problem not addressed by revision. As suggested before, there are various strategies that might be employed. For example, one might choose the simplest knowledge base, according to some application of Occam's razor. Or one might select an arbitrary knowledge base from the set, or take their union, or employ some other strategy.

Alternately, one might decide that a revision function should have as value a single knowledge base. This could come about indirectly, as a result of imposing various conditions on the similarity metric. Or it could come about directly; one could stipulate that the ordering $\preceq$ is in fact a total order on knowledge bases. Or one could stipulate that similarity is closed under unions, in the sense that if $|K_1|$ and $|K_2|$ are equally similar, then they are both equally similar also to $|K_1| \cup |K_2|$. In this case there would be a maximal element in $K \dot{\square} \alpha$ that could be selected as the revised knowledge base.

For either strategy, the imposition of additional constraints should not be ad hoc, but rather should reflect reasonable assumptions in the semantics. Thus for example, if $\preceq$ were a total order on knowledge bases, then one would be compelled to buy into the assumption that there are no "ties" in similarity of knowledge bases. If one decided that revision is closed under unions, then presumably one should be able to justify this choice.

4 DISCUSSION

The intent of this approach is to provide a very basic framework in which to investigate revision of knowledge bases. The central intuition is that the revision of a knowledge base $|K|$ by a sentence α is the knowledge base most similar to $|K|$ in which α is true. The resultant approach is quite basic, in that many of the AGM postulates don't hold, or only hold in a weaker form. Arguably the approach is not too basic, in that interesting properties still obtain (as given in the set of KB revision postulates). Moreover, the approach provides very fine-grained control over the properties of a revision operator. This is illustrated by the fact that of the basic AGM postulates that don't hold in the approach, each is independently satisfied in some augmentation of the approach. Perhaps the most interesting of the postulates is the first, seemingly the most basic and obvious of the postulates. As the discussion at the end of the preceding section shows, there are several alternatives and subtleties involved in moving from a revision operator that may have a set of knowledge bases as its value, to an operator that has a single knowledge base as value.

There are several directions in which this work can be extended. First, iterated revision is not addressed here. It may prove to be the case that iteration of revisions may be more easily addressed here than (say) beginning with the AGM approach, primarily because here we have stepped back from some of the commitments of the AGM approach. One plausible intuition, for example, is to try to retain as much as one can of a similarity ordering. This could be realised by: if according to $|K|$ we have $|K_1| \preceq |K_2| \preceq |K_3|$ then according to $|K_1|$ we have $|K_2| \preceq |K_3|$.

Second, *contraction* of knowledge bases has not been addressed. The contraction of $|K|$ by α is easily enough defined in this framework: this would just be the set of knowledge bases most similar to $|K|$ that fail to imply α. While the properties of this operator haven't been investigated, it is clear that the Levi and Harper identities will fail to hold in general. In this case, it becomes an interesting question then to ask why these relations fail to obtain here, and what this tells us about revision and contraction.

5 PROOFS OF THEOREMS

Proof. [of Theorem 12]

1. Since $\vdash \neg\alpha$, so $KB(\alpha) = \{L\} = \{K_\perp\}$. By $(K \dot{\square} 2)$, $K \dot{\square} \alpha \subseteq KB(\alpha)$ and by $(K \dot{\square} 1)$ we have $K \dot{\square} \alpha$ is nonempty.

2. Left to right is trivial: Since $K \dot{\square} \alpha \subseteq KB(\alpha)$ and $K \dot{\square} \alpha = K \dot{\square} \beta$ so $K \dot{\square} \beta \subseteq KB(\alpha)$. Similarly we obtain $K \dot{\square} \alpha \subseteq KB(\beta)$.

   For right to left, assuming $K \dot{\square} \alpha \subseteq KB(\beta)$ gives $K \dot{\square} \alpha = K \dot{\square} (\alpha \wedge \beta)$ via $(K \dot{\square} 7)$. Similarly we obtain that $K \dot{\square} \beta = K \dot{\square} (\alpha \wedge \beta)$ from which we conclude. ■

Proof [of Theorem 13]

1. If $K \dot{\square} \alpha \cap KB(\beta) = \emptyset$ then, since $K \dot{\square} (\alpha \wedge \beta) \subseteq KB(\beta)$, so $K \dot{\square} \alpha \cap K \dot{\square} (\alpha \wedge \beta) = \emptyset$.

2. Immediate from $(K \dot{\square} 7)$.

3. Immediate from $(K \dot{\square} 7)$.

4. If $K \dot{\square} \alpha \cap K \dot{\square} \beta \neq \emptyset$ then $K \dot{\square} \alpha \cap KB(\beta) \neq \emptyset$ and $K \dot{\square} \beta \cap KB(\alpha) \neq \emptyset$. So from $(K \dot{\square} 7)$, we obtain $K \dot{\square} (\alpha \wedge \beta) = K \dot{\square} \alpha \cap KB(\beta) = K \dot{\square} \beta \cap KB(\alpha) = K \dot{\square} \alpha \cap KB(\beta) \cap K \dot{\square} \beta \cap KB(\alpha) = K \dot{\square} \alpha \cap K \dot{\square} \beta$. ■

Proof. [of Theorem 14]

1. Assume that $K \dot{\square} \alpha_i \subseteq KB(\alpha_{i+1})$ for $0 \leq i < n$ and $K \dot{\square} \alpha_n \subseteq KB(\alpha_0)$. Consequently, via Theorem 13.3, we obtain that $K \dot{\square} (\alpha_i \wedge \alpha_{i+1}) = K \dot{\square} \alpha_i$ for $0 \leq i < n$ and $K \dot{\square} (\alpha_n \wedge \alpha_0) = K \dot{\square} \alpha_n \quad (1)$.

   From the antecedent conditions we also obtain $K \dot{\square} \alpha_i \cap KB(\alpha_{i+1}) \neq \emptyset$ for $0 \leq i < n$ and $K \dot{\square} \alpha_n \cap KB(\alpha_0) \neq \emptyset$. Repeated application of $(K \dot{\square} 8)$ yields $K \dot{\square} (\alpha_i \wedge \alpha_{i+1}) \subseteq K \dot{\square} \alpha_{i+1}$ for $0 \leq i < n$ and $K \dot{\square} (\alpha_n \wedge \alpha_0) \subseteq K \dot{\square} \alpha_0$. Combining this with (1) gives $K \dot{\square} \alpha_0 \subseteq K \dot{\square} \alpha_1 \subseteq \ldots \subseteq K \dot{\square} \alpha_n \subseteq K \dot{\square} \alpha_0$ from which we obtain $K \dot{\square} \alpha_i = K \dot{\square} \alpha_{i+1}$ for $0 \leq i < n$.

2. I prove the contrapositive. Assume that $K \dot{\square} \alpha \cap K \dot{\square} (\alpha \wedge \beta \wedge \gamma) \neq \emptyset$. So $K \dot{\square} \alpha \cap KB(\alpha \wedge \beta \wedge \gamma) \neq \emptyset$ and so $K \dot{\square} \alpha \cap KB(\beta) \neq \emptyset$. By Theorem 13.2 we obtain $K \dot{\square} (\alpha \wedge \beta) \subseteq K \dot{\square} \alpha$ and so with $(K \dot{\square} 1)$ we get $K \dot{\square} \alpha \cap K \dot{\square} (\alpha \wedge \beta) \neq \emptyset$.

3. I prove the contrapositive. Assume that $K \dot{\square} \alpha \cap K \dot{\square} (\alpha \wedge \beta \wedge \gamma) \neq \emptyset$ (1). We have that $K \dot{\square} (\alpha \wedge \beta \wedge \gamma) \subseteq KB(\beta)$. Hence $K \dot{\square} \alpha \cap KB(\beta) \neq \emptyset$, so via Theorem 13.2, $K \dot{\square} \alpha \subseteq K \dot{\square} (\alpha \wedge \beta)$ and so from (1) we obtain $K \dot{\square} (\alpha \wedge \beta) \cap K \dot{\square} (\alpha \wedge \beta \wedge \gamma) \neq \emptyset$.

4. Since $K \dot{\square} (\alpha \wedge \beta \wedge \gamma) \subseteq K \dot{\square} \alpha$ so $K \dot{\square} \alpha \cap KB(\beta) \neq \emptyset$, so via Theorem 13.2 we obtain so $K \dot{\square} (\alpha \wedge \beta) \subseteq K \dot{\square} \alpha$.

   Assuming $K \dot{\square} (\alpha \wedge \beta \wedge \gamma) \subseteq K \dot{\square} \alpha$ gives $K \dot{\square} (\alpha \wedge \beta \wedge \gamma) \subseteq K \dot{\square} \alpha \cap KB(\beta)$. But by $(K \dot{\square} 7)$ we have $K \dot{\square} \alpha \cap KB(\beta) = K \dot{\square} (\alpha \wedge \beta)$, whence $K \dot{\square} (\alpha \wedge \beta \wedge \gamma) \subseteq K \dot{\square} (\alpha \wedge \beta)$. ■

Proof. [of Theorem 15]

1. Obviously: $K \dot{\square} \alpha \cap KB(\beta) \neq \emptyset$ or $K \dot{\square} \beta \cap KB(\alpha) \neq \emptyset$ or: $K \dot{\square} \alpha \cap KB(\beta) = \emptyset$ and $K \dot{\square} \beta \cap KB(\alpha) = \emptyset$. Theorem 13.2 applied to the first two disjuncts gives us $K \dot{\square} (\alpha \wedge \beta) \subseteq K \dot{\square} \alpha$ or $K \dot{\square} (\alpha \wedge \beta) \subseteq K \dot{\square} \beta$. For the third disjunct, if we have $K \dot{\square} \alpha \cap KB(\beta) = \emptyset$ and $K \dot{\square} \beta \cap KB(\alpha) = \emptyset$ then clearly $K \dot{\square} \alpha$ and $K \dot{\square} \beta$ are disjoint, whence $K \dot{\square} \alpha \cap K \dot{\square} \beta = \emptyset$.

2. We have via Theorem 13.4 that if $K \dot{\square} (\alpha \wedge \beta) \cap K \dot{\square} \alpha \neq \emptyset$ then $K \dot{\square} (\alpha \wedge \beta) \subseteq K \dot{\square} \alpha$ This can be rewritten as: $K \dot{\square} (\alpha \wedge \beta) \subseteq K \dot{\square} \alpha$ or $K \dot{\square} (\alpha \wedge \beta) \cap K \dot{\square} \alpha = \emptyset$. An instance is: $K \dot{\square} ((\alpha \vee \beta) \wedge \beta) \subseteq K \dot{\square} (\alpha \vee \beta)$ or $K \dot{\square} ((\alpha \vee \beta) \wedge \beta) \cap K \dot{\square} (\alpha \vee \beta) = \emptyset$ or: $K \dot{\square} \beta \subseteq K \dot{\square} (\alpha \vee \beta)$ or $K \dot{\square} \beta \cap K \dot{\square} (\alpha \vee \beta) = \emptyset$ (1). Similarly we obtain $K \dot{\square} \alpha \subseteq K \dot{\square} (\alpha \vee \beta)$ or $K \dot{\square} \alpha \cap K \dot{\square} (\alpha \vee \beta) = \emptyset$ (2). The result is a consequence of (1) combined with (2). ■

Proof. [of Theorem 16] Straightforward. ■

Proof. [of Theorem 17] Define $M = \langle W, \preceq, P \rangle$ where W and P are as in the original definition for a similarity order model. Let $\mathcal{KB} = \{|K'| \mid \exists \alpha \text{ such that } K' \in K \dot{\square} \alpha\}$.

Define $\preceq'$ by: For $|K_1| \in \mathcal{KB}$ if $|K_1| \models \beta$ then for every $K_2 \in K \dot{\square} \beta$ we have $|K_2| \preceq' |K_1|$.

Let $\preceq$ be the transitive closure of $\preceq'$.

We have:

1. $\preceq$ is reflexive: For $|K_1| \in \mathcal{KB}$ there is α such that $K_1 \in K \dot{\square} \alpha$. Via ($K \dot{\square}$ 2) we obtain that $|K_1| \models \alpha$ so $|K_1| \preceq' |K_1|$ by the definition of $\preceq'$, and so $|K_1| \preceq |K_1|$ by the definition of $\preceq$.

2. $\preceq$ is transitive by definition.

3. $\preceq$ is centred on $|K|$: First, if $I \preceq |K|$ then for some α we have $K \vdash \alpha$ and $I \in K \dot{\square} \alpha$. But by ($K \dot{\square}$ 3), $K \dot{\square} \alpha = \{K\}$, and since $I \in K \dot{\square} \alpha$ so $I = K$.

   Second, for $|K_1| \in \mathcal{KB}$ there is α such that $K_1 \in K \dot{\square} \alpha$. Now, $|K_1| \models \top$ so via ($K \dot{\square}$ 1) and the definition of $\mathcal{KB}$ we obtain $K \in K \dot{\square} \top$, which is $\{K\}$ via ($K \dot{\square}$ 3), so by the definition of $\preceq$ we have $|K| \preceq |K_1|$.

4. By the definition of $\preceq'$ (and so $\preceq$) for arbitrary α, if $K_1 \in K \dot{\square} \alpha$ then $|K_1|$ is a minimum among those knowledge bases in $\mathcal{KB}$ in which α is believed.

Consequently $\preceq$ satisfies the conditions given in Definition 8 and so we have a similarity order model centred on $|K|$. To finish we need to show that $K \dot{\square} \alpha = kb(min_M(\alpha))$.

One half, namely $K \dot{\square} \alpha \subseteq kb(min_M(\alpha))$, is straightforward: Let $K_1 \in K \dot{\square} \alpha$, and let $|K_2| \in \mathcal{KB}$. If $|K_2| \models \alpha$ then by the definition of $\preceq'$ we have $|K_1| \preceq |K_2|$ for all such $|K_2|$. Thus from Definition 9, $|K_1| \in min_M(\alpha)$ and so $K_1 \in kb(min_M(\alpha))$.

$kb(min_M(\alpha)) \subseteq K \dot{\circ} \alpha$ is shown as follows. Assume, contrary to what is to be proved that $K' \in kb(min_M(\alpha))$ and $K' \notin K \dot{\circ} \alpha$. Let $K'' \in K \dot{\circ} \alpha$, so $|K''| \models \alpha$. Hence $|K'| \preceq |K''|$. Since $\preceq$ is the transitive closure of $\preceq'$ there must be K_i, $1 \leq i < n$ where $|K'| = |K_n| \preceq' |K_{n-1}| \preceq' \ldots \preceq' |K_2| \preceq |K_1| = |K''|$. That is, there are $\alpha_1, \ldots, \alpha_n$ where $\alpha = \alpha_1$ and $|K_1| \in K \dot{\circ} \alpha_1$, $K_1 \vdash \alpha_2$, and $|K_2| \in K \dot{\circ} \alpha_2$, $K_2 \vdash \alpha_3$, $\ldots$, $|K_n| \in K \dot{\circ} \alpha_n$, $K_n \vdash \alpha_1$. So $K \dot{\circ} \alpha_i \cap KB(\alpha_{i+1}) \neq \emptyset$ for $1 \leq i < n$, and $K \dot{\circ} \alpha_n \cap KB(\alpha_1) \neq \emptyset$, and so $K \dot{\circ} (\alpha_1 \wedge \alpha_n) \subseteq K \dot{\circ} \alpha_1$ via $(K \dot{\circ} 8)$.

Since $K_n \in K \dot{\circ} \alpha_n$ and $K_n \vdash \alpha_1$, so $K_n \in K \dot{\circ} \alpha_n \cap KB(\alpha_1)$. But since $K \dot{\circ} \alpha_n \cap KB(\alpha_1) \neq \emptyset$ we have $K \dot{\circ} \alpha_n \cap KB(\alpha_1) = K \dot{\circ} (\alpha_1 \wedge \alpha_n)$ via $(K \dot{\circ} 7)$. So $K_n \in K \dot{\circ} (\alpha_1 \wedge \alpha_n)$ and since $K \dot{\circ} (\alpha_1 \wedge \alpha_n) \subseteq K \dot{\circ} \alpha_1$ we obtain $K_n \in K \dot{\circ} \alpha_1$ which is the same as $K' \in K \dot{\circ} \alpha$ ■

Proof. [of Theorems 18–20] Straightforward. ■

ACKNOWLEDGEMENTS

I thank Maurice Pagnucco and a referee for extensive and very helpful comments on this paper.

Simon Fraser University, Burnaby, Canada.

REFERENCES

[Alchourrón *et al.*, 1985] C. E. Alchourrón, P. Gärdenfors and D. Makinson. On the logic of theory change: Partial meet contraction and revision functions. *Journal of Symbolic Logic*, **50**, 510–530, 1985.

[Gärdenfors, 1988] P. Gärdenfors. *Knowledge in Flux: Modelling the Dynamics of Epistemic States*. The MIT Press, Cambridge, MA, 1988.

[Gärdenfors and Makinson, 1988] P. Gärdenfors and D. Makinson. Revisions of knowledge systems using epistemic entrenchment. In *Proceedings of the Second Theoretical Aspects of Reasoning About Knowledge Conference*, pp. 83–95, Monterey, CA, 1988.

[Grove, 1988] A. Grove. Two modellings for theory change. *Journal of Philosophical Logic*, **17**, 157–170, 1988.

[Hughes and Cresswell, 1984] G. E. Hughes and M. J. Cresswell. *A Companion to Modal Logic*. Methuen and Co., 1984.

[Lewis, 1973] D. Lewis. *Counterfactuals*. Harvard University Press, 1973.

A. BOCHMAN

CONTRACTION OF EPISTEMIC STATES: A GENERAL THEORY

1 INTRODUCTION

We are going to describe a general framework for representing belief change based on the notion of an epistemic state. The latter subsumes essential, though implicit, features of the current representations, and in this way is intended to provide foundations for a (future) general theory of belief change.

Two main approaches to representing belief change have been suggested in the literature. The first is a so-called AGM theory of belief change (see [Alchourrón *et al.*, 1985] and Peter Gärdenfors' book [Gärdenfors, 1988]), a starting point in the formal study of the problem. It suggested a systematic approach to the problem both in terms of general rationality postulates that a belief change should satisfy and in developing semantic representations that conform to these postulates.

The AGM theory was intended to give a representation for a process of revising *belief states* considered simply as deductively closed sets of propositions. The basic setting of the AGM representation, however, is a pair consisting of a belief set and some *preference mechanism* allowing to choose among admissible maximal subtheories of the belief set. In [Alchourrón *et al.*, 1985] this is achieved using a suitable *selection function* on maximal subsets of the source belief set that are consistent with the new data. The authors of [Alchourrón *et al.*, 1985] have considered also an important special case of the formalism in which the selection function is *relational*, that is, based on a certain preference order among the maximal subtheories. However, the problem of giving a complete description of the corresponding relational belief change operations has turned out to be difficult in the general case (see [Rott, 1993]). Some reasons for this difficulty will become clearer later in the paper.

A major alternative solution to the problem of belief revision is based on the assumption that our corpus of beliefs is usually generated by some set of *basic* propositions (see, e.g., [Fuhrmann, 1991; Hansson, 1992; Nebel, 1989]). This base-generation approach embodies an important structural aspect of our beliefs that does not find its proper place in the AGM theory, namely that some our beliefs are purely derivative and arise simply as logical consequences of other beliefs we have. It would be natural to require that such derived beliefs should be withdrawn when we remove beliefs that served as their justification. As a result, changes of belief sets are determined in this case by changes in their underlying bases. Still, the resulting belief set on most of these accounts is also determined by imposing preference relations on such alternatives. As argued by Hansson [1992], the role of the latter amounts to resolving residual choice problems that are not decided by bases alone.

M.-A. Williams and H. Rott (eds.), Frontiers in Belief Revision, 195–220.

To begin with, we will claim that belief change operations on belief sets should not be seen as primary objects, but rather as 'by-products' of corresponding operations on the underlying epistemic states that explicitly include in some form or other the above mentioned preference mechanisms and the base generating a given belief set (if the belief set is seen as base-generated). As we argue in more details in [Bochman, 1999c], this is the most reasonable possibility open to us, if we want to preserve what is called in [Gärdenfors and Rott, 1995] *the principle of categorial matching*, according to which the representation of the epistemic state after a change should be of the same kind as that before the change.

Now, a common feature of the AGM and base representations is a preference structure on certain subsets of the belief set. In the case of the AGM paradigm, it is a preference structure on maximal deductively closed subsets of the belief set, while for the base representation it is a preference structure on the subtheories of the belief set that are generated by subsets of the base. Thus, the role of bases amounts to restricting the set of subtheories of the belief set that are considered as 'serious' alternatives for a choice. The notion of an epistemic state introduced in the next section will reflect this common structure of the two representations.

2 EPISTEMIC STATES AND THEIR BELIEF SETS

We will adhere in this study to the claim that "a rational choice should be a relational choice" (see [Rott, 1993]). In other words, unlike the AGM approach and some more general studies in base-generated change (e.g. [Hansson, 1993b]), we will insist from the very beginning that a proper selection mechanism should be based on the underlying preference relation among admissible alternatives. In this case the common structure of the AGM and base representations will amount to a structure consisting of (some) subtheories of the belief set, ordered by a preference relation. In order to be precise, however, we need to fix first the underlying language.

Let $\mathcal{L}$ be a propositional language containing the usual classical connectives, and $\vDash$ the associated classical entailment relation. Sets of propositions closed with respect to $\vDash$ will be called deductively closed.

DEFINITION 1. An *epistemic state* $\mathbb{E}$ in the language $\mathcal{L}$ is a pair $(\mathbb{B}, \prec)$, where $\mathbb{B}$ is a a set of deductively closed theories in $\mathcal{L}$ called *admissible belief states*, while $\prec$ is a strict preference relation on $\mathbb{B}$.

If $s \prec t$, we will say that the state t is *preferred* to the state s. Notice that our epistemic states are language-relative entities. This fact will have important consequences for our subsequent deliberations.

It turns out that the preference relation can be used to determine propositions that are believed in an epistemic state:

DEFINITION 2. A proposition will be said to be *believed* in an epistemic state $\mathbb{E}$ if it holds in all maximally preferred admissible belief states from $\mathbb{E}$. The set of all propositions believed in $\mathbb{E}$ will be called the *belief set* of $\mathbb{E}$, and it will be denoted by $[\mathbb{E}]$.

Thus, even if an epistemic state contains conflicting preferred belief states, we can still believe in propositions that hold in all of them. As to other potential beliefs, the belief set is a result of suspending judgment between preferred 'serious' possibilities.

It is important to observe that the AGM theory of belief change presupposes our understanding of belief acceptance, though with respect to propositions that 'survive' a change: thus, a proposition will belong to a contracted belief state if it belongs to all preferred maximal sub-theories of the initial state that do not include the proposition being contracted. On our approach, this is how we should accept our beliefs from the very beginning.

An epistemic state determines also propositions that are considered to be known (or 'firmly believed', if you prefer) by the agent. Namely, a proposition will be said to be *known* in an epistemic state $\mathbb{E}$ if it holds in all admissible belief states from $\mathbb{E}$; otherwise it will be called *contingent*. As we will see later, the set of known propositions determines the 'internal logic' of epistemic states and associated belief change operations[1].

2.1 AGM states and base-generated states

We will establish now a formal correspondence between our notion of an epistemic state and the two major existing representations of belief change.

The AGM states. As we said, in the case of a relational selection function, the AGM framework consists of a belief set K and a strict preference relation R such that, for any set $K\bot A$ of maximal subtheories of K that do not contain A, the set $\gamma(K\bot A)$ of 'preferred' theories from $K\bot A$ is the set of R-maximal elements from $K\bot A$ (see [Alchourrón *et al.*, 1985; Rott, 1993]). Now, this construction can be seen as an epistemic state $(K\bot, R)$, where $K\bot$ is a set of all maximal deductively closed subsets of K, plus K itself. It is important to note that the same effect can be achieved by considering an epistemic state $(\mathbb{K}, R)$, where $\mathbb{K}$ is a set of *all* subtheories of K and R is a strict preference relation on $\mathbb{K}$ that satisfies a monotonicity ('maximizing') property with respect to set inclusion:

Monotonicity If $u \subset v$, then uRv.

Given monotonicity, preferred alternatives will always be among maximal subtheories of K, so the two representations will be 'revision-equivalent'. The monotonicity requirement can be seen as another characteristic feature of the AGM approach that amounts to the principle of *informational economy* (see [Gärdenfors,

[1]Note that our framework is thoroughly epistemic (subjective), so the above notion of knowledge does not presuppose *objective* truth; it refers, instead, to what an agent considers as known (and hence as not susceptible to change).

1988]): any information is valuable, so belief sets preserving more information should be preferred.

Base-generated states. Let K be a belief set generated by some underlying base $\mathbf{B}$, that is, $K = Th(\mathbf{B})$. This base generates a set of admissible belief states $\mathbb{B}$ which is a set of theories determined by subsets of the base:

$$\mathbb{B} = \{Th(\mathbf{B}_0) \mid \mathbf{B}_0 \subseteq \mathbf{B}\}$$

As we show elsewhere [Bochman, 1999c], the set of theories $\mathbb{B}$ provides a 'descriptively equivalent' representation for the base $\mathbf{B}$, since the latter can be restored from the structure of $\mathbb{B}$. In this way base-generated belief states can be identified with another special class of epistemic states in our sense. Notice that the majority of current approaches in the base-generation 'camp' eventually impose some kind of preference structure on the subsets of the base, which gives an epistemic state of the form $(\mathbb{B}, \prec)$, where $\prec$ is some preference relation on $\mathbb{B}$ – see, e.g., [Fuhrmann, 1991; Hansson, 1993b; Nebel, 1989]. Moreover, in most cases this preference relation is also assumed to satisfy the monotonicity property, mentioned above, though it is restricted now to the theories from $\mathbb{B}$. An important special case is obtained when no preferences are imposed on the elements or subsets of the base. In this case base change operations involve choosing maximal subsets of the base that are consistent with the new data. In other words, set inclusion becomes then the only guiding principle of choice, so the relevant 'pure' epistemic state can be identified with a pair $(\mathbb{B}, \subset)$, where $\subset$ is a relation of set inclusion.

Summing up the above descriptions, it can be said that the two major paradigms of belief change representation give raise to epistemic states in which the preference relation satisfies the monotonicity property. Another important common feature of these two paradigms is that admissible belief states belong in both cases to the subsets of the source belief set. This property can be formalized in our framework as follows.

An epistemic state $\mathbb{E}$ will be called *determinate*[2] if it has a unique preferred admissible belief state that includes also all other admissible states. Clearly, the preferred belief state will coincide with the belief set of $\mathbb{E}$. It is also easy to see that the two main belief change paradigms give rise to determinate epistemic states.

As we argued in [Bochman, 1999c], determination should not be taken as a 'rationality constraint' on epistemic states. First, because it creates problems when combined with the principle of categorial matching, mentioned in the introduction; adherence to this principle requires revised epistemic states to be determinate also, and this often leads to an unjustified loss of information (see below). Moreover, we argued also that incoherent epistemic states suggest a more realistic representation of quite common epistemic situations that involve conflicting potential beliefs. Notice, for example, that an inconsistent set of basic propositions can be naturally

[2]Such epistemic states were called coherent in [Bochman, 1999a], which creates unnecessary association with coherentism in the present context.

seen as forming an incoherent epistemic state generated by its consistent subsets. Such situations are actually quite common in theories of commonsense reasoning (see, e.g., [Poole, 1988]) that involve reasoning with incompatible default assumptions.

2.2 *Abstract epistemic states*

Recall that epistemic states are language-relative objects, that is, they depend on the language in which they are formulated. Assume now that our language $\mathcal{L}$ is a restriction of another propositional language $\mathcal{L}_0$, and let $\mathbb{E}$ be some epistemic state in $\mathcal{L}_0$. This epistemic state does not always correspond to an epistemic state in $\mathcal{L}$, since different admissible theories of $\mathbb{E}$ may 'collapse' to the same theory in $\mathcal{L}$. This means that the language $\mathcal{L}$ is insufficient to differentiate distinct states in $\mathbb{E}$. However, we will see later that natural belief change operations on epistemic states in the language $\mathcal{L}_0$ generate corresponding operations in the restricted language $\mathcal{L}$. In order to describe such operations *within* the restricted language, our notion of an epistemic state should be generalized to permit situations in which different admissible belief states correspond to the same deductively closed belief sets. This move is actually well known in the theory of nonmonotonic inference which is closely related to belief revision. Previous experience with nonmonotonic inference formalisms (see especially [Kraus *et al.*, 1990]) has shown the importance of models in which different states may correspond to the same set of supported propositions. The following definition provides the corresponding generalization for the notion of an epistemic state.

DEFINITION 3. An *abstract epistemic state* $\mathbb{E}$ in a language $\mathcal{L}$ is a triple $(\mathbb{B}, l, \prec)$, where $\mathbb{B}$ is a set of objects called *admissible belief states*, l is a function assigning a deductively closed theory in $\mathcal{L}$ (called *an admissible belief set*) to every state from $\mathbb{B}$, while $\prec$ is a preference relation on $\mathbb{B}$.

The above definition allows for a possibility that two admissible belief states (which are treated now as arbitrary objects) are associated with the same set of beliefs. We will call an abstract epistemic state *standard* if the labeling function is injective, that is, no two admissible belief states are labeled with the same belief set. Standard abstract epistemic states can be identified with ordinary epistemic states, as defined earlier.

It should be clear that the main notions associated with ordinary epistemic states, such as belief and knowledge sets, monotonicity and determination, etc., can be immediately extended to abstract epistemic states. So, in what follows we will use these notions also for abstract states.

As we have seen, both the AGM and base representation give raise to standard epistemic states. In fact, this restriction can be seen as responsible for the difficulties arising in an attempt to give a complete characterization of relational belief change operations (see below).

3 CONTRACTIONS OF EPISTEMIC STATES

As we said in the introduction, belief change operations should be defined primarily as functions from epistemic states to epistemic states. In other words, though any epistemic state determines an associated belief set, changes of the latter will be determined by changes made to the underlying epistemic state. Below we will demonstrate this for the case of contractions.

On the suggested understanding of an epistemic state, its admissible belief states constitute all potential alternatives that are considered as 'serious possibilities' by the agent. In accordance with this, a contraction of a proposition from an epistemic state should amount simply to a removal of all admissible belief states that include the proposition.

DEFINITION 4. A *contraction* of an abstract epistemic state $\mathbb{E} = (\mathbb{B}, l, \prec)$ with respect to a proposition A is an epistemic state, denoted by $\mathbb{E} - A$, determined by restricting $\mathbb{B}$ to the set of belief states that do not support A.

Thus, a contraction of A from an epistemic state $\mathbb{E}$ is obtained by removing admissible belief states that contain A and restricting $\prec$ to the reduced set of admissible belief states. Consequently, contraction is a function that transforms epistemic states into new epistemic states. As a by-product, it can change what is believed in an epistemic state, an in this sense it generates a certain change in its belief set $[\mathbb{E}]$. Accordingly, the belief set of $\mathbb{E} - A$, that is, $[\mathbb{E} - A]$ can be seen as a result of contracting the belief set $[\mathbb{E}]$ with respect to A. Such *belief contraction functions* will be the main subject of our study in what follows. But first we will consider briefly how our contraction operation is related to the two main approaches to belief change.

Contracting AGM states. If the AGM framework is represented by what we have called AGM states above, then, for any proposition A, $[\mathbb{E} - A]$ will be precisely the contracted belief set $K \div A$ according to the AGM definition. In this respect, the AGM contraction function can be seen as a special case of our general construction. Still, there is an important difference between the two, since what we obtain in our construction is not only the new belief set, but also a new epistemic state. Consequently, our contraction operation can be iterated, which is impossible in the original AGM framework. Note also that in some sense the new epistemic state runs against the basic assumption of the AGM approach, since in most cases it will not already be determinate.

Contracting base-generated states. A more complex situation arises when comparing our contraction operation with base-generated contractions. Let K be a belief set generated by a base $\mathbf{B}$, A a proposition being contracted and $(\mathbb{B}, \prec)$ the associated standard epistemic state, as described earlier, where $\mathbb{B}$ is the set of theories determined by the subsets of the base. According to the general construction given in [Hansson, 1993b], the first step in performing a base-generated contraction of A consists in finding preferred (selected) subsets of the base that do not imply A. So far, this fits well with our 'reconstruction', since the latter subsets exactly correspond to preferred admissible theories of the associated contracted epistemic state. Our definition then says, in effect, that the contracted belief set should be equal to the intersection of all these preferred theories. However, such a solution cannot be considered as a principled solution from the point of view of the base-generation paradigm. The reason is that the latter sees belief change operations primarily as operations on bases. In other words, bases serve exactly the same role in this approach as epistemic states in our present account. Accordingly, a contraction of a base should result first of all in a new base, and only this latter base will determine the resulting belief set. Accordingly, Hansson [1993b] defines first the new 'contracted' base as the intersection of all preferred subsets of the base ('partial meet base contraction'), and then the contracted belief set is defined as the set of all propositions that are implied by the new base.

As can be easily seen, adherence to base representation as an invariant of belief change operations implies, in particular, adherence to determination. In the latter case, however, this may lead to an unjustified loss of information, as shows a simple and well-worn example of contracting $p \wedge q$ from a belief set generated by the base $\{p, q\}$. If there are no preferences between the two elements of the base, then the first step will give us $\{p\}$ and $\{q\}$ as preferred subsets of the base, and then the second step will leave us with an empty set as the 'contracted' base. Our construction, however, gives for this case a quite reasonable and expected new belief set $Th(p \vee q)$, as well as a new epistemic state consisting of two theories, $Th(p)$ and $Th(q)$.

The above example can be seen as an illustration of the fact that contractions do not preserve the property of base-generation (and even determination), and consequently bases are simply inadequate as a general framework for representing belief change. As we argue in more details in [Bochman, 1999c], a more plausible representation that is already invariant with respect to the main belief change operations was suggested, in fact, in [Fagin *et al.*, 1986] and consists in replacing bases by what they called *flocks of theories*. The latter representation will already agree with the general contraction operation described above.

Failure. Contractions are definable for all epistemic states and all propositions being contracted. Note, however, that if A is known, that is, if it holds in all admissible belief states, then $\mathbb{E} - A$ will be an empty epistemic state. In order to avoid this situation, we can redefine the above contraction operation by stipulating that if A is known, then $\mathbb{E} - A$ should coincide with $\mathbb{E}$. In other words, when requiring to do the impossible, we decide to do nothing. This 'opportunistic' strategy is actually implicit in both the AGM and base-generation approaches to belief change. We will also accept this stipulation in what follows.

4 BELIEF CONTRACTION FUNCTIONS

Thus, contractions of epistemic states generate corresponding contraction operations on their belief sets. Below we will give a formal characterization of such belief contraction functions in terms of 'rationality postulates' they satisfy.

4.1 Postulates of contraction

For a future reference and comparison, we give first the AGM postulates for contraction.

(K–1) $Th(K \div A) = K \div A$ (closure)

(K–2) $K \div A \subseteq K$ (inclusion)

(K–3) If $A \notin K$, then $K \div A = K$ (vacuity)

(K–4) If $A \notin Th(\emptyset)$, then $A \notin K \div A$ (success)

(K–5) If $Th(A) = Th(B)$, then $K \div A = K \div B$ (extensionality)

(K–6) $K \subseteq Th((K \div A) \cup \{A\})$ (recovery)

(K–7) $(K \div A) \cap (K \div B) \subseteq K \div (A \wedge B)$ (conjunction1)

(K–8) If $A \notin K \div (A \wedge B)$, then $K \div (A \wedge B) \subseteq K \div A$ (conjunction2)

To begin with, our notation is essentially different from the above one, mainly because the source belief set no longer plays the main role in determining the contracted belief set; this role is relegated to the underlying epistemic state. Accordingly, instead of the function $K \div A$ on belief sets, we have now the function $[\mathbb{E} - A]$ from epistemic states to belief sets. Still, the correspondence between the two kinds of notation is immediate, so the AGM postulates can be easily 'translated' into our terminology and vice versa. We will implicitly use this correspondence in what follows. But even if we ignore these conceptual and notational differences, it turns out that only three of the above postulates are valid for contractions of epistemic states, namely closure (K–1), extensionality (K–5) and conjunction1 (K–7).

Now we are going to describe the postulates that characterize our belief contraction functions. By a *contraction function* we will mean any function satisfying the following conditions:

(E–1) $[\mathbb{E} - A]$ is a deductively closed set (closure)

(E–2) If $\models A \leftrightarrow B$, then $[\mathbb{E} - A] = [\mathbb{E} - B]$ (extensionality)

(E–3) If $A \in [\mathbb{E} - A]$, then $[\mathbb{E} - A] = [\mathbb{E} - \bot]$ (failure)

(E–4) If $A \in [\mathbb{E} - A \wedge B]$, then $A \in [\mathbb{E} - A \wedge B \wedge C]$ (partial antitony)

(E–5) $[\mathbb{E} - A] \cap [\mathbb{E} - B] \subseteq [\mathbb{E} - A \wedge B]$ (distributivity)

(E–6) If $A \in [\mathbb{E} - A \wedge B]$, then $[\mathbb{E} - A \wedge B] = [\mathbb{E} - B]$ (cumulativity)

The first postulate (E–1) corresponds to the AGM postulate of closure (K–1). The second postulate, extensionality, corresponds to the AGM postulate (K–6); it says that logically equivalent propositions generate identical contracted belief sets[3]. The third postulate (E–3) corresponds to the *postulate of failure* introduced by Fuhrmann and Hansson in [1994]. As we shall see, the effect of the failure postulate consists in identifying the result of contracting a known proposition with the original belief set. Thus, it embodies, in effect, the above mentioned 'opportunistic' stipulation that contractions of known propositions do not change epistemic states. In fact, the postulate is valid both for AGM contractions and base-generated contractions.

The first three postulates constitute our counterpart of the 'basic postulates' of AGM contractions (more exactly, what is left of them). The rest of the postulates above can be called supplementary ones. Their role consists, in effect, in restricting the notion of contraction to *relational* contractions that are determined by the preference structure of the underlying epistemic state[4]. Fortunately, it turns out that all these postulates are also known from the literature on belief change. Postulate (E–5) is an exact counterpart of the AGM postulate (K–7). We have also partial antitony (E–4) that can be found already in the initial AGM study [Alchourrón *et al.*, 1985], where it was shown to be equivalent to (K–7). The proof, however, depended essentially on the recovery postulate (K–5) which is absent from our list. Partial antitony was also used by Hansson in [1993a] under the name 'conjunctive trisection'. Finally, cumulativity (E–6) corresponds to a combination of the two 'AGM-like' postulates introduced by Hans Rott in [1992]:

(K–7c) If $A \in K \div (A \wedge B)$, then $K \div B \subseteq K \div (A \wedge B)$

(K–8c) If $A \in K \div (A \wedge B)$, then $K \div (A \wedge B) \subseteq K \div B$

These postulates are extensively used in [Rott, 1993] for describing contraction functions definable by relational AGM frames (see below).

As can be seen, our postulates preserve much of the 'rationality' behind AGM contractions. In what follows we will see also that the rest of the AGM postulates can be satisfied by imposing additional constraints on epistemic states. Among other things, this will help us to reveal some constitutive principles underlying the AGM approach.

[3]Actually, the conclusion of this postulate can be strengthened to the identity of the contracted epistemic states themselves, that is, to $\mathbb{E} - A = \mathbb{E} - B$. However, this stronger version will not be needed in our present context.

[4]So, our notion of contraction is more specific in this respect than partial meet contractions of AGM.

We define now two notions that will play an important role in our analysis of contractions. It turns out that any contraction function allows to 'restore' the sets of propositions that are, respectively, believed and known in any epistemic state that generates it.

Even AGM contractions allow for a situation in which the contracted proposition is still retained in the contracted belief set. This is what is happening, for example, when we try to delete a logically valid proposition. This abnormal behavior points out that the proposition in question is considered as belonging to our knowledge rather than to our beliefs, and hence as impossible to retract. To make the discussion of such propositions more precise, let us introduce the following definition:

DEFINITION 5. A proposition A will be said to be *known* with respect to a contraction function, if $A \in [\mathbb{E} - A]$; otherwise, it will be called *contingent*. The set of known propositions will be called the *knowledge set of* the contraction function and denoted by $\mathcal{K}_-$.

According to the intended interpretation, $\mathcal{K}_-$ consists of propositions that are known in the associated epistemic state. As we will show in the next section, this set determines, in effect, the internal logic that governs the behavior of contractions.

DEFINITION 6. A proposition A will be said to be *believed* with respect to a contraction function, if $A \in [\mathbb{E} - \bot]$. The set of all such propositions will be called the *belief set of* the contraction function.

As can be seen, $[\mathbb{E} - \bot]$ is a set of propositions that are believed in the absence of falsity $\bot$. Note that if the underlying epistemic state $\mathbb{E}$ has a consistent belief set, then $[\mathbb{E} - \bot]$ is precisely the belief set of $\mathbb{E}$. As can be anticipated, it will play an important role in characterizing AGM contractions.

4.2 The internal logic of contractions and the success postulate

Following the lead of [Alchourrón *et al.*, 1985], the logic presupposed in practically all current studies of belief change is taken to be an arbitrary Tarski consequence relation satisfying compactness, supraclassicality and the deduction theorem. We will call such relations *classical consequence relations* in what follows, and will denote by Th the associated provability operator.

Any classical consequence relation can be seen as a classical entailment augmented with some auxiliary non-logical axioms. And as we will see now, the underlying logic of any contraction function is uniquely determined by taking the knowledge set $\mathcal{K}_-$ as a set of such non-logical axioms. Below we will denote by $Th_{\mathcal{K}_-}$ the least classical consequence relation that includes $\mathcal{K}_-$.

Only three AGM postulates depend on the underlying consequence relation: closure (K–1), success (K–4) and equivalence (K–6). Translated into our language, they read as follows:

(EC) $Th([\mathbb{E} - A]) = [\mathbb{E} - A]$;

(ES) If $A \notin Th(\emptyset)$, then $A \notin [\mathbb{E} - A]$;

(EE) If $A \leftrightarrow B \in Th(\emptyset)$, then $[\mathbb{E} - A]) = [\mathbb{E} - B]$.

Accordingly, we will say that a contraction function *respects* a consequence relation Th, if it satisfies the above three conditions. Then the following result, proved in [Bochman, 1999a], shows that $Th_{\mathcal{K}_-}$ provides an adequate description of the logic underlying a given contraction function.

THEOREM 7.

1. *Any contraction function respects* $Th_{\mathcal{K}_-}$.
2. *If a contraction function satisfies (EC) and (ES) with respect to a classical consequence relation* Th*, then the latter coincides with* $Th_{\mathcal{K}_-}$.

As the above result shows, instead of the classical entailment, we could as well choose $Th_{\mathcal{K}_-}$ as our underlying logic. Moreover, in the latter case we would have that our contraction function satisfies the success postulate (ES). Thus, the effect of the latter postulate amounts to 'fixing' the underlying logic of contraction.

5 CANONICAL EPISTEMIC STATES

In this section we will outline the construction of a *canonical epistemic state* for a given contraction function, given in [Bochman, 1999a]. The construction was used there in the proof of a number of representation theorems for belief contraction functions that we will describe in the next section. Also, we will use such canonical epistemic states later in giving some new, 'refined' representation results.

So far we have imposed no restrictions on potential epistemic states that generate belief contraction functions. It can happen, however, that an abstract epistemic state contains no admissible belief states that would be maximally preferred. In order to exclude such cases, we will require below that both the original epistemic state and all its contractions should have preferred admissible states. Such epistemic states will be called *smooth*. The smoothness restriction is actually well-known in the literature on nonmonotonic reasoning (see [Kraus *et al.*, 1990]).

For a proposition A and an abstract epistemic state $\mathbb{E}$, we will denote by $]A[$ the set of all admissible belief states from $\mathbb{E}$ that do not support A.

DEFINITION 8. An abstract epistemic state will be called *smooth* if, for any contingent proposition A and a state $s \in]A[$, either s is maximal preferred in $]A[$, or there exists a state t such that $s \prec t$ and t is maximal preferred in $]A[$.

It is easy to check that any smooth epistemic state produces a belief contraction function in our sense. Moreover, it was shown in [Bochman, 1999a] that any contraction function is generated by some abstract epistemic state. Below we will recast the relevant construction from [Bochman, 1999a] in the terminology of belief contraction functions.

To begin with, for a given contraction function, we define the following relation among propositions:

$$A \leq B \quad \equiv \quad A \to B \in [\mathbb{E} - A \wedge B]$$

This relation turns out to be important in its own right: as we show in [Bochman, 1999b], it is a Tarski consequence relation that is intimately connected (actually, interdefinable) with the generalized epistemic entrenchment from [Rott, 1992]. For our present purposes, however, it is sufficient to note that this relation is a partial order.

Now, for any contingent proposition A, we define a set of theories that are normal for A.

DEFINITION 9. A deductively closed theory u will be called *normal for* a contingent proposition A if $A \notin u$ and, for any B such that $A \leq B$, either $B \in u$ or $[\mathbb{E} - B] \subseteq u$.

As was noted in [Bochman, 1999a], the set of normal theories can actually be restricted to normal theories that are either worlds (maximal deductively closed sets) or intersections of pairs of worlds $\alpha \cap \beta$ such that $\neg A \in \alpha$ and $A \in \beta$. This restriction will be extensively used in what follows.

Now we can define a *canonical epistemic state* for a given contraction function as follows:

- Admissible belief states are pairs (u, A), where A is contingent and u is a normal theory for A.
- $(v, B) \prec (u, A) \equiv A \leq B$ and $B \in u$.
- The labeling function l is defined as $l : (u, A) \mapsto u$.

As is shown in [Bochman, 1999a], the above description determines a smooth epistemic state, where $\prec$ is a strict partial order. Moreover, it provides a 'canonical epistemic state' for a given contraction function. As a result, we obtain

REPRESENTATION THEOREM 1. Any contraction function is generated by a smooth abstract epistemic state.

6 DETERMINATE, RECOVERING AND RATIONAL CONTRACTIONS

Using epistemic states as our semantic representation, we acquire an opportunity to determine the meaning of the postulates for contraction suggested by the AGM theory. As we will see, these postulates can be seen as conditions reflecting various restrictions on underlying epistemic states.

6.1 *Determinate contractions*

As we mentioned, common representations presuppose that the underlying epistemic state is determinate. Such states make valid the following two conditions for associated belief contraction functions:

(EI) *Inclusion*: $[\mathbb{E} - A] \subseteq [\mathbb{E} - \bot]$,

(EV) *Vacuity*: If $A \notin [\mathbb{E} - \bot]$, then $[\mathbb{E} - \bot] \subseteq [\mathbb{E} - A]$.

The above postulates correspond, respectively, to the AGM postulates of inclusion (K–2) and vacuity (K–3). A contraction function will be called *determinate* if it satisfies them.

An abstract epistemic state will be called *determinate* if it contains a unique preferred admissible belief state k that includes all admissible belief sets in the sense that, for any admissible state s, $l(s) \subset l(k)$. Clearly, the state k will determine the belief set of the epistemic state.

As shows the following result from [Bochman, 1999a], determinate epistemic states provide an adequate representation for determinate belief contraction functions:

REPRESENTATION THEOREM 2. A contraction function is determinate if and only if it is generated by a determinate epistemic state.

Though determinate epistemic states constitute a most common case we can meet in practice, we have argued earlier that determination should not be considered as a rationality constraint on our epistemic states. But if an epistemic state is not determinate, it may include a number of preferred belief states, and then contraction of some of these possibilities may actually result in a growth of information. Consequently, such epistemic states provide a natural and 'rational' way of violating both Inclusion and Vacuity. The example below illustrates how this could happen.

EXAMPLE 10. Let us consider a standard epistemic state $\mathcal{E}$ containing the following theories: $\{Th(p \to q), Th(p \vee q), Th(p), Th(q)\}$, with set inclusion as its preference order. This epistemic state is not determinate and, as is easy to see, $[\mathcal{E}] = Th(p \vee q)$. Contracting p from this state, however, will give us a new (and greater) belief set $Th(q)$. Thus, both inclusion and vacuity fail.

6.2 *Recovering contractions*

The famous and much disputed AGM postulate of recovery amounts in our setting to the following condition:

(ER) *Recovery* If $B \in [\mathbb{E} - \bot]$, then $A \to B \in [\mathbb{E} - A]$.

A contraction function will be called a *recovering contraction*, if it is determinate and satisfies Recovery. Note that if Th is an arbitrary classical consequence relation, then Recovery implies the more familiar AGM postulate of recovery with respect to Th:

(ER′) $[\mathbb{E} - \bot] \subseteq Th(A, [\mathbb{E} - A])$.

Accordingly, recovering contractions will satisfy already all the basic postulates for the AGM contraction functions. Moreover, for AGM contractions, partial antitony (E–4) is already equivalent to (K–7), while (K–7c) is a consequence of (K–7) — see [Alchourrón *et al.*, 1985; Rott, 1992]. Consequently, recovering contractions can also be characterized as contraction functions satisfying all the AGM postulates, except the last (K–8) which is replaced by Rott's (K–8c).

Let K be a deductively closed theory and $K\bot$ the set of its maximal subtheories, plus K itself.

DEFINITION 11. A determinate epistemic state $\mathbb{E}$ with a belief set K will be called an *AGM-state* if $l(s) \in K\bot$, for any admissible belief state s from $\mathbb{E}$.

It is easy to check that contraction functions determined by AGM-states satisfy recovery. Moreover, we show in [Bochman, 1999a] that such epistemic states provide an adequate representation of recovering contractions:

REPRESENTATION THEOREM 3. A contraction function is a recovering contraction iff it is generated by an epistemic AGM state.

Notice that the above representation result refers to arbitrary AGM states, not only to standard ones. This additional freedom (as compared with the standard AGM setting) is essential, as follows from a similar result for relational AGM-contractions proved by Hans Rott in [1993]. As is shown, in effect, by Rott, in order to have a representation in terms of AGM-states that are standard, we need further conditions. Rott gives the following sufficient condition that turns out also to be necessary in the finite case:

(K–8r) $K \div (A \wedge B) \subseteq Th(K \div A \cup K \div B)$

Thus, even in the finite case there are recovering contractions that are not representable by standard AGM models. Notice also that (K–8r) is a quite unusual condition, which can be anticipated on the basis of our subsequent results (see Corollary 14 below).

6.3 Rational contractions

An epistemic state will be called *modular* if its preference order is modular (ranked):

Modularity If $s \prec t$, then either $r \prec t$, or $s \prec r$, for any r.

Contraction functions determined by modular epistemic states satisfy already the last AGM postulate (K–8). Accordingly, 'full' AGM contractions belong to this class. However, the class of such contractions is larger, since it includes also contractions that do not satisfy the recovery postulate. It includes, for example, contraction functions called *Levi contractions* in [Hansson and Olsson, 1995].

A contraction function will be called *rational* if it satisfies the following two additional postulates:

ER1 If $A \notin [\mathbb{E} - A \wedge B]$, then $[\mathbb{E} - A \wedge B] \subseteq [\mathbb{E} - A]$.

ER2 If $B \in [\mathbb{E} - A]$ and $A \notin [\mathbb{E} - B]$, then $B \in [\mathbb{E} - A \wedge B]$.

As can be seen, (ER1) is nothing other than the last AGM postulate (K-8). As to (ER2), it seems to be new. For recovering contractions, however, it is a consequence of (ER1).

Any modular epistemic state determines a rational contraction function. Moreover, we show in [Bochman, 1999a] that any rational contraction function is determined by some *standard and monotonic* modular epistemic state.

REPRESENTATION THEOREM 4. A contraction function is rational iff it is generated by an epistemic state which is standard, monotonic and modular.

So rational contractions have a pleasant property that they can be always represented by standard monotonic epistemic states in the same language. If we add now recovery to the postulates of rational contractions, we obtain precisely contraction functions satisfying all the AGM postulates. In fact, the representation of full AGM contractions, given in [Alchourrón *et al.*, 1985] can be easily obtained by combining the results, stated above.

7 REFINED REPRESENTATION: WEAK MONOTONICITY AND SATURATEDNESS

The construction of a canonical epistemic state for a given contraction function, described earlier, allows to single out a number of special classes of epistemic states that would still be adequate for representing all contraction functions. For example, the preference relation of the canonical epistemic state is a strict partial order, so partially ordered epistemic states are sufficient for representing any contraction function. The result stated below establishes a number of further interesting conditions that can be safely imposed on the notion of an epistemic state in this sense.

Isaac Levi has given in [1991] an outline of an alternative coherentist theory of belief change that involves, in particular, weakening of some of the assumptions underlying the AGM approach (see also [Hansson and Olsson, 1995] for a formal representation of Levi's ideas). One of Levi's claims was that the monotonicity condition (see above) should be rejected, since not all growth in accepted beliefs constitutes a growth in informational value. Accordingly, he suggested that the monotonicity principle should be replaced by *weak monotonicity* that requires only that a 'bigger' belief set should not be worse that the given one. In addition, he suggested that instead of taking the set $K\bot$ of all maximal subsets of a belief set

K as a primary set of alternatives for choice, we should consider a broader class of 'saturatable' theories that satisfy only the condition that adding $\neg A$ transform them into worlds. More exactly, a deductive theory u will be called *A-saturatable* for some proposition A, if $Th(u, \neg A)$ is a world. Such theories can also be characterized by the condition that, for any proposition B, either $A \vee B$ or $A \vee \neg B$ should belong to u.

Generalizing a bit these ideas, we introduce the following definitions.

DEFINITION 12. An epistemic state $\mathbb{E}$ will be called

1. *weakly monotonic* if $s \prec t$ holds only when $l(t) \not\subseteq l(s)$;
2. *saturatable* if, for any state s that is preferred in $]A[$, $l(s)$ is an A-saturatable theory.

The following result shows that the above conditions can be safely imposed on epistemic states without changing the class of generated contraction functions.

COROLLARY 13. *Any contraction function is generated by some weakly monotonic and saturatable epistemic state.*

Proof. If $(u, A) \prec (v, B)$ holds in the canonical epistemic state, then, by the definition of the preference relation, $A \notin u$ and $A \in v$, and hence $v \not\subseteq u$. Thus, the canonical epistemic state is already weakly monotonic. Moreover, we have noted earlier that the set of normal theories for A can be restricted to either worlds or intersections of pairs of worlds $\alpha \cap \beta$ such that $\neg A \in \alpha$ and $A \in \beta$. As can be seen, each such theory will be A-saturated, and this immediately implies that the 'reduced' canonical epistemic state generated by such theories will be saturatable. ■

8 STANDARD EPISTEMIC STATES AND HIDDEN INFORMATION

To begin with, let us consider an abstract epistemic state $\mathbb{E}_0$ in the finite language $\{p, q\}$ determined by four states $\{s_1, s_2, s_3, s_4\}$ such that $s_3 \prec s_1$, $s_4 \prec s_2$, and the labeling function defined as follows: $l(s_1) = Th(p \wedge \neg q)$, $l(s_2) = Th(\neg p \wedge \neg q)$, and $l(s_3) = l(s_4) = Th(p \wedge q)$.

Actually, the above example was used in [Kraus *et al.*, 1990] for demonstrating that not all preferential inference relations are definable by injective models. We invite the reader to check also that there is no standard epistemic state *in the same language* that determines the same contraction function as $\mathbb{E}_0$. This will demonstrate that not all contraction functions are representable by standard epistemic states.

As has been said, a most plausible way of understanding non-standard abstract epistemic states consists in the assumption that such states involve information that is not expressible in the current language. We consider now this assumption in more details.

Assume that a language $\mathcal{L}$ is a restriction of another propositional language $\mathcal{L}_0$, and let $\mathbb{E}$ be some standard epistemic state in $\mathcal{L}_0$. This epistemic state generates some contraction function in $\mathcal{L}_0$, and hence *a certain contraction function in the restricted language* $\mathcal{L}$. However, as we already said, a standard epistemic state $\mathbb{E}$ may give raise to a non-standard epistemic state in the restricted language $\mathcal{L}$. Furthermore, it may well happen that the contraction function in the language $\mathcal{L}$ generated by this standard state $\mathbb{E}$ is not representable by any standard epistemic state *in* $\mathcal{L}$.

It seems completely unreasonable to exclude the above 'language-restricted' contraction functions from consideration: they can be seen as giving a partial description of some perfectly legitimate contraction operations on epistemic states. Hence we have to live with the possibility that some quite natural contraction functions are not representable by standard epistemic states *in the same language*. Fortunately, we will show now that this assumption of language restriction is sufficient for our contraction functions; namely, it turns out that any such function is determined by a standard epistemic state in a certain extended language. Moreover, we may require even that this epistemic state will satisfy, in addition, the Monotonicity property.

REPRESENTATION THEOREM 5. For any contraction function $\sim$ in the language $\mathcal{L}$ there exists a standard monotonic epistemic state $\mathbb{E}$ in some language $\mathcal{L}_0$ extending $\mathcal{L}$ such that its generated contraction function, restricted to $\mathcal{L}$, coincides with $\sim$.

Proof.[A sketch of the proof] We will construct an alternative canonical epistemic state as follows. First, for any formula A in $\mathcal{L}$, we will introduce a new propositional variable p_A. Then we define admissible states in the resulting extended language as theories having either the form $Th(\alpha \cup \{p_A\})$, where α is a normal world for A, or the form $Th(\alpha \cap \beta \cup \{\neg p_A\})$, where α, β are worlds and $\alpha \cap \beta$ is a normal theory for A.

Let $\tilde{p}_A$ denote either p_A or $\neg p_A$. We will define a preference relation $\prec_0$ on our new admissible states as follows:

$$Th(u \cup \{\tilde{p}_A\}) \prec_0 Th(v \cup \{\tilde{p}_B\}) \equiv (u, A) \prec (v, B)$$

Notice that our belief states are incomparable with respect to set inclusion. Indeed, if it were the case that $Th(u \cup \{\tilde{p}_A\}) \subset Th(v \cup \{\tilde{p}_B\}$, then, first of all, $\tilde{p}_A$ would coincide with $\tilde{p}_B$, and hence $A = B$. Now, if $\tilde{p}_A$ is p_A, then u and v should both be normal worlds for A, and hence the above inclusion is impossible. Similarly, if $\tilde{p}_A$ is $\neg p_A$, then u and v are pairs of distinct worlds, which also blocks the above inclusion.

Since our theories are incomparable with respect to set inclusion, the above defined preference order will vacuously satisfy monotonicity. Hence we need only to show that the constructed epistemic state is adequate for our contraction function. It is easy to check, however, that, on formulas from $\mathcal{L}$, the above 'extended' epistemic state will give the same results as the original canonical epistemic state. In particular, if A, B are formulas from $\mathcal{L}$, then $A \dashv B$ will be valid in the new epistemic state iff it is valid in the canonical epistemic state. But the canonical epistemic state is adequate for our contraction function, and we are done. ■

An important technical consequence of the above result is that restriction to standard monotonic epistemic states cannot be characterized using some 'simple' postulates for contractions.

By a general *inference rule* for contractions we will mean a rule of the form $\Gamma \vdash \Delta$, where Γ and Δ are sets of assertions of the form $B \in [\mathbb{E} - A]$[5]. The intended meaning of such inference rules is "If all assertions from Γ hold, then one of the assertions from Δ should hold". As can be shown, all our postulates for contraction functions, as well as all the AGM postulates, can be translated into inference rules in this sense.

An inference rule $\Gamma \vdash \Delta$ will be said to be *admissible* with respect to a set of contraction functions $\mathcal{K}$ if, for any contraction function $\sim \in \mathcal{K}$, if all assertions from Γ hold for $\sim$, then at least one assertion from Δ will also hold for $\sim$. Then we have

COROLLARY 14. *An inference rule is admissible for all contraction functions determined by monotonic standard epistemic states iff it is admissible for all contraction functions.*

Proof. If an inference rule $\Gamma \vdash \Delta$ does not hold for some contraction function $\sim$, the canonical abstract epistemic state for $\sim$ makes valid all assertions from Γ, but invalidates all Δ. This abstract epistemic state can be transformed into a standard monotonic epistemic state by the above theorem, and hence the inference rule will not hold for a certain contraction function determined by an ordinary monotonic epistemic state. ■

The above corollary implies, in particular, that a characterization of contraction functions determined by (monotonic) standard states in the same language cannot be achieved using simple additional conditions. This does not exclude, however, a possibility of a more complex characterization. Thus, the results of Rott [1993], mentioned earlier, show that such a characterization is often possible.

9 COHERENTISM VERSUS FOUNDATIONALISM

The destiny of derived beliefs in belief change, and the role of justification in belief acceptance lie at the heart of the dispute between coherentist and foundational approaches to belief and knowledge (see, e.g., [Harman, 1986; Gärdenfors, 1990; Val, 1994]). In this respect, the AGM theory is usually interpreted as a realization of the coherentist approach, while the theory of base change is seen as an

[5]Such assertions correspond to *contraction rules* used in [Bochman, 1999a] as an alternative representation of belief contraction functions.

embodiment of the foundational approach. It should be noted, however, that the understanding of both coherentism and foundationalism when applied to the problem of belief change is somewhat different from the traditional view of these notions. Given earlier description of the AGM and base-generation approaches, we can describe the distinction between these doctrines of belief change as follows.

A 'pure' coherentist approach is based on an assumption that belief sets are formed only on the basis of an overall coherence among potential beliefs. So the only guiding principles in this setting are consistency and preference relations among alternative sets of beliefs that reflect the level or degree of their coherence. In particular, *no set of beliefs should be excluded as a potential option for choice* (though it can be excluded as a solution to the choice task, being a less 'coherent' option than others). This latter claim, called the *homogeneity principle* in what follows, can be seen as a guiding principle behind the AGM theory. The principle is also forcefully advocated by Isaac Levi [1991; 1997] who suggested an alternative theory of belief change. Accordingly, we will consider the homogeneity principle as the characteristic property of the coherentist approach.

The foundationalist approach to belief change explicitly accounts for the fact that some of the beliefs are derivative and depend on other, more basic, beliefs. Consequently it reduces the set of admissible options to 'well-formed' ones that are generated as deductive closures of basic propositions. In other words, the essence of this approach can be seen in rejecting the above-mentioned homogeneity principle. Note that the preference relation among the alternatives is no longer essential in this setting. Moreover, a 'pure' foundationalist approach could be expressed by the claim that the dependence structure among beliefs (that is determined, in particular, by singling out a set of basic beliefs) should be seen as the only principle guiding our choice decisions in belief change. The preference relation is reduced in this case simply to the relation of set inclusion among admissible options, and hence is wholly determined by the underlying dependence structure.

In order to make the relevant differences more vivid, we will introduce below two 'extreme' kinds of epistemic states that can be seen as corresponding, respectively, to a purely coherentist and purely foundationalist paradigm.

DEFINITION 15. A standard and determinate epistemic state $\mathbb{E}$ will be called

1. *homogeneous* if the set of admissible belief sets coincides with the set of all deductively closed theories that include the knowledge set and are included in the belief set of $\mathbb{E}$.

2. *pure* if $\prec$ coincides with the set inclusion on the theories from $\mathbb{E}$.

Homogeneous epistemic states presuppose, in effect, that no dependence relations hold among believed propositions, except for logical ones, and hence any deductively closed subset of the belief set is admissible. Consequently, the structure of such a state is determined solely by a preference relation on all subtheories of the belief set. Notice that the AGM paradigm belongs to this class, but involves an additional 'maximizing' property that the preference relation should satisfy monotonicity. This additional assumption is rejected in another coherentist approach to belief change suggested by Isaac Levi [1991] (see above). As we will show below, homogeneous epistemic states turn out to be adequate for representing a broad range of belief contraction functions.

Pure epistemic states, on the other hand, 'trivialize' the preferential component of the notion of an epistemic state by reducing it to set inclusion among admissible theories. So, a pure epistemic state can be identified, in effect, with a set of deductively closed theories. A theory of belief change on such states is the main subject of [Bochman, 1999c]. It shown, in particular, that pure epistemic states can be described in terms of dependence relations holding among propositions. This representation can be viewed as reflecting a rigid foundationalist position according to which dependence relations among propositions is the only essential factor in determining our epistemic states and changes made to it.

Below we will consider in more details expressive capabilities of these two kinds of representations.

9.1 *The coherentist paradigm*

As we said, a purely coherentist approach is characterized by the assumption that all deductively closed subsets of the belief set should be considered as admissible options for choice. This is reflected in our notion of a homogeneous determinate epistemic state. We will show now that this kind of approach is reasonable also for epistemic states in general. For *fully homogeneous* epistemic state, described below, the preference relation is defined, in effect, on all theories of the language.

DEFINITION 16. An abstract epistemic state $\mathbb{E}$ in the language $\mathcal{L}$ will be called *fully homogeneous* if any deductively closed theory in $\mathcal{L}$ that includes the knowledge set of $\mathbb{E}$ is an admissible belief set in $\mathbb{E}$.

The following important result shows, in effect, that the coherentist approach can be always used in giving representation for contraction functions.

REPRESENTATION THEOREM 6. Any contraction function in the language $\mathcal{L}$ is generated by some fully homogeneous epistemic state in $\mathcal{L}$.

Proof. Let $\mathbb{E}_0$ be the canonical epistemic state for a given contraction function. We will extend $\mathbb{E}_0$ to a fully homogeneous epistemic state. Let $\mathcal{U}$ be the set of all deductively closed theories u including the knowledge set $\mathcal{K}_-$ that are not admissible belief sets of $\mathbb{E}_0$. We will consider all such theories as new admissible belief states and extend the preference order as follows. First, if $u \in \mathcal{U}$ is not a world in $\mathcal{L}$, we will subordinate it to all worlds in $\mathcal{U}$ that include u, as well as to all states of the form (α, B), where α is a world containing u. Then any world in $\mathcal{U}$ will be subordinated to all worlds α such that $\alpha = l(s)$, for some state s in $\mathbb{E}_0$. In this way we will obtain a new state $\mathbb{E}$ that is already fully homogeneous. We will show now that $\mathbb{E}$ and $\mathbb{E}_0$ generate the same contraction function. If $s \in \mathbb{E}$ is an 'old' state, then it is easy to see that it has the same more preferred states in $\mathbb{E}$ as it had in $\mathbb{E}_0$. Consequently, for any A, such a state will be maximal in $]A[$ with respect to $\mathbb{E}$ iff it was maximal in $\mathbb{E}_0$. Moreover, we will show that no new state $u \in \mathcal{U}$ can be maximal in $]A[$. Indeed, if u is such a new state and $A \notin u$, then there must exist a world α including u such that $\neg A \in \alpha$. Now if α does not coincide with u, then u will always be subordinated to some world or state that does not satisfy A, and hence u is not maximal in $]A[$. Assume now that $u = \alpha$. Since $\mathcal{K}_-$ is included in u, A does not belong to $\mathcal{K}_-$ and hence it is contingent. Consequently there must exist a world β that is normal for A. But then $s = (\beta, A)$ should be an admissible state of $\mathbb{E}_0$, and $u \prec s$. Thus, in this case also u cannot be maximal in $]A[$.

Thus, we have shown, in effect, that a state s is maximal in $]A[$ with respect to $\mathbb{E}$ iff s is a state of $\mathbb{E}_0$ and is also maximal in $]A[$ with respect to $\mathbb{E}_0$. Consequently, both states should produce the same contraction function. Now the result follows from the fact that $\mathbb{E}_0$ is adequate for representing our contraction function. ∎

The importance of the above result lies primarily in demonstrating that the coherentist approach turns out to be sufficiently expressive to capture all reasonable kinds of contraction functions in our sense. Moreover, we can combine this result with previous ones and obtain then that conditions of weak monotonicity and saturatedness can be also imposed on such states without changing the generated contraction functions.

As a special case of the above result, the following theorem shows that determinate homogeneous epistemic states are sufficient to provide a representation for any determinate contraction. We omit the proof.

REPRESENTATION THEOREM 7. Any determinate contraction function is generated by a determinate homogeneous epistemic state.

Thus, any determinate contraction is generated by some determinate homogeneous epistemic state. We can require also that the relevant preference relation should satisfy weak monotonicity. Note, however, that we cannot impose strong monotonicity in this setting, since this would immediately imply the validity of the recovery postulate. Thus, the generality of our coherentist representation essentially depends on non-acceptance of the strong maximization principle.

9.2 *Pure foundationalist approach*

As is shown in [Bochman, 1999c], pure epistemic states can be alternatively described in terms of *dependence relationships* holding between believed propositions. In this way the framework of pure epistemic states allows to represent a general foundationalist approach to belief change. Still, our version of foundationalism is very moderate, since the net of dependencies is not assumed in general to have a well-founded structure starting with universally acceptable self-justified 'basic' propositions. In this way the version of foundationalism we suggested avoids much of the criticism raised against the foundationalist approach.

Pure epistemic states generate a special class of belief contraction functions that we call *foundational contractions*. Unfortunately, the problem of a complete characterization of such contraction functions remains open. Still, it can be easily checked that all such functions satisfy the following additional postulate:

(EP) If $B \in [\mathbb{E} - A]$, then $[\mathbb{E} - A \wedge B] \subseteq [\mathbb{E} - A]$ (persistence)

Actually, there are some reasonable grounds for conjecturing that adding this postulate to our characterization of general contraction functions, given earlier, would provide the required complete characterization for foundational belief contractions. Anyway, the validity of the persistence postulate is sufficient for establishing that *foundational belief contractions are incomparable with AGM contractions*: on the one hand, the former do not satisfy, in general, recovery (K–6) and the last AGM postulate (K–8); on the other hand, persistence (EP) does not follow even from the full list of the AGM postulates. Thus, there are 'fully rational' AGM contractions that are not foundational contractions. Moreover, it can be shown that persistence cannot even be added to the AGM postulates, on pain of triviality: as is shown in [**?**; **?**][Bochman, 1998], a contraction function satisfies the basic AGM postulates and persistence only if it is a full meet contraction. So, foundational contractions constitute an alternative understanding of belief contraction that is not subsumed by the AGM theory.

As we have shown, the coherentist paradigm provides a powerful representation framework allowing to capture all contraction functions in our sense. In particular, it allows in principle to represent foundational contractions that we have considered as paradigmatic for a purely foundationalist approach. Speaking more generally, an appropriately chosen preference relation can incorporate all the relevant information embodied in the dependence structure of an epistemic state. The foundationalist approach turns out to be inferior in this respect, since the class of contraction functions representable by pure epistemic states is restricted to foundational contractions.

All these facts notwithstanding, the above picture should not be construed as demonstrating the 'final victory' of coherentism.

To begin with, a prerequisite for a successful implementation of a coherentist representation consists in determining an adequate preference relation on all subsets of the belief set. It seems, however, that in many cases such a task poses an unbearable burden on our capabilities. If we know, however, that the belief state is base-generated, or even has a more general dependence structure, as described in [Bochman, 1999c], we can drastically reduce the set of alternatives for choice, and in this way would obtain a much more feasible (and computable) representation for subsequent belief changes. As was aptly remarked by Hansson in [1992], the base of a belief set can relieve the preference mechanism of the majority of its functions.

A further support for the viability of the foundationalist approach can be found in [Rott, 1993; Val, 1994], where it has been shown that a large class of AGM contraction and revision functions admit a base-generated representation. In addition, it is shown in [Bochman, 1999c; Bochman, 1998] that pure epistemic states turn out to be sufficiently expressive for a large class of belief change operations found in the literature. In particular, recovering contractions (see above) as well as a broad range of AGM revision functions are representable in this framework. For such functions, the foundational approach turns out to be no less expressive than the traditional AGM approach.

Severe withdrawal

As we said, foundational contraction functions do not satisfy, in general, the last AGM postulate (K–8). However, this postulate will hold for pure epistemic states in which the admissible belief sets are linearly ordered by inclusion. We will call such pure epistemic states and their associated foundational contractions *linear* in what follows.

It turns out that linear foundational contractions coincide with *severe withdrawals* suggested recently by Rott and Pagnucco [1997]. A similar notion, called *mild contraction* has been introduced by Levi in [1997]. It is interesting to note, however, that though these studies give quite a different description for this kind of contraction, in both cases the authors suggest a broadly coherentist justification for this notion.

As is shown, in effect, in [Rott and Pagnucco, 1997], severe withdrawals can be characterized as determinate contractions satisfying the following postulate:

(EL) If $B \notin [\mathbb{E} - A]$, then $[\mathbb{E} - A] \subseteq [\mathbb{E} - B]$ (linearity)

The following representation result has been proved in [Bochman, 1998].

THEOREM 17. *A contraction function is a severe withdrawal iff it is a linear foundational contraction.*

Linearity is a severe constraint on epistemic states. For example, severe withdrawals satisfy the following *Expulsiveness* property (see [Rott and Pagnucco, 1997]): if A and B are arbitrary contingent propositions, then either $A \notin [\mathbb{E} - B]$ or $B \notin [\mathbb{E} - A]$. So, in the linear case any two sentences may affect one another in contractions. We agree here with Rott and Pagnucco that this is an undesirable property. However, as can be easily checked, this property is not germane to foundational contractions, so we can simply turn Expulsiveness into an argument against taking linearity as a 'rationality constraint' on epistemic states.

10 CONCLUSIONS

In order to have a more adequate and uniform representation of belief change, we need a notion of an epistemic state more complex than simply a set of beliefs. Such an epistemic state should embody various dependencies and preferences among believed propositions that would be sufficient for determining the results of its rational revision in response to new data.

We have demonstrated that the suggested explication of the notion of an epistemic state subsumes the major existing approaches to representing belief change. Despite this generality, it determines natural belief change operations preserving much of the 'rationality' embodied in the traditional AGM approach. Moreover, it allows to give a precise semantic interpretation for the rest of the AGM postulates, including those that are considered as basic in the AGM framework.

It should be stressed, however, that the suggested notion of an epistemic state is more versatile and general than what is strictly needed for a representation of the two major approaches to belief change, namely the AGM theory and the base-generation paradigm. We have seen, in particular, that many alternative approaches, such as Levi's coherentist theory [Levi, 1991; Levi, 1997] or a foundational theory of flock-generated change [Fagin *et al.*, 1986], can be naturally represented in this framework. In short, the suggested explication of the notion of an epistemic state gives us a very broad view on the problem of belief change that indicates also some plausible alternative ways of dealing with it.

Our framework has allowed us to provide a more exact setting for studying the relation between coherentist and foundationalist approaches to belief change. We have shown, in particular, that a (reasonably generalized) coherentist approach gives a comprehensive representation for a broad range of belief contraction functions. We have singled out also the class of foundational belief contraction functions that can be seen as representing a 'purely foundational' view of belief change.

The present study can be seen as a contribution to a general theory of belief change. Looking from this standpoint, there is clearly much to be done in order to transform our framework into a full-fledged theory. To begin with, we have considered here only one operation on epistemic states, namely contraction. Contraction is rightly seen by many as one of the most important belief change operations. But there are at least two other operations that are commonly considered as essential for a comprehensive theory of belief change, namely expansions and revisions (see [Gärdenfors, 1988; Levi, 1991]). It turns out, however, that the task of describing corresponding operations on epistemic states is far from being trivial or unequivocal. Some initial steps in this direction are made in [Bochman, 1999c; Bochman, 1998], where we introduce a number of such operations in the framework of pure epistemic states. Further work is needed, however, in order to account for the mutual influence of these operations and the preference order among admissible states.

ACKNOWLEDGEMENT

I am grateful to the anonymous reviewer for his extensive and instructive comments.

Computer Science Department, Technological Academic Institute, Holon, Israel.

REFERENCES

[Alchourrón *et al.*, 1985] C. Alchourrón, P. Gärdenfors and D. Makinson. On the logic of theory change: Partial meet contraction and revision functions. *Journal of Symbolic Logic*, **50**, 510–530, 1985.

[Bochman, 1998] A. Bochman. A foundationalist view of the AGM theory of belief change. To appear in *Artificial Intelligence*.

[Bochman, 1999a] A. Bochman. Belief conraction as nonmonotonic inference. To appear in the *Journal of Symbolic Logic*, 1999.

[Bochman, 1999b] A. Bochman. Entrenchment versus dependence: Coherence and foundations in belief change. (In preparation), 1999.

[Bochman, 1999c] A. Bochman. A foundational theory of belief and belief change. *Artificial Intelligence*, **108**, 309–352, 1999.

[Fagin *et al.*, 1986] R. Fagin, J. D. Ullman, G. M. Kuper and M. Y. Vardi. Updating logical databases. In *Advances in Computing Research*, volume 3, pp. 1–18. 1986.

[Fuhrmann and Hansson, 1994] A. Fuhrmann and S. O. Hansson. A survey of multiple contractions. *Journal of Logic, Language and Information*, **3**, 39–76, 1994.

[Fuhrmann, 1991] A. Fuhrmann. Theory contraction through base contraction. *Journal of Philosophical Logic*, **20**, 175–203, 1991.

[Gärdenfors and Rott, 1995] P. Gärdenfors and H. Rott. Belief revision. In *Handbook of Logic in Artificial Intelligence and Logic Programming*, Vol. 4, D. M. Gabbay *et al.*, eds. pp. 35–132. Clarendon Press, Oxford, 1995.

[Gärdenfors, 1988] P. Gärdenfors. *Knowledge in Flux: Modeling the Dynamics of Epistemic States*. Bradford Books, MIT Press, 1988.

[Gärdenfors, 1990] P. Gärdenfors. The dynamics of belief systems: Foundations vs. coherence theories. *Revue Internationale de Philosophie*, **44**, 24–46, 1990.

[Hansson and Olsson, 1995] S. O. Hansson and E. J. Olsson. Levi contractions and AGM contractions: a comparison. *Notre Dame Journal of Formal Logic*, **36**, 103–119, 1995.

[Hansson, 1992] S. O. Hansson. In defense of base contraction. *Synthese*, **91**, 239–245, 1992.

[Hansson, 1993a] S. O. Hansson. Changes of disjunctively closed bases. *Journal of Logic, Language and Information*, **2**, 255–284, 1993.

[Hansson, 1993b] S. O. Hansson. Theory contraction and base contraction unified. *Journal of Symbolic Logic*, **58**, 602–625, 1993.

[Harman, 1986] G. Harman. *Change in View*. Bradford Books, MIT Press, 1986.

[Kraus *et al.*, 1990] S. Kraus, D. Lehmann, and M. Magidor. Nonmonotonic reasoning, preferential models and cumulative logics. *Artificial Intelligence*, **44**, 167–207, 1990.

[Levi, 1991] I. Levi. *The Fixation of Belief and Its Undoing*. Cambridge University Press, 1991.

[Levi, 1997] I. Levi. Contraction and Informational Value. Columbia University, fifth version, August 1997.

[Nebel, 1989] B. Nebel. A knowledge level analysis of belief revision. In *Proceedings of the First International Conference on Principles of Knowledge Representation and Reasoning*, R. J. Brachman et al., eds. pp. 301–311. Morgan Kauffman, 1989.

[Poole, 1988] D. Poole. A logical framework for default reasoning. *Artificial Intelligence*, **36**, 27–47, 1988.

[Rott and Pagnucco, 1997] H. Rott and M. Pagnucco. Severe withdrawal (and recovery). (to appear), 1997.

[Rott, 1992] H. Rott. Preferential belief change using generalized epistemic entrenchment. *Journal of Logic, Language and Information*, **1**, 45–78, 1992.

[Rott, 1993] H. Rott. Belief contraction in the context of the general theory of rational choice. *Journal of Symbolic Logic*, **58**, 1426–1450, 1993.

[Val, 1994] A. Del Val. On the relation between the coherence and foundations theories of belief revision. In *Proceedings AAAI-94*, pages 909–914, 1994.

JOHN CANTWELL

TWO NOTIONS OF EPISTEMIC ENTRENCHMENT

1 INTRODUCTION

A powerful feature of the tradition of belief change that loosely can be called the AGM tradition (after [Alchourrón *et al.*, 1985]) is the multitude of seemingly quite distinct semantic intuitions that all converge on the same theory. Notions such as the partial meet of remainder sets, systems of spheres, similarity relations on worlds and a relation of epistemic entrenchment on sentences or propositions have all been shown to be closely related both directly in terms of direct constructions of one notion from the other, and indirectly, through providing representation theorems for the Gärdenfors postulates for contraction and revision (see [Gärdenfors, 1988]).

In fact, most of these relationships were well established prior to their application in belief change. David Lewis established in [1973] the close connection between similarity relations on possible worlds, systems of spheres and a relation closely related to that of epistemic entrenchment. A system of spheres construction appropriate for the Gärdenfors postulates was given by [Grove, 1988], who established the connection between partial meet approach in the original AGM paper and systems of spheres. (c.f. [Gärdenfors, 1988]).

All these results depend on rather strong assumptions on the structures involved. In particular, systems of spheres are usually taken to be linearly ordered by inclusion, this corresponds to the assumption that the similarity relation on possible worlds be connected: any two worlds are comparable as regards similarity. In [Lindström and Rabinowicz, 1991] (henceforth L&R) the linearity assumption on system of spheres was challenged. Dropping the linearity assumption on systems of spheres has as a result that in general there will be several different minimal spheres on which to base a contraction or a revision operation. As a result the notion of a system of "spheres" becomes rather inappropriate and so I shall call these more general structures *hypertheories* after [Segerberg, 1995] and the elements of the hypertheory *fallbacks* after L&R.

L&R suggested that, in the more general framework provided by hypertheories, contraction and revision operations should be viewed as relational: there can be several possible outcomes of a contraction or a revision operation–each based on a minimal fallback–and the hypertheory does not contain information regarding which outcome to choose. Of course, this is not the only way of treating the fact that there are multiple minimal fallbacks on which to base belief change operations. A different approach, pursued in [Cantwell, 199y] is to consider the union of these fallbacks as the appropriate unit on which to base belief change operations. This corresponds to the wide-spread intuition that whenever there are several equally good but irreconcilable theories to choose from, one should defer

M.-A. Williams and H. Rott (eds.), Frontiers in Belief Revision, 221–245.

judgement and accept only what they have in common until further evidence can adjudicate between them–this I call the *sceptical* approach. Thus dropping linearity on systems of spheres need not result in a relational notion of belief change. In this paper I will only be concerned with sceptical belief-change, mainly with contraction.

L&R showed that the assumption that systems of spheres be linearly ordered by inclusion corresponded precisely to the assumption that the relation of epistemic entrenchment considered by them be connected. When each of these assumptions are dropped, the two constructions still stand in a one-to-one relation. However, when we drop connectedness on epistemic entrenchment several of the appealing direct relationships between epistemic entrenchment and belief change are lost. In [Cantwell, 199y] it was shown that there is no simple way (this is made precise in the paper) of constructing operations such as revision and contraction on the basis of the weakened notion of epistemic entrenchment. Furthermore, it was shown that if we give up linearity on hypertheories and insist that belief change operations be sceptical, then the epistemic entrenchment relation can no longer be elicited from belief-changing behaviour. Thus, in the latter case, the close relationship between belief change operations and the theory of rational choice, a relationship extensively studied in [Rott, 1996; Rott, 1993], as applied to epistemic entrenchment is lost.

Hans Rott [1992] has proposed a different way of weakening the assumptions put on the original notion epistemic entrenchment than L&R. His proposal has precisely the virtues that L&R's proposal lack: there is a simple way of constructing contractions and revisions from an entrenchment relation and entrenchment can be elicited from contraction behaviour. Prima facie, at least, these virtues speak in favour of Rott's conception of epistemic entrenchment. However, Rott's proposal does not include any way of relating epistemic entrenchment to systems of spheres or hypertheories. It would seem then that there are two distinct directions in which we can proceed when weakening the assumptions on our semantics for belief change operations: one which abides by the "minimal spheres" intuition, and one which abides by the "rational choice" intuition.

In fact, I will show that these two directions are closely related, in some important cases equivalent. The two notions of epistemic entrenchment are related, but in a rather roundabout manner, which seems easiest to explicate by their mutual relationship to hypertheories. The analysis of this relationship is the core of this paper.

In [Cantwell, 199y] I made use of a version of DDL (Dynamic Doxastic Logic, see [Segerberg, 1995]), roughly, a propositional logic containing a belief operator, dynamic operators for belief change and a binary relation of epistemic entrenchment. Although sceptical belief change was axiomatised, it was also shown that both sceptical and relational belief change gave rise to logics that were not compact, and thus hard to work with. Here I shall study a less expressive version of DDL: one that does not contain a relation of epistemic entrenchment. A strongly complete finitary axiomatisation of sceptical, recovery-style contractions will be presented, in the weakened language.

This paper can be seen as a continuation of an earlier paper concerning logics of belief change without linearity [Cantwell, 199y]. I have attempted to keep the present paper self-contained, so to some extent I will cover the same ground as the earlier paper, however, for obvious reasons some older material will be presented in a more condensed form.

2 SOME PRELIMINARIES

Let U denote a set of points representing the possible states in some domain of enquiry. A *proposition* is some subset of U. The set of propositions relative to U is denoted by $\mathcal{B}$. I shall assume that $\mathcal{B}$ is denumerable, that it is closed under finite intersections, unions and complement, and, finally, is compact. For any subset X of U define the *closure* of X as:

$$\mathcal{C}(X) = \bigcap\{P \in \mathcal{B} : X \subseteq P\}$$

X is *closed* if and only if $X = \mathcal{C}(X)$. I shall make use of a number of well-known properties of propositional algebras of this kind, one that perhaps deserves special mention is: if $X, Y \subseteq U, P \in \mathcal{B}$ and $X \cap Y \subseteq P$, then there are $Q, R \in \mathcal{B}$ such that $X \subseteq Q, Y \subseteq R$ and $Q \cap R \subseteq P$.

The following also needs mentioning:

THEOREM 1 (Cantwell, 1999). *If C is a non-empty inclusion chain of closed sets, then $\forall P \in \mathcal{B}$, if $\bigcap C \subseteq P$, then $\exists Y \in C, Y \subseteq P$.*

3 DDL AND ITS SEMANTICS

Below I shall consider a number of different semantic ideas for contraction. It will be helpful to employ a fixed language to speak of contractions but to allow the semantics to vary. The language I shall use is a variant of Dynamic Doxastic Logic.

It consists of an at most denumerably infinite set of propositional letters, denoted by $p, q, r, \ldots$ and the standard Boolean connectives: $\wedge, \neg, \vee, \rightarrow$ and $\leftrightarrow$. $\bot$ denotes the inconsistent sentence and $\top$ the tautology. The formulas generated by the propositional letters and the Boolean connectives are called *Boolean*. The set of Boolean formulas will be denoted by $\mathcal{L}_{PC}$.

The basic idea is that Boolean expressions are *objective*: they pertain to those aspects of the world about which the agent has beliefs. To simplify things I assume that the agent has no higher-order beliefs: beliefs about beliefs and so on. Accordingly the language contains an operator for B belief, constrained so that it only operates on *Boolean* formulas.

The language also contains a set of *action terms* $\div\phi$, defined for each *Boolean* formula ϕ. An action term α will occur inside a dynamic operator: $[\alpha]$, which is subject to no restrictions other than those imposed on α. $< \div\phi > \psi$ is defined as $\neg[\div\phi]\neg\psi$.

Note that $< \div\phi > \psi$ should be understood as stating that there is some way of contracting ϕ such that ψ holds, while an expression like $[\div\phi]B\psi$ should be understood roughly as: if there is a way of contracting ϕ, then ψ is believed after the contraction. The expression $[\div\phi]\bot$ will mean that there is no way of contracting ϕ. This will happen, for instance, if ϕ is a logical truth.

The reader should keep in mind the difference between expressions like $[\div\phi]\neg\phi$ which states that if there is a way of contracting ϕ, ϕ comes out false, as opposed to expressions like $[\div\phi]\neg B\phi$ which states that if there is a way of contracting ϕ, ϕ will no longer be believed. The former statement will not in general be true, while the latter will come out valid in all the models considered: it is the way to formulate the postulate of *success* in DDL.

The Boolean formulae are mapped onto the propositional structure $\mathcal{B}$ as follows. Let V be a function such that for each propositional letter p in $\mathcal{L}_{PC}$, $V(p) \in \mathcal{B}$. The *intension* of a Boolean formula ϕ is given by the function $||\phi||_{V,U,\mathcal{B}}$ and is defined in the usual fashion (suppressing the sub-scripts):$||p|| = V(p)$, for each propositional constant p; $||\phi \wedge \psi|| = ||\phi|| \cap ||\psi||$; $||\neg\phi|| = U - ||\psi||$, and so on for the other Boolean connectives. To simplify the exposition I will assume that the models are *expressive*: if $P \in \mathcal{B}$, then there is some ϕ such that $||\phi|| = P$.

One can think of U as determining the domain of enquiry of the agent, i.e. those aspects of the world about which the agent has beliefs. These could, for instance, be the different possible outcomes of some experiment. As already indicated I assume that the agent's own beliefs and contraction strategies are not part of the agent's domain of enquiry, that is, the agent forms no "second-order" beliefs about his or her beliefs or about contraction behaviour. Let W denote a set of *possible worlds* that determines not only the current domain of enquiry but also the agent's current beliefs and doxastic dispositions. When $x \in W$ let $wst\,(x) \in U$ denote that part of the current state of the world that is included in the agent's domain of enquiry. Let *bst* (x) denote the belief *set* of the agent at x, that is, *bst* (x) is a closed subset of U.

A contraction with a proposition P is regarded as a *doxastic action* an action that changes the belief state of the agent but not the belief-independent state of the world. This is represented with a binary relation $R^{\div P}$ on the elements of W. If $(x, y) \in R^{\div P}$, then *bst* (x) is the original belief set and *bst* (y) is the new belief set after the contraction. I shall throughout assume that if there is a way of contracting P, then this is uniquely defined. That is, a standing assumption will be:

$$\text{If } (x, y) \in R^{\div P} \text{ and } (x, z) \in R^{\div P}, \text{ then } y = z.$$

Below I shall consider a number of different kinds of models but they will all have these elements in common: U, $\mathcal{B}$, V, wst, bst and $R^{\div}$.

A *basic frame* is a structure $\mathcal{F} = (W, U, \mathcal{B}, wst\,, bst\,, R^{\div})$ and a basic *model* $\mathcal{M}$ is a basic frame augmented with a valuation V.

The truth definition will be the same regardless of the kind of model considered:

1. $\mathcal{M} \models_x p$ iff $wst\,(x) \in V(p)$, for any propositional letter p.

2. $\mathcal{M} \models_x \phi \wedge \psi$ iff $\mathcal{M} \models_x \phi$ and $\mathcal{M} \models_x \psi$

3. $\mathcal{M} \models_x \neg\phi$ iff $\mathcal{M} \not\models_x \phi$, and so on for the other connectives.

4. $\mathcal{M} \models_x B\phi$ iff $bst\,(x) \subseteq ||\phi||$

5. $\mathcal{M} \models_x [\div\phi]\psi$ iff $\forall y \in W$, if $(x, y) \in R^{\div||\phi||}$, then $\mathcal{M} \models_y \psi$

A formula ϕ is *valid* with respect to a class of frames $\mathfrak{F}$, if for every frame $\mathcal{F} \in \mathfrak{F}$ and for all models $\mathcal{M}$ based on $\mathcal{F}$ and for all $x \in W$, $\mathcal{M} \models_x \phi$.

Important: when I below consider different extensions to the basic model, the notations $\mathcal{M}_{\mathfrak{H}}$, $\mathcal{M}_{\leq}$ and $\mathcal{M}_{\ll}$ will signify a basic model $\mathcal{M}$ extended with $\mathfrak{H}$, $\leq$ and $\ll$ respectively. They will, within the same context, all share the same basic model $\mathcal{M}$. As a basic model determines the truth-values of all formulae: what is believed at a world x, what the result of a contraction will be, etc., the main focus of interest is how these truth-values are related to conditions on the structures $\mathfrak{H}$, $\leq$ and $\ll$.

4 HYPERTHEORIES

If $\mathcal{H}$ is a set of subsets of U, P is a proposition and $X \in \mathcal{H}$, then X is a *fallback* for P if and only if $X \not\subseteq P$.

DEFINITION 2. $\mathcal{H} \subseteq \wp\wp U$ is a *hypertheory* if and only if

1. For all $G \in \mathcal{H}$, $G = \mathcal{C}(G)$.

2. $\bigcap \mathcal{H} \in \mathcal{H}$.

3. If $X \subseteq \mathcal{H}$ and $X \neq \emptyset$, then $\mathcal{C}(\bigcup X) \in \mathcal{H}$.

4. If C is a maximal non-empty chain of fallbacks for P in $\mathcal{H}$, then $\bigcap C \in \mathcal{H}$.

$\bigcap \mathcal{H}$ is the *belief set* of the agent, the set of states consistent with the agent's beliefs. I shall sometimes refer to the whole $\mathcal{H}$ as the *belief state* of the agent: it contains not only the belief *set*, but also the doxastic dispositions of the agent, clues to how the agent will go about changing his beliefs.

Note that in the light of Theorem 1 (4) is a limit assumption. We can thus let $min(P, \mathcal{H})$ denote the set of minimal fallbacks for P in $\mathcal{H}$. This will be non-empty if there are any fallbacks for P in $\mathcal{H}$, furthermore, from (4), $min(P, \mathcal{H}) \subseteq \mathcal{H}$.[1]

(LIN) A hypertheory $\mathcal{H}$ is *linearly ordered by inclusion* if and only if for all $G, G' \in \mathcal{H}$, either $G \subseteq G'$ or $G' \subseteq G$.

[1]For a discussion and analysis on appropriate conditions for hypertheories, see [Cantwell, 199y], the present conditions have been choosen so as to simplify the exposition.

4.1 Contraction recipes for hypertheories

An hyper-frame (model) is a basic frame (model) augmented with a function $\mathfrak{H}$ that to each $x \in W$ assigns the hypertheory of the agent at x with the restriction that $\bigcap \mathfrak{H}(x) = bst\,(x)$.

The next conditions states necessary and sufficient conditions when contraction is possible:[2]

(HYPA) $\mathcal{M}_{\mathfrak{H}} \models_x \neg[\div\phi]\bot$ if and only if $min(||\phi||, \mathfrak{H}(x)) \neq \emptyset$.

Two different contraction recipes will receive most attention:

(HYPB) $\mathcal{M}_{\mathfrak{H}} \models_x [\div\phi]B\psi$ if and only if $min(||\phi||, \mathfrak{H}(x)) = \emptyset$ or $bst\,(x) \cup (-\,||\phi|| \cap \bigcup min(||\phi||, \mathfrak{H}(x))) \subseteq ||\phi||$

(HYPC) $\mathcal{M}_{\mathfrak{H}} \models_x [\div\phi]B\psi$ if and only if $\bigcup min(P, \mathfrak{H}(x)) \subseteq ||\psi||$.

(HYPB) contains several ingredients: (1) contractions are weakenings of the original belief set; (2) the contraction should include all and only those $-\,||\phi||$ states that are elements of $(-\,||\phi|| \cap \bigcup min(||\phi||, \mathfrak{H}(x)))$. Roughly, the elements of $(-\,||\phi|| \cap \bigcup min(||\phi||, \mathfrak{H}(x)))$ are the "best" (most plausible, likely or, perhaps, most probable) $-\,||\phi||$ states from the perspective of $\mathfrak{H}(x)$. If one includes any $-\,||\phi||$ state in the new belief set, then the principle of sufficient reason suggests that we should include any other $-\,||\phi||$ state that is just as good, while the principle of minimal change suggests that we should only include the best $-\,||\phi||$ states.

It is easy to see that any contraction function satisfying (HYPB) will satisfy *recovery*:

$$\mathcal{M}_{\mathfrak{H}} \models_x [\div\phi]B(\phi \to \psi).$$

(HYPC) Can be seen as making use of another more inclusive concept of the principle of sufficient reason. Not only should the contraction contain the best $-\,||\phi||$ states, it should also contain any other state (not necessarily a $-\,||\phi||$ state) that is just as good. It is thus in general incompatible with (HYPB).

Despite their differences (HYPB) and (HYPC) are *revision equivalent* if revision with a proposition P is defined via the *Levi-identity*: first one contracts $-P$ and then one expands with P. When revision is defined in this way all that matters are the P states in $\bigcup min(-P, \mathcal{H})$ and these will be the same in (HYPB) and (HYPC).

5 EPISTEMIC ENTRENCHMENT: L&R

Here I shall rehearse what is in essence the notion of epistemic entrenchment introduced in L&R. Let $\leq$ be a binary relation on propositions.

DEFINITION 3. $\leq$ is an *Epistemic Entrenchment* relation on a closed set G if and only if each of the following hold:

[2] An equivalent way of stating (HYPA) would be: $\exists y(x, y) \in R^{\div ||\phi||}$ if and only if $min(||\phi||, \mathfrak{H}(x)) \neq \emptyset$. This way of phrasing (HYPA) would bring out the fact that (HYPA) imposes a condition on $R^{\div}$. However, the present format of (HYPA) seems more readable. Similar comments apply to all conditions considered below.

(DOMINANCE)	If $P \subseteq Q$, then $P \leq Q$.
(TRANSITIVITY)	If $P \leq Q$ and $Q \leq S$, then $P \leq S$.
(CONJUNCTIVE CLOSURE)	If $P \leq Q$ and $P \leq S$, then $P \leq Q \cap S$.
(BOTTOM)	If $G \neq \emptyset$, then $G \subseteq P$ if and only if $\emptyset < P$.

An entrenchment relation $\leq$ is *connected* if and only if:

$$\forall P, Q \in \mathcal{B}, P \leq Q \text{ or } Q \leq P$$

$P < Q$ to denotes the strict counterpart of $\leq$: $P \leq Q$ and $Q \not\leq P$.

When an EE relation is connected I shall sometimes refer to it as a "traditional" notion of epistemic entrenchment, that is, essentially the notion of epistemic entrenchment introduced in [Gärdenfors and Makinson, 1988]. This is not quite true as they have (what corresponds to) the additional requirement that if $P \subset U$, then $P < U$.

5.1 *From EE relations to hypertheories and back*

Starting from a hypertheory $\mathcal{H}$ we can define an EE-relation:

$$P \leq_{\mathcal{H}} Q \text{ iff } \forall G \in \mathcal{H}, \text{ if } G \subseteq P, \text{ then } G \subseteq Q$$

THEOREM 4 (L&R). *Let $\mathcal{H}$ be any hypertheory:*

1. *$\leq_{\mathcal{H}}$ is an EE relation on $\bigcap \mathcal{H}$,*
2. *$\mathcal{H}$ satisfies* (LIN) *if and only if $\leq_{\mathcal{H}}$ is connected.*

We can also go the other way by means of an auxilliary notion of a $\leq$-*stable* set. When $\leq$ is an EE-relation on G:

DEFINITION 5. A subset X of U is $\leq$-*stable* if and only if $X = \mathcal{C}(X)$, $G \subseteq X$ and for every proposition P and Q, if $X \subseteq P$ and $P \leq Q$, then $X \subseteq Q$.

The main intuition is this: a closed set X is stable if, whenever it supports (is a subset of) a belief P, it also supports any belief that is at least as entrenched as P. As X becomes larger, fewer beliefs will be supported by X and those that are supported will be those that are highly entrenched. Let $\leq$ be an EE-relation on G. Define:

$$F_{\mathrm{H}}(\leq, G) = \{X \subseteq U : X \text{ is stable w.r.t } \leq \text{ on } G\}$$

In [Cantwell, 199y] the following was shown:

THEOREM 6 ([Cantwell, 199y], L&R).

1. $F_H(\leq, G)$ *is a hypertheory, if* $\leq$ *is an EE-relation on* G.
2. $\leq_{F_H(\leq,G)} = \leq$, *if* $\leq$ *is an EE-relation on* G.
3. $\mathcal{H} = F_H(\leq_{\mathcal{H}}, \bigcap \mathcal{H})$, *if* $\mathcal{H}$ *is a hypertheory.*

Theorems 6 and 4 show that there is a one-one relationship between EE-relations and hypertheories. A hypertheory $\mathcal{H}$ and an EE-relation $\leq$ on $\bigcap \mathcal{H}$ will be said to be *interdefinable* if $\mathcal{H}_{\leq} = \leq$ or, equivalently, $F_{\mathrm{H}}(\leq, \bigcap \mathcal{H}) = \mathcal{H}$.

5.2 *Contraction recipes for EE relations*

An EE-frame (model) is a basic frame (model) extended so that for $x \in W$, $\leq_x$ is an EE-relation on $bst\,(x)$.

(EEA) $\mathcal{M}_{\leq} \models_x \neg[\div\phi]\bot$ if and only if $||\phi|| <_x U$.

When we are dealing with connected epistemic entrenchment orderings we have different recipes for constructing a contraction operation $\div$ using $\leq$, the first due to [Gärdenfors and Makinson, 1988] and the second due to [Rott, 1991]:

(EEB) $\mathcal{M}_{\leq} \models_x [\div\phi]B\psi$ if and only if $U \leq ||\phi||$ or $bst\,(x) \subseteq ||\psi||$ and $||\phi|| <_x ||\phi|| \cup ||\psi||$.

(EEC) $\mathcal{M}_{\leq} \models_x [\div\phi]B\psi$ if and only if $U \leq ||\phi||$ or $||\phi|| <_x ||\psi||$.

OBSERVATION 7. Given an EE-model $\mathcal{M}_{\leq}$ and a hyper-model $\mathcal{M}_{\mathfrak{H}}$ such that for all $x \in W$, $\leq_x$ and $\mathfrak{H}(x)$ are interdefinable and $\leq_x$ is connected (and so $\mathfrak{H}(x)$ is linearly ordered by inclusion):

1. $\mathcal{M}_{\leq}$ satisfies (EEA) if and only if $\mathcal{M}_{\mathfrak{H}}$ satisfies (HYPA).
2. $\mathcal{M}_{\leq}$ satisfies (EEA) and (EEB) if and only if $\mathcal{M}_{\mathfrak{H}}$ satisfies (HYPA) and (HYPB).
3. $\mathcal{M}_{\leq}$ satisfies (EEA) and (EEC) if and only if $\mathcal{M}_{\mathfrak{H}}$ satisfies (HYPA) and (HYPC).

For a more extensive analysis of the relationship contraction recipes on EE-relations and their corresponding hypertheories, I refer the reader to [Cantwell, 199y]. There it was shown that as soon as we drop the assumption that $\leq$ be connected (2) and (3) fail to hold. While constructions such as (HYPB) on hypertheories have a high intuitive appeal even after linearity is dropped, constructions such as (EEB) and (EEC) break down completely as reasonable bases for contraction (when the L&R notion of entrenchment is employed). Here is a simple example:

EXAMPLE 8. Consider a hyper-model where $U = \{1,2,3\}$, $\mathcal{B} = \wp U$ and $\mathfrak{H}(x) = \{\{1\},\{1,2\},\{1,3\},\{1,2,3\}\}$. Assuming (HYPA) and (HYPB) to hold and that $(x, y) \in R^{\div\{1\}}$ we have $bst(y) = \{1, 2, 3\}$ which seems reasonable given that the minimal fallbacks for $\{1\}$ are $\{1, 2\}$ and $\{1, 3\}$. However we have $\{1\} <_{\mathfrak{H}(x)} \{1\} \cup \{1, 2\}$ and $\{1\} <_{\mathfrak{H}(x)} \{1\} \cup \{1, 3\}$ and so assuming (EEA) and (EEB) to hold, $bst(y) = \{1\}$. This is a contradiction, moreover the result we get from (EEA) together with (EEB) is clearly counterintuitive. Similar examples can be given for (EEC).

(EEB) and (EEC) are of little use when we drop connectedness. In [Cantwell, 199y] it was shown how these could be replaced with the following conditions

(EEB′) $\mathcal{M}_{\leq} \models_x [\div\phi]B\psi$ if and only if $bst(x) \subseteq ||\psi||$ and $\forall S \in \mathcal{B}\,((||\phi \vee \psi|| \cap S \leq_x ||\phi|| \Rightarrow S \leq_x ||\phi||)$.

(EEC′) $\mathcal{M}_{\leq} \models_x [\div\phi]B\psi$ if and only if and only if $\forall S \in \mathcal{B}(||\psi|| \cap S \leq_x ||\phi|| \Rightarrow S \leq_x ||\phi||)$.

OBSERVATION 9 (Cantwell, 199y). Given an EE-model $\mathcal{M}_{\leq}$ and a hyper-model $\mathcal{M}_{\mathfrak{H}}$ such that $\leq_x$ and $\mathfrak{H}(x)$ are interdefinable:

1. $\mathcal{M}_{\leq}$ satisfies (EEA) and (EEB′) if and only if $\mathcal{M}_{\mathfrak{H}}$ satisfies (HYPA) and (HYPB).
2. $\mathcal{M}_{\leq}$ satisfies (EEA) and (EEC′) if and only if $\mathcal{M}_{\mathfrak{H}}$ satisfies (HYPA) and (HYPC).

5.3 *Elicitation of preferences*

Consider the following:

OBSERVATION 10. If $\leq_x$ is a connected EE-relation and satisfies (EEA) and either (EEB) or (EEC), then

$$\mathcal{M}_{\leq} \models_x [\div(\phi \wedge \psi)]\neg B\phi \text{ if and only if } ||\phi|| \leq_x ||\psi||.$$

This suggests that we can interpret a contraction of $||\phi|| \cap ||\psi||$ as giving the agent a choice of contracting $||\phi||$, $||\psi||$ or both and that the choice depends on if $||\phi||$ is less entrenched than, more entrenched than or equally entrenched as $||\psi||$, respectively. This property gives us a way of understanding the relative entrenchment of propositions: entrenchment encodes how disposed the agent is to give up one proposition rather than another. Thus on the one hand we can discuss coherence constraints on the relationship between different contractions. We might perhaps consider the relationship between the three potential contractions of $||\phi|| \cap ||\psi||$, $||\psi|| \cap ||\chi||$ and $||\phi|| \cap ||\chi||$. On the present reading this correponds to three different choice situations: giving up $||\phi||$ or $||\psi||$, giving up $||\psi||$ or $||\chi||$, and giving up $||\phi||$ or $||\chi||$. One might insist, perhaps, that the agent's choices across these choice situations satisfy some general properties of rational choice (e.g. Sen's property α, which corresponds to transitivity on $\leq$). Thus here is a direct connection to rational choice. The connection goes deeper than so, for when giving up $||\phi||$, one must choose between, among other things, giving up $||\phi|| \cup ||\psi||$ or giving up $||\phi|| \cup - ||\psi||$ (for if both are kept then $||\phi||$ can be inferred). In contraction recipes such as (EEB) or (EEC) these choices are made on the basis of the EE relation. Here then is another level at which we can impose coherence constraints. First one decides which proposition or propositions to be contracted. Once this choice is made the contraction needs to be performed. The performance itself involves further choices governing which propositions to give up and these choices are based on the same relation of epistemic entrenchment as the top-level choices.

This is only a rough picture, deeper analyses can be found in Rott (1996,1993). It should indicate however the importance of the rational choice perspective in belief change in general and of the relationship expressed in Observation 10 in particular. It is thus worrying that as soon as we drop the requirement that hypertheories be linearly ordered by inclusion in Observation 10, the relationship no longer holds: the right-to-left direction fails (as shown in [Cantwell, 199y]). Again, an important connection between contraction and the traditional notion of epistemic entrenchment is lost.

6 GENERALISED EPISTEMIC ENTRENCHMENT

Hans Rott [1992] has introduced a different notion of epistemic entrenchment: *Generalised Epistemic Entrenchment*. Starting with a *strict* relation $P \ll Q$ read "P is less entrenched than Q" he gives the following definition:

DEFINITION 11. $\ll$ is a relation of Generalised Epistemic Entrenchment on the theory T if and only if $\ll$ satisfies

(GEE1) $U \not\ll U$.
(GEE2↑) If $P \ll Q$ and $Q \subseteq R$, then $P \ll R$.
(GEE2↓) If $P \ll Q$ and $R \subseteq P$, then $R \ll Q$.
(GEE3↑) If $P \ll Q$ and $P \ll R$, then $P \ll R \cap Q$.
(GEE3↓) If $P \cap Q \ll Q$, then $P \ll Q$.

OBSERVATION 12 ([Rott, 1992]). If $\ll$ satisfies (GEE1-3) then it satisfies:

1. If $P \ll Q$ and $Q \ll R$, then $P \ll R$.
2. (GEEDR2) If $P \ll Q$ and $R \ll S$, then $P \cap R \ll Q \cap S$.
3. (GEEDR3) If $P \cap R \ll Q \cap R$, then $P \ll Q$.
4. (GEEDR4) $P \not\ll P$.

The notion of generalised epistemic entrenchment I will study here will be assumed to satisfy three additional limiting conditions also considered by Rott:

(GEE4) If $T \neq \emptyset$, then $\emptyset \ll P$ if and only if $T \subseteq P$.
(GEE4′) If $T \subseteq P$ and $T \not\subseteq Q$, then $Q \ll P$.
(GEE5) If $P \ll U$ and $Q \not\ll U$, then $P \ll Q$.

6.1 Contraction recipes for GEE relations

A GEE-frame (model) is a basic frame (model) extended with a GEE-relation.

(GEEA) $\mathcal{M}_{\ll} \models_x \neg[\div\phi]\bot$ if and only if $||\phi|| \ll_x U$.

Consider the following conditions:

(GEEB) $\mathcal{M}_{\ll} \models_x [\div\phi]B\psi$ if and only if $||\phi|| \not\ll_x U$ or $bst\,(x) \subseteq ||\psi||$ and $||\phi|| \ll_x ||\phi|| \cup ||\psi||$.

(GEEC) $\mathcal{M}_{\ll} \models_x [\div\phi]B\psi$ if and only if $||\phi|| \not\ll_x U$ or $||\phi|| \ll_x ||\psi||$.

Note the close resemblance between (GEEB) and (EEB) on the one hand and (GEEC) and (EEC) on the other.

THEOREM 13. *For any GEE-model such that (GEEA) and either (GEEB) or (GEEC) is satisfied:*

$$\mathcal{M}_{\ll} \models_x [\div(\phi \wedge \psi)]B\psi \text{ if and only if } ||\phi|| \ll_x ||\psi|| \text{ or } ||\phi \wedge \psi|| \not\ll_x U$$

Proof. If $||\phi \wedge \psi|| \not\ll_x U$, then trivially by (GEEA) $\mathcal{M}_{\ll} \models_x [\div(\phi \wedge \psi)]B\psi$. Assume that $||\phi|| \ll_x ||\psi||$. By (GEE4) $bst\,(x) \subseteq ||\psi||$. By (GEE2↓) $||\phi|| \cap ||\psi|| \ll_x ||\psi||$, while by (GEE2↑) $||\phi|| \cap ||\psi|| \ll_x (||\phi|| \cap ||\psi||) \cup ||\psi||$. So by either of (GEEB) or (GEEC), $\mathcal{M}_{\ll} \models_x [\div(\phi \wedge \psi)]B\psi$.

Next assume that $\mathcal{M}_{\ll} \models_x [\div(\phi \wedge \psi)]B\psi$ and that $||\phi \wedge \psi|| \ll_x U$. If $\mathcal{M}_{\ll}$ satisfies (GEEC), then $||\phi|| \cap ||\psi|| \ll_x ||\psi||$ and so by (GEE3↓), $||\phi|| \ll_x ||\psi||$. If $\mathcal{M}_{\ll}$ satisfies (GEEB), then $||\phi|| \cap ||\psi|| \ll_x (||\phi|| \cap ||\psi||) \cup ||\psi||$, i.e. $||\phi|| \cap ||\psi|| \ll_x ||\psi||$ and so by (GEE3↓), $||\phi|| \ll_x ||\psi||$. ■

This means that here, as opposed to the case of the L&R generalisation of traditional EE-relations, considerations of rational choice are directly applicable. Furthermore whereas the recipes for EE relations break down when connectedness is dropped, the corresponding recipes for GEE relations are robust. But Rott does not show this by appealing to an equivalence between these recipes and, say, the properties that emerge from contractions based on hypertheories. Rather, Rott relies on a representation theorem between the constructions and a set of postulates on $\div$. I shall return to this issue in Section 7.2. In the following sections I shall explore the relationship between EE-relations and GEE-relations on the one hand and in particular between hypertheories and GEE-relations on the other.

7 GEE-RELATIONS, EE-RELATIONS AND HYPERTHEORIES

Let us first see why we cannot use the "natural" equivalence between GEE relations and EE relations:

$$P \ll Q \text{ if and only if } P < Q$$

To see why this will not work, recall (GEE3↑): if $P \ll Q$ and $P \ll R$, then $P \ll Q \cap R$. The corresponding property for $<$ does *not* hold in general. Let

U, $\mathcal{B}$ and $\mathcal{H}$ be as in Example 8. Consider $\leq_{\mathcal{H}}$. Clearly $\{1\} <_{\mathcal{H}} \{1,2\}$ and $\{1\} <_{\mathcal{H}} \{1,3\}$, yet $\{1\} \not<_{\mathcal{H}} \{1,2\} \cap \{1,3\}$.

A related difference is that while the following always holds $\bigcap\{Q : P \ll Q\} \not\subseteq P$, we might have $\bigcap\{Q : P < Q\} \subseteq P$. This is the reason why (EEB) and (EEC) do not work as contraction recipes when connectedness is given up: the fact that a belief is more entrenched than P is not a sufficient condition for keeping the belief after contracting P.

Yet another difference between employing GEE-relations and EE-relations is that the latter, but not the former distinguishes between the situation where two propositions are *incomparable* (neither $P \leq Q$ nor $Q \leq P$) from the situation where two propositions are *equally* entrenched (both $P \leq Q$ and $Q \leq P$). One might say that when employing GEE-relations there is a tacit assumption that the difference between two propositions being incomparable and their being equally entrenched is immaterial. This is an assumption that might need justification, however, I shall not pursue this here.

Hans Rott interprets a GEE-relation as the converse complement of an EE-relation:

$P \ll Q$ if and only if $Q \not\leq P$

Consider:

(VIRTUAL CONNECTIVITY) If $P \ll Q$, then $P \ll R$ or $R \ll Q$

OBSERVATION 14 ([Rott, 1992]). When $\ll$ is the converse complement of $\leq$

1. $\leq$ is connected and satisfies (DOMINANCE), (TRANSITIVITY) and (CONJUNCTIVE CLOSURE) if and only if $\ll$ satisfies (VIRTUAL CONNECTIVITY) and (GEE1-3).
2. $\leq$ is virtually connected if and only if $\ll$ is transitive.
3. If $\ll$ is virtually connected, then $\leq$ is transitive.

While these results are sound I shall not follow Rott's interpretation here. Rott wants to consider what happens when we drop the virtual connectivity of $\ll$, but this amounts to dropping transitivity on the corresponding EE-relation $\leq$. On the other hand Rott wants to keep transitivity for $\ll$ but this amounts to keeping connectedness for $\leq$ (in the presence of (EE1)). By contrast the EE-relations studied in the previous sections have satisfied transitivity but not connectedness. Thus in the present setting it will not do to take $\ll$ to be the converse complement of $\leq$.

I shall treat $P \ll Q$ and $P < Q$ (where $<$ is the strict part of $\leq$) as two competing ways of capturing the (admittedly loose) notion "P is less entrenched than Q". In the end we shall see that in fact the two notions are closely related, although not fully interdefinable and that one might say, very loosely, that $P \ll Q$ expresses the idea "P is *considerably less* entrenched than Q". To get there I shall first look at the relationship between GEE relations and hypertheories.

7.1 From GEE relations to hypertheories

Define for any hypertheory $\mathcal{H}$:[3]

$$P \ll_{\mathcal{H}} Q \text{ if and only if } \bigcup min(P \cap Q, \mathcal{H}) \subseteq Q \text{ and } min(P \cap Q, \mathcal{H}) \neq \emptyset$$

THEOREM 15. *If $\mathcal{H}$ is a hypertheory, then $\ll_{\mathcal{H}}$ is a GEE-relation on $\bigcap \mathcal{H}$.*

The leading idea behind the next construction, whereby a hypertheory is generated from a GEE-relation is analogous to the construction of Section 5.1 where a hypertheory was generated from an EE-relation. In particular the auxilliary notions of an EE-stable set and GEE-stable set are quite close, however, the present construction is a bit more elaborate.

When $\ll$ is a GEE relation with respect to T let $TOP_{\ll} = \bigcap\{P : P \not\ll U\}$, $TOP_{\ll}$ will be the maximal element of $F_{\mathrm{H}}(\ll, T)$ defined below.

For any closed set G: G is *$\ll$-stable* with respect to T if and only if $T \subseteq G \subseteq TOP_{\ll}$ and $\forall P, Q \in \mathcal{B}$ if $G \subseteq P$ and $P \ll Q$, then $G \subseteq Q$.

Define

$$F_{\mathrm{H}}(\ll, T) = \{G : G \text{ is } \ll\text{-stable with respect to } T\}$$

THEOREM 16. *$F_H(\ll, T)$ is a hypertheory such that $\bigcap F_H(\ll, T) = T$*

Thus a hypertheory gives rise to a GEE-relation and a GEE-relation gives rise to a hypertheory. The next task is to show to what extent hypertheories and GEE-relations are interdefinable. First some auxilliary results.

LEMMA 17. *For any GEE-relation $\ll$ on T:*

1. *If $P \ll U$, then $\bigcap\{Q \in B : P \ll Q\} \subseteq R$ if and only if $P \ll R$*
2. *$\bigcap\{Q \in B : P \ll Q\}$ is $\ll$-stable with respect to T, if $P \ll U$*
3. *$\bigcap\{Q \in B : P \ll Q\} \cap P$ is $\ll$-stable with respect to T, if $T \subseteq P$ and $P \ll U$*

For the next theorem, note that $\ll_{F_{\mathrm{H}}(\ll,T)}$ is the GEE-relation generated from the hypertheory generated from $\ll$, while $F_{\mathrm{H}}(\ll_{\mathcal{H}}, \bigcap \mathcal{H})$ is the hypertheory generated from the GEE-relation generated from $\mathcal{H}$.

THEOREM 18.

1. *$\ll_{F_H(\ll,T)} = \ll$, if $\ll$ is a GEE-relation on T.*
2. *$\mathcal{H} \subseteq F_H(\ll_{\mathcal{H}}, \bigcap \mathcal{H})$ and $\bigcap \mathcal{H} = \bigcap F_H(\ll_{\mathcal{H}}, \bigcap \mathcal{H})$, if $\mathcal{H}$ is a hypertheory.*

[3] The proofs of this section are relegated to the appendix.

So: (1) Every GEE-relation generates a hypertheory from which we can recover the GEE-relation. (2) Every hypertheory generates a GEE-relation from which we can generate a hypertheory in which the original hypertheory is *included*. The new hypertheory need not, however, be identical to the old hypertheory.

To see this consider: $\mathcal{H} = \{\{1\}, \{1,2,3\}, \{1,2,4\}, \{1,2,3,4\}\}$ where $U = \{1,2,3,4\}$ and $\mathcal{B} = \wp U$. Note that $\{1,2\}$ is $\ll_{\mathcal{H}}$-stable (as there is only one proposition P such that $\{1,2\} \ll_{\mathcal{H}} P$, namely $P = \{1,2,3,4\}$ and $\{1,2\} \subseteq \{1,2,3,4\}$). But $\{1,2\} \notin \mathcal{H}$, thus $F_{\mathrm{H}}(\ll_{\mathcal{H}}, \bigcap \mathcal{H}) \not\subseteq \mathcal{H}$.

COROLLARY 19.

1. *The GEE-relation generated from $\mathcal{H}$ and the GEE-relation generated from $F_{H}(\ll_{\mathcal{H}}, \bigcap \mathcal{H})$ are identical.*

2. *For any GEE-model $\mathcal{M}_{\ll}$, there is a hyper-model $\mathcal{M}_{\mathfrak{H}}$ such that for all $x \in W$, $\ll_x$ is generated from $\mathfrak{H}(x)$*

Proof. (1) Let $\ll = \ll_{\mathcal{H}}$. By Theorem 18 $\ll_{F_{\mathrm{H}}(\ll, \bigcap \mathcal{H})} = \ll$, thus the GEE-relation generated from $\mathcal{H}$ and the GEE-relation generated from $F_{\mathrm{H}}(\ll_{\mathcal{H}}, \bigcap \mathcal{H})$ are identical.

(2) Immediately from Theorem 18. ■

Two different hypertheories can generate the same GEE-relation. However, one can show that these hypertheories are, under certain conditions, *contraction equivalent*, and thus that any difference between them is immaterial.

LEMMA 20. *Take any hyper-model $\mathcal{M}_{\mathfrak{H}}$, if $\mathfrak{H}(x)$ and $\mathfrak{H}(y)$ are two hypertheories that generate the same GEE-relation (i.e. $\ll_{\mathfrak{H}(x)} = \ll_{\mathfrak{H}(y)}$) and (HYPA) and (HYPB) is satisfied, then:*

$$\mathcal{M}_{\mathfrak{H}} \models_x [\div\phi]B\psi \text{ if and only if } \mathcal{M}_{\mathfrak{H}} \models_y [\div\phi]B\psi$$

What remains to be shown is that the contraction recipes for GEE-relations and hypertheories –the way these structures are put to use– are equivalent.

THEOREM 21. *For any GEE-model $\mathcal{M}_{\ll}$ and hyper-model $\mathcal{M}_{\mathfrak{H}}$ such that for all $x \in W$, $\ll_x$ is generated from $\mathfrak{H}(x)$: $\mathcal{M}_{\ll}$ satisfies (GEEA) and (GEEB) if and only if $\mathcal{M}_{\mathfrak{H}}$ satisfies (HYPA) and (HYPB).*

Proof. First note that $min(P, \mathfrak{H}(x)) \neq \emptyset$ if and only if $P \ll_x U$. So $\mathcal{M}_{\mathfrak{H}}$ satisfies (HYPA) if and only if $\mathcal{M}_{\ll}$ satisfies (GEEA).

Assume that $min(P, \mathfrak{H}(x)) \neq \emptyset$. Note that $\bigcup min(P, \mathfrak{H}(x)) \cap -P \subseteq Q$ if and only if $\bigcup min(P, \mathfrak{H}(x)) \subseteq P \cup Q$ if and only if $\bigcup min(P \cap (P \cup Q), \mathfrak{H}(x)) \subseteq P \cup Q$ if and only if $P \ll_x P \cup Q$. But then $\mathcal{M}_{\mathfrak{H}}$ satisfies (HYPC) if and only if $\mathcal{M}_{\ll}$ satisfies (GEEC). ■

The above theorem only applies to recovery contractions. What about contractions that do not satisfy recovery? Consider the following example where we have a hyper-model $\mathcal{M}_{\mathfrak{H}}$ based on a basic model $\mathcal{M}$. Let U, $\mathcal{B}$ and $\mathfrak{H}(x)$ be as in Example 8, that is $\mathfrak{H}(x) = \{\{1\},\{1,2\},\{1,3\},\{1,2,3\}\}$. Assume that (HYPA) and (HYPC) holds. Thus there is a unique y such that $(x,y) \in R^{\div\{1,2\}}$ and $bst\,(y) = \{1,3\}$. Consider now a GEE-model $\mathcal{M}_{\ll}$ also based on $\mathcal{M}$. Assume that $\ll_x = \ll_{\mathfrak{H}(x)}$. Note that there is only one proposition P, namely $\{1,2,3\}$, such that $\bigcup min(\{1,2\} \cap P, \mathfrak{H}(x)) \subseteq P$. To see that $\{1,2,3\}$ indeed satisfies this, note that $\bigcup min(\{1,2\} \cap \{1,2,3\}, \mathfrak{H}(x)) = \bigcup min(\{1,2\}, \mathcal{H}) = \{1,3\}$. Thus $\{1,2\} \ll_x \{1,2,3\}$. To check that $\{1,2,3\}$ is the only proposition P such that $\{1,2\} \ll_x P$ we need to check all the remaining propositions. A quick inspection, however, makes it clear that the only other plausible candidate is $\{1,3\}$. But $\bigcup min(\{1,2\} \cap \{1,3\}, \mathfrak{H}(x)) = \bigcup min(\{1\}, \mathfrak{H}(x)) = \{1,2\} \cup \{1,3\} = \{1,2,3\} \not\subseteq \{1,3\}$, so $\{1,2\} \not\ll_x \{1,3\}$. So by (GEEC), $bst\,(y) \not\subseteq \{1,3\}$ which shows that while our present hyper-model satisfies (HYPC) the corresponding GEE-model does not satisfy (GEEC).

In fact, (GEEC) (together with (GEEA)) constitutes a quite different contraction recipe than we have hitherto considered. Consider:

(HYPD) $\mathcal{M}_{\mathfrak{H}} \models_x [\div\phi]B\psi$ if and only if
$$\bigcup min(\|\phi\|, \mathfrak{H}(x)) \cup \bigcup\{G \in \mathfrak{H}(x) : G \subseteq \|\phi\|\} \subseteq \|\psi\|$$

From the preceeding example we see that this condition violates the condition that if $\bigcup min(\|\phi\|, \mathfrak{H}(x)) \subseteq \|\psi\|$, then $\mathcal{M}_{\mathfrak{H}} \models_x [\div\phi]B\psi$. It may seem condemning that a contraction recipe thus violates what seems to be a basic constraint of minimal change, however, the violation of minimal change involved is quite controlled. If the hypertheory is linearly ordered by inclusion, (HYPD) will be equivalent to (HYPC). Even if the hypertheory is not linearly ordered by inclusion, no non-minimal fallback for a proposition will be used in the contraction of that proposition. Finally as:

$$-\|\phi\| \cap \mathcal{C}(\bigcup min(\|\phi\|, \mathfrak{H}(x)) \cup \bigcup\{G \in \mathfrak{H}(x) : G \subseteq \|\phi\|\}) = -\|\phi\| \cap (\mathcal{C}(\bigcup min(\|\phi\|, \mathfrak{H}(x)))$$

that is, as the $-\|\phi\|$ area is identical for (HYPD), (HYPB) and (HYPC), these are all revision equivalent. Thus (HYPD) is not without its virtues. A similar contraction recipe was suggested in [Meyer *et al.*, 1998].

THEOREM 22. *Consider any GEE-model $\mathcal{M}_{\ll}$ and hyper-model $\mathcal{M}_{\mathfrak{H}}$ such that $\ll_x$ is generated from $\mathfrak{H}(x)$ for each $x \in W$: $\mathcal{M}_{\mathfrak{H}}$ satisfies (HYPA) and (HYPD) if and only if $\mathcal{M}_{\ll}$ satisfies (GEEA) and (GEEC).*

Finally, one can establish some connections between EE-relations and GEE-relations.

THEOREM 23. *If $\leq$ and $\ll$ are generated from the same hypertheory $\mathcal{H}$, then*

1. *if* $P \ll Q$, *then* $P < Q$;

2. *if* $P < U$ *and* $\forall S(Q \cap S \leq P \cap Q \Rightarrow S \leq P \cap Q)$, *then* $P \ll Q$;

3. *if* $P \ll Q$ *and* $P \ll R$, *then* $P < Q \cap R$.

(3) is a weakening of the principle: if $P < Q$ and $P < R$, then $P < Q \cap R$. At the top of Section 7, the latter principle was shown not to hold for EE-relations in general.

7.2 *Axiomatics*

In this section the logic induced by the class of frames satisfying (HYPA)+(HYPB) (and thus by (GEEA)+(GEEB) and by (EEA)+(EEB′)) will be completely axiomatised. Let $\vdash_R$ be the smallest normal modal logic closed under the following rules and axioms:[4]

(PE)	If $\vdash_{PC} \phi \leftrightarrow \psi$, then $\vdash_R [\div\phi]\chi \leftrightarrow [\div\psi]\chi$.
(success)	$\vdash_R [\div\phi]\neg B\phi$
(inclusion)	$\vdash_R \neg B\psi \rightarrow [\div\phi]\neg B\psi$
(vacuity)	$\vdash_R \neg B\phi \wedge B\psi \rightarrow <\div\phi> B\psi$
(recovery)	$\vdash_R B\psi \rightarrow [\div\phi]B(\phi \rightarrow \psi)$
(7)	$\vdash_R <\div\phi> B\chi \wedge <\div\psi> B\chi \rightarrow <\div\phi \wedge \psi> B\chi$
(7c+8c)	$\vdash_R <\div\phi \wedge \psi> B\psi \rightarrow (<\div\phi> B\chi \leftrightarrow <\div\phi \wedge \psi> B\chi)$
(max 1)	$\vdash_R [\div\phi]\bot \rightarrow [\div\psi]B\phi$
(max 2)	$\vdash_R [\div\phi \wedge \psi]\bot \rightarrow [\div\phi]\bot$
(func)	$\vdash_R <\div\phi> \psi \rightarrow [\div\phi]\psi$

The axioms (PE), (success), (inclusion), (vacuity), (recovery), (7) all have their immediate counterpart in the standard Gärdenfors postulates. (7c+8c) constitue a weakening of Gärdenfors (8) postulate; it is borrowed from [Rott, 1992]. The "new" axioms are (max 1), (max 2) and (func). Recall that $< \div\phi > \psi$ states that there is a way of contracting ϕ, while $[\div\phi]\bot$ states that there is no way of contracting ϕ. Thus (max 1) states that if one cannot contract ϕ, then in every contraction, ϕ is believed; while (max 2) states that if one cannot contract $\phi \wedge \psi$, then one cannot contract ϕ either. (func) states that contraction, if it can be applied, has a unique result.

As the above logic is normal, we can make use of a great number of well-known results and techniques for normal modal logics. In proofs I will refer to these simply by: "from modal logic". The following result is useful in the completeness proof:

LEMMA 24.

$$\vdash_R <\div\phi \wedge \psi> B\psi \rightarrow <\div\phi \wedge \psi \wedge \chi> B\psi$$

[4]Here and elsewhere $\vdash_{PC}$ denotes the standard classical logic of the propositional calculus.

Proof. Assume that $< \div\phi \wedge \psi > B\psi$. By (inclusion), $B\psi$. By (recovery), $< \div(\phi\wedge\psi) \to \chi > B(((\phi\wedge\psi) \to \chi) \to \psi)$, by simple truth-functional reasoning and modal logic $< \div(\phi\wedge\psi) \to \chi > B\psi$. Thus by (7), $< \div((\phi\wedge\psi) \to \chi)\wedge\phi\wedge\psi > B\psi$ and so by PE $< \div\phi \wedge \psi \wedge \chi > B\psi$. ■

7.3 Soudness and Completeness of the axioms

Although a number of important details are different, a large part of the credit for the soundness and completeness proof of this axiomatisation is really Hans Rott's. In his [1992] paper he gives a representation theorem between a set of postulates analogous to the present axioms (minus (max 1), (max 2) and (func)) and GEE-relations. For the completeness result I shall make use of the results established in the previous sections showing how GEE-relations and hypertheories are related.

THEOREM 25. *Each of the above axioms are valid in the set of frames satisfying (HYPA)+(HYPB), (GEEA)+(GEEB) or (EEA)+(EEB′).*

Let U_R be the set of maximal PC-consistent sets of *Boolean* formulae, $V_R(p) = \{u \in U_R : p \in u\}$, let $||\phi||$ be induced by V_R and let $\mathcal{B}_R = \{||\phi|| : \phi \text{ Boolean}\}$ (clearly $\mathcal{B}$ is a compact Boolean algebra of propositions satisfying. Furthermore let W_R be the set of maximal R-consistent sets of formulae. Define (for maximal R-consistent sets x, y):

$$(x, y) \in R_R^{\div||\phi||} \text{ iff } \forall\psi([\div\phi]\psi \in x \Rightarrow \psi \in y)$$

$$bst\,(x) = \bigcap\{||\phi|| : B\phi \in x\}$$

$$wst_R(x) = \{\phi \in x : \phi \text{ Boolean}\}$$

Note that by standard methods of modal logic $bst\,(x) \subseteq ||\phi||$ if and only if $B\phi \in x$, also wst is a function from W_R onto U_R. Finally, by (func), if $(x, y), (x, z) \in R^{\div||\phi||}$, then $y = z$. Thus, $\mathcal{M}_R = (W_R, U_R, \mathcal{B}_R, wst_R, R_R^{\div}, V_R)$ is a basic model. Now define:

$$||\phi|| \ll_{R,x} ||\psi|| \text{ if and only if } < \div\phi \wedge \psi > B\psi \in x$$

THEOREM 26. *$\ll_{R,x}$ is a GEE-relation on $bst\,(x)$.*

Define:

$$\mathfrak{H}_R(x) = F_{\mathrm{H}}(\ll_{R,x}, bst\,(x))$$

$$\leq_{R,x} = \leq_{\mathfrak{H}_R(x)}$$

THEOREM 27. *Let $\mathcal{M}_\ll$, $\mathcal{M}_\mathfrak{H}$ and $\mathcal{M}_\leq$ be extensions of the basic model $\mathcal{M}_R$ with $\ll_R$, $\mathfrak{H}_R$ and $\leq_R$, respectively.*

1. *$\mathcal{M}_\ll$ is a GEE-model satisfying (GEEA) and (GEEB).*

2. *$\mathcal{M}_{\mathfrak{H}}$ is a hyper-model satisfying (HYPA) and (HYPB).*

3. *$\mathcal{M}_{\leq}$ is an EE-model satisfying (EEA) and (EEB$'$).*

Using standard methods of modal logic we then have:

COROLLARY 28. *Every formula valid in the class of frames satisfying (GEEA)+(GEEB) ((HYPA)+(HYPB), (EEA)+(EEB$'$)) is a theorem of the logic R.*

COROLLARY 29. *The logic R is decidable.*

Sketch of proof: When we consider the satisfiability of a finite set of sentences it is sufficient to consider the finite sublanguage based on whatever propositional letters that occur in the set. U_R, $\mathcal{B}_R$, W_R and $\mathfrak{H}_R(x)$ will then all contain finitely many elements. Using Lindenbaums Lemma, the constructions of this section and Theorem 18 it then follows that every consistent finite set of sentences can be satisfied in a finite model.

8 CONCLUSION

We have seen that hypertheories provide a kind of semantics for GEE-relations: every GEE-relation can be described as a hypertheory. We have also seen that while the converse does not hold: one and the same GEE-relation may correspond to two different hypertheories, these hypertheories will be contraction equivalent as long as contraction satisfies recovery. Given the contraction recipes for GEE-relations and the fact that a GEE-relation can be elicited from contraction behaviour, given that contraction satisfies the axioms of section 7.2, it seems that GEE-relations have nicer properties than the EE-relations considered by L&R. Combining these features, I think we have a case for focusing further research on epistemic entrenchment on GEE-relations.

The formal (object) language used in this paper is the same as the one considered in [Cantwell, 199y], with one very important exception: it does not contain any EE-operator $\phi \preceq \psi$ stating that ψ is at least as entrenched as ϕ. In [Cantwell, 199y] it was noted that as long as we are dealing with relational contraction, one can always express that ψ is at least as entrenched as ϕ using the construction $[\div\phi\wedge\psi]\neg B\phi$. As noted in Section 5.3 above, this avenue is not in general available when we consider sceptical contraction. Thus in the sceptical approach, removing the entrenchment relation means reducing the expressive power of the language. In [Cantwell, 199y] a completeness result for sceptical contraction was given in a language containing an EE operator, but, it was shown that this logic was not compact and so needed an infinitary axiom. By omitting the EE operator from the object language and thus lessening its expressive power, we have gained compactness and a more pliable axiomatisation.

APPENDIX

PROOF OF MAIN THEOREMS AND LEMMAS

Proof of Theorem 15. (GEE1): Clearly $min(U, \mathcal{H}) = \emptyset$ so $U \not\ll_{\mathcal{H}} U$.
(GEE2↑): Assume that $\bigcup min(P \cap Q, \mathcal{H}) \subseteq Q$, that $min(P \cap Q, \mathcal{H}) \neq \emptyset$ and that $Q \subseteq R$. Clearly for some $G \in \mathcal{H}, G \not\subseteq P$. Thus $min(P \cap R, \mathcal{H}) \neq \emptyset$. Take any $G \in min(P \cap R, \mathcal{H})$ and assume for reductio that $G \not\subseteq R$, then $G \not\subseteq Q$. So $G \not\subseteq P$, but then for some $G' \in min(P \cap Q, \mathcal{H})$, $G' \subseteq G$. However, $G' \subseteq Q$ and so $G' \subseteq R$. As $G' \not\subseteq P$, $G' \in min(P \cap R, \mathcal{H})$, but $G' \subset G$ – contradicting the assumption that $G \in min(P \cap R, \mathcal{H})$. So $\bigcup min(P \cap R, \mathcal{H}) \subseteq R$.
(GEE2↓): Assume that $\bigcup min(P \cap Q, \mathcal{H}) \subseteq Q$, that $min(P \cap Q, \mathcal{H}) \neq \emptyset$ and that $R \subseteq P$. Clearly for some $G \in \mathcal{H}, G \not\subseteq P$. Thus $G \not\subseteq R$ and so $min(R \cap Q, \mathcal{H}) \neq \emptyset$. Take any $G \in min(R \cap Q, \mathcal{H})$ and assume for reductio that $G \not\subseteq Q$, thus $G \not\subseteq P \cap Q$. But then for some $G' \in min(P \cap Q, \mathcal{H})$, $G' \subseteq G$. But $G' \subseteq Q$ so $G' \not\subseteq P$ and so $G' \not\subseteq R$ so $G \notin min(R \cap Q, \mathcal{H})$ contrary to assumption. Thus $\bigcup min(R \cap Q, \mathcal{H}) \subseteq Q$.
(GEE3↑): Assume that $\bigcup min(P \cap Q, \mathcal{H}) \subseteq Q$, that $min(P \cap Q, \mathcal{H}) \neq \emptyset$, that $\bigcup min(P \cap R, \mathcal{H}) \subseteq R$ and that $min(P \cap R, \mathcal{H}) \neq \emptyset$. We immediately have $min(P \cap R \cap Q, \mathcal{H}) \neq \emptyset$. Asssume that $G \in min(P \cap R \cap Q, \mathcal{H})$ and assume for reductio that $G \not\subseteq R \cap Q$, thus either (i) $G \not\subseteq R$ or (ii) $G \not\subseteq Q$. It is sufficient to consider the first case. Then there is a $G' \in min(P \cap R, \mathcal{H})$ such that $G' \subseteq G$, $G' \subseteq R$ and $G' \not\subseteq P$. So $G' \subset G$, but then $G \notin min(P \cap R \cap Q, \mathcal{H})$ and we have a contradiction. Thus $G \subseteq R \cap Q$ and so $\bigcup min(P \cap R \cap Q, \mathcal{H}) \subseteq R \cap Q$.
(GEE3↓): Assume that $\bigcup min(P \cap Q \cap Q, \mathcal{H}) \subseteq Q$ and that $min(P \cap Q \cap Q, \mathcal{H}) \neq \emptyset$. But then it is immediate that $\bigcup min(P \cap Q, \mathcal{H}) \subseteq Q$ and that $min(P \cap Q, \mathcal{H}) \neq \emptyset$.
(GEE4): Assume that $\bigcap \mathcal{H} \neq \emptyset$ and that $\emptyset \ll_{\mathcal{H}} P$. Then $\bigcup min(P \cap \emptyset, \mathcal{H}) \subseteq P$, i.e. $\bigcup min(\emptyset, \mathcal{H}) \subseteq P$ and $min(\emptyset, \mathcal{H}) \neq \emptyset$. But as $\bigcap \mathcal{H} \neq \emptyset$, $\bigcap \mathcal{H} = \bigcup min(\emptyset, \mathcal{H})$ and so $\bigcap \mathcal{H} \subseteq P$. Next assume that $\bigcap \mathcal{H} \subseteq P$. As $\bigcap \mathcal{H} = \bigcup min(\emptyset, \mathcal{H})$, $min(\emptyset, \mathcal{H}) \neq \emptyset$ and so $\bigcup min(\emptyset \cap P, \mathcal{H}) \subseteq P$.
(GEE4′): Assume that $\bigcap \mathcal{H} \subseteq P$ and that $\bigcap \mathcal{H} \not\subseteq Q$.
But then $\bigcup min(P \cap Q, \mathcal{H}) = \bigcap \mathcal{H} \subseteq P$. So $Q \ll_{\mathcal{H}} P$.
(GEE5): Assume that $\bigcup min(P, \mathcal{H}) \subseteq U$, that $min(P, \mathcal{H}) \neq \emptyset$ and that $\bigcup min(Q, \mathcal{H}) = \emptyset$. But then clearly, $min(P \cap Q, \mathcal{H}) \neq \emptyset$ and $\bigcup min(P \cap Q, \mathcal{H}) \subseteq Q$. ■

LEMMA 30. *If* $TOP_{\ll} \subseteq R$, *then* $R \not\ll U$.

Proof. Assume that $\bigcap\{P : P \not\ll U\} \subseteq R$. By compactness there are $Q_1, \ldots, Q_n$ such that $Q_i \not\ll U$ and $Q_1 \cap \cdots \cap Q_n \subseteq R$. Assume for reductio that $Q_1 \cap \cdots \cap Q_n \ll U$, but then $Q_1 \cap \cdots \cap Q_n \ll Q_n$, by (GEE5). By (GEE3↓), $Q_1 \cap \cdots \cap Q_{n-1} \ll Q_n$, so by (GEE2↑), $Q_1 \cap \cdots \cap Q_{n-1} \ll U$, so by (GEE5) $Q_1 \cap \cdots \cap Q_{n-1} \ll Q_{n-1}$ and so by (GEE3↓), $Q_1 \cap \cdots \cap Q_{n-2} \ll Q_{n-1}$.

Repeating this procedure we eventually get $Q_1 \ll Q_2$, but then $Q_1 \ll U$ by (GEE2↑) contrary to assumption. So $Q_1 \cap \cdots \cap Q_n \not\ll U$ and so $R \not\ll U$, by (GEE2↓). ■

Proof of Theorem 16. We first show that T is $\ll$-stable with respect to T. Assume that $TOP_{\ll} \subseteq P$, if $T = \emptyset$ then clearly $T \subseteq TOP_{\ll}$ so assume that $T \neq \emptyset$. As $TOP_{\ll} \subseteq P$, $P \not\ll U$ by Lemma 30. Now $T \subseteq U$ so by (GEE4), $\emptyset \ll U$ and so by (GEE5), $\emptyset \ll P$ and so by (GEE4), $T \subseteq P$. So $T \subseteq TOP_{\ll}$.

Assume that $T \subseteq P$. Two cases: (i) $T = \emptyset$, in which case $T \subseteq Q$ for all Q and so T is $\ll$-stable or (ii) $T \neq \emptyset$. So $\emptyset \ll P$ by (GEE4). Assume that $P \ll Q$, by transitivity and (GEE4), $\emptyset \ll Q$ and so by (GEE4), $T \subseteq Q$. So T is $\ll$-stable and so $T \in F_{\mathrm{H}}(\ll, T)$ and so clearly $T = \bigcap F_{\mathrm{H}}(\ll, T)$, but then $\bigcap F_{\mathrm{H}}(\ll, T) \in F_{\mathrm{H}}(\ll, T)$.

For the limit assumption we show that for all non-empty chains C of $F_{\mathrm{H}}(\ll, T)$, $\bigcap C \in F_{\mathrm{H}}(\ll, T)$. So take any non-empty chain C. It is sufficient to show that $\bigcap C$ is $\ll$-stable with respect to T. We know that $T = \bigcap F_{\mathrm{H}}(\ll, T) \subseteq \bigcap C$. We also know that $\forall G \in C$, $G \subseteq TOP_{\ll}$, so $\bigcap C \subseteq TOP_{\ll}$. So assume that $\bigcap C \subseteq P$ and that $P \ll Q$. By Theorem 1, there is a $G \in C$ such that $G \subseteq P$ and so $G \subseteq Q$ but then $\bigcap C \subseteq Q$ and we are done.

Finally we show that if $W \subseteq F_{\mathrm{H}}(\ll, T)$ and $W \neq \emptyset$, then $\mathcal{C}(\bigcup W) \in F_{\mathrm{H}}(\ll, T)$. Make the requisite assumptions for W. Clearly $T \subseteq \mathcal{C}(\bigcup W) \subseteq TOP_{\ll}$. Assume that $\mathcal{C}(\bigcup W) \subseteq P$, i.e. $\bigcup W \subseteq P$, and that $P \ll Q$. But then for any $G \in W, G \subseteq P$ and so $G \subseteq Q$. Thus, $\bigcup W \subseteq Q$ and so $\mathcal{C}(\bigcup W) \subseteq Q$. ■

Proof of Lemma 17. (1) Assume that $P \ll U$ and that $\bigcap\{Q \in B : P \ll Q\} \subseteq R$. As $\bigcap\{Q \in B : P \ll Q\} \neq \emptyset$, it follows from compactness that there are $Q_1, \ldots, Q_n$ such that $P \ll Q_i$ and $Q_1 \cap \cdots \cap Q_n \subseteq R$. By iterated application of (GEE3↑), $P \ll Q_1 \cap \cdots \cap Q_n$ and so by (GEE2↑), $P \ll R$. The opposite direction is trivial.

(2) Assume that $P \ll U$. Clearly $\bigcap\{Q \in B : P \ll Q\}$ is closed. Assume that $\bigcap\{Q \in B : P \ll Q\} \subseteq R$, we show that $T \subseteq R$. Two cases: (i) $T = \emptyset$ in which case $T \subseteq R$ follows immediately, (ii) $T \neq \emptyset$. From (1) of this lemma it follows that $P \ll R$. But then by (GEE2↓) $\emptyset \ll R$ and so $T \subseteq R$ by (GEE4). Assume that $TOP_{\ll} \subseteq S$. By Lemma 30, $S \not\ll U$ and so by (GEE5), $P \ll S$ and so $\bigcap\{Q \in B : P \ll Q\} \subseteq S$. Thus $T \subseteq \bigcap\{Q \in B : P \ll Q\} \subseteq TOP_{\ll}$.

Assume that $\bigcap\{Q \in B : P \ll Q\} \subseteq R$ and that $R \ll S$. As $P \ll R$ by transitivity $P \ll S$ and so $\bigcap\{Q \in B : P \ll Q\} \subseteq S$. Thus $\bigcap\{Q \in B : P \ll Q\}$ is $\ll$-stable.

(3) Assume that $T \subseteq P$ and that $P \ll U$. Clearly $\bigcap\{Q \in B : P \ll Q\} \cap P$ is closed. Assume that $\bigcap\{Q \in B : P \ll Q\} \cap P \subseteq R$, we show that $T \subseteq R$. Two cases: (i) $T = \emptyset$ in which case $T \subseteq R$ follows immediately, (ii) $T \neq \emptyset$, thus $\emptyset \ll P$ by (GEE4). From (1) of this Lemma it follows that $P \ll -P \cup R$ so by transitivity and (GEE3↑), $\emptyset \ll P \cap (-P \cup R)$, i.e. $\emptyset \ll P \cap R$ and so by (GEE2↑) $\emptyset \ll R$ and so by (GEE4), $T \subseteq R$. Assume that $\bigcap\{Q \in B : Q \not\ll U\} \subseteq R$. From

Lemma 30 $R \not\ll U$ and so by (GEE5), $P \ll R$ and so $\bigcap\{Q \in B : P \ll Q\} \subseteq R$. But then $\bigcap\{Q \in B : P \ll Q\} \cap P \subseteq R$. Thus $T \subseteq \bigcap\{Q \in B : P \ll Q\} \cap P \subseteq TOP_{\ll}$.

Assume that $\bigcap\{Q \in B : P \ll Q\} \cap P \subseteq R$ and that $R \ll S$. From (1) of this lemma $P \ll -P \cup R$ and by (GEEDR2) $P \cap R \ll S \cap (-P \cup R)$, i.e. $P \cap (-P \cup R) \ll S \cap (-P \cup R)$ and so by (GEEDR3) $P \ll S$ and so $\bigcap\{Q \in B : P \ll Q\} \cap P \subseteq S$. ■

Proof of Theorem 18. (1) Right-to-left. Assume that $P \ll Q$ (thus $P \ll U$ by (EE2↑)). Consider $\bigcap\{R \in \mathcal{B} : P \ll R\}$, by Lemma 17, $\bigcap\{R \in \mathcal{B} : P \ll R\} \in F_{\mathrm{H}}(\ll, T)$. Also by Lemma 17 and (GEEDR4), $\bigcap\{R \in \mathcal{B} : P \ll R\} \not\subseteq P$, thus $min(P \cap Q, F_{\mathrm{H}}(\ll, T)) \neq \emptyset$.

Assume that $G \in min(P \cap Q, F_{\mathrm{H}}(\ll, T))$. Let $Y = \{R \in \mathcal{B} : \exists S \in \mathcal{B}, G \subseteq S$ and $S \cap Q \ll R\}$. Two cases: (i) $Y = \emptyset$. Then for each S, if $G \subseteq S$, then $S \cap Q \not\ll U$, i.e. by (GEE2↓), $S \not\ll U$. So $TOP_{\ll} \subseteq G$ and so $G = TOP_{\ll}$. Now by Lemma 17, $\bigcap\{S : P \ll S\} \in F_{\mathrm{H}}(\ll, T)$ so $\bigcap\{S : P \ll S\} \subseteq TOP_{\ll}$. Again by Lemma 17, and (GEEDR4) $\bigcap\{S : P \ll S\} \not\subseteq P$, so $\bigcap\{S : P \ll S\} = TOP_{\ll}$ (as $TOP_{\ll} = G \in min(P \cap Q, F_{\mathrm{H}}(\ll, T))$). By Lemma 17, $\bigcap\{S : P \ll S\} \subseteq Q$, so $G \subseteq Q$ and so $\bigcup min(P \cap Q, F_{\mathrm{H}}(\ll, T)) \subseteq Q$, thus $P \ll_{F_{\mathrm{H}}(\ll, T)} Q$ by definition.

(ii) $Y \neq \emptyset$. We are first going to show that $G \cap Q \cap \bigcap Y \in F_{\mathrm{H}}(\ll, T)$. As $G \in F_{\mathrm{H}}(\ll, T), T \subseteq G \subseteq TOP_{\ll}$. Furthermore as $P \ll Q$, $\emptyset \ll Q$ by (GEE2↓) and so $T \subseteq Q$ by (GEE4). So $T \subseteq G \cap Q \subseteq TOP_{\ll}$. For each $R \in Y$ there is some S such that $S \ll R$, thus $\emptyset \ll R$ by (GEE2↓) and so $T \subseteq R$ by (GEE4) and so $T \subseteq \bigcap Y$ thus $T \subseteq G \cap Q \cap \bigcap Y \subseteq TOP_{\ll}$.

Assume now that $G \cap Q \cap \bigcap Y \subseteq R$ and that $R \ll S$. Thus there are α and β such that $G \subseteq \alpha$, $\bigcap Y \subseteq \beta$ and $\alpha \cap Q \cap \beta \subseteq R$ and thus by (GEE3↓), $\alpha \cap Q \cap \beta \ll S$. There are $\gamma_1, \ldots, \gamma_n, \sigma_1, \ldots, \sigma_n \in \mathcal{B}$ such that $G \subseteq \gamma_i$ and $\gamma_i \cap Q \ll \sigma_i$ and $\sigma_1 \cap \cdots \cap \sigma_n \subseteq \beta$.

By iterated application of (GEEDR2), $\gamma_1 \cap \cdots \cap \gamma_n \cap Q \ll \sigma_1 \cap \cdots \cap \sigma_n$ and by (GEE2↑), $\gamma_1 \cap \cdots \cap \gamma_n \cap Q \ll \beta$. Recall that $\alpha \cap Q \cap \beta \ll S$. By (GEEDR2), $\alpha \cap Q \cap \beta \cap \gamma_1 \cap \cdots \cap \gamma_n \ll S \cap \beta$. By (GEEDR3), $\alpha \cap Q \cap \gamma_1 \cap \cdots \cap \gamma_n \ll S$. Clearly $G \subseteq \alpha \cap \gamma_1 \cap \cdots \cap \gamma_n$, so $S \in Y$ and so $\bigcap Y \subseteq S$, but then $G \cap Q \cap \bigcap Y \subseteq S$ and so $G \cap Q \cap \bigcap Y \in F_{\mathrm{H}}(\ll, T)$.

We now show that $G \cap Q \cap \bigcap Y \not\subseteq P$. For assume the contrary. Thus there is an α and a β such that $G \subseteq \alpha$ and $\bigcap Y \subseteq \beta$ and $\alpha \cap Q \cap \beta \subseteq P$, i.e. $\alpha \cap \beta \subseteq -Q \cup P$. Note that as $P \ll Q$, $P \cap Q \ll Q$ by (GEE2↓), i.e. $Q \cap (-Q \cup P) \ll Q \cap Q$. By (GEEDR3), $(-Q \cup P) \ll Q$. So by (GEE2↓), $\alpha \cap \beta \ll Q$. There must be $\gamma_1, \ldots, \gamma_n, \sigma_1, \ldots, \sigma_n \in \mathcal{B}$ such that $G \subseteq \gamma_i$ and $\gamma_i \cap Q \ll \sigma_i$ and $\sigma_1 \cap \cdots \cap \sigma_n \subseteq \beta$. By iterated application of (GEEDR2), $Q \cap \gamma_1 \cap \cdots \cap \gamma_n \ll \sigma_1 \cap \cdots \cap \sigma_n$. Thus $Q \cap \gamma_1 \cap \cdots \cap \gamma_n \ll \beta$ by (GEE2↑). By (GEEDR2), $\alpha \cap \beta \cap Q \cap \gamma_1 \cap \cdots \cap \gamma_n \ll Q \cap \beta$. By (GEEDR3), $\alpha \cap \beta \cap \gamma_1 \cap \cdots \cap \gamma_n \ll \beta$, by (GEE3↓), $\alpha \cap \gamma_1 \cap \cdots \cap \gamma_n \ll \beta$. As $G \subseteq \alpha \cap \gamma_1 \cap \cdots \cap \gamma_n$ and G is $\ll$-stable, $G \subseteq \beta$. As $G \subseteq \alpha \cap \beta$ and G is $\ll$-stable, $G \subseteq -Q \cup P$ and $G \subseteq Q$, but then $G \subseteq Q \cap (-Q \cup P)$, i.e. $G \subseteq P$.

But then $G \subseteq P \cap Q$ and so $G \notin min(P \cap Q, \mathcal{H}^T_{\ll})$ contrary to assumption.

So $G \cap Q \cap \bigcap Y \nsubseteq P$. As $G \cap Q \cap \bigcap Y \subseteq G$, $G \cap Q \cap \bigcap Y \in F_{\mathrm{H}}(\ll, T)$ and $G \in min(P \cap Q, \mathcal{H}^T_{\ll})$, $G = G \cap Q \cap \bigcap Y$. So $G \subseteq Q$ for each $G \in min(P \cap Q, \mathcal{H}^T_{\ll})$, thus $\bigcup min(P \cap Q, \mathcal{H}^T_{\ll}) \subseteq Q$ and so $P \ll_{F_{\mathrm{H}}(\ll,T)} Q$.

Left-to-right. Assume that $P \ll_{F_{\mathrm{H}}(\ll,T)} Q$, i.e. $min(P \cap Q, F_{\mathrm{H}}(\ll, T)) \neq \emptyset$ and $\bigcup min(P \cap Q, F_{\mathrm{H}}(\ll, T)) \subseteq Q$.

Two cases: (i) $T \nsubseteq P$. Then $T = \mathcal{C}(\bigcup min(P \cap Q, F_{\mathrm{H}}(\ll, T)))$, thus $T \subseteq Q$ and so by (GEE4′), $P \ll Q$.

(ii) $T \subseteq P$. Assume for reductio that $P \not\ll -P \cup Q$. Consider $Y = \bigcap\{R : P \ll R\}$. If $P \not\ll U$, then $TOP_{\ll} \subseteq P$, by Lemma 30, but then $\bigcup min(P \cap Q, \mathcal{H}^T_{\ll}) \subseteq P$ which gives us a contradiction. So $P \ll U$. By Lemma 17, $Y \cap P \in F_{\mathrm{H}}(\ll, T)$. Assume for reductio that $Y \cap P \subseteq Q$, then $Y \subseteq -P \cup Q$ and then, by Lemma 17 $P \ll -P \cup Q$ contrary to assumption. Thus $Y \cap P \nsubseteq Q$ and so for some $G \in min(P \cap Q, F_{\mathrm{H}}(\ll, T))$, $G \subseteq Y \cap P$, but $G \nsubseteq P \cap Q$ so $G \nsubseteq Q$ but then $\bigcup min(P \cap Q, F_{\mathrm{H}}(\ll, T)) \nsubseteq Q$ contrary to assumption.

So $P \ll -P \cup Q$. Consider $Y = \bigcap\{R : -Q \cup P \ll R\}$. By Lemma 17, $Y \cap (-Q \cup P) \in F_{\mathrm{H}}(\ll, T)$. Assume for reductio that $Y \cap (-Q \cup P) \nsubseteq P$. So $Y \cap (-Q \cup P) \nsubseteq Q$. Thus for some $G \in min(P \cap Q, F_{\mathrm{H}}(\ll, T))$, $G \subseteq Y \cap (-Q \cup P)$. By assumption $G \subseteq Q$, but as $G \subseteq -Q \cup P$, $G \subseteq P$, but then $G \subseteq P \cap Q$ and so $G \notin min(P \cap Q, F_{\mathrm{H}}(\ll, T))$ – a contradiction.

So $Y \cap (-Q \cup P) \subseteq P$. Then $Y \subseteq -(-Q \cup P) \cup P$, i.e. $Y \subseteq (Q \cap -P) \cup P$, i.e. $Y \subseteq Q \cup P$ and so by Lemma 17, $-Q \cup P \ll Q \cup P$. But then by (GEE2↓), $P \ll Q \cup P$ and so by (GEE3↑), $P \ll (Q \cup P) \cap (Q \cup -P)$, i.e. $P \ll Q$.

(2) Assume that $G \in \mathcal{H}$, thus $\bigcap \mathcal{H} \subseteq G$. Assume that $TOP_{\ll_{\mathcal{H}}} \subseteq P$, then $P \not\ll_{\mathcal{H}} U$, so $min(P \cap U, \mathcal{H}) = \emptyset$. But then $G \subseteq P$. So $G \subseteq TOP_{\ll_{\mathcal{H}}}$.

Assume that $G \subseteq P$, that $P \ll_{\mathcal{H}} Q$ and, for reductio that, $G \nsubseteq Q$. But then there is a $G' \in min(P \cap Q, \mathcal{H})$ such that $G' \subseteq G \subseteq P$. So then $\bigcup min(P \cap Q, \mathcal{H}) \nsubseteq Q$ and so $P \not\ll_{\mathcal{H}} Q$ contrary to assumption. So $G \subseteq Q$ thus G is $\ll$-stable and so $G \in F_{\mathrm{H}}(\ll_{\mathcal{H}}, \bigcap \mathcal{H})$. As $\bigcap \mathcal{H} \in \mathcal{H}$, $\bigcap \mathcal{H} \in F_{\mathrm{H}}(\ll_{\mathcal{H}}, \bigcap \mathcal{H})$ and furthermore for all $G \in F_{\mathrm{H}}(\ll_{\mathcal{H}}, \bigcap \mathcal{H})$, $\bigcap \mathcal{H} \subseteq G$ so $\bigcap \mathcal{H} = \bigcap F_{\mathrm{H}}(\ll_{\mathcal{H}}, \bigcap \mathcal{H})$. ■

Proof of Lemma 20. Make the requisite assumptions. It follows that $bst\,(x) = bst\,(y)$ and that $min(P, \mathfrak{H}(x)) = \emptyset$ if and only if $min(P, \mathfrak{H}(y)) = \emptyset$.

Assume that $min(P, \mathfrak{H}(x)) \neq \emptyset$. Note that $(-P \cap \mathcal{C}(\bigcup min(P, \mathfrak{H}(x)))) \subseteq Q$ if and only if $\bigcup min(P, \mathfrak{H}(x)) \subseteq P \cup Q$ if and only if $\bigcup min(P \cap (P \cup Q), \mathfrak{H}(x)) \subseteq P \cup Q$ if and only if $P \ll_{\mathfrak{H}(x)} P \cup Q$ if and only if $P \ll_{\mathfrak{H}(y)} P \cup Q$ if and only if $(-P \cap \mathcal{C}(\bigcup min(P, \mathfrak{H}(y)))) \subseteq Q$.

By (HYPA) and (HYPB), $\mathcal{M}_{\mathfrak{H}} \models_x [\div\phi]B\psi$ if and only if $bst\,(x) \subseteq ||\psi||$ and $(-\,||\phi|| \cap \mathcal{C}(\bigcup min(||\phi||, \mathfrak{H}(x)))) \subseteq ||\psi||$. But as we have seen this is equivalent to $bst\,(y) \subseteq ||\psi||$ and $(-\,||\phi|| \cap \mathcal{C}(\bigcup min(||\phi||, \mathfrak{H}(y)))) \subseteq ||\psi||$ which by (HYPA) and (HYPB) gives us $\mathcal{M}_{\mathfrak{H}} \models_y [\div\phi]B\psi$. ■

Proof of Theorem 22. As (HYPA) and (GEEA) are equivalent it will be sufficient to prove that, whenever $\ll = \ll_{\mathcal{H}}$: $\bigcup min(P, \mathcal{H}) \subseteq Q$ and $\bigcup\{G \in \mathcal{H} : G \subseteq P\} \subseteq Q$ if and only if $P \ll Q$. Assume throughout that $min(P, \mathcal{H}) \neq \emptyset$.

Assume that $\bigcup min(P, \mathcal{H}) \subseteq Q$ and $\bigcup\{G \in \mathcal{H} : G \subseteq P\} \subseteq Q$. Take any $G \in min(P \cap Q, \mathcal{H})$. If $G \not\subseteq P$, then $G \in min(P, \mathcal{H})$ and so $G \subseteq Q$, but if $G \subseteq P$, then again $G \subseteq Q$. Thus $\bigcup min(P \cap Q, \mathcal{H}) \subseteq Q$ As $\bigcup min(P, \mathcal{H}) \neq \emptyset$, $\bigcup min(P \cap Q, \mathcal{H}) \neq \emptyset$. So $P \ll Q$.

Assume instead that $P \ll Q$. Then $\bigcup min(P \cap Q, \mathcal{H}) \subseteq Q$. Thus $\bigcup min(P, \mathcal{H}) \subseteq Q$ and if $G \subseteq P$, then $G \subseteq Q$. So $\bigcup\{G \in \mathcal{H} : G \subseteq P\} \subseteq Q$. ■

Proof of Theorem 23. Let $\leq$ and $\ll$ be generated from $\mathcal{H}$. (1) Assume that $P \ll Q$, then $\bigcup min(P \cap Q, \mathcal{H}) \subseteq Q$ and $min(P \cap Q, \mathcal{H}) \neq \emptyset$, but then $P < Q$. (2) Assume that $\forall S(Q \cap S \leq P \cap Q \Rightarrow S \leq P \cap Q)$ and $P < U$. Thus $min(P \cap Q, \mathcal{H}) \neq \emptyset$. From Observation 9, $\bigcup min(P \cap Q, \mathcal{H}) \subseteq Q$, but then $P \ll Q$. (3) Assume that $\bigcup min(P \cap Q, \mathcal{H}) \subseteq Q$ and that $\bigcup min(P \cap R, \mathcal{H}) \subseteq R$, where $min(P \cap Q, \mathcal{H}) \neq \emptyset$ and $min(P \cap R, \mathcal{H}) \neq \emptyset$. Then $\bigcup min(P \cap Q \cap R, \mathcal{H}) \subseteq Q \cap R$ and $min(P \cap Q \cap R, \mathcal{H}) \neq \emptyset$ and so $P < Q \cap R$. ■

Proof of Theorem 25. I omit proofs for (success), (inclusion), (vacuity), (recovery), (min 2) and (func).

Take any hyper-model such that (HYPA) and (HYPB) are satisfied. For (7) assume that $\models_x < \div\phi > B\chi \wedge < \div\psi > B\chi$. By the truth-conditions, there is some y and y' such that $(x, y) \in R^{\div\|\phi\|}$ and $(x, y') \in R^{\div\|\psi\|}$. Thus $min(\|\phi\|, \mathfrak{H}(x)) \neq \emptyset$, $bst\,(y) = bst\,(x) \cup (-\|\phi\| \cap \bigcup min(\|\phi\|, \mathfrak{H}(x)))$, $min(\|\phi\|, \mathfrak{H}(x)) \neq \emptyset$ and $bst\,(y') = bst\,(x) \cup (-\|\psi\| \cap \bigcup min(\|\psi\|, \mathfrak{H}(x)))$. Furthermore, $bst\,(y) \subseteq \|\chi\|$ and $bst\,(y') \subseteq \|\chi\|$. Thus, $(-\|\phi\| \cap \bigcup min(\|\phi\|, \mathfrak{H}(x))) \subseteq \|\chi\|$ and $(-\|\psi\| \cap \bigcup min(\|\psi\|, \mathfrak{H}(x))) \subseteq \|\chi\|$. Clearly $min(\|\phi \wedge \psi\|, \mathfrak{H}(x))) \neq \emptyset$ so by (HYPA), there is some y'' such that $(x, y'') \in R^{\div\|\phi\wedge\psi\|}$. Assume that $G \in min(\|\phi \wedge \psi\|, \mathfrak{H}(x))$. Two cases, either: (i) $G \in min(\|\phi\|, \mathfrak{H}(x))$ or (ii) $G \in min(\|\psi\|, \mathfrak{H}(x))$. (i) Either $G \subseteq \|\psi\|$, in which case, as $G \cap -\|\phi\| \subseteq \|\chi\|$, $G \cap -\|\phi \wedge \psi\| \subseteq \|\chi\|$. Or $G \not\subseteq \|\psi\|$, but then $G \in min(\|\psi\|, \mathfrak{H}(x))$ and so again $G \cap -\|\phi \wedge \psi\| \subseteq \|\chi\|$. (ii) is analogous to (i). So $(-\|\phi \wedge \psi\| \cap \bigcup min(\|\phi \wedge \psi\|, \mathfrak{H}(x))) \subseteq \|\chi\|$ and as $bst\,(x) \subseteq \|\chi\|$, by (HYPB) and the truth-conditions $\models_x < \div\phi \wedge \psi > B\chi$.

(7c+8c) Assume that $\models_x < \div\phi \wedge \psi > B\psi$. Thus there is a y such that $(x, y) \in R^{\div\|\phi\wedge\psi\|}$. Furthermore $min(\|\phi \wedge \psi\|, \mathfrak{H}(x)) \neq \emptyset$, $bst\,(y) = bst\,(x) \cup (-\|\phi \wedge \psi\| \cap \bigcup min(\|\phi \wedge \psi\|, \mathfrak{H}(x)))$ and $bst\,(y) \subseteq \|\psi\|$. We will show that $min(\|\phi \wedge \psi\|, \mathfrak{H}(x)) = min(\|\phi\|, \mathfrak{H}(x))$, from which the rest follows by truth-conditions and simple set-theory. Assume that $G \in min(\|\phi \wedge \psi\|, \mathfrak{H}(x))$. Then $-\|\phi \wedge \psi\| \cap G \subseteq \|\psi\|$ and so $G \subseteq \|\psi\|$ and so $G \in min(\|\phi\|, \mathfrak{H}(x))$. Assume instead that $G \in min(\|\phi\|, \mathfrak{H}(x))$. Assume that for some that for some $G' \in min(\|\phi \wedge \psi\|, \mathfrak{H}(x))$, $G' \subset G$. Then $G' \subseteq \|\phi\|$, but as $-\|\phi \wedge \psi\| \cap G' \subseteq \|\psi\|$, $G' \subseteq \|\psi\|$ and we have a contradiction. Thus $G \in min(\|\phi \wedge \psi\|, \mathfrak{H}(x))$.

(max 1) Assume that $\models_x [\div\phi]\bot$. Thus $min(\|\phi\|, \mathfrak{H}(x)) = \emptyset$. Assume that $(x, y) \in R^{\div\|\psi\|}$. Thus $min(\|\psi\|, \mathfrak{H}(x)) \neq \emptyset$ and so for some $G \in min(\|\psi\|, \mathfrak{H}(x))$, $G \not\subseteq \|\phi \wedge \psi\|$. But clearly $G \subseteq \|\phi\|$ as otherwise there would be some $G' \in min(\|\phi\|, \mathfrak{H}(x))$ such that $G' \subseteq G$. But then $bst\,(y) \subseteq \|\phi\|$, so $\models_x [\div\psi]B\phi$.

To see that these axioms are also valid in the class of GEE-models satisfying (GEEA)+(GEEB), take any such model $\mathcal{M}_{\ll}$. By Corollary 19 there is a hyper-model $\mathcal{M}_{\mathfrak{H}}$ such that for all $x \in W$, $\ll_x$ is generated from $\mathfrak{H}(x)$ and from Theorem 21, $\mathcal{M}_{\mathfrak{H}}$ satisfies (HYPA)+(HYPB). But we know from the above proofs that the axioms are true in hyper-models satisfying (HYPA)+(HYPB) and so in all GEE-models satisfying (GEEA)+(GEEB). A similar argument can be given for EE-models using Theorem 6 and Observation 9. ■

Proof of Theorem 26. (GEE1) By (success) $[\div\top \wedge \top]\neg B(\top \wedge \top) \in x$ and so by modal logic $\neg <\div\top \wedge \top> B\top \in x$ and so $\|\top\| \not\ll_x \|\top\|$. (GEE2↑) Assume that $<\div\phi \wedge \psi> B\psi \in x$ and that $\|\psi\| \subseteq \|\chi\|$. By PE $<\div(\phi \wedge \chi) \wedge \psi> B\psi \in x$. By modal logic $<\div(\phi \wedge \chi) \wedge \psi> B\chi \in x$ and so by (7c+8c), $<\div\phi \wedge \chi> B\chi \in x$ so $\|\phi\| \ll_x \|\chi\|$. (GEE2↓) Assume that $<\div\phi \wedge \psi> B\psi \in x$ and that $\|\chi\| \subseteq \|\phi\|$. By Lemma 24, $<\div\phi \wedge \psi \wedge \chi> B\psi \in x$ and so by PE $<\div\chi \wedge \psi> B\psi \in x$. So $\|\chi\| \ll_x \|\psi\|$. (GEE3↑) Assume that $<\div\phi \wedge \psi> B\psi \in x$ and that $<\div\phi \wedge \chi> B\chi \in x$. By two applications of Lemma 24 and modal logic $<\div\phi \wedge \psi \wedge \chi> B(\psi \wedge \chi) \in x$. So $\|\phi\| \ll_x \|\psi\| \cap \|\chi\|$. (GEE3↓) Assume that $<\div(\phi \wedge \psi) \wedge \psi> B\psi \in x$. By PE $<\div\phi \wedge \psi> B\psi \in x$ and so $\|\phi\| \ll_x \|\psi\|$. (GEE4) Assume that $\neg B \perp \in x$. So $\neg B(\perp \wedge\phi) \in x$. Assume that $<\div\perp \wedge\phi> B\phi \in x$. By (inclusion), $B\phi \in x$. Assume instead that $B\phi \in x$. By (vacuity) $<\div\perp \wedge\phi> B\phi \in x$. (GEE4′) Assume that $\neg B\psi \in x$ but that $B\phi \in x$. Thus $\neg B(\phi \wedge \psi) \in x$. By (vacuity) $<\div\psi \wedge \phi> B\phi \in x$. (GEE5) Assume that $<\div\phi \wedge \top> B\top \in x$, thus $\neg[\div\phi]\perp \in x$, and that $\neg <\div\psi \wedge \top> B\top \in x$. Thus by modal logic $[\div\psi \wedge \top]\perp \in x$ and by PE $[\div\psi]\perp \in x$. So by (max 1) and PE $[\div\phi \wedge \psi]B\psi \in x$. By (max 2), $\neg[\div\phi \wedge \psi]\perp \in x$ so by modal logic, $<\div\phi \wedge \psi> B\psi \in x$. Thus $\|\phi\| \ll_x \|\psi\|$. ■

Proof of Theorem 27. (1) (GEEA) Assume that $\neg[\div\phi]\perp \in x$. Thus by PE and modal logic $<\phi \wedge \top> B\top \in x$ and so $\|\phi\| \ll_x \|\top\|$. Conversely, assume that $\|\phi\| \ll_x \|\top\|$, i.e. $<\div\phi> B\top \in x$ but by modal logic $\neg[\div\phi]\perp \in x$.

(GEEB) If $[\div\phi]\perp \in x$, then by the above argument $\|\phi\| \not\ll_x \|\top\|$ and so (GEEB) is satisfied. Assume then that $[\div\phi]B\psi \in x$ and that $\neg[\div\phi]\perp \in x$. So $<\div\phi> B\psi \in x$, thus by PE and modal logic $<\div\phi \wedge (\phi \vee \psi)> B(\phi \vee \psi) \in x$. Thus $\|\phi\| \ll_x \|\phi\| \cup \|\psi\|$. By (inclusion) $B\psi \in x$ so $bst(x) \subseteq \|\psi\|$.

Next, if $\|\phi\| \not\ll_x \|\top\|$, then $[\div\phi] \perp \in x$ and so by modal logic $[\div\phi]B\psi \in x$. So assume that $bst(x) \subseteq \|\psi\|$, i.e. $B\psi \in x$ and that $\|\phi\| \ll_x \|\phi\| \cup \|\psi\|$, i.e. $<\div\phi \wedge (\phi \vee \psi)> B(\phi \vee \psi) \in x$. By PE $<\div\phi> B(\phi \vee \psi) \in x$. By (recovery), $[\div\phi]B(\neg\phi \vee \psi) \in x$ and so by modal logic $<\div\phi> B\psi \in x$, but then $[\div\phi]B\psi \in x$ by (func). So (GEEB) is satisfied.

(2) Follows from Theorems 18 and 21. (3) Follows from (2) and Observation 9. ■

Department of Philosophy, Uppsala University, Sweden.

REFERENCES

[Alchourrón *et al.*, 1985] Alchourrón, C., P. Gärdenfors, and D. Makinson. On the logic of theory change: Partial meet functions for contraction and revision. *Journal of Symbolic Logic* **50**, 510–530, 1985.

[Cantwell, 1999] Cantwell, J. Some logics of iterated revision. *Studia Logica*, **63**, 49–84..

[Cantwell, 199y] Cantwell, J. Logics of belief change without linearity. To appear in *Journal of Symbolic Logic*, 1999.

[Gärdenfors, 1988] Gärdenfors, P. *Knowledge In Flux*. The MIT Press, 1988.

[Gärdenfors and Makinson, 1988] Gärdenfors, P. and D. Makinson. Revisions of knowledge systems using epistemic entrenchment. In M. Vardi (Ed.), *Theoretical Aspects of Reasoning About Knowledge*, pp. 83–95. Los Altos, CA: Morgan Kaufman, 988.

[Grove, 1988] Grove, A. Two modellings for theory change. *Journal of Philosophical Logic* **17**, 157–170, 1988.

[Lewis, 1973] Lewis, D. *Counterfactuals*. Cambridge, Massachusetts: Harvard University Press, 1973.

[Lindström and Rabinowicz, 1991] Lindström, S. and W. Rabinowicz. Epistemic entrenchment with incomparabilities and relational belief revision. In A. Fuhrmann and M. Morreau (Eds.), *The Logic of Theory Change*, pp. 93–126. Berlin: Springer-Verlag, 1991.

[Meyer *et al.*, 1998] Meyer, T. A., W. A. Labuschagne, and J. Heidema. A semantic weakening of the recovery postulate for theory contraction. To appear, 1998.

[Rott, 1991] Rott, H. Two methods of constructing contractions and revisions of knowledge systems. *Journal of Philosophical Logic* **20**, 149–173, 1991.

[Rott, 1992] Rott, H. Preferential belief change using generalised epistemic entrenchment. *Journal of Logic, Language and Information* **1**, 45–78, 1992.

[Rott, 1993] Rott, H. Belief contraction in the context of the general theory of rational choice. *Journal of Symbolic Logic* **58**, 1426–50, 1993.

[Rott, 1996] Rott, H. *Making up ones mind: Foundations, Coherence, Nonmonotonicity*. Habilitation thesis: Dept. of Philosophy, University of Konstanz, 1996.

[Segerberg, 1995] Segerberg, K. Some questions about hypertheories. In S. O. Hansson and W. Rabinowicz (Eds.), *Logic for a change*. Uppsala: Uppsala Prints and Preprints in Philosophy, 1995.

EDUARDO L. FERMÉ

FIVE FACES OF RECOVERY

1 INTRODUCTION

One of the basic principles of the AGM theory [Alchourrón *et al.*, 1985] is that belief changes should take place with minimal loss of previous beliefs. In the opinion of the AGM trio, the postulate of recovery guarantees minimal loss of contents in the contraction process.[1] However, several authors have criticised the recovery postulate [Fermé, 1998; Makinson, 1987; Levi, 1991; Levi, 1997; Lindström and Rabinowicz, 1991; Hansson, 1991; Niederée, 1991; Nayak, 1994; Makinson, 1997]. The present work describes recovery from five angles or models in which it is possible to define the AGM contraction: *Postulates, partial meet functions, epistemic entrenchment, safe/kernel contraction* and *sphere-systems*. It also shows how the intuitions or non-intuitions that surround recovery appear or disappear in each of them and consequently, the status of recovery turns out to differ substantially among the five approaches.

In Section 2 we introduce AGM contraction in its five presentations, and in Sections 3 to 7 we analyse recovery in the five AGM presentations.

2 THE AGM ACCOUNT

In the AGM [Alchourrón *et al.*, 1985] account the beliefs of a rational agent are represented by a belief set $\mathbf{K}$, which is a set of sentences in a language $\mathcal{L}$ closed under logical consequence Cn, where Cn satisfies: $A \subseteq Cn(A)$, $Cn(Cn(A)) \subseteq Cn(A)$ and $Cn(A) \subseteq Cn(B)$ if $A \subseteq B$, as well as supraclassicality, deduction and compactness. We use $\vdash \alpha$ as an alternative notation for $\alpha \in Cn(\emptyset)$, $\mathbf{H} \vdash \alpha$ for $\alpha \in Cn(\mathbf{H})$, $\alpha \vdash \beta$ for $\beta \in Cn(\{\alpha\})$. $\mathbf{K}_\perp$ denotes the inconsistent belief set. $\mathbf{K}{+}\alpha$ denotes the expansion of $\mathbf{K}$ by α and is defined by $\mathbf{K}{+}\alpha = Cn(\mathbf{K} \cup \{\alpha\})$. A set of sentences that is no closed under logical consequence is called a belief base.

2.1 Axioms

The AGM axioms for contraction are:

[1]'When contracting K with respect to A, the loss of information should be as small as possible. The recovery postulate $(K-5)$ [recovery] *is one way of guaranteeing this.*'[Gärdenfors, 1988, p. 65]. '*Clearly $A \div x$ will have to be 'fairly big' as a subset of A in order to satisfy this.* [recovery]'[Makinson, 1985, p. 352].
'*...we are thus free to appreciate the considerations in its favour, notably its appeal as a sign of 'minimality' of the change made to the belief set,...*'[Makinson, 1997, p. 478].

M.-A. Williams and H. Rott (eds.), Frontiers in Belief Revision, 247–259.

Closure $\mathbf{K}-\alpha$ is a belief set whenever $\mathbf{K}$ is a belief set.
Success If $\not\vdash \alpha$, then $\mathbf{K}-\alpha \not\vdash \alpha$.
Inclusion $\mathbf{K}-\alpha \subseteq \mathbf{K}$.
Vacuity If $\mathbf{K} \not\vdash \alpha$, then $\mathbf{K} \subseteq \mathbf{K}-\alpha$.
Extensionality If $\vdash \alpha \leftrightarrow \beta$ then $\mathbf{K}-\alpha = \mathbf{K}-\beta$.
Recovery $\mathbf{K} \subseteq (\mathbf{K}-\alpha) + \alpha$.
Conjunctive overlap $\mathbf{K}-\alpha \cap \mathbf{K}-\beta \subseteq \mathbf{K}-(\alpha \wedge \beta)$.
Conjunctive inclusion If $\mathbf{K}-(\alpha \wedge \beta) \not\vdash \alpha$, then $\mathbf{K}-(\alpha \wedge \beta) \subseteq \mathbf{K}-\alpha$.

2.2 *Partial meet contraction*

A second way of constructing an AGM contraction function is by means of a selection among the maximal subsets of $\mathbf{K}$ that do not imply the sentence to be contracted. This construction, *partial meet contraction*, is defined as follows:

DEFINITION 1. [Alchourrón *et al.*, 1985] Let $\mathbf{K}$ be a belief set. Let $\mathbf{K}\perp\alpha$ be the set of all maximal subsets of $\mathbf{K}$ that does not imply α. Let γ be a selection function that satisfies: $\gamma(\mathbf{K}\perp\alpha)$ is a non-empty subset of $\mathbf{K}$ if $\mathbf{K}\perp\alpha$ is non-empty, in which case $\gamma(\mathbf{K}\perp\alpha) = \{\mathbf{K}\}$.
The *partial meet contraction* on $\mathbf{K}$ that is generated by γ is the operation $\sim_\gamma$ such that for all sentence α:

$$\mathbf{K} \sim_\gamma \alpha = \cap\gamma(\mathbf{K}\perp\alpha)$$

An operation $-$ on $\mathbf{K}$ is a partial meet contraction if and only if there is a selection function γ for $\mathbf{K}$ such that for all sentences $\alpha : \mathbf{K}-\alpha = \mathbf{K} \sim_\gamma \alpha$.

Furthermore, $-$ is (transitively) relational if and only if it can be generated from a (transitively) relational selection function.

2.3 *Epistemic Entrenchment*

The notion of epistemic entrenchment for theories was introduced in [Gärdenfors, 1988] by Gärdenfors to define the properties that an order between sentences of the language should satisfy. Gärdenfors proposed the following set of axioms:

(EE1) Transitivity If $\alpha \leq_{\mathbf{K}} \beta$ and $\beta \leq_{\mathbf{K}} \delta$, then $\alpha \leq_{\mathbf{K}} \delta$.
(EE2) Dominance If $\alpha \vdash \beta$, then $\alpha \leq_{\mathbf{K}} \beta$.
(EE3) Conjunctiveness $\alpha \leq_{\mathbf{K}} (\alpha \wedge \beta)$ or $\beta \leq_{\mathbf{K}} (\alpha \wedge \beta)$.
(EE4) Minimality If $\mathbf{K} \not\vdash \bot$, then $\alpha \notin \mathbf{K}$ if and only if $\alpha \leq_{\mathbf{K}} \beta$ for all β.
(EE5) Maximality If $\beta \leq_{\mathbf{K}} \alpha$ for all β, then $\vdash \alpha$.

Gärdenfors and Makinson [1988] investigated the connections between orders of epistemic entrenchment and contraction functions. The two are connected by the following equivalences, where we write $\alpha <_{\mathbf{K}} \beta$ when $\alpha \leq_{\mathbf{K}} \beta$ and $\beta \not\leq_{\mathbf{K}} \alpha$:

$(C \leq)$ $\alpha \leq_{\mathbf{K}} \beta$ if and only if $\alpha \notin \mathbf{K}-(\alpha \wedge \beta)$ or $\vdash (\alpha \wedge \beta)$.
$(-_{\mathrm{G}})$ $\beta \in \mathbf{K}-\alpha$ if and only if $\beta \in \mathbf{K}$ and either $\vdash \alpha$ or $\alpha <_{\mathbf{K}} (\alpha \vee \beta)$.

2.4 Safe/Kernel contraction

Safe Contraction [Alchourrón and Makinson, 1985] and its generalisation Kernel Contraction [Hansson, 1994] are based on a selection among the sentences of a belief set $\mathbf{K}$ that contribute effectively to imply α; and how to use this selection in contracting by α.

DEFINITION 2. [Hansson, 1994] Let $\mathbf{K} \perp\!\!\!\perp \alpha$ be the set of all minimal subsets of $\mathbf{K}$ that implies α. An *incision function* σ for $\mathbf{K}$ is a function such that for all sentences α:

$$\begin{cases} \sigma(\mathbf{K} \perp\!\!\!\perp \alpha) \subseteq \bigcup(\mathbf{K} \perp\!\!\!\perp \alpha) \\ \emptyset \neq A \in \mathbf{K} \perp\!\!\!\perp \alpha, \text{ then } A \cap \sigma(\mathbf{K} \perp\!\!\!\perp \alpha) \neq \emptyset \end{cases}$$

An incision function σ for a belief set $\mathbf{K}$ is *smooth* if and only if it holds for all subsets A of $\mathbf{K}$ that: *if* $A \vdash \beta$ and $\beta \in \sigma(\mathbf{K} \perp\!\!\!\perp \alpha)$, *then* $A \cap \sigma(\mathbf{K} \perp\!\!\!\perp \alpha) \neq \emptyset$.

DEFINITION 3. [Hansson, 1994] Let $\mathbf{K}$ be a belief set and σ an incision function for $\mathbf{K}$. The *smooth kernel contraction* $-_\sigma$ for $\mathbf{K}$ is defined as follows:

$$\mathbf{K}-_\sigma\alpha = \mathbf{K} \setminus \sigma(\mathbf{K} \perp\!\!\!\perp \alpha).$$

An operator $-$ for a belief set $\mathbf{K}$ is a smooth kernel contraction if and only if there is an smooth incision function σ for $\mathbf{K}$ such that $\mathbf{K} \sim \alpha = \mathbf{K}-_\sigma\alpha$ for all sentences α.

DEFINITION 4. [Alchourrón and Makinson, 1985] Any sentence β in a belief set $\mathbf{K}$ is safe with respect to α if and only if β is not minimal under $\prec$ with respect to the elements of any $\mathbf{A} \in \mathbf{K} \perp\!\!\!\perp \alpha$ The set of all *safe* sentences of $\mathbf{K}$ respect to α is denoted $\mathbf{K}/\alpha$. Safe Contraction is defined by the following identity:

$$\mathbf{K} \sim \alpha = Cn(\mathbf{K} \cap \mathbf{K}/\alpha)$$

DEFINITION 5. [Alchourrón and Makinson, 1986] Let $\mathbf{K}$ be a belief set and $\prec$ a hierarchy over $\mathbf{K}$. Then, for all α, β and $\delta \in \mathbf{K}$, $\prec$ is virtually connected over $\mathbf{K}$ if and only if: *if* $\alpha \prec \beta$ *then either* $\alpha \prec \delta$ *or* $\delta \prec \beta$.

2.5 Possible worlds and Grove's sphere-system

The last construction is based on possible worlds models. A proposition (set of possible worlds) can represent either a belief set or an input sentence. The belief set $\mathbf{K}$ can be replaced, as a belief state representation, by $||\mathbf{K}|| = \{X \mid \mathbf{K} \subseteq X \in \mathcal{L} \perp\!\!\!\perp\}$, which is the set of worlds that contain $\mathbf{K}$. Similarly, each sentence α can be represented by the set $||\alpha|| = ||Cn(\{\alpha\})||$. Contraction by α takes the form of adding new possible worlds in which $\neg\alpha$ holds, i.e.:

DEFINITION 6. [Hansson, 1999] Let X be a proposition. A *propositional selection function* for X is a function f such that for all sentences α:
(I) $f(||\alpha||) \subseteq ||\alpha||$
(II) If $||\alpha|| \neq \emptyset$ then $f(||\alpha||) \neq \emptyset$.
(III) If $X \cap ||\alpha|| \neq \emptyset$, then $f(||\alpha||) = X \cap ||\alpha||$.

DEFINITION 7. Let X be a proposition. An operator $\ominus$ is a *propositional contraction operator* for X if and only if there is a propositional selection function f for X such that for all α, $X \ominus ||\alpha|| = X \cup f(||\neg\alpha||)$

The *Grove's sphere-system* makes use of a system of concentric spheres around the proposition. Intuitively, each sphere represents a degree of closeness or similarity to $||\mathbf{K}||$. In contraction by α, the closest $\neg\alpha$-worlds are added to $||\mathbf{K}||$.

DEFINITION 8. [Grove, 1988] \$ is a *system of spheres* if and only if it satisfies:
\$1 $\emptyset \neq \$ \subseteq \mathcal{P}(\mathcal{L} \perp\perp)$,
\$2 $\cap\$ \in \$$,
\$3 If $\mathbf{G}, \mathbf{G}' \in \$$, then $\mathbf{G} \subseteq \mathbf{G}'$ or $\mathbf{G}' \subseteq \mathbf{G}$,
\$4 $\cup\$ \in \$$,
\$5 If $||\alpha|| \cap (\cup\$) \neq \emptyset$, then $\mathbf{S}_\alpha \in \$$ and $\mathbf{S}_\alpha \cap ||\alpha|| \neq \emptyset$, and
\$6 $\mathcal{L} \perp\perp \in \$$,

where $\mathbf{S}_\alpha = \bigcap\{\mathbf{G} \in \$ \mid \mathbf{G} \cap ||\alpha|| \neq \emptyset\}$.

DEFINITION 9. [Grove, 1988] A propositional selection function f for a proposition X is *sphere-based* if and only if there is a system of spheres \$ such that for all α: If $||\alpha|| \neq \emptyset$, then $f(||\alpha||) = \mathbf{S}_\alpha \cap ||\alpha||$. A propositional contraction operator is sphere-based if and only if it is based on a sphere-based propositional selection function.

2.6 The interconnection among the five presentations

THEOREM 10. *Let* **K** *be a belief set and* $-$ *an operator on* **K**. *Then the following conditions are equivalent:*
1. $-$ *satisfies* closure, inclusion, vacuity, success, extensionality *and* recovery.
2. $-$ *is a* partial meet contraction function.
3. $-$ *is a* smooth kernel contraction function.
4. *There exists a function f such that for all α, $f(\alpha) \subseteq ||\alpha||$ and* $\mathbf{K}-\alpha = Th(||\mathbf{K}|| \cup f(\neg\alpha))$.

THEOREM 11. *Let* **K** *be a belief set and* $-$ *an operator on* **K**. *Then the following conditions are equivalent:*
1. $-$ *satisfies* closure, inclusion, vacuity, success, extensionality, recovery, disjunctive inclusion, *and* disjunctive overlap.
2. $-$ *is a* transitively relational partial meet contraction *function.*
3. $-$ *is a safe contraction function, based on a virtually connected hierarchy* $\prec$.

4. *$-$ is a Gärdenfors entrenchment-based contraction based on a relation $\leq_{\mathbf{K}}$ defined from $-$ by condition $(C \leq)$ and $\leq_{\mathbf{K}}$ satisfies the standard entrenchment postulates.*
5. *There exists a propositional sphere-based selection function f such that for all α, $\mathbf{K}{*}\alpha = Th(f(\neg\alpha))$.*

3 RECOVERY AND MINIMAL CHANGE IN THE AGM AXIOMATIC

The debate on recovery has focused mainly on the axiomatic presentation. Consequently, this is the best known of the fives faces of recovery.

One possible first approach to the notion of minimal loss of previous beliefs is the following: A sentence β must be discarded in the contraction of $\mathbf{K}$ by α, only if its presence in the contracted set leads to α being inferred. This reasoning is reflected in the following postulate:

Fullness [Alchourrón *et al.*, 1985] If $\beta \in \mathbf{K}$ and $\beta \notin \mathbf{K}{-}\alpha$ then $\not\vdash \alpha$ and $\beta \to \alpha \in \mathbf{K}{-}\alpha$.

However, in the presence of closure, fullness implies the following principle [Makinson, 1985]:

Saturability If $\alpha \in \mathbf{K}$, then for any $\beta \in \mathcal{L}$, either $\alpha \vee \beta \in \mathbf{K}{-}\alpha$ or $\alpha \vee \neg\beta \in \mathbf{K}{-}\alpha$.

The following example shows the implausibility of this property:

EXAMPLE 12. I believe that 'my floppy disk is empty' (α). Then I also believe that 'my floppy disk is empty or there is life after death'($\alpha \vee \beta$) and 'my floppy disk is empty or there is no life after death'($\alpha \vee \neg\beta$). I discover later that my floppy drive is broken. Then I must contract my belief α (but not revise it by $\neg\alpha$). According to *saturability* I must retain either $\alpha \vee \beta$ or $\alpha \vee \neg\beta$, but I have no reason to do this.

The AGM theory proposes, as a rule of minimality, the postulate of recovery, according to which it is enough to add (by expansion) the contracted sentence to recover the whole of the original theory.

LEMMA 13. *[Gärdenfors, 1988] Fullness implies Recovery.*

The following example shows a situation where recovery is reasonable:

EXAMPLE 14. [Hansson, 1999] I believed that I had my latchkey on me (α). Then I felt in my left pocket, where I usually keep it, and did not find it. I lost my belief in α (but without starting to believe in $\neg\alpha$ instead). Half a second later, I found the key, and regained my belief in α.

Hansson showed that recovery gives rise to unintuitive results as we can see in the following examples:

EXAMPLE 15. [Hansson, 1993] 'I believe that 'Cleopatra had a son' (α) and that 'Cleopatra had a daughter' (β), and thus also 'Cleopatra had a child' ($\alpha \vee \beta$, briefly δ). Then I receive information that makes me give up my belief in δ, and contract my belief set accordingly, forming $\mathbf{K}-\delta$. Soon afterwards I learn from a reliable source that 'Cleopatra had a child'. It seems perfectly reasonable for me to then add δ ($\alpha \vee \beta$) to my set of beliefs without also reintroducing either α or β.'

In this example, the problem appears because when we contract $\mathbf{K}$ by $\alpha \vee \beta$, by recovery the sentence $(\alpha \vee \beta) \to (\alpha \wedge \beta)$ must remain in the contraction.

EXAMPLE 16. [Hansson, 1993][2] 'I previously entertained the two beliefs, '*x is divisible by 2*' (α) and '*x is divisible by 6*' (β). When I received new information that induced me to give up the first of these beliefs (α), the second (β) had to go as well (since α would otherwise follow from β).
I then received new information that made me accept the belief '*x is divisible by 8.*' (ϵ). Since α follows from ϵ, $(\mathbf{K}-\alpha) + \alpha$ is a subset of $(\mathbf{K}-\alpha) + \epsilon$, then by recovery I obtain that '*x is divisible by 24*' (δ), contrary to the intuition.'

In the above example we show that retaining the sentence $\mu = \alpha \to \beta$ in the contraction of $\mathbf{K}$ by α gives rise to unintuitive results. Therefore μ must be removed in the process of contraction by α. Due to recovery, AGM contraction cannot eliminate μ. However not all the $\alpha \to \beta$ sentences are undesirable.

Makinson [1997, p. 478] noted that *'as soon as contraction makes use of the notion 'y is believed only because of x', we run into counterexamples to recovery'*. He argued that this is provoked by the use of a justificatory structure that is not represented in the belief set and that, without this structure, recovery can be accepted; or, in Makinson's words, it can be accepted in a 'naked' theory. In [Hansson, 1998], Hansson replied that *'Actual human beliefs always have such a justificatory structure (...). It is difficult if not impossible to find examples about which we can have intuitions, and in which the belief set is not associated with a justificatory structure that guides our intuitions. Against this background, it is not surprising that, as Makinson says, recovery 'appears to be free of intuitive counterexamples' (...). It also seems to be free of confirming examples of this kind.'*

In [Fermé and Rodríguez, 1997; Fermé, 1998] a selection mechanism to determine which $\alpha \to \beta$ sentences must be discarded is proposed. This mechanism represents the justificatory structure referred to by Makinson. The result is a contraction function without recovery.

Niederée [1991] found several unintuitive properties that follow from recovery:

OBSERVATION 17. [Niederée, 1991] Let $\mathbf{K}$ be a belief set and $\alpha \in \mathbf{K}$. Then, regardless of whether or not β is in $\mathbf{K}$, recovery together with *closure* implies that:

1. $\alpha \to \beta \in \mathbf{K}-(\alpha \vee \beta)$,

[2] 'We use here the modified version introduced in [Fermé and Rodríguez, 1997].

2. $\alpha \in (\mathbf{K}-(\alpha \vee \beta)) + \beta$,

3. $\neg\beta \in (\mathbf{K}-(\alpha \vee \beta)) + \neg\alpha$.

Another significant point is the relationship from contraction to revision defined via the Levi identity ($\mathbf{K}{*}\alpha = (\mathbf{K}-\neg\alpha + \alpha)$. Makinson [1987] pointed out that via the Levi identity, recovery is not needed to obtain the six basic AGM revision postulates. However, as we have noted in [Fermé, 1999], recovery is needed for the supplementary postulates. In particular:

OBSERVATION 18. [Alchourrón *et al.*, 1985; Makinson, 1987] Let **K** be a theory and $-$ an operator for **K** that satisfies the contraction postulates *closure, inclusion, success, vacuity* and *extensionality*. Let $*$ be an operator for **K** defined from $-$ via the Levi identity. Then $*$ satisfies the revision postulates *closure, success, inclusion, vacuity, consistency* and *extensionality*. If $-$ also satisfies *conjunctive inclusion*, then $*$ satisfies *subexpansion*.

OBSERVATION 19. [Alchourrón *et al.*, 1985] Let **K** be a theory and $-$ an operator for **K** that satisfies the contraction postulates *closure, inclusion, success, vacuity, extensionality,* **recovery** and *conjunctive overlap*. Let $*$ be an operator for **K** defined from $-$ via the Levi identity. Then $*$ satisfies *superexpansion*.

OBSERVATION 20. [Fermé, 1999] Let **K** be a theory and $-$ an operator for **K** that satisfies the contraction postulates *closure, inclusion, success, vacuity, extensionality* and *conjunctive overlap*, but not *recovery*. Let $*$ be an operator for **K** defined from $-$ via the Levi identity. Then $*$, in general, does not satisfy *superexpansion*.

Levi [1996] proposed another identity that he called 'Ramsey Revision' ($\mathbf{K}{*}\alpha = ((\mathbf{K}-\neg\alpha - \alpha) + \alpha)$. Ramsey revision coincides with the AGM revision when recovery is satisfied.

To replace recovery, Hansson proposed to relax the fullness condition in the following sense: If a sentence β was removed in the contraction of **K** by α, then β contributes to the fact that α will be deduced in **K**:

Core-retainment [Hansson, 1991] If $\beta \in K$ and $\beta \notin \mathbf{K}-\alpha$ then there is some set **H** such that $\mathbf{H} \subseteq \mathbf{K}$ and $\alpha \notin Cn(\mathbf{H})$ but $\alpha \in Cn(\mathbf{K} \cup \{\beta\})$.

This *intuitive way* leads again to recovery, since core-retainment is equivalent to recovery in presence of the other basic AGM postulates [Hansson, 1991]. [3]

For the last proposal we quote a comment by Makinson with respect to saturability [Makinson, 1985, page 357]: 'in general, neither $\alpha \vee \beta$ nor $\alpha \vee \neg\beta$ should be retained in the process of eliminating α from **K**, unless there is 'some reason' in **K** for their continued presence'. The proposal is to extend this idea in the sense that *in general, no β should be retained in the process of eliminating α from* **K**, *unless there is 'some reason' in* **K** *for their continued presence*. This condition was explored by Fuhrmann [1991] and gives rise to the filtering condition:

[3] However this equivalence disappears in belief bases.

> 'If β has been retracted from a base B in order to bar derivations of α from B, then the contraction of Cn(B) by α should not contain any sentences which were in Cn(B) 'just because' β was in Cn(B).'

The filtering condition is a different notion of minimal change from that of recovery, since $\alpha \rightarrow \beta$ maybe is in $\mathbf{K}$ 'just because' β is in $\mathbf{K}$.

First Conclusion: In the axiomatic, rather than in the other presentations, recovery is an explicit property. Consequently, it is in this section where we can analyse recovery in a more independent way.

The counterexamples show the implausibility of the use of recovery as a general property. However, it is also clear that it is not a good idea to reject it completely. At this point, the 'filtering condition' appears as the best candidate to be used as a rule of minimality and the greatest challenge is to find postulates that allow to differentiate among the '$\alpha \rightarrow \beta$' sentences that are in $\mathbf{K}$ *just because* β is in $\mathbf{K}$, from those '$\alpha \rightarrow \beta$' sentences believed by their proper value. The open problem is to find an axiomatic that reflects the spirit of the filtering condition.

4 RECOVERY IN PARTIAL MEET CONTRACTION

In the original development of partial meet contraction [Alchourrón and Makinson, 1981; Alchourrón and Makinson, 1982], the first approach was to select only one element of $\mathbf{K}\bot\alpha$. This approach, originally called Choice and later Maxichoice produces constructions that are 'too large'; in fact it corresponds to the basic AGM postulates plus fullness. In the other extreme, we can consider a function that returns only the propositions that are common to all the elements of $\mathbf{K}\bot\alpha$; but this function, full meet contraction, returns only $Cn(\{\neg\alpha\}) \cap \mathbf{K}$ when $\alpha \in \mathbf{K}$ and $\not\vdash \alpha$. Full meet contraction also satisfies the basic AGM postulates. Partial meet contraction takes the common elements of a selected subset of $\mathbf{K}\bot\alpha$ and corresponds exactly to the basic AGM postulates. If the selection is based on a transitively relational function between the members of $\mathbf{K}\bot\alpha$, then it corresponds to the basic and supplementary postulates.

Full meet contraction is the *lower bound* for contractions satisfying recovery, in the sense that if a contraction satisfies recovery, then it must be a superset of full meet contraction. In a superficial reading, recovery is reasonable since it appears in all possible combinations of $\mathbf{K}\bot\alpha$. However the following question remains: If recovery is defended as the postulate that guarantees minimal change, how is it possible to have both *too large* (maxichoice) and *too small* (full meet) contractions that both satisfy recovery? Due to this possibility, it appears that recovery does not guarantee minimal change. It is arguable that minimal change is not only a 'quantitative' concept (as it appears to be when we consider full meet and maxichoice). Under this supposition, minimal change must be evaluated considering the epistemic value of the sentences to be discarded. However, the use of 'remainder sets' reflected that the 'quantitative' concept it is intrinsically present in this approach.

In this way, we can note that the elements of $\mathbf{K}\bot\alpha$ become saturated (i.e., become maximal consistent subsets of the language) by adding $\neg\alpha$ [Alchourrón and Makinson, 1981]. In [Levi, 1991, p. 134], Levi argued that not only the elements of $\mathbf{K}\bot\alpha$ guarantee minimal loss but all the saturatable sets do; and presented an alternative contraction, based on a selection among all the saturatable subsets of $\mathbf{K}$ with respect to α instead of $\mathbf{K}\bot\alpha$. Hansson and Olsson [Hansson and Olsson, 1995] proved that this contraction corresponds exactly to a contraction function that satisfies *failure* and all the AGM postulates (except recovery) (If $\vdash \alpha$, then $\mathbf{K}-\alpha = \mathbf{K}$).

The main problem of the Levi contraction is that the rule of 'minimality' is too weak, as we see in the following example:

$$\mathbf{K}-\alpha = \begin{cases} \mathbf{K} & \text{if } \alpha \notin \mathbf{K} \text{ or } \vdash \alpha \\ Cn(\emptyset) & \text{otherwise} \end{cases}$$

The above function seems to be extreme, since for all non-limiting cases of contraction it returns only the minimal theory. However, it is a possible Levi contraction.

Second Conclusion: In both AGM contraction and Levi contraction, the notion of 'minimality' seems to be deposited in the selection among the remainder/saturatable sets and not in the proper sets. In this way, the plausibility of recovery (and consequently its acceptance) is deposited in select to use remainder or saturatable sets. As we see, both constructions appear to be equally (im)plausible.

5 RECOVERY IN EPISTEMIC ENTRENCHMENT

In Section 2 we presented the epistemic entrenchment postulates and its relation to the AGM axiomatic, via $(C\ \leq)$ and $(-_{\mathrm{G}})$. The crucial clause of $(-_{\mathrm{G}})$ is $\alpha <_{\mathbf{K}} (\alpha \vee \beta)$. It does not seem possible to intuitively justify this relation unless one accepts the recovery postulate.[4] In fact Gärdenfors admitted 'The comparison is somewhat counterintuitive' [Gärdenfors, 1992]. When we relate the AGM axioms with epistemic entrenchment, recovery is not needed to prove the entrenchment postulates, but only to prove the rule $(-_{G})$. Consequently, the role of recovery in epistemic entrenchment is deposited in the definition of the rule of contraction. Rott [1991] proposed an alternative definition, later called *Severe Contraction* [Rott and Pagnucco, 1999]:

$(-_{\mathrm{R}})$ $\quad \beta \in \mathbf{K}-\alpha$ if and only if $\beta \in \mathbf{K}$ and, either $\vdash \alpha$ or $\alpha <_{\mathbf{K}} \beta$.

Rott proved that severe contraction satisfies all the AGM postulates except recovery [Rott, 1991]. This construction was later independently axiomatised in

[4] 'Perhaps the best way to motivate this condition $[(-_{G})]$ ... *(Note that this argument does not stand completely on its own feet, since it presumes* $(C\ \leq)$ *and the validity of several of the basic postulates for contraction including most conspicuously* $(K-5)$ [recovery])' [Gärdenfors and Makinson, 1988, pp. 89-90]

[Pagnucco, 1996], [Fermé and Rodríguez, 1998] and [Rott and Pagnucco, 1999]. Rott [Rott, 1991] proved that for all α, $\mathbf{K} -_{\mathrm{R}} \alpha \subseteq \mathbf{K} -_{\mathrm{G}} \alpha$.

The rule of selection of the Rott contraction appears, at first, more plausible than the Gärdenfors proposal. However, Hansson [1999] proved that Severe contraction satisfies the implausible postulate of expulsiveness. If $\nvdash \alpha$ and $\nvdash \beta$, then either $\alpha \notin \mathbf{K}{-}\beta$ or $\beta \notin \mathbf{K}{-}\alpha$.

Lindström and Rabinowicz have proposed [Lindström and Rabinowicz, 1991, p. 115]:

> *'One would like to say that the truth lies somewhere in between the two extremes: the original proposal* [in this case equivalently with the severe contraction]*and Grove's definition* [in this case equivalently with Gärdenfors' entrenchment-based contraction]*seem to give us the* lower *and* upper *limit for contraction.'*

This condition was called *Lindström and Rabinowicz's interpolation thesis* [Rott, 1995]. According to this thesis, a *reasonable* entrenchment-based contraction operation should lie between Rott's and Gärdenfors' operators; and consequently, should not, in general, satisfy recovery.

Third Conclusion: The rule of $(-_G)$ is closely related to the recovery postulate. This rule seems to be unexplainable without its relation to recovery. If we suppress this constraint, the intuitions used to define $(-_G)$ are the some as those used by Rott to define $(-_{\mathrm{R}})$: 'When I contract by α, I discarded all the sentences that are less entrenched than α'. But this principle also provokes undesirable consequences. There are two ways of defining reasonable contraction functions in this approach: By finding new possible rules of contraction, preferably satisfying the Lindström and Rabinowicz's interpolation thesis, or by preserving the rule proposed by Rott, but changing the entrenchment postulates [Lindström and Rabinowicz, 1991; Rott, 1992; Rott, 1996]. In all cases, the result will be a contraction without recovery.

6 RECOVERY IN SAFE/KERNEL CONTRACTION

On the one hand, we saw that recovery in the epistemic entrenchment approach is rather implausible. On the other hand, recovery appears as a logical consequence in safe/kernel contraction.

As we have seen in Section 2, safe/kernel contraction are based on the identification of the minimal subsets of $\mathbf{K}$ that imply α and on the elimination in the contraction of at least one sentence from each such subset. We have first noted that recovery can be expressed as:

If $\beta \in \mathbf{K}$, then $\alpha \rightarrow \beta \in \mathbf{K}{-}\alpha$

It is trivial to show that sentences of the form $\alpha \rightarrow \beta$ are never used in a minimal set of sentences that imply α; and consequently recovery is guaranteed in safe/kernel contraction, and therefore it appears impossible to define any kind of kernel contraction without it.

Fourth Conclusion: This conclusion is extremely simple. To accept contraction functions based on the safe/kernel approach is to accept recovery.

7 RECOVERY IN GROVE'S SPHERE-SYSTEM

In the possible worlds' approach or Grove's sphere-system [Grove, 1988], we will make a difference between the model corresponding to partial meet contraction and that corresponding to transitively relational partial meet contraction. If we translate recovery to the possible worlds' context, it means that only $\neg\alpha$-worlds will be added in the contraction by α. In this context recovery appears as intuitive. What is the reason to add α-worlds (that verify and enforce the belief in α) in the process of discarding α? It is not an easy question to answer for critics of recovery.

In the second case, the situation is quite different. We can see that the contraction function extends the actual set $||\mathbf{K}||$ of possible worlds to reach the $\neg\alpha$-worlds. Why not extend it to encompass all the possible worlds that are at least as close as the $\neg\alpha$-worlds, i.e., all the smallest spheres that contain $\neg\alpha$-worlds? If there exists a reason to reach the $\neg\alpha$-worlds, then there are reasons to extend $||\mathbf{K}||$ to the nearest α worlds. In this analysis, recovery appears as implausible. The proposed contraction corresponds exactly to severe contraction [Rott and Pagnucco, 1999] as introduced in Section 5.

Fifth Conclusion: Again, the conclusion is simple. In the possible worlds' approach, recovery is a plausible property. However, in a sphere-system it does not seem to exist an important reason to be inclined by functions with or without recovery.

8 GENERAL CONCLUSION

We have exhibited the faces of recovery in five presentations of the AGM theory and found arguments to accept or reject recovery in all of them. Probably the main result of this paper is to have shown that recovery has different status in five approaches that, curiously, are equivalent.

9 ACKNOWLEDGEMENTS

The author would like to thank specially Sven Ove Hansson for corrections and remarks on a draft. The author is also grateful to Carlos Areces, Verónica Becher,

Isaac Levi, Ricardo Rodríguez, Tor Sandqvist and the anonymous referees for their stimulating suggestions on an earlier version of the article. The text has also benefited from discussions at Krister Segerberg's seminar in Uppsala.

University of Buenos Aires, Argentina.

REFERENCES

[Alchourrón and Makinson, 1981] C. Alchourrón and D. Makinson. Hierarchies of regulations and their logic. In *New Studies in Deontic Logic: Norms, Actions, and the Foundations of Ethics*, R. Hilpinen, ed. pp. 125–148, 1981.

[Alchourrón and Makinson, 1982] C. Alchourrón and D. Makinson. On the logic of theory change: Contraction functions and their associated revision functions. *Theoria*, *48*, 14–37, 1982.

[Alchourrón and Makinson, 1985] C. Alchourrón and D. Makinson. On the logic of theory change: Safe contraction. *Studia Logica*, **44**, 405–422, 1985.

[Alchourrón and Makinson, 1986] C. Alchourrón and D. Makinson. Maps between some differents kinds of contraction functions: The finite case. *Studia Logica*, **45**, 187–198, 1986.

[Alchourrón *et al.*, 1985] C. Alchourrón, P. Gärdenfors and D. Makinson. On the logic of theory change: Partial meet contraction and revision functions. *Journal of Symbolic Logic*, **50**, 510–530, 1985.

[Fermé and Rodríguez, 1997] E. Fermé and R. Rodríguez. Semi-contraction: Axioms and construction. 1997. To appear *Notre Dame Journal of Formal Logic*.

[Fermé and Rodríguez, 1998] E. Fermé and R. Rodríguez. A brief note about the Rott contraction. *Logic Journal of the IGPL*, **6**, 835–842, 1998.

[Fermé, 1998] E. Fermé. On the logic of theory change: Contraction without recovery. *Journal of Logic, Language and Information*, **7**, 127–137, 1998.

[Fermé, 1999] E. Fermé. *Revising the AGM postulates*. PhD thesis, University of Buenos Aires, April 1999.

[Fuhrmann, 1991] A. Fuhrmann. Theory contraction through base contraction. *Journal of Philosophical Logic*, **20**, 175–203, 1991.

[Gärdenfors and Makinson, 1988] P. Gärdenfors and D. Makinson. Revisions of knowledge systems using epistemic entrenchment. In *Proceedings of the Second Conference on Theoretical Aspects of Reasoning About Knowledge*, M. Y. Vardi, ed. pp. 83–95, Morgan Kaufmann, Los Altos, 1988.

[Gärdenfors, 1988] P. Gärdenfors. *Knowledge in Flux: Modeling the Dynamics of Epistemic States*. The MIT Press, Cambridge, 1988.

[Gärdenfors, 1992] P. Gärdenfors. Belief revision: An introduction. In *Belief Revision*, P. Gärdenfors, ed. pp. 1–28. Vol. 29 of Cambridge Tracts in Theoretical Computer Science, Cambridge University Press, 1992.

[Grove, 1988] A. Grove. Two modellings for theory change. *Journal of Philosophical Logic*, **17**, 157–170, 1988.

[Hansson and Olsson, 1995] S. O. Hansson and E. Olsson. Levi contraction and AGM contraction: A comparision. *Notre Dame Journal of Formal Logic*, **36**, 103–119, 1995.

[Hansson, 1991] S. O. Hansson. Belief contraction without recovery. *Studia Logica*, **50**, 251–260, 1991.

[Hansson, 1993] S. O. Hansson. Changes of disjunctively closed bases. *Journal of Logic, Language and Information*, **2**, 255–284, 1993.

[Hansson, 1994] S. O. Hansson. Kernel contraction. *Journal of Symbolic Logic*, **59**, 845–859, 1994.

[Hansson, 1998] S. O. Hansson. Recovery and epistemic residue. *Journal of Logic, Language and Information*, 1998. (In press).

[Hansson, 1999] S. O. Hansson. *A Textbook of Belief Dynamics*. Kluwer Academic Publishers, Dordrecht, 1999.

[Levi, 1991] I. Levi. *The fixation of belief and its undoing: changing beliefs through inquiry*. Cambridge University Press, Cambridge, 1991.

[Levi, 1996] I. Levi. *For the Sake of Argument*. Cambridge University Press, Cambridge, 1996.

[Levi, 1997] I. Levi. Contraction and informational value. (manuscript), 1997.

[Lindström and Rabinowicz, 1991] S. Lindström and W. Rabinowicz. Epistemic entrenchment with incomparabilities and relational belief revision. In *The Logic of Theory Change*, A. Fuhrmann and M. Morreau, eds. pp. 93–126, Springer-Verlag, Berlin, 1991.

[Makinson, 1985] D. Makinson. How to give it up: a survey of some recent work on formal aspects of the logic of theory change. *Synthese*, **62**, 347–363, 1985.

[Makinson, 1987] D. Makinson. On the status of the postulate of recovery in the logic of theory change. *Journal of Philosophical Logic*, **16**, 383–394, 1987.

[Makinson, 1997] D. Makinson. On the force of some apparent counterexamples to recovery. In *Normative Systems in Legal and Moral Theory: Festschrift for Carlos Alchourrón and Eugenio Bulygin*, E. Garzón Valdéz *et al.*, eds. pp. 475–481, Dunker and Humblot, Berlin, 1997.

[Nayak, 1994] A. Nayak. Foundational belief change. *Journal of Philosophical Logic*, **23**, 495–533, 1994.

[Niederée, 1991] R. Niederée. Multiple contraction: A further case against Gärdenfors' principle of recovery. In *The Logic of Theory Change*, A. Fuhrmann and M. Morreau, eds.pp. 322–334, Springer-Verlag, Berlin, 1991.

[Pagnucco, 1996] M. Pagnucco. *The Role of Abductive Reasoning Within the Process of Belief Revision*. PhD thesis, Department of Computer Science, University of Sydney, February 1996.

[Rott, 1996] H. Rott. Making up one's mind: Foundations, coherence, nonmonotonicity. Technical report. Habilitationsschrift, Philosophische Fakultät, Universität Konstanz, October 1996. Also to be published by Oxford University Press, 1998.

[Rott and Pagnucco, 1999] H. Rott and M. Pagnucco. Severe withdrawal (and recovery). *Journal of Philosophical Logic*, **28**, 501–547, 1999.

[Rott, 1991] H. Rott. Two methods of constructing contractions and revisions of knowledge systems. *Journal of Philosophical Logic*, **20**, 149–173, 1991.

[Rott, 1992] H. Rott. Preferential belief change using generalized epistemic entrenchment. *Journal of Logic, Language and Information*, **1**, 45–78, 1992.

[Rott, 1995] H. Rott. 'Just because'. Taking belief bases very seriously. In *Logic for a change*, S. O. Hansson and W. Rabinowicz, eds. pp. 106–124. Vol. 9 of Uppsala Prints and Preprints in Philosophy, Dep. of Philosophy, Uppsala University, 1995.

CARLOS ARECES & VERÓNICA BECHER

ITERABLE AGM FUNCTIONS

1 INTRODUCTION

The issue of iterated theory change is indeed interesting. Legal codes are under constant modification, new discoveries shape scientific theories, and robots ought to update their representation of the world each time a sensor gains new data. A pertinent criticism to the AGM formalism of theory change [Alchourrón *et al.*, 1985] is its lack of definition with respect to iterated change. Let's start by introducing the basic elements in the AGM framework

Informally, let K be a collection of data (which we call a theory), and α a piece of information, then the AGM model characterizes three different kinds of theory change: expansion $(K + \alpha)$ when information is *simply added* to the theory, revision $(K * \alpha)$ when information is *consistently added* to the theory, and contraction $(K - \alpha)$ when information is *eliminated* from the theory. The iteration of each of these operations separately is significant, and even more so the consideration of sequences of different kinds of change. Although the AGM formalism does not forbid the iteration of change functions, it omits any specification of how it should be performed or what the properties of successive change are.

The aim of the present work is to define the simplest scheme of iteration for AGM: *iterable functions*, binary functions whose behaviour is specified for any theory K and formula α. The basic idea of this article dates back to Alchourrón and Makinson's work on safe contractions [Alchourrón and Makinson, 1985]. In that article they briefly discuss properties of the contraction function with respect to the intersection and union of theories, and they present some properties of "multiple contractions." Following this idea we elaborate upon the definition of an iterable function for each of the five AGM presentations: postulates [Alchourrón *et al.*, 1985], systems of spheres [Grove, 1988], meet functions [Alchourrón and Makinson, 1982], epistemic entrenchments [Gärdenfors and Makinson, 1988] and safe hierarchies [Alchourrón and Makinson, 1985].

In this work we assume knowledge of the AGM model as well as basic knowledge of classical logic. About notation, we fix a propositional language $\mathcal{L}$ and a consequence operation Cn that includes the classical one, is compact and satisfies disjunction in the antecedent. We use Greek letters α, β, γ for sentences of $\mathcal{L}$, capital Roman letters K, K', H for theories of $\mathcal{L}$ (subsets of $\mathcal{L}$ closed under Cn), and denote with $\mathbb{K}$ the class of all theories of $\mathcal{L}$. For the purposes of this work we consider the terms possible world, maximal consistent subset of $\mathcal{L}$ and valuation on $\mathcal{L}$ interchangeable. The letters U, V, W range over sets of possible worlds. M is the set of all possible worlds. $[\alpha]$ denotes the set of all possible worlds containing

M.-A. Williams and H. Rott (eds.), Frontiers in Belief Revision, 261–277.

α. If K is a theory, $[K]$ denotes the set of possible worlds containing K. Given U a set of possible worlds, $\mathrm{Th}(U)$ returns the associated theory.

2 AGM AND THE NOTION OF ITERATION

The AGM model has as points of departure a theory to be modified, a formula to be considered the new information and change functions. The framework seems then to be naturally that of binary functions $\bullet$ which when applied to a theory K and a formula α return a new theory K'. In infix notation, $K \bullet \alpha = K'$. However, when we study the AGM model, we immediately realize that change functions are *relative to the original theory*. This is an important issue: although change functions are presented as binary operators they are characterized only for a given fixed theory K. I.e., the first argument (the theory to be modified) has been fixed obtaining in such a way a family of functions $\bullet^K$. The binary approach has been abandoned and AGM only aims to study one of the indexed unary functions without trying to correlate it with the rest of the family.

Turning to iterated change now, once that we have understood that AGM change functions are really indexical (relative to the theory to be changed), an obvious first attempt to deal with iteration presents itself. If we possess *beforehand* the complete set of change functions, one for each possible theory, we can freely perform successive changes. Consider any pair of formulas α, β and a particular theory K. In order to calculate the successive changes of K, first by α and then by β, we need the change function $\bullet_1$ for K, and also the change function $\bullet_2$ relative to $(K \bullet_1 \alpha)$. The result of the successive change is the theory $(K \bullet_1 \alpha) \bullet_2 \beta$. But beware, if there are no properties linking the different change functions the result obtained can be unexpected and the corresponding behavior erratic. The whole point is then to investigate ways to coordinate these different change functions.

These facts have already been recognized and discussed in the theory change community and many proposals have in common the following characteristic: the AGM model is expanded in such a way that change functions return not only the modified theory but also a modified version of the change function (or equivalently, return enough information to build a new change function). Usually, a method or algorithm to construct the new change function based on the original theory, the input formula and the *previous change function* is specified. This can be done in a qualitative way as in [Boutilier, 1996; Hansson, To come; Nayak, 1994; Lehmann, 1995], or by enriching the model with numbers [Darwiche and Pearl, 1997; Spohn, 1987; Williams, 1995]. Notice that in these approaches we are not really going back to a binary function $\bullet$ and returning the theory K to its original role of argument. The "construction" method is more flexible than considering a binary function. Given a theory K and a formula α, change functions associated to $K \bullet \alpha$ are not uniquely determined and depend really on a third argument: the change function for K. These approaches are very rich —they can circumvent the problem of functional behaviour of the change function with respect to the theory under change, discussed for example in [Lehmann, 1995]. But they are usually complex.

We will consider in this paper the case of binary change functions. More specifically, AGM binary (non indexical) functions which are total in their two arguments. Any such function can trivially be iterated, $(K \bullet \alpha) \bullet \beta$ is well defined. We will call these functions *iterable AGM functions*. Notice that iterable functions can be considered a particular case of the construction method described above: after applying it to a theory, the same function is "returned" and can be applied again to the resulting theory. Some advantages of this approach are evident: it is mathematically elegant, simple and remains close to the AGM model (each time the theory argument is fixed a standard AGM indexical function is obtained). But, while formally attractive, an iterable function makes a strong simplifying assumption since it lacks historic memory; each theory is modified in a predetermined way independently of how we have obtained such a theory. An iterable function $\bullet$ is deterministic with respect to the theory to be modified. I.e., it satisfies:

$$\text{If } K = (\ldots(H \bullet \alpha_1)\ldots \bullet \alpha_n) \text{ then } K \bullet \alpha = (\ldots(H \bullet \alpha_1)\ldots \bullet \alpha_n) \bullet \alpha,$$

which is posed as undesirable in [Lehmann, 1995] (where it is referred to as a non-postulate.) But if K is really considered an *argument* of the function $\bullet$, this is to be expected. If f is a function, it is required that $f(a) = f(b)$ whenever $a = b$.

In spite of the modesty of functional change operators they vary in the sophistication of their fixed structures and associated behavior. A quite elaborate one, outside the AGM framework, is Katsuno and Mendelzon's account of *update* [Katsuno and Mendelzon, 1991], which is based on a fixed set of orders of possible worlds (one order relative to each possible world). The update function is obtained as a fixed combination of such multiple orders. With the same spirit of update, Becher's lazy update [Becher, 1995; Becher, 1998] formalizes an iterable version of the AGM model defined in terms of a fixed set of wellfounded orders over possible worlds.

In the simplest case we have binary change functions that depend on no order at all, as the original AGM expansion and the full meet contraction function [Alchourrón and Makinson, 1982]. The AGM representation theorem for the function $+$ states that $K + \alpha = \mathrm{Cn}(K \cup \{\alpha\})$. Expansion inherits its capacity of iteration from the consequence relation, which is applicable to any set of formulas. For any theory K and formulas α, β, $(K + \alpha) + \beta = \mathrm{Cn}(\mathrm{Cn}(K \cup \{\alpha\}) \cup \{\beta\}) = \mathrm{Cn}(K \cup \{\alpha\} \cup \{\beta\})$. As indicated by its signature, expansion is a total binary function $+ : \mathbb{K} \times \mathcal{L} \to \mathbb{K}$. While, as it stands in the original partial meet construction presented in [Alchourrón *et al.*, 1985], contraction is a unary function relative to a theory K, $-^{K} : \mathcal{L} \to \mathbb{K}$, based on a selection function s^{K} depending on K.

$$\text{Partial Meet: } -^{K}(\alpha) = \begin{cases} \bigcap s^{K}(K \perp \alpha) & \text{if } K \perp \alpha \neq \emptyset \\ K & \text{otherwise} \end{cases}$$

where the set $K \perp \alpha$ contains the maximal subsets of K that do not imply α and the function $s^K : \mathcal{L} \to \mathcal{P}(\mathcal{P}(K)) \setminus \{\emptyset\}$ selects a nonempty subset of $K \perp \alpha$.

The limiting case in which the function s^K returns the whole set $K \perp \alpha$ originates the full meet contraction function. The selection function s^K relative to K disappears, yielding a contraction that solely depends on the explicit argument K and α, i.e. if $-$ is a full meet, again we have a binary total function $- : I\!K \times \mathcal{L} \to I\!K$. Moreover, for full meet contraction functions $K - \alpha = K \cap \mathrm{Cn}(\neg\alpha)$. As expansion functions, they depend on no underlying structure, relative order or selection function, and are applicable to any theory.

But there exists important differences between expansion and full meet contraction. While expansion is appropriately modeled via the consequence relation, full meet contraction is ultimately unsatisfactory. The following two properties reveal its over-simplicity.

Elimination: $(K - \alpha) - \beta = K - (\alpha \wedge \beta)$, from which
Commutativity: $(K - \alpha) - \beta = (K - \beta) - \alpha$ follows.

Alchourrón, Gärdenfors and Makinson argue that full meet contraction functions suffer from too much loss of information and take them as a demarcation of the limiting case. The aim of the next section is to provide iterable AGM functions which are more interesting than full meet functions.

3 ITERABLE AGM FUNCTIONS

In [Alchourrón and Makinson, 1985] the authors define a new kind of contraction function called safe contraction, based on a hierarchical order of the elements of a theory K according to what they call their "degree of safety". They show that every safe contraction over a theory K is a partial meet contraction function over K. They also prove the converse result for finite theories (in the sense that the consequence relation Cn partitions the elements of K into a finite number of equivalence classes). The general case for infinite theories was solved by Rott in [1992a].

Interestingly, Alchourrón and Makinson study in their paper some properties of safe contraction with respect to the intersection or union of theories and also properties of "multiple contractions". They say ([Alchourrón and Makinson, 1985], p. 419):

"[...] we shall turn to questions that arise when A (the set of propositions) is allowed to vary. [...] But in the case of safe contraction the way of dealing with variations of A is quite straightforward. As we are working with a relation $<$ over A the natural relation to consider over a subset A' of A is simply the restriction $< \cap\, (A' \times A')$ of $<$ to A'."

They obtain a general result relating $A' - \alpha$ to $A - \alpha$, when $A' \subseteq A$. As a special case they apply it to $(A - \beta) - \gamma$, since $A - \beta \subseteq A$ always holds. Although not explicit in their article a particular case of Alchourrón and Makinson's proposal is to start with a hierarchical order over all the formulas of the language. The simple restriction of the hierarchy over $\mathcal{L}$ to the elements of any theory K provides for a hierarchy over such a theory, hence, an appropriate relation for the definition of a safe contraction function for K. This setting yields an iterable contraction function based on a unique fixed order of all the formulas, the safe hierarchy.

Reusing the same fixed order makes sense, for example, when involved in tentative reasoning: a fixed set of facts and laws which are known beforehand constitute the background knowledge from which a sequence of consistent, but tentative, inference steps are performed to reach a conclusion[1]. We will come back to this idea in Section 3.5.

The following subsections are devoted to the definition of iterable AGM functions in each of the classical presentations, following the ideas we just explained for safe contractions. Notice that since contraction and revision are inter-definable in the AGM framework via the Levi and Harper identities, the task of providing iterable change functions can be reduced to defining just one of them (see Section 4 for further details).

3.1 Extended Safe Contraction Functions

A relation $<_{sf}$ over a set A is a *hierarchy* if it is acyclic: for any set of elements $\alpha_1, \ldots, \alpha_n \in A, n \geq 1$, it is not the case that $\alpha_1 <_{sf} \alpha_2 <_{sf} \ldots \alpha_n <_{sf} \alpha_1$. A relation $<_{sf}$ over A *continues up* Cn if for every $\alpha_1, \alpha_2, \alpha_3 \in A$, if $\alpha_1 <_{sf} \alpha_2$ and $\alpha_3 \in \mathrm{Cn}(\alpha_2)$ then $\alpha_1 <_{sf} \alpha_3$. A relation $<_{sf}$ over A is *virtually connected* if for every $\alpha_1, \alpha_2, \alpha_3 \in A$ if $\alpha_1 <_{sf} \alpha_2$ then either $\alpha_1 <_{sf} \alpha_3$ or $\alpha_3 <_{sf} \alpha_2$. Let $<_{sf}$ be a virtually connected hierarchy over a theory K that continues up Cn, and let α be a sentence. The safe contraction function $-^K$ is defined as

$$-^K(\alpha) = K \cap \mathrm{Cn}(\{\beta \mid \forall K' \subseteq K, \text{ s.t. } \alpha \in \mathrm{Cn}(K') \text{ and } K' \text{ is } \subseteq\text{-minimal} \\ \text{with this property, } \beta \notin K' \text{ or there is } \gamma \in K' \text{ s.t. } \gamma <_{sf} \beta\}).$$

The elements of $-^K(\alpha)$ are called the safe elements of K with respect to α since they can not be "blamed" for implying α. An element is safe for α if it does not belong to any of the $\subseteq$-minimal subsets of K that imply α, or else it is not $<_{sf}$-minimal in the hierarchy in such subsets.

Following Alchourrón and Makinson's idea of restricting the hierarchical order, we can define the iterable safe contraction function $-_{sf}$ based on a hierarchy over all the sentences of $\mathcal{L}$.

DEFINITION 1 (Derived Order). Let $<_{sf}$ be a hierarchy over the language $\mathcal{L}$. Then for any theory K the derived hierarchy $<_{sf}^K$ is defined as $<_{sf}^K = <_{sf}|K$ (where $R|X$ is the restriction of R to the elements in X).

[1]This interpretation was pointed out to us by Isaac Levi.

PROPOSITION 2. *Let* $<_{sf}$ *be a virtually connected hierarchy that continues up* Cn *in* $\mathcal{L}$, *then for any theory* K *the relation* $<^K_{sf}$ *is a virtually connected hierarchy and continues up* Cn *in* K.

Proof. Trivial. The properties of being acyclic, virtually connected and continuing up Cn are preserved under taking restrictions to theories. ■

Once this result is obtained, to define an iterable safe contraction is straightforward.

DEFINITION 3 (Iterable Safe Contraction). Let $<_{sf}$ be a virtually connected hierarchy that continues up Cn in $\mathcal{L}$. The iterable AGM contraction $-_{sf} : \mathbb{K} \times \mathcal{L} \to \mathbb{K}$ is defined as

$$K -_{sf} \alpha = K \cap \mathrm{Cn}(\{\beta \mid \forall K' \subseteq K, \text{ s.t. } \alpha \in \mathrm{Cn}(K') \text{ and } K' \text{ is } \subseteq\text{-minimal with this property, } \beta \notin K' \text{ or there is } \gamma \in K' \text{ s.t. } \gamma <^K_{sf} \beta\}),$$

where $<^K_{sf}$ is the derived safe hierarchy for K.

That $-_{sf}$ satisfies the AGM postulates $K-1$ to $K-8$ follows from Alchourrón and Makinson's original results stating that every safe contraction function generated by a virtually connected hierarchy $<$ that continues up Cn over a theory K is a transitively relational partial meet contraction function.

As a side remark, notice that definitions 1 and 3 can be merged in a unique definition and $-_{sf}$ defined then directly over $<_{sf}$ instead of over $<^K_{sf}$. This is just a matter of notation, as in both cases $-_{sf}$ is really a binary function as required. This remark applies as well to the definitions of iterable functions in the remaining presentations.

In the definitions above we started from a hierarchy $<_{sf}$ for $\mathcal{L}$ and defined its restriction $<^K_{sf}$. A valid question is whether the converse can also be achieved. Given a hierarchy for K can a hierarchy for $\mathcal{L}$ be defined such that the iterable function agrees with $-^K$ when applied to K?

PROPOSITION 4. *Let* $-^K$ *be an AGM safe contraction function for a given theory* K. *Then* $-^K$ *can be extended to an iterable AGM safe contraction* $-_{sf}$, *such that for every* α, $K -_{sf} \alpha = -^K(\alpha)$.

Proof. Given $<^K_{sf}$ the order associated to $-^K$, define $<_{sf}$ as follows: $\alpha <_{sf} \beta$ iff either $(\alpha \notin K)$ or $(\alpha, \beta \in K$ and $\alpha <_{sf} \beta)$. Intuitively, when extending the order to the whole language, elements in K are promoted in their safeness while elements outside K are minimally safe. From the definition $<^K_{sf} = <_{sf}|K$, and it is not hard to check that $<_{sf}$ is a virtually connected hierarchy that continues up over Cn in $\mathcal{L}$. ■

In [Hansson, 1994] the safe contraction approach is generalized in the kernel contraction approach. Instead of implementing a relational way of defining "safe elements", selection functions (called incision functions) are introduced. Our results for safe contraction can be extended to kernel contraction easily.

3.2 Extended Partial Meet Contraction Functions

The principle of information economy requires that $K - \alpha$ contains as much as possible from K without entailing α. For every theory K and sentence α, the set $K \perp \alpha$ of maximal subsets of K that fail to imply α are the definitional basis for partial meet contraction functions.

$$K \perp \alpha = \{K' \subseteq K \mid \alpha \notin \mathrm{Cn}(K') \text{ and } K' \text{ is } \subseteq\text{-maximal with this property}\}.$$

A selection function s is a function which returns a nonempty subset of a given nonempty set. Let K be a theory, we note as $s^K : \mathcal{L} \to \mathcal{P}(\mathcal{P}(K)) \setminus \{\emptyset\}$, a selection function for $K \perp \alpha$, for $\alpha \in \mathcal{L}$. We furthermore require that $s^K(\alpha) = \{K\}$ whenever $K \perp \alpha = \emptyset$. The original AGM partial meet contraction function $-^K$ is then defined, for a theory K, as

$$-^K(\alpha) = \bigcap s^K(\alpha), \text{ where } s^K \text{ is a selection function for } K.$$

Under this definition the contraction function $-^K$ satisfies the basic AGM postulates $K-1$ to $K-6$. To satisfy the extended set of postulates, $K-1$ to $K-8$, s^K must be *transitively relational*, i.e. for each $\alpha \in \mathcal{L}$ the selection function returns the smallest elements according to some transitive relation defined over $K \perp \alpha$.

In order to define an iterable version of $-^K$ richer than the full meet contraction, we need to obtain somehow the selections functions s^K, one for each eventual K. Of course, we might assume to have all the selection functions beforehand. But following the ideas presented in the extension of safe contraction functions, we would rather synthesize the different s^K out of a unique structure.

The largest possible theory is $\mathcal{L}$, the whole language. Then $s^{\mathcal{L}}$ provides for each formula α a selection function over all the maximal consistent sets of $\mathcal{L}$ that do not imply α. It is possible to extract from $s^{\mathcal{L}}$ the corresponding s^K for each theory K. This is a consequence of the following two observations: (a) If $\alpha \notin K$, then, trivially, the maximal consistent subset of K that fails to imply α is K itself. (b) If $\alpha \in K$, each maximal consistent subset of K that fails to imply α is included in a maximal consistent subset of $\mathcal{L}$ that fails to imply α (by a Lindenbaum style argument each element in $K \perp \alpha$ can be extended to an element of $\mathcal{L} \perp \alpha$). Therefore, we can derive a selection function $s^K(\alpha)$ by just restricting the result of $s^{\mathcal{L}}(\alpha)$ to its common part with K.

DEFINITION 5 (Derived Selection Functions). Let $s^{\mathcal{L}}$ be a selection function for $\mathcal{L}$. Then, for any theory K the selection function s^K is

$$s^K(\alpha) = \begin{cases} \{K\} & \text{if } \alpha \notin K \\ \{K' \in K \perp \alpha \mid K' = K \cap H' \text{ with } H' \in s^{\mathcal{L}}(\alpha)\} & \text{otherwise.} \end{cases}$$

It is immediate to see that each derived s^K is indeed a selection function. What is more interesting is to check whether each s^K is transitively relational whenever $s^{\mathcal{L}}$ is.

PROPOSITION 6. *If $s^{\mathcal{L}}$ is a transitively relational selection function, then for any theory K, s^{K} is a transitively relational selection function.*

Proof. The intuition is as follows, as $s^{\mathcal{L}}$ is transitively relational there is a transitive relation R defined over $\mathcal{L} \perp \alpha$ whose smallest elements are selected by $s^{\mathcal{L}}(\alpha)$. This relation R can be projected over each $K \perp \alpha$ to show that $s^{K}(\alpha)$ selects the smallest elements of a transitive relation. ■

Given that $s^{\mathcal{L}}$ is a transitively relational selection function we are able to define an iterable AGM contraction function $-_{pm}$ based on the partial meet construction.

DEFINITION 7 (Iterable Partial Meet Contraction). Let $s^{\mathcal{L}}$ be a transitively relational selection function over $\mathcal{L}$. The iterable AGM contraction $-_{pm} : \mathbb{K} \times \mathcal{L} \to \mathbb{K}$ is defined as $K -_{pm} \alpha = \bigcap s^{K}(\alpha)$, where s^{K} is the derived selection function for K.

By construction $-_{pm}$ is an AGM transitively relational partial meet contraction. It is iterable as it is applicable to any theory K. We now prove that every AGM partial meet contraction function can be extended to an iterable partial meet.

PROPOSITION 8. *Let $-^{K}$ be an AGM transitively relational partial meet contraction function for a given theory K. Then $-^{K}$ can be extended to an iterable AGM partial meet contraction $-_{pm}$, such that for every α, $K -_{pm} \alpha = -^{K}(\alpha)$.*

Proof. Given a selection function s^{K} we have to come up with a selection function $s^{\mathcal{L}}$. As we previously said, for each $H \in K \perp \alpha$ there is $H' \in \mathcal{L} \perp \alpha$ such that $H \subseteq H'$. Hence, we can define $s^{\mathcal{L}}(\alpha) = \{H' \in \mathcal{L} \perp \alpha \mid \exists H \in s^{K}(K \perp \alpha) \text{ and } H \subseteq H'\}$. Notice that there can be some $H' \in \mathcal{L} \perp \alpha$ such that there exists no subset H of K and $H \subseteq H'$, then H' is not selected.

Since s^{K} is transitively relational there is a relation R over $K \perp \alpha$ which can be lifted to $\mathcal{L} \perp \alpha$. If $R(H_1, H_2)$ then $R'(H_1', H_2')$ for $H_1', H_2' \in \mathcal{L} \perp \alpha$ such that $H_i \subseteq H_i'$. For every $H' \in \mathcal{L} \perp \alpha$ such that there exists no subset H of K and $H \subseteq H'$, we define $R'(H'', H')$ for every $H'' \in \mathcal{L} \perp \alpha$. Now $s^{\mathcal{L}}(\alpha)$ selects the smallest elements of R'. It follows from the definition that R' is transitive, hence $s^{\mathcal{L}}$ is transitively relational. ■

3.3 Extended Systems of Spheres

In this section we develop a definition of an iterable contraction function based on Systems of Spheres, which turns out to be equivalent to an early unpublished result of Makinson.[2]. We first turn to Grove's original framework [Grove, 1988].

A system of spheres S for a theory K is a set of sets of possible worlds that verifies the properties

S1. If $U, V \in S$ then $U \subseteq V$ or $V \subseteq U$. (Totally Ordered.)
S2. For every $U \in S$, $[K] \subseteq U$. (Minimum.)

[2]Personal communication.

S3. $M \in S$. (Maximum.)

S4. For every sentence α such that there is a sphere U in S with $[\alpha] \cap U \neq \emptyset$, there is a $\subseteq$-minimal sphere V in S such that $[\alpha] \cap V \neq \emptyset$. (Limit Assumption.)

For any sentence α, if $[\alpha]$ has a non-empty intersection with some sphere in S then by $S4$ there exists a minimal such sphere in S, say $c_s(\alpha)$. But, if $[\alpha]$ has an empty intersection with all spheres, then it must be the empty set (since $S3$ assures M is in S), in this case $c_s(\alpha)$ is just M. Given a system of spheres S and a formula α, $c_s(\alpha)$ is defined as:

$$c_s(\alpha) = \begin{cases} M & \text{if } [\alpha] = \emptyset \\ \text{the } \subseteq \text{-minimal sphere } S' \text{ in } S \text{ s.t. } S' \cap [\alpha] \neq \emptyset & \text{otherwise.} \end{cases}$$

Using the function c_s, the function $f_s : \mathcal{L} \to \mathcal{P}(M)$ is defined as $f_s(\alpha) = [\alpha] \cap c_s(\alpha)$. Given a sentence α, $f_s(\alpha)$ returns the closest elements (with respect to theory K) where α holds. Grove shows that the function defined as $-^{K}(\alpha) = \text{Th}([K] \cup f_s(\neg\alpha))$ is an AGM contraction function. And conversely, for any AGM contraction function relative to a theory K there is a system of spheres S centered in $[K]$ that gives rise to the same function.

We shall now extend Grove's construction to obtain an iterable function using the same strategy we used for partial meet. Again, the central idea is to consider the inconsistent theory. A system of spheres for $\mathcal{L}$ has the particular property that its innermost sphere is the empty set, since $[\mathcal{L}] = \emptyset$. Given a system of spheres S centered in $\emptyset$ we define for any theory K a derived system S^K centered in $[K]$ simply by "filling in" the innermost sphere of S with $[K]$.

DEFINITION 9 (Derived System of Spheres). Let S be a system of spheres for $\mathcal{L}$. Then for any theory K the derived system of spheres S^K is defined as $S^K = \{[K] \cup S_i \mid S_i \in S\}$.

PROPOSITION 10. *Let S be a system of spheres for $\mathcal{L}$. Then for any theory K, S^K is a system of spheres centered in K.*

Having defined the method to derive a system of spheres S^K, the functions c^K_S and f^K_S are as above. We can now define the iterable contraction function $-_{ss} : I\!K \times \mathcal{L} \to I\!K$, applicable to every theory K and every formula α.

DEFINITION 11 (Iterable Sphere Contraction). Let S be a system of spheres for $\mathcal{L}$. The iterable AGM contraction $-_{ss} : I\!K \times \mathcal{L} \to I\!K$ is defined as $K -_{ss} \alpha = \text{Th}([K] \cup f^K_S(\neg\alpha))$, where f^K_S is the derived function for K.

It is clear that $-_{ss}$ is iterable. By Grove's characterization result it follows that $-_{ss}$ is an AGM contraction function. We prove that every AGM contraction function can be extended to an iterable sphere contraction function.

PROPOSITION 12. *Let $-^K$ be an AGM contraction functions based on systems of spheres. Then $-^K$ can be extended to an iterable AGM contraction $-_{ss}$ based on systems of spheres, such that for every α, $K -_{ss} \alpha = -^K(\alpha)$.*

Proof. It is enough to prove that if S^K is a system of spheres for K, then it can be extended to a system of spheres for $\mathcal{L}$. Define S centered in $\emptyset$ as $S = S^K \cup \{\emptyset\}$. Clearly, S validates $S1$ to $S4$ for $\mathcal{L}$. ■

3.4 *Extended Epistemic Entrenchments*

An *epistemic entrenchment* for a theory K is a total relation among the formulas in the language reflecting their degree of relevance in K and their usefulness when performing inference. Gärdenfors and Makinson [1988] specify the following five conditions for an epistemic entrenchment relation $\leq_{ee}$ for a theory K:

EE1. If $\alpha \leq_{ee} \beta$ and $\beta \leq_{ee} \delta$ then $\alpha \leq_{ee} \delta$.
EE2. If $\beta \in \mathrm{Cn}(\alpha)$ then $\alpha \leq_{ee} \beta$.
EE3. $\alpha \leq_{ee} (\alpha \wedge \beta)$ or $\beta \leq_{ee} (\alpha \wedge \beta)$.
EE4. If theory K is consistent then $\alpha \notin K$ iff $\alpha \leq_{ee} \beta$ for every β.
EE5. If $\beta \leq_{ee} \alpha$ for every β then $\alpha \in \mathrm{Cn}(\emptyset)$.

The AGM contraction function $-^K$ based on an epistemic entrenchment relation $\leq_{ee}$ for K, is defined as follows. For every formula α in $\mathcal{L}$,

$$-^K(\alpha) = \{\beta \in K \mid \alpha \in \mathrm{Cn}(\emptyset) \text{ or } \alpha <_{ee} (\alpha \vee \beta)\},$$

where $<_{ee}$ is the strict relation obtained from $\leq_{ee}$.

For any given relation $\leq_{ee}$ for a consistent theory K, the formulas in K are ranked in $\leq_{ee}$, while all the formulas outside K have the $\leq_{ee}$-minimal epistemic value. That is, by $EE4$ for a consistent theory K, all formulas outside K are zeroed in $\leq_{ee}$. However, $EE4$ is vacuous for the contradictory theory $\mathcal{L}$. If we consider as a point of departure an epistemic entrenchment over the contradictory theory $\mathcal{L}$, there is an obvious way to derive an entrenchment order for any theory K: just depose the formulas not in K to a minimal rank.

DEFINITION 13 (Derived Epistemic Entrenchment). Let $\leq_{ee}$ be an epistemic entrenchment relation for $\mathcal{L}$. Then for any theory K the derived epistemic entrenchment relation $\leq^K_{ee}$ is defined as:

$$\alpha \leq^K_{ee} \beta \text{ iff either } (\alpha \notin K) \text{ or } (\alpha, \beta \in K \text{ and } \alpha \leq_{ee} \beta).$$

Again the first step is to establish that our definition is sound.

PROPOSITION 14. *Let $\leq_{ee}$ be an epistemic entrenchment relation for $\mathcal{L}$, then for any theory K, $\leq^K_{ee}$ is an epistemic entrenchment relation for K.*

DEFINITION 15 (Iterable Epistemic Entrenchment Contraction). Let $\leq_{ee}$ be an epistemic entrenchment relation for $\mathcal{L}$. The iterable AGM contraction $-_{ee} : \mathbb{K} \times \mathcal{L} \to \mathbb{K}$ is defined as $K -_{ee} \alpha = \{\beta \in K \mid \alpha \in \mathrm{Cn}(\emptyset) \text{ or } \alpha <^K_{ee} (\alpha \vee \beta)\}$, where $<^K_{ee}$ is the strict part of $\leq^K_{ee}$, for $\leq^K_{ee}$ the derived epistemic entrenchment relation for K.

It remains to show that every contraction function based on epistemic entrenchments can be extended to an iterable contraction function.

PROPOSITION 16. *Let* $-^K$ *be an AGM contraction function based on epistemic entrenchments for a given theory* K. *Then* $-^K$ *can be extended to an iterable AGM contraction* $-_{ee}$ *based on epistemic entrenchments such that for every* α, $K -_{ee} \alpha = -^K(\alpha)$.

Proof. The key point is to prove that an epistemic entrenchment relation for $K \leq^K_{ee}$ can be extended to a relation for $\mathcal{L}$.

If $K = \mathcal{L}$ then we are done. Suppose $K \neq \mathcal{L}$. We claim that $\leq^K_{ee}$ is also an epistemic entrenchment relation for $\mathcal{L}$. Conditions $EE1$, $EE2$, $EE3$ and $EE5$ do not refer to the specific theory so they hold also trivially for $\mathcal{L}$, while condition $EE4$ does not apply as $\mathcal{L}$ is inconsistent. ■

3.5 Extended Postulates

One of the hallmarks of the AGM formalism is that a contraction operation always returns a consistent theory. The largest possible theory is the inconsistent theory $\mathcal{L}$, the whole language. The contraction function over the inconsistent theory can be regarded as a generic removal procedure leading to consistency. As every theory is a subset of the inconsistent theory this generic removal procedure can be applied to any theory. We propose the following postulate:

$$\mathbf{K-9}.\ \text{If } \alpha \in K, \text{ then } K - \alpha = (\mathcal{L} - \alpha) \cap K.$$

Postulate $K - 9$ is extremely simple and reveals the unsophisticated behavior of our iterable contraction function. Its dual iterable revision postulate is defined as:

$$\mathbf{K*9}.\ \text{If } \neg\alpha \in K, \text{ then } K * \alpha = (\mathcal{L} * \alpha)$$

In Section 4 we elaborate on the inter-definability of K*9 and K–9 via the Levi and Harper identities. It becomes obvious that a revision function $*$ satisfying $K * 1$-$K*9$ is in fact iterable: for any $\alpha, \beta \in \mathcal{L}$, $K * \alpha * \beta$ is well defined: If $\neg\beta \in K * \alpha$ then $K * \alpha * \beta = (\mathcal{L} * \beta)$; else $K * \alpha * \beta = (K * \alpha) + \beta$. An immediate observation is that $K*9$ forces independence between two arbitrary revision steps. Namely, the result of revising a theory is independent of the preceding steps that lead to it, only the actual theory being revised matters. This is what we have described as lack of historic memory in Section 2, or as reported in [Friedman and Halpern, 1996], the qualitative analogue of the Markov Assumption.

The revision postulate $K * 9$ is sound with the interpretation of revision as a kind of tentative reasoning. The revision function for $\mathcal{L}$ encodes a fixed and pre-established criteria, "the way things are" (facts) and "the way things work" (laws) in the actual world. A sequence of revisions is then performed in search of tentative explanations (of the facts) and conclusions (derived from them). When we detect an inconsistency between the hypothesis elaborated up to now and a new supposition we are trying to adjust to the reasoning, we lose confidence in the chain of hypothesis. We should then start it all over, and accommodate the latest piece of our tentative chain in accordance with our (fixed and pre-established) criteria, leaving behind our previous wrong conjectures.

We take $K-1$ to $K-9$ as defining iterable AGM contraction functions via postulates. We show in the next section that these functions coincide with the iterable AGM contraction functions defined above.

Lemma 7.4 in [Alchourrón and Makinson, 1985] can be considered as the first reference to the ideas put forward in postulate $K-9$. But the connection with iteration is first elucidated by Rott in [Rott, 1992b]. He mentions explicitly $K-9$ in connection with generalized entrenchment relations and considers it as a policy of iteration. He also proves that iterated theory change according to this method reduces to change of the inconsistent theory. Remarkably, [Freund and Lehmann, 1994] proposes precisely the same postulate $K*9$ and shows the correspondence between an AGM revision operation satisfying it and a rational consistency preserving consequence relation. Freund and Lehmann also show that such a revision function admits iteration. Although their postulate and ours turned out to be identical, the two works are indeed complementary. In the attempt to elucidate the meaning and effect of $K-9$ we were driven to recast it in the four other standard presentations of AGM (safe hierarchies, partial meet functions, systems of spheres and epistemic entrenchments) and in the next section we will prove that they are indeed equivalent. Freund and Lehmann chose instead to consider the connection existing between theory change and non-monotonic reasoning [Gärdenfors and Makinson, 1991] and study the effect of the new postulate on the (non-monotonic) inference relation. The main result in their paper is the proof that revisions satisfying $K*1$ to $K*9$ stand in one-to-one correspondence with rational, consistency-preserving non-monotonic inference relations.

3.6 Equivalences

In this section we will prove the equivalence of the five systems presented. We first prove that postulates $K-1$ to $K-9$ characterize the iterable AGM contractions based on systems of spheres.

THEOREM 17 (Postulates/Systems of Spheres). *Given an iterable AGM contraction $-$ satisfying $K-1$ to $K-9$, there exists a system of spheres S for $\mathcal{L}$ such that for every K and every α, $K-\alpha = \mathrm{Th}([K] \cup f_S^K(\neg\alpha))$. Conversely, every $-_{ss}$ based on a system of spheres S for $\mathcal{L}$ satisfies postulates $K-1$ to $K-9$.*

Proof. As $-_{ss}$ is a contraction based on systems of spheres it satisfies $K-1$ to $K-8$. It is trivial to check that it also satisfies $K-9$.

By Grove's original result, for any AGM function for $\mathcal{L}$ that satisfies $K-1$ to $K-8$ there is a system of spheres S for $\mathcal{L}$ such that $\mathcal{L}-\alpha = \mathrm{Th}(f_S(\neg\alpha))$. By definition $S^K = \{[K] \cup S_i \mid S_i \in S\}$. There are two cases. For any $\alpha \notin K$, clearly $f_S^K(\neg\alpha) = [K] \cap [\neg\alpha]$, then $\mathrm{Th}([K] \cup f_S^K(\neg\alpha)) = K$ and by postulate

$K-3$, $K = K - \alpha$, so we are done. For $\alpha \in K$, $f_s^K(\neg\alpha) = f_s^{\mathcal{L}}(\neg\alpha)$, then $\mathrm{Th}([K] \cup f_s^K(\neg\alpha)) = \mathrm{Th}([K] \cup f_s^{\mathcal{L}}(\neg\alpha)) = K \cap \mathrm{Th}(f_s^K(\neg\alpha)) = K \cap (\mathcal{L} - \alpha)$, and we are done. ■

We shall prove that $-_{ee}$ and the extended postulates are equivalent.

THEOREM 18 (Postulates/Epistemic Entrenchments). *Given an iterable AGM contraction $-$ that satisfies $K-1$ to $K-9$, there exists an epistemic entrenchment relation $\leq_{ee}$ for $\mathcal{L}$ such that for every K and every α, $K-\alpha = \{\beta \in K \mid \alpha \in \mathrm{Cn}(\emptyset)$ or $\alpha <_{ee}^K (\alpha \vee \beta)\}$. Conversely, every $-_{ee}$ satisfies $K-1$ to $K-9$.*

Proof. Again, by previous results, $-_{ee}$ satisfies $K-1$ to $K-8$ and it is easy to verify that it also satisfies $K-9$.

Let $\leq_{ee}$ be the epistemic entrenchment guaranteed to exist for any contraction function satisfying $K-1$ to $K-8$. We already proved that it is an epistemic entrenchment for $\mathcal{L}$.

If $\alpha \notin K$ then by $K-3$, $K - \alpha = K$. As $\leq_{ee}$ satisfies $EE1$ and $EE4$, $\alpha <_{ee}^K (\alpha \vee \beta)$ for all $\beta \in K$. Hence $K - \alpha = \{\beta \in K \mid \alpha \in \mathrm{Cn}(\emptyset)$ or $\alpha <_{ee}^K (\alpha \vee \beta)\}$.

Suppose $\alpha \in K$. As $\leq_{ee}^K$ is the restriction of $\leq_{ee}$, $K -_{ee} \alpha = \{\beta \in K \mid \alpha \in \mathrm{Cn}(\emptyset)$ or $\alpha <_{ee}^K (\alpha \vee \beta)\} = K \cap \{\beta \in \mathcal{L} \mid \alpha \in \mathrm{Cn}(\emptyset)$ or $\alpha <_{ee} (\alpha \vee \beta)\} = (\mathcal{L} - \alpha) \cap K = K - \alpha$, if $-$ satisfies $K-9$. ■

We have presented $-_{pm}$ and $-_{ss}$, and showed that they are both iterable AGM functions relative to some fixed order for the inconsistent theory $\mathcal{L}$. We now prove that $-_{pm}$ and $-_{ss}$ are in fact equivalent.

THEOREM 19 (Meet Functions/Systems of Spheres). *For each iterable partial meet contraction $-_{pm}$ there exists a system of spheres S for $\mathcal{L}$ such that for every theory K and every α, $K -_{pm} \alpha = \mathrm{Th}([K] \cup c_S^K(\neg\alpha))$. Conversely, for each iterable contraction $-_{ss}$ defined by a system of spheres there exists a selection functions $s^{\mathcal{L}}$ such that for every theory K and every α, $K -_{ss} \alpha = \bigcap s^K(\alpha)$.*

Proof. The theorem is a direct consequence of the "Grove connection" [Makinson, 1993] relating consistent complete theories in the language of K containing α and the elements in $\{A \cup \mathrm{Cn}(\alpha) | A \in K \perp \neg\alpha\}$ by a total injective mapping. In the particular case when we consider the inconsistent theory $\mathcal{L}$, this mapping can be recast as a bijection between the set of all consistent complete theories (worlds) and $\bigcup_\alpha \cup(\mathcal{L} \perp \alpha)$. Once this connection has been established, the order provided by a system of spheres centered in $\emptyset$ defines a transitively relational selection function $s^{\mathcal{L}}$ and vice versa. ■

Finally, by using results in [Rott, 1992a] we can establish the equivalence between iterated epistemic entrenchment contractions and iterated safe contractions functions, proving that the five approaches to iteration presented in the article are indeed five faces of the same phenomenon.

THEOREM 20 (Epistemic Entrenchments/Safe Hierarchies). *For each iterable epistemic entrenchment contraction* $-_{ee}$ *there exists a virtually connected hierarchy* $<_{sf}$ *that continues up* Cn *in* $\mathcal{L}$*, such that for every theory* K *and every* α, $K -_{ee}\alpha = K \cap \mathrm{Cn}(\{\beta \mid \forall K' \subseteq K,$ *s.t.* $\alpha \in \mathrm{Cn}(K')$ *and* K' *is a* $\subseteq$*-minimal with this property,* $\beta \notin K'$ *or there is* $\gamma \in K'$ *s.t.* $\gamma <^K_{sf} \beta\})$. *Conversely, for each safe iterable contraction* $-_{sf}$ *there exists an epistemic relation* $\leq_{ee}$ *for* $\mathcal{L}$*, such that for every theory* K *and every* α $K -_{sf} \alpha = \{\beta \in K \mid \alpha \in \mathrm{Cn}(\emptyset)$ *or* $\alpha <^K_{ee} (\alpha \vee \beta)\}$.

Proof. The first part is immediate. As it is proved in [Rott, 1992a], an epistemic entrenchment is also a safe hierarchy. Furthermore the relativization to K used during iteration is preserved. For the second part, let $<_{sf}$ be the hierarchy for $\mathcal{L}$ associated to $-_{sf}$. Now using the main result in [Rott, 1992a] we can obtain an epistemic entrenchment relation $\leq_{ee}$ such that the associated contraction function behaves as $-_{sf}$ for $\mathcal{L}$. Take $\leq_{ee}$ as the basis for our epistemic entrenchment iterable contraction function $-_{ee}$. If $\alpha \in \mathrm{Cn}(\emptyset)$ or $\alpha \notin K$, then as both $-_{sf}$ and $-_{ee}$ are AGM functions, $K -_{sf} \alpha = K = \{\beta \in K \mid \alpha \in \mathrm{Cn}(\emptyset)$ or $\alpha <^K_{ee} (\alpha \vee \beta)\}$. If $\alpha \notin \mathrm{Cn}(\emptyset)$ and $\alpha \in K$, as the functions satisfy $K-9$, $K -_{sf} \alpha = (\mathcal{L} -_{sf} \alpha) \cap K = (\mathcal{L} -_{ee} \alpha) \cap K = \{\beta \in K \mid \alpha \in \mathrm{Cn}(\emptyset)$ or $\alpha <^K_{ee} (\alpha \vee \beta)\}$. ■

4 PROPERTIES OF ITERABLE AGM FUNCTIONS

As we already argued, AGM full meet operations are the most elementary iterable constructions that comply with the AGM postulates, but they are commutative. However, despite their modest definition our iterable AGM functions do not validate commutativity: in general, $(K - \alpha) - \beta$ is different from $(K - \beta) - \alpha$.

Just as AGM contraction and revision are inter-definable via the Levi and Harper identities, so are iterable AGM contractions and revisions. Specifically, the Levi identity let us define iterable revision functions:

$$\textbf{Levi.} \quad K * \alpha = (K - \neg\alpha) + \alpha.$$

This is important since it allows for sequences of different kinds of changes, like for example $(\ldots((K + \alpha) - \beta) * \delta \ldots * \gamma)$. In [Hansson, To come] Hansson proposes reversing the Levi identity as an alternative and plausible way to define revision when change functions are applied to sets of formula that are not closed under logical consequence (bases).

$$\textbf{R-Levi.} \quad K * \alpha = (K + \alpha) - \neg\alpha.$$

Originally, this property was studied in [Alchourrón and Makinson, 1982] as an intuitive property for change functions. Functions satisfying

$$(K - \neg\alpha) + \alpha = (K + \alpha) - \neg\alpha$$

were called *permutable* and the question under which condition an AGM function is permutable was left open in that paper. In [Alchourrón and Makinson, 1985] they show that safe contractions are permutable under the appropriate conditions (Lemma 7.1).

Given K-9, an iterable revision function $*$ can be defined in terms of an iterable contraction function equivalently via **Levi** or **R-Levi**.

PROPOSITION 21. *Iterable AGM contraction functions are permutable.*

A direct proof of the above is immediate but the result derives from Lemma 7.1 in [Alchourrón and Makinson, 1985].

As iterable AGM contractions induce safe contractions functions for each theory K, the results proved in [Alchourrón and Makinson, 1985] carry over:

PROPOSITION 22.
i.) If $\alpha \in K_1 \cap K_2$ *then* $(K_1 \cap K_2) - \alpha = (K_1 - \alpha) \cap (K_2 - \alpha)$ *and* $(K_1 \cup K_2) - \alpha = (K_1 - \alpha) \cup (K_2 - \alpha)$.
ii.) If $\alpha \in K - \beta$ *and* $\beta \in K - \alpha$ *then* $(K - \alpha) - \beta = (K - \alpha) \cap (K - \beta) = (K - \beta) - \alpha$.

And similarly for iterable revisions. These properties hold not just for two theories but also for indefinitely many.

Darwiche and Pearl present in [1997] a number of properties for iterated change. In our notation, they are:

C1. If $\alpha \in \mathrm{Cn}(\beta)$ then $(K * \alpha) * \beta = K * \beta$.
C2. If $\neg\alpha \in \mathrm{Cn}(\beta)$ then $(K * \alpha) * \beta = K * \beta$.
C3. If $\alpha \in K * \beta$ then $\alpha \in (K * \alpha) * \beta$.
C4. If $\neg\alpha \notin K * \beta$ then $\neg\alpha \notin (K * \alpha) * \beta$.
C5. If $\neg\beta \in K * \alpha$ and $\alpha \notin K * \beta$ then $\alpha \notin (K * \alpha) * \beta$.
C6. If $\neg\beta \in K * \alpha$ and $\neg\alpha \in K * \beta$ then $\neg\alpha \in (K * \alpha) * \beta$.

Properties $C1$ to $C4$ are considered in that paper as plausible for iterated change, while $C5$ and $C6$ (satisfied by iterated functions like those in [Boutilier, 1996]) are considered too demanding. In [Lehmann, 1995] property $C2$ was proved inconsistent with AGM postulates $K*7$ and $K*8$. It is not difficult to prove the following.

PROPOSITION 23.
i) All iterable AGM functions, satisfy $C1$, $C3$ *and* $C4$.
ii) There exist iterable AGM functions violating $C2$, $C5$ *and* $C6$.

Most noticeably, our iterable AGM functions validate six of the seven postulates of Lehmann's widening ranked models [Lehmann, 1995]. He argues that these structures are suitable for iterative change and proposes seven postulates that fully characterize revision functions based on these structures. His postulates in our notation are:

I1. $K * \alpha$ is a consistent theory.
I2. $\alpha \in K * \alpha$.
I3. If $\beta \in K * \alpha$, then $\alpha \supset \beta \in K$.

I4. If $\alpha \in K$ then $K * \beta_1 * \ldots * \beta_n \equiv K * \alpha * \beta_1 * \ldots * \beta_n$ for $n \geq 1$.
I5. If $\alpha \in Cn(\beta)$, then $K * \alpha * \beta * \beta_1 * \ldots * \beta_n \equiv K * \beta * \beta_1 * \ldots * \beta_n$.
I6. If $\neg\beta \notin K * \alpha$ then $K * \alpha * \beta * \beta_1 * \ldots * \beta_n \equiv K * \alpha * (\alpha \wedge \beta) * \beta_1 * \ldots * \beta_n$.
I7. $K * \neg\beta * \beta \subseteq Cn(K \cup \beta)$.

The last property, when β is in K, forces dependency between two proper revision steps (in the sense that it constrains a given revision operation on the base of a previous one). Consequently, $I7$ introduces historic memory (at least to some extent), which iterable AGM revisions lack.

PROPOSITION 24.
i) All iterable AGM functions, satisfy $I1$*-*$I6$.
ii) There exist iterable AGM functions violating $I7$.

Finally, in [Lehmann *et al.*, 1996] the following three properties are suggested as natural properties for iterated change, which can be shown to hold when change functions are defined on "pseudo-distances". For any pair of theories K_1, K_2 and sentences α, β, γ, δ

D1. $(K_1 \cap K_2) * \alpha \in \{(K_1 * \alpha) \cap (K_2 * \alpha), K_1 * \alpha, K_2 * \alpha\}$.
D2. If $\delta \in (K * \alpha) * \gamma$ and $\delta \in (K * \beta) * \gamma$ then $\delta \in (K * (\alpha \vee \beta)) * \gamma$.
D3. If $\delta \in (K * (\alpha \vee \beta)) * \gamma$ then $\delta \in (K * \alpha) * \gamma$ or $\delta \in (K * \beta) * \gamma$.

Although property $D1$ is a variation of one of the properties appearing in Proposition 22, in general it is not validated by our iterable AGM functions. We can prove the following proposition:

PROPOSITION 25.
i) All iterable AGM functions satisfy $D2$ *and* $D3$.
ii) There exist iterable AGM functions violating $D1$.

Modest as they are, it is surprising that iterable AGM functions satisfy a good number of the standard properties put forward as relevant for iterated change.

ACKNOWLEDGMENTS

This work has benefited from invaluable discussions with David Makinson and Hans Rott. We are indebted to one of the anonymous referees for his very careful review of the paper. We also acknowledge Eduardo Fermé for his helpful comments on previous versions of this work.

Carlos Areces
University of Amsterdam, The Netherlands.

Verónica Becher
University of Buenos Aires, Argentina.

REFERENCES

[Alchourrón and Makinson, 1982] C. Alchourrón and D. Makinson. On the logic of theory change: Contraction functions and their associated revision functions. *Theoria*, **48**, 14–37, 1982.

[Alchourrón and Makinson, 1985] C. Alchourrón and D. Makinson. The logic of theory change: Safe contraction. *Studia Logica*, **44**, 405–422, 1985.

[Alchourrón *et al.*, 1985] C. Alchourrón, P. Gärdenfors and D. Makinson. On the logic of theory change: Partial meet contraction and revision functions. *Journal of Symbolic Logic*, **50**, 510–530, 1985.

[Becher, 1995] V. Becher. Unified semantics for revision and update, or the theory of lazy update. In *Annals of the 24 Jornadas Argentinas de Informática e Investigación Operativa (JAIIO)*, 1995.

[Becher, 1998] V. Becher. Iterable AGM revision based on fixed orderings. Technical report, Departamento de Computación. FCEyN. UBA, January 1998.

[Boutilier, 1996] C. Boutilier. Iterated revision and minimal revision of conditional beliefs. *Journal of Philosophical Logic*, **25**, 263–305, 1996.

[Darwiche and Pearl, 1997] A. Darwiche and J. Pearl. On the logic of iterated belief revision. *Artificial Intelligence*, **89**, 1–29, 1997.

[Freund and Lehmann, 1994] M. Freund and D. Lehmann. Belief revision and rational inference. Technical Report 94-16, The Leibniz Center. Hebrew University, Jerusalem, Israel, 1994.

[Friedman and Halpern, 1996] N. Friedman and J. Halpern. A qualitative Markov assumption and its implications for belief change. In *Uncertainty in artificial intelligence (Portland, OR, 1996)*, pp. 263–273. Morgan Kaufmann, San Francisco, CA, 1996.

[Gärdenfors and Makinson, 1988] P. Gärdenfors and D. Makinson. Revisions of knowledge systems using epistemic entrenchment. In *Proceedings of the Second Conference on Theoretical Aspects of Reasoning about Knowledge (Pacific Grove, CA, 1988)*, pp. 83–95, Los Altos, CA, 1988. Morgan Kaufmann.

[Gärdenfors and Makinson, 1991] P. Gärdenfors and D. Makinson. Relations between the logic of theory change and nonmonotonic logic. In *The logic of theory change (Konstanz, 1989)*, pp. 185–205. Springer, Berlin, 1991.

[Grove, 1988] A. Grove. Two modellings for theory change. *Journal of Philosophical Logic*, **17**, 157–170, 1988.

[Hansson, 1994] S. Hansson. Kernel contraction. *The Journal of Symbolic Logic*, **59**, 845–859, 1994.

[Hansson, To come] S. Hansson. *A Textbook of Belief Dynamics*. Kluwer Academic Publisher, To come. Manuscript.

[Katsuno and Mendelzon, 1991] H. Katsuno and A. Mendelzon. On the difference between updating a knowledge database and revising it. In *Proceedings of the Second International Conference on Principles of Knowledge Representation and Reasoning*, pp. 387–394, Cambridge, 1991.

[Lehmann *et al.*, 1996] D. Lehmann, M. Magidor and K. Schlechta. Distance semantics for belief revision. In *Proceedings of the Sixth Conference of Theoretical Aspects of Rationality and Knowledge*, Y. Shoham, ed. pp. 137–146, San Francisco, 1996. Morgan Kaufmann.

[Lehmann, 1995] D. Lehmann. Belief revision, revised. In *IJCAI-95, Vol. 1, 2 (Montreal, PQ, 1995)*, pp. 1534–1540. Morgan Kaufmann, San Francisco, CA, 1995.

[Makinson, 1993] D. Makinson. Five faces of minimality. *Studia Logica. An International Journal for Symbolic Logic*, **52**, 339–379, 1993.

[Nayak, 1994] A. Nayak. Iterated belief change based on epistemic entrenchment. *Erkenntnis. An International Journal of Analytic Philosophy*, **41**, 353–390, 1994.

[Rott, 1992a] H. Rott. On the logic of theory change: More maps between different kinds of contraction functions. In *Belief Revision*, volume 29, P. Gärdenfors, ed. pp. 122–141. Cambridge Univ. Press, Cambridge, 1992.

[Rott, 1992b] H. Rott. Preferential belief change using generalized epistemic entrenchment. *Journal of Logic, Language and Information*, **1**, 45–78, 1992.

[Spohn, 1987] W. Spohn. Ordinal conditional functions: A dynamic theory of epistemic states. In *Causation in Decision, Belief Change and Statistics*, volume 2, W. Harper and B. Skyrms, eds. pp. 105–134. D. Reidel, Dordrecht, 1987.

[Williams, 1995] M. Williams. Iterated theory base change: A computational model. In *IJCAI-95 Proceeding of the 14th International Joint Conference on Artificial Intelligence*, pp. 1541–1550. Morgan Kauffman, 1995.

ODILE PAPINI

ITERATED REVISION OPERATIONS STEMMING FROM THE HISTORY OF AN AGENT'S OBSERVATIONS

1 INTRODUCTION

Knowledge bases can be used to represent an agent's perception of the world. As an agent often has to deal with incomplete, uncertain or vague information, she has to revise her beliefs about the world. In order to model revision, one has to provide a mechanism to support the modification of the knowledge base in the presence of a new item of information. Since revision is a central topic in knowledge representation, it has been tackled in the literature according to several points of view, symbolic or numerical, logical or probabilistic. Among the logical approaches, the AGM paradigm [Alchourron *et al.*, 1985], in which revision is interpreted as beliefs change, has become a standard. Although very elegant, this framework does not support iterated revision because the underlying preference relation between beliefs is lost in the process of change. In fact, in this approach an epistemic state is represented by a beliefs set, i.e. a deductively closed set of sentences of a logical language, that represents the agent's current beliefs. However, an epistemic state does not only consist of the agent's current beliefs but also encodes the strategy that the agent uses to modify his beliefs after learning a new piece of information. A revision operator satisfying the AGM postulates is equivalent to a set of preorders $\leq_\Psi$, where each pre-order corresponds to an epistemic state Ψ and is used for the revision of this state in the presence of a new observation. However the total pre-orders associated with two successive epistemic states are not related, the only requirement is that these pre-orders are faithful.

Iterated revision has been recently brought into focus by several authors, some proposing a framework for iterated revision like Williams [1994; 1995] with transmutations, Boutilier [1993] with natural revision, Friedman and Halpern [1994] with Belief Change Systems. Other approaches start with the AGM postulates and augment them in order to characterize iterated revision. Boutilier [1993] opts for an absolute minimization strategy. Lehmann [1995] considers the agent's epistemic state as a sequence of observations. Darwiche and Pearl [1997] show that the AGM postulates are too weak and propose additional postulates which constrain the relationship between the total pre-orders associated with two successive epistemic states. Intuitively, in terms of pre-orders, the DP postulates preserve the relative ordering between the models of the added formula. Furthermore, the relative ordering between the countermodels of the added formula is preserved, and the ordering between models and countermodels of the added formula does not change.

M.-A. Williams and H. Rott (eds.), Frontiers in Belief Revision, 279–301.

We propose revision operations at the epistemic state level, in the special case where the revision process takes the history of the agent's observation into account. The underlying intuition is that the agent remembers all her previous information. This information is not at the same level, according to whether the last observation is preferred or not in the next epistemic state. These revision operations are performed at the epistemic state level. Each epistemic state, as in [Darwiche and Pearl, 1997], denoted Ψ, has an associated belief state which is represented by a propositional formula, denoted $Bel(\Psi)$. For each epistemic state Ψ, we define a function that assigns each interpretation of the propositional calculus, denoted $\mathcal{L}_{\mathcal{PC}}$, a weight. The function assigning interpretations a weight induces a ranking on the interpretations of $\mathcal{L}_{\mathcal{PC}}$. The revision operation provides the construction of a new ranking on the interpretations of $\mathcal{L}_{\mathcal{PC}}$ which stems from the stategy that preferred interpretations are those that satisfy as many formulas as possible in the sequence of observations. The function that assigns each interpretation of $\mathcal{L}_{\mathcal{PC}}$ a weight provides a function that assigns each formula of $\mathcal{L}_{\mathcal{PC}}$ a total pre-order on interpretations of $\mathcal{L}_{\mathcal{PC}}$ which is a faithful assignment. In the revision process this assignment preserves the relative ordering between models of the preferred formula and also preserves the relative ordering between interpretations which are not models of the preferred formula.

We first define a $\circ_{\triangleright}$ revision operator where the last observation is preferred in the next epistemic state, in this case, the more recent an observation is the more reliable it is. However, this revision operator attempts to satisfy as many previous observations as possible. The way in which the proposed revision operation assigns each interpretation a weight is shown in the following figures where the weights are represented by ordinals.[1]

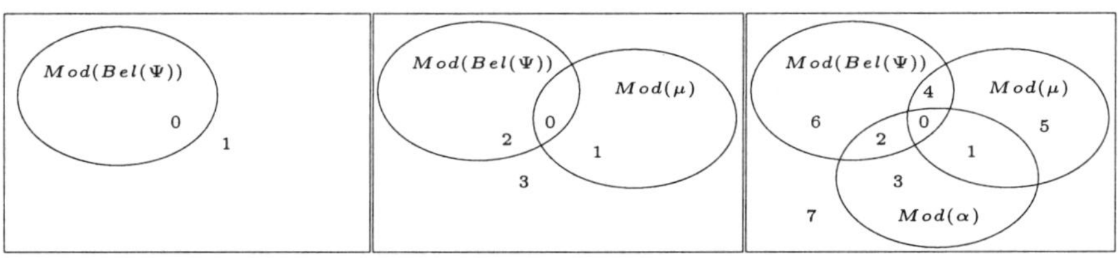

(a) Ψ (b) $\Psi \circ_{\triangleright} \mu$ (c) $(\Psi \circ_{\triangleright} \mu) \circ_{\triangleright} \alpha$

In figure (a) the models[2] of $Bel(\Psi)$ are assigned weight 0, and the models of $\neg Bel(\Psi)$ are assigned weight 1. In figure (b) the models of the added formula μ are assigned weight 0 or 1 according to whether they are or are not models of $Bel(\Psi)$ respectively. The models of $\neg\mu$ are assigned weight 2 or 3 according

[1]For a better understanding of the underlying intuitions, ordinals are used in the figures below, however in the computation of weights polynomial on natural numbers are used. Polynomials allow for a suitable and elegant representation of operations that weaken the weights, i.e. they are analogous to right shifts, and they are useful to distinguish among the interpretations, the models from the countermodels of the added formula.

[2]The set of models of a formula x is denoted $Mod(x)$.

to whether they are or are not models of $Bel(\Psi)$ respectively, and the models of $Bel(\Psi \circ_\triangleright \mu)$ are the minimal weight models. In figure (c) the process is iterated with a new added formula α.[3]

We then define a dual $\circ_\triangleleft$ revision operator where the oldest observation is preferred in the next epistemic state, in this case, the older an observation is the more reliable it is. However, this revision operator attempts to satisfy as many new observations as possible. The way in which the proposed revision operation assigns each interpretation a weight is shown in the following figures where the weights are represented by ordinals.

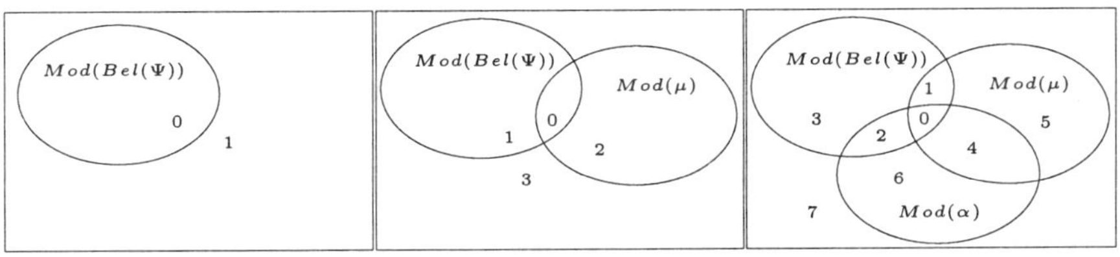

(a) Ψ (b) $\Psi \circ_\triangleleft \mu$ (c) $(\Psi \circ_\triangleleft \mu) \circ_\triangleleft \alpha$

In figure (a) the models of $Bel(\Psi)$ are assigned weight 0, and the models of $\neg Bel(\Psi)$ are assigned weight 1. In figure (b) the models of $Bel(\Psi)$ are assigned weight 0 or 1 according to whether they are or are not models of the added formula μ respectively. The models of $\neg Bel(\Psi)$ are assigned weight 2 or 3 according to whether they are or are not models of μ respectively, and the models of $Bel(\Psi \circ_\triangleleft \mu)$ are the minimal weight models. In figure (c) the process is iterated with a new added formula α.

We finally show that we can alternatively use the revision operators together.

The paper is organized as follows. In Section 2 we define a function that assigns each interpretation a weight. The revision operator $\circ_\triangleright$ is presented in Section 3, we show that the revision operation satisfies the AGM postulates reformulated for epistemic states, and that a faithful assignment can be defined leading to a representation theorem. We then show that this operation satisfies the DP postulates for iterated revision. The revision operator $\circ_\triangleleft$ is then presented in Section 4, we show that this revision operation satisfies most of the AGM postulates reformulated for epistemic states and some DP postulates for iterated revision. In Section 5, we show how we use $\circ_\triangleright$ and $\circ_\triangleleft$ together before concluding in Section 6.

2 DEFINITION OF A WEIGHTING ON $\mathcal{W}$

The proposed revision operation is performed at the epistemic state level. Each epistemic state Ψ has an associated belief set which represents the agent's current

[3] The figures illustrate the case where the added formula is consistent with the initial epistemic state. It is also possible to illustrate the inconsistent case occuring when the intersection between the set of the models of the added formula and the set of models of $Bel(\Psi)$ is empty.

beliefs. A belief set is represented by a propositional formula, denoted $Bel(\Psi)$. Each epistemic state has an associated ranking on the set of all interpretations of the propositional calculus $\mathcal{L}_{\mathcal{PC}}$, denoted $\mathcal{W}$. This ranking is used for the revision of the epistemic state in the presence of a new observation. As a new observation modifies the previous ranking, we define a method that constructs a new ranking associated with the new epistemic state.

2.1 Polynomials and natural numbers

In order to provide a constructive method of a ranking that keeps track of a sequence of observations, we assign each interpretation of $\mathcal{W}$ a weight. For the sake of computation, the information held by an agent is finite, since an agent's current beliefs are represented by a propositional formula, the number of propositional variables occurring in it, is finite, thus the number of interpretation of $\mathcal{L}_{\mathcal{PC}}$ is finite.

Suppose a weight is represented by a natural number, denoted n, there exists an integer i such that $n \leq 2^i$. We assign n the tuple corresponding to its binary decomposition $(p_0, p_1, \ldots, p_{i-1})$ where $p_j \in \{0,1\}\ \forall j, 0 \leq j \leq i-1$. As there is a one to one correspondence between tuple and polynomials, n corresponds to the polynomial $p(x) = \sum_{j=0}^{i-1} p_j\ x^j$. Conversely to each polynomial whose coefficients belong to the set $\{0,1\}$ corresponds an integer which binary representation corresponds to the coefficients of the polynomial, we denote this integer $N(p(x))$. Suppose that the degree of $p(x)$ is r, $N(p(x)) = \sum_{i=0}^{r} p_i 2^i$. A weight can be represented either by a natural number or by a polynomial where coefficients belong to the set $\{0,1\}$. In the following, we denote B, the set $\{0,1\}$, and $B[x]$, the set of polynomials whose coefficients belong to $\{0,1\}$, we define an ordering between polynomials of $B[x]$ which is a total order, denoted $<_B$ induced by the total order on natural numbers as follows:

DEFINITION 1. Let $p(x), p'(x) \in B[x]$.

$$p(x) <_B p'(x) \text{ iff } \exists i \in \mathbb{N} \text{ such that } \forall j,\ j < i,\ \ p_j = p'_j \ \textit{and}\ \ p_i < p'_i.$$

(The reflexive closure of $<_B$ is denoted $\leq_B$.[4])

REMARK 2. Definition 1 introduces the lexicographical ordering between polynomials.

EXAMPLE 3. Let $a(x) = 1, b(x) = x, c(x) = x^2, d(x) = x^2 + x$ be polynomials of $B[x]$ and let $<_B$ denotes the total pre-order between these polynomials. The correspondence between polynomials and integers is illustrated by the following array:

[4]For simplify notation we denote $=$ the equality between polynomials.

$N(p(x))$	2^0	2^1	2^2	$p(x)$	$<_B$
1	1	0	0	$a(x) = 1$	4
2	0	1	0	$b(x) = x$	2
4	0	0	1	$c(x) = x^2$	1
6	0	1	1	$d(x) = x^2 + x$	3

As illustrated in this example, the defined correspondence between polynomials and integers does not reflect the ordering between polynomials, $N(a(x)) < N(b(x)) < N(c(x)) < N(d(x))$ while $c(x) <_B b(x) <_B d(x) <_B a(x)$. When the array representing the coefficients of polynomials is read from right to left, these coefficients correspond to the binary decomposition of an integer reflecting the ordering between polynomials. More formally, let $(p_0, p_1, \ldots, p_{i-1})$ be the coefficients of $p(x)$, the coefficients read in reverse order are $(p_{i-1}, \ldots, p_1, p_0)$. They correspond to the polynomial $p'(x) = \sum_{j=0}^{i-1} p_{(i-1)-j}\, x^j$ which can be written $x^{i-1}p(x^{-1})$, where $p(x^{-1}) = p_0 + p_1x^{-1} + \ldots + p_{i-1}x^{-(i-1)}$ is called the reciprocal polynomial of $p(x)$.

As we use a finite set of polynomials, since the polynomials may have different degrees, let u be the maximum degree of these polynomials. The coefficients of $x^u p(x^{-1})$, where $p(x^{-1})$ is the reciprocal polynomial of $p(x)$, provide the binary decomposition of an integer reflecting the ordering between polynomials, as shown by the following property:

PROPERTY 4. Let $p(x)$ and $p'(x)$ be two polynomials of $B[x]$, let u be the maximum degree of $p(x)$ and $p'(x)$.

$$p(x) <_B p'(x) \text{ iff } N(x^u p(x^{-1})) < N(x^u p'(x^{-1})).$$

EXAMPLE 5. The maximum degree of the polynomials $a(x) = 1$, $b(x) = x$, $c(x) = x^2$, $d(x) = x^2 + x$ is $u = 2$, thus the binary decomposition of an integer reflecting the ordering between polynomials is:

$N(p(x))$	2^0	2^1	2^2	$p(x)$
1	1	0	0	$a(x) = 1$
2	0	1	0	$b(x) = x$
4	0	0	1	$c(x) = x^2$
6	0	1	1	$d(x) = x^2 + x$

$N(p(x))$	$N(x^u p(x^{-1}))$	2^0	2^1	2^2	$x^u p(x^{-1})$
1	4	0	0	1	$x^2 a(x^{-1}) = x^2$
2	2	0	1	0	$x^2 b(x^{-1}) = x$
4	1	1	0	0	$x^2 c(x^{-1}) = 1$
6	3	1	1	0	$x^2 d(x^{-1}) = 1 + x$

We now have $N(a(x)) < N(b(x)) < N(c(x)) < N(d(x))$ and $x^2a(x^{-1}) <_B x^2b(x^{-1}) <_B x^2c(x^{-1}) <_B x^2d(x^{-1})$.

2.2 Weight

For each epistemic state Ψ we assign a weighting on $\mathcal{W}$. In the case where the initial epistemic state has a ranking on $\mathcal{W}$, we define an initial weighting as follows. Let n be number of ranks of the initial epistemic state, there exists an integer j such that $n \leq 2^j$. To each integer i which indexes a rank, $0 \leq i \leq n-1$, we assign the tuple corresponding to its binary decomposition $(p_0, p_1, \ldots, p_{j-1})$ where $p_k \in \{0,1\}$ for $0 \leq k \leq j-1$. In order to reflect the ordering between polynomials, to each integer i we assign a weight which is the polynomial $x^{j-1}p(x^{-1}) = \sum_{i=0}^{j-1} p_{(j-1)-i}\, x^i$.

In the special case where the initial epistemic state has no specified ranking on $\mathcal{W}$ we define a ranking between the interpretations which are models of $Bel(\Psi)$ from those which are countermodels of $Bel(\Psi)$. In this case, there are two ranks (in this case $j = 1$) and the weighting of the initial epistemic state is defined as follows : $\forall \omega \in \mathcal{W}$, if $\omega \in Mod(Bel(\Psi))$ then $p_0 = 0$ otherwise $p_0 = 1$.

More formally a function that maps each epistemic state to weighting on $\mathcal{W}$ is defined by:

DEFINITION 6. Let Ψ be an epistemic state. The *weight* corresponding to an interpretation of $\mathcal{L}_{PC}$ is a polynomial of $B[x]$ defined by :

$$\begin{aligned} \mathcal{W} &\rightarrow B[x] \\ \omega &\rightarrow p^{\omega}(\Psi)(x) = \sum_{i=0}^{m} p_i^{\omega}(\Psi)\, x^i \end{aligned}$$

where $m = j-1$ corresponds to the initial ranking associated with Ψ.

The weight corresponding to an interpretation is a polynomial of $B[x]$. The use of polynomials allows us to make a clear distinction between interpretations that are models of $Bel(\Psi)$ from those which are countermodels of $Bel(\Psi)$, the weight corresponding to a model of $Bel(\Psi)$ is a polynomial whose smallest coefficient is zero and the weight corresponding to a countermodel of $Bel(\Psi)$ is a polynomial whose smallest coefficient is one. In the revision process, polynomials provide a simple means to represent the construction of a new weighting from a previous one. In the case where the last observation is preferred, the weight corresponding to a model of both current beliefs and a new observation, will be right shifted and the weight corresponding to a countermodel of the new observation will be right shifted and translated with 1. In the case where the last observation is not preferred, the weight corresponding to a model of both current beliefs and a new observation, will be left shifted and the weight corresponding to a countermodel of the new observation will be left shifted and translated with 1. It seems natural to use polynomials since they allow for a suitable representation of right shifts and left shifts, i.e. multiplication by x and multiplication by x^{-1}. Moreover, polynomials allow us to come back to previous weightings. Binary sequences can't be used because after shifts operations their length grows, this involves difficulties for computation and comparison.

2.3 Weak and strong equivalences

We are now able to define weak and strong equivalences between two epistemic states.
The weak equivalence between two epistemic states expresses that the associated beliefs sets have the same models.

DEFINITION 7. Let Ψ and Φ be two epistemic states. Ψ and Φ are *weakly equivalent*, denoted $\Psi \equiv_w \Phi$, iff $Bel(\Psi) \equiv Bel(\Phi)$.[5]

Strong equivalence expresses that the epistemic states have the same weighting on $\mathcal{W}$.

DEFINITION 8. Let Ψ and Φ be two epistemic states. Ψ and Φ are *strongly equivalent*, denoted $\Psi \equiv_s \Phi$, iff $\Psi \equiv_w \Phi$ and $\forall \omega \in \mathcal{W}, p^\omega(\Psi)(x) = p^\omega(\Phi)(x)$.

One of the problems with revision at the beliefs set level is that two equivalent knowledge bases are revised in the same way. We formulate revision at the epistemic state level. The definition of a weighting on $\mathcal{W}$ allows for the introduction of two kinds of equivalences, that makes it possible to resolve this problem. Two weakly equivalent epistemic states shall be differently revised, on the other hand two strongly equivalent epistemic states shall be equally revised. The notion of strong equivalence is analogous to Darwiche and Pearl's equality between epistemic states [Darwiche and Pearl, 1997].

3 A REVISION OPERATOR $\circ_\triangleright$

We first define a revision operation which prefers the last item of information. The general philosophy is that an old assertion is less reliable than a new one, such as, for example, a robot moving according to observations of the environment. We believe that in many cases it seems reasonable to decrease the confidence that one has in an item of information, as time goes by. However, this revision operation attempt to satisfy as many previous observations as possible. That is an old observation persists until it becomes contradictory with a more recent ones. The revision operation uses the history of the sequence of previous observations to perform revision.

DEFINITION 9. The revision of an epistemic state Ψ by a formula $\mu \in \mathcal{L}_{PC}$, leads to a new epistemic state denoted $\Psi \circ_\triangleright \mu$. The modification of the weighting after revision by μ is:

$$\text{if } \omega \in Mod(\mu) \text{ then } p^\omega(\Psi \circ_\triangleright \mu)(x) = xp^\omega(\Psi)(x)\ ,$$
$$\text{otherwise } p^\omega(\Psi \circ_\triangleright \mu)(x) = xp^\omega(\Psi)(x) + 1.$$

The weights corresponding to the models of μ are right shifted and the weights corresponding to the countermodels of μ are right shifted and translated by 1.

[5] As $Bel(\Psi)$ and $Bel(\Phi)$ are propositional formulas $\equiv$ denotes the propositional equivalence.

The models of $Bel(\Psi \circ_{\triangleright} \mu)$ are such that:

$$\forall \omega \in Mod(Bel(\Psi \circ_{\triangleright} \mu)),\ \forall \omega' \in \mathcal{W},\ p^{\omega}(\Psi \circ_{\triangleright} \mu)(x) \leq_B p^{\omega'}(\Psi \circ_{\triangleright} \mu)(x).$$

REMARK 10. If $\mu \neq \bot$ and if $\omega \in Mod(Bel(\Psi \circ_{\triangleright} \mu))$ then $\omega \in Mod(Bel(\Psi \circ_{\triangleright} \mu))$, $p^{\omega}(\Psi \circ_{\triangleright} \mu)(x) <_B 1$.[6] If $\mu = \bot$, then $Mod(Bel(\Psi \circ_{\triangleright} \mu)) = Mod(Bel(\Psi))$ and the total pre-order on $\mathcal{W}$ is preserved.

It follows from the definition:

PROPOSITION 11. *Let Ψ be an epistemic state and μ be a formula of $\mathcal{L}_{PC}$, if $Mod(Bel(\Psi)) \cap Mod(\mu) \neq \emptyset$ then $\omega \models Bel(\Psi \circ_{\triangleright} \mu)$ iff $\omega \models Bel(\Psi)$ and $\omega \models \mu$.*

We reformulate the AGM postulates for epistemic states as follows:

Modified AGM postulates for epistemic states Let Ψ be an epistemic state[7] and, ϕ and μ be formulas of $\mathcal{L}_{PC}$.

- $(R1\triangleright)$ $Bel(\Psi \circ_{\triangleright} \mu) \models \mu$.
- $(R2\triangleright)$ If $Bel(\Psi) \wedge \mu$ is satisfiable, then $\Psi \circ_{\triangleright} \mu \equiv_w \Psi \wedge \mu$.
- $(R3\triangleright)$ If μ is satisfiable, then so is $Bel(\Psi \circ_{\triangleright} \mu)$.
- $(R4\triangleright)$ If $\Psi_1 \equiv_s \Psi_2$ and $\mu_1 \equiv \mu_2$, then, $\Psi_1 \circ_{\triangleright} \mu_1 \equiv_s \Psi_2 \circ_{\triangleright} \mu_2$.
- $(R5\triangleright)$ $Bel(\Psi \circ_{\triangleright} \mu) \wedge \phi \models Bel(\Psi \circ_{\triangleright} (\mu \wedge \phi))$.
- $(R6\triangleright)$ If $Bel(\Psi \circ_{\triangleright} \mu) \wedge \phi$ is satisfiable, then $Bel(\Psi \circ_{\triangleright} (\mu \wedge \phi)) \models Bel(\Psi \circ_{\triangleright} \mu) \wedge \phi$.

$(R1\triangleright)$, $(R2\triangleright)$, $(R3\triangleright)$, $(R5\triangleright)$ and $(R6\triangleright)$ are the straightforward translation of the corresponding original AGM postulates. For $(R5\triangleright)$ and $(R6\triangleright)$ we assume that $\not\models \neg\mu$. In contrast, $(R4\triangleright)$ is a weaker version of original AGM postulate; it requires the epistemic states to be strongly equivalent in order to be equally revised. If the weak equivalence is used the postulate is not satisfied. It can be noticed that Darwiche and Pearl [1997] also weaken this postulate using the equality instead of the equivalence between epistemic states. The following result can be established:

THEOREM 12. *The operator $\circ_{\triangleright}$ verifies the postulates $(R1\triangleright) - (R6\triangleright)$.*

We then reformulate the Katsuno and Mendelzon's definition of faithful assignment [Katsuno and Mendelzon, 1991], for epistemic states:

DEFINITION 13. Let $\mathcal{W}$ be the set of all interpretations of $\mathcal{L}_{PC}$. A function that maps each epistemic state Ψ to a total pre-order $\leq_{\Psi}$ on interpretations $\mathcal{W}$ is said to be a *faithful assignment* if and only if:

(1) If $\omega_1, \omega_2 \models Bel(\Psi)$ then $\omega_1 =_{\Psi} \omega_2$;
(2) if $\omega_1 \models Bel(\Psi)$ and $\omega_2 \not\models Bel(\Psi)$ then $\omega_1 <_{\Psi} \omega_2$;
(3) if $\Psi \equiv_s \Phi$ then $\leq_{\Psi} = \leq_{\Phi}$.

[6] 1 is the polynomial $\sum_{i=0}^{n} p_i\, x^i$, where $p_0 = 1$ and $p_i = 0, \forall i, 1 \leq i \leq n$.

[7] Each epistemic state has an associated propositional formula, denoted $Bel(\Psi)$ which represents a beliefs set.

Here, $\omega_1 <_\Psi \omega_2$ is defined as $\omega_1 \leq_\Psi \omega_2$ and $\omega_2 \not\leq_\Psi \omega_1$; $\omega_1 =_\Psi \omega_2$ is defined as $\omega_1 \leq_\Psi \omega_2$ and $\omega_2 \leq_\Psi \omega_1$.

Condition (3) is weakened, the stong equivalence is used. Darwiche and Pearl [1997] also weaken this condition using the equality instead of the equivalence between epistemic states. In the previous Section, we defined a function that assigns to each epistemic state Ψ a weighting on interpretations of $\mathcal{L}_{\mathcal{PC}}$. This function yields a function that assigns to each epistemic state a total pre-order on interpretations of $\mathcal{L}_{\mathcal{PC}}$ which is a faithful assignment.

PROPOSITION 14. *Let Ψ be an epistemic state, let ω_1 and ω_2 be interpretations of $\mathcal{L}_{\mathcal{PC}}$. A total pre-order on interpretations of $\mathcal{L}_{\mathcal{PC}}$, denoted $\leq_\Psi$, is defined by:*

$$\omega_1 \leq_\Psi \omega_2 \text{ iff } p^{\omega_1}(\Psi)(x) \leq_B p^{\omega_2}(\Psi)(x).$$

The function that assigns to each epistemic state Ψ this total pre-order on interpretations of $\mathcal{L}_{\mathcal{PC}}$ is a faithful assignment.

Thus the following theorem holds:

THEOREM 15. *Let Ψ be an epistemic state, μ be a formula of $\mathcal{L}_{\mathcal{PC}}$ and let $\leq_\Psi$ be the total pre-order on interpretations of $\mathcal{L}_{\mathcal{PC}}$ defined in the previous proposition, we then have*

$$Mod(Bel(\Psi \circ_\triangleright \mu)) = min(Mod(\mu), \leq_\Psi).$$

Here, $Mod(Bel(\Psi \circ_\triangleright \mu))$ denotes the set of all models of $\Psi \circ_\triangleright \mu$ and $Mod(\mu)$ is the set of all models of μ.[8]

The defined weighting for the revision process leads to the construction of an ordering on interpretations that preserves the relative ordering between models of the added formula. Furthermore it also preserves the relative ordering between the interpretations which are not models of the added formula.

EXAMPLE 16. Let Ψ be an epistemic state with associated belief set represented by $Bel(\Psi) = a \vee b$, and a ranking between interpretations of $\mathcal{W}$, $\omega_4 <_\Psi \omega_3 =_\Psi \omega_2 <_\Psi \omega_1$. Let $\mu = \neg b$ and $\alpha = \neg a$ be formulas of $\mathcal{L}_{\mathcal{PC}}$. The following array shows the evolution of the ranking after a revision first by μ then by α:

$\mathcal{W}$	a	b	$p^\omega(\Psi)(x)$	p_0	p_1	$p^\omega(\Psi \circ_\triangleright \mu)(x)$	p_0	p_1	p_2
ω_1	0	0	1	1	0	x	0	1	0
ω_2	0	1	x	0	1	$1 + x^2$	1	0	1
ω_3	1	0	x	0	1	x^2	0	0	1
ω_4	1	1	0	0	0	1	1	0	0

[8] $min(Mod(\mu), \leq_\Psi)$ contains all models that are minimal in $Mod(\mu)$ according to the total pre-order $\leq_\Psi$.

$\mathcal{W}$	a	b	$p^{\omega}((\Psi \circ_{\rhd} \mu) \circ_{\rhd} \alpha)(x)$	p_0	p_1	p_2	p_3
ω_1	0	0	x^2	0	0	1	0
ω_2	0	1	$x + x^3$	0	1	0	1
ω_3	1	0	$1 + x^3$	1	0	0	1
ω_4	1	1	$1 + x$	1	1	0	0

$\omega_3 <_{\Psi \circ_{\rhd} \mu} \omega_1 <_{\Psi \circ_{\rhd} \mu} \omega_4 <_{\Psi \circ_{\rhd} \mu} \omega_2$ and $\omega_1 <_{(\Psi \circ_{\rhd} \mu) \circ_{\rhd} \alpha} \omega_2 <_{(\Psi \circ_{\rhd} \mu) \circ_{\rhd} \alpha} \omega_3 <_{(\Psi \circ_{\rhd} \mu) \circ_{\rhd} \alpha} \omega_4$ The weight corresponding to ω_i is $p^{\omega_i}((\Psi \circ_{\rhd} \mu) \circ_{\rhd} \alpha)(x) = p_0 + p_1 x + p_2 x^2 + p_3 x^3$. The coefficients of the polynomial provide some information, the last columns of the previous array $p_0\ p_1\ p_2\ p_3$ give the total pre-order corresponding to the current epistemic state $(\Psi \circ_{\rhd} \mu) \circ_{\rhd} \alpha$, the columns $p_1\ p_2\ p_3$ give the total pre-order corresponding to the previous epistemic state $\Psi \circ_{\rhd} \mu$ and the columns $p_2\ p_3$ give the total pre-order corresponding to the initial epistemic state Ψ. The values of coefficients of the polynomials show that the interpretation satisfies (value 0) or not (value 1) the successive observations. For example, for the polynomial $p^{\omega_2}((\Psi \circ_{\rhd} \mu) \circ_{\rhd} \alpha)(x)$, $p_0 = 0$ thus $\omega_2 \models \alpha$, $p_1 = 1$ thus $\omega_2 \not\models \mu$.

The iteration of the revision process leads to the following property:

PROPOSITION 17. *Let Ψ be an epistemic state, μ and α be formulas of $\mathcal{L}_{\mathcal{PC}}$, if $Mod(Bel(\Psi)) \cap Mod(\mu) \cap Mod(\alpha) \neq \emptyset$ then $\omega \models Bel((\Psi \circ_{\rhd} \mu) \circ_{\rhd} \alpha)$ iff $\omega \models Bel(\Psi)$ and $\omega \models \mu$ and $\omega \models \alpha$.*

DP postulates for iterated revision Let Ψ be an epistemic state, α and μ[9] be formulas of $\mathcal{L}_{\mathcal{PC}}$,

$(C1\rhd)$ If $\alpha \models \mu$ then $(\Psi \circ_{\rhd} \mu) \circ_{\rhd} \alpha \equiv_w \Psi \circ_{\rhd} \alpha$.
$(C2\rhd)$ If $\alpha \models \neg\mu$ then $(\Psi \circ_{\rhd} \mu) \circ_{\rhd} \alpha \equiv_w \Psi \circ_{\rhd} \alpha$.
$(C3\rhd)$ If $Bel(\Psi \circ_{\rhd} \alpha) \models \mu$ then $Bel((\Psi \circ_{\rhd} \mu) \circ_{\rhd} \alpha) \models \mu$.
$(C4\rhd)$ If $Bel(\Psi \circ_{\rhd} \alpha) \not\models \neg\mu$ then $Bel((\Psi \circ_{\rhd} \mu) \circ_{\rhd} \alpha) \not\models \neg\mu$.

The following result holds:

THEOREM 18. *The operator $\circ_{\rhd}$ verifies: $(C1\rhd)$, $(C2\rhd)$, $(C3\rhd)$ and $(C4\rhd)$.*

In the previous Section, we defined a function that assigns to each formula of $\mathcal{L}_{\mathcal{PC}}$ a pre-order on the interpretations of $\mathcal{L}_{\mathcal{PC}}$, denoted $\leq_{\Psi}$. We showed that this function is a faithful assignment. The postulates $(C1\rhd)$, $(C2\rhd)$, $(C3\rhd)$ and $(C4\rhd)$ in relationship with total pre-orders associated to two succesive epistemic states are the following:
Let Ψ be an epistemic state, α and μ be formulas of $\mathcal{L}_{\mathcal{PC}}$,

$(CR1\rhd)$ If $\omega_1 \models \mu$ and $\omega_2 \models \mu$ then $\omega_1 \leq_{\Psi} \omega_2$ iff $\omega_1 \leq_{\Psi \circ_{\rhd} \mu} \omega_2$.
$(CR2\rhd)$ If $\omega_1 \models \neg\mu$ and $\omega_2 \models \neg\mu$ then $\omega_1 \leq_{\Psi} \omega_2$ iff $\omega_1 \leq_{\Psi \circ_{\rhd} \mu} \omega_2$.
$(CR3\rhd)$ If $\omega_1 \models \mu$ and $\omega_2 \models \neg\mu$ then $\omega_1 <_{\Psi} \omega_2$ only if $\omega_1 <_{\Psi \circ_{\rhd} \mu} \omega_2$.
$(CR4\rhd)$ If $\omega_1 \models \mu$ and $\omega_2 \models \neg\mu$ then $\omega_1 \leq_{\Psi} \omega_2$ only if $\omega_1 \leq_{\Psi \circ_{\rhd} \mu} \omega_2$.

[9]We assume $\not\models \neg\mu$

The defined $\circ_\triangleright$ revision operator satisfies the following theorem:

THEOREM 19. *If the operator $\circ_\triangleright$ satisfies the postulates $(R1\triangleright) - (R6\triangleright)$ and $(C1\triangleright) - (C4\triangleright)$, then the revision operator and its corresponding faithful assignment verify $(CR1\triangleright)$, $(CR2\triangleright)$, $(CR3\triangleright)$ and $(CR4\triangleright)$.*

The proof stems from the followings facts. $(CR1\triangleright)$: the operator $\circ_\triangleright$ does not change the relative ordering of models in $Mod(\mu)$. $(CR2\triangleright)$: the operator $\circ_\triangleright$ does not change the relative ordering of models in $Mod(\neg\mu)$. $(CR3\triangleright)$ and $(CR4\triangleright)$: a model in $Mod(\mu)$ is assigned a lower weight than a model in $Mod(\neg\mu)$.

The $\circ_\triangleright$ revision operator does not satisfy the straightforward translation of the postulates (CB), $(C5)$ and $(C6)$ i. e. $(CB\triangleright)$: If $Bel(\Psi \circ_\triangleright \mu) \models \neg\alpha$ then $(\Psi \circ_\triangleright \mu) \circ_\triangleright \alpha \equiv_w \Psi \circ_\triangleright \alpha$; $(C5\triangleright)$: If $Bel(\Psi \circ_\triangleright \mu) \models \neg\alpha$ and $Bel(\Psi \circ_\triangleright \alpha) \not\models \mu$ then $Bel((\Psi \circ_\triangleright \mu) \circ_\triangleright \alpha) \not\models \mu$; $(C6\triangleright)$: If $Bel(\Psi \circ_\triangleright \mu) \models \neg\alpha$ and $Bel(\Psi \circ_\triangleright \alpha) \models \neg\mu$ then $Bel((\Psi \circ_\triangleright \mu) \circ_\triangleright \alpha) \models \neg\mu$.

4 A REVISION OPERATOR $\circ_\triangleleft$

Preferring the last item of information is not always desirable, it may, in certain cases, lead to unacceptable conclusions. Consider booking problems, like, for example, taxi booking calls. In the case where all taxis are busy, preferring the last booking call, may lead to the eviction of one of the customers from one of the busy taxis before the end of the fare, this is absolutely unacceptable. As, in certain circumstances the last observation has not to be preferred in the next epistemic state. We define a new revision operation which is a dual revision operation of the one introduced in the previous section. The general philosophy is that a new observation is less reliable than an old one. We increase the confidence that one has in an item of information, as time goes by. However, this revision operation attempts to satisfy as many new observations as possible. A new observation is accepted if it is not contradictory with a less recent ones. The revision operation uses the history of the sequence of previous observations to perform revision.

4.1 Weight

In order to define a dual revision operator of $\circ_\triangleright$, we have to slightly modify the definition of the weight:

DEFINITION 20. Let Ψ be an epistemic state. The *weight* corresponding to an interpretation of $\mathcal{L}_{\mathcal{PC}}$ is a polynomial of $B[x]$ defined by :

$$\begin{array}{rcl} \mathcal{W} & \rightarrow & B[x] \\ \omega & \rightarrow & p^\omega(\Psi)(x) = \sum_{k=1}^{n} p^\omega_{-k}(\Psi)\, x^{-k} + \sum_{i=0}^{m} p^\omega_i(\Psi)\, x^i \end{array}$$

The notion of *support* of polynomial, i.e. the set of indexes where the coefficients are non zero is required in order to compare weights, more formally:

DEFINITION 21. Let $p^\omega(\Psi)(x)$ be a weight. The support of a weight is

$$S(p^\omega(\Psi)(x)) = \{i,\ i \in \mathbb{Z} \text{ such that } p_i^\omega(\Psi) \neq 0\}.$$

The set of polynomials is finite, let U be the union of the supports of the polynomials, $U = \cup_{\omega \in \mathcal{W}} S(p^\omega(\Psi)(x))$. We denote min the smallest element of U and max the greatest element of U.

DEFINITION 22. Let $p^\omega(\Psi)(x), p^{\omega'}(\Psi)(x) \in B[x]$. $p^\omega(\Psi)(x) <_B p^{\omega'}(\Psi)(x)$ iff $\exists i \in U$ such that $\forall j,\ j < i,\ p_j^\omega(\Psi) = p_j^{\omega'}(\Psi)$, and $p_i^\omega(\Psi) < p_i^{\omega'}(\Psi)$. (The reflexive closure of $<_B$ is denoted $\leq_B$.[10])

The weighting corresponding to the initial epistemic state is such that $min = 0$ and $max = j - 1$, where j corresponds to the initial ranking associated with Ψ.

DEFINITION 23. The revision of an epistemic state Ψ by a formula $\mu \in \mathcal{L}_{PC}$, leads to a new epistemic state denoted $\Psi \circ_\triangleleft \mu$. The modification of the weighting after revision by μ is:

$$\text{if } \omega \in Mod(\mu) \text{ then } p^\omega(\Psi \circ_\triangleleft \mu)(x) = x^{-1} p^\omega(\Psi)(x)\,,$$
$$\text{otherwise } p^\omega(\Psi \circ_\triangleleft \mu)(x) = x^{-1} p^\omega(\Psi)(x) + x^{max}.$$

min, (resp. max) is the smallest (resp. the greatest) element of the union of the supports of the polynomials $p^\omega(\Psi)(x)$. The weights corresponding to the models of μ are left shifted and the weights corresponding to the countermodels of μ are left shifted and translated by 1.

The models of $Bel(\Psi \circ_\triangleleft \mu)$ are such that:

$$\forall \omega \in Mod(Bel(\Psi \circ_\triangleleft \mu))\ \forall \omega' \in \mathcal{W},\ p^\omega(\Psi \circ_\triangleleft \mu)(x) \leq_B p^{\omega'}(\Psi \circ_\triangleleft \mu)(x).$$

REMARK 24. If $\omega \in Mod(Bel(\Psi \circ_\triangleleft \mu))$ then $x^{|min|+1}(p^\omega(\Psi \circ_\triangleleft \mu)(x)) <_B 1$,[11] where min is the smallest element of the union of the supports, $U = \cup_{\omega \in \mathcal{W}} S(p^\omega(\Psi)(x))$. The smallest element of $U = \cup_{\omega \in \mathcal{W}} S(p^\omega(\Psi \circ_\triangleleft \mu)(x))$ is $min - 1$ and as $min < 0$ thus $|min - 1| = |min| + 1$.

It follows from the definition:

PROPOSITION 25. *Let Ψ be an epistemic state and μ be a formula of $\mathcal{L}_{PC}$, if $Mod(Bel(\Psi)) \cap Mod(\mu) \neq \emptyset$ then $\omega \models Bel(\Psi \circ_\triangleleft \mu)$ iff $\omega \models Bel(\Psi)$ and $\omega \models \mu$.*

Since the new onservation is not preferred in the new epistemic state, we reformulate the AGM postulates for epistemic states as follows:

[10] To simplify notation we denote $=$ the equality between polynomials.

[11] 1 is the polynomial $\sum_{i=0}^{n} p_i\, x^i$, where $p_0 = 1$ and $p_i = 0$, for all i, $1 \leq i \leq n$.

Modified AGM postulates for epistemic states Let Ψ be an epistemic state[12] and, ϕ and μ be formulas of $\mathcal{L}_{\mathcal{PC}}$.

$(R1\triangleleft)$ $Bel(\Psi \circ_\triangleleft \mu) \models Bel(\Psi)$.

$(R2\triangleleft)$ If $Bel(\Psi) \wedge \mu$ is satisfiable, then $\Psi \circ_\triangleleft \mu \equiv_w \Psi \wedge \mu$.

$(R3\triangleleft)$ If $Bel(\Psi)$ is satisfiable, then so is $Bel(\Psi \circ_\triangleleft \mu)$.

$(R4\triangleleft)$ If $\Psi_1 \equiv_s \Psi_2$ et $\mu_1 \equiv \mu_2$, then, $\Psi_1 \circ_\triangleleft \mu_1 \equiv_s \Psi_2 \circ_\triangleleft \mu_2$.

$(R5\triangleleft)$ $Bel(\Psi \circ_\triangleleft \mu) \wedge \phi \models Bel(\Psi \circ_\triangleleft (\mu \wedge \phi))$.

$(R1\triangleleft)$ and $(R3\triangleleft)$ express that older observations have to be preferred in the next epistemic state, the part of μ and $Bel(\Psi)$ is inverted. $(R2\triangleleft)$ and $(R5\triangleleft)$ are the straightforward translation of the corresponding original AGM postulates. For $(R5\triangleleft)$ we assume that $\not\models \neg\mu$. In contrast, $(R4\triangleleft)$ is a weaker version of original AGM postulate; it requires the epistemic states to be strongly equivalent in order to be equally revised. The following result can be established :

THEOREM 26. *The operator $\circ_\triangleleft$ verifies the postulates $(R1\triangleleft) - (R5\triangleleft)$.*

The straightforward translation of the original postulate $(R6)$ is not satisfied by the $\circ_\triangleleft$ operation, it requires an additional condition that is: if $Bel(\Psi \circ_\triangleleft \mu) \wedge \phi$ is satisfiable and $Bel(\Psi \circ_\triangleleft (\mu \wedge \phi)) \models \phi$, then $Bel(\Psi \circ_\triangleleft (\mu \wedge \phi)) \models Bel(\Psi \circ_\triangleleft \mu) \wedge \phi$.

Moreover, the revision $\circ_\triangleleft$ operation verifies the following properties:

PROPOSITION 27. *Let Ψ be an epistemic state and μ be a formula of $\mathcal{L}_{\mathcal{PC}}$.*

$(R2 \triangleleft\ bis)$ *If $Bel(\Psi) \wedge \mu$ is not satisfiable, then $\Psi \circ_\triangleleft \mu \equiv_w \Psi$.*

$(R3 \triangleleft\ bis)$ *If $Bel(\Psi \circ_\triangleleft \mu)$ is satisfiable, then so is $Bel(\Psi)$.*

EXAMPLE 28. Let Ψ be an epistemic state with associated belief set represented by $Bel(\Psi) = a \vee b$, and a ranking between interpretations of $\mathcal{W}$, $\omega_4 =_\Psi \omega_3 =_\Psi \omega_2 <_\Psi \omega_1$. Let $\mu = \neg b$ and $\alpha = \neg a$ be formulas of $\mathcal{L}_{\mathcal{PC}}$. The following array shows the evolution of the ranking after a revision first by μ then by α:

$\mathcal{W}$	a	b	$p^\omega(\Psi)(x)$	p_0	$p^\omega(\Psi \circ_\triangleleft \mu)(x)$	p_{-1}	p_0
ω_1	0	0	1	1	x^{-1}	1	0
ω_2	0	1	0	0	1	0	1
ω_3	1	0	0	0	0	0	0
ω_4	1	1	0	0	1	0	1

$\mathcal{W}$	a	b	$p^\omega((\Psi \circ_\triangleleft \mu) \circ_\triangleleft \alpha)(x)$	p_{-2}	p_{-1}	p_0
ω_1	0	0	x^{-2}	1	0	0
ω_2	0	1	x^{-1}	0	1	0
ω_3	1	0	1	0	0	1
ω_4	1	1	$x^{-1}+1$	0	1	1

$\omega_3 <_{\Psi \circ_\triangleleft \mu} \omega_2 =_{\Psi \circ_\triangleleft \mu} \omega_4 <_{\Psi \circ_\triangleleft \mu} \omega_1$ and $\omega_3 <_{(\Psi \circ_\triangleleft \mu) \circ_\triangleleft \alpha} \omega_2 <_{(\Psi \circ_\triangleleft \mu) \circ_\triangleleft \alpha} \omega_4 <_{(\Psi \circ_\triangleleft \mu) \circ_\triangleleft \alpha} \omega_1$. The weight corresponding to ω_i is $p^{\omega_i}((\Psi \circ_\triangleleft \mu) \circ_\triangleleft \alpha)(x) =$

[12] Each epistemic state has an associated propositional formula, denoted $Bel(\Psi)$ which represent a beliefs set.

$p_{-2}x^{-2} + p_{-1}x^{-1} + p_0$. The coefficients of the polynomial provide some information, for example, for $p^{\omega_3}((\Psi \circ_{\triangleleft} \mu) \circ_{\triangleleft} \alpha)(x)$, $p_0 = 1$ thus $\omega_3 \not\models \alpha$, $p_{-1} = 0$ thus $\omega_3 \models \mu$ and p_{-2} allows to keep a track of the initial ranking. After revision first by μ then by α, the array consisting in the coefficients of the polynomials gives some information. The columns $p_{-2}\, p_{-1}\, p_0$ give the total pre-order corresponding to the current epistemic state $(\Psi \circ_{\triangleleft} \mu) \circ_{\triangleleft} \alpha$, the columns $p_{-2}\, p_{-1}$ give the total pre-order corresponding to the previous epistemic state $\Psi \circ_{\triangleleft} \mu$ and the column p_{-2} gives the total pre-order corresponding to the initial epistemic state Ψ. The previous $\circ_{\triangleright}$ revision operation uses right shifts thus the rightest column of the polynomial gives the total pre-order corresponding to the initial epistemic state. The $\circ_{\triangleleft}$ revision operation now uses left shifts thus the leftest column of the polynomial gives the total pre-order corresponding to the initial epistemic state.

The iteration of the revision process leads to the following property:

PROPOSITION 29. *Let Ψ be an epistemic state, μ and α be formulas of $\mathcal{L}_{\mathcal{PC}}$, if $Mod(Bel(\Psi)) \cap Mod(\mu) \cap Mod(\alpha) \neq \emptyset$ then $\omega \models Bel((\Psi \circ_{\triangleleft} \mu) \circ_{\triangleleft} \alpha)$ iff $\omega \models Bel(\Psi)$ and $\omega \models \mu$ and $\omega \models \alpha$.*

DP postulates for iterated revision Let Ψ be an epistemic state, α and μ [13] be formulas of $\mathcal{L}_{\mathcal{PC}}$,

$(C3\triangleleft)$ If $Bel(\Psi \circ_{\triangleleft} \alpha) \models \mu$ then $Bel((\Psi \circ_{\triangleleft} \mu) \circ_{\triangleleft} \alpha) \models \mu$.
$(C4\triangleleft)$ If $Bel(\Psi \circ_{\triangleleft} \alpha) \not\models \neg\mu$ then $Bel((\Psi \circ_{\triangleleft} \mu) \circ_{\triangleleft} \alpha) \not\models \neg\mu$.

The following result holds:

THEOREM 30. *The operator $\circ_{\triangleleft}$ verifies: $(C3\triangleleft)$ and $(C4\triangleleft)$.*

The operator $\circ_{\triangleleft}$ does not verify the straightforward translation of postulate $(C1)$, i.e. $(C1\triangleleft)$: If $\alpha \models \mu$ then $(\Psi \circ_{\triangleleft} \mu) \circ_{\triangleleft} \alpha \equiv_w \Psi \circ_{\triangleleft} \alpha$. $(C1\triangleleft)$ does not hold when $Bel(\Psi) \wedge \mu$ is satisfiable and $Bel(\Psi) \wedge \alpha$ is not satisfiable, because in this case $(\Psi \circ_{\triangleleft} \mu) \circ_{\triangleleft} \alpha \equiv_w \Psi \wedge \mu$ and $\Psi \circ_{\triangleleft} \alpha \equiv_w \Psi$.
The operator $\circ_{\triangleleft}$ does not verify the straightforward translation of postulate $(C2)$, i.e. $(C2\triangleleft)$: If $\alpha \models \neg\mu$ then $(\Psi \circ_{\triangleleft} \mu) \circ_{\triangleleft} \alpha \equiv_w \Psi \circ_{\triangleleft} \alpha$. $(C2\triangleleft)$ does not hold when $Bel(\Psi) \wedge \mu$ is satisfiable and $Bel(\Psi) \wedge \alpha$ is satisfiable because in this case $(\Psi \circ_{\triangleleft} \mu) \circ_{\triangleleft} \alpha \equiv_w \Psi \wedge \mu$ and $\Psi \circ_{\triangleleft} \alpha \equiv_w \Psi \wedge \alpha$.

We previously defined a function that assigns to each formula of $\mathcal{L}_{\mathcal{PC}}$ a pre-order on the interpretations of $\mathcal{L}_{\mathcal{PC}}$, denoted $\leq_{\Psi}$. We showed that this function is a faithful assignment. The DP postulates in relationship with total pre-orders associated to two succesive epistemic states are the following:
Let Ψ be an epistemic state, α and μ be formulas of $\mathcal{L}_{\mathcal{PC}}$,

[13] We assume $\not\models \neg\mu$

$(CR1\triangleleft)$	If $\omega_1 \models \mu$ and $\omega_2 \models \mu$ then $\omega_1 \leq_\Psi \omega_2$ iff $\omega_1 \leq_{\Psi\circ_\triangleleft\mu} \omega_2$.
$(CR2\triangleleft)$	If $\omega_1 \models \neg\mu$ and $\omega_2 \models \neg\mu$ then $\omega_1 \leq_\Psi \omega_2$ iff $\omega_1 \leq_{\Psi\circ_\triangleleft\mu} \omega_2$.
$(CR3\triangleleft)$	If $\omega_1 \models \mu$ and $\omega_2 \models \neg\mu$ then $\omega_1 <_\Psi \omega_2$ only if $\omega_1 <_{\Psi\circ_\triangleleft\mu} \omega_2$.
$(CR4\triangleleft)$	If $\omega_1 \models \mu$ and $\omega_2 \models \neg\mu$ then $\omega_1 \leq_\Psi \omega_2$ only if $\omega_1 \leq_{\Psi\circ_\triangleleft\mu} \omega_2$.

The defined $\circ_\triangleleft$ revision operator satisfies the following proposition:

PROPOSITION 31. *The revision operator $\circ_\triangleleft$ and its corresponding faithful assignment verify $(CR1\triangleleft)$, $(CR2\triangleleft)$, $(CR3\triangleleft)$ and $(CR4\triangleleft)$.*

Proof: *The proof stems from the followings facts. $(CR1\triangleleft)$: the operator $\circ_\triangleleft$ does not change the relative ordering of models in $Mod(\mu)$. $(CR2\triangleleft)$: the operator $\circ_\triangleleft$ does not change the relative ordering of models in $Mod(\neg\mu)$. $(CR3\triangleleft)$ and $(C4\triangleleft)$: a model in $Mod(\mu)$ is assigned a lower weight than a model in $Mod(\neg\mu)$.*

The $\circ_\triangleleft$ revision operator does not satisfy the straightforward translation of the postulates (CB), $(C5)$ and $(C6)$.

5 REVISION USING OPERATORS $\circ_\triangleright$ AND $\circ_\triangleleft$ TOGETHER

In certain situations it seems reasonable to prefer a new observation and in others, the oldest observation has to be preferred. It may be supposed that they come from different sources. Let S_1 be the source of the most recent information to be preferred in the next epistemic state and S_2 be the source of the oldest information to be preferred in the next epistemic state, we perform revision alternatively using $\circ_\triangleright$ operator if the observation comes from S_1 and $\circ_\triangleleft$ operator if the observation comes from S_2.

In order to use $\circ_\triangleright$ and $\circ_\triangleleft$ operators together, the weights assigned an interpretation ω of $\mathcal{W}$ is a polynomial of $B[x]$ of the form $p^\omega(\Psi)(x) = \sum_{k=1}^{n} p^\omega_{-k}(\Psi)\, x^{-k} + \sum_{i=0}^{m} p^\omega_i(\Psi)\, x^i$ We recall that min (max) denotes the smallest (the greatest respectively) element of the union of the supports of the polynomials. We thus have to generalize some definitions when the $\circ_\triangleright$ is used. We have to slightly modify the definition of the weighting assiociated with two successive epistemic states. In the case where $\omega \notin Mod(\mu)$ $p^\omega(\Psi \circ_\triangleright \mu)(x) = xp^\omega(\Psi)(x) + x^{min}$. This generalizes definition 9 given in Section 3 where the weights were defined as $p^\omega(\Psi)(x) = \sum_{i=0}^{m} p^\omega_i(\Psi)\, x^i$, the smallest element of the support was $min = 0$. The definition of models of $Bel(\Psi \circ_\triangleright \mu)$ is the same, but we now have $\forall\omega \in Mod(\Psi \circ_\triangleright \mu)$, $x^{|min|}(p^\omega(\Psi \circ_\triangleright \mu)(x)) <_B 1$. We are now able to give the definition of the revision operation using $\circ_\triangleright$ and $\circ_\triangleleft$ operators together:

DEFINITION 32. Let Ψ be an epistemic state, S_1 and S_2 be two sources of information. The revision of an epistemic state Ψ by a formula $\mu \in \mathcal{L}_{\mathcal{PC}}$, leads to a new epistemic state denoted $\Psi \circ \mu$:

$$\text{if } \mu \in S_1 \text{ then } \Psi \circ \mu = \Psi \circ_\triangleright \mu,$$
$$\text{if } \mu \in S_2 \text{ then } \Psi \circ \mu = \Psi \circ_\triangleleft \mu.$$

PROPOSITION 33. *Let Ψ be an epistemic state, and two formulas μ, $\alpha \in \mathcal{L}_{\mathcal{PC}}$*

$$(\Psi \circ_{\triangleright} \mu) \circ_{\triangleleft} \alpha \equiv_s (\Psi \circ_{\triangleleft} \alpha) \circ_{\triangleright} \mu$$

This result shows that the order with which the operators are used has no importance as illustrated in the following figures.

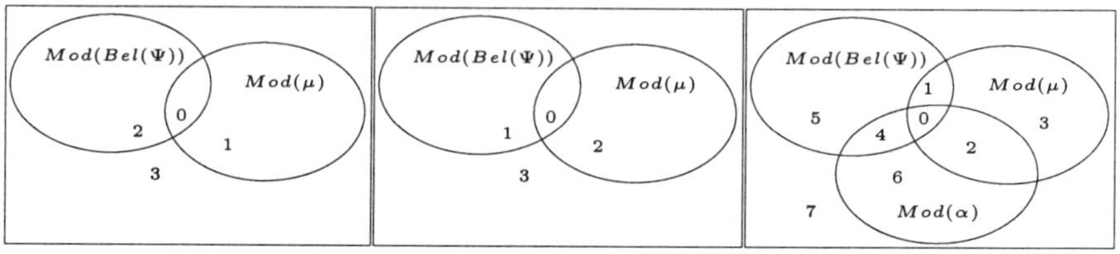

(a) $\Psi \circ_{\triangleright} \mu$ (b) $\Psi \circ_{\triangleright} \mu$ (c) $(\Psi \circ_{\triangleright} \mu) \circ_{\triangleleft} \alpha \equiv_s (\Psi \circ_{\triangleleft} \mu) \circ_{\triangleright} \alpha$

It follows from the definition that the models of $Bel((\Psi \circ_{\triangleright} \mu) \circ_{\triangleleft} \alpha)$ are such that:

$\forall \omega \in Mod(Bel((\Psi \circ_{\triangleright} \mu) \circ_{\triangleleft} \alpha))\ \forall \omega' \in \mathcal{W}$,

$$p^{\omega}((\Psi \circ_{\triangleright} \mu) \circ_{\triangleleft} \alpha)(x) \leq_B p^{\omega'}((\Psi \circ_{\triangleright} \mu) \circ_{\triangleleft} \alpha)(x).$$

REMARK 34. $\forall \omega \in Mod(Bel((\Psi \circ_{\triangleright} \mu) \circ_{\triangleleft} \alpha)), x^{|min|-1}(p^{\omega}((\Psi \circ_{\triangleright} \mu) \circ_{\triangleleft} \alpha)(x)) <_B 1$.

EXAMPLE 35. Let Ψ be an epistemic state with associated belief set represented by $Bel(\Psi) = a \vee b$, and a ranking between interpretations of $\mathcal{W}$, $\omega_4 =_\Psi \omega_3 =_\Psi \omega_2 <_\Psi \omega_1$. Let $\mu = \neg b$ and $\alpha = \neg a$ be formulas of $\mathcal{L}_{\mathcal{PC}}$. The following array shows the evolution of the ranking after a revision first by μ with $\circ_{\triangleright}$ operator then by α with $\circ_{\triangleleft}$ operator:

$\mathcal{W}$	a	b	$p^{\omega}(\Psi)(x)$	$p^{\omega}(\Psi \circ_{\triangleright} \mu)(x)$		$p^{\omega}((\Psi \circ_{\triangleright} \mu) \circ_{\triangleleft} \alpha)(x)$	
ω_1	0	0	1	x	01	1	010
ω_2	0	1	0	1	10	x^{-1}	100
ω_3	1	0	0	0	00	x	001
ω_4	1	1	0	1	10	$x + x^{-1}$	101

The minimal and the maximal element of the union of the supports of the polynomials $p^{\omega}(\Psi)(x)$ are $min(\cup_{\omega \in \mathcal{W}} S(p^{\omega}(\Psi)(x))) = 0$ and $max(\cup_{\omega \in \mathcal{W}} S(p^{\omega}(\Psi)(x))) = 0$ and the minimal and the maximal element of the union of the supports of the polynomials $p^{\omega}(\Psi \circ_{\triangleright} \mu)(x)$ are $min(\cup_{\omega \in \mathcal{W}} S(p^{\omega}(\Psi \circ_{\triangleright} \mu)(x))) = 0$ and $max(\cup_{\omega \in \mathcal{W}} S(p^{\omega}(\Psi \circ_{\triangleright} \mu)(x))) = 1$.

The following array shows the evolution of the ranking after a revision first by α with $\circ_{\triangleleft}$ operator then by μ with $\circ_{\triangleright}$ operator:

$\mathcal{W}$	a	b	$p^\omega(\Psi)(x)$	$p^\omega(\Psi \circ_\triangleleft \alpha)(x)$		$p^\omega((\Psi \circ_\triangleleft \alpha) \circ_\triangleright \mu)(x)$	
ω_1	0	0	1	x^{-1}	10	1	010
ω_2	0	1	0	0	00	x^{-1}	100
ω_3	1	0	0	1	01	x	001
ω_4	1	1	0	1	01	$x + x^{-1}$	101

The minimal and the maximal element of the union of the supports of the polynomials $p^\omega(\Psi)(x)$ are $min(\cup_{\omega \in \mathcal{W}} S(p^\omega(\Psi)(x))) = 0$ and $max(\cup_{\omega \in \mathcal{W}} S(p^\omega(\Psi)(x))) = 0$ and the minimal and the maximal element of the union of the supports of the polynomials $p^\omega(\Psi \circ_\triangleleft \alpha)(x)$ are $min(\cup_{\omega \in \mathcal{W}} S(p^\omega(\Psi \circ_\triangleleft \alpha)(x))) = -1$ and $max(\cup_{\omega \in \mathcal{W}} S(p^\omega(\Psi \circ_\triangleleft \alpha)(x))) = 0$.

It can be seen on the last column of the previous arrays that $(\Psi \circ_\triangleright \mu) \circ_\triangleleft \alpha \equiv_s (\Psi \circ_\triangleleft \alpha) \circ_\triangleright \mu$. The resulting ranking on the interpretations is: $\omega_3 <_{(\Psi \circ_\triangleright \mu) \circ_\triangleleft \alpha} \omega_1 <_{(\Psi \circ_\triangleright \mu) \circ_\triangleleft \alpha} \omega_2 <_{(\Psi \circ_\triangleright \mu) \circ_\triangleleft \alpha} \omega_4$ and $\omega_3 \models Bel(\Psi)$ and $\omega_3 \models \mu$, $\omega_1 \models \alpha$ and $\omega_1 \models \mu$, $\omega_2 \models Bel(\Psi)$ and $\omega_2 \models \alpha$, $\omega_4 \models Bel(\Psi)$.

The following property holds:

PROPOSITION 36. *Let Ψ be an epistemic state, μ and α be a formulas of $\mathcal{L}_{\mathcal{PC}}$, if $Mod(Bel(\Psi)) \cap Mod(\mu) \cap Mod(\alpha) \neq \emptyset$ then*
(1) $\omega \models Bel((\Psi \circ_\triangleleft \mu) \circ_\triangleright \alpha)$ iff $\omega \models Bel(\Psi)$ and $\omega \models \mu$ and $\omega \models \alpha$.
(2) $\omega \models Bel((\Psi \circ_\triangleright \mu) \circ_\triangleleft \alpha)$ iff $\omega \models Bel(\Psi)$ and $\omega \models \mu$ and $\omega \models \alpha$.

Using alternatively $\circ_\triangleleft$ and $\circ_\triangleright$ operators, the following result holds:

PROPOSITION 37. *Let Ψ be an epistemic state, α and μ [14] be formulas of $\mathcal{L}_{\mathcal{PC}}$,*
$(C1 \triangleleft \triangleright)$ If $\alpha \models \mu$ then $(\Psi \circ_\triangleleft \mu) \circ_\triangleright \alpha \equiv_w \Psi \circ_\triangleright \alpha$.
$(C3 \triangleleft \triangleright)$ If $Bel(\Psi \circ_\triangleright \alpha) \models \mu$ then $Bel((\Psi \circ_\triangleleft \mu) \circ_\triangleright \alpha) \models \mu$.
$(C4 \triangleleft \triangleright)$ If $Bel(\Psi \circ_\triangleright \alpha) \not\models \neg\mu$ then $Bel((\Psi \circ_\triangleleft \mu) \circ_\triangleright \alpha) \not\models \neg\mu$.
$(C3 \triangleright \triangleleft)$ If $Bel(\Psi \circ_\triangleleft \alpha) \models \mu$ then $Bel((\Psi \circ_\triangleright \mu) \circ_\triangleleft \alpha) \models \mu$.
$(C4 \triangleright \triangleleft)$ If $Bel(\Psi \circ_\triangleleft \alpha) \not\models \neg\mu$ then $Bel((\Psi \circ_\triangleright \mu) \circ_\triangleleft \alpha) \not\models \neg\mu$.

Proof : *The proof follows from the properties of $\circ_\triangleleft$ and $\circ_\triangleright$ operators.*

$(C1 \triangleright \triangleleft)$: If $\alpha \models \mu$ then $(\Psi \circ_\triangleright \mu) \circ_\triangleleft \alpha \equiv_w \Psi \circ_\triangleleft \alpha$. $(C1 \triangleright \triangleleft)$ does not hold because if $Bel(\Psi) \wedge \mu$ is satisfiable and $Bel(\Psi) \wedge \alpha$ is not satisfiable then $(\Psi \circ_\triangleright \mu) \circ_\triangleleft \alpha \equiv_w \Psi \wedge \mu$ and $\Psi \circ_\triangleleft \alpha \equiv_w \Psi$.
$(C2 \triangleleft \triangleright)$: If $\alpha \models \neg\mu$ then $(\Psi \circ_\triangleleft \mu) \circ_\triangleright \alpha \equiv_w \Psi \circ_\triangleright \alpha$. $(C2 \triangleleft \triangleright)$ does not hold because if $Bel(\Psi) \wedge \mu$ is satisfiable and $Bel(\Psi) \wedge \alpha$ is satisfiable then $(\Psi \circ_\triangleleft \mu) \circ_\triangleright \alpha \equiv_w \alpha$ and $\Psi \circ_\triangleright \alpha \equiv_w \Psi \wedge \alpha$.
$(C2 \triangleright \triangleleft)$: If $\alpha \models \neg\mu$ then $(\Psi \circ_\triangleright \mu) \circ_\triangleleft \alpha \equiv_w \Psi \circ_\triangleleft \alpha$. $(C2 \triangleright \triangleleft)$ does not hold because either $(\Psi \circ_\triangleright \mu) \circ_\triangleleft \alpha \equiv_w \mu$ or $(\Psi \circ_\triangleright \mu) \circ_\triangleleft \alpha \equiv_w \Psi \wedge \mu$, and either $\Psi \circ_\triangleleft \alpha \equiv_w \Psi$ or $\Psi \circ_\triangleleft \alpha \equiv_w \Psi \wedge \alpha$.

[14] We assume $\not\models \neg\mu$

6 CONCLUSION

We define revision operations at the epistemic state level, that keep track of a sequence of observations. These revision operations attempt to satisfy as many observations as possible. In the case where these observations do not conflict, the interpretations that satisfy them are preferred. The revision operation $\circ_{\triangleright}$ satisfies all the AGM postulates and all the DP postulates, the revision operation $\circ_{\triangleleft}$ satisfies most of the AGM postulates and only some DP postulates. We show that these operations can be used together and that the order with which they are used has no importance.

In order to provide total pre-orders on interpretations of $\mathcal{L}_{\mathcal{PC}}$ we construct a weighting on interpretations of $\mathcal{L}_{\mathcal{PC}}$ by means of polynomials which are suitable, simple and elegant tools to represent the constructive ranking of the dual revision operators. Moreover, they allow for a computational efficiency since right shifts and left shifts can be implemented.

Konieczny [1998] independently proposes revision operations with memory, stemming from the principle of "strong primacy of the new item of information", $\circ_{\triangleright}$ operation is a special case of these operations. He shows that these operations have good properties concerning the iteration of the process of revision and gives a method of constructing such operations from "classical" revision operations. He focuses on properties while the present work focuses on the construction of the total pre-order corresponding to the revised epistemic state, by means of polynomials.

Given an initial epistemic state Ψ and its corresponding total pre-order $\leq_\Psi$, we give a constructive method that provides the total pre-order $\leq_{\Psi\circ\mu}$ corresponding to the revised epistemic state $\Psi \circ \mu$, however we didn't provide a syntactic representation of its corresponding beliefs set, denoted $Bel(\Psi \circ \mu)$. In a future work, the belief set corresponding to revised epistemic state $\Psi \circ \mu$ could be provided using the stratified knowledge bases approach proposed by Benferhat, Dubois and Prade [1998].

The dual operators $\circ_{\triangleright}$ and $\circ_{\triangleleft}$ stem from two opposite and extreme strategies. Concerning the status of observations, in Spohn's Conditional Ordinal Function [1987], the observation is represented by a pair (μ, m), where μ is a propositional formula and m is the post-revision degree of plausibility of μ. Revising an epistemic state by a new observation, also called (μ, m)-conditionalization, involves changing the ranking of interpretations. Extending Spohn's work, Williams [1994; 1995] refers to the process of changing an underlying preference relation as a transmutation. The observation is a formula α and an ordinal i which represents the information to be accepted with a degree of firmness i. The (α, i)-transmutation of a ranking involves minimal change to the initial ranking such that the formula α is accepted with degree of firmness i. In order to deal with degrees of firmness for the observations, we have to study how our framework could be modified.

APPENDIX

PROOFS

Proof of property 4:

- We first show that if $p(x) <_B p'(x)$ then $N(x^u p'(x^{-1})) - N(x^u p(x^{-1})) > 0$.

If $p(x) <_B p'(x)$ then there exists i such that $\forall j, j < i\ p_j = p'_j$, and $p_i < p'_i$.
Thus $N(x^u p'(x^{-1})) - N(x^u p(x^{-1})) = 2^{u-i}(p'_i - p_i) + 2^{u-i-1}(p'_{i+1} - p_{i+1}) + \ldots + 2^0(p'_u - p_u)$.
As $p(x) < p'(x)$ then $(p'_i - p_i) > 0$, by definition, p_i and p'_i belong to $\{0,1\}$ $(p'_i - p_i) = 1$ anxd $2^{u-i} > 0$. As the rest of the sum may be negative, we have to prove that :
$|2^{u-i-1}(p'_{i+1} - p_{i+1}) + \ldots + 2^0(p'_u - p_u)| < 2^{u-i}$.
$|2^{u-i-1}(p'_{i+1} - p_{i+1}) + \ldots + 2^0(p'_u - p_u)| \leq 2^{u-i-1}|(p'_{i+1} - p_{i+1})| + \ldots + 2^0|(p'_u - p_u)|$. As, by definition, p_j and p'_j belong to $\{0,1\}$ thus $2^{u-i-1}|(p'_{i+1} - p_{i+1})| + \ldots + 2^0|(p'_u - p_u)| \leq \sum_{j=0}^{u-i-1} 2^j$.
As $\sum_{j=0}^{u-i-1} 2^j = 2^{u-i} - 1$, therefore $|2^{u-i-1}(p'_{i+1} - p_{i+1}) + \ldots + 2^0(p'_u - p_u)| \leq 2^{u-i} - 1$ consequently, $N(x^u p'(x^{-1})) - N(x^u p(x^{-1})) > 0$.

- We then show that if $N(x^u p(x^{-1})) < N(x^u p'(x^{-1}))$ then $p(x) <_B p'(x)$.

If $N(x^u p(x^{-1})) < N(x^u p'(x^{-1}))$ then $N(x^u p'(x^{-1})) - N(x^u p(x^{-1})) > 0$. By definition, $N(x^u p'(x^{-1})) - N(x^u p(x^{-1})) = \Sigma_{j=0}^{u} x^{u-j}(p'_j - p_j)$. If $p'(x) \leq_B p(x)$, either $\forall j, p'_j \leq p_j$ and consequently $N(x^u p'(x^{-1})) - N(x^u p(x^{-1})) \leq 0$ or there exists j such that $\forall j, j < i\ p_j = p'_j$, and $p'_i < p_i$. In this case $N(x^u p'(x^{-1})) - N(x^u p(x^{-1})) = -2^{u-i} + 2^{u-i-1}(p'_{i+1} - p_{i+1}) + \ldots + 2^0(p'_u - p_u)$. By definition, p_j and p'_j belong to $\{0,1\}$ thus $2^{u-i-1}|(p'_{i+1} - p_{i+1})| + \ldots + 2^0|(p'_u - p_u)| \leq \sum_{j=0}^{u-i-1} 2^j$. As $\sum_{j=0}^{u-i-1} 2^j = 2^{u-i} - 1$, therefore $N(x^u p'(x^{-1})) - N(x^u p(x^{-1})) < 0$ which contradicts the hypothesis.

Proof of proposition 11:

($\Rightarrow$) $\forall \omega \in Mod(Bel(\Psi \circ_\triangleright \mu))$, if $\omega \not\models \mu$ then $p^\omega(\Psi \circ_\triangleright \mu)(x) = xp^\omega(\Psi)(x) + 1$, then by definition of the revision operation $p^\omega(\Psi \circ_\triangleright \mu)(x) \not\leq_B 1$ thus $\omega \not\models Bel(\Psi \circ_\triangleright \mu)$, which contradicts the hypothesis, therefore $\omega \models \mu$. As $\omega \models \mu$, $p^\omega(\Psi \circ_\triangleright \mu)(x) = xp^\omega(\Psi)(x)$, if $\omega \not\models Bel(\Psi)$, as $Mod(Bel(\Psi)) \cap Mod(\mu) \neq \emptyset$ there exists $\omega' \in Mod(Bel(\Psi)) \cap Mod(\mu)$ and as $\omega' \models Bel(\Psi)$ thus $p^{\omega'}(\Psi)(x) \leq p^\omega(\Psi)(x)$ therefore $\omega \not\models Bel(\Psi \circ_\triangleright \mu)$ which contradicts the hypothesis, in consequence $\omega \models Bel(\Psi)$.

($\Leftarrow$) if $\omega \models Bel(\Psi)$ and $\omega \models \mu$ then $p^\omega(\Psi \circ_\triangleright \mu)(x) = xp^\omega(\Psi)(x)$ thus $p^\omega(\Psi \circ_\triangleright \mu)(x) \leq_B 1$ as $\omega \models Bel(\Psi)$ there is no $\omega' \in \mathcal{W}$ such that $p^{\omega'}(\Psi \circ_\triangleright \mu)(x) \leq_B p^\omega(\Psi \circ_\triangleright \mu)(x)$ therefore $\omega \models Bel(\Psi \circ_\triangleright \mu)$.

Proof of theorem 12:

($R1\triangleright$) $\forall \omega \in Mod(Bel(\Psi \circ_\triangleright \mu))$, if $\omega \notin Mod(\mu)$ then $p^\omega(\Psi \circ_\triangleright \mu)(x) = xp^\omega(\Psi)(x) + 1$ then by definition of the operator $\circ_\triangleright$, $\omega \notin Mod(Bel(\Psi \circ_\triangleright \mu))$, therefore $\omega \in Mod(\mu)$ and $Bel(\Psi \circ_\triangleright \mu) \models \mu$.

($R2\triangleright$) If $Bel(\Psi) \wedge \mu$ is satisfiable, then there exists $\omega \in \mathcal{W}$ such that $\omega \models Bel(\Psi)$ and $\omega \models \mu$. By proposition 1, $\Psi \circ_\triangleright \mu \equiv_w \Psi \wedge \mu$.

$(R3\triangleright)$ If μ is satisfiable, then there exists $\omega \in \mathcal{W}$ such that $\omega \models \mu$, by definition of the operator $\circ_{\triangleright}$, $p^{\omega}(\Psi \circ_{\triangleright} \mu)(x) = xp^{\omega}(\Psi)(x)$, thus $\omega \in Mod(Bel(\Psi \circ_{\triangleright} \mu))$.

$(R4\triangleright)$ $\forall \omega$ such that $\omega \models Bel(\Psi_1 \circ_{\triangleright} \mu_1)$, as by $(R1\triangleright)$ $\omega \models \mu_1$, $p^{\omega}(\Psi_1 \circ_{\triangleright} \mu_1)(x) = xp^{\omega}(\Psi_1)(x)$. As $\Psi_1 \equiv_s \Psi_2$ then $p^{\omega}(\Psi_1)(x) = p^{\omega}(\Psi_2)(x)$ and $\mu_1 \equiv \mu_2$ thus $\omega \models \mu_2$ therefore $\omega \models Bel(\Psi_2 \circ_{\triangleright} \mu_2)$. The converse proof is similar.

$(R5\triangleright)$ $\forall \omega \in Mod(Bel(\Psi \circ_{\triangleright} \mu) \wedge \phi)$, $\omega \models \phi$ and $\omega \models Bel(\Psi \circ_{\triangleright} \mu)$ then by $(R1\triangleright)$, $\omega \models \mu$ thus $\omega \models (\mu \wedge \phi)$ thus $p^{\omega}(\Psi \circ_{\triangleright} (\mu \wedge \phi))(x) = xp^{\omega}(\Psi)(x)$. If $\omega \not\models Bel(\Psi \circ_{\triangleright} (\mu \wedge \phi))$ then either $p^{\omega}(\Psi \circ_{\triangleright} (\mu \wedge \phi))(x) \not<_B 1$ or there exists $\omega' \in \mathcal{W}$ such that $\omega' \models \mu$ and $p^{\omega'}(\Psi \circ_{\triangleright} (\mu \wedge \phi))(x) < p^{\omega}(\Psi \circ_{\triangleright} (\mu \wedge \phi))(x)$.

Since $\omega \models (\mu \wedge \phi)$ thus $p^{\omega}(\Psi \circ_{\triangleright} (\mu \wedge \phi))(x) = xp^{\omega}(\Psi)(x)$ therefore $p^{\omega}(\Psi \circ_{\triangleright} (\mu \wedge \phi))(x) <_B 1$. On the other hand if $p^{\omega'}(\Psi)(x) <_B p^{\omega}(\Psi)(x)$ then $p^{\omega'}(\Psi \circ_{\triangleright} \mu)(x) <_B p^{\omega}(\Psi \circ_{\triangleright} \mu)(x)$ which contradicts the fact $\omega \models Bel(\Psi \circ_{\triangleright} \mu)$, therefore $Bel(\Psi \circ_{\triangleright} \mu) \wedge \phi \models Bel(\Psi \circ_{\triangleright} (\mu \wedge \phi))$.

$(R6\triangleright)$ $\forall \omega \in Mod(Bel(\Psi \circ_{\triangleright} (\mu \wedge \phi)))$, by then $(R1\triangleright)$, $\omega \models \mu \wedge \phi$ thus $\omega \models \mu$ and $\omega \models \phi$. By hypothesis $Bel(\Psi \circ_{\triangleright} \mu) \wedge \phi$ is satisfiable and if $\omega \notin Mod(Bel(\Psi \circ_{\triangleright} \mu) \wedge \phi)$, as $\omega \models \phi$ thus $\omega \notin Mod(Bel(\Psi \circ_{\triangleright} \mu))$. Either $p^{\omega}(\Psi \circ_{\triangleright} \mu)(x) \not<_B 1$ or there exists $\omega' \in Mod(Bel(\Psi \circ_{\triangleright} \mu))$ such that $p^{\omega'}(\Psi \circ_{\triangleright} \mu)(x) < p^{\omega}(\Psi \circ_{\triangleright} \mu)(x)$. As $\omega \models \mu$ then $p^{\omega}(\Psi \circ_{\triangleright} \mu)(x) = xp^{\omega}(\Psi)(x)$, thus $p^{\omega}(\Psi \circ_{\triangleright} \mu)(x) <_B 1$ and if there exists ω' such that $p^{\omega'}(\Psi)(x) <_B p^{\omega}(\Psi)(x)$ this contradicts the fact that $\omega \in Mod(Bel(\Psi \circ_{\triangleright} (\mu \wedge \phi)))$, therefore $Bel(\Psi \circ_{\triangleright} (\mu \wedge \phi)) \models Bel(\Psi \circ_{\triangleright} \mu) \wedge \phi$.

Proof of proposition 14:

(1) If $\omega_1 \models Bel(\Psi)$ then $\forall \omega_i \in \mathcal{W}$, $p^{\omega_1}(\Psi)(x) \leq_B p^{\omega_i}(\Psi)(x)$. If $\omega_2 \models Bel(\Psi)$ then $\forall \omega_i \in \mathcal{W}$, $p^{\omega_2}(\Psi)(x) \leq_B p^{\omega_i}(\Psi)(x)$. As $\omega_1, \omega_2 \models Bel(\Psi)$ then $p^{\omega_1}(\Psi)(x) \leq_B p^{\omega_2}(\Psi)(x)$ and $p^{\omega_2}(\Psi)(x) \leq_B p^{\omega_1}(\Psi)(x)$ thus $p^{\omega_1}(\Psi)(x) = p^{\omega_2}(\Psi)(x)$, therefore $\omega_1 =_{\Psi} \omega_2$.

(2) If $\omega_1 \models Bel(\Psi)$ and $\omega_2 \not\models Bel(\Psi)$ then $p^{\omega_1}(\Psi)(x) \leq_B p^{\omega_2}(\Psi)(x)$, and $p^{\omega_2}(\Psi)(x) \not\leq_B p^{\omega_1}(\Psi)(x)$ thus $p^{\omega_1}(\Psi)(x) <_B p^{\omega_2}(\Psi)(x)$, therefore $\omega_1 <_{\Psi} \omega_2$.

(3) Follows immediately from the definition of $\equiv_s$.

Proof of theorem 15:

• $Mod(Bel(\Psi \circ_{\triangleright} \mu)) \subseteq min(Mod(\mu), \leq_{\Psi})$. $\forall \omega \in Mod(Bel(\Psi \circ_{\triangleright} \mu))$, The corresponding weight is $p^{\omega}(\Psi \circ_{\triangleright} \mu)(x)$ with $p^{\omega}(\Psi \circ_{\triangleright} \mu)(x) <_B 1$ and $\forall \omega' \in \mathcal{W}$, $p^{\omega}(\Psi \circ_{\triangleright} \mu)(x) \leq_B p^{\omega'}(\Psi \circ_{\triangleright} \mu)(x)$. By $(R1_{\triangleright})$ $\omega \models \mu$. The corresponding weight is $p^{\omega}(\Psi \circ_{\triangleright} \mu)(x) = xp^{\omega}(\Psi)(x)$. Suppose $\omega' \models \mu$ ¿From $p^{\omega}(\Psi \circ_{\triangleright} \mu)(x) \leq_B p^{\omega'}(\Psi \circ_{\triangleright} \mu)(x)$ we have $xp^{\omega}(\Psi)(x) \leq_B xp^{\omega'}(\Psi)(x)$ thus $p^{\omega}(\Psi)(x) \leq_B p^{\omega'}(\Psi)(x)$ therefore $\omega \leq_{\Psi} \omega'$ and $\omega \in min(Mod(\mu), \leq_{\Psi})$.

• $min(Mod(\mu), \leq_{\Psi}) \subseteq Mod(Bel(\Psi \circ_{\triangleright} \mu))$. $\forall \omega \in min(Mod(\mu), \leq_{\Psi})$ then $\omega \leq_{\Psi} \omega'$ for all ω' such that $\omega' \models \mu$. By definition of $(\circ_{\triangleright})$ if $\omega \models \mu$ and $\omega' \models \mu$ thus $p^{\omega}(\Psi \circ_{\triangleright} \mu)(x) = xp^{\omega}(\Psi)(x)$ and $p^{\omega'}(\Psi \circ_{\triangleright} \mu)(x) = xp^{\omega'}(\Psi)(x)$. By definition of $\leq_{\Psi}$ and as $\omega \leq_{\Psi} \omega'$ it follows that $xp^{\omega}(\Psi)(x) \leq_B xp^{\omega'}(\Psi)(x)$ therefore $p^{\omega}(\Psi \circ_{\triangleright} \mu)(x) \leq_B p^{\omega'}(\Psi \circ_{\triangleright} \mu)(x)$ for all $\omega' \in \mathcal{W}$ such that $\omega' \models \mu$, in consequence $\omega \models Bel(\Psi \circ_{\triangleright} \mu)$ and $\omega \in Mod(Bel(\Psi \circ_{\triangleright} \mu))$.

Proof of proposition 17:

$(\Rightarrow)$ $\forall \omega \in Mod(Bel((\Psi \circ_{\triangleright} \mu) \circ_{\triangleright} \alpha))$, $p^{\omega}((\Psi \circ_{\triangleright} \mu) \circ_{\triangleright} \alpha)(x) <_B 1$, by $(R1\triangleright)$ $\omega \models \alpha$ thus the corresponding weight is $p^{\omega}((\Psi \circ_{\triangleright} \mu) \circ_{\triangleright} \alpha)(x) = xp^{\omega}((\Psi \circ_{\triangleright} \mu))(x)$. If $\omega \not\models \mu$

or $\omega \not\models Bel(\Psi)$, by hypothesis there exists $\omega' \in Mod(Bel(\Psi)) \cap Mod(\mu) \cap Mod(\alpha)$ such that $p^{\omega'}((\Psi \circ_{\triangleright} \mu) \circ_{\triangleright} \alpha)(x) <_B p^{\omega}((\Psi \circ_{\triangleright} \mu) \circ_{\triangleright} \alpha)(x)$, by definition of weights. This contradicts the hypothesis.

($\Leftarrow$) If $\omega \models Bel(\Psi)$ and $\omega \models \mu$ and $\omega \models \alpha$ then $p^{\omega}((\Psi \circ_{\triangleright} \mu) \circ_{\triangleright} \alpha)(x) = xp^{\omega}(\Psi \circ_{\triangleright} \mu)(x) = x^2 p^{\omega}(\Psi)(x)$. If $\omega \not\models Bel((\Psi \circ_{\triangleright} \mu) \circ_{\triangleright} \alpha)$ then there exists $\omega' \in \mathcal{W}$ such that $p^{\omega'}(\Psi)(x) <_B p^{\omega}(\Psi)(x)$ which contradicts the hypothesis.

Proof of theorem 18:

$(C1\triangleright)$ ($\Rightarrow$) If $\omega \models Bel((\Psi \circ_{\triangleright} \mu) \circ_{\triangleright} \alpha)$, by $(R1\triangleright)$, $\omega \models \alpha$ thus $p^{\omega}((\Psi \circ_{\triangleright} \mu) \circ_{\triangleright} \alpha)(x) = xp^{\omega}(\Psi \circ_{\triangleright} \mu)(x)$. As by hypothesis, $\alpha \models \mu$, $p^{\omega}(\Psi \circ_{\triangleright} \mu)(x) = xp^{\omega}(\Psi)(x)$. Therefore $p^{\omega}((\Psi \circ_{\triangleright} \mu) \circ_{\triangleright} \alpha)(x) = x^2 p^{\omega}(\Psi)(x)$ and and $p^{\omega}((\Psi \circ_{\triangleright} \mu) \circ_{\triangleright} \alpha)(x) <_B 1$ and $p^{\omega'}((\Psi \circ_{\triangleright} \mu) \circ_{\triangleright} \alpha)(x) \leq_B p^{\omega'}((\Psi \circ_{\triangleright} \mu) \circ_{\triangleright} \alpha)(x), \forall \omega' \in \mathcal{W}$. If $\omega \not\models Bel(\Psi \circ_{\triangleright} \alpha)$ then either $p^{\omega}(\Psi \circ_{\triangleright} \alpha)(x) \not<_B 1$ or there exists ω' such that $p^{\omega'}(\Psi \circ_{\triangleright} \alpha)(x) <_B p^{\omega}(\Psi \circ_{\triangleright} \alpha)(x)$. As $p^{\omega}(\Psi \circ_{\triangleright} \alpha)(x) = xp^{\omega}(\Psi)(x)$ thus $p^{\omega}(\Psi \circ_{\triangleright} \alpha)(x) <_B 1$. If there exists ω' such that $p^{\omega'}(\Psi \circ_{\triangleright} \alpha)(x) <_B p^{\omega}(\Psi \circ_{\triangleright} \alpha)(x)$ then $p^{\omega'}(\Psi)(x) <_B p^{\omega}(\Psi)(x)$ and $\omega \not\models Bel((\Psi \circ_{\triangleright} \mu) \circ_{\triangleright} \alpha)$, therefore $\omega \models Bel(\Psi \circ_{\triangleright} \alpha)$. ($\Leftarrow$) the proof is similar.
The proofs of $(C2\triangleright)$ and $(C3\triangleright)$ are similar and the proofs of $(C4\triangleright)$ results from proposition 17.

The proof of proposition 25 is similar to the proof of proposition 11.

Proof of theorem 26:

$(R1\triangleleft)$ $\forall \omega \in Mod(Bel(\Psi \circ_{\triangleleft} \mu))$, $x^{|min|+1}(p^{\omega}(\Psi \circ_{\triangleleft} \mu)(x)) <_B 1$. If $\omega \not\models Bel(\Psi)$ then there are two cases according to either $\omega \not\models \mu$ or $\omega \models \mu$.

If $\omega \not\models \mu$ then $p^{\omega}(\Psi \circ_{\triangleleft} \mu)(x) = x^{-1}p^{\omega}(\Psi)(x) + x^{max}$ and $x^{|min|+1}(p^{\omega}(\Psi \circ_{\triangleleft} \mu)(x)) = x^{|min|}p^{\omega}(\Psi)(x) + x^{max+|min|+1}$. As min is the smallest element of $S(p^{\omega}(\Psi)(x))$ and as $\omega \not\models Bel(\Psi)$ it follows that $x^{|min|+1}(p^{\omega}(\Psi \circ_{\triangleleft} \mu)(x)) \not<_B 1$ wich contradicts the hypothesis, therefore $\omega \models Bel(\Psi)$.

If $\omega \models \mu$ then $p^{\omega}(\Psi \circ_{\triangleleft} \mu)(x) = x^{-1}p^{\omega}(\Psi)(x)$ and $x^{|min|+1}(p^{\omega}(\Psi \circ_{\triangleleft} \mu)(x)) = x^{|min|}p^{\omega}(\Psi)(x)$. As min is the smallest element of $S(p^{\omega}(\Psi)(x))$ and as $\omega \not\models Bel(\Psi)$ it follows that $x^{|min|+1}(p^{\omega}(\Psi \circ_{\triangleleft} \mu)(x)) \not<_B 1$ wich contradicts the hypothesis, therefore $\omega \models Bel(\Psi)$.

$(R2\triangleleft)$ If $Bel(\Psi) \wedge \mu$ is satisfiable, then there exists $\omega \in \mathcal{W}$ such that $\omega \models Bel(\Psi)$ and $\omega \models \mu$. By proposition 4, $\Psi \circ_{\triangleleft} \mu \equiv_w \Psi \wedge \mu$.

$(R3\triangleleft)$ If Ψ is satisfiable, then there exists $\omega \in \mathcal{W}$ such that $\omega \models Bel(\Psi)$, by definition of the operator $\circ_{\triangleleft}$,there are two cases according to either $\omega \not\models \mu$ or $\omega \models \mu$.

If $\omega \not\models \mu$ then $p^{\omega}(\Psi \circ_{\triangleleft} \mu)(x) = x^{-1}p^{\omega}(\Psi)(x) + x^{max}$ and $x^{|min|+1}(p^{\omega}(\Psi \circ_{\triangleleft} \mu)(x)) = x^{|min|}p^{\omega}(\Psi)(x) + x^{max+|min|+1}$. As min is the smallest element of $S(p^{\omega}(\Psi)(x))$ and as $\omega \models Bel(\Psi)$ it follows that $x^{|min|+1}(p^{\omega}(\Psi \circ_{\triangleleft} \mu)(x)) <_B 1$.

If $\omega \models \mu$ then $p^{\omega}(\Psi \circ_{\triangleleft} \mu)(x) = x^{-1}p^{\omega}(\Psi)(x)$ and $x^{|min|+1}(p^{\omega}(\Psi \circ_{\triangleleft} \mu)(x)) = x^{|min|}p^{\omega}(\Psi)(x)$. As min is the smallest element of $S(p^{\omega}(\Psi)(x))$ and as $\omega \models Bel(\Psi)$ it follows that
$x^{|min|+1}(p^{\omega}(\Psi \circ_{\triangleleft} \mu)(x)) <_B 1$.

$(R4\triangleleft)$ $\forall \omega \in Mod(\Psi_1 \circ_{\triangleleft} \mu_1)$, if $\omega \models \mu_1$ then $p^{\omega}(\Psi_1 \circ_{\triangleleft} \mu_1)(x) = x^{-1}p^{\omega}(\Psi)(x)$ and $x^{|min|+1}(x^{-1}p^{\omega}(\Psi_1)(x)) <_B 1$. As min is the smallest element of $S(p^{\omega}(\Psi_1)(x))$ and as by $(R1\triangleleft)$ $\omega \models Bel(\Psi_1)$ then $x^{|min|}p^{\omega}(\Psi_1)(x)) <_B 1$. As $\Psi_1 \equiv_s \Psi_2$ then $p^{\omega}(\Psi_1)(x) = p^{\omega}(\Psi_2)(x)$ and $\mu_1 \equiv \mu_2$ thus $\omega \models \mu_2$ therefore $\omega \models Bel(\Psi_2 \circ_{\triangleleft} \mu_2)$. In the case where $\omega \not\models \mu_1$ the proof is similar. The proof of the converse is similar.

($R5\triangleleft$) $\forall\omega \in Mod((\Psi \circ_{\triangleleft} \mu) \wedge \phi)$, $\omega \models \phi$ and $\omega \models Bel(\Psi \circ_{\triangleleft} \mu)$, by ($R1\triangleleft$), $\omega \models Bel(\Psi)$. There are two cases according to either $\omega \models \mu$ or $\omega \not\models \mu$.
If $\omega \models \mu$ then by ($R2\triangleleft$), $\Psi \circ_{\triangleleft} \mu \equiv_w \Psi \wedge \mu$ thus $(\Psi \circ_{\triangleleft} \mu) \wedge \phi \equiv_w \Psi \wedge (\mu \wedge \phi)$. Since $Bel(\Psi) \wedge (\mu \wedge \phi)$ is satisfiable then $\Psi \circ_{\triangleleft} (\mu \wedge \phi) \equiv_w \Psi \wedge (\mu \wedge \phi)$ therefore $Bel(\Psi \circ_{\triangleleft} \mu) \wedge \phi \models Bel(\Psi \circ_{\triangleleft} (\mu \wedge \phi))$.
If $\omega \not\models \mu$ thus $\omega \not\models \mu \wedge \phi$ and $p^{\omega}(\Psi \circ_{\triangleleft} (\mu \wedge \phi))(x) = x^{-1}p^{\omega}(\Psi)(x) + x^{max}$ Since $\omega \models Bel(\Psi)$ thus $p^{\omega}(\Psi \circ_{\triangleleft} (\mu \wedge \phi))(x) <_B 1$ and if there exists ω' such that $p^{\omega'}(\Psi \circ_{\triangleleft} (\mu \wedge \phi))(x) <_B p^{\omega}(\Psi \circ_{\triangleleft} (\mu \wedge \phi))(x)$ thus $p^{\omega'}(\Psi)(x) <_B p^{\omega}(\Psi)(x)$ which contradicts the fact that $\omega \models Bel(\Psi)$.

Proof of proposition 27:

($R2 \triangleleft$ bis) $Bel(\Psi \circ_{\triangleleft} \mu) \models Bel(\Psi)$ by ($R2\triangleleft$), we have to show that $Bel(\Psi) \models Bel(\Psi \circ_{\triangleleft} \mu)$. $\forall\omega \in Mod(Bel(\Psi))$ as $Bel(\Psi) \wedge \mu$ is not satisfiable, $\omega \notin Mod(\mu)$, in terms of weights $p^{\omega}(\Psi \circ_{\triangleleft} \mu)(x) = x^{-1}p^{\omega}(\Psi)(x) + x^{max}$ since $\omega \in Mod(Bel(\Psi))$ then $p^{\omega}(\Psi)(x) <_B 1$ so $x^{-1}p^{\omega}(\Psi)(x) <_B 1$ and $p^{\omega}(\Psi \circ_{\triangleleft} \mu)(x) <_B 1$.
Since $\omega \in Mod(Bel(\Psi))$ if $\exists\omega' \in \mathcal{W}$ such that $p^{\omega'}(\Psi \circ_{\triangleleft} \mu)(x) <_B p^{\omega}(\Psi \circ_{\triangleleft} \mu)(x)$ then $p^{\omega'}(\Psi)(x) <_B p^{\omega}(\Psi)(x)$ therefore ω is not a model of Ψ which contradicts the hypothesis.

($R3 \triangleleft$ bis) If $\Psi \circ_{\triangleleft} \mu$ is satisfiable $\exists\omega \in \mathcal{W}$ such that $\omega \in Mod(Bel(\Psi \circ_{\triangleleft} \mu))$, in terms of weights $p^{\omega}(\Psi \circ_{\triangleleft} \mu)(x) <_B 1$ and since $p^{\omega}(\Psi \circ_{\triangleleft} \mu)(x) = x^{-1}p^{\omega}(\Psi)(x) + x^{max}$ then $p^{\omega}(\Psi)(x) <_B 1$. On the other hand $\forall\omega' \in \mathcal{W}$, $p^{\omega}(\Psi \circ_{\triangleleft} \mu)(x) \leq_B p^{\omega'}(\Psi \circ_{\triangleleft} \mu)(x)$ thus $p^{\omega}(\Psi)(x) \leq_B p^{\omega'}(\Psi)(x)$ therefore $\omega \in Mod(Bel(\Psi))$.

The proof of proposition 29 is similar to the proof of proposition 17.

Proof of theorem 30:

($C3\triangleleft$) If $Bel(\Psi) \wedge \alpha$ is satisfiable then $\Psi \circ_{\triangleleft} \alpha \equiv_w \Psi \wedge \alpha$. By hypothesis, $Bel(\Psi \circ_{\triangleleft} \alpha) \models \mu$ thus $Bel(\Psi) \wedge \alpha \models \mu$ therefore $Bel(\Psi) \wedge \mu$ is satisfiable and $(\Psi \circ_{\triangleleft} \mu) \circ_{\triangleleft} \alpha \equiv_w (\Psi \wedge \mu) \wedge \alpha$ thus $Bel((\Psi \circ_{\triangleleft} \mu) \circ_{\triangleleft} \alpha) \models \mu$.
If $Bel(\Psi) \wedge \alpha$ is not satisfiable then by ($R2 \triangleleft$ bis), $\Psi \circ_{\triangleleft} \alpha \equiv_w \Psi$. Since, by hypothesis, $Bel(\Psi \circ_{\triangleleft} \alpha) \models \mu$ thus $Bel(\Psi) \models \mu$ therefore $(\Psi \circ_{\triangleleft} \mu) \circ_{\triangleleft} \alpha \models \mu$.

($C4\triangleleft$) If $Bel(\Psi) \wedge \alpha$ is satisfiable then $\Psi \circ_{\triangleleft} \alpha \equiv_w \Psi \wedge \alpha$. By hypothesis, $Bel(\Psi) \wedge \alpha \not\models \neg\mu$ thus $Bel(\Psi) \wedge \mu$ is satisfiable therefore $(\Psi \circ_{\triangleleft} \mu) \circ_{\triangleleft} \alpha \equiv_w (\Psi \wedge \mu) \wedge \alpha$ and $Bel((\Psi \circ_{\triangleleft} \mu) \circ_{\triangleleft} \alpha) \not\models \neg\mu$.
If $Bel(\Psi) \wedge \alpha$ is not satisfiable then by ($R2 \triangleleft$ bis), $\Psi \circ_{\triangleleft} \alpha \equiv_w \Psi$. Since, by hypothesis, $Bel(\Psi \circ_{\triangleleft} \alpha(\not\models \neg\mu$ thus $Bel(\Psi) \wedge \mu$ is satisfiable therefore $(\Psi \circ_{\triangleleft} \mu) \circ_{\triangleleft} \alpha \equiv_w \Psi \wedge \mu$ and $Bel((\Psi \circ_{\triangleleft} \mu) \circ_{\triangleleft} \alpha) \not\models \neg\mu$.

Proof of proposition 33:

Applying the definition of the revision operators leads to the following array:

$Mod(\phi)$	$Mod(\mu)$	$p^{\omega}((\Psi \circ_{\triangleright} \mu) \circ_{\triangleleft} \phi)(x)$
X	X	$p^{\omega}(\Psi)(x)$
X	.	$p^{\omega}(\Psi)(x) + x^{min-1}$
.	X	$p^{\omega}(\Psi)(x) + x^{MAX}$
.	.	$p^{\omega}(\Psi)(x) + x^{min-1} + x^{MAX}$

$Mod(\phi)$	$Mod(\mu)$	$p^{\omega}((\Psi \circ_{\triangleleft} \phi) \circ_{\triangleright} \mu)(x)$
X	X	$p^{\omega}(\Psi)(x)$
X	.	$p^{\omega}(\Psi)(x) + x^{MIN}$
.	X	$p^{\omega}(\Psi)(x) + x^{max+1}$
.	.	$p^{\omega}(\Psi)(x) + x^{MIN} + x^{max+1}$

The first line of the array is read if $\omega \in Mod(\phi)$ and $\omega \in Mod(\mu)$ then $p^{\omega}((\Psi \circ_{\triangleright} \mu) \circ_{\triangleleft} \phi)(x) = p^{\omega}(\Psi)(x)$ and $p^{\omega}((\Psi \circ_{\triangleleft} \phi) \circ_{\triangleright} \mu)(x) = p^{\omega}(\Psi)(x)$. MAX is the greatest element of $\cup_{\omega \in \mathcal{W}} S(p^{\omega}(\Psi \circ_{\triangleright} \mu)(x))$ and $MAX = max + 1$. MIN is the smallest element of $\cup_{\omega \in \mathcal{W}} S(p^{\omega}(\Psi \circ_{\triangleleft} \phi)(x))$ and $MIN = min - 1$.

The proof of proposition 36 is similar to the proof of proposition 17.

ACKNOWLEDGEMENTS

Many thanks to D. Cukierman, J. Delgrande, D. Dubois, T. Meyer, S. Konieczny and C. Schwind for their fruitful discussions and helpful comments.

Université de Marseille, France.

REFERENCES

[Alchourron *et al.*, 1985] C. Alchourron, P. Gärdenfors and D. Makinson. On the Logic of Theory Change: Partial Meet Functions for Contraction and Revision. *Journal of Symbolic Logic*, **50**, 510–530, 1985.

[Benferhat *et al.*, 1998] S. Benferhat, D. Dubois, J. Lang, H. Prade, A. Saffiotti and P. Smets. A general approach for inconsistency handling and merging information in prioritized knowledge bases. In *Proccedings of KR98*, pp. 466–477, 1998.

[Boutilier, 1993] C. Boutilier. Revision Sequences and Nested Conditionals. In *Proccedings of IJ-CAI93*, pp. 519–531, 1993.

[Darwiche and Pearl, 1997] A. Darwiche and J. Pearl. On the logic of iterated revision. *Artificial Intelligence*, **89**, 1–29, 1997.

[Friedman and Halpern, 1994] N. Friedman and J. Halpern. Conditional Logics of Belief Change. In *Proceedings of the AAAI International Conference*, pp. 915–921, 1994.

[Katsuno and Mendelzon, 1991] H. Katsuno and A. Mendelzon. Propositional knowledge base revision and minimal change. *Artificial Intelligence*, **52**, 263–294, 1991.

[Konieczny, 1998] S. Konieczny. Operators with memory for iterated revision. Technical Report No IT-314, LIFL, 1998.

[Lehmann, 1995] D. Lehmann. Belief revision revisited. In *Proceedings of 14th International Joint Conference on Artificial Intelligence*, pp. 1534–1539, 1995.

[Spohn, 1987] W. Spohn. Ordinal conditiona functions: a dynamic theory of epistemic states. *Causation in Decision, Belief Change, and Statistics*, **2**, 105–134, 1987.

[Williams, 1994] M. A. Williams. Transmutations of Knowledge Systems. In *Proceedings of 4th Principle of Knowledge Representation and Reasoning Conference*, pp. 619–629, 1994.

[Williams, 1995] M. A. Williams. Iterated Theory Base Change:A Computational Model. In *Proceedings of 14th International Joint Conference on Artificial Intelligence*, pp. 1541–1547, 1995.

MICHAEL FREUND

ON A FULL MEET BASE REVISION THAT SATISFIES THE CATEGORIAL MATCHING PRINCIPLE

1 INTRODUCTION

Belief revision theory is concerned with the problem of revising a set of beliefs K with a new belief represented by a formula α. When the set K is supposed to represent the totality of the current beliefs of an agent, it is usually taken to be closed under classical consequence, since necessary consequences of beliefs are themselves beliefs. This closure assumption nevertheless leads to important problems: Hansson, for instance, invokes in [Hansson, 1996] the disadvantages of dealing with a belief set that contains "myriads of sentences that the believer has never thought of", and also notes that the *recovery postulate* problem and the problem of *inconsistent belief states* may find solutions that are more satisfying when the revision operation is performed on belief bases than when it is performed on belief sets. Another argument in favour of the *foundations theory*, which focuses on belief bases rather than on belief sets, is that it conforms with the intuistic notion that a set of beliefs most commonly consists of a rough collection B of several pieces of knowledge, put together without any structure, and treated as elementary beliefs. In order to revise the resulting theory $K = Cn(B)$ by an information α, it is therefore natural in this perspective to first try to revise the base B by α, and it is only at a second stage that the effect of this revision on the logical closure K of B should be examined (for a more detailed discussion on the difference between the *justifications theory and the coherence theory*, see [Gärdenfors and Rott, 1995]).

Several attempts have been made in order to define a satisfying notion of revision on knowledge bases, and different sets of postulates for belief base revision have been proposed. An overview on these approaches may be found in [Gärdenfors and Rott, 1995]. Some of the solutions use an additional selection mechanism, similar to the Gärdenfors–Makinson selection functions used in the revision of closed theories [Gärdenfors and Makinson, 1994]. The most "objective" of these functions is obtained when one selects and intersects **all** the subsets of the theory K that can be retained, but it turns out that the resulting revision operation (full meet revision) is of little use in closed theories (Alchourron-Makinson triviality theorem, [Alchourrón and Makinson, 1982]). The question therefore naturally arises whether it is possible to define a suitable notion of full meet revision in the framework of belief **bases**, where the revision process is performed on a (typically finite) set B such that $K = Cn(B)$. This question was examined by Fagin, Kuper, Ullman and Vardi [1986], Nebel [1989] and Rott [1993], but no really satisfactory answer was provided. Let us briefly explain what are the main

M.-A. Williams and H. Rott (eds.), Frontiers in Belief Revision, 303–313.

problems encountered in this kind of base revision :
The most natural way to define the full meet base revision of a knowledge base B by a formula α consists in simply replacing B by the base $B * \alpha = \{\alpha\} \cup (\cap X)$, where the intersection is taken over all the subsets X of B that are maximally consistent with α. Note, however, that this intersection may be empty, like in the example where $B = \{p, q\}$ and $\alpha = \neg(p \wedge q)$. In this case, the resulting belief base trivially consists of the set $\{\alpha\}$, so that all the information encoded in B becomes lost. This shortcoming may be avoided if, instead of taking the intersection $\cap X$, one considers the set $B_\alpha = \cap Cn(X)$, and take for $B * \alpha$ the union $\{\alpha\} \cup B_a$. But in the trivial case where α is an element of B (or of $Cn(B)$), the effect of this revision is simply to replace the knowledge base B by its closure $Cn(B)$. Rather than having to deal with knowledge bases that might sometimes become closed theories and sometimes not, it seems then preferable to require the output always to be a closed theory, and define the revision of B by α to be the closed theory $B * \alpha = Cn(\{\alpha\}, B_\alpha)$. This is indeed the base revision that authors like Fagin *et al.* and Rott studied, but, as can be seen in their work, this version of full meet base revision suffers from two major shortcomings. The first one is that the above construction provides no natural base for the revised set $B * \alpha$, and therefore violates the *categorial matching principle* recalled in [Gärdenfors and Rott, 1995, section 1.2]. According to this principle, "the representation of a belief state after a belief change has taken place should be of the same format as the representation of the belief state before the change". This principle is therefore violated when, starting with a belief base B or a belief set K with known justifications B, one obtains a closed theory in which the track of any such justification is lost. As a pratical consequence, note that the Alchourron–Makinson triviality theorem forbids in this case the use of iterated full meet revision: once the base B has been revised by α, one gets a closed theory $B*\alpha$, and the full meet revision of $B*\alpha$ by any formula β gives a trivial output : the resulting set $B * \alpha * \beta$ is either $Cn(B * \alpha, \beta)$ or $Cn(\beta)$, depending whether β is or not consistent with $B * \alpha$. Thus, the violation of the categorial matching principle is compensated by no material advantage.

The second drawback of this version of full meet revision is that even when B is consistent, its natural extension to justified belief sets, that is to sets of the form $K = Cn(B)$, does not satisfy the postulate of rational monotony $K * 8$ (This postulate, referred to as "*Conjunction 2*", "*Rational Monotony*" or "*Rationality*", reads : if $\neg\beta \notin K * \alpha$, then $Cn(K * \alpha, \beta) \subseteq K * (\alpha \wedge \beta)$). This fact is well-known (for example cf. [Rott, 1993, theorem 5]). As a simple example, consider for instance, in the propositional language $\mathcal{L}$ built on the two propositions p and q, the belief base $B = p \wedge q, p, q, p \vee \neg q$, with closure $K = Cn(B) = Cn(p \wedge q)$. Let $*$ be the full meet revision on K induced by the full meet base revision of B ; for any formula α, one has therefore $K * \alpha = Cn(B * \alpha) = Cn(\alpha, B_\alpha)$. It is not difficult to see that $p \vee q$ is an element of $K * (\neg p \vee q)$, while p is not. By $K * 8$, this should imply that $p \vee q$ is an element of the set $K * (\neg p \vee \neg q) \wedge \neg p = K * \neg p$. But this latter set is the theory $Cn[\neg p, Cn(q) \cap Cn(p \vee \neg q)] = Cn(\neg p)$, which does not contain the formula $p \vee q$. Thus we see in this example that the extension of the full meet base revision defined above does not, in general, satisfy the extended set of AGM postulates.

The above considerations show that the most natural procedure of full meet base revision suffers from important drawbacks. Nevertheless, full meet revision is quite an interesting example of revision: its main feature is that it directly provides a mechanism of revision for every knowledge base, without the need of any extraneously given selection procedure. Furthermore, as we shall see, the universality of full meet revision is emphasized by the fact that, given any closed belief set K and any AGM revision $\odot$ on K, there exists a base B for K such that $\odot$ coincides with the full meet revision operator $*$ of B. Thus one has $K \odot \alpha = B * \alpha$ for any formula α. In this perspective, the problem of defining a suitable full meet base revision that obeys the principle of categorial matching, with closure satisfying the extended set of AGM postulates, appears to be a fundamental one in belief revision theory. In this paper, we shall propose a solution to this problem. To do so, we shall first introduce and study the "improper" full meet revision operator $*$ defined, for any base B and any formula α, by $B * \alpha = Cn(\alpha, B_\alpha)$. This operator induces a non-trivial revision on the closed theory $K = Cn(B)$ defined by $K * \alpha = B * \alpha$, and we shall characterize the belief bases B for which the induced revision is an AGM revision. These bases will be called *stratified*. We will then be ready to define a proper full meet base revision operator $\diamondsuit$ with closure equal to $*$, such that, for every formula α and every stratified base B, the output $B\diamondsuit\alpha$ will be again a stratified base. Finally, in the last section, we shall list and discuss the main properties of $\diamondsuit$, and study the special case of iterated revision.

2 STRATIFIED BELIEF BASES AND RATIONAL BELIEF REVISION

Let B be a belief base, that is an arbitrary subset of a propositional language $\mathcal{L}$. For any formula α, we denote by B_α the intersection of all the sets $Cn(X)$ where X is a subset of B that is maximally consistent with α. *The improper full meet base revision* of B by α is the set $B * \alpha = Cn(\alpha, B_\alpha)$. We call it "improper" as it does not satisfy the categorial matching principle. Since one has readily $B * \alpha = (B \cup \{True\}) * \alpha$, we shall assume that our belief bases always contain the element **True**. Note that while B is a belief base, $B * \alpha$ is a closed theory, so that the principle of categorial matching is violated.

It is convenient to consider the inference relation $|\sim_B$ defined by : $\alpha |\sim_B$ iff $\beta \in B * \alpha$. In the framework of belief change theory, this inference relation is understood as follows : given the base B that represents the beliefs of an agent, β may be concluded from α iff the agent cannot incorporate the information encoded by α in his set of beliefs without also incorporating in this set the information represented by β. In the particular case where $*$ is taken, as above, to be the full meet revision operation, a slightly different point of view may identify the inference relation $|\sim_B$ with that induced by a Poole system with set of defaults B and empty set of constraints [Freund, 1998; Makinson, 1994]. As such, this inference relation was shown to satisfy the properties of a preferential inference relation [Makinson, 1994]; furthermore, when B is a consistent set, this preferential relation satisfies the property of *weak rationality*, corresponding, in the belief revision framework, to the AGM postulate $K * 4$ ("*Expansion 2*"). It follows directly from these considerations—but an alternative proof may be found in [Rott, 1993]—that **the extension of the operation $*$ to the set $K = Cn(B)$, defined, for any formula α, by $K * \alpha = B * \alpha$, satisfies all the AGM postulates of belief revision, except $K * 8$.** The prominent role played in belief change theory by the full meet base revision operator $*$ is now shown by the following

THEOREM 1. *Let K be a closed subset of a logically finite language $\mathcal{L}$, and $\odot$ a revision operation on K that satisfies the extended set $K * 1 - K * 8$ of AGM postulates. Then there exists a base B for K such that, for any formula α, one has $K \odot \alpha = B * \alpha$.*

The above result is no longer true if the finiteness hypothesis is removed. In a slightly different form, this theorem is due to Rott [1993]. In the framework of preferential inference relations, we proved a more general result and established a characterization of the family of all inference relations that can be induced by a Poole system [Freund, 1998]. As remarked in [Freund, 1998, section 4], Theorem 1 may be easily interpreted in terms of Grove [1988] theory of spheres: consider indeed the Grove spheres associated with the revision $\odot$ of K. These are subtheories $K_0 = K \supseteq K_1 \supseteq K_2 \supseteq \ldots \supseteq K_n = Cn(True)$ of K such that, for every consistent formula α, $K \odot \alpha = Cn(\alpha, K_i)$ where i is the first index such that α is consistent with K_i. If the language is finite, we can write $K_i = Cn(\delta_i)$, and we have $\delta_0 \vdash \delta_1 \vdash \ldots \vdash \delta_n = True$. It is then immediate to check that the set $B = \{\delta_i, 0 \leq i \leq n\}$ is a base for K and that one has $K \odot \alpha = B * \alpha$ for every formula α.

From now on, we will suppose that the language is logically finite. This hypothesis is essential for the validity of the results of this section, and it will be determinant in the construction of the proper full meet base revision operator proposed in the next section.

Our first task is to characterize the belief bases B for which the extension of the improper full meet base revision operator $*$ satisfies the postulate $K * 8$. We shall then use this characterization in the next section to construct an operation of base revision that will satisfy the categorial matching principle. For any world m, we shall denote by form(m) the set of all formulae α that are satisfied by m.

DEFINITION 2. Let Y be any set of formulae and X a subset of Y. Then X is determinable in Y iff there exists a world m such that $X = form(m) \cap Y$.

A set X is therefore determinable in a superset Y iff there exists a world m such that, for any formula $\alpha \in Y$, m satisfies α iff $\alpha \in X$. Clearly, a set X is determinable in Y iff the set $X \cup \{\neg\gamma / \gamma \in Y - X\}$ is consistent. As we shall see, the notion of **maximal determinable** sets is a central one when looking for bases that induce a **rational** full meet revision.

DEFINITION 3. A base B is said to be stratified iff it can be written as a disjoint union of non-empty subsets $B_1, B_2, ..., B_h = \{True\}$, for which the following two conditions hold:

1. $\alpha \vdash \beta$ for any formula $\alpha \in B_i$ and $\beta \in B_{i+1}$
2. any non-empty proper subset of B_i that is determinable in B_i is maximally so.

Note that condition 2 may be equivalently reformulated in

2$'$. there are no worlds m, n such that
$\emptyset \subset form(m) \cap B_i \subset form(n) \cap B_i \subset B_i$.

The information encoded by a stratified base may be gathered in a set of graded sheaves. Every element of a given sheaf dominates all the elements that belong to sheaves of higher rank, and, inside each sheaf, the traces of two worlds are never comparable. We will refer to the sequence $(B_1, B_2, \ldots, B_h)$ as to a stratification of the base B.

EXAMPLES:

a) The simplest example of a non-trivial stratified base is given by the logical chain $\delta_1 \vdash \delta_2 \vdash ... \vdash \delta_n = True$. These singletons form a stratification of the base $B = \delta_i, 1 \leq i \leq h$.

b) Any closed theory K satisfies the condition 2 of the above definition: indeed, if X and Y are two determinable non-empty subsets of K such that X is strictly embedded in Y, there exists two worlds n and m such that $X = form(n) \cap K$ and $Y = form(m) \cap K$. Let α be an arbitrary element of K, and β an element in Y that does not lie in X; the world n satisfies $\neg\beta$, and therefore satisfies the formula $\alpha \vee \neg\beta$. Since K is closed, this formula is an element of K, and it follows that $\alpha \vee \neg\beta \in X$. This implies that $\alpha \vee \neg\beta \in Y$, hence that m satisfies $\alpha \vee \neg\beta$. It follows that m satisfies α. Since this is true for any element α of K, we see that m satisfies K, and we have shown that $Y = K$.

   Note that the same argument shows that the set $K_1 = K - \{True\}$ satisfies condition 2. It follows that any closed theory K may be considered as a stratified base, writing $K = K_1 \cup \{True\}$.

c) Any set B_i that has cardinality ≤ 2 satisfies condition 2. It follows that the base
$B = \{p \wedge q, q \wedge r, q, p \vee r, p \vee q \vee r, True\}$ is stratified, setting
$B_0 = \{p \wedge q, q \wedge r\}$,
$B_1 = \{q, p \wedge r\}, B_2 = \{p \vee q \vee r, True\}$.

When the belief base B is stratified, the improper full meet revision operation on B can be directly evaluated, using a given stratification of B:

PROPOSITION 4. *Let B be a stratified belief base and (B_j) a stratification of B. For any consistent formula α, let i be the first index such that B_i is consistent with α. Then the improper full meet base revision $*$ on B is given by $B*\alpha = Cn(\alpha, B_i)$ if no element of B_{i-1} is consistent with α, and $B * \alpha = Cn(\alpha, \beta_1 \vee \beta_2 \vee ... \vee \beta_n)$ otherwise, where the β_k's are the formulae of B_{i-1} that are consistent with α.*

EXAMPLE: If the base B satisfies the condition 2 of Definition 3, we can use the decomposition $B = B_1 \cup \{True\}$, and apply the above result. We have then $B * \alpha = Cn(\alpha)$ iff α is inconsistent with B, and $B * \alpha = Cn(\alpha, B)$ otherwise. In the particular case where B is a closed theory, this is the Alchourrón–Makinson triviality theorem.

The main feature of the improper full meet revision operator is that it satisfies postulate $K * 8$ when applied to a stratified base:

COROLLARY 5. *For any stratified base B, the improper full meet revision operator $*$ satisfies the AGM postulate $K * 8$ of rational monotony.*

The postulate $K * 8$ requires that one has $B*\alpha \subseteq B*(\alpha \wedge \beta)$ for any formula β such that $\neg\beta \notin B * \alpha$. The proof of corollary 5 follows directly from Proposition 4.

The main result of this paper is a converse of the above corollary : if the improper full meet revision operator applied on a base B satisfies $K * 8$, then B is a stratified base:

THEOREM 6. *The improper full meet revision $*$ of a base B satisfies $K * 8$ if and only if B is a stratified base.*

Proof. If B is stratified, we know by Corollary 5 that $*$ satisfies $K * 8$. Conversely, suppose that the revision $*$ satisfies Rational Monotony. Let $\prec$ be the strict partial order defined over the subset $\mathcal{L}_c$ of consistent formulae of $\mathcal{L}$ by $\alpha \prec \beta$ iff $\neg\beta \in B*(\alpha \vee \beta)$. Note that $\prec$ is related to the epistemic entrenchment relation $\prec'$ introduced in [Gärdenfors and Makinson, 1994] by the identity : $\alpha \prec \beta$ iff $\neg\alpha \prec' \neg\beta$. For any consistent formulae γ and δ, we have therefore $\gamma \in B * \delta$ iff $\delta \prec \delta \wedge \neg\gamma$. Since the revision operator $*$ satisfies the extended set of AGM postulates, we can associate with $\prec$ a normalized ranking function κ ; for any consistent formula α, $\kappa(\alpha)$ is a thus a non-negative integer that satisfies $\kappa(\gamma \vee \delta) = Min(\kappa(\gamma), \kappa(\delta))$, and $\kappa(\alpha) < \kappa(\beta)$ iff $\alpha \prec \beta$. Note that $\beta \in B * \alpha$ iff $\alpha \vdash \beta$ or $\kappa(\alpha) < \kappa(\alpha \wedge \neg\beta)$. We denote by h the **height** of κ, so that the range of this ranking function is the set $\kappa(\mathcal{L}_c) = \{0, 1, 2, ..., h-1\}$.

For any integer $i \leq h-1$, denote by δ_i the conjunction of all the consistent formulae β such that $\kappa(\neg\beta) > i$. Observe that the formulae thus defined form a logical chain $\delta_0 \vdash \delta_1 \vdash \delta_2 \vdash ... \vdash \delta_{h-1} =$ **True**, with $\kappa(\neg\delta_i) = i+1$, and that, for any consistent formula α, one has $\beta \in B * \alpha$ iff there exists an index i such that δ_i is consistent with α and $\alpha \wedge \delta_i \vdash \beta$.

Now, let α be a formula of B, and $i = \kappa(\neg\alpha)$. We have $\neg\alpha \prec \neg\delta_i$, that is $\delta_i \in B * (\neg\alpha \vee \neg\delta_i)$. By definition of the operator $*$, this implies that any subset T of B that is consistent with δ_i must be consistent with $\neg\alpha$, and it follows that $\alpha \vdash \delta_i$. If furthermore we suppose $i > 0$, we have, by definition of δ_{i-1}, $\delta_{i-1} \vdash \alpha$. We have therefore shown that, given any formula $\alpha \in B$, either $\alpha \vdash \delta_0$, or $\delta_{i-1} \vdash \alpha \vdash \delta_i$ for some index $i > 0$.

The sets B_i are defined as follows : for each index i for which there exists an element α of B with $\kappa(\neg\alpha) = i$, denote by B'_i be the subset of formulae $\alpha \in B$ such that $\kappa(\neg\alpha) = i$. After renumerating the sets, we obtain a sequence $(B_1, B_2, ..., B_n)$ of non-empty sets such that $B = \cup B_i$.

By what precedes, condition 1) is clearly satisfied. To show that condition 2) holds, we use the fact (see [Freund, 1998] for details) that there exists a ranking function κ' on the set of worlds W attached to the language, that satisfies $\kappa'(m) < \kappa'(n)$ iff $form(n) \cap B$ is a strict subset of $form(m) \cap B$. Furthermore the inequality $\kappa'(m) < \kappa'(n)$ holds iff there exists an index κ such that δ_k is satisfied by m and not by n. Let X be a proper non-empty set determinable in B_i, so that there exists a world n such that $form(n) \cap B_i = X$. We know that either $B_i \vdash \delta_0$, or there exists an index j such that $\delta_j \vdash B_i \vdash \delta_{j+1}$; in this latter case, we see that n satisfies $\neg\delta_j \wedge \delta_{j+1}$. Note that $form(n) \cap B$ is then equal to $X \cup_{k \geq j} B_k$. If Y is a strict determinable subset of B_i that strictly contains X, there exists a world m that satisfies $\neg\delta_j \wedge \delta_{j+1}$, with $form(n) \cap B$ is strictly embedded in $form(m) \cap B$. Now, this latter condition implies $\kappa'(m) < \kappa'(m)$, hence the existence of an index k such that δ_k is satisfied by m and not by n. This leads to a contradiction, since we have $form(n) \cap \{\delta_1, ..., \delta_{h-1}\} = form(n) \cap \{\delta_1, ..., \delta_{h-1}\} = \{\delta_i, i > j\}$.

This proves that condition 2) is satisfied for every B_i such that $\delta_j \vdash B_i \vdash \delta_{j+1}$. A similar proof shows that this result holds in the case where $B_i \vdash \delta_0$. We have therefore proven that if the improper revision operator $*$ on B satisfies $K * 8$, there exists a partition (B_i) of B for which conditions 1 and 2 of the theorem are fulfilled. ∎

We shall now proceed to the construction of a proper full meet revision operator, whose closure agrees with the operator $*$ defined in this section.

3 THE RATIONAL FULL MEET BASE REVISION $\Diamond$

Let B be a stratified belief base and (B_i) a stratification of B. For any formula α and any integer k, we denote by $\alpha \wedge B_k$ the set $\alpha \wedge B_k = \{\alpha \wedge \beta / \beta \in B_k\}$.

DEFINITION 7. The rational full meet base revision operator $\Diamond$ of a stratified base B is defined by,
$B \Diamond \alpha = \{False, True\}$ if α is a contradiction, and
$B \Diamond \alpha = \{\alpha \wedge (\beta_1 \vee \beta_2 \vee \ldots \vee \beta_n)\} \cup_{k \geq i} (\alpha \wedge B_k) \cup \{True\}$, if α is consistent, where i is the first index such that α is consistent with B_i, and $\beta_1, \ldots, \beta_n$ $(n \geq 0)$ are the elements of B_{i-1} that are consistent with α.

This operator turns out to be independent of the chosen stratification.

Thus $B\Diamond\alpha$ is a belief base that, up to classical equivalence, contains α. The fact that the rational full meet base revision $B\Diamond\alpha$ defined above does not depend on the choice of the sequence (B_i) is rather surprising. It may be proven *via* a tedious analysis of the equality

$$B_0 \cup B_1 \cup \ldots \cup (B_{i-1} - \{\beta_1, \ldots, \beta_n\} = B'_0 \cup B'_1 \cup \ldots \cup (B'_{j-1} - \{\beta'_1, \ldots, \beta'_m\}$$

that is obtained when one stratifies the set $X = \{\delta \in B/\delta$ inconsistent with $\alpha\}$ through two different statifications (B_i) and (B'_j) of B.

We first note that the operator $\Diamond$ respects the categorial matching principle:

PROPOSITION 8. *If B is a stratified base, the same is true for $B\Diamond\alpha$.*

The link between the improper full meet base revision $*$ defined in the preceding section and the rational full meet base revision $\Diamond$ is given by the following

PROPOSITION 9. *For any formula α and any stratified base B, one has $Cn(B\Diamond\alpha) = B * \alpha$.*

Proof. Straightforward using Proposition 4 and the definition of $\Diamond$. ■

It follows from the above proposition that, given a stratified base B, the closure of the rational full meet base revision operator on B satisfies the AGM extended set of postulates $K{*}1 - K{*}8$. More precisely, Theorem 6 together with Proposition 9 show that, for any stratified base B with closure $K = Cn(B)$, the revision $*$ of K defined by $K * \alpha = Cn(B\Diamond\alpha)$ is an AGM revision.

Let us compute the value of $B\Diamond\alpha$ in an example

EXAMPLE
Let $\mathcal{L}$ be the language built on the two propositions p and q, B be the base $\{p, q, True\}$ and α the formula $\neg(p \wedge q)$. Revising B by α means that one at least of the formulae p or q has to be removed. The classical question "*which one ?*", is easily solved by the full meet revision operator : the unique decomposition of B is $B_0 = \{p, q\}$ and $B_1 = \{True\}$.
The formula α is inconsistent with B_0, and we have $B\Diamond\alpha = \{\neg(p \wedge q) \wedge (p \vee q), \neg(p \wedge q) \wedge True, True\}$, that is $B\Diamond\alpha = \{(p \wedge \neg q) \vee (\neg p \wedge q), \neg p \vee \neg q, True\}$. Note that the theory-revision $*$ induced on $K = Cn(p \wedge q)$ by $\Diamond$ yields $K * \neg(p \wedge q) = Cn((p \wedge \neg q) \vee (\neg p \wedge q))$. In this example, full meet revision appears to provide the most intuitive solution.

By the above properties, the rational full meet revision operator $\Diamond$ clearly provides a solution to the problem stated in the introduction : it satisfies the principle of categorial matching and yields an AGM revision on all closed theories K of the form $K = Cn(B)$ where B is a stratified base. Furthermore, the solution proposed by this operator is universal in the framework of belief base revision : given any belief base B' and any revision $\odot$ of B' whose closure satisfies the extended set of AGM postulates, there exists a stratified base B of $Cn(B')$ such that, for all formulae α, one has $Cn(B' \odot \alpha) = Cn(B \Diamond \alpha)$. This is a straightforward consequence of Theorem 1 and Proposition 9. We shall now study some properties of $\Diamond$.

4 BASIC PROPERTIES OF THE RATIONAL FULL MEET REVISION OPERATOR AND ITERATED REVISIONS

In belief change theory, one usually starts with a collection of "reasonable" postulates, studies their consequences and, eventually, proposes a belief change operator that satisfies these postulates. In this paper, our approach was slightly different: we started with a specific operator—the full meet revision operator—and tried to characterize the bases for which this operator satisfies the categorial matching principle together with the extended set of AGM postulates. We did not present a set of base revision postulates, analogue to those studied by Gärdenfors–Rott [1995], Hansson [1993] or Katsuno–Mendelzon [1992]. In this section, we shall study some elementary properties of the operator $\Diamond$, but we emphasize that these properties are not to be considered as a set of necessary postulates that should govern belief base revision.

We first list some properties of the rational full meet revision operator and then discuss their meaning. These properties only apply to stratified bases. We denote by B a stratified belief base, and use the equality sign between to sets X and Y when these sets contain the same elements up to classical equivalence.

R.F.M.1 $B \Diamond \alpha$ is a consistent stratified base for all consistent formulae α

R.F.M.2 $\alpha \in B \Diamond \alpha$

R.F.M.3 $B \Diamond \alpha = (\alpha \wedge B) \cup \{True\}$ if α is consistent with B

R.F.M.4 $(B \Diamond \alpha) \Diamond \alpha = B \Diamond \alpha$

R.F.M.5 $B \Diamond (\alpha \wedge \beta) = \beta \wedge (B \Diamond \alpha) \cup \{True\}$ if β is consistent with $B \Diamond \alpha$

R.F.M.6 For all $\beta \in B$, $\alpha \wedge \beta \in B \Diamond \alpha$ or $\alpha \wedge \beta \vdash B \Diamond \alpha$

R.F.M.7 If β is consistent with α, $B \Diamond \alpha \Diamond \beta = \{\beta\} \cup B \Diamond (\alpha \wedge \beta)$.

The two first properties are self-explanatory. Note that the vacuity postulate is not satisfied : if α is already an element of the belief base, the revision of B by α does not yield B; rather, as shown by R.F.M.3, its effect is to yield a set, equivalent to B, but in which the agent's belief in α is strengthened. The *rationale* of this is that the revision of a base B (or of a theory K) by formula α is a non-trivial decision process. As pointed out by Friedman and Halpern [1996], one may well have $K * \alpha \neq K$ although $\alpha \in K$, since being informed of α raises the agent's strength of belief in α. Practically, the only reason why an agent should decide to proceed to the revision of his set of beliefs by a formula α that already lies in this set, is that, for this agent, the confirmation of the information represented by α has to be emphasized in its original belief state.

The property R.F.M.5 exactly corresponds to the rationality postulate $K * 8$. The rather surprising R.F.M.6 seems to be connected with a minimality principle that characterizes the *sceptical* approach of full meet revision: if $\beta \in B$ is inconsistent with α, then, trivially, $\alpha \wedge \beta \vdash B\Diamond\alpha$. On the other hand, if β is consistent with α, then either β lies in the "α-strenghtenable" set $\cup_{k \geq i} B_k$, where i is the first index such that B_i is consistent with α, and in this case $\alpha \wedge \beta$ will be in the revised set, or β is one of the formulae $\beta_j \in B_{i-1}$, in which case $\beta \vdash B\Diamond\alpha$. For instance, in the example where $B = \{p, q, True\}$ and $\alpha = \neg(p \wedge q)$, the formula $\alpha \wedge p = p \wedge \neg q$, which is not an element of the revised set, classically implies the whole set $B\Diamond\alpha = \{(p \wedge \neg q) \vee (\neg p \wedge q), \neg p \vee \neg q, True\}$.

The categorial matching property of the rational full meet revision $\Diamond$ provides a simple solution to the problem of iterated revisions. Since the rational full meet revision of a stratified base by a formula α is again a stratified base, it is possible to use the revised base $B\Diamond\alpha$ as an input and apply again the operator $\Diamond$. The property R.F.M.7 shows that the resulting set $B\Diamond\alpha\Diamond\beta$ is equivalent to that obtained by the revision $B\Diamond(\alpha \wedge \beta)$ of B by the conjunction $\alpha \wedge \beta$. This may be seen as a triviality result for rational iterated full meet revisions. Nevertheless, the order in which the revisions are performed is not without importance, as the bases $B\Diamond\alpha\Diamond\beta$ and $B\Diamond\beta\Diamond\alpha$ generally differ.

5 CONCLUSION

We have seen that it is possible to construct a base revision operation that satisfies the categorial matching principle and whose closure yields a AGM revision. This operation cannot be performed on arbitrary bases, without the loss of the rationality postulate $K * 8$, and it is only defined on stratified bases. The question naturally arises whether it could be possible to transform an arbitrary base into a stratified base, so that the rational full meet base revision could be then applied. This problem seems to be linked with that of the rationalization of the inference process determined by a Poole system, which we evoked in [Freund, 1998] and [Freund, submitted]. Although several solutions were proposed to transform a belief base into a logical chain, thus yielding a rational full meet base revision, none of these solutions provide a satisfactory answer because they fail to leave invariant the belief bases that are already stratified.

ACKNOWLEDGEMENTS

Thanks are due to David Makinson for his accurate comments, suggestions and corrections. I also wish to thank the anonymous referees whose remarks and critics greatly helped to improve the presentation of this paper.

Department of Mathematics, University of Orleans, France.

REFERENCES

[Alchourrón and Makinson, 1982] C. E. Alchourron and D. Makinson. On the logic of theory change: contraction functions and their associated revision functions, *Theoria*, **48**, 14–37, 1982.

[Fagin *et al.*, 1986] R. Fagin, J. D. Ulmann, G. M. Kuper and M. Y. Vardi. Updating logical databases, *Advances in Computing Research*, **3**, 1–18, 1986.

[Freund, 1998] M. Freund. Preferential reasoning in the perspective of Poole default logic, *Artificial Intelligence*, **98**, 209–235, 1998.

[Freund, submitted] M. Freund. Statics and dynamics of induced inferences. Submitted.

[Friedman and Halpern, 1996] N. Friedman and J. Y. Halpern. Belief revision: a critique. In *Principles of Knowledge Representation and Reasoning, Proceedings of the 5th International Conference, KR' 96*, pp. 421-431, 1996.

[Gärdenfors and Makinson, 1994] P. Gärdenfors and D. Makinson. Nonmonotonic inference based on expectations, *Artificial Intelligence*, **65**, 197–245, 1994.

[Gärdenfors and Rott, 1995] P. Gärdenfors and H. Rott. Belief revision. In *Handbook of Logic in Artificial Intelligence and Logic Programming*, Vol 4, D. M. Gabbay *et al.*, eds. pp. 35–132. Clarendon Press, Oxford, 1995.

[Grove, 1988] A. Grove. Two modellings for theory change, *Journal of Philosophical Logic*, **17**, 157–170, 1988.

[Hansson, 1993] S. O. Hansson. Reversing the Levi identity, *Journal of Philosophical Logic*, **22**, 637–669, 1993.

[Hansson, 1996] S. O. Hansson. Knowledge-level analysis of belief base operations, *Artificial Intelligence*, **82**, 225–235, 1996.

[Katsuno and Mendelzon, 1992] H. Katsuno and A. O. Mendelzon. On the difference between updating a knowledge base and revising it. In *Belief Revision*, P. Gärdenfors, ed. pp. 183–203. Cambridge University Press, 1992.

[Makinson, 1994] D. Makinson. General patterns in nonmonotonic reasoning. In *Handbook of Logic in Artificial Intelligence and Logic Programming*, Vol 3, D. M. Gabbay *et al.*, eds. pp. 35–110, Oxford University Press, 1994.

[Nebel, 1989] B. Nebel. A knowledge-level Analysis of belief revision. In *Principles of Knowledge Representation and Reasoning : Proceedings of the First International Conference*, R. Brachman, H. Levesque and R. Reiter eds. pp. 2301–311. Morgan Kaufmann, San Mateo, CA, 1989.

[Rott, 1993] H. Rott. Belief contraction in the context of the general theory of rational choice, *Journal of Symbolic Logic*, **58**, 1426–1450, 1993.

HASSAN BEZZAZI

REVISION AND UPDATE BASED ON STRATIFIED FORWARD CHAINING

1 INTRODUCTION

In this work we reconsider some of the properties of nonmonotonic logic [Gabbay, 1985; Kraus *et al.*, 1990] and change operators [Alchourrón *et al.*, 1985; Katsuno and Mendelzon, 1990; Darwiche and Pearl, 1994] which were established using classical logic as being the object language in a less rich framework but yet enough expressive to consider some interesting situations. Pieces of knowledge are represented as literals and rules. The inference engine we propose to represent the underlying logic of the agent is based on an ordered stratification of the set of literals appearing in the knowledge base which consists of a finite set of rules. Given such a stratification, elementary forward chaining steps are achieved along its strata starting from the first one which is taken to be the input set of literals (the basic facts). The literals generated this way are combined in such a way that the specific information is privileged over less specific information when they conflict each other. Forward chaining allows for efficient computations as it is the case with inheritance systems which are known to be efficient nonmonotonic systems. An eminent property of stratified forward chaining is Consistency Preservation which makes the consistency of the consequences depend only on the consistency of the set of literals which the inference operation starts from.

This work was motivated by previous work on change operators and forward chaining [Bezzazi *et al.*, 1997] which in its turn was motivated by the concern to extend the set of conclusions obtained from a knowledge base and an exceptional information by extending the so called ranked revision. Ranked revision consists in computing the consequences of a set of literals by forward chaining using a subset of the set of rules for which it is consistent. This subset is computed in a precise way using forward chaining. However the conclusions it yields miss many others one would intuitively expect by using some kind of transitivity for instance [Bezzazi *et al.*, 1996]. It is precisely this kind of say cautious transitivity that we are attempting to catch by stratified forward chaining.

The paper is organized as follows: In Section 2 we give basic definitions and notations. In particular we recall the conditions usually required to be satisfied by a consequence operation [Makinson, 1994]. These conditions are relativized to our framework and the Consistency Preservation condition is then introduced. In Section 3 we define an operation called cautious extension which roughly speaking extends a consistent set of literals by those literals of another set that preserve consistency. This operation is used to define in Section 4 an inference operation called

M.-A. Williams and H. Rott (eds.), Frontiers in Belief Revision, 315–331.

stratified forward chaining. We describe in this section how to construct the stratification upon which the inference is based. In Section 5 we emphasize the nonmonotonic properties of stratified forward chaining by relativizing to our framework the rules of preferential logic [Kraus *et al.*, 1990]. In Section 6 we show that given any syntactical consequence operation satisfying our relativized version of Inclusion, Idempotence, Cautious Monotony and Consistency Preservation a natural revision operator is defined which satisfy our relativized version of AGM postulates for revision operators. This revision operator makes a fundamental use of cautious extension. It is also shown that iterated revision is rather well supported. In section 6 we do the same as in Section 7 by considering update operators instead of revision operators with respect to the Katsuno and Mendelzon postulates [Katsuno and Mendelzon, 1990]. In Section 8 we show the consistency and the completeness of stratified forward chaining for the well known inference in inheritance systems based on preemption when these systems are unambiguous[Horty *et al.*, 1990; Gregoire, 1989]. Finally in our conclusion we outline some of the issues that have drawn our attention while writing this paper.

2 PRELIMINARIES

Let At be the set of atoms. A literal is an atom or a negation of an atom. The set of literals is $Lit = At \cup \neg At$. However we may use a succession of $\neg$ before an atom which is to be reduced in the usual way by erasing the occurrences of two successive $\neg$.

A rule is a sentence of the shape $l_1, l_2, \ldots, l_n \to l_{n+1}$ where $n > 0$ and l_i is a literal for $i = 1, \ldots, n+1$.

A knowledge base is a finite set rules.

The fact that we do not consider rules with empty body is due to the fact that these particular rules denote actually literals for which we have reserved a special treatment through revision and update processes as we shall see in related sections. However, in the more general case where these rules are allowed, R will be partitioned into $R_0 \cup R_1$ where R_0 is the set of rules with empty body and we will focus on R_1 as being the set of rules and think of R_0 as a set of literals representing the input information over which the inference procedure will start.

A set of literals is said to be consistent if it does not contain two opposite literals, *i.e.* an atom and its negation.

The consistent part of a set of literals L is the set $\tilde{L}$ which is obtained by removing from L all opposite literals.

Let R and L be a finite set of rules and a finite set of literals respectively.

A rule $r \in R$ is L-fireable iff its body is in L.

We define the set of consequences of L by one-step forward chaining with respect to R as:

$fc(R, L) = L \cup \{l \in Lit : l_1, l_2, \ldots, l_n \to l$ is an L-fireable rule of $R\}$.

Let $\{L_i\}_{i\in\omega}$ be the sequence defined by:
(i) $L_0 = L$
(ii) $L_{i+1} = fc(R, L_i)$
The closure of L by forward chaining w.r.t. R is defined by:

$$C_{fc}(R, L) = \cup_{i\in\omega} L_i$$

Notice that it is easily established that if $L' \subseteq C_{fc}(R, L)$ then $C_{fc}(R, L \cup L') = C_{fc}(R, L)$

In the AGM classical framework, the beliefs of the agent are represented in a propositional language closed under the usual connectives $\neg, \wedge, \vee$ and $\rightarrow$ and any consequence operation used to represent the underlying logic of the agent is required to satisfy some conditions called Inclusion, Idempotence, Monotony, Supraclassicality, Deduction and Compactness [Makinson, 1994]. However when we take instead of the propositional language a language which is closed only under conjunction starting from literals and when we consider a syntactical consequence operation $\mathcal{C}$, Supraclassicality turns out to be equivalent to Inclusion and Deduction doesn't make sense anymore because of the absence of implication as a connective in our language. Therefore in our framework the conditions above reduce to the four conditions:

Inclusion: $L \subseteq \mathcal{C}(L)$
Idempotence: $\mathcal{C}(\mathcal{C}(L)) = \mathcal{C}(L)$
Monotony: $\mathcal{C}(L) \subseteq \mathcal{C}(L')$ whenever $L \subseteq L'$
Compactness: If $l \in \mathcal{C}(L)$ then $l \in \mathcal{C}(L')$ for some finite $L' \subseteq L$.

As a matter of fact forward chaining satisfy the four of these conditions[1] and was investigated as a consequence operation underlying the definition of syntactical revision operators in [Bezzazi *et al.*, 1997]. The main idea in this paper is to investigate consequence operations which satisfy these conditions except eventually the monotony condition (so it is a nonmonotonic consequence operation). Instead we will require Cautious Monotony [Makinson, 1994] and an additional condition called Consistency Preservation:

Cautious Monotony: If $L \subseteq \mathcal{C}(L')$ then $\mathcal{C}(L') \subseteq \mathcal{C}(L \cup L')$
Consistency Preservation: If L is consistent then $\mathcal{C}(L)$ is consistent.

Notice that when $\mathcal{C}$ satisfies Inclusion then Consistency Preservation is equivalent to saying that L is consistent iff $\mathcal{C}(L)$ is consistent. In the sequel we will refer to a consequence operation that satisfies Inclusion, Idempotence, Cautious Monotony and Consistency preservation as an **admissible** consequence operation. It is easily established that if $\mathcal{C}$ satisfies Inclusion, Idempotence and Cautious

[1]Compactness is true for any syntactic consequence when the set of rules is finite as long as propositional calculus is concerned which will be always the case in this paper.

Monotony then it also satisfies the Cut property and hence the property of cumulativity:

Cut: If $L \subseteq \mathcal{C}(L')$ then $\mathcal{C}(L \cup L') \subseteq \mathcal{C}(L')$
Cumulativity: If $L \subseteq \mathcal{C}(L')$ then $\mathcal{C}(L') = \mathcal{C}(L \cup L')$

3 CAUTIOUS EXTENSION

We will use in the sequel of this paper an operation on sets of literals called cautious extension. This is a simple and yet a fundamental operation for the stratified forward chaining as well as for the revision operation we shall define. Cautious extension denoted by $\oplus$ is the non commutative binary operation on sets of literals defined by:

$$L \oplus L' = L \cup (L' - \{l \in L' : \neg l \in L\})$$

So $L \oplus L'$ is the extension of L by literals of L' that are not opposite to literals in L.

Some of the properties of this operation are listed in the following lemma. Their proof is quite straightforward.

LEMMA 1 (Properties of $\oplus$). *The following properties hold for any sets of literals L, L', L'':*
(i) $L \subseteq L \oplus L'$
(ii) $L \oplus L' \subseteq L \cup L'$
(iii) $\oplus$ *is associative:* $(L \oplus L') \oplus L'' = L \oplus (L' \oplus L'')$
(iv) If $L' \subseteq L \oplus L''$ *then* $L' \subseteq L \oplus (L' \oplus L'')$
(v) If $L' \cup L''$ *is consistent then* $(L \oplus L') \cup L'' = (L \cup L'') \oplus L'$
(vi) If $(L \oplus L') \cup L''$ *is consistent then* $(L \oplus L') \cup L'' = (L \cup L'') \oplus L'$

Proof.

(i) and (ii) are immediate by definition of $L \oplus L'$

(iii) We show only one inclusion namely $(L \oplus L') \oplus L'' \subset L \oplus (L' \oplus L'')$, the other inclusion has a similar proof.

let $l \in (L \oplus L') \oplus L''$.

If $l \in L$ then $l \in L \oplus (L' \oplus L'')$ else necessarily $\neg l \notin L$ and if $l \in L'$ then $l \in L' \oplus L''$ and so $l \in L \oplus (L' \oplus L'')$. If $l \in L''$ and $l \notin L \cup L'$ then $\neg l \notin L'$ otherwise $\neg l \in L \oplus L'$ and then $l \notin (L \oplus L') \oplus L''$. But then $l \in L' \oplus L''$ and since $\neg l \notin L, l \in L \oplus (L' \oplus L'')$

(iv) let $L' \subset L \oplus L''$ and $l \in L'$. If $l \in L$ then $l \in L \oplus (L' \oplus L'')$. If $l \notin L$ then necessarily $l \in L''$ and $\neg l \notin L$. Now since $l \in L' \oplus L''$ and $\neg l \notin L$, $l \in L \oplus (L' \oplus L'')$. So $L' \subset L \oplus (L' \oplus L'')$. Conversely, let L' be a set of literals such that $L' \subset L \oplus (L' \oplus L'')$ and $l \in L'$. If $l \in L$ then $l \in L \oplus L''$ else necessarily $l \in L' \oplus L''$

(v) This is easily seen.

(vi) $(L \oplus L') \cup L'' = L \cup L' - \{l \in L' : \neg l \in L\} \cup L'' = (L \cup L'') \cup L' - \{l \in L' : \neg l \in L\}$. Since $(L \oplus L') \cup L''$ is consistent by hypothesis the set $\{l \in L : \neg l \in L''\}$ is empty and we can write $(L \oplus L') \cup L'' = (L \cup L'') \cup L' - \{l \in L' : \neg l \in L\} - \{l \in L' : \neg l \in L''\}$ which can be written again $(L \oplus L') \cup L'' = (L \cup L'') \cup L' - \{l \in L' : \neg l \in (L \cup L'')\} = (L \cup L'') \oplus L'$ ■

4 STRATIFIED FORWARD CHAINING

The inference engine we propose to produce the deductions of the agent is based on a particular ordered stratification of the set of literals appearing in the knowledge base. Given this stratification, elementary forward chaining steps are achieved in a way to be described later along its strata in an ascending order. This inference works in such a way that more specific knowledge overrides less specific knowledge as dictated by the specificity principle.

DEFINITION 2 (Stratification). Let R be a non-empty set of rules. Let $Lit(R)$ be the set of literals that appear in R. We say that the sequence $\langle S_1, \ldots, S_n \rangle$ is a stratification for R iff it is a partition of $Lit(R)$ such that if $l_1, l_2, \ldots, l_p \to l$ is a rule of R then: $\forall k \in [1..p] : stratum(l_k) < stratum(l)$ where $stratum(l) = i$ iff $l \in S_i$. R is said to be stratified iff its set of stratifications is not empty. A stratification is said to be based on a set of literals L iff it is a stratification for R/L which is the subset of R that consists of all $C_{fc}(R, L)$-fireable rules of R[2].

In general, we have many stratifications for a given set of rules. We will define an ordering over these stratifications where, roughly speaking, a stratification is preferred to another one when it is more compact and specific, that is the second one can be obtained from the first one by exploding some of its strata into subsets (so it is less compact) and/or by shifting some of its strata to the right (so it is less specific).

EXAMPLE 3. Take for example the set of rules which codes the knowledge that bats are animals that fly, animals that fly are typically birds and bats are not birds (actually mammals): $R = \{bat \to animal, bat \to fly, animal \wedge fly \to bird, bat \to \neg bird\}$. Four of the stratifications of R are: $\Sigma_1 = \langle \{bat\}, \{animal\}, \{fly\}, \{bird\}, \{\neg bird\} \rangle$
$\Sigma_2 = \langle \{bat\}, \{animal\}, \{fly\}, \{\neg bird\}, \{bird\} \rangle$
$\Sigma_3 = \langle \{bat\}, \{animal\}, \{fly, \neg bird\}, \{bird\} \rangle$
$\Sigma_4 = \langle \{bat\}, \{animal, fly, \neg bird\}, \{bird\} \rangle$
Σ_4 will be preferred to Σ_3 which is preferred to Σ_2 which itself is preferred to Σ_1. Σ_1 is obtained from Σ_2 by shifting $\{\neg bird\}$, Σ_2 is obtained from Σ_3 by exploding $\{fly, \neg bird\}$ into $\{fly\}$, $\{\neg bird\}$ and Σ_3 is obtained from Σ_4 by exploding $\{animal, fly, \neg bird\}$ into $\{animal\}$, $\{fly, \neg bird\}$.

---

[2]It is a simple fact that if R is stratified then so is R/L.

The following definition formalizes these ideas through a partial ordering over stratifications.

DEFINITION 4 (Ordering). We now define the decreasing lexicographical ordering $\prec$ on the set of stratifications augmented by the empty sequence ε of a stratified set of rules.
(i) $\varepsilon \prec \Sigma$ for any stratification Σ,
(ii) if $\Sigma = \langle S_1, \ldots, S_n \rangle$ and $\Sigma' = \langle S'_1, \ldots, S'_p \rangle$ are two non empty stratifications then $\Sigma \prec \Sigma'$ iff $S'_1 \subseteq S_1$ and $S_1 \neq S'_1$ or $S_1 = S'_1$ and $\langle S_2, \ldots, S_n \rangle \prec \langle S'_2, \ldots, S'_p \rangle$

Stratification will generate an order in the application of rules in accordance with the specificity principle. Among the many stratifications of R one is of first importance for our inference engine. It is the "most preferred" stratification in the sense described above.

PROPOSITION 5. *Let R be a stratified set of rules. The ordering $\prec$ over its stratifications has a least element.*

Proof. We are going to give an algorithm that computes a stratification which we shall prove is the least stratification w.r.t. $\prec$. ■

DEFINITION 6 (Best stratification). The best stratification of a stratified set of rules R is the least stratification of R according to $\prec$.

We will denote the best stratification of a stratified set of rules R by $\Sigma(R) = \langle S_1(R), \ldots, S_n(R) \rangle$

4.1 *Computing the best stratification of a stratified set of rules*

We give in this subsection an algorithm that assigns to the literals appearing in R the rank of their stratum. The definition of the function $stratum$ is extended to sets of literals as $stratum(L) = \{stratum(l) : l \in L\}$. $head(\Delta)$ is the set of literals that appear in the head of a rule of Δ.

```
Algorithm:
Input:  A non empty set of rules R={Lᵢ →lᵢ:1≤i≤n}
Output:  the best stratification of R if it is stratified
let Δ=R
for all l∈Lit(Δ) let stratum(l)=0
let h=1
repeat
   for all l∈Lit(Δ)
      if l∉head(Δ)and stratum(l)=0 then set stratum(l)=h
   Let Δ'={L→l∈ Δ:max(stratum(L))=h and min(stratum(L))≠0}
   set Δ = Δ − Δ' and set h=h+1
   for all l∈head(Δ') if l∉Lit(Δ) then set stratum(l)=h
until Δ' is empty
```

```
if Δ is empty then
   %define the best stratification%
   for all j∈[1..h] set Sj={l∈Lit(R):stratum(l)=j}
else R is not stratified.
```

To make clear the way this algorithm works, think of a dependance graph where nodes represent the different literals that appear in R and where each directed link from a literal l' to another literal l represents the dependance of l on l', *i.e.* the occurrence of l' in the body of a rule of R which head is l. The algorithm will recognize if this graph is acyclic by forming strata in a bottom-up way. First, all literals that depend on no literal are put in the first stratum, secondly among the remaining literals all those that depend only on those of the first stratum are put in the second stratum, thirdly among the remaining literals all those that depend only on those of the first and second strata are put in the third stratum ...and so on. If R is stratified this construction will succeed in assigning a stratum to all the literals of R, otherwise the corresponding graph is cyclic and the literals that are implied in cycles would not be assigned a stratum.

PROPOSITION 7. *The algorithm above computes the least stratification of R w.r.t. $\prec$.*

Proof. (Sketch of proof.) The repeat loop terminates because at each step of the loop Δ' is set to a subset of Δ which cardinal is strictly decreased if Δ' is not empty by setting Δ to $\Delta - \Delta'$. If after the repeat loop Δ is not empty then it contains precisely those rules that prevent the stratification by forming cycles. If it is empty then it is easy to see that the sequence $\langle S_1, \ldots, S_h \rangle$ computed by the algorithm is a partition of $Lit(R)$ since each literal of $Lit(R)$ has been assigned a unique stratum by the algorithm. It is also easy to see that it is a stratification since given a rule $l_1, l_2, \ldots, l_p \rightarrow l$ of R all of the literals of its body are assigned a stratum in the algorithm before l. Indeed, for the current set of rules Δ, this assignment is done for the literals that do not appear as a head of a rule. Now we show that it is the best stratification. Let $\langle S'_1, \ldots, S'_n \rangle$ be some stratification of R. It is easy to see that $S'_1 \subseteq S_1$. If $S_1 \neq S'_1$ we are done, otherwise let $k > 1$ be the least integer s.t. $S_k \neq S'_k$ and let l be a literal in S'_k. We denote by $head^{-1}(l)$ the set of rules r of R s.t. $head(r) = l$ and we denote by Since $\langle S'_1, \ldots, S'_n \rangle$ is a stratification $body(head^{-1}(l)) \subseteq \cup_{1 \leq i \leq j} S'_i$ for some $j < k$. So $body(head^{-1}(l)) \subset \cup_{1 \leq i \leq j} S_i$ by hypothesis. Now the algorithm runs precisely s.t. $j = k - 1$ since $l \notin \cup_{1 \leq i \leq j} S_i$. So $l \in S_{j+1} = S_k$. Indeed, the assignment of a stratum to a literal l is achieved inside the repeat loop of the algorithm either in the body of the first for statement or in the body of the second for statement. Notice then that this assignment is done once and it is done as soon as all the literals in $body(head^{-1}(l))$ have been assigned a stratum. Thus $S'_k \subset S_k$ and $\langle S_1, \ldots, S_n \rangle \prec \langle S'_1, \ldots, S'_p \rangle$ ■

REMARK 8. In the sequel we shall abbreviate for convenience $fc(R, L)$, $C_{fc}(R, L)$ and $S_i(R/L)$, to respectively $fc(L)$, $C_{fc}(L)$ and $S_i(L)$ as long as no ambiguity is encountered. We will also use the following notations:

$\mathbf{S}_{<i+1}(L) = \mathbf{S}_{\leq i}(L) = \cup_{1\leq j\leq i} S_j(L)$,
$\mathbf{S}_{>i}(L) = \mathbf{S}_{\geq i+1}(L) = \cup_{i<j\leq n} S_j(L)$.

The following central definition describes the application of stratified forward chaining to a set of literals L according to a set of rules R. It uses three ingredients which are the best stratification of R/L, cautious extension and forward chaining. Intuitively, stratified forward chaining is based on a succession of elementary forward chaining steps along the strata of the best stratification. At each step, forward chaining is applied to the cautious union of the results of previous steps. Cautious extension ensures that, at a given step, if a result contradicts previous results, it is ignored.

DEFINITION 9. Let R and L be respectively a set of rules and a set of literals. We define the stratified forward chaining of L with R, denoted $C_s(L)$ in two steps. First we define the sequence $\bar{\Sigma}(L) = \langle \bar{S}_1(L), \ldots, \bar{S}_n(L)\rangle$ by:
$\bar{S}_1(L) = L$
$\bar{S}_{i+1}(L) = \widetilde{fc}(\bar{\mathbf{S}}_{\leq i}(L) \cap \mathbf{S}_{\leq i}(L))$ for $i = 1, ..., n-1$
where $\bar{\mathbf{S}}_{\leq i}(L) = \oplus_{1\leq j\leq i} \bar{S}_j(L)$
Then we put:

$$C_s(L) = \bar{\mathbf{S}}_{\leq n}(L) = \oplus_{1\leq i\leq n} \bar{S}_i(L)$$

REMARK 10. Given a stratified set of rules R and a set of literals L, it is easy to see that, by definition, stratified forward chaining satisfies the Inclusion and the Consistency Preservation condition and therefore the only case where $C_s(L)$ is inconsistent is when L is inconsistent. Notice also that if $l \in C_s(L)$ and $stratum(l) = p$ then $l \in \oplus_{1\leq i\leq p} \bar{S}_i(L)$.

LEMMA 11. *If* $L' \subseteq Lit(R/L)$ *then* $R/(L \cup L') = R/L$

Proof. $R/(L \cup L')$ consists of all $C_{fc}(L \cup L')$-fireable rules of R. Since $L' \subseteq Lit(R/L)$ and $Lit(R/L) = C_{fc}(R, L)$ we have $L' \subseteq C_{fc}(L)$. So $C_{fc}(L \cup L') = C_{fc}(L)$ and then $R/L \cup L' = R/L$ ■

REMARK 12. Restraining the stratification operation to R/L when computing $C_s(L)$ instead of stratifying the entire R is a technical point. If we just use the stratification of R, this computation may be complicated by literals which are irrelevant for the information in L and which alter the stratification based on L. Consider for example $R = \{a \to b, a' \to b, a \to \neg b, c \to c', c' \to \neg b\}$ and $L = \{a, a'\}$. The best stratification for R yields three strata, $S_1 = \{a, a', c\}$, $S_2 = \{b, c'\}$ and $S_3 = \{\neg b\}$ while the best stratification based on L yields two strata, $S_1 = \{a, a'\}$ and $S_2 = \{b, \neg b\}$.

LEMMA 13. *If* $l \in C_s(L)$ *then* $\bar{S}_i(L \cup l) = \bar{S}_i(L)$ *for* $i = 2, ..., n$

Proof. Suppose $stratum(l) = k$. $\bar{S}_i(L \cup l) = \widetilde{fc}(\bar{\mathbf{S}}_{<i}(L \cup l) \cap \mathbf{S}_{<i}(L \cup l))$ for $i = 2, ..., n$. Since by the previous lemma $R/(L \cup l) = R/L$ we have: $\bar{S}_i(L \cup l) = \widetilde{fc}(\bar{\mathbf{S}}_{<i}(L \cup l) \cap \mathbf{S}_{<i}(L))$ for $i = 2, ..., n$

case $i = 2$: By definition we have $\bar{S}_1(L \cup l) = L \cup l$, so $\bar{S}_2(L \cup l) = \widetilde{fc}(\bar{\mathbf{S}}_{\leq 1}(L \cup l) \cap \mathbf{S}_{\leq 1}(L)) = \widetilde{fc}(L \cup l \cap S_1(L))$. If $k \geq 2$ then $\widetilde{fc}(L \cup l \cap S_1(L)) = \widetilde{fc}(\bar{S}_1(L) \cap S_1(L)) = \bar{S}_2(L)$.

Suppose the equality $\bar{S}_i(L \cup l) = \bar{S}_i(L)$ true for $2 \leq i \leq p$ with $p < n$ and let us prove it is also true for $p+1$.We have $\bar{S}_{p+1}(L \cup l) = \widetilde{fc}(\bar{\mathbf{S}}_{\leq p}(L \cup l) \cap \mathbf{S}_{\leq p}(L \cup l))$ and by induction hypothesis:
$\bar{S}_{p+1}(L \cup l) = \widetilde{fc}((\oplus_{1 \leq j \leq p} \bar{S}_j(L) \cup l) \cap \mathbf{S}_{\leq p}(L))$. If $k > p$ then $\bar{S}_{p+1}(L \cup l) = \widetilde{fc}(\oplus_{1 \leq j \leq p} \bar{S}_j(L) \cap \mathbf{S}_{\leq p}(L))$. If $k \leq p$ then $l \in \oplus_{1 \leq j \leq p} \bar{S}_j(L)$ since $l \in \oplus_{1 \leq i \leq k} \bar{S}_i(L)$ by the remark above and $\oplus_{1 \leq i \leq k} \bar{S}_i(L) \subset \oplus_{1 \leq j \leq p} \bar{S}_j(L)$. So in both cases we have $\bar{S}_{p+1}(L \cup l) = \bar{S}_{p+1}(L)$ ■

PROPOSITION 14. *If $L' \subseteq C_s(L)$ then $\bar{S}_i(L \cup L') = \bar{S}_i(L)$ for $i = 2, ..., n$*

Proof. The property is trivially true when $L' = \emptyset$.

Suppose the property true for any set $L' \subseteq C_s(L)$ of cardinality k and let us prove that it is also true for $L' \cup l$ when $l \in C_s(L) = C_s(L \cup L')$. We have $\bar{S}_i(L \cup L' \cup l) = \bar{S}_i(L \cup L')$ for $i = 2, ..., n$ by the previous lemma and then $\bar{S}_i(L \cup L' \cup l) = \bar{S}_i(L)$ for $i = 2, ..., n$ by hypothesis ■

5 CONNECTION WITH NONMONOTONIC LOGICS

In this section we check some of the properties similar to those of nonmonotonic logic as stated in preferential logics [Kraus *et al.*, 1990]. We are interested in literals one can infer from the set of rules R according to the inference relation defined by $L \mid\!\sim_s L'$ iff $L' \subseteq C_s(L)$.

DEFINITION 15. The four properties called Reflexivity, And, Cautious Monotony and Cut for an inference relation $\mid\!\sim$ are given respectively by the following rules:

$$\textbf{REF} \quad \frac{}{L \mid\!\sim L}$$

$$\textbf{AND} \quad \frac{L \mid\!\sim L' \quad L \mid\!\sim L''}{L \mid\!\sim L' \cup L''}$$

$$\textbf{CM} \quad \frac{L \mid\!\sim L' \quad L \mid\!\sim L''}{L \cup L'' \mid\!\sim L'}$$

$$\textbf{CUT} \quad \frac{L \cup L' \mid\!\sim L'' \quad L \mid\!\sim L'}{L \mid\!\sim L''}$$

PROPOSITION 16. *The inference relation $\mid\!\sim_s$satisfies* **REF**, **AND**, **CM** *and* **CUT**.

Proof.

REF and AND are easily established.

CM: Suppose $L'' \subseteq C_s(L)$ and, without loss of generality, that $L'' \cap L = \emptyset$. By definition, $C_s(L \cup L'') = \oplus_{1 \leq i \leq n} \bar{S}_i(L \cup L'')$. Then by proposition 14 $C_s(L \cup L'') = (L \cup L'') \oplus (\oplus_{2 \leq i \leq n} \bar{S}_i(L))$. Now by 1 *(v)* we have $C_s(L \cup L'') = (L \oplus (\oplus_{2 \leq i \leq n} \bar{S}_i(L))) \cup L''$ since $L'' \subseteq \oplus_{2 \leq i \leq n} \bar{S}_i(L)$ given that $\oplus_{2 \leq i \leq n} \bar{S}_i(L)$ is consistent by construction. So $C_s(L \cup L'') = C_s(L) \cup L'' = C_s(L)$. Thus if $L' \subseteq C_s(L)$ and $L'' \subseteq C_s(L)$ then $L' \subseteq C_s(L \cup L'') = C_s(L)$.

CUT: Suppose that $L' \subseteq C_s(L \cup L'')$ and $L'' \subseteq C_s(L)$. We have just seen in CM above that in this case $C_s(L \cup L'') = C_s(L)$. So $L' \subseteq C_s(L)$ ■

The following corollary shows that the stratified forward chaining satisfies the Idempotence property and therefore it is an admissible consequence operation.

COROLLARY 17. $C_s(L) = C_s(C_s(L))$

Proof. In our proof of **CM** we have stated that if $L'' \subseteq C_s(L)$ then $C_s(L \cup L'') = C_s(L)$. So $C_s(L \cup C_s(L)) = C_s(L)$ because $C_s(L) \subseteq C_s(L)$ but we have also $C_s(L \cup C_s(L)) = C_s(C_s(L))$ because $L \subseteq C_s(L)$ ■

6 CONNECTION WITH REVISION THEORY

Instead of taking the propositional logic for representing the beliefs of the agent and instead of considering the classical consequence to be the logic of the agent as in AGM framework, we investigate an approach to belief revision where beliefs are expressed as literals and rules and the underlying logic is some admissible consequence operation $\mathcal{C}$ (*i.e.* satisfying the four properties of the introduction Inclusion, Idempotence, Cautious Monotony and Consistency preservation) *e.g.* stratified forward chaining.

We define the absolute revision of a set of literals L by another set of literals L' as follows

$$L \circ L' = L' \oplus \tilde{L}$$

Actually the revision operation should apply to a set of literals closed by the underlying consequence relation. Such a set is taken to be the belief set which represent the agent's epistemic state. In our setting we should focus on the definition of the operation $\mathcal{C}(L) * L'$ which returns a new belief set. In the definition we are to give for this operator the set L in $\mathcal{C}(L)$ is distinguished from the rest of the literals of $\mathcal{C}(L)$ as being its generator, a similar differentiation is done in [Williams, 1994]. The operator $*$ is defined by

$$\mathcal{C}(L) * L' = \mathcal{C}(L \circ L')$$

Similarly, we define the expansion operation of the knowledge base $\mathcal{C}(L)$ by the set of literals L as:

$$\mathcal{C}(L) + L' =_{def} \mathcal{C}(L \cup L')$$

Notice that this definition of expansion is not the same as with the classical one which would state: $\mathcal{C}(L) + L' = \mathcal{C}(L \cup \mathcal{C}(L'))$which does not hold in general with $\mathcal{C}$ being nonmonotonic.

The postulates we are about to give now ensure in particular that the revision of $\mathcal{C}(L)$ by L' coincides with its expansion by the same set when they are consistent to each other. These postulates constitute a relativized version to our framework of the classical revision postulates. We call them syntactical revision postulates because they define operators which are in general syntax-sensitive. In particular the postulate for irrelevance of syntax does not hold in general for these operators. $\bullet$ is an operation that takes as argument a couple of sets of literals. the first set is closed under the consequence operation of interest and represents the belief set to be revised by the second set. The result of this operation is a new belief set.

(SR1) $L' \subseteq \mathcal{C}(L) \bullet L'$

(SR2) If $\mathcal{C}(L) \cup L'$ is consistent, then $\mathcal{C}(L) \bullet L' = \mathcal{C}(L) + L'$

(SR3) If L' is consistent then $\mathcal{C}(L) \bullet L'$ is also consistent

(SR4) If $(\mathcal{C}(L) \bullet L') \cup L''$ is consistent then $\mathcal{C}(L) \bullet (L' \cup L'') = (\mathcal{C}(L) \bullet L') + L''$

PROPOSITION 18. *The operation $*$ satisfies the syntactical revision postulates.*

Proof. SR1: $L' \subseteq L' \oplus \tilde{L} \subseteq \mathcal{C}(L' \oplus \tilde{L}) = \mathcal{C}(L) * L'$ by the Inclusion property.

SR2: If $\mathcal{C}(L) \cup L'$ is consistent, then $L \circ L' = L' \cup L$. Now, since by definition of expansion, $\mathcal{C}(L) + L' = \mathcal{C}(L \cup L')$, we have $\mathcal{C}(L) + L' = \mathcal{C}(L \circ L') = \mathcal{C}(L) * L'$.

SR3: $\mathcal{C}(L) * L' = \mathcal{C}(L' \oplus \tilde{L})$ is consistent iff $L' \oplus \tilde{L}$ is consistent by the Consistency Preservation property and this is true iff L' is consistent by definition of cautious extension.

SR4: Suppose $(\mathcal{C}(L) * L') \cup L'' = \mathcal{C}(L \circ L') \cup L''$ is consistent. Since $(L' \oplus \tilde{L}) \cup L''$ is consistent by the Consistency Preservation property we have $(L \circ L') \cup L'' = (L' \oplus \tilde{L}) \cup L'' = (L' \cup L'') \oplus \tilde{L} = L \circ (L' \cup L'')$ by virtue of lemma 1 *(vi)*. So $\mathcal{C}(L) * (L' \cup L'') = \mathcal{C}(L \circ (L' \cup L'')) = \mathcal{C}((L \circ L') \cup L'')$ and then $\mathcal{C}(L) * (L' \cup L'') = \mathcal{C}(L \circ L') + L'' = (\mathcal{C}(L) * L') + L''$ ■

6.1 *Iterated revision*

Our definition for the revision operation makes very natural the definition of iterated revision since the input for revising by a given set of literals is a belief set as described above and the result of the revision is a new belief set which may in its turn be subject to revision by another set of literals and so on. The four relativized postulates proposed by Darwiche and Pearl [Darwiche and Pearl, 1994] to account for the iterated belief change are given below for a revision operation $\bullet$ defined as above.

(SR5) If $L' \subseteq L''$ then $(\mathcal{C}(L) \bullet L') \bullet L'' = \mathcal{C}(L) \bullet L''$

(SR6) If $L' \cup L''$ is inconsistent, then $(\mathcal{C}(L) \bullet L') \bullet L'' = \mathcal{C}(L) \bullet L''$

(SR7) If $L' \subseteq \mathcal{C}(L) \bullet L''$ then $L' \subseteq (\mathcal{C}(L) \bullet L') \bullet L''$

(SR8) If $\neg l \notin \mathcal{C}(L){\bullet}L''$ and $l \in L'$ then $\neg l \notin (\mathcal{C}(L){\bullet}L'){\bullet}L''$

PROPOSITION 19. *Supposing that all of* L, L' *and* L'' *are consistent the revision operation* $*$ *satisfies three of the four relativized postulates above and fails to satisfy* ***(SR6)****.*

Proof. SR5: Indeed $(\mathcal{C}(L) * L') * L'' = \mathcal{C}(L'' \oplus \widetilde{(L' \oplus \tilde{L})}) = \mathcal{C}(L'' \oplus (L' \oplus L)) = \mathcal{C}((L'' \oplus L') \oplus L)$ and so $(\mathcal{C}(L) * L') * L'' = \mathcal{C}(L'' \oplus L) = \mathcal{C}(L) * L''$.

SR6: This rule is not satisfied. Take L, L' and L'' to be respectively $\{t\}, \{b, s\}$, $\{\neg s\}$ for example and consider $R = \emptyset$. Clearly $L' \cup L''$ is inconsistent and $(\mathcal{C}(L) * L') * L'' = \{t, b, \neg s\}$ and $\mathcal{C}(L) * L'' = \{t, \neg s\}$. This rule is actually counterintuitive for this example if we think of t as tweety, b as bird and s as singing in that there is no reason to reject b.

SR7: Suppose $L' \subseteq \mathcal{C}(L) * L''$, then $L' \cup L''$ is consistent by Consistency Preservation. $(\mathcal{C}(L) * L') * L'' = \mathcal{C}(L \circ (L' \circ L'')) = \mathcal{C}((L'' \oplus L') \oplus L) = \mathcal{C}((L'' \cup L') \oplus L)$. So by the lemma 1 *(v)* $(\mathcal{C}(L) * L') * L'' = \mathcal{C}((L'' \oplus L) \cup L')$ and then $(\mathcal{C}(L) * L') * L'' = \mathcal{C}(L'' \oplus L)$ by Cumulativity since $L' \subseteq \mathcal{C}(L) * L'' = \mathcal{C}(L'' \oplus L)$ by hypothesis.

SR8: Suppose $\neg l \in (\mathcal{C}(L) * L') * L'' = \mathcal{C}(L'' \oplus (L' \oplus L))$ and $l \in L'$. Then by Consistency Preservation $\neg l \in L''$. So $\neg l \in L'' \oplus L$ and then $\neg l \in \mathcal{C}(L'' \oplus \tilde{L}) = \mathcal{C}(L) * L''$. ■

REMARK 20. A property satisfied by $*$ and which has not been proposed as a postulate for iterated revision which generally deals with different operators is relative associativity:

(SR9) $(\mathcal{C}(L) * L') * L'' = \mathcal{C}(L) * (L' \circ L'')$

Indeed, $(\mathcal{C}(L) * L') * L'' = \mathcal{C}(L'' \oplus (L' \oplus L)) = \mathcal{C}((L'' \oplus L') \oplus L)$ and so $(\mathcal{C}(L) * L') * L'' = \mathcal{C}(L) * (L'' \oplus L') = \mathcal{C}(L) * (L' \circ L'')$

7 CONNECTION WITH UPDATE THEORY

We consider in this section our relativized version of the postulates proposed by Katsuno and Mendelzon [Katsuno and Mendelzon, 1990] to characterize the operation of updating a knowledge base. Here again as with the revision operation and for the same reasons we have dropped the postulate concerning the syntax independence. We have also dropped from the original setting two postulates (the two last ones) which deal with disjunctive formulas since in our setting formulas are only conjunction of literals. Consider an operation $\diamond$ that takes as argument a couple of sets of literals. The first set represents the data base to be updated by the second data set. The result of this operation is a new data base.$\diamond$ is said to be a syntactical update operator iff it satisfies the following postulates:

(SU1) $L' \subset \mathcal{C}(L \diamond L')$

(SU2) If $L' \subset \mathcal{C}(L)$ then $\mathcal{C}(L \diamond L') = \mathcal{C}(L)$

(SU3) If both L and L' are consistent then $L \diamond L'$ is also consistent.

(SU4) If $(L \diamond L') \cup L''$ is consistent then $\mathcal{C}(L \diamond (L' \cup L'')) \subset \mathcal{C}((L \diamond L') \cup L'')$

(SU4') If $(L \diamond L') \cup L''$ is inconsistent then so is $\mathcal{C}((L \diamond L') \cup L'')$

(SU5) Suppose both of $L \diamond L'$ and $L \diamond L''$ are consistent then if $L'' \subset \mathcal{C}(L \diamond L')$ and $L' \subset \mathcal{C}(L \diamond L'')$ then $\mathcal{C}(L \diamond L') = \mathcal{C}(L \diamond L'')$

We now check that the absolute revision operator $\circ$ defined above satisfies these postulates when $\mathcal{C}$ is a syntactical consequence operation that satisfies the four properties above.

PROPOSITION 21. *The operator* $\circ$ *defined by* $L \circ L' = L' \oplus \tilde{L}$ *is a syntactical update operator*

Proof.

SU1: $L' \subset \mathcal{C}(L \circ L') = \mathcal{C}(L) * L'$ is an immediate consequence of (R1) above.

SU2: Suppose $L' \subset \mathcal{C}(L)$. It follows that $L \circ L' = L \cup L'$ and then $\mathcal{C}(L \circ L') = \mathcal{C}(L \cup L') = \mathcal{C}(L)$ since $\mathcal{C}$ is cumulative.

SU3: This is trivial since $L \circ L' = L' \oplus \tilde{L}$ is consistent iff L' is consistent.

SU4: This is an immediate consequence of (SR4).

SU4': This is immediate from the property of consistency preservation enjoyed by $\mathcal{C}$.

SU5: If $L'' \subset \mathcal{C}(L \circ L')$ and $L' \subset \mathcal{C}(L \circ L'')$ then $\mathcal{C}(L \circ L') = \mathcal{C}((L \circ L') \cup L'')$ and $\mathcal{C}(L \circ L'') = \mathcal{C}((L \circ L'') \cup L')$ by the property of cumulativity enjoyed by $\mathcal{C}$. Now if $L \circ L'$ and $L \circ L''$ are supposed consistent then all of $(L \circ L') \cup L''$, $(L \circ L'') \cup L'$ and $L' \cup L''$ are consistent and hence $(L \circ L') \cup L'' = (L \circ L') \circ L'' = L \circ (L' \circ L'') = L \circ (L' \cup L'')$ and similarly $(L \circ L'') \cup L' = (L \circ L'') \circ L' = L \circ (L'' \circ L') = L \circ (L'' \cup L')$ and so $\mathcal{C}(L \circ L') = \mathcal{C}(L \circ (L' \cup L'')) = \mathcal{C}(L \circ L'')$ ■

8 CONNECTION WITH INFERENCE IN INHERITANCE SYSTEMS

Inheritance systems are directed acyclic graphs where links between nodes may be positive ($x \rightarrow y$) or negative ($x \not\rightarrow y$). A path is a sequence of positive links and is then called positive or a sequence of positive links followed by a negative link and is then called negative. A path is conflicted in a given inheritance network if there exists another path of apposite sign with the same starting and ending nodes. Preemption resp. preclusion is the strategy that helps resolving this kind of conflict in favor of the path with more direct information about the ending node, *i.e.* with a direct link from an earlier node in the path. Here again, which actually motivates the definition of stratified forward chaining, the central idea is that arguments based on more specific knowledge override arguments based on less specific knowledge. In order to compare stratified forward chaining to the inference in an inheritance system based on preemption, we give the following definition for inheritance systems.

DEFINITION 22. A set of rules Γ is an inheritance system (or inheritance network) iff all of its rules (or links) are of the shape $l \rightarrow l'$ where l is a positive literal and for any positive literal $l \in lit(\Gamma), \neg l \notin \widetilde{fc}(l)$. A path over Γ is a finite sequence $\{l_i \rightarrow l_{i+1}\}_{1 \leq i \leq n}$ henceforth denoted as $l_1 \rightarrow l_2 \rightarrow ... \rightarrow l_{n+1} (n \geq 1)$ where all of the literals are positive except possibly the last. Two rules are said to be contradictory iff they have the same body and opposite heads. An inheritance network Γ is said to be non contradictory iff it does not contain contradictory rules.

We give now the definition of a valid path σ in an inheritance network Γ which is denoted by $\Gamma \models \sigma$. This definition is at the basis of the inference mechanism in inheritance systems.

DEFINITION 23.

1. If $l \rightarrow l' \in \Gamma$ then $\Gamma \models l \rightarrow l'$

2. Let $\sigma = l \rightarrow \sigma_1 \rightarrow l_1 \rightarrow l'$ be a path in Γ, then $\Gamma \models \sigma$ iff

- **(i)** $\Gamma \models l \rightarrow \sigma_1 \rightarrow l_1$
- **(ii)** $l_1 \rightarrow l' \in \Gamma$
- **(iii)** $l \rightarrow \neg l' \notin \Gamma$
- **(iv)** for any node $l'' \in lit(\Gamma)$ such that $\Gamma \models l \rightarrow \tau \rightarrow l''$ and $l'' \rightarrow \neg l' \in \Gamma$ there is a node l_0 such that $\Gamma \models l \rightarrow \tau_1 \rightarrow l_0 \rightarrow \tau_2 \rightarrow l''$ and $l_0 \rightarrow l'$.

Let $\mid\!\sim_\Gamma$ be the inference relation defined on $lit(\Gamma)$ by $l \mid\!\sim_\Gamma l'$ iff $\Gamma \models l \rightarrow \sigma \rightarrow l'$ for some (possibly empty) path σ. Non contradictory inheritance networks enjoy the soundness property [Horty *et al.*, 1990]:

PROPOSITION 24. *If Γ is a non contradictory inheritance network then:*
$l \mid\!\sim_\Gamma l' \Rightarrow l \not\mid\!\sim_\Gamma \neg l'$

DEFINITION 25. The inheritance network Γ is said to be unambiguous iff it is non contradictory and:
$(l \mid\!\sim_\Gamma l_0 \text{ and } l_0 \rightarrow l'' \in \Gamma) \Rightarrow (\, l \not\mid\!\sim_\Gamma \neg l'' \Leftrightarrow l \mid\!\sim_\Gamma l''\,)$.

The following proposition states that stratified forward chaining is coherent with the inference relation defined by Horty et al. [Horty *et al.*, 1990] when the underlying network is unambiguous.

PROPOSITION 26. *Let Γ be a non ambiguous inheritance network and let $\mid\!\sim_\Gamma$ be the inference relation defined on $lit(\Gamma)$ by $l \mid\!\sim_\Gamma l'$ iff $\Gamma \models l \rightarrow \sigma \rightarrow l'$ for some (possibly empty) path σ, then $l \mid\!\sim_\Gamma l'$ iff $l' \in C_s(l)$ and $l \neq l'$*

Proof. l being fixed the proof is done by induction on $stratum(l')$. If $l \mid\!\sim_\Gamma l'$ or $l' \in C_{sfc}(l)$ then $stratum(l') \geq 2$. (base case) Suppose $stratum(l') = 2$ then necessarily $l \rightarrow l' \in \Gamma$ and so $l \mid\!\sim_\Gamma l'$ by definition of $\mid\!\sim_\Gamma$. On the other hand $l' \in \widetilde{fc}(l)$ since Γ is non contradictory. Now $C_{sfc}(l) = \cup_{1 \leq i \leq n} \bar{S}_i(l)$ with

$\bar{S}_1(l) = \{l\}$ and $\bar{S}_2(l) = \widetilde{fc}(\bar{S}_1(l) \cap S_1(l)) = \widetilde{fc}(l)$ because $\bar{S}_1(l) = S_1(l) = \{l\}$. So $l' \in \bar{S}_2(l)$ and therefore $l' \in \bar{S}_1(l) \cup \bar{S}_2(l) \subset C_{sfc}(l)$.
(induction step) Suppose that the equivalence $l \mid\!\sim_\Gamma l'$ iff $l' \in C_{sfc}(l)$ and $l \neq l'$ holds for all l' such that $stratum(l') \leq p$ with $p \geq 2$. ($\Rightarrow$) Consider an l'' such that $l \mid\!\sim_\Gamma l''$ and $stratum(l'') = p + 1$. We have $\Gamma \models l \rightarrow \sigma \rightarrow l''$ for some non empty path $\sigma = \sigma_1 \rightarrow l'$. Let then σ be such a path with l' s.t. $stratum(l')$ is minimal. This implies that $\Gamma \models l \rightarrow \sigma$ and $l' \rightarrow l'' \in \Gamma$. Since $stratum(l') \leq p$ and $l \mid\!\sim_\Gamma l'$ we have $l' \in C_{sfc}(l)$. Let k be the least integer such that $l' \in \bar{S}_k(l)$ (we have then $k \leq stratum(l')$). Then $l'' \in \widetilde{fc}(\bar{\mathbf{S}}_{\leq k}(l) \cap \mathbf{S}_{\leq k}(l))$ unless $l_0 \rightarrow \neg l'' \in \Gamma$ for some $l_0 \in \bar{\mathbf{S}}_{\leq k}(l) \cap \mathbf{S}_{\leq k}(l)$. If this were the case then $l_0 \in C_{sfc}(l)$ and $stratum(l_0) \leq k \leq p$. Then by induction hypothesis $l \mid\!\sim_\Gamma l_0$. Now by the definition above for inference in inheritance networks there exists a literal l_1 such that $\Gamma \models l \rightarrow \tau_1 \rightarrow l_1 \rightarrow \tau_2 \rightarrow l_0$ and $l_1 \rightarrow l''$ for some paths τ_1 and τ_2. Notice then that $l \mid\!\sim_\Gamma l_1$ and $l_1 \rightarrow l''$ with $stratum(l_1) < k \leq stratum(l')$ which contradicts the fact that $stratum(l')$ is minimal. Thus $l'' \in \widetilde{fc}(\bar{\mathbf{S}}_{\leq k}(l) \cap \mathbf{S}_{\leq k}(l)) = \bar{S}_{k+1}(l) \subset C_{sfc}(l)$.

($\Leftarrow$) Conversely suppose $l'' \in C_{sfc}(l)$ and $l \neq l''$ then there is a rule $l_0 \rightarrow l'' \in \Gamma$ with $l_0 \in \bar{\mathbf{S}}_{\leq k}(l) \cap \mathbf{S}_{\leq k}(l)$ and $stratum(l_0) < p + 1$ minimal. So $l_0 \in C_{sfc}(l)$ and by induction hypothesis $l \mid\!\sim_\Gamma l_0$. Now since Γ is unambiguous $l \mid\!\sim_\Gamma l''$ unless $l \mid\!\sim_\Gamma \neg l''$. If this were the case then there is a node l_1 such that $\Gamma \models l \rightarrow \tau_1 \rightarrow l_1 \rightarrow \tau_2 \rightarrow l_0$ and $l_1 \rightarrow \neg l''$. We have then by induction hypothesis $l \mid\!\sim_\Gamma l_1$ since $stratum(l_1) < stratum(l_0) < p + 1$ and $l_1 \in \bar{S}_{k_1}(l)$ with $k_1 \leq stratum(l_1)$. Now $\neg l'' \in \widetilde{fc}(\bar{\mathbf{S}}_{\leq k_1}(l) \cap \mathbf{S}_{\leq k_1}(l))$ since $k_1 < stratum(l_0)$ and then $\neg l'' \in \widetilde{fc}(\bar{\mathbf{S}}_{\leq k_1}(l) \cap \mathbf{S}_{\leq k_1}(l)) \subset C_{sfc}(l)$ since $k_1 \leq stratum(l_1) < stratum(\neg l'')$ but we have supposed $l'' \in C_{sfc}(l)$ so necessarily $l \mid\!\sim_\Gamma l''$ ■

9 CONCLUSION

In this paper, we begun the investigation of a special kind of consequence operations for representing the rational agent underlying logic by strengthening a weaken version of the classical definition of such operations where the monotony property is dropped. Indeed, these consequence operations enjoy the Consistency Preservation condition which reduces the requirements on the theory inferred to requirements on the generator of the theory. In particular we presented one such consequence operation named stratified forward chaining which is close to reasoning over inheritance networks. Actually, we have generalized the idea of preemption as defined in the theory of inheritance systems as rules may have a set of literals as body and not only one positive literal. We think that such a generalization is desirable to avoid introducing artificial nodes in the inheritance system to represent the conjunction of concepts. It is clear that the knowledge base of our example would not be directly translated into an inheritance network *i.e.* by simply associating nodes to the literals. This is due precisely to the rule $animal \wedge fly \rightarrow bird$ which suggests the use of an extra node to represent its body.

Still much work has to be done. In this respect we list some of the issues for future work:

• Compare different stratified forward chaining with respect to the different stratifications they are based on.

• Investigate the combining of ranked revision and revision with stratified forward chaining.

• Define and investigate revision operators starting as we did in this paper from absolute revision but in the more general framework of propositional logic.

• Investigate the extension to the predicate case.

• Investigate the addition of priorities to the rules [Brewka, 1994].

As mentioned in the introduction, the main motivation in defining stratified forward chaining was the shortcoming of ranked revision in handling cautious transitivity also known as inheritance sanction [Benferhat *et al.*, 1995] which is a real drawback of many of the nonmonotonic logics proposed in the literature was it based on classical logic or forward chaining [Bezzazi *et al.*, 1996; Bezzazi *et al.*, 1997]. However this is not the only motivation since we were looking at the same time for a nonmonotonic system with a polynomial complexity. This is why we took the forward chaining as a basis for the inference mechanism. Our current work is dealing with the expressive power of stratified forward chaining in comparison with ranked revision an its extensions.

ACKNOWLEDGMENTS

Many thanks to the anonymous referees for their valuable comments which helped improving this paper.

University of Lille I, France.

REFERENCES

[Alchourrón *et al.*, 1985] C.E. Alchourrón, P. Gärdenfors and D. Makinson. On the logic of theory change. *Journal of Symbolic Logic*, **50**, 510–530, 1985.

[Bezzazi *et al.*, 1996] H. Bezzazi, D. Makinson, and R. Pino Pérez. Beyond rational monotony: some strong non-horn rules for nonmonotonic inference relations. *Journal of Logic and Computation*, **6**, 605–631, 1997

[Bezzazi *et al.*, 1997] H. Bezzazi, S. Janot, S. Konieczny and R. Pino Pérez. Analysing rational properties of change operators based on forward chaining. To appear in *Transactions and change in logic databases*. LNCS, Springer, 1998.

[Brewka, 1994] G. Brewka. Reasoning about priorities in default logic. In *Proceedings of AAAI-94*, Seattle, 1994.

[Darwiche and Pearl, 1994] A. Darwiche and J. Pearl. On the logic of iterated belief revision. In *Proceedings of the Fifth Conference on Theoretical Aspects of Reasoning about Knowledge*, R. Fagin, ed. pp. 5–23. Morgan Kauffman, Pacific Grove, CA. 1994.

[Benferhat *et al.*, 1995] S. Benferhat, D. Dubois and H. Prade. Connaissances conditionnelles et exceptions: du raisonnement non-monotone à la théorie des possibilités. *Revue d'intelligence artificielle*, **9**, 475–521, 1995.

[Gabbay, 1985] D. M. Gabbay. Theoretical foundations for non-monotonic reasoning in expert systems. In *Logics and Models of Concurrent Systems,* K. R. Apt, ed. pp. 439–457. Springer Verlag, Berlin, 1985.

[Gregoire, 1989] E. Gregoire. About the relationship between the skeptical theory of inheritance in semantic networks and general nonmonotonic logics. In *Proceedings of AAI Workshop on Formal Aspects of Semantic Networks*, Santa Catalina Island. pp. 37–50. 1989.

[Horty *et al.*, 1990] J. Horty, R. Thomason and D. Touretzky. A skeptical theory of inheritance in nonmonotonic networks.*Artificial Intelligence*, **42**, 311–348, 1990.

[Katsuno and Mendelzon, 1990] H. Katsuno and A. O. Mendelzon. On the difference between updating a knowledge database and revising it. In *Belief Revision*. P. Gärdenfors, ed. Cambridge University Press, Cambridge, 1990.

[Kraus *et al.*, 1990] S. Kraus, D. Lehmann and M. Magidor. Nonmonotonic reasoning, preferential models and cumulative logics. *Artificial Intelligence*, **44**,167–207, 1990.

[Makinson, 1994] D. Makinson. General patterns in nonmonotonic reasoning. *In Handbook of Logic in Artificial Intelligence and Logic Programming*, Vol 3: Non Monotonic Reasoning and Uncertain Reasoning, D. Gabbay, C. J. Hogger and J. A. Robinson, eds. pp. 35–110. Clarendon Press, Oxford, 1994.

[Williams, 1994] M. A. Williams. Transmutations of Knowledge Systems. In *Principles of Knowledge Representation and Reasoning*, J. Doyle, E. Sandewall, and P. Torasso, eds. pp. 619–629. Morgan Kaufmann Publishers, San Mateo, CA, 619-629, 1994.

LAURENT AUDIBERT AND KARL SCHLECHTA

DEFEASIBLE INHERITANCE AND REFERENCE CLASSES

1 INTRODUCTION

Throughout, we work in a defeasible reasoning framework, and in finite propositional languages.

1.1 Motivation

This paper has two aims: First, to formalize, in a defeasible setting, the use of a reference class to augment information of a base class (Section 2). Second, to argue that there is an important interplay between the concept of a reference class and defeasible inheritance formalisms. On the one hand, the simple framework of inheritance diagrams allows us to find the "right" reference classes and to decide which information shall be inherited from the reference classes (via valid paths, see the end of Section 3). On the other hand, our concept allows us to argue in favour of an upward chaining, on-path formalism (see the end of Section 3, too). Even if there are still many existing and imaginable inheritance formalisms which are upward chaining and on-path, we think that any systematic argument in favour of one or the other formalism is a welcome contribution to clarification. The lack of a convincing semantics has allowed a multitude of formalisms, which are often distinguished essentially by the more or less satisfactory way in which some examples are solved, and not by systematic arguments.

We use the concept of a reference class in the following sense. Let X be a set, and ϕ be some information that holds defeasibly for X, in the sense that "most $x \in X$ satisfy ϕ", or "normally, $\phi(x)$ for $x \in X$" etc. Sometimes, we shall then say "in X, things satisfy normally ϕ" etc. "Most" is used in this article in a qualitative, not necessarily probabilistic sense, and only for the intuition. Let Y be another set, and most $y \in Y$ satisfy ψ. Suppose further that the language of ϕ is disjoint from the language of ψ. We use Y as a reference class for the base class X by augmenting the information about the normal state of affairs of X by the information about the normal state of affairs of Y (giving priority to the base class information). Thus, in our example, we will now conclude that most $x \in X$ satisfy ψ, too. Note that X might be a singleton $\{x\}$, and $x \in Y$, this is a special case.

We thus depart somewhat from the philosophical tradition, see e.g. the work of Reichenbach, [1949], and also Kyburg and Pollock, [1974; 1983; 1990]—we have neither the intention nor the competence to give a detailed comparison here. We just want to give a specific formal interpretation of the notion of reference class.

M.-A. Williams and H. Rott (eds.), Frontiers in Belief Revision, 333–348.

We keep the languages of base and reference class disjoint for four reasons: First, this seems to suffice in the context of defeasible inheritance. Second, this seems to correspond to the organization of human knowledge bases at least in some cases. Third, keeping languages separate favours small databases. Fourth, it seems a justifiable initial simplification.

This might be the place to compare our approach informally with theory revision. Revising T with ϕ, $T * \phi$, presupposes that both T and ϕ are formulated in the same language. In general, however, the language of A used as reference class for B, is different from—in our approach even disjoint to—the language of B. On the other hand, both approaches treat the in some sense minimal modification of one information by another one. The information imported from the reference class will usually be considered less reliable, because subject to some reasoning by analogy, than direct information, i.e. information of the base class. Thus, the reference class information can be compared to the old theory T in theory revision, and the direct information to ϕ.

As said above, one of the aims of this paper is to formalize how reference class information is used to augment the base information. We want to "add" reference class information formulated in a reference class language $\mathcal{L}_R$ to base information in a base language $\mathcal{L}_B$, resulting in some theory in a language $\mathcal{L}_{B+R}$. As we work in a defeasible setting, there are two natural semantical approaches. If both theories are expressed by preferential structures (over different languages)—see e.g. [Kraus *et al.*, 1990; Lehman and Magidor, 1992; Schlechta, 1992; Schlechta, 1997] for motivation, discussion and results for preferential structures—we will construct a preferential structure in the augmented language $\mathcal{L}_{B+R}$ which in a reasonable way expresses the joint information. (Definitions 4, 5), In a more general case, defeasible information corresponds to coherent systems of filters or orders over formulas (= sets of models)—essentially by a definition like $\alpha < \beta$ iff $Con(\beta)$ and $\alpha \vee \beta \mid\sim \neg\alpha$, where $\mid\sim$ expresses the defeasible information—see [Ben-David and Ben-Eliyau, 1994; Friedman and Halpern, 1998; Schlechta, 1997b]. In that case, we have to construct in a reasonable way an order (or coherent system of filters) on the augmented language from the orders (or systems) of the base and the reference languages. (Definition 17). In both cases, augmentation corresponds to the construction of a product structure from the individual structures representing the base and the reference class information. Abstractly, we take two nonmonotonic databases, transform them into semantical form (as preferential structures or partial orders), compute the product structure, and transform it back into the resulting joint nonmonotonic database.

As a preferential structure generates a partial order on formulas, it is a natural and basic formal question whether passing from preferential structures to the product structure and then to the partial order on the product gives the same result as going first from the preferential structures to the partial orders and then to the partial order on the product. This is answered positively in Proposition 18(2). Thus, our definitions are in a certain way natural, as they seem well-behaved in elementary algebraic operations.

An important problem of reference classes is to determine which classes are the reference classes for a given base class. If we know that Tweety is a bird and a penguin, shall we take the candidate "birds" or the candidate "penguins" as reference class for Tweety's flying abilities? We give an answer in the simple case of defeasible inheritance diagrams: Y is a reference class for X iff there is a valid positive path from X to Y.

A defeasible inheritance diagram Γ is a finite directed acyclic graph whose nodes stand (roughly) for sets, with two types of arrows $X \to Y$ and $X \not\to Y$, where $X \to Y$ ($X \not\to Y$) expresses roughly "elements of X are normally (not) elements of Y", or "most $X's$ are (not) $Y's$". We can reformulate this as "in the class X, things are normally (not) in Y", or "in the class X, most things are (not) $Y's$". Recall that our "most" is a qualitative and not necessarily probabilistic one, which is not made precise and is there for intuitive purposes only.

The problem of inheritance diagrams is to find the "valid paths" in the diagram, and their conclusions. If, for instance, Γ is the diagram $X \to Y \to Z$, then it is universally accepted that the paths $X \to Y, Y \to Z, X \to Y \to Z$ are valid in Γ, and we conclude from the third path that in X, things are normally in Z. We justify this reasoning as follows: As the path $X \to Y$ is valid, not only "most $X's$ are $Y's$", but also Y is a reference class for X. Otherwise, why should X inherit from Y that things are normally in Z? Transitivity of reasoning is not admissible in a defeasible setting, and we see no other possible justification. Thus, we think that a suitable concept of reference class has to be at the basis of reasoning in inheritance diagrams, and we hope that our approach is a first step in this direction. On the other hand, in reasoning in inheritance diagrams - at least in the upward chaining variants - information "flows" only via valid (positive) paths, so reference classes seem to be found via such valid paths.

Consider now the diagram Γ' consisting of the arrows $X \to Y \to Z, Y \to Z'$, $X \not\to Z'$. Even if there is valid path $X \to Y$, there is no valid path $X \to Y \to Z'$ in Γ', as the arrow $X \not\to Z'$ precludes it. So, not all information is inherited from a reference class, but only information corresponding again to valid paths.

In this interpretation, we need a valid initial segment ($X \to Y$) to inherit "most things are in Z" from Y by the valid path $X \to Y \to Z$, so we are led to an upward chaining formalism.

In Γ, the base class X has the information that things are normally in Y, the reference class Y has the information that things are normally in Z, the language of the class X is (determined by) $Y(x)$, the language of Y is $Z(x)$, and the languages are disjoint, so we can apply our formalism. In Γ', the languages of X and Y are not disjoint, but we can easily make them so.

1.2 Overview of the paper

In the remainder of this Section 1 we will introduce the basic definitions of preferential structures and of inheritance diagrams.

In Section 2, we will define the augmented preferential structure (Definitions 4 and 5), and the order on the augmented language (Definition 17), examine some formal properties of our definitions (Facts 6–16) and show their equivalence when appropriate (Proposition 18). Proposition 18 contains our main formal results. Section 2 is written almost entirely in an abstract algebraic style, we do not speak about sets of models there, but about arbitrary sets. Thus, our results are valid independent of logic and models. Note also that we restrict our discussion there to the case of one reference class, which is already sufficiently nasty, as can be seen in the proof of Proposition 18.

In Section 3, we will look at defeasible inheritance diagrams and analyse them using the concept of a reference class. In particular, this will allow us to decide in favour of an upward chaining formalism, our cautious approach will lead to on-path preclusion only. We will thus have good reasons to decide two questions in the multitude of inheritance formalisms.

1.3 Basic definitions

We will work in a finite situation, the base logic will be classical propositional logic (in a language with finitely many propositional variables).

NOTATION 1. We use $\mathcal{P}$ to denote the power set operator.

Let $\mathcal{L}$ be a propositional language, we denote by $v(\mathcal{L})$ the set of its variables, by $M_{\mathcal{L}}$ the set of its classical models, ϕ etc. shall denote formulas, T etc. theories (sets of formulas) in $\mathcal{L}$ and $M(T) \subseteq M_{\mathcal{L}}$ the models of T, likewise $M(\phi)$. $Con(.)$ stands for (classical) consistency.

DEFINITION 2. (Preferential structures, simplified: the labelling function is the identity, or, equivalently, no multiple copies of models.)

1. $\mathcal{Z} =< X, \prec>$ is called a preferential structure iff X is a set, and $\prec$ a binary relation on X.

2. If $\mathcal{Z} =< X, \prec>$ is a preferential structure, then $x \in X$ is called a minimal element of X iff $x \in X$ and there is no $x' \in X$ s.t. $x' \prec x$.

3. If $\mathcal{Z} =< X, \prec>$ is a preferential structure, and X a set, then $\mu_{\mathcal{Z}}(X) := \{x \in X : x \text{ is a minimal element of } X\}$. When the context is clear, we write μ for $\mu_{\mathcal{Z}}$.

   Note: If A is finite, $\prec$ acyclic, $A \neq \emptyset$, then $\mu(A) \neq \emptyset$.

4. A relation $\prec$ on X is called ranked iff there is a set O totally ordered by a relation $<$ and a function $f : X \to O$ s.t. $x \prec y$ iff $f(x) < f(y)$ for all $x, y \in X$.

5. A preferential structure $\mathcal{Z} =< X, \prec>$ s.t. all $x \in X$ are classical models for some (propositional) language $\mathcal{L}$ is called a classical preferential struc-

ture. It defines a (in general nonmonotonic) logic $\models_{\mathcal{Z}}$ for $\mathcal{L}$ by $T \models_{\mathcal{Z}} \phi$ iff $\mu(M(T)) \subseteq M(\phi)$.

6. A structure $< X, \prec>$ is called transitive etc. iff $\prec$ is transitive etc.

Note: We will work on finite sets here, and our relations will be transitive, so the structures will be smooth (see e.g. [Kraus *et al.*, 1990]). Moreover, the relations will be acyclic.

We now turn to defeasible inheritance diagrams. For more details and motivation the reader is referred e.g. to [Horty *et al.*, 1987; Schlechta, 1997; Selman and Levesque, 1989; Touretzky *et al.*, 1987].

DEFINITION 3.

1. A defeasible inheritance diagram is a finite directed acyclic graph with two types of arrows or links, $\rightarrow$ and $\not\rightarrow$, and no parallel arrows, i.e. there is at most one arrow from any X to any Y. Such diagrams will be denoted Γ etc.

2. $\mapsto$ will stand for $\rightarrow$ or $\not\rightarrow$.

   Let now Γ be fixed, subsequent definitions are relative to Γ.

3. A (generalized) path in Γ is a sequence of concatenated arrows pointing the same way. So $X \rightarrow Y \not\rightarrow Z$ is a generalized path, neither $X \rightarrow Y \leftarrow Z$ nor $X \rightarrow Y\ Z \rightarrow U$ is one.

4. A positive (generalized) path ends with $\rightarrow$, a negative one with $\not\rightarrow$.

5. An arrow is called an atomic path, other paths are called composite.

6. Potential paths in Γ are defined inductively:

   - An arrow is a potential path.
   - If $X \ldots \rightarrow Y$ is a positive potential path, then $X \ldots \rightarrow Y \mapsto Z$ is a potential path.

   Thus $X \rightarrow Y \not\rightarrow Z$ is a potential path, $X \not\rightarrow Y \rightarrow Z$ is not. This is intuitively justified, from the latter we cannot conclude anything about X and Z.

7. Two paths $\sigma : X \ldots \mapsto Y$, $\sigma' : X \ldots \mapsto Y$ are called contradictory iff one is positive, and the other negative.

8. A subpath of a path σ with the same beginning as σ is called an intial segment of σ. Thus, $X \rightarrow Y$ and $X \rightarrow Y \rightarrow Z$ are initial segments of $X \rightarrow Y \rightarrow Z \rightarrow U$.

The main problem of defeasible inheritance diagrams is to define in a coherent and intuitively appealing way the set of "valid" paths and their results. If a path $X \ldots \rightarrow Y$ ($X \ldots \not\rightarrow Y$) is accepted as valid, we say the result "most $X's$ are $Y's$" (" most $X's$ are not $Y's$") is valid in the diagram. There is a multitude of definitions of validity of paths, with sometimes very subtle differences.

We will now present some of the basic ideas and alternatives.

Let again a diagram Γ be given.

(1) Concatenation. All potential paths are candidates for valid paths.

(2) The concept of preclusion (= preemption). Some paths are considered "stronger" than others, and if a stronger path contradicts a weaker one, the first one might be accepted as valid, but not the second. Example: In the diagram $X \rightarrow Y \rightarrow Z, X \not\rightarrow Z$, the direct arrow $X \not\rightarrow Z$ is considered stronger than the composite one $X \rightarrow Y \rightarrow Z$, the latter will not be valid (and the former will, all arrows will be valid paths).

(3) Extension based versus directly sceptical approach. There are, however, conflicts which cannot be resolved this way. Example: In the diagram $X \rightarrow Y \rightarrow Z, X \rightarrow U \not\rightarrow Z$, both paths from X to Z have equal strength, but they contradict each other. The extension based approach makes two extensions, in one extension $X \rightarrow Y \rightarrow Z$ is valid, in the other one $X \rightarrow U \not\rightarrow Z$ is valid. Usually, one will then take the intersection of extensions, formed either over the set of valid paths, or of accepted results (" most $X's$ are $Z's$" in the first one, "most $X's$ are not $Z's$" in the second one etc.). A directly sceptical approach will not accept any of $X \rightarrow Y \rightarrow Z, X \rightarrow U \not\rightarrow Z$ as valid, as they are in unresolvable conflict (and neither the result "most $X's$ are $Z's$" nor "most $X's$ are not $Z's$").

(4) Upward versus downward chaining. Upward chaining formalisms require that initial segments of valid paths be valid, downward chaining formalisms that terminal segments of valid paths be valid. For example, in the diagram $A \rightarrow B \rightarrow C \rightarrow D$, if the path $A \rightarrow B \rightarrow C \rightarrow D$ is to be valid, the subpath $A \rightarrow B \rightarrow C$ ($B \rightarrow C \rightarrow D$) has to be valid in upward (downward) chaining formalisms. This leads naturally to an inductive definition of validity.

(5) On-path versus off-path preclusion. A path $\sigma : X \ldots \rightarrow Y \ldots \rightarrow Z$ and an arrow $Y \not\rightarrow U$ is an off-path preclusion of the path $\tau : X \ldots \rightarrow Z \ldots \rightarrow U$, but an on-path preclusion only iff all nodes on τ between X and Z are on σ. A preclusion will be called valid if the precluding path σ is valid.

Example: In the classical Tweety diagram $Tweety \rightarrow birds \rightarrow flying - things, Tweety \rightarrow penguins \not\rightarrow flying - things, penguins \rightarrow birds, \sigma : Tweety \rightarrow penguins, penguins \not\rightarrow flying - things$ is an on-path preclusion of $Tweety \rightarrow penguins \rightarrow birds \rightarrow flying - things$, but $\sigma' : Tweety \rightarrow$

$penguins \to birds, penguins \not\to flying - things$ is only an off-path preclusion of $Tweety \to birds \to flying - things$. (The node $Tweety$ stands here for an element, not a set, but this is no serious problem.)

Our formal definition of valid paths will be given below in Definition 20.

2 THE FORMALISM OF REFERENCE CLASSES

Recall that our formal approach is semantical, we work either with the preferential semantics or the abstract partial order semantics of nonmonotonic logics - and abstract even further by working with arbitrary sets. This liberates us immediately from all considerations about equivalence of formulas, and, in general, we consider the semantical approach the better one. Recall further that we take two nonmonotonic databases, transform them into semantical form (as preferential structures or partial orders), compute the product structure, and transform it back into the resulting joint nonmonotonic database. This section deals with the computation of the product structure. Some basic and natural formal properties are developped in Proposition 18.

2.1 *Reference classes and preferential structures*

We formalize now the importation of information from a reference class in the preferential structure approach. For illustration, we first treat a simple example.

Let $v(\mathcal{L}_b) := \{p\}$, $v(\mathcal{L}_r) := \{q\}$, and the defeasible base theory be given by the preferential structure $m' \models p \prec m \models \neg p$, the reference class theory by $n' \models q \prec n \models \neg q$. The joint language is then defined by $\{p, q\}$, and we have to define a preferential structure on the four models of p and q. It seems clear that $m_0 \models p \wedge q \prec m_1 \models \neg p \wedge q$ and that $m_2 \models p \wedge \neg q \prec m_3 \models \neg p \wedge \neg q$, as by the base information p is preferred to $\neg p$. Likewise, we should have $m_0 \models p \wedge q \prec m_2 \models p \wedge \neg q$ and $m_1 \models \neg p \wedge q \prec m_3 \models \neg p \wedge \neg q$, as the reference class information prefers q to $\neg q$. But, we will also have $m_2 \models p \wedge \neg q \prec m_1 \models \neg p \wedge q$, even though the reference class prefers q to $\neg q$, as the information (and preferences) of the base class—which prefers p to $\neg p$—are considered stronger.

This leads to the following basic definition:

DEFINITION 4. Let $\mathcal{L}_b$ and $\mathcal{L}_r$ be two disjoint (propositional) languages. A model m of the joint language can be uniquely decomposed into m_b and m_r , the parts of the base and the reference class language. Let further $\prec_b$ and $\prec_r$ be preferential relations on the base and reference class models. We then define a preference relation on the models of the joint language by

$m \prec m'$ iff $m_b \prec_b m'_b$ or ($m_b = m'_b$ and $m_r \prec_r m'_r$).

In the abstract algebraic setting of Section 2.2, we will use the following notation:

If $\prec_X$ is a binary relation on X, $\prec_Y$ a binary relation on Y, we define $\prec_{X \times Y}$ on $X \times Y$ by $(x, y) \prec_{X \times Y} (x', y')$ iff $x \prec_X x'$ or ($x = x'$ and $y \prec_Y y'$).

Note that our definition encodes priority of the base class.

We generalize this definition to the case with multiple reference classes:

DEFINITION 5. Let $\mathcal{L}_b$ and $\mathcal{L}_{r_i}$ be pairwise disjoint (propositional) languages, and m_b (m_{r_i}) the components of a model m of the joint language as above, let $\prec_b$ ($\prec_{r_i}$) be preferential relations on the base and reference class models. We then define a preference relation on the models of the joint language by

$m \prec m'$ iff $m_b \prec_b m'_b$ or ($m_b = m'_b$ and there is i s.t. $m_{r_i} \prec_{r_i} m'_{r_i}$, and for all j $m_{r_j} \prec_{r_j} m'_{r_j}$ or $m_{r_j} = m'_{r_j}$).

We note the following properties:

FACT 6. If the relations $\prec_b$ and $\prec_{r_i}$ are irreflexive (transitive, acyclic), then so is $\prec$ as defined above.

Rankedness is not preserved, however, as the following example shows:

EXAMPLE 7. Let $\mathcal{L}_b$ be defined by p,q, $\mathcal{L}_r$ by r, $\prec_b$ be the transitive closure of $p \wedge q \prec_b p \wedge \neg q \prec_b \neg p \wedge \neg q$, $p \wedge q \prec_b \neg p \wedge q \prec_b \neg p \wedge \neg q$, and $\prec_r$ by $r \prec_r \neg r$ (both structures are obviously ranked), then the resulting $\prec$ is the transitive closure of $p \wedge q \wedge r \prec p \wedge q \wedge \neg r \prec p \wedge \neg q \wedge r \prec p \wedge \neg q \wedge \neg r \prec \neg p \wedge \neg q \wedge r \prec \neg p \wedge \neg q \wedge \neg r$ and $p \wedge q \wedge \neg r \prec \neg p \wedge q \wedge r \prec \neg p \wedge q \wedge \neg r \prec \neg p \wedge \neg q \wedge r$. So $p \wedge \neg q \wedge r$ and $\neg p \wedge q \wedge r$ are incomparable, $p \wedge \neg q \wedge r \prec p \wedge \neg q \wedge \neg r$, but not $\neg p \wedge q \wedge r \prec p \wedge \neg q \wedge \neg r$.

DEFINITION 8. Let $A \subseteq X \times Y$.

1. $A^X := \{x \in X : \exists y \in Y.(x, y) \in A\}$,
2. $A^Y := \{y \in Y : \exists x \in X.(x, y) \in A\}$,
3. for $y \in Y$, $A^X(y) := \{x \in X : (x, y) \in A\}$,
4. for $x \in X$, $A^Y(x) := \{y \in Y : (x, y) \in A\}$.

FACT 9.

1. $A \subseteq B \rightarrow A^X \subseteq B^X$,
2. $A \subseteq B \rightarrow A^X(y) \subseteq B^X(y)$,
3. $(A \cup B)^X = A^X \cup B^X$,
4. $(A \cup B)^X(y) = A^X(y) \cup B^X(y)$,
5. $(A \cap B)^X(y) = A^X(y) \cap B^X(y)$,
6. $(A - B)^X(y) = A^X(y) - B^X(y)$.

(likewise, of course, for A^Y etc.)

FACT 10. Let $A \subseteq X \times Y$, $\prec_{X \times Y}$ be defined from $\prec_X$, $\prec_Y$ as in Definition 4. Then $\mu_{X \times Y}(A) = \{(x, y) : x \in \mu_X(A^X),\ y \in \mu_Y(A^Y(x))\}$—where μ_X stands for $\mu_{<X, \prec_X>}$ etc.

Proof. Let $B := \{(x,y) : x \in \mu(A^X), y \in \mu(A^Y(x))\}$.

$'' \subseteq''$: Suppose $(x,y) \notin B$, we show $(x,y) \notin \mu(A)$. Case 1: $x \notin \mu(A^X)$. If $x \notin A^X$, then $(x,y) \notin A$, so $(x,y) \notin \mu(A)$. Suppose $x \in A^X$, but $x \notin \mu(A^X)$, so there is $x' \in A^X$, $x' \prec x$. Thus there is y' s.t. $(x',y') \in A$, but then $(x',y') \prec (x,y)$. Case 2: $y \notin \mu(A^Y(x))$. If $y \notin A^Y(x)$, then $(x,y) \notin A$. If $y \in A^Y(x)$, but $y \notin \mu(A^Y(x))$, then there is $y' \prec y$, $y' \in A^Y(x)$, so $(x,y') \in A$ and $(x,y') \prec (x,y)$.

$'' \supseteq''$: Let $(x,y) \in B$. (1) $(x,y) \in A : y \in \mu(A^Y(x)) \subseteq A^Y(x) \rightarrow (x,y) \in A$. (2) Suppose $(x,y) \in A$, but there is $(x',y') \in A$, $(x',y') \prec (x,y)$. Consider the cases of Definition 8. Case 1: $x' \prec x$. Then $x \notin \mu(A^X)$. Case 2: $x = x'$, but $y' \prec y$. Then $y \notin \mu(A^Y(x))$. ■

FACT 11. If $A = X' \times Y'$, then $\mu(A) = \mu(X') \times \mu(Y')$.

2.2 *Reference classes and orders between formulas*

Recall that we work here in a purely algebraic setting over some finite sets X, Y, Z, which are to be understood as the sets of models of some languages $\mathcal{L}_X$, $\mathcal{L}_Y$, $\mathcal{L}_Z$. The relations $\prec$ will be transitive and acyclic.

DEFINITION 12. Define from a relation $\prec$ on Z a relation $<_\prec$ on $\mathcal{P}(Z)$ by $A <_\prec B :\leftrightarrow B \neq \emptyset$ and $\mu(A \cup B) \cap A = \emptyset$.

FACT 13. $<_\prec$ as defined in Definition 12 is equivalent to the (model-variant of the) definition $\alpha <' \beta :\leftrightarrow Con(\beta)$ and $\alpha \vee \beta \models_Z \neg\alpha$.

CONDITION 14. We recall the usual filter (or ideal) and coherence properties:

1. $\emptyset < A$ if $A \neq \emptyset$,
2. $A, B < C \rightarrow A \cup B < C$,
3. $A \subseteq B < C \subseteq D \rightarrow A < D$,
4. $A, B < C \rightarrow A < C - B$,
5. $A < B \rightarrow B \neq \emptyset$.

FACT 15. $<_\prec$ as defined in Definition 12 satisfies the properties of Condition 14.

Proof.

1. Trivial.
2. We show $\mu(A \cup B \cup C) \cap (A \cup B) = \emptyset$. Suppose there is $x \in (A \cup B)$ s.t. there is no $x' \prec x$, $x' \in A \cup B \cup C$, but this contradicts the hypotheses $\mu(A \cup C) \cap A = \emptyset$ and $\mu(B \cup C) \cap B = \emptyset$.
3. We show $\mu(A \cup D) \cap A = \emptyset$. But if $x \in A \subseteq B$, then by $\mu(B \cup C) \cap B = \emptyset$ there is (by finiteness of Z and transitivity of $\prec$) $x'' \in \mu(B \cup C) \subseteq C \subseteq D$, $x'' \prec x$, so $x \notin \mu(A \cup D)$.

4. We first show $C - B \neq \emptyset$. As $B < C$, $C \neq \emptyset$, and $\mu(B \cup C) \neq \emptyset$. But $\mu(B \cup C) \subseteq C - B$. It remains to show $\mu((C - B) \cup A) \cap A = \emptyset$. Let $x \in A$. By $\mu(C \cup A) \cap A = \emptyset$, there is $x' \in C$, $x' \prec x$. If $x' \notin B$, we are done, suppose $x' \in B$. As $\mu(B \cup C) \cap B = \emptyset$, there must be $x'' \in C - B$, $x'' \prec x'$. So $x'' \prec x$.

5. Trivial by definition. ■

FACT 16. If $<$ on $\mathcal{P}(Z)$ satisfies the properties (2)–(4) of Condition 14, then the following hold:

1. If $A, B \subseteq C$, $C - A < A$, $C - B < B$, then $C - (A \cap B) < A \cap B$,

2. If $A < C - A$, $B < C - B$, then $A \cup B < C - (A \cup B)$.

Proof.

1. $C - A < A \rightarrow$ (by property (3)) $C - A < C$, likewise $C - B < C$, so by (2) $C - (A \cap B) = ((C - A) \cup (C - B)) < C$, so by (4) $C - (A \cap B) < C - (C - (A \cap B)) = A \cap B$.

2. $A < C - A \subseteq C$, $B < C - B \subseteq C$, so by (2) $A \cup B < C$, so by (4) $A \cup B < C - (A \cup B)$. ■

The following definition seems at first sight somewhat complicated, but we do not see a simpler one which gives the same Proposition 18. Moreover, intuitively it seems to be the right one. Roughly, $A < B$ iff there is $W \subseteq B - A$ which is a "big" subset of $A \cup B$ in both coordinates.

DEFINITION 17. Let $<_X$ be a binary relation on $\mathcal{P}(X)$, $<_Y$ a binary relation on $\mathcal{P}(Y)$. We then define a binary relation $<_{X \times Y}$ on $X \times Y$ by

$A < B$ iff there is $W \subseteq B - A$ s.t.

$(A \cup B)^X - W^X <_X W^X$ and for all $x \in W^X . (A \cup B)^Y(x) - W^Y(x) <_Y W^Y(x)$.

We call such W a witness for $A < B$.

PROPOSITION 18.

1. If $<_X$ and $<_Y$ satisfy the properties of Condition 14, then so does $<_{X \times Y}$.

2. If $<_{\prec_X}$ is generated from $\prec_X$, $<_{\prec_Y}$ from $\prec_Y$ as in Definition 12, $\prec_{X \times Y}$ from $\prec_X$ and $\prec_Y$ as in Definition 4, then $<_{X \times Y}$ as defined in Definition 17 from $<_{\prec_X}$ and $<_{\prec_Y}$ is the relation $<_{\prec_{X \times Y}}$ on $\mathcal{P}(X \times Y)$ generated by $\prec_{X \times Y}$ as in Definition 12 (commutativity of definitions).

3. If $A \cup B = X' \times Y'$ and $B \neq \emptyset$, then $A <_{X \times Y} B$ iff $(\mu(X') \times \mu(Y')) \cap A = \emptyset$.

Proof.

1. The proof is surprisingly tedious—but perhaps there is a much nicer one we just did not see!

   (1.1) Let $A \neq \emptyset$, we have to show $\emptyset < A$. $W := A$ witnesses $\emptyset < A$.

   (1.2) Let $A < C, B < C$, we have to show $A \cup B < C$. Let W_A witness $A < C$, W_B witness $B < C$. Define $W_{A \cup B} := \{(x, y) : x \in W_A^X \cap W_B^X, (x, y) \in C - (A \cup B)\}$. $W_{A \cup B}$ witnesses $A \cup B < C$:
   Note $W_{A \cup B} \subseteq C - (A \cup B)$.
   We first show $\forall x \in W_A^X \cap W_B^X \; W_{A \cup B}^Y(x) > (A \cup B \cup C)^Y(x) - W_{A \cup B}^Y(x)$. By $W_A \subseteq C - A$, we have $C^Y(x) - A^Y(x) = (C - A)^Y(x) \supseteq W_A^Y(x) > (A \cup C)^Y(x) - W_A^Y(x) \supseteq (A \cup C)^Y(x) - (C - A)^Y(x) = A^Y(x)$, likewise $C^Y(x) - B^Y(x) > B^Y(x)$. So by Fact 16, (2) $W_{A \cup B}^Y(x) = C^Y(x) - (A \cup B)^Y(x) > (A \cup B)^Y(x) = (A \cup B \cup C)^Y(x) - W_{A \cup B}^Y(x)$.
   Consequently, by property (5), $\forall x \in W_A^X \cap W_B^X . W_{A \cup B}^Y(x) \neq \emptyset$, so $W_{A \cup B}^X = W_A^X \cap W_B^X$.
   We now show $W_{A \cup B}^X > (A \cup B \cup C)^X - W_{A \cup B}^X$. By prerequisite, $W_B^X > (C \cup B)^X - W_B^X$. Note that $W_B \subseteq C$, so $C^X \supseteq W_B^X > (C \cup B)^X - W_B^X = (C^X \cup B^X) - W_B^X \supseteq B^X - C^X \supseteq B^X - (C^X \cup A^X)$, so $C^X > B^X - (C^X \cup A^X)$. Likewise, $C^X \supseteq W_A^X > (A^X \cup C^X) - W_A^X \supseteq C^X - W_A^X$, so $C^X > C^X - W_A^X$. So by property (4) of Condition 14 $W_A^X = C^X - (C^X - W_A^X) > B^X - (C^X \cup A^X)$. So by $W_A^X > (A^X \cup C^X) - W_A^X$, $W_A^X > B^X - (C^X \cup A^X)$, and by property (2) of Condition 14, $W_A^X > ((A^X \cup C^X) - W_A^X) \cup (B^X - (C^X \cup A^X)) = (A^X \cup B^X \cup C^X) - W_A^X$. For the latter equality: "$\subseteq$": $((A^X \cup C^X) - W_A^X) \subseteq (A^X \cup B^X \cup C^X) - W_A^X$, and $B^X - (C^X \cup A^X) \subseteq (A^X \cup B^X \cup C^X) - W_A^X$ by $W_A \subseteq C$. "$\supseteq$": If $x \in (A^X \cup C^X) - W_A^X$, this is ok. If $x \in B^X - (A^X \cup C^X \cup W_A^X) = B^X - (A^X \cup C^X)$, this is ok, too. Thus, $W_A^X > (A \cup B \cup C)^X - W_A^X$. Likewise, $W_B^X > (A \cup B \cup C)^X - W_B^X$, so by Fact 16, (1) $W_A^X \cap W_B^X > (A \cup B \cup C)^X - (W_A^X \cap W_B^X)$.

   (1.3) We first show $A \subseteq B < C \to A < C$. Let W_B witness $B < C$. Then $W_B \subseteq C - B$, so $W_B \subseteq C - A$. By property (3), the other properties of W_B hold to witness $A < C$.
   We now show $A < B \subseteq C \to A < C$. Let W_A witness $A < B$, and define $W := \{(x, y) : x \in W_A^X, (x, y) \in W_A \cup (C - (A \cup B))\} \cup \{(x, y) \in C : x \in C^X - (A \cup B)^X\}$. Thus, $W^X = W_A^X \cup (C^X - (A \cup B)^X)$ and $W \subseteq C - A$. We now show $(A \cup C)^X - W^X = (A \cup B)^X - W_A^X$, and conclude that $W^X > (A \cup C)^X - W^X$: $(C^X - (A \cup B)^X) \cup (A \cup B)^X = C^X \cup A^X \cup B^X = C^X \cup A^X = (A \cup C)^X$, so $(A \cup C)^X - W^X = ((C^X - (A \cup B)^X) \cup (A \cup B)^X) - (W_A^X \cup (C^X -$

$(A \cup B)^X)) = (A \cup B)^X - W_A^X$, as $(A \cup B)^X \cap (C^X - (A \cup B)^X) = \emptyset$. But now $W^X \supseteq W_A^X > (A \cup B)^X - W_A^X = (A \cup C)^X - W^X$. It remains to show that $W^Y(x) > (A \cup C)^Y - W^Y(x)$ for $x \in W^X$. Case 1: $x \in C^X - (A \cup B)^X$, then $(A \cup C)^Y(x) = C^Y(x)$, so $(A \cup C)^Y(x) - W^Y(x) = C^Y(x) - C^Y(x) = \emptyset < C^Y(x) = W^Y(x)$ (as $x \in C^X$, $C^Y(x) \neq \emptyset$). Case 2: $x \in W_A^X$. By prerequisite, $W_A^Y(x) > (A \cup B)^Y(x) - W_A^Y(x)$. $W^Y(x) = W_A^Y(x) \cup (C - (A \cup B))^Y(x) \supseteq W_A^Y(x) > (A \cup B)^Y(x) - W_A^Y(x) =$ (as $(A \cup B)^Y(x) \cap (C - (A \cup B))^Y(x) = \emptyset$) $(A \cup B)^Y(x) - (W_A^Y(x) \cup (C - (A \cup B))^Y(x)) =$ (as $(A \cup B) - (C - (A \cup B)) = (A \cup C) - (C - (A \cup B))$) $(A \cup C)^Y(x) - (W_A^Y(x) \cup (C - (A \cup B))^Y(x)) = (A \cup C)^Y(x) - W^Y(x)$.

(1.4) We have to show $A, B < C \rightarrow A < C - B$. Choose $W_{A \cup B}$ as in the construction for (1.2). Then $W_{A \cup B} \subseteq (C - B) - A$. As shown above, $W_{A \cup B}^X > (A \cup B \cup C)^X - W_{A \cup B}^X \supseteq (A \cup (C - B))^X - W_{A \cup B}^X$. Likewise for $x \in W_{A \cup B}^X$ $W_{A \cup B}^Y(x) > (A \cup B \cup C)^Y(x) - W_{A \cup B}^Y(x) \supseteq (A \cup (C - B))^Y(x) - W_{A \cup B}^Y(x)$.

(1.5) If W witnesses $A < B$, then $W \subseteq B - A$, $W^X > (A \cup B)^X - W^X$, so $W^X \neq \emptyset$, so $B \supseteq W \neq \emptyset$.

2. We have to show for $A, B \subseteq X \times Y$ $A <_{\prec_{X \times Y}} B$ iff $A <_{X \times Y} B$. Now, $A <_{\prec_{X \times Y}} B$ iff $B \neq \emptyset$ and $\mu_{X \times Y}(A \cup B) \cap A = \emptyset$, where by Fact 10 $\mu_{X \times Y}(A \cup B) = \{(x, y) : x \in \mu_X((A \cup B)^X), y \in \mu_Y((A \cup B)^Y(x))\}$. Moreover, $A <_{X \times Y} B$ iff there is $W \subseteq B - A$ s.t. $(A \cup B)^X - W^X <_{\prec_X} W^X$ and for all $x \in W^X$ $(A \cup B)^Y(x) - W^Y(x) <_{\prec_Y} W^Y(x)$.

   Note that by $B \neq \emptyset$, $A \cup B \neq \emptyset$, $\mu(A \cup B) \neq \emptyset$ etc.

   "$\rightarrow$": Let $W := \mu_{X \times Y}(A \cup B)$. Then $W \subseteq B - A$, and $W = \{(x, y) : x \in \mu_X((A \cup B)^X), y \in \mu_Y((A \cup B)^Y(x))\}$, so $W^X = \mu_X((A \cup B)^X)$, and for $x \in W^X$ $W^Y(x) = \mu_Y((A \cup B)^Y(x))$. Thus by $W^X \neq \emptyset$, $W^X >_{\prec_X} (A \cup B)^X - W^X$. Moreover, if $x \in W^X$, then $W^Y(x) \neq \emptyset$, and thus $W^Y(x) >_{\prec_Y} (A \cup B)^Y(x) - W^Y(x)$. So W witnesses $A <_{X \times Y} B$.

   "$\leftarrow$": Let $A <_{X \times Y} B$, we have to show $B \neq \emptyset$ and $\mu_{X \times Y}(A \cup B) \cap A = \emptyset$. By Fact 15, $<_{\prec_X}$ and $<_{\prec_Y}$ satisfy the properties of Condition 14, thus so does $<_{X \times Y}$ (by (1)), so if $A <_{X \times Y} B$, then $B \neq \emptyset$. Let now W witness $A <_{X \times Y} B$. Thus $W \subseteq B - A$ and $(A \cup B)^X - W^X <_{\prec_X} W^X$, so $\mu_X((A \cup B)^X) \subseteq W^X$. Likewise, for all $x \in W^X$ $(A \cup B)^Y(x) - W^Y(x) <_{\prec_Y} W^Y(x)$, so $\mu_Y((A \cup B)^Y(x)) \subseteq W^Y(x)$. By Fact 10, $\mu_{X \times Y}(A \cup B) = \{(x, y) : x \in \mu_X((A \cup B)^X), y \in \mu_Y((A \cup B)^Y(x))\}$, so $\mu_{X \times Y}(A \cup B) \subseteq W$. Thus by $W \cap A = \emptyset$, $\mu_{X \times Y}(A \cup B) \cap A = \emptyset$.

3. Trivial by Fact 11. ■

3 REFERENCE CLASSES AND DEFEASIBLE INHERITANCE

As said above, one of the problems with reference classes is how to find them. Recall that we will say in an inheritance diagram that Y is a reference class for X iff there is a good argument (in the diagram) that Xs behave like Ys, or, that "most Xs are Ys", or, that there is valid positive path (argument) from X to Y. (A negative valid path gives no direct information about reference classes.)

Direct versus indirect inheritance, direct versus indirect information In the simple diagram $A \to B \to C \to D$ (in which all potential paths will be valid in all inheritance diagram formalisms), e.g. A has the direct information from the direct arrow $A \to B$ that As are Bs, and the indirect information that As are Cs (from the composite valid path $A \to B \to C$). On the other hand, A inherits directly from B via the direct arrow $A \to B$ that Bs are Cs and indirectly from C via the valid path $A \to B \to C$ that Cs are Ds.

Direct inheritance of direct information is too weak to account for such diagrams, as we cannot conclude this way that As are Ds; with this reasoning, we cannot go beyond paths of length 2.

Add now to the above diagram the path $A \to E \not\to C$. If we accept the idea that reference classes for X are those to which there is a valid positive path, in a directly sceptical framework, B and E are the only reference classes for A. On the other hand, C is a reference class for B. Thus, B has the indirect information that Bs are Ds, or, that things are normally in D. So, if we inherit indirect information, A will inherit from B that things are normally Ds and thus conclude that As are Ds too, which is not acceptable. Moreover, if we accept to inherit indirect information, the base class has no control where the information comes from, which seems contradictory to the spirit of inheritance networks.

Thus, the only correct way seems to have indirect inheritance of direct information. This leads naturally to upward chaining, as discussed at the end of this Section.

Valid paths The main rule of preference is that direct links have priority over composite paths, as a direct link gives more reliable information than a composite path. Warning: The word "preference" is used here in colloquial style, and not in the sense of preferential structures.

We now give an auxiliary definition, followed by the formal definition of validity.

Again, we fix a diagram Γ, definitions will be relative to Γ.

DEFINITION 19. $deg(X, Y)$ is the maximal length of all generalized paths from X to Y in Γ.

Fix now an arbitrary enumeration ρ_X of the nodes $\neq X$ in Γ to which there is a generalized path from X, and which respects deg, i.e. $deg(X, Y) < deg(X, Z) \to \rho_X(Y) < \rho_X(Z)$.

DEFINITION 20. (Inductive definition of valid paths in Γ.) Let Y be the $\rho_X - first$ node not yet treated. Let Φ^0_{XY} be the set of potential paths from X to Y. Let Φ^1_{XY} be the set of paths in Φ^0_{XY} from X to Y which are direct arrows or whose initial segments are valid (this has already been decided by induction, as ρ_X respects deg). Let Φ^2_{XY} be the set of paths in Φ^1_{XY} from X to Y for which there is no valid on-path preclusion in Γ (again, this has already been decided by induction). Let Φ_{XY} be the set of paths in Φ^2_{XY} from X to Y for which there is no contradictory path in Φ^2_{XY}. Φ_{XY} is the set of valid paths from X to Y.

We note: Our approach is directly sceptical (by the final step of the definition), and upward chaining (but in general not downward chaining) by the definition of Φ^1_{XY}. An example which shows that downward chaining need not hold, is: $A \to B \to C \to E, B \to D \not\to E, A \not\to D$. $A \to B \to C \to E$ is valid, $B \to C \to E$ is not.

We do not necessarily consider more specific information to be more reliable—our only preference is for direct links over composite paths. That's why we did not adopt off-path preclusion.

We now define formally:

DEFINITION 21. Y is a reference class for X in the diagram Γ, iff there is a valid positive path from X to Y in Γ.

We have not yet specified which information shall be inherited from the reference classes of a given class X. To see the problem, consider the following diagram: $A \to B \to C \to E, B \not\to D, C \to D$. The defeasible information of node B, "most things are in C, but not in D", in partial order representation $C \wedge \neg D > C \wedge D > \neg C \wedge D, C \wedge \neg D > \neg C \wedge \neg D > \neg C \wedge D$, that of node C "most things are in D and E", or $D \wedge E > D \wedge \neg E > \neg D \wedge \neg E$, $D \wedge E > \neg D \wedge E > \neg D \wedge \neg E$. So B prefers $\neg D$, and C prefers D, obviously, we want to inherit the information that $\neg D$ is preferred.

Thus, to solve the problem which information will be inherited from a reference class Y, we will inherit the information which corresponds to a valid path from X via Y to the node which corresponds to that information. In our example, there is a valid path $A \to B \not\to D$, but no valid path $A \to B \to C \to D$, and the resulting languages can be chosen disjoint.

It is now evident that we have to take an upward chaining approach. We first need a valid path $\sigma : X \ldots \to Y$ to the reference class, which is contained in a valid path $\sigma' : X \ldots \to Y \to Z$ to the node corresponding to the information. The fact that we showed that Y is a reference class for X (via validity of σ) justified the result that Xs behave like Ys.

4 CONCLUSION

We have clarified the use of reference classes (in our sense) in a defeasible setting, examined two formal definitions of this use, one in the framework of preferential structures, the other in the framework of orders defined by a nonmonotonic database. We have shown that both approaches are equivalent, in the sense that the preferential approach is the same as the one which first transforms the preference relations into orders, and then operates on the orders.

We have, we think, clarified the concepts of defeasible inheritance by analyzing such diagrams using the notion of reference class, which led us to adopt an upward chaining, on-path preclusion approach. The simple setting of inheritance diagrams permits a clear choice of the reference classes and the information inherited from such classes.

Our approach to the use of reference classes seems broad enough to treat other situations than simple inheritance diagrams, for instance those where other defeasible information, not only class-inclusion, is appended to an inheritance diagram, similar to KL-ONE situations.

We have not addressed the first order problem, so this is a subject of further research. We did not investigate either whether our formalism - though different— can help to clarify the use of reference classes in philosophy of science.

ACKNOWLEDGEMENTS

Three anonymous referees have helped to make the paper much more readable (we hope).

Laboratoire d'Informatique de Marseille, Marseille, France.

REFERENCES

[Ben-David and Ben-Eliyau, 1994] S. Ben-David and R. Ben-Eliyahu. A modal logic for subjective default reasoning. In *Proceedings LICS-94*, 1994.

[Friedman and Halpern, 1998] N. Friedman and J. Halpern. Plausibility Measures and Default Reasoning. IBM Almaden Research Center Tech.Rept. 1995, to appear in *Journal of the ACM*.

[Horty *et al.*, 1987] J. F.Horty, D. S.Touretzky and R. H.Thomason. A sceptical theory of inheritance in nonmonotonic semantic networks. In *Proceedings AAAI-87*, pp. 358–363, 1987.

[Kraus *et al.*, 1990] S. Kraus, D. Lehmann and M. Magidor. Nonmonotonic reasoning, preferential models and cumulative logics, *Artificial Intelligence*, **44**, 167–207, 1990.

[Lehman and Magidor, 1992] D. Lehmann and M. Magidor. What does a conditional knowledge base entail? *Artificial Intelligence*, **55**, 1–60, 1992.

[Kyburg, 1974] H. E. Kyburg. *The Logical Foundations of Statistical Inference*. Reidel, 1974.

[Kyburg, 1983] H. E. Kyburg. The reference class, *Philos. Sci.*, **50**, 374–397, 1983.

[Pollock, 1990] J. L. Pollock. *Nomic Probabilities and the Foundations of Induction*. Oxford University Press, 1990.

[Reichenbach, 1949] H. Reichenbach. *Theory of Probability*, Univ. of California Press, Berkeley, 1949.

[Schlechta, 1992] K. Schlechta. Some results on classical preferential models, *Journal of Logic and Computation*, **2**, 675–686, 1992.

[Schlechta, 1997] K. Schlechta. *Nonmonotonic Logics: Basic Concepts, Results, and Techniques*, Springer, 1997.

[Schlechta, 1997b] K. Schlechta. Filters and partial orders, *Journal of the Interest Group in Pure and Applied Logic*, **5**, 753–772, 1997.

[Shoham, 1987] Y. Shoham. A semantical approach to nonmonotonic logics. In *Proceedings of Logics in Computer Science*, pp. 275–279, Ithaca, NY, 1987.

[Selman and Levesque, 1989] B. Selman and H. Levesque. The tractability of path-based inheritance. In *Proceedings IJCAI 1989*, pp. 1140–1145, 1989.

[Touretzky *et al.*, 1987] D. S. Touretzky, J. F. Horty and R. H. Thomason. A clash of intuition: The current state of nonmonotonic multiple inheritance systems. In *Proceedings IJCAI 1987*, pp. 476–482, 1987.

RENATA WASSERMANN

ON STRUCTURED BELIEF BASES

1 INTRODUCTION

Intelligent agents must have some way of revising their beliefs. Even though the AGM paradigm [Alchourrón *et al.*, 1985] provides a very elegant and powerful framework for reasoning about how a rational agent should change his beliefs when confronted with new information, it tells us very little about how that agent could really perform such belief changes. Moreover, the rational agent described is a highly idealized one, a perfect reasoner with infinite memory, logical ability, no inconsistent beliefs and no time constraints.

In the AGM paradigm, the belief state of an agent is represented by a *belief set*, a set of logical formulas that is closed under logical consequence. The use of belief sets has received several criticisms, the two most important being that they are usually to big to be (computationally) dealt with, and that they are not expressive enough, not allowing for example for distinctions between beliefs with an independent standing and merely derived ones.

One alternative for the use of belief sets if to represent the belief state of an agent by means of a set that is not closed under logical consequence, called *belief bases*. This alternative has been extensively studied and AGM-like operations have been defined for belief bases. However the term "belief base" has been used by two different communities with different meanings. Most authors interested in implementing AGM belief revision [Nebel, 1990; Williams, 1994; Dixon, 1994] use belief bases to represent the belief set of an agent. A belief base in these approaches is a finite axiomatization of the theory (belief set) representing the agent's commitments. The fact that a formula of the belief set is an element of the belief base does not distiguish it from other formulas that are not part of the belief base but follow logically from it. There are just two possibilities for a formula: either it follows from the belief base, and so the agent is commited to it, or it does not. Authors following this approach usually try to avoid redundancies in the belief base. In databases, for example, this is a desirable property, since it makes alterations of the data easier. On the other hand, adding new information becomes much more complex, since one has to check for redundancies.

The approach that we follow in this paper is in line with another use of the term "belief base", defended for example by [Fuhrmann, 1991; Rott, 1996; Hansson, 1999]. According to this line, a belief base is an arbitrary set of formulas representing those beliefs of an agent that have independent standing. Some authors [Fagin and Halpern, 1988] call these the *explicit beliefs*. Beliefs that follow from the ones in the belief base but are not part of it have a different status, being merely derived beliefs. The set of formulas to which the agent is commited, also called *implicit beliefs*, is formed by taking the logical closure of the agent's belief base. A

M.-A. Williams and H. Rott (eds.), Frontiers in Belief Revision, 349–367.

model of the belief state of a resource-bounded agent is presented in [Wassermann, 1999], which includes explicit, implicit and active beliefs. The set of active beliefs is the set of formulas that is relevant for use at a certain moment. In [Hansson and Wassermann, 1999] we present one way of retrieving the active beliefs from the belief base. This method and its shortcomings are detailed in section 2.

While in the first notion of belief base the stress is on keeping a non-redundant base, and thus requiring a non-trivial operation of expansion, in the second notion what matters is the justification of an agent for believing the formulas of the base. In this case, adding new information to the belief base via expansion is a trivial operation. The complexity arises when one has to give up beliefs (contraction) or use the beliefs for reasoning, since they may well be inconsistent.[1]

When trying to model more realistic agents, one should take into account some limitations of the agents. We may hold inconsistent beliefs without even realizing it, and this does not prevent us from being able to reason about other topics. Realistic agents should not try to keep their whole set of beliefs consistent, but only solve inconsistencies when they become relevant for a line of reasoning.

Even if real agents (natural or artificial) had the ability to calculate all the consequences of their beliefs, they would not have any interest in doing so. Some consequences are useful, but an agent should not waste resouces calculating that $p \vee q$, $p \wedge p$, $p \wedge p \vee q$ and $p \wedge p \wedge p \vee q$ all follow from his belief in p. In approaches to belief revision that use belief bases [Fuhrmann, 1991; Hansson, 1994; Nebel, 1990] instead of logically closed belief sets, the operations defined usually depend on finding maximal subsets of the belief base not implying some formula α, or minimal subsets of the base implying α.[2]Exploring all subsets of a reasonably sized belief base is a very expensive operation.

One way to attack the problem is to try to reduce the size of the set to be explored. Intuitively, not all of an agent's beliefs are relevant for deciding what to do with new information. There should be a way of isolating the subset of a belief base that contains the relevant beliefs for an operation of belief change. In [Hansson and Wassermann, 1999], this approach is explored. A notion of *compartment* is presented for retrieving the relevant part of a belief base and then local operations of belief change are defined that act only on the relevant part of the beliefs. The problem is that the way the compartments are defined uses the notion of minimal subsets of the base implying some formula, that is, finding a compartment is as expensive as performing a traditional operation of belief change. However, the representation results obtained in [Hansson and Wassermann, 1999] for the local

[1] In [Rott, 1996], two ways of using belief bases are distinguished. Either the belief base is a finite axiomatization of a belief set, which can be obtained by applying Cn on the base (the horizontal perspective), or the belief base is an arbitrary set of formulas, possibly inconsistent, and the commitments of the agent are obtained by applying a more sophisticated inference operator on the base (the vertical perspective). We follow in this paper the vertical perspective.

[2] Alternative approaches based on epistemic entrenchments (E-bases [Rott, 1991]; "ensconcements" [Williams, 1994]) rely on a well behaved pre-order of the beliefs in the base to construct operations of belief change. Given the pre-order, the operations become less complex, but constructing and maintaining this pre-order can be computationally very costly.

versions of the belief change operations are very general and do not depend on the particular way the compartment is defined, but only on certain properties of the resulting compartments.

In this paper we present more efficient ways of retrieving the relevant part of a belief base. The retrieved set can then be "plugged" into the constructions of local operations. Even though the local operations also rely on finding minimal or maximal subsets implying or not implying certain formulas, the set to be explored is reduced to a manageable size.

The paper proceeds as follows: in the next section the basic definitions and results of [Hansson and Wassermann, 1999] are summarized. In section 3, a computer system is presented which has a very efficient mechanism for retrieving relevant beliefs from a belief base with extra structure. The ideas of the system inspired some considerations on more general ways of structuring the base and on formalizing the notion of retrieving the most relevant beliefs for a certain input. These considerations are presented in section 4. In section 5, some examples of relatedness relations are presented that can be used for structuring the belief base. Computational aspects are examined in section 6. Some related work is discussed in section 7, and conclusions are presented in section 8.

In the rest of the paper we will be working within a propositional framework, with a language $\mathcal{L}$ containing the basic boolean connectives. We will assume that a belief base is a finite set of formulas of $\mathcal{L}$.

It is possible to ignore differences in the syntactical form of formulas, although we do not do it here, by assuming (i) a logical approach: when we say "p occurs in φ" we actually mean "for all ψ such that $\vdash \varphi \leftrightarrow \psi$, p occurs in ψ"; or (ii) a computational approach: the formulas are all represented in some normal form, and equivalent formulas have equal representation.

We will use the terms " belief base" and "database" indiscriminately to refer to a set of formulas of $\mathcal{L}$.

2 LOCAL CHANGE

In [Hansson and Wassermann, 1999], we presented a framework for performing local reasoning. The key idea is that not all of an agent's beliefs are relevant for an operation of belief change. As an example, suppose that I wake up and see that the sun is shining in Amsterdam. This contradicts my previous beliefs about the weather, like the one that it always rains in Holland, and leads to revision. However, the revision process does not have to take my beliefs about mathematics into account. These beliefs are completely irrelevant for the change taking place and should not play any role in it.

How do we determine which of the beliefs from a belief base are relevant for a certain operation? We are interested in the concept of a *compartment* around a formula or a set of formulas. In [Hansson and Wassermann, 1999], given two sets of formulas A and B, we define the relevant formulas in B for A as those that contribute for proving or disproving any formula of A. We formalize this using the notion of *kernel sets* - minimal subsets implying a given sentence:

DEFINITION 1. [Hansson, 1994] Let C be an inference operation on $\mathcal{L}$. Then the kernel operation $\perp\!\!\!\perp_C$ is the operation such that for all subsets B and elements α of $\mathcal{L}$, $X \in B \perp\!\!\!\perp_C \alpha$ if and only if:

1. $X \subseteq B$
2. $\alpha \in C(X)$
3. for all Y, if $Y \subset X$ then $\alpha \notin C(Y)$

The elements of $B \perp\!\!\!\perp_C \alpha$ are called α-kernels.

We write $\perp\!\!\!\perp$ as an abbreviation of $\perp\!\!\!\perp_{Cn}$, where Cn is a classical consequence operation.

The compartment of B around a set of sentences A is given by the union of the α and $\neg\alpha$-kernels of B for all elements α of A. We discard the inconsistent kernels, since we do not want an inconsistent kernel like $\{p, \neg p\}$ to be included in the compartment around q only because it implies every sentence in the language.

DEFINITION 2. [Hansson and Wassermann, 1999] The A-compartment of B, where A and B are sets of sentences is defined as:

$c(A, B) = \bigcup_{\alpha \in A}(\bigcup((B \perp\!\!\!\perp \alpha) \cup (B \perp\!\!\!\perp \neg\alpha) \setminus (B \perp\!\!\!\perp \perp))$

We call c a compartmentalization function.

Note that the compartments defined above are usually overlapping and should not be seen as a partition of the belief base into different topics or subjects.

Note also that the definition of compartment around a set as the union of the compartments around each of its elements has some limitations. It may be the case that for some formulas α, β and γ, α is not relevant for β or for γ, but is relevant for the set $\{\beta, \gamma\}$. An example due to Dubois and cited in [Herzig, 1997] lets α be "I take a bath", β be "I use a hairdryer" and γ be "I die".

OBSERVATION 3.

(1) For all sets A and B of sentences, $c(A, B) = c(A, c(A, B))$.

(2) If $A \subseteq A'$ and $B \subseteq B'$, then $c(A, B) \subseteq c(A', B')$.

Even though the way the compartments are defined is purely logical, they depend on the belief base (and hence, additions or subtractions change the compartments) and on the set around which the compartment is built, which can be seen as giving the context in which the relevant formulas have to be retrieved.

Given the notion of compartment around a set A, we can define the localization of a given inference operation C to A as:

DEFINITION 4. [Hansson and Wassermann, 1999] Let C be an inference operation on $\mathcal{L}$ and let c be a compartmentalization function as in definition 2. Then for any set A, the A-localization of C is the inference operation C_A such that for all sets B of sentences: $C_A(B) = C(c(A, B))$.

A set B is *A-locally consistent* if and only if $\bot \notin C_A(B)$

THEOREM 5. *[Hansson and Wassermann, 1999] Let be C_A the A-localization of an inference operation C. Then:*

1. *If C satisfies monotony, then so does C_A.*

2. *If C satisfies monotony and compactness, then so does C_A.*

We also showed how local versions of the operations of contraction, revision, consolidation and semi-revision can be constructed and characterized by means of postulates. I reproduce below one of the results obtained in [Hansson and Wassermann, 1999], namely the characterization of local kernel contraction, which can be used for deriving the others.

The idea behind kernel contraction is that, if we remove from the belief base at least one element of each α-kernel (minimal subset of the base that implies α), we obtain a belief base that does not imply α. In the case of the local operation, we are interested in obtaining a belief base that does not A-locally imply α, where A is a set of sentences. We consider then only those kernel sets that A-locally imply α and use an *incision function* to select the formulas from the kernel sets to be removed. An incision function is a function defined from sets of sets of sentences into sets of sentences, selecting at least one sentence from each set of the argument.

DEFINITION 6. [Hansson, 1994] An *incision function* is any function $\sigma : \mathcal{P}(\mathcal{P}(\mathcal{L})) \rightarrow \mathcal{P}(\mathcal{L})$ such that for any subset S of $\mathcal{P}(\mathcal{L})$:

1. $\sigma(S) \subseteq \bigcup S$

2. If $\emptyset \neq X \in S$, then $X \cap \sigma(S) \neq \emptyset$

Example: Let $S = \{\{a, b\}, \{c\}, \{d, e, f\}\}$. Then we may have an incision function σ such that $\sigma(S) = \{b, c, e\}$.

DEFINITION 7. [Hansson, 1994] Let C be an inference operation on $\mathcal{L}$ and σ an incision function. The local kernel contraction of B determined by C and σ is the operation $\dot{-}_{C,\sigma}$ such that for all sets of sentences B:

$B \dot{-}_{C,\sigma} \alpha = B \setminus \sigma(B \perp\!\!\!\perp_C \alpha)$

The following theorem characterizes the operation of local kernel contraction and is a generalization of the result obtained in [Hansson, 1994]. The intended interpretation is that C should be a localization C_A of an inference operator, as defined above. However, the formal result is more general and is therefore stated in terms of an operation C of a more general type.

THEOREM 8. *[Hansson and Wassermann, 1999] Let C be an inference operation satisfying monotony and compactness. An operation $\dot{-}$ is an operation of local kernel contraction determined by C and some incision function if and only if for all sets of sentences B:*

- *If* $\alpha \notin C(\emptyset)$*, then* $\alpha \notin C(B\dot{-}\alpha)$ *(success)*
- $B\dot{-}\alpha \subseteq B$ *(inclusion)*
- *If* $x \in B \setminus B\dot{-}\alpha$*, then there is some* $B' \subseteq B$ *such that* $\alpha \notin C(B')$ *and* $\alpha \in C(B' \cup \{x\})$ *(core-retainment)*
- *If for all subsets* B' *of* B $\alpha \in C(B')$ *if and only if* $\beta \in C(B')$*, then* $B\dot{-}\alpha = B\dot{-}\beta$ *(uniformity)*

The problem with this approach is that the way the compartments are calculated is extremely inefficient. On the whole, the local change operations are computationally as costly as the original versions, although intuitively more appropriate.

However, the representation results proven in [Hansson and Wassermann, 1999] do not rely on the way the compartments are defined, but only on properties of the local inference operation obtained, namely, monotony and compactness. The compartment construction in definition 2 can be seen as an example, as one way of constructing a compartment such that the localization of the consequence operator to the compartment satisfies the requirements. This means that if we find another way of retrieving the relevant beliefs from a base such that the associated local inference operation is also monotonic and compact, the results in [Hansson and Wassermann, 1999] go through.

In the rest of the paper, some ideas for efficient ways of retrieving relevant information are presented.

Note that even if we apply traditional constructions for belief change on the set of relevant beliefs, since this set can be kept much smaller than the belief base as a whole, the operations become more feasible.

3 RABIT

In this section we briefly discuss the system RABIT (**R**easoning **A**bout **B**eliefs **I**n **T**ime). For details, the reader is referred to [Gary, 1993; Gary and Elgot-Drapkin, 1996].

RABIT is intended to simulate commonsense reasoning in an efficient, psychologically based way.

The system consists of four modules, each one representing another sort of memory: LTM (Long-Term Memory), STM (Short-Term Memory), ITM (Intermediate-Term Memory) and RTM (Relevant-Term Memory). The idea is that all the information (the beliefs) is stored in the LTM component, but the reasoning is performed on a small subset of the beliefs in LTM, the STM. This reasoning is based on the step-logic formalism [Drapkin and Perlis, 1986]. The ITM component stores the history of the reasoning process and the RTM works as a kind of context, storing the relevant concepts (in RABIT, any symbol in the language, like predicate names and constants, represent a concept). The idea of working on a small subset of the belief base is psychologically as well as computationally motivated.

RABIT has a very efficient algorithm for retrieving the relevant information from the LTM. The LTM is organized as a bipartite graph where the nodes are either formulas or concepts. Each formula is linked to all the concepts that occur in it. So, (example from [Gary and Elgot-Drapkin, 1996] the formula *penguin(tweety)* is linked to the nodes *penguin* and *tweety*. If one wants to retrieve every formula that mentions Tweety, one only needs to take all nodes adjacent to Tweety in the graph.

A method of marker-passing is used for determining which formulas of the LTM go to STM. The system chooses the relevant concepts to start with (for example, the concepts occurring in a new belief acquired) and "spreads" the activation through the edges of the graph. The activation level decreases every time it passes a new edge. Every belief with an activation level above a certain threshold is copied into the STM. By regulating the different parameters, like the initial activation, the decrease function and the threshold of activation, one can keep the STM small.

The LTM may contain contradictions, that are only solved when they become evident in the STM. Beliefs in the LTM as well as in the STM have their source attached. When a contradiction arises in the STM, a precedence order of the sources determines which belief should be given up from the STM. But nothing is deleted from the LTM. This means that a contradiction may be retrieved over and over again due to the same input. In a more recent version of RABIT, there is an "adaptive behaviour" that increases the distance between the formula that "lost" in the contradiction solving procedure and any node, so that it becomes less and less likely that the contradiction will be retrieved again.

The RABIT architecture is intuitively very appealing, but there are some aspects of it that prevent it from being useful for our purposes:

1. The retrieval mechanism is very efficient, but what happens after the relevant part of the LTM has been retrieved is that the system starts inferring everything it can from the beliefs in the STM, that is, it is not goal-directed.

2. The LTM only grows, new beliefs are added, but nothing is deleted. Besides the fact that this presents obvious disadvantages from the computational point of view, it does not seem very intuitive that an agent, after concluding that a belief is false, continues to hold it for the same reasons. The belief could certainly be reinferred by another line of reasoning but we do not want a system that follows always the same (doomed to failure) line of reasoning.

3. The way in which the LTM is organized is purely syntactical. There are no links between concepts, for example. If we know that Paul is a lecturer, that a lecturer is a member of the staff and that members of the staff are people,

there is no "short path" between beliefs about people in general and beliefs about Paul.

The aspects above show that the reasoning part of RABIT is not adequated for our purposes. Nevertheless, the architecture of the program is going to be used in the rest of the paper. RABIT's architecture is based on cognitive models of memory and the fact that these models use the notions of small short term memory and relevance links between beliefs provides an independent motivation for our model of a rational agent's belief state. In the next two sections, we will explore and generalize those aspects of the RABIT architecture that will allow us to construct more efficient operations for belief change.

4 STRUCTURING THE BELIEF BASE

As we have seen, if we have an efficient method of retrieving relevant beliefs from a belief base, such that the inference relation obtained by localizing some inference operator C is monotonic and compact, we can use it together with the representation results in [Hansson and Wassermann, 1999] and get efficient, well defined operations of belief change.

In this section we show how to use extra structure of belief bases in order to make the retrieval of the relevant beliefs more efficient.

We begin by assuming that a relatedness relation between formulas of the language is given, with the intended meaning as follows:

$\mathcal{R}(\varphi, \psi)$ if and only if φ and ψ are directly related.

For the moment we leave open what we mean by "directly related". It may have a psychological interpretation given by statements or concepts that individuals associate, or a semantic interpretation - φ and ψ are assertions about the same (or related) topic. In section 5 we give some examples of relatedness relation.

Some desirable properties of $\mathcal{R}$ are:

1. reflexivity - $\mathcal{R}(\varphi, \varphi)$
2. symmetry - $\mathcal{R}(\varphi, \psi) \Leftrightarrow \mathcal{R}(\psi, \varphi)$
3. negation invariance - $\mathcal{R}(\varphi, \neg\varphi)$

Transitivity is not desirable, for two reasons: first, we want to be able to model agents with limited resources, who may be unable to calculate the transitive closure of the relatedness function. Second, we want to be able to talk about degrees of relatedness.

Given a relatedness relation, we can represent a belief base as a (possibly disconnected) graph where each node is a formula and there is an edge between φ and ψ if and only if $\mathcal{R}(\varphi, \psi)$. This graph representation gives us 'immediately a notion of degrees of relatedness: the shorter the path between two formulas of the base is, the closer related they are. Another notion made clear is that of connectedness: the connected components partition the graph into unrelated "topics" or "subjects". Sentences in the same connected component are somehow related, even if far apart.

Formally:

DEFINITION 9. Let B be a belief base and $\mathcal{R}$ be a relation between formulas. A $\mathcal{R}$-path between two formulas φ and ψ in a belief base B is a sequence $P = (\varphi_0, \varphi_1, ..., \varphi_n)$ of formulas such that:

1. $\varphi_0 = \varphi$ and $\varphi_n = \psi$
2. $\{\varphi_1, ..., \varphi_{n-1}\} \subseteq B$
3. $\mathcal{R}(\varphi, \varphi_1), \mathcal{R}(\varphi_1, \varphi_2)$, ..., and $\mathcal{R}(\varphi_n, \psi)$.

If it is clear from the context to which relation we refer we will talk simply about a path in B.

We represent the fact that P is a path between φ and ψ by $\varphi \overset{P}{\leadsto} \psi$.

The length of a path $P = (\varphi_0, \varphi_1, ..., \varphi_n)$ is $l(P) = n$

Note that the extremities of a path in B are not necessarily elements of B.

DEFINITION 10. Let B be a belief base and $\mathcal{R}$ a relation between formulas of the language. We say that two formulas φ and ψ are related in B by $\mathcal{R}$ if and only if there is a path P in B such that $\varphi \overset{P}{\leadsto} \psi$.

Given two formulas φ and ψ and a belief base B, we can use the length of the shortest path between them in B as the degree of unrelatedness of the formulas. If the formulas are not related in B, the degree of unrelatedness is set to infinity. Formulas with a shorter path between them in B are closer related in B.

DEFINITION 11. Let B be a belief base, $\mathcal{R}$ a relation between formulas of the language and φ and ψ formulas. The unrelatedness degree of φ and ψ in B is given by:

$$u(\varphi, \psi) = \begin{cases} 0 & \text{if } \varphi = \psi \text{ and } \varphi \in B \\ \min\{l(P) | \varphi \overset{P}{\leadsto} \psi, P in\ B\} & \text{if } \varphi \text{ and } \psi \text{ are related in B by } \mathcal{R} \\ \infty & \text{otherwise} \end{cases}$$

OBSERVATION 12. A distance function on a set U is a function $d : U \times U \to I\!R$ such that: (i) $d(x, y) \geq 0$; (ii) $d(x, y) = 0$ iff $x = y$; (iii) $d(x, y) = d(y, x)$; and (iv) $d(x, y) \leq d(x, z) + d(z, y)$. The unrelatedness degree u restricted to the connected subgraphs of B is a distance function.

In Figure 1 we see an example of a belief base structured by a relation $\mathcal{R}$ defined by:

$\mathcal{R}(\varphi, \psi)$ if and only if φ and ψ share an atom

This is just an example of a relatedness relation. This relation is clearly too simplistic to capture a cognitive notion of relevance. Nevertheless, it has some

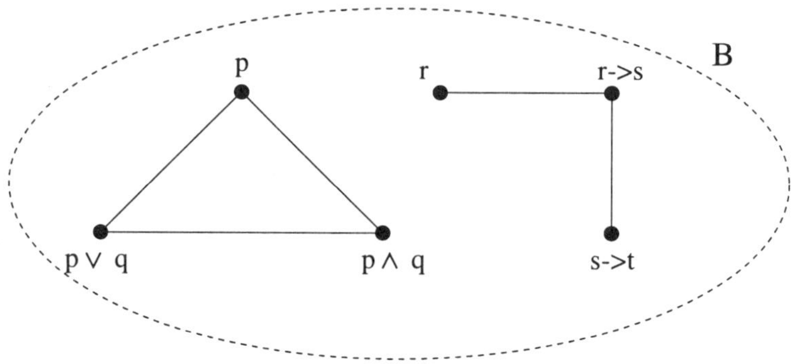

Figure 1. Structured belief base

interesting properties which make it a good starting point for studying relevance. The intended interpretation of $\mathcal{R}(\varphi, \psi)$ is: “Given a formula φ, take every formula ψ in which we believe and that involves the atoms in φ”.

The edges in the figure represent the relation $\mathcal{R}$ between the elements of the belief base. The graph representing the structured base has two disconnected components. The formulas $p \wedge q$ and $r \rightarrow s$ are not related in B. The formula $q \wedge r$ is related to all formulas in the belief base, since it is possible to find a path between it and all formulas in the base. Remember that the initial and final nodes of the path do not have to be elements of the base. This means that if one adds the formula $q \wedge r$ to the base, all the other elements become related to each other in B. This can be interpreted in the following way: the two disconnected components of the original base represent beliefs about unrelated subjects. As soon as one introduces a belief mentioning the subjects of both components, all beliefs in the two componnents become related to each other. There is an implicit assumption here that if one choses to add a belief $p \wedge q$ instead of two beliefs p and q, then there is some relation between p and q.

We now show, given the structure of a belief base, how to retrieve the set of formulas relevant for a given formula α:

DEFINITION 13. The set of formulas of B which are relevant for α with degree i is given by:

$\Delta^i(\alpha, B) = \{\varphi \in B | u(\alpha, \varphi) = i\}$ for $i \geq 0$

DEFINITION 14.

The set of formulas of B which are relevant for α up to degree n is given by:

$\Delta^{\leq n}(\alpha, B) = \bigcup_{0 \leq i \leq n} \Delta^i(\alpha, B)$ for $n \geq 0$

We say that $\Delta^{\leq \omega}(\alpha, B) = \bigcup_{i \geq 0} \Delta^i(\alpha, B)$ is the set of relevant formulas for α.

In section 2 we presented a notion of compartment around a sentence. In definition 2 the α-compartment of a belief base B was defined as the set of formulas of B that contribute to proving either α or its negation. These were the formulas of B that were relevant for an operation of belief change. As we mentioned before, for the representation results obtained in [Hansson and Wassermann, 1999] the particular construction of the compartments does not matter, but only the properties of the inference relation obtained. We now show some properties of the inference operation obtained using $\Delta^{\leq n}$ instead of c (definition 2) as a compartmentalization function.

PROPOSITION 15. *Let B be a belief base and α a formula. For every natural number n and any inference operator C, if C is monotonic and compact, then the local inference operations defined as $C^n_\alpha(B) = C(\Delta^{\leq n}(\alpha, B))$ are monotonic and compact.*

Proof. Since all sets considered are finite, compactness follows trivially. For monotony, let B and D be sets of formulas such that $B \subseteq D$. Let $\beta \in C^n_\alpha(B)$, i.e., $\beta \in C(\Delta^{\leq n}(\alpha, B))$. It is easy to see that $\Delta^{\leq n}(\alpha, B) \subseteq \Delta^{\leq n}(\alpha, D)$. Hence, since C is monotonic, $\beta \in C(\Delta^{\leq n}(\alpha, D))$, i.e., $\beta \in C^n_\alpha(D)$. ■

This means that for any n, $\Delta^{\leq n}$ can be used as a compartmentalization function to define local operations characterized by the results presented in [Hansson and Wassermann, 1999] and summarized in section 2. In the case of an ideal agent, that is, an agent with no limits in its capacity of retrieval, all of the agent's relevant beliefs are retrieved, that is, $\Delta^{\leq \omega}$ is used as a compartmentalization function. Otherwise, we can limit the size of the set retrieved by the choice of n.

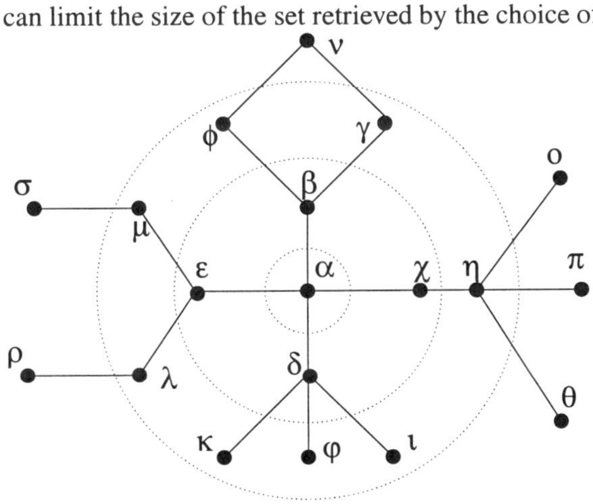

Figure 2. Degrees of relevance

In figure 2, we see an example of a structured belief base $B = \{\alpha, \beta, \gamma, \delta, \varepsilon, \eta, \theta, \iota, \kappa, \lambda, \mu, \nu, o, \pi, \rho, \sigma, \phi, \varphi, \chi\}$. The dotted circles represent different levels of relevance for α. We have:

$$\Delta^0(\alpha, B) = \{\alpha\}$$
$$\Delta^1(\alpha, B) = \{\beta, \chi, \delta, \varepsilon\}$$
$$\Delta^2(\alpha, B) = \{\gamma, \eta, \iota, \varphi, \kappa, \lambda, \mu, \phi\}$$
$$\Delta^3(\alpha, B) = \{\nu, o, \pi, \theta, \rho, \sigma\}$$
$$\Delta^{\leq\omega}(\alpha, B) = \Delta^0(\alpha, B) \cup \Delta^1(\alpha, B) \cup \Delta^2(\alpha, B) \cup \Delta^3(\alpha, B) = B$$

5 WHERE DOES THE STRUCTURE COME FROM?

In the previous section we assumed that a relation of relatedness between elements of the language was given. In this section we will present some ways of deriving such a relation from the belief base.

5.1 Database definitions

In many real applications, there is a part of the database dedicated to the definition of concepts which can be used to generate a relatedness relation.

Let B be a database and A be the subset of B where all the definitions are made. We can say that atoms appearing in the same formula of A are related. We can say that two formulas φ and ψ are related if they share an atom or if there are atoms p in φ and q in ψ such that p and q are related.

Formally:

DEFINITION 16. Let A be a set of formulas. We define a relation R_A on atoms by:

$R_A(p, q)$ if and only if either $p = q$ or p and q occur in the same formula of A.

The relation R_A can be extended to a relation on the language:

DEFINITION 17. Let $\mathcal{R}_A$ be a relation on formulas defined as:

$\mathcal{R}_A(\varphi, \psi)$ iff there are atoms p in φ and q in ψ such that $R_A(p, q)$.

It is easy to see that $\mathcal{R}_A$ is symmetric and reflexive and that for every φ, $\mathcal{R}_A(\varphi, \neg\varphi)$.

The transitive closure of the relation $\mathcal{R}_A$ gives an equivalence relation that determines a partition of the belief base. Each member of the partition is completely independent from the others with respect to the definitions in A.

We can also have $A = B$, that is, use the whole belief base for deriving the relatedness relation.

5.2 *The syntactic approach*

Rodrigues [1997] claims that to ask for a primitive relation between propositional variables or a primitive subject matter assignment may be to strong a requirement. He proposes instead to use directly the relation introduced in Figure 1, i.e.:

$\mathcal{R}(\varphi, \psi)$ if and only if φ and ψ share an atom

He shows that this is actually the smallest relation satisfying the conditions given in [Epstein, 1990] for a relatedness relation.[3]

Epstein [1990] takes the topic or subject matter of a proposition as a primitive and says two propositions are related if they share a subject matter. He considers a set of topics $\mathcal{S}$ and supposes that each propositional variable has a non-empty set of topics associated with it. The set of topics associated with a proposition is simply the union of the sets of topics associated to each variable appearing in it. Epstein shows that one can also take a relatedness relation $\mathcal{R}$ as a primitive and derive a topic assignment from it by taking the subject matter of a formula φ to be $s(\varphi) = \{\{\varphi, \psi\} | \mathcal{R}(\varphi, \psi)\}$. Clearly, the result of applying the definition of relatedness to this topic assignment, i. e., $\mathcal{R}(\varphi, \psi)$ if and only if $s(\varphi) \cap (\psi)$ is non-empty is the relation $\mathcal{R}$.

Another way of deriving the relatedness structure from the given data is to consider the knowledge base as a whole and create a graph that has as nodes formulas and atoms. Each formula is then linked to the atoms that occur in it. This is the approach followed by the RABIT system. The derived structure is that of a (possibly disconnected) bipartite graph. Atoms can be related to each other only via some formula in the database that contains them. In the same way, formulas are only related to other formulas via some atom they share. This has the advantage that it is very easy to insert a new formula in the graph, one only has to link it to the atoms it contains. On the other hand, since there is no link between atoms, even if the atoms p and q are intuitively directly related, the formulas p and q will only be related if there is any formula in the belief base containing both. One could use tricks, like adding some formula *related(p,q)* to the belief base if the agent believes that p and q are related or adding a tautology like $(p \vee \neg p) \vee (q \vee \neg q)$ to the belief base in order to relate p and q.

Epstein's and RABIT's approaches have the property that the relatedness relation is defined on the whole language and is independent from the particular belief base. This means that adding beliefs to the structure consists of adding the input formula α to the set of nodes and adding an edge between α and every node β such that $\mathcal{R}(\alpha, \beta)$. Deleting a belief α from thee set of nodes and removing all

[3] According to [Epstein, 1990], any relatedness relation R should satisfy:
R1 - $R(\varphi, \varphi)$
R2 - $R(\varphi, \psi)$ iff $R(\neg\varphi, \psi)$
R3 - $R(\varphi, \psi)$ iff $R(\psi, \varphi)$
R4 - $R(\varphi, \gamma \rightarrow \psi)$ iff $R(\varphi, \gamma)$ or $R(\varphi, \psi)$
R5 - $R(\varphi, \gamma \wedge \psi)$ iff $R(\varphi, \gamma \rightarrow \psi)$.

the edges leaving from it. After adding or deleting a belief, the result is another structured base. The relation $\mathcal{R}$ does not have to be recalculated.

5.3 *The logical approach*

We can define a relatedness relation $\mathcal{R}$ that captures a notion closer to the logical compartments in section 2 as:

$\mathcal{R}(\varphi, \psi)$ if and only if there is a set $A \subseteq B$ such that $A \cup \{\varphi\} \nvdash \bot$ and either $A \nvdash \psi$ and $A \cup \{\varphi\} \vdash \psi$ or $A \nvdash \neg\psi$ and $A \cup \{\varphi\} \vdash \neg\psi$

or:

$\mathcal{R}(\varphi, \psi)$ if and only if $\varphi \in c(\psi, B)$

where c is a compartmentalization function as in definition 2.

Note that this relation is not symmetric. The definitions of path, unrelatedness degree and relevant set of formulas (Δ^ω) in section 4 can be maintained. The obvious problem of this approach is that it may be very hard to find the related pairs, but if the relation is given, this problem is avoided. If the language is finite, one way in which the relation can be given is as follows: All sets of formulas can be listed. For each pair of formulas φ and ψ, one can select all sets where φ occurs, check whether they imply ψ or $\neg\psi$ and if so, check their subsets to see whether they also imply ψ or $\neg\psi$. If not, then $\mathcal{R}(\varphi, \psi)$. This is of course very costly, but if the same language is going to be used several times, one can pre-compute this relation and use it for all belief bases.

5.4 *The hybrid approach*

A fourth alternative is to combine the database or the syntactic approach with the logical one. If the database is such that it contains several (small) independent modules, this can be a good strategy. One can first apply the first notion of relatedness and find a partition of the database. Then one only has to consider the partition members related to the input formula and look for the relevant formulas inside them using the logic formulation of compartments given in section 2. It can be shown that the compartment obtained is the same that would be obtained checking the whole set.

Let B be a belief base and let $\mathcal{R}$ be the relatedness relation introduced in figure 1, i. e.: $\mathcal{R}(\varphi, \psi)$ if and only if φ and ψ share an atom. Since $\mathcal{R}$ is reflexive and symmetric, its transitive closure defines a partition of the elements of B. Let $\{B_1, B_2, ..., B_n\}$ be the elements of the partition. We say that a set B_i is related to a formula α ($\mathcal{R}(\alpha, B_i)$)if and only if $\mathcal{R}(\alpha, \beta)$ for some $\beta \in B_i$. We denote by P_α the set of elements of the partition that are related to α, i.e., $P_\alpha = \{B_i | \mathcal{R}(\alpha, B_i)\}$.

THEOREM 18. *Let B be a belief base, α be a contingent formula and c be the compartmentalization function as in definition 2.Then $c(\alpha, B) = c(\alpha, \bigcup P_\alpha)$.*

Proof. From $\bigcup P_\alpha \subseteq B$ and observation 3 it follows that $c(\alpha, \bigcup P_\alpha) \subseteq c(\alpha, B)$. For the other side of the inclusion, let $\beta \in c(\alpha, B)$. This means that there is $X \subseteq B$ such that X is consistent, inclusion minimal and $\alpha \in Cn(X)$ or $\neg\alpha \in Cn(X)$. Suppose by contradiction that $X \not\subseteq \bigcup P_\alpha$. Then, there is $\gamma \in X$ such that for all $B_i \in P_\alpha, \gamma \notin B_i$. From this it follows that α is not related to γ, i.e., there is no $\mathcal{R}$ path from α to γ. Since X is consistent it follows that $\alpha \in Cn(X \setminus \{\gamma\})$ or $\neg\alpha \in Cn(X \setminus \{\gamma\})$, contradicting the minimality of X. Hence, $\beta \in X \subseteq \bigcup P_\alpha$ and from parts 1 and 2 of observation 3 it follows that $c(\alpha, B) \subseteq c(\alpha, \bigcup P_\alpha)$. ■

As an example, let $B = \{p, q, p \to q, s, t \vee v, s \to v, w \wedge x, x \to z, z \vee w\}$ and let c be a compartmentalization function as in definition 2. The compartment around $p \vee w$ is given by $c(p \vee w, B) = \{p, w \wedge x\}$. The set B can be clearly divided into three unrelated components: $B_1 = \{p, q, p \to q\}$, $B_2 = \{s, t \vee v, s \to v\}$ and $B_3 = \{w \wedge x, x \to z, z \vee w\}$. The formula $p \vee w$ is only related to two of these components, namely B_1 and B_3. We can then disconsider B_2 and calculate the compartment by: $c(p \vee w, B) = c(p \vee w, B_1 \cup B_3) = \{p, w \wedge x\}$.

6 COMPUTATIONAL ASPECTS

In this section we discuss the complexity of the operation described for retrieving the set of relevant beliefs from a base.

An *anytime algorithm* is one that whenever it is interrupted has built an approximate solution for a problem, and the longer it runs, the better the approximation gets.

The good thing about the method for retrieving the relevant beliefs is that it is an anytime method, that is, whenever it is interrupted, it has retrieved the most relevant beliefs, and the longer it runs, the closer it gets to retrieving all the relevant beliefs (the maximal connected subgraph). This is a very desirable property for modeling agents that may not have enough time or memory to find all the related beliefs. In the ideal case, if there is no resource limitation, the method succeeds in retrieving a maximal connected subgraph.

Below we present a sketch of an algorithm that takes as input a formula α and a belief base and returns the set of formulas of the base that are relevant for α. The algorithm can be stopped at anytime, always returning the set of most relevant beliefs for α. The algorithm is a modification of the algorithm BFS for breadth first search in [Cormen *et al.*, 1990].

The belief base is represented by a vector of formulas, each one with a list of pointers to the adjacent nodes in the graph. The nodes adjacent to a formula α are given by Adjacent(α). The complexity of the construction of the list of adjacent nodes depends on the relatedness relation used. For the relation used in figure 1, we can use extra, invisible nodes corresponding to the atoms of the language. Every formula added to the belief base is linked to all atoms appearing on it. Constructing the list has then complexity $O(m \times n)$, where m is the number of occurences of atoms in the formulas involved (the "size" of the belief base) and n is the number of atoms in the language. If the atoms are organized in some kind of lexicographical order, this complexity becomes $O(m \times \log n)$.

Retrieve(α,B,Relevant):
1. If $\alpha \in B$, then mark(α)
2. $\Delta^1(\alpha, B)$:= Adjacent(α)
3. i := 1; stop := false
4. While not stop do
    4.1. For all $\beta \in \Delta^i(\alpha, B)$ mark(β)
    4.2. i := i+1
    4.3 For all $\beta \in \Delta^{i-1}(\alpha, B)$,
        $\Delta^i(\alpha, B) := \Delta^i(\alpha, B) \cup \{\varphi \in$Adjacent($\beta$) s.t. not marked($\varphi$)$\}$
    4.4 If $\Delta^i(\alpha, B) = \emptyset$, then stop := true
5. Relevant := $\{\beta \in B$ s.t. marked(β)$\}$

At each step, the algorithm looks at the set retrieved at the previous step and gets all the neighbours that have not been visited yet. When all nodes of a connected component have been visited, it halts. Depending on how the information is encoded, the algorithm runs in linear time.

After retrieving the relevant beliefs, traditional belief change constructions can be applied to it, provided the set is small enough (one can stop the algorithm once the relevant set gets bigger than a certain limit).

7 RELATED WORK

The idea of isolating inconsistencies by means of compartments has been studied by several authors. Most of these did not use the notion of relevance to create the compartments.

Jaśkowski introduced his discursive logics as a way of formalizing "what some participant of a discourse is committed to" [Jaśkowski, 1969]. If participant x asserts α and participant y asserts β, then α and β are true in his logics, but not $\alpha \wedge \beta$, since there may be no participant of the discourse that is committed to both assertions α and β. Assertions associated to different participants of the discourse cannot be mixed.

Lewis [1982] also defended the idea of fragments that cannot be mixed, but the different (possibly overlapping) fragments were part of a single agent's beliefs.

Fagin and Halpern [1988] formalized a similar idea. In their Logic of Local Reasoning, an agent may have several "frames of mind". An agent believes α if he beliefs α in some frame of mind. This idea is formalized via an extended Kripke structure, where instead of one accessibility relation between worlds, there is a relation $\mathcal{C}$ between worlds and sets of worlds. If $\mathcal{C}(s) = \{T_1, ..., T_n\}$, then an agent in state s sometimes takes the set of worlds T_1 as possible, sometimes T_2, etc.

Benferhat *et al.* [1997] use yet another approach to isolate inconsistencies, which is very similar to the approach known in AI as WIDTIO (When In Doubt Throw It Out) [Winslett, 1990]. They define a free (or sound) inference operator that disconsiders all formulas belonging to a minimal inconsistent subset. So, $B \vdash_{free} \alpha$ if and only if $Free(B) \vdash \alpha$, where $Free(B)$ is the result of deleting every minimal inconsistent subset from B.

There are in the literature several attempts to define the concepts of relevance and dependence. In [del Cerro and Herzig, 1996] a set of postulates is presented that any dependence relation should satisfy. They show then how a contraction operation satisfying the Gärdenfors postulates can be obtained from a dependence relation.

Their dependence relations are syntax independent and only logically independent formulas can be related. From this it seems clear that the notion of relevance captured by the postulates is very different from the one we are trying to model. Our notion is independent of the logic.

The idea of using graphs representing dependency relations for finding the relevant part of a database is well-known in the field of logic programming (see, for example, [Kowalski, 1979]). In the case of logic programs, the dependency relation is not symmetric and the graph obtained is a directed one.

8 CONCLUSIONS AND FURTHER WORK

We have presented a way of introducing more
indexstructured be;oefs structure to belief bases so that relevant beliefs can be retrieved in an efficient way. The belief bases are represented by a graph, instead of by a set of formulas, where the formulas the agent believes are the nodes and the edges represent a relatedness relation. We have shown some example of relatedness relations and how they can be obtained.

We presented an algorithm to retrieve the most relevant beliefs from a structured belief base and showed that the algorithm could be used instead of the compartmentalization function defined in [Hansson and Wassermann, 1999]. In this way, we obtained efficient and well characterized operations of belief change.

In more realistic agents, the whole belief base may be connected, that is, it may be impossible to isolate a small connected component. In such cases, one can think about more sophisticated notions of connectedness, like finding connected "chunks" in the graph and preferring edges internal to a chunk over the others (see, for example, [van Dongen, 1997]).

The structure of the belief base is used now only to retrieve the most relevant beliefs. Then traditional operations for belief change are applied on the set of beliefs retrieved. Further work includes investigating how to use the structure of the belief base also for implementing more efficient operations of belief change.

ACKNOWLEDGMENTS

I would like to thank Chris Albert, Kevin Gary, Hans Rott and Frans Voorbraak for comments on an earlier draft. This research is sponsored by a grant from the Brazilian funding agency CAPES and the Dutch Research Council PIONIER-project Reasoning With Uncertainty.

University of Amsterdam, The Netherlands.

REFERENCES

[Alchourrón *et al.*, 1985] Carlos Alchourrón, Peter Gärdenfors, and David Makinson. On the logic of theory change. *Journal of Symbolic Logic*, 50, 1985.

[Benferhat *et al.*, 1997] Salem Benferhat, Didier Dubois, and Henri Prade. Some syntactic approaches to the handling of inconsistent knowledge bases: A comparative study. part 1: The flat case. *Studia Logica*, pages 17–45, 1997.

[del Cerro and Herzig, 1996] Luis Fariñas del Cerro and Andreas Herzig. Belief change and dependence. In Yohav Shoham, editor, *Proceedings of TARK 96*, 1996.

[Cormen *et al.*, 1990] Thomas H. Cormen, Charles E. Leiserson, and Ronald L. Rivest. *Introduction to Algorithms*. MIT Press, 1990.

[Dixon, 1994] Simon E. Dixon. *Belief Revision: a Computational Approach*. PhD thesis, Basser Department of Computer Science, University of Sidney, 1994.

[van Dongen, 1997] Stijn van Dongen. Graph clustering and information structuring. In E. Kraak and R. Wassermann, editors, *Proceedings of the Accolade 97*. Dutch Graduate School in Logic, 1997.

[Drapkin and Perlis, 1986] Jennifer Drapkin and Don Perlis. Step-logics: An alternative approach to limited reasoning. In Wolfgang Wahlster, editor, *Proceedings of the European Conference on Artificial Intelligence (ECAI)*. Wiley, 1986.

[Epstein, 1990] Richard L. Epstein. *The semantic foundations of logic, volume 1: Propositional Logic*. Nijhoff International Philosophy Series. Kluwer Academic Publishers, 1990.

[Fagin and Halpern, 1988] Ronald Fagin and Joseph Halpern. Belief, awareness, and limited reasoning. *Artificial Intelligence*, 34:39–76, 1988.

[Fuhrmann, 1991] André Fuhrmann. Theory contraction through base contraction. *Journal of Philosophical Logic*, 20:175–203, 1991.

[Gary and Elgot-Drapkin, 1996] Kevin Gary and Jennifer Elgot-Drapkin. RABIT- Bridging formal and implementational approaches to commonsense reasoning. Technical report, Arizona State University, 1996.

[Gary, 1993] Kevin Gary. RABIT - A spreading activation approach to real-time commonsense reasoning. Master's thesis, Arizona State University, Tempe, Arizona, 1993.

[Hansson and Wassermann, 1999] Sven Ove Hansson and Renata Wassermann. Local change. In preparation (a preliminary version was presented at the Fourth Symposium on Logical Formalizations of Commonsense Reasoning, London, 1998), 1999.

[Hansson, 1994] Sven Ove Hansson. Kernel contraction. *Journal of Symbolic Logic*, 59:845–859, 1994.

[Hansson, 1999] Sven Ove Hansson. *A Textbook of Belief Dynamics*. Kluwer Academic Press, 1999.

[Herzig, 1997] Andreas Herzig. How to change factual beliefs using laws and independence information. In Dov M. Gabbay, Rudolf Kruse, Andreas Nonnengart, and Hans Juergen Ohlbach, editors, *Qualitative and Quantitative Practical Reasoning - First Int. Joint Conf. on Qual. and Quant. Practical Reasoning; ECSQARU-FAPR'97*, number 1244 in LNCS, pages 311–321. Springer, jun 1997.

[Jaśkowski, 1969] Stanislaw Jaśkowski. Propositional calculus for contradictory deductive systems. *Studia Logica*, XXIV:143–157, 1969. Translation from the Polish original that appeared in Studia Societatis Scientiarum Torunensis, Vol I, No. 5, 1948.

[Kowalski, 1979] Robert Kowalski. *Logic for Problem Solving*. North Holland, 1979.

[Lewis, 1982] David Lewis. Logic for equivocators. *Noûs*, 16:431–441, 1982.

[Nebel, 1990] Bernhard Nebel. *Reasoning and Revision in Hybrid Representation Systems*, volume 422 of *Lecture Notes in Artificial Intelligence*. Springer-Verlag, 1990.

[Rodrigues, 1997] Odinaldo T. Rodrigues. *A Methodology for Iterated Information Change*. PhD thesis, Imperial College, University of London, 1997.

[Rott, 1991] Hans Rott. A nonmonotonic conditional logic for belief revision. In André Fuhrmann and Michael Morreau, editors, *The logic of theory change*. Springer Verlag, 1991. LNAI 465.

[Rott, 1996] Hans Rott. Making up one's mind: Foundations, coherence, nonmonotonicity. Habilitationsschrift, University of Konstanz. To appear as *Change, Choice, and Inference*, Oxford University Press, October 1996.

[Wassermann, 1999] Renata Wassermann. Resource-bounded belief revision. *Erkenntnis*, 50:429–446, 1999.

[Williams, 1994] Mary-Anne Williams. On the logic of theory base change. In *Proceedings of the European Workshop on Logics in Artificial Intelligence (JELIA'95)*, 1994.

[Winslett, 1990] Marianne Winslett. *Updating Logic Databases*. Number 9 in Cambridge Tracts in Theoretical Computer Science. Cambridge University Press, 1990.

BRIGITTE BESSANT, ERIC GRÉGOIRE, PIERRE MARQUIS AND LAKHDAR SAÏS

ITERATED SYNTAX-BASED REVISION IN A NONMONOTONIC SETTING

1 INTRODUCTION

Various approaches to belief revision have been proposed this last decade. Most of them have been investigated from a knowledge-level theoretical perspective [Newell, 1982], mainly. Despite a few noticeable exceptions (e.g. [Papini, 1991] [Nebel, 1992] [Eiter and Gottlob, 1992] [Liberatore and Schaerf, 1996]), their computational counterparts have rarely been considered. Worse, due to worst case complexity results, they are often believed to be intractable when large-scale applications are addressed. However, recent impressive empirical progress in propositional reasoning and search [Selman *et al.*, 1997] does open real computational perspectives for syntax-based approaches to belief revision with respect to large applications. Also, many efforts have been devoted to establish formal connections between nonmonotonic logics and belief revision (see e.g. [del Val, 1984] [Makinson and Gärdenfors, 1991] [Moinard, 1994] [Liberatore and Schaerf, 1995]). In this paper, a knowlege[1] engineering-motivated approach to belief revision is adopted, showing that belief revision and nonmonotonic logics are not only two sides of the same coin [Gärdenfors, 1992] but that they can play useful synergetic roles in a unified framework that proves empirically computationally viable. More precisely, a two-steps policy to syntax-based revision of inconsistent beliefs is proposed. On the one hand, nonmonotonic ingredients are provided within a belief representation language giving rise to a gain of expressiveness, allowing a careful knowledge engineer to avoid many future inconsistencies that would occur if a standard deductive representation and inference of beliefs were selected. Inconsistencies that are not forecast and prevented in this way are then the object of a syntax-based belief revision process. In this respect, we can envision a whole family of syntax-based revision approaches: from a *full-meet* cautious one that weakens each formula in each minimally inconsistent subbase to regain consistency, to a *maxichoice* change policy that just weakens one smallest subset of formulas to restore consistency. In this paper, an empirically viable computational technique for the first approach is proposed. It makes use of a specific heuristic in the trace of local search techniques to check (in)consistency. Interestingly enough, it is shown that the nonmonotonic ingredients do not significantly affect the computational complexity results with respect to the revision process, neither from a worst case point of view, nor from an empirical one.

[1] In this paper, *knowledge* is used for *belief*.

M.-A. Williams and H. Rott (eds.), Frontiers in Belief Revision, 369–391.

The paper is organized as follows. After some formal preliminaries, a specific nonmonotonic representation setting is described. Then, a new syntax-based approach to iterated belief base revision is introduced and motivated in this framework, together with a preferred-models inference relation for the resulting logic. The complexity and rationality issues for this cautious, full-meet approach to base revision are analyzed. Local search techniques for SAT are then specialized to match our specific needs. Typical results from extensive tests are reported. Finally, the specific position adopted in this paper with respect to the various facets of belief revision is summarized, and perspectives for further research are briefly exposed. Basic elements of computational complexity can be found in an appendix.

2 SOME FORMAL PRELIMINARIES

Let PS denote a denumerable set of *propositional symbols* (also called *variables* or *atoms*). For every subset V of PS, $PROP_V$ denotes the *propositional language* built up from the symbols of PS, the boolean constants $true$ and $false$ and the connectives $\neg$, $\wedge$, $\vee$, $\Rightarrow$, $\Leftrightarrow$ in the standard way. The elements of $PROP_{PS}$ are called *formulas*.

Every propositional symbol of PS is also called a *positive literal* and a negated one a *negative literal*. The boolean constants are also viewed as positive literals. A *literal* is either a positive literal or a negative literal. Every finite disjunction of literals is called a *clause*. $Var(KB)$ denote the set of propositional variables occurring in the formula KB. For every propositional symbol v from PS, $KB_{v\leftarrow true}$ (resp. $KB_{v\leftarrow false}$) denotes the formula KB in which every occurrence of v is replaced by $true$ (resp. $false$).

An *interpretation* I (over $PROP_{PS}$) is a mapping that associates every propositional symbol to one of the two truth values of $BOOL = \{0, 1\}$ and $I(true) = 1$ and $I(false) = 0$. $[\![KB]\!](I)$ denotes the truth value taken by KB within I; it is defined in the usual compositional way. When I is s.t. $[\![KB]\!](I) = 1$, I is said to be a *model* of KB, noted $I \models KB$; otherwise, I is a *counter-model* of KB. The set of all models of KB is noted $\mathcal{M}(KB)$. When a formula has a model, it is said *consistent*. When a formula has no model (resp. no counter-model), it is said *inconsistent* (resp. *valid*). The binary relation $\models$ over $PROP_{PS}$ is defined by $KB \models f$ iff $\mathcal{M}(KB) \subseteq \mathcal{M}(f)$ holds. The *deductive closure* of KB is the set of all formulas that are logical consequences of KB. Whenever $KB \models f$ and $f \models KB$ both hold, KB and f are said *logically equivalent*, noted $KB \equiv f$.

Every set of formulas is interpreted conjunctively; especially, when it is finite, a set of formulas is also considered as the formula that is the conjunction of its elements. It is well-known that every formula admits a conjunction of clauses equivalent to it; such a conjunction of clauses is called a *conjunctive normal form* (CNF for short) of the formula.

3 A NONMONOTONIC REPRESENTATION FRAMEWORK

This paper is more concerned with the knowledge engineering branch of artificial intelligence than with its cognitive and philosophical sides; building effective practical systems is here the main goal. In this respect, it is generally agreed that some trade-off can be required between the expressiveness of the representation language and the inference efficiency. Similarly, a specific combination of belief revision and nonmonotonic representation of beliefs and inference can be beneficial, especially when software quality properties are required.

Accordingly, a two-steps handling of inconsistent beliefs is advocated in this paper. First, the knowledge engineer is provided with a nonmonotonic language allowing him to prevent many future inconsistencies that would occur if a purely standard deductive logic were used. This language should be expressive enough to represent (prioritized) rules of default reasoning and exceptions, preventing these last ones from leading to inconsistency when they actually occur. In this respect, it is claimed here that when real-world large-scale applications are undertaken, the knowledge engineer can be required a disciplined use of nonmonotonic ingredients that are restricted, in exchange for the hope for predictable system behavior and good computational performance in many cases. However, the knowledge engineer cannot be required to forecast all such exceptions in this way. This is exactly where belief revision has to play a role in our framework. Belief revision will thus here just concern a mere remainder of the inconsistencies that would occur if a purely deductive logic were selected. This point will allow specific revision policies to be justified.

In the following, any belief base KB will be represented as a finite set (interpreted conjunctively) of propositional formulas from $PROP_{PS}$. The set of propositional symbols PS is partitioned into three denumerable sets, P, AB_{KB} and $AB_{Revision}$. P is used to represent the core knowledge of KB, while the two disjoint sets AB_{KB} and $AB_{Revision}$ contain McCarthy's prioritized Abnormality propositions, noted respectively by Ab_i and Ab_{R_i} [McCarthy, 1986]. Elements from AB_{KB} allow prioritized rules of default reasoning to be expressed together with exceptions (they encode structural abnormalities) while $AB_{Revision}$ is actually a sequence and is devoted to the revision policy. Typically, a default rule expressing that a bird can fly (unless exceptions) will be of the form $\neg Bird \vee Ab_{flying\_bird} \vee Fly$, representing the formula $Bird \wedge \neg Ab_{flying\_bird} \Rightarrow Fly$. Ab_i propositions are intended to allow for exceptions without the need of expressing them explicitly. Such a framework will be interpreted under model-preference semantics *à la* Shoham [Shoham, 1987]: $KB \mid\!\sim_{\leq} f$ iff $[\![f]\!](I) = 1$ in all preferred models I of KB, where the preferred models of KB are those that are minimal w.r.t. a given pre-order $\leq$. Intuitively, models where Ab_i propositions are minimized (i.e. are interpreted as 0) will be preferred. Many minimization schemata (especially prioritizing ones) giving rise to preferred-models inference relations $\mid\!\sim_{\leq}$ can be adopted in this context. The approaches of revision that will be developed in this paper are compatible with all of them.

4 BASE REVISION BY WEAKENING: THE FULL-MEET APPROACH

As the last example illustrates it, the knowledge engineer may not forecast possible exceptions to all rules (assume that he has asserted that all birds fly and that now we are given a penguin). When inconsistency does occur, several possible approaches to restore consistency can be devised. As we adopt here a knowledge engineering approach to artificial intelligence, we claim that the syntax of the encoded beliefs is important and that this should appear in the revision process. Accordingly, in our approach, the epistemic state of an agent (i.e. the set of all its beliefs) is represented as a belief base, i.e. a finite set of propositional formulas: the pieces of knowledge that can be inferred from such a set are the agent's beliefs. While such an approach to belief revision is syntax-sensitive (at least to the extent that it cannot be guaranteed that two equivalent KBs will always be revised in the same way), it is representationally feasible; this contrasts with the belief set approach and the model-based approach to belief revision: due to space considerations, representing the epistemic state of an agent by a deductively closed set of formulas, or by the corresponding set of models, is typically out of reach.

Our cautious approach to belief revision is based on the logical concept of weakening. Indeed, we believe that throwing out some beliefs in order to restore consistency is unnecessary destructive. Accordingly, we prefer "hidding" these beliefs by logically weakening them, allowing interesting perspectives with respect to iterated belief revision.

Intuitively, the way according to which beliefs are weakened amounts to considering these beliefs as exceptional ones that do not hold in regard of the newly introduced formula f.

Assume KB to be a nonmonotonic propositional belief base to be interpreted under some preferred-models semantics, given by a pre-order $\leq$ among interpretations. Initially, KB does not contain any occurrence of a symbol from $AB_{Revision}$. Let f be the so-called *revision formula*, i.e. a new piece of knowledge to be added into KB. A *severe revision* has to occur whenever $KB \cup \{f\}$ is inconsistent. The sequence of Abnormality propositions $AB_{Revision} = \{Ab_{R_1}, \ldots, Ab_{R_j}, \ldots\}_{(j<\omega)}$ is used to remove inconsistencies. More precisely, each time a severe revision is to be conducted, a subset of formulas in KB are weakened using the next available Ab_{R_j} in the sequence $AB_{Revision}$ as an additional disjunct in each of these clauses. Note that the elements of $AB_{Revision}$ are ordered in such a way that AB_{R_j} is after AB_{R_i} whenever $i < j$, so as to ensure that the most recently introduced abnormality symbol Ab_{R_j} occurs after Ab_{R_i} in $AB_{Revision}$.

Now, several revision policies can be defined depending on the way this set of formulas to be weakened is selected. Indeed, in order to break all inconsistencies, it is sufficient to weaken one formula in every of the possibly many subbases of KB that are inconsistent with f. Accordingly, several hitting sets of such subbases can be elected for being weakened in the general case. For the case where no additional information (e.g. an epistemic relevance ordering [Nebel, 1990]) enables chosing one such hitting set, a *cautious* policy is proposed: in this situation, all the formulas in the set-theoretic union of the smallest subsets of KB inconsistent with f are weakened. But let us formalize this.

DEFINITION 1 (Minimally inconsistent subbase). A *minimally inconsistent* subbase of KB w.r.t. f is any subset S of KB s.t. $S \cup \{f\}$ is inconsistent and no proper subset of it satisfies the same property.

Such subbases are sometimes called *entailment sets* for $\neg f$ (indeed, $S \cup \{f\}$ is inconsistent iff $\neg f$ is entailed by S).

DEFINITION 2 (Kernel). The *kernel* $Ker(KB, f)$ of KB w.r.t. f is the set-theoretic union of all minimally inconsistent subbases of KB w.r.t. f

$Ker(KB, f)$ can also be defined in a dual way, focusing on the maximally consistent subbases of KB w.r.t. f (also called *remainders* of KB by $\neg f$). Indeed, $Ker(KB, f)$ is the set-theoretic complement in KB of the intersection of all such subbases (see Theorem 7.1 from [Nebel, 1998]).

We are now ready to define our full-meet base revision operation:

DEFINITION 3 (Full-meet revision). Assume that KB is the result of i previous severe revisions. $KB \circ_{full-meet} f = (Ker(KB, f) \vee Ab_{R_{i+1}}) \cup (KB \setminus Ker(KB, f)) \cup \{f\}$

In this definition, $Ker(KB, f) \vee Ab_{R_{i+1}}$ denotes the set of formulas $g \vee Ab_{R_{i+1}}$, where g is a formula from $Ker(KB, f)$. Clearly enough, the rank $i + 1$ of the current revision can be determined in time linear in the size of KB (it is sufficient to filter out the greatest i s.t. AB_{R_i} occurs in KB, and to increment it).

EXAMPLE 4. Let us illustrate the previous definition through a very simple example. Let $KB = \{\neg Bird \vee Fly, Bird\}$. This corresponds to the case where the knowledge engineer does not envision any exceptional bird, i.e. a bird that does not fly. We have:

1. $KB \circ_{full-meet} \neg Fly = \{\neg Bird \vee Fly \vee Ab_{R_1}, Bird \vee Ab_{R_1}, \neg Fly\}$.
2. $(KB \circ_{full-meet} \neg Fly) \circ_{full-meet} Fly = \{\neg Bird \vee Fly \vee Ab_{R_1}, Bird \vee Ab_{R_1}, \neg Fly \vee Ab_{R_2}, Fly\}$.

In our approach, every formula from KB that belongs to the intersection of all maximally consistent subbases of KB w.r.t. f is kept in the revised base, while the remaining formulas are weakened. Thus, instead of focusing on the intersection of the *logical closures* of all (preferred[2]) maximally consistent subbases of KB w.r.t. f (as it is the case in many base revision approaches), we focus on the subbases themselves. This has two immediate, favourable consequences:

[2]Several criteria based on subset maximality or cardinality maximality can be used to select some maximally consistent subbases in presence of an information preference, i.e. assuming that the KB is stratified.

- Revised KBs can be efficiently represented in our approach (since the size of the revised KBs cannot exceed the size of the corresponding original KB plus the size of the revision formula plus the number of formulas occurring in the original KB).
- Revised KBs do not reduce to a single formula. Accordingly, iterated belief revision can be achieved without trivializing as soon as the first severe revision has been achieved.

These two valuable features are not shared by many syntax-based approaches to base revision. On the one hand, it is shown [Cadoli *et al.*, 1995] that representations of revised KBs that are compact, i.e. of size polynomially bounded by the size of the original KB plus the size of the revision formula, are very unlikely to exist in the general case for various revision policies. Especially, while there can be exponentially many maximally consistent subbases of KB w.r.t. f, the size of their set-theoretic union is necessarily bounded by the size of KB. On the other hand, while the intersection of the logical closures of all maximally consistent subbases of KB w.r.t. f can be finitely encoded as the disjunction of all such subbases, the resulting revised base contains only one formula[3]; thus, the whole content of KB would be removed, would a second severe revision occur.

Because it is based on the computation of $Ker(KB, f)$, our approach is closely related to both WIDTIO base revision [Winslett, 1990], and safe base revision [Alchourrón and Makinson, 1985] (that coincide when no preference information is available [Nebel, 1998], and share the two valuable features listed above). Indeed, in [Winslett, 1990], a purely standard logic approach to revision (namely, WIDTIO, i.e. "When In Doubt Throw It Out") requires $Ker(KB, f)$ to be discarded in case of a severe revision:
$KB \circ_{WIDTIO} f$ is defined as $KB \circ_{WIDTIO} f = (KB \setminus Ker(KB, f)) \cup \{f\}$.

Instead, we propose to weaken $Ker(KB, f)$. As we will see in the next section, this may have a great influence on the revised epistemic state in the context of iterated revisions.

5 INFERRING FROM A REVISED KNOWLEDGE BASE

Let $\leq$ be any pre-order among interpretations from which a preferred-models inference relation can be defined. Let us now define an inference relation $\mid\!\sim_{R,\leq}$ under which revised KBs will be interpreted. Actually, the inference relation will be nonmonotonic; it will interpret the Abnormality propositions from $AB_{Revision}$ and AB_{KB} separately, and successively. From a semantical point of view, the inference relation will use a concept of *preferred revision-preferred model*. Such models minimize abnormality according to two principles:

[3]Or two, if the pair formed by such a disjunction and f is considered as the revised base.

Principle 1.
Elements from $AB_{Revision}$ have a higher priority than elements from AB_{KB}. Elements of $AB_{Revision}$ encode unexpected abnormalities, corresponding to severe revisions. They must be interpreted in such a way that consistency is restored. This can easily constrain the set of possible truth values of the elements of AB_{KB}. Structural abnormalities from this latter set must also be minimized.

Principle 2.
The elements of $AB_{Revision}$ are prioritized, *à la* prioritized circumscription [McCarthy, 1986] but with one abnormality symbol per stratum, only. A higher priority is given to more recently introduced Abnormality propositions. Accordingly, every Ab_{R_i} is preferred $false$ (except the most recently introduced Abnormality proposition, which must be $true$ to revise the last state of inconsistency).

Formally, let us assume without loss of generality that PS is totally ordered (using any order) and that interpretations I over $PROP_{PS}$ are represented as words over $\{0,1\}$ s.t. the ith bit of I is 1 iff the ith symbol of PS is interpreted as 1 in I. For every subset E of PS, let $I[E]$ denote the restriction of I to the symbols of E. On this ground, we can define a total pre-order among the models of KB:

DEFINITION 5 (Revision-preference). Let I and J be two models of KB. I is said at least as *revision-preferred* as J, noted $I \leq_R J$, iff $I[AB_{Revision}] \leq_{lex} J[AB_{Revision}]$ holds, where $\leq_{lex}$ is the reverse lexicographic ordering on words over $\{0,1\}$, induced by $0 < 1$.

The revision-preferred models of KB are the minimal models of KB w.r.t. $\leq_R$.

DEFINITION 6 (Revision-preferred model). The set of all revision-preferred models of KB is defined by $\mathcal{M}_R(KB) = min(\mathcal{M}(KB), \leq_R)$.

It is worth noting that all revision-preferred models I of KB coincide on $AB_{Revision}$. Such models can be characterized in the following constructive way. Let Ab_{R_z} be the lastly introduced symbol of $AB_{Revision}$ in KB:

Procedure Revision-preferred-models
Input: KB, $AB_{Revision}$, Ab_{R_z}
Output: an interpretation I over $PROP_{AB_{Revision}}$

```
begin
 for every AbR_i in ABRevision from AbR_z downto AbR_1 do
  if KB_{AbR_i ← false} is consistent
   then [[AbR_i]](I) = 0
   else [[AbR_i]](I) = 1
 return I
end
```

All the remaining symbols from $AB_{Revision}$ are set to 0 in the revision-preferred models I of KB^4. Now, among the revision-preferred models, the preferred ones are those that minimize the structural abnormalities, according to any preset preferred-models semantics:

DEFINITION 7 (Preferred revision-preferred model). Let $\leq$ be any pre-order among the models of KB. The set of all preferred revision-preferred models of KB is defined by $\mathcal{M}_{R,\leq}(KB) = min(\mathcal{M}_R(KB), \leq)$.

Finally, the corresponding preferred-models inference relation $\mid\!\sim_{R,\leq}$ can be defined as follows:

DEFINITION 8 (Preferred revision-preferred inference). Let $\leq$ be any pre-order among the models of KB. $KB \mid\!\sim_{R,\leq} f$ iff f is satisfied in all preferred revision-preferred models of KB.

Clearly enough, in the situation where no severe revision has been performed, no symbol from $AB_{Revision}$ occurs in KB. Thus, every model is a revision-preferred one and the preferred revision-preferred models of KB are just the preferred models of KB, i.e. those that are minimal w.r.t. $\leq$. Contrastingly, in the situation where no structural abnormalities have been envisioned (i.e. $AB_{KB} = \emptyset$), the preferred revision-preferred models of KB are its revision-preferred models.

EXAMPLE 9 (continued). For simplicity, let us assume that $AB_{KB} = \emptyset$. Let $KB = \{\neg Bird \vee Fly, Bird\}$. We have:

1. $KB \mid\!\sim_{R,\leq} Fly \wedge Bird$. The (preferred) revision-preferred models of KB coincide with the models of KB.

2. $KB \circ_{full-meet} \neg Fly = \{\neg Bird \vee Fly \vee Ab_{R_1}, Bird \vee Ab_{R_1}, \neg Fly\} \mid\!\sim_{R,\leq} \neg Fly$. Once again, the (preferred) revision-preferred models I of $KB \circ_{full-meet} \neg Fly$ coincide with its models and satisfy $[\![Ab_{R_1}]\!](I) = 1$.

3. $(KB \circ_{full-meet} \neg Fly) \circ_{full-meet} Fly = \{\neg Bird \vee Fly \vee Ab_{R_1}, Bird \vee Ab_{R_1}, \neg Fly \vee Ab_{R_2}, Fly\} \mid\!\sim_{R,\leq} Fly \wedge Bird$. This time, the (preferred) revision-preferred models I of the revised base do not coincide with its models. Every I is s.t. $[\![Ab_{R_2}]\!] = 1$ and $[\![Ab_{R_1}]\!] = 0$.

As evoked before, our framework does not enable taking into account preference information about what subbases should be kept. Indeed, the two revision principles given above are to be applied to any KB, thus the way unexpected abnormalities from $AB_{Revision}$ are minimized does not depend on KB. Nevertheless, some preference information about structural abnormalities can be incorporated within our framework; it is supported by the given pre-order $\leq$, and different pre-orders can easily give rise to different inference relations $\mid\!\sim_{R,\leq}$ from revised KBs. Furthermore, some flexibility can be achieved in our framework by modifying the status of some occurrences of Abnormality propositions. Indeed,

[4]This is required by the definition but is not very significant since such remaining symbols do not occur in KB.

when an unexpected, revision-generated exception has been revealed, the knowledge engineer can easily decide to view it afterwards as a structural abnormality. This modification can easily change what can be inferred.

6 RATIONALITY AND COMPLEXITY ISSUES

It is time now to weight the pros and the cons of our approach, especially w.r.t. rationality and complexity issues.

From a formal point of view, it is not easy to check our non-standard approach against usual rationality postulates for belief revision. On the one hand, we use a nonmonotonic inference framework instead of the standard deductive one. On the other hand, the ontology is not constant since additional Abnormality propositions are introduced during the successive severe revision steps. As a consequence, our approach does not satisfy the inclusion postulate proposed by [Hansson, 1993]: in the general case, $KB^{\circ_{full-meet}} f$ is not a subset of $KB \cup \{f\}$. Also, standard AGM rationality postulates apply to *belief sets*, i.e. deductively closed sets of beliefs, whereas we consider *belief bases* (more precisely finite sets of formulas).

Adapting Nebel's technique [Nebel, 1989] to our nonmonotonic framework, we can associate a belief set revision operator $*_{full-meet}$ to our belief base one. Let $Cn(KB) = \{h \text{ s.t. } KB \mid\!\sim_{R,\leq} h\}$ the nonmonotonic closure of KB given $\mid\!\sim_{R,\leq}$. A belief set, i.e. the set of beliefs of some agent, is the nonmonotonic closure of a belief base KB. The belief set operator $*_{full-meet}$ generated by $\circ_{full-meet}$ is given by $Cn(KB)^{*_{full-meet}} f = Cn(KB^{\circ_{full-meet}} f)$.

It is easy to show that $*_{full-meet}$ obeys the six basic rationality postulates by Alchourrón *et al.* [Alchourrón *et al.*, 1985]. However, the two supplementary postulates are not satisfied in the general case. This is not very surprising since WIDTIO base revision typically exhibits the same behaviour w.r.t. rationality postulates.

As evoked previously, our revision process does not entail an exponential increase of size for the revised KB as in many syntax-based approaches, especially [Fagin *et al.*, 1983], and it allows for iterated belief revision in a non-trivial way (unlike some techniques proposed so far, see e.g. [Nebel, 1989]). Moreover, as it will be shown in the next section, it is far less destructive than WIDTIO in presence of iterated revision, hence adhering more closely to the principle of minimal change.

We believe that the way we hide pieces of information by weakening them can open new alternative research directions in the study of rationality postulates for iterated belief revision, which currently gives rise to an unsettled controversy (see e.g. [Darwiche and Pearl, 1997] [Lehman, 1995] [Williams, 1995] and [Friedman and Halpern, 1996]).

Let us now turn to computational aspects. Propositional belief base revision is intractable in the general case. This intractability concerns both the complexity of deciding whether a formula is implied by a revised belief base, and the complexity of representing a revised belief base. Thus, [Nebel, 1998] analyzes in depth the first issue and shows that inference from a revised KB typically is at the first level or even at the second level of the polynomial hierarchy.

Like (full-meet) WIDTIO [Winslett, 1990] and safe base revision [Alchourrón and Makinson, 1985], our approach suffers from a high worst case complexity. In order to simplify things, let us first assume that $AB_{KB} = \emptyset$ (in this situation, the chosen pre-order $\leq$ over models is not significant).

PROPOSITION 10. *Let KB, f be two formulas and $AB_{KB} = \emptyset$. Checking whether $KB \mid\!\sim_{R,\leq} f$ holds is Π_2^p-complete.*

Sketch of proof: In order to check that $KB \not\mid\!\sim_{R,\leq} f$, it is sufficient to guess a model I of KB, then check that it is a revision-preferred one, and that $I \not\models f$ holds. Clearly enough, checking that a given model I of KB is a revision-preferred one can be achieved in polynomial time on a Turing machine equipped with an NP oracle. Indeed, showing that I is not a revision-preferred model of KB can be achieved easily in nondeterministic polynomial time by guessing a model J of KB and checking that $J \leq_R I$ and $I \not\leq_R J$. Equivalently, I is a revision-preferred model of KB iff it coincides with all the revision-preferred models of KB on the symbols of $AB_{Revision}$, and the required truth values of these symbols can be computed thanks to a number of calls to SAT that is bounded by the size of KB (see the procedure `Revision-preferred-models` in the previous section). Accordingly, determining whether $KB \mid\!\sim_{R,\leq} f$ is in Π_2^p. Because inference from WIDTIO revised bases is a restriction of inference w.r.t. $\mid\!\sim_{R,\leq}$ (cf. next section), and inference from WIDTIO revised bases is Π_2^p-hard (lee Lemma 6.2 from [Eiter and Gottlob, 1992]), the Π_2^p-completeness of inference from $\mid\!\sim_{R,\leq}$ follows.

Now, in the case where AB_{KB} is not empty (so that the given pre-order $\leq$ is significant), the complexity upper bound of the inference problem will be given by the complexity of checking whether a model I of KB is a preferred revision-preferred model of KB. If such a model checking problem belongs to coNP (which is the case for many preference relations $\leq$), checking $KB \mid\!\sim_{R,\leq} f$ still belongs to Π_2^p, hence it is Π_2^p-complete.

Focusing on the computation of revised KBs only, the main difficulty of both WIDTIO and our technique is the computation of $Ker(KB, f)$. Indeed, computing minimally inconsistent subbases of KB w.r.t. f can be hard; especially, we can easily prove that, given a finite set KB of propositional formulas and a revision formula f, checking whether a given subset of KB is a minimally inconsistent subbase of KB w.r.t. f is BH_2-complete. Moreover, from a worst case computational complexity point of view, checking the membership of a formula g from KB to $Ker(KB, f)$ is Σ_2^p-complete (this is a consequence of Theorem 8.2 from [Eiter and Gottlob, 1992]). This makes the full-meet approach impractical in the worst case. Fortunately, from the practical side, things are not so bad.

7 APPROXIMATING KERNELS THANKS TO LOCAL SEARCH

A computationally valuable feature of our approach is the existence of an efficient local search-based heuristic for approximating kernels when KB and f are two CNF formulas (which is not so much an unrealistic assumption) [Mazure *et al.*, 1998].

Since this is just a heuristic technique, we cannot guarantee that the output of the proposed algorithm will actually be $Ker(KB, f)$ when the inputs are KB and f. Nevertheless, this does not question the practical utility of the technique. While local search techniques for SAT are not guaranteed to find out a model for every consistent KB, they enable proving the consistency of many of them, which cannot be achieved using a systematic method. In the same vein, experiments show that our heuristic technique can be used to derive or, at least, to focus the search on kernels in many situations.

Since our heuristic technique is based on local search, let us first recall the most representative local search algorithm, namely Selman *et al.*'s GSAT [Selman *et al.*, 1992] [Selman *et al.*, 1993]. This algorithm performs a greedy local search for a satisfying assignment of a set of propositional clauses. The algorithm starts with a randomly generated truth assignment. It then changes ("flips") the assignment of the variable that leads to the largest increase in the total number of satisfied clauses. Such flips are repeated until either a model is found or a preset maximum number of flips (MAX-FLIPS) is reached. This process is repeated as needed up to a maximum of MAX-TRIES times.

```
Procedure GSAT
Input: a set of clauses S, MAX − FLIPS, and MAX − TRIES
Output: a satisfying truth assignment $I$ of S, if found
begin
 for i := 1 to MAX − TRIES do
  I := a randomly generated truth assignment
  for j := 1 to MAX − FLIPS do
   if I is a model of S then return I
   x := a propositional variable s.t. a change in its truth
        assignment gives the largest increase (possibly negative)
        in the number of clauses of S that are satisfied by I
   I := I with the truth assignment of x reversed
 return ''no satisfying assignment found''
end
```

Let us stress that some variant (e.g. random) moves are inserted in order to escape from local minima. In the following, TSAT, a local search technique of our own, is used [Mazure *et al.*, 1997]. It makes use of a tabu list forbidding recurrent flips and appears competitive in most situations. One of the nice features of TSAT is that it drops many stochastic properties of other local search techniques and is purely deterministic as far as the initial interpretation is selected in a non-random way. However, the following experimental results can be obtained using most local search techniques, and are not TSAT specific.

Although such techniques prove efficient in showing the consistency of hard propositional CNF belief bases, they are clearly logically incomplete in the sense that they do not cover the whole search space and cannot thus directly prove that a formula is inconsistent. In this respect, when KB is inconsistent, GSAT-like algorithms provide us with a way to approximate $MAXSAT$, i.e. finding a cardinality maximal subbase of KB. Indeed, at each step, the unsatisfied clauses form a hitting set of the minimally inconsistent subbases of KB. Such a powerful computational approach to a maxi-choice base revision policy is not investigated here (see [Grégoire, 1999]), as we focus on the full-meet one.

Some of us have discovered recently that the trace of local search algorithms can allow one to determine kernels very often when they fail to prove consistency within a preset amount of computing time [Mazure *et al.*, 1998]. More precisely, for each clause, taking each flip as a step of time, the number of times during which this clause is falsified is updated. A similar trace is also recorded for each literal occurring in the belief base, counting the number of times it has appeared in the falsified clauses. All the clauses from KB that are falsified t times more than the mean number of falsification per clause are delivered. t is an empirically fixed threshold. When the local search technique fails to prove consistency, it appears extremely often that the most often falsified clauses from KB form a superset of the set-theoretic union of the minimally inconsistent subbases of KB when KB is actually inconsistent. Likewise, literals that exhibit the highest scores take part in these subbases.

Accordingly, our heuristic is based on the following assumption:

Heuristic: The set S_{TSAT} of clauses from KB delivered by TSAT when it fails in finding a model of $KB \cup \{f\}$ is a superset of $Ker(KB, f)$.

Depending on the computational effort we are ready to spend, the validity of the heuristic can be tested by:

1. Checking that $KB \setminus S_{TSAT} \cup \{f\}$ is consistent. If this is not the case, the heuristic is wrong.

2. Checking that $S_{TSAT} \cup \{f\}$ is inconsistent. If this is not the case, the heuristic is wrong.

The consistency checks can be performed exactly (using a complete algorithm for SAT, e.g. a Davis–Putnam one [Davis *et al.*, 1962]) or approximately using a local search algorithm (assuming that the input formula is inconsistent if no model has been found within a preset time). Note that the test phase can be achieved in practice quite efficiently.

In the case where the heuristic is found wrong, we can turn to a systematic, more computationally expensive technique, to compute $Ker(KB, f)$. Alternatively, we can modify the threshold or modify the parameters of TSAT (the maximum numbers of tries and flips) and, in this latter case, run it again.

It is worth noticing that replacing $Ker(KB, f)$ by a superset S_{TSAT}, as it can be delivered by the first phase of our technique, does not question the consistency of the revised KB. It would just lead to an over-cautious revision policy that would weaken too many pieces of information. Such a policy could be adopted when limited computational resources justify a trade-off between the computational cost and a distance between the probable kernels and the real ones.

Let us stress that in the general case the heuristic provides us with an *approximation* of $Ker(KB, f)$ in the following sense: some formulas from $Ker(KB, f)$ might not appear in S_{TSAT} and S_{TSAT} might contain formulas that do not belong to $Ker(KB, f)$. Clearly enough, if the heuristic is not found wrong, we cannot be sure that S_{TSAT} actually is a superset of $Ker(KB, f)$ (the test phase enables identifying *some* situations where the heuristic is wrong, but *not all of them*). However, under severe time constraints, such an approximation can prove useful as such.

Empirically, the validity of the heuristic depends on several aspects. First, in our nonmonotonic framework, inconsistency is the exception and should normally concern a few formulas, only. Moreover, in large real-world KBs, inconsistency is often due to a limited number of contradictory rules and data (unless total inconsistency of the modeled agent!), which allow a small $Ker(KB, f)$ to emerge very often. Such a phenomenon matches most philosophical and psychological models of beliefs. Also, the local search algorithm should "cover" the space of interpretations in the most uniform and systematic way. This can be achieved partly by a large number of tries, with initial interpretations that are sufficiently distant. Clearly, the accuracy of the heuristic depends also on the consumed computation time. We are currently working on an improved system that stops its computation when a stable (probable) $Ker(KB, f)$ has clearly emerged. Obviously enough, the accurracy of the heuristic also depends on the interdependence level between formulas from $Ker(KB, f)$ and the other ones: whenever a formula from $Ker(KB, f)$ is falsified, not too many formulas from $KB \setminus Ker(KB, f)$ should be falsified at the same time. This is related to a *knowledge locality* principle, which is often a valid assumption in actual KBs.

Finally, let us note that whenever the revision formula f does not contain any Abnormality proposition, no formula from KB among those that have been weakened so far can belong to $Ker(KB, f)$. Indeed, in this situation, every Ab_{R_i} literal occurs only positively in KB. Thus, it cannot be the case that a weakened formula belongs to a minimally inconsistent subbase of KB w.r.t. f (assuming that every Ab_{R_i} is $true$ is always possible and sufficient to satisfy the weakened formulas). This remark is valuable from a computational point of view since it means that whenever sufficiently many severe revisions have been done, computing $Ker(KB, f)$ can be easier since the number of candidate formulas from KB

will be smaller (all the formulas that have been weakened so far can be omitted).

The main remarkable feature of this approach lies in its effective tractability for very large applications. In spite of the fact that it does not require a subset of propositional clausal logic to be used (like the Horn one) as it is sometimes required and that it is nonmonotonic, it proves empirically efficient for very large KBs, at least when inconsistency can be related to a small subpart of KB.

Very comprehensive experimentations have been conducted to test the heuristic, using standard benchmarks for propositional reasoning and consistency checking that are taken from [DIMACS, 1993] or have been proposed in the meantime. All experiments have been conducted on Pentium 166 PCs. Let us just give a typical example. First, let us illustrate our approach when a purely monotonic knowledge is considered (i.e. $AB_{KB} = \emptyset$). We mixed a very large consistent propositional problem proposed by [Kautz and Selman, 1996] representing a planning-related knowledge base with a globally inconsistent one proposed by [DIMACS, 1993]. These problems contain 37388 and 24 clauses (2883 and 9 variables), respectively. In our framework, we can interpret the first problem together with some clauses of the second one as representing a consistent KB, while the remaining part of the second one represents the clausal formula f to be inserted into KB. Clearly, $KB \wedge f$ is inconsistent.

TSAT (with a weight option [Morris, 1993] [Selman *et al.*, 1993]) was run on $KB \wedge f$. Figure 1 shows (using a logarithmic scale) the trace (i.e. the score of the clauses) delivered after 2 seconds CPU computation time. The inconsistent subbase clearly emerges and is easily recognized. It consists of the 24 clauses with the highest scores. Weakening the subpart of this subbase that belongs to KB is now a straightforward task.

Let us now move to the nonmonotonic case. To our best knowledge, we are not aware of *large* propositional benchmarks in the nonmonotonic area representing real-world problems. Benchmarks in this domain have been defined mainly in order to check the principles guiding the logics and not their computational properties. Therefore, we had to define our own benchmarks. For instance, we transformed monotonic ones so that they actually incorporate Abnormality propositions in some of their rules. Accordingly, the above knowledge base has been enriched in the following way. 10 % of clauses have been given their own additional literals Ab_i from AB_{KB}, representing possible future exceptions to the rules. TSAT was run again during 2 seconds. Figure 2 gives the trace of the computation. The introduction of Abnormality propositions does not modify the empirical results.

8 RELATED WORKS

As evoked previously, our approach to belief base revision is closely related to WIDTIO [Winslett, 1990]. Especially, in the basic monotonic case and when only one-step of revision is considered, both our approach and WIDTIO coincide from an inferential point of view.

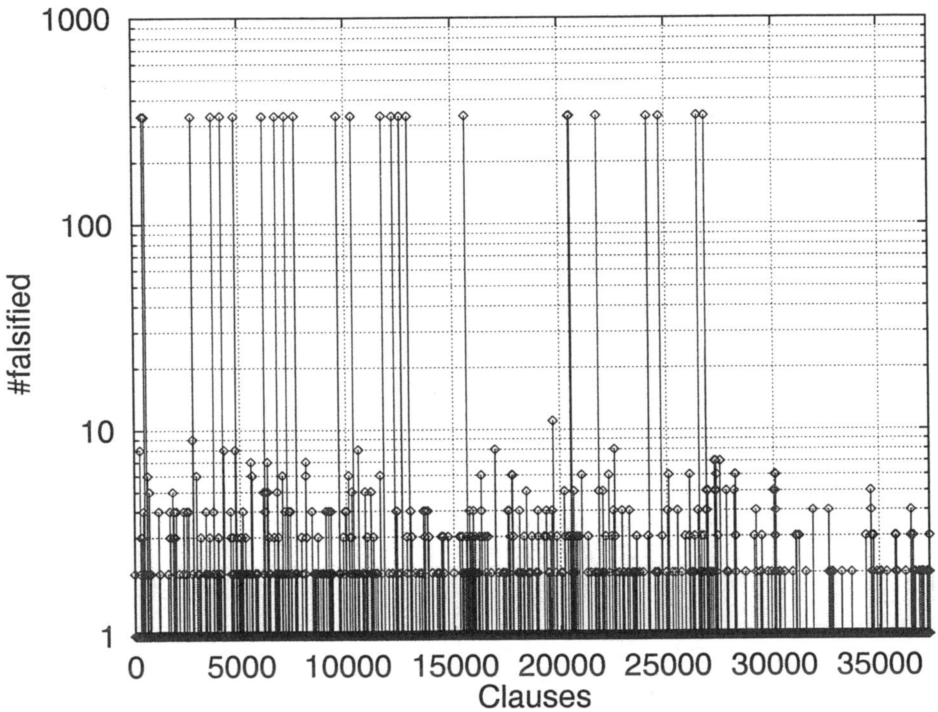

Figure 1. Monotonic framework.

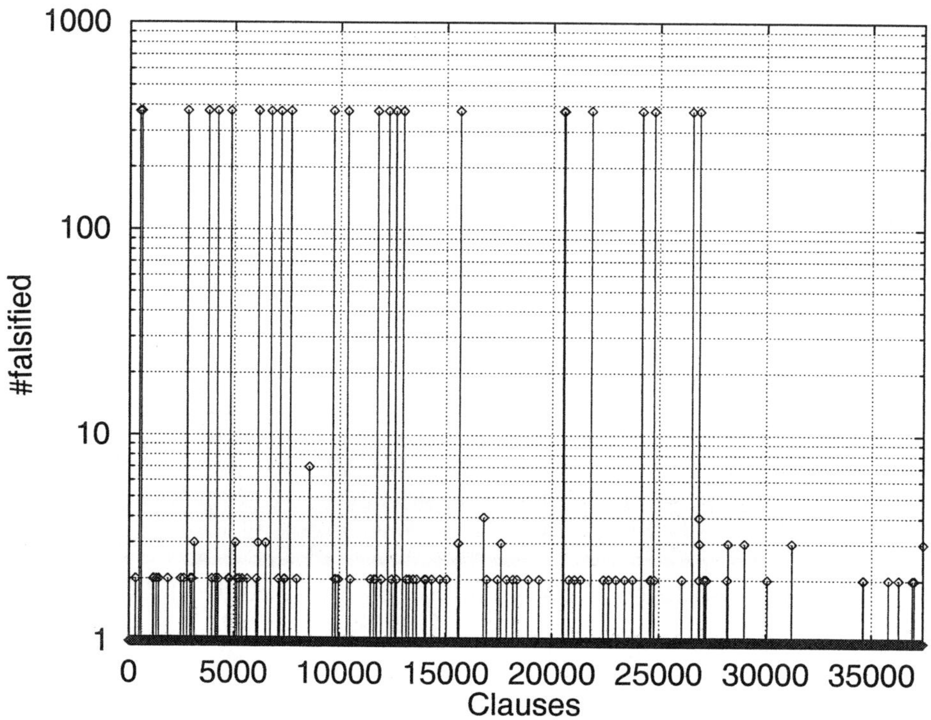

Figure 2. Nonmonotonic framework.

PROPOSITION 11. *Assume that KB, f and g do not contain any Abnormality proposition.* $KB^{\circ_{WIDTIO}} f \models g$ *iff* $KB^{\circ_{full-meet}} f \mid\!\sim_{R,\leq} g$

Sketch of proof: If $KB \cup \{f\}$ is consistent, then $Ker(KB, f) = \emptyset$, so $\mathcal{M}(KB^{\circ_{WIDTIO}} f) = \mathcal{M}_{R,\leq}(KB^{\circ_{full-meet}} f)$. Otherwise, every formula removed in the WIDTIO approach is weakened by Ab_{R_1} in our approach, and the converse also holds. Since Ab_{R_1} is necessarily $true$ in the revised KB, the weakened formulas do not participate to inference. More formally, for every preferred revision-preferred model I of $KB^{\circ_{full-meet}} f$, there exists a model J of $KB^{\circ_{WIDTIO}} f$ s.t. for every symbol p of P, $[\![p]\!](I) = [\![p]\!](J)$, and *vice-versa*. The fact that g does not contain any Abnormality symbol is sufficient to end up the proof.

EXAMPLE 12 (continued). Let $KB = \{\neg Bird \vee Fly, Bird\}$. We have:

1. $KB \models Fly \wedge Bird$.
2. $KB^{\circ_{WIDTIO}} \neg Fly = \{\neg Fly\} \models \neg Fly$.

However, our approach extends WIDTIO in at least two directions. First, WIDTIO is based on a purely standard logic framework. Second, our cautious approach is less "destructive" than WIDTIO in the sense that sources of inconsistency are "hidden" instead of being cancelled. This may lead to more "rationality", especially with respect to the principle of minimal change when iterated belief revision steps are processed. Indeed, WIDTIO is unnecessarily too much destructive.

EXAMPLE 13 (continued). $(KB^{\circ_{WIDTIO}} \neg Fly)^{\circ_{WIDTIO}} Fly = \{Fly\}$. Compared with our approach, let us note that $Bird$ is lost; actually when WIDTIO gives up a piece of information, it is forever (unless it is added again).

It is worth noting that the gain in expressiveness and "rationality" achieved by our approach (compared with WIDTIO) does neither necessarily lead to a degradation of the worst case complexity, with respect to inference from the revised KB. Indeed, inference from (full-meet) WIDTIO revised bases is Π_2^p-complete as well (see Theorem 5.21 from [Nebel, 1998]). Moreover, once $Ker(KB, f)$ is derived, the revised base w.r.t. WIDTIO and our technique can be computed in polynomial time. Especially, removing inconsistency by weakening all its possible causes is not more expensive than deleting them.

Our approach can also be related to *linear base revision* from stratified bases [Nebel, 1994]. In this approach, only one subbase of KB consistent with f has to be considered.

Let us associate to every (revised) belief base considered in our approach a stratified belief base s.t.:

- Originally (i.e. when no revision formula has been considered), all the formulas from KB are given the same priority, namely priority 0.

- Afterwards, when the ith revision formula f is considered, every formula of $KB \setminus Ker(KB, f)$ is given priority i, f is also given priority i and all the remaining formulas keep their previous priorities.

Let KB_i denote the subset of KB consisting of all the formulas of priority i. Let z be the highest priority among the formulas in KB.

Procedure Inference-from-prioritized-KB
Input: a stratified KB
Output: a subset S_{max} of KB

```
begin
 S_max ← KB_z
 for every i from z − 1 downto 1 do
  if S_max ∪ KB_i is consistent
   then S_max ← S_max ∪ KB_i
 return S_max
end
```

A formula g is viewed as a consequence of such a stratified belief base KB iff it is a logical consequence of S_{max}. Interestingly, this occurs exactly when $KB \mid\!\sim_{R,\leq} g$, provided that $AB_{KB} = \emptyset$ and that the successive revision formulas f do not contain any Abnormality proposition. In other words, under these restrictive assumptions, inference in our approach and inference from such linearly revised stratified bases coincide. This can be easily explained by the fact that $AB_{Revision}$ is linearly ordered, and to each symbol Ab_{R_i} of $AB_{Revision}$ is associated a subset of the original KB, those formulas that are weakened by Ab_{R_i}, in so far as all the formulas from the subset can be considered as present in the revised KB when Ab_{R_i} is interpreted as $false$, and absent otherwise.

EXAMPLE 14 (continued).

1. We associate to the original $KB = \{\neg Bird \vee Fly, Bird\}$ the stratified base $KB^0 = \{\neg Bird \vee Fly(0), Bird(0)\}$. The corresponding set S^0_{max} is KB^0, from which $Bird$ and Fly are inferrable.
2. Now, KB is revised by $\neg Fly$. The corresponding revised base is associated to $KB^1 = \{\neg Bird \vee Fly(0), Bird(0), \neg Fly(1)\}$. The associated set S^1_{max} is $\{\neg Fly\}$, from which only $\neg Fly$ is inferrable.
3. Lastly, the resulting base is revised by Fly. The corresponding revised base is associated to $KB^2 = \{\neg Bird \vee Fly(2), Bird(2), \neg Fly(1), Fly(2)\}$. The associated set S^2_{max} is $\{\neg Bird \vee Fly, Bird, Fly\}$, from which both $Bird$ and Fly are inferrable.

While they give equivalent results in this restricted situation, our approach and linear base revision do not necessarily coincide in the general case, especially when AB_{KB} is not empty, or when the revision formulas may contain Abnormality symbols. Moreover, the fact that the ontology increases while severe revisions are performed enables *reasoning about the revision process itself* : the Ab_{R_i} symbols also play the role of temporal markers, allowing one to decide efficiently whether or not some initial piece of knowledge has been severely revised. For instance, the presence of the formula $\neg Bird \vee Fly \vee Ab_{R_1}$ in $(KB^{\circ_{full-meet}} \neg Fly)^{\circ_{full-meet}} Fly$ shows that the original piece of knowledge $\neg Bird \vee Fly$ has been subject to a severe revision.

9 CONCLUSIONS AND PERSPECTIVES

Most of the times, belief revision has been investigated from a theoretical point of view. As such, this domain has sometimes been criticized for its lack of computational theory-validating large-size applications. On the one hand, this paper is a modest contribution towards filling this missing facet of belief revision. On the other hand, non-conventional positions are adopted in this paper with respect to various facets of belief revision. As conclusive remarks, let us summarize and motivate them briefly again. We believe that each of them could open new fruitful paths of research.

- Belief revision should not be studied from the philosophical and cognitive sides of artificial intelligence only, but also from its (knowledge) engineering one. As such, specific new revision theories can be proposed that are guided by specific motivations: empirical computational efficiency, importance of the syntax and software quality properties, mainly.

- In this respect, we propose a combined use of nonmonotonic logics and belief revision. The nonmonotonic logic ingredients should be simple enough to allow an easy encoding of priorities, rules of default reasoning and exceptions. Inconsistencies should be prevented in advance as much as possible by an adequate encoding using this logic; severe revisions should concern inconsistencies that form a mere remainder of all inconsistencies that could occur if a standard representation and deductive logic were selected.

- Throwing out beliefs to restore consistency is unnecessary destructive. We propose to weaken beliefs instead. Quite remarkably, the weakening ingredients that we propose coincide with the nonmonotonic ones. Actually, beliefs that are inconsistent with respect to the newly introduced ones are interpreted as exceptional cases that do not actually occur. Weakening instead of throwing out opens new perspectives with respect to iterated belief revision considerations.

- Bad worst case complexity results for belief revision should not be misinterpreted. They do not prevent computational efficiency from being reached in many actual large-size applications.

- On the contrary, techniques based on local search techniques offer efficient heuristic tools to implement belief revisions techniques for very large propositional knowledge bases. The power of these techniques is currently unmatched, and offers interesting anytime properties that can be essential when time-critical belief revision processes are under consideration.

APPENDIX: BASIC ELEMENTS OF COMPUTATIONAL COMPLEXITY

One of the main purposes of complexity theory[5] is to classify problems according to their worst case requirements on computational resources depending on the size of the input. In this framework, a problem is a generic question, i.e., a set of specific instances. Specifically, a *decision problem* is one that has only "yes" and "no" as possible answers. Formally, a decision problem can be considered as a formal language consisting of the set of all its "yes" instances.

It is usually acknowledged that an *efficient algorithm* is one that runs in time polynomial in the size of the input (assuming a standard model of computation, e.g., a sequential deterministic Turing machine). Accordingly, a decision problem is considered *efficiently solvable* iff there exists an algorithm that can classify every instance of it in a number of computational steps that is polynomially bounded.

The class of all decision problems that are solvable in polynomial time is denoted by P. All the remaining ones require exponential time and are considered not efficiently solvable. In order to determine whether a problem is efficiently solvable or not, it is sufficient to point out an efficient algorithm to solve it, or to prove that such an algorithm cannot exist.

Unfortunately, for many problems, no polynomial time algorithms are known but it seems to be impossible to prove that super-polynomial time is actually required. For all these problems, the separation efficiently solvable vs. non-efficiently solvable is not fine-grained enough to classify them in a computationally valuable way: there is a need for more refined classes for problems that are not known in P.

The notion of non-deterministic Turing machine is an important tool to achieve this goal. Thus, the class of all languages (encoding decision problems) that can be recognized in polynomial time by such a non-deterministic machine is denoted by NP. Because a deterministic Turing machine can be considered as a non-deterministic one, the inclusion $\mathsf{P} \subseteq \mathsf{NP}$ is established; however, the converse is the famous open problem: $\mathsf{P} \stackrel{?}{=} \mathsf{NP}$ (that is conjectured false). Among all the problems in NP, the hardest ones are those from which every problem in NP can be

[5]See e.g. [Papadimitriou, 1994] for details.

polynomially many-one reduced: such problems are referred to as NP-*complete*. If any of them has a polynomial algorithm, then P = NP holds. Accordingly, it is believed that it is impossible to solve NP-complete problems in polynomial time. SAT, the problem of determining whether a propositional formula in conjunctive normal form is satisfiable, is the prototypical NP-complete problem [Cook, 1971]. Its complementary problem $UNSAT$ (consisting of determining whether a propositional formula in conjunctive normal form is unsatisfiable) is not necessarily in NP (in contrast to P, NP is not known to be closed under complementation). It is assigned to the class coNP that contains the complementary problems to problems of NP. It is conjectured that NP $\neq$ coNP. In the following, let us note $\bar{L}$ the complementary problem of L.

To go further into the classification of non-efficiently solvable problems, another important tool is the notion of Turing machine (deterministic or non-deterministic) *with oracle*. Let X be a class of decision problems. P^X (resp. NP^X) is the class of all decision problems that can be solved in polynomial time using a deterministic (resp. non-deterministic) Turing machine that can use an oracle for deciding a problem $Q \in X$ for "free" (i.e., within a constant, unit time). On this basis, the classes Δ_k^p, Σ_k^p and Π_k^p are defined by:

- $\Delta_0^p = \Sigma_0^p = \Pi_0^p = \mathsf{P}$,
- $\Delta_{k+1}^p = \mathsf{P}^{\Sigma_k^p}$,
- $\Sigma_{k+1}^p = \mathsf{NP}^{\Sigma_k^p}$,
- $\Pi_{k+1}^p = \mathsf{co}\Sigma_{k+1}^p$.

Thus, $\Sigma_1^p = \mathsf{NP}$ and $\Pi_1^p = \mathsf{coNP}$. The *polynomial hierarchy* PH is the union of all Σ_k^p (for k non-negative integer). While it is easy to check that both $\Delta_k^p \subseteq \Sigma_{k+1}^p$, $\Delta_k^p \subseteq \Pi_{k+1}^p$, $\Sigma_k^p \subseteq \Delta_{k+1}^p$, and $\Pi_k^p \subseteq \Delta_{k+1}^p$ hold for every k, it is unknown whether the inclusions are proper or not (but it is conjectured that it is the case). Thus, it is strongly believed that the polynomial hierarchy does not collapse, i.e., is a truly infinite hierarchy.

In order to discriminate further among the problems from Δ_2^p, one can focus on the number of calls to an NP-oracle that are used. Thus, the classes BH_k and coBH_k are defined in the following way:

- $\mathsf{BH}_0 = \mathsf{P}$,
- $\mathsf{BH}_1 = \mathsf{NP}$,
- $\mathsf{BH}_2 = \{L_1 \cap \bar{L}_2 | L_1 \in \mathsf{NP}, L_2 \in \mathsf{NP}\}$,
- $\mathsf{BH}_{2k+1} = \{L_1 \cup L_2 | L_1 \in \mathsf{BH}_{2k}, L_2 \in \mathsf{NP}\}$ with $k \geq 1$,
- $\mathsf{BH}_{2k+2} = \{L_1 \cap L_2 | L_1 \in \mathsf{BH}_{2k+1}, L_2 \in \mathsf{NP}\}$, with $k \geq 1$,
- $\mathsf{coBH}_k = \{L | \bar{L} \in \mathsf{BH}_k\}$.

Thus, $\mathsf{BH}_1 = \mathsf{NP}$ and $\mathsf{coBH}_1 = \mathsf{coNP}$. The *boolean hierarchy* BH is the union of all BH_k (for k non-negative integer). It turns out that BH is equivalent to the class of problems that can be solved in deterministic polynomial time using a constant number of calls to an NP-oracle.

ACKNOWLEDGMENTS

This paper has been supported in part by a *"Contrat d'Objectifs de la Région Nord/Pas-de-Calais"* and by the IUT de Lens. We are indebted to Salem Benferhat for so many interesting comments about a preliminary version of this paper and to Bertrand Mazure for his help with respect to the implementation side.

CRIL, Université d'Artois, France.

REFERENCES

[Alchourrón and Makinson, 1985] C. E. Alchourrón and D. Makinson. On the logic of theory change: safe contractions. *Studia logica*, **44**, 405–422, 1985.

[Alchourrón *et al.*, 1985] C.E. Alchourrón, P. Gärdenfors and D. Makinson. On the logic of theory change: partial meet functions for contraction and revision. *Journal of Symbolic Logic*, **50**, 510–530, 1985.

[Benferhat *et al.*, 1995] S. Benferhat, D. Dubois and H. Prade. How to infer from inconsistent beliefs without revising. In *IJCAI'95*, pp. 1449–1455, 1995.

[Bessant *et al.*, 1998] B. Bessant, É. Grégoire, P. Marquis and L. Saïs. Combining nonmonotonic reasoning and belief revision: a practical approach. In *AIMSA'98*, volume 1480 of *Lecture Notes in Artificial Intelligence*, pp. 115–128. Springer-Verlag, 1998.

[Cadoli *et al.*, 1995] M. Cadoli, F. Donini, P. Liberatore and M. Schaerf. The size of a revised knowledge base. In *PODS'95*, pp. 151–162, 1995.

[Cook, 1971] S. A. Cook. The complexity of theorem-proving procedures. In *Third Annual ACM Symposium on Theory of Computing*, pp. 151–158, 1971.

[Darwiche and Pearl, 1997] A. Darwiche and J. Pearl. On the logic of iterated belief revision. *Artificial Intelligence*, **89**, 1–30, 1997.

[Davis *et al.*, 1962] M. Davis, G. Logemann and D. Loveland. A machine program for theorem proving. *Journal of the Association for Computing Machinery*, **5**, 394–397, 1962.

[del Val, 1984] A. del Val. On the relation between the coherence and foundations theories of belief revision. In *AAAI'94*, pp. 909–914, 1984.

[DIMACS, 1993] DIMACS, 1993. Second SAT challenge organized by the Center for Discrete Mathematics and Computer Science of Rutgers University, `http://dimacs.rutgers.edu/Challenges`.

[Eiter and Gottlob, 1992] T. Eiter and G. Gottlob. On the complexity of propositional knowledge base revision, updates, and counterfactual. *Artificial Intelligence*, **5**, 227–270, 1992.

[Fagin *et al.*, 1983] R. Fagin, J. D. Ullman and M. Y. Vardi. On the semantics of updates in databases. In *PODS'83*, pp. 352–365, 1983.

[Friedman and Halpern, 1996] N. Friedman and J. Y. Halpern. Belief revision: a critique. In *KR'96*, pp. 429–431, 1996.

[Gärdenfors, 1992] P. Gärdenfors. Belief revision and nonmonotonic logic: Two sides of the same coin? In *ECAI'92*, pp. 768–773, 1992.

[Grégoire, 1999] É. Grégoire. Handling inconsistency efficiently in the incremental construction of stratified belief bases. Technical report, CRIL, 1999.

[Hansson, 1993] S. O. Hansson. Reversing the Levi identity. *Journal of Phiolosophical Logic*, **22**, 637–669, 1993.

[Kautz and Selman, 1996] H. Kautz and B. Selman. Pushing the envelope: planning, propositional logic, and stochastic search. In *AAAI'96*, pp. 1194–1201, 1996.

[Lehman, 1995] D. Lehman. Belief revision revisited. In *IJCAI'95*, pp. 1534–1540, 1995.

[Liberatore and Schaerf, 1995] P. Liberatore and M. Schaerf. Relating belief revision and circumscription. In *IJCAI'95*, pp. 1557–1553, 1995.

[Liberatore and Schaerf, 1996] P. Liberatore and M. Schaerf. The complexity of model checking for belief revision and update. In *AAAI'96*, pp. 556–561, 1996.

[Makinson and Gärdenfors, 1991] D. Makinson and P. Gärdenfors. Relations between the logic of theory change and nonmonotonic logic. In *Workshop on the logic of theory change*, Fuhrmann and Moreau, eds. pp. 185–205. LNCS 465, Springer, 1991.

[Mazure *et al.*, 1997] B. Mazure, L. Saïs and É. Grégoire. Tabu search for sat. In *AAAI'97*, pp. 281–285, 1997.

[Mazure *et al.*, 1998] B. Mazure, L. Saïs and É. Grégoire. Boosting complete techniques thanks to local search. *Annals of Mathematics and Artificial Intelligence*, **22**, 319–322, 1998.

[McCarthy, 1986] J. McCarthy. Applications of circumscription to formalizing common-sense knowledge. *Artificial Intelligence*, **2**, :89–116, 1986.

[Moinard, 1994] Y. Moinard. Revision and nonmonotonicity. *International Journal of Intelligent Systems*, **9**, 1994.

[Morris, 1993] P. Morris. The breakout method for escaping from local minima. In *AAAI'93*, pp. 40–45, 1993.

[Nebel, 1989] B. Nebel. A knowledge level analysis of belief revision. In *KR'89*, pp. 301–311, 1989.

[Nebel, 1990] B. Nebel. *Reasoning and revision in hybrid representation systems*, volume 422 of *Lecture Notes in Artificial Intelligence*. Springer-Verlag, 1990.

[Nebel, 1992] B. Nebel. *Belief Revision*, chapter Syntax-based approaches to belief revision, pp. 53–88. Cambridge University Press, 1992.

[Nebel, 1994] B. Nebel. Base revision operations and schemes: semantics, representation and complexity. In *ECAI'94*, pp. 341–345, 1994.

[Nebel, 1998] B. Nebel. *How hard is it to revise a belief base?*, volume 3 of *Handbook of Defeasible Reasoning and Uncertainty Management Systems*, chapter Belief Change, pp. 77–145. Kluwer Academic, 1998.

[Newell, 1982] A. Newell. The knowledge level. *Artificial Intelligence*, **18**, 87–127, 1982.

[Papadimitriou, 1994] C. H. Papadimitriou. *Computational complexity*. Addison-Wesley, 1994.

[Papini, 1991] O. Papini. Revision in propositional calculus. In *ECSQAU'91*, volume 548 of *Lecture Notes in Artificial Intelligence*, pp. 272–276. Springer-Verlag, 1991.

[Selman and Kautz, 1993] B. Selman and H. Kautz. An empirical study of greedy local search for satisfiability testing. In *AAAI'93*, 1993.

[Selman *et al.*, 1992] B. Selman, H. Levesque, and D. Mitchell. A new method for solving hard satisfiability problems. In *AAAI'92*, pp. 440–446, 1992.

[Selman *et al.*, 1993] B. Selman, H. A. Kautz and B. Cohen. Local search strategies for satisfiability testing. In *DIMACS Workshop on Maximum Clique, Graph Coloring, and Satisfiability*, 1993.

[Selman *et al.*, 1997] B. Selman, H. Kautz and D. McAllester. Computational challenges in propositional reasoning and search. In *IJCAI'97*, pp. 50–54, 1997.

[Shoham, 1987] Y. Shoham. *Readings in Non-Monotonic Reasoning*, chapter A semantical approach to non-monotonic logics. Morgan Kaufmann, 1987.

[Williams, 1995] M.A. Williams. Iterated theory base change: a computational model. In *IJCAI'95*, pp. 1541–1550, 1995.

[Winslett, 1990] M. Winslett. *Updating Logical Databases*. Cambridge University Press, 1990.

GABRIELE KERN-ISBERNER

REVISING AND UPDATING PROBABILISTIC BELIEFS

1 INTRODUCTION

Besides the representation of knowledge, the handling of its dynamics in the light of new information, generally termed *belief change*, is one of the fundamental problems in Artificial Intelligence. The great variety of approaches that has been set forth up to now, usually each method coming along with a descriptive axiom scheme (for a survey, cf. [Gärdenfors and Rott, 1994]), corresponds to the many different interpretations and names the term *change* has been given. Gärdenfors [1988] identified three fundamental types of belief change, *revision, expansion* and *update*. Katsuno and Mendelzon [1991] argued that the axioms of Gärdenfors for revision are only adequate to describe a change in knowledge about a *static* world, but not for recording changes in an *evolving* world. They called this latter type of change *update*, with *erasure* being its inverse operation (cf. [Katsuno and Mendelzon, 1991]). *Conditioning* has been regarded as an adequate method for revising probabilistic beliefs (cf. e.g. [Paris, 1994; Gärdenfors, 1988]), but Dubois and Prade [1997] emphasize that actually, conditioning does not correspond to revision but rather to *focusing*.

Most of the work in describing and classifying belief change operations has been done for belief sets based on classical logics (cf. e.g. [Gärdenfors and Rott, 1994]). Probabilistic knowledge is much more difficult to deal with because of its too solid structure when being represented by a probability distribution (representing a complete knowledge base), or, even worse, because of its too weak structure when being represented only by a set of probabilistic constraints – usually, there will be a myriad of different distributions all satisfying the constraints specified.

In this paper, we will show how updating and revision may be realized within a (generalized) probabilistic framework. We will open up probabilistic structures by distinguishing between *belief states* represented by distributions reflecting states of belief in equilibrium (cf. [Gärdenfors, 1988; Paris, 1994]), and *belief bases* separating background knowledge from uncertain contextual knowledge. The transition from belief bases to belief states is achieved by using probabilistic inference operations which are assumed to be nonmonotonic to yield nontrivial inferences. Based on this approach, we present axiom schemata and representation results for probabilistic revision and updating. Revision operates on belief bases, while updating is defined on belief states. To realize updating, we make use of the inference operation underlying knowledge representation. This establishes a strong connection between nonmonotonic logics and probabilistic belief change, similar to that in more classical approaches. The notion of a *universal inference operation*,

M.-A. Williams and H. Rott (eds.), Frontiers in Belief Revision, 393–408.

generalizing usual inference operations and introduced here as an expressive counterpart for belief change operations, allows a more adequate comparison between characteristics of nonmonotonic logics and of belief change.

As an example for an adequate and powerful universal inference operation, we present reasoning based on the techniques of maximum entropy resp. minimum cross-entropy. And we show that in this case, revision is different from focusing, thus revealing a behavior of probabilistic inference analogous to that proved by Dubois and Prade in [1997] for upper and lower probabilities.

This paper is organized as follows: Section 2 lists fundamental definitions and terms of probabilistic knowledge representation. In section 3, two ways of representing probabilistic knowledge, *belief bases* and *belief states*, are motivated and introduced. Section 4 describes the transition from belief bases to belief states. We begin section 5 with a short review of related work and develop the appropriate ideas for revision and updating within a probabilistic framework. In the following two sections 6 and 7 we make both notions concrete by setting up axiom schemata, and we state representation results. Section 8 compares both belief change operations directly, and section 9 shows that within the framework of optimum entropy, focusing is different from revision but akin to updating. Section 10 concludes this paper.

2 PROBABILISTIC LOGICS

We consider probability distributions P over a finite set of atomic propositions $\mathcal{V}$. Let Ω denote the set of all elementary events ω (also called complete conjunctions), and let $\mathcal{L}$ be the propositional language over the alphabet $\mathcal{V}$ with logical connectives $\vee, \wedge$ resp. juxtaposition and $\neg$. Thus each propositional formula $\mathrm{A} \in \mathcal{L}$ corresponds to an event and has probability $P(\mathrm{A}) = \sum_{\omega:\mathrm{A}(\omega)=1} P(\omega)$, where $\mathrm{A}(\omega) = 1$ resp. $= 0$ means that A is true resp. false in the world described by ω.

A *probabilistic conditional* or *probabilistic rule* has the form $\mathrm{A} \rightsquigarrow \mathrm{B}[x]$ with $\mathrm{A}, \mathrm{B} \in \mathcal{L}, x \in [0,1]$. Let $\mathcal{L}^*$ denote the set of all probabilistic conditionals over $\mathcal{L}$: $\mathcal{L}^* = \{\mathrm{A} \rightsquigarrow \mathrm{B}[x] | \mathrm{A}, \mathrm{B} \in \mathcal{L}, x \in [0,1]\}$. Their semantics is based on a distribution P via conditional probabilities: We write $P \models \mathrm{A} \rightsquigarrow \mathrm{B}[x]$ iff $P(\mathrm{A}) > 0$ and $P(\mathrm{B}|\mathrm{A}) = \dfrac{P(\mathrm{AB})}{P(\mathrm{A})} = x$. *Probabilistic facts* are probabilistic rules $\top \rightsquigarrow \mathrm{B}[x]$ with tautological antecedent, written as $\mathrm{B}[x]$. Thus $\mathcal{L}^*$ comprises the formulas of the classical language $\mathcal{L}$ by identifying a propositional formula B with the probabilistic conditional $\top \rightsquigarrow \mathrm{B}[1]$. Let $Th(P)$ denote the set of all conditionals that may be entailed from P: $Th(P) = \{\mathrm{A} \rightsquigarrow \mathrm{B}[x] | P \models \mathrm{A} \rightsquigarrow \mathrm{B}[x]\}$.

A set $\mathcal{R}$ of probabilistic conditionals is *consistent* iff it has a *model*, i.e. iff there is a distribution Q with $Q \models \mathcal{R}$. Let $Mod(\mathcal{R}) = \{Q \mid Q \models \mathcal{R}\}$ denote the set of (probabilistic) models of $\mathcal{R}$. If P is a distribution, then $\mathcal{R}$ is called *P-consistent* iff there is a distribution Q with $Q \ll P$ (meaning Q is P-continuous, i.e. $P(\omega) = 0$ implies $Q(\omega) = 0$) and $Q \models \mathcal{R}$. P-consistency ensures a compatibility between prior knowledge P and new information $\mathcal{R}$. In particular, a P-consistent set $\mathcal{R} \subseteq \mathcal{L}^*$ does not contain any conditional $\mathrm{A} \rightsquigarrow \mathrm{B}[x]$ with $P(\mathrm{A}) = 0$. For two sets $\mathcal{R}_1, \mathcal{R}_2 \subseteq \mathcal{L}^*$, $\mathcal{R}_2$ is said to *probabilistically entail* $\mathcal{R}_1$, $\mathcal{R}_2 \models^{prob} \mathcal{R}_1$, iff $Mod(\mathcal{R}_2) \subseteq Mod(\mathcal{R}_1)$. $\mathcal{R}_1$ and $\mathcal{R}_2$ are *probabilistically equivalent* iff $Mod(\mathcal{R}_1) = Mod(\mathcal{R}_2)$.

Probabilistic conditionals constitute quite a general and popular form of probabilistic constraints. Thus in this paper, we base probabilistic knowledge representation upon $\mathcal{L}^*$. Many of the results to be derived, however, will also hold for more general probabilistic languages.

3 PROBABILISTIC BELIEF

A *state of belief* (or *epistemic state*, as Gärdenfors calls it in [Gärdenfors, 1988]) is characterized as a state of equilibrium which contains all explicitly stated as well as all implicitly derived knowledge. So in a probabilistic setting, probability distributions are usually considered to represent state of beliefs adequately (cf. also [Paris, 1994]). They are complete in the sense that to any (conditional) proposition, a probability is assigned. Therefore, however, speaking of *revision* as a knowledge adding process does not really make sense. Moreover, no distinction is made between explicit and implicit knowledge. All knowledge is considered on the same level, though e.g. adding evidential knowledge should be contrasted clearly to revising background knowledge (cf. [Dubois and Prade, 1997]).

Voorbraak [1996] uses *partial probabilistic models*, i.e. classes of probability functions, to study *conditioning* and *constraining* appropriately. If, however, one is not willing to give up the convenience of having a single distribution as "best" knowledge base, a way to overcome both restrictions described above may be offered by taking (properly defined) *probabilistic belief bases* as primitive representations of probabilistic knowledge from which *probabilistic belief states*, i.e. probability distributions, may be calculated. In [Dubois and Prade, 1997] it is argued that belief sets arise from applying generic knowledge to evidence as sets of plausible consequences. There, as usual, evidential knowledge is restricted to certain facts, representing knowledge about a present *case*. This approach may be generalized quite easily by considering evidence as reflecting knowledge about the *context* under consideration, thus being again of a probabilistic nature. So the harsh distinction between background and evidential knowledge is mitigated, and fluctuation of knowledge is modelled more naturally: Our prior knowledge serves as a base for obtaining an adequate probabilistic description of the present context which may be used again as background knowledge.

DEFINITION 1. A *(probabilistic) belief state* is a distribution P (over the set of atomic propositions $\mathcal{V}$). A *(probabilistic) belief base* is a pair $(P, \mathcal{R})$, where P is a belief state (*background knowledge*), and $\mathcal{R} \subseteq \mathcal{L}^*$ is a P-consistent set of probabilistic rules (*contextual* or *evidential knowledge*).
Let $\mathcal{BB}$ resp. $\mathcal{BS}$ be the set of all belief bases resp. of all belief states.

Besides the distinction between background and context knowledge two points have to be emphasized with this definition: Firstly, a probabilistic belief state, i.e. a distribution, represents an epistemic state, not only a *belief set* which is to contain merely propositional beliefs. Darwiche and Pearl [1997] also pointed out the importance of taking epistemic states as starting points for belief change operations. Secondly, certain beliefs, i.e. propositions or conditionals of probability 1, are not of major interest here. On principle, all information is assumed to be probabilistic, with probabilities $x \in [0, 1]$, so that certain knowledge is dealt with as a borderline case.

In the following, the components of a belief base $(P, \mathcal{R})$ will serve as a prior distribution (P) and posterior constraints ($\mathcal{R}$), respectively.

EXAMPLE 2. A psychologist has worked with addicted people for a couple of years. His experiences concerning the propositions

$\mathcal{V}$: A : addicted to Alcohol
D : addicted to Drugs
Y : being Young

may be summarized by the following distribution P that expresses his belief state probabilistically (where negation is indicated by barring the corresponding letter):

ω	$P(\omega)$	ω	$P(\omega)$	ω	$P(\omega)$	ω	$P(\omega)$
ADY	0.050	$\overline{A}DY$	0.333	$AD\overline{Y}$	0.053	$\overline{A}D\overline{Y}$	0.052
$A\overline{D}Y$	0.093	$\overline{A}\,\overline{D}Y$	0.102	$A\overline{D}\,\overline{Y}$	0.225	$\overline{A}\,\overline{D}\,\overline{Y}$	0.091

The following probabilistic conditionals may be entailed from P:

$$\begin{array}{ll} A \rightsquigarrow D[0.242] & (\text{i.e.} \quad P(D \mid A) = 0.242) \\ \overline{A} \rightsquigarrow D[0.666] & (\text{i.e.} \quad P(D \mid \overline{A}) = 0.666) \\ Y \rightsquigarrow A[0.246] & \overline{Y} \rightsquigarrow A[0.660] \\ Y \rightsquigarrow D[0.662] & \overline{Y} \rightsquigarrow D[0.251] \end{array}$$

4 FROM BELIEF BASES TO BELIEF STATES BY PROBABILISTIC INFERENCE

The transition from belief bases to belief states has to be achieved by an adequate inference operation.

A *(probabilistic) inference operation* is an operation $C : 2^{\mathcal{L}^*} \to 2^{\mathcal{L}^*}$ on sets of probabilistic conditionals. C is called *reflexive* iff $\mathcal{R} \subseteq C(\mathcal{R})$, and *cumulative* iff $\mathcal{R} \subseteq \mathcal{R}' \subseteq C(\mathcal{R})$ implies $C(\mathcal{R}) = C(\mathcal{R}')$ for $\mathcal{R}, \mathcal{R}' \subseteq \mathcal{L}^*$. It satisfies *left logical equivalence* iff $C(\mathcal{R}) = C(\mathcal{S})$ whenever the sets $\mathcal{R}, \mathcal{S} \subseteq \mathcal{L}^*$ are probabilistically equivalent (cf. [Makinson, 1994]). We call C *complete* iff it specifies for each set $\mathcal{R} \subseteq \mathcal{L}^*$ with $C(\mathcal{R}) \neq \emptyset, \mathcal{L}^*$ a unique distribution, i.e. iff there is a (unique) distribution $Q_{\mathcal{R}}$ such that $C(\mathcal{R}) = Th(Q_{\mathcal{R}})$.

So to generate belief states from belief bases $(P, \mathcal{R})$, we need inference operations that depend in a reasonable way upon the background knowledge P. The following definition generalizes the well-known notion of an inference operation by taking prior knowledge explicitly into account:

DEFINITION 3. A *universal probabilistic inference operation* $\mathbf{C}$ assigns a complete probabilistic inference operation C_P to each distribution P: $\mathbf{C} : P \mapsto C_P$. It is said to be *reflexive*, resp. *cumulative*, resp. to satisfy *left logical equivalence*, iff all its involved inference operations have the corresponding property. $\mathbf{C}$ *preserves consistency* iff for each distribution P and for each P-consistent set $\mathcal{R} \subseteq \mathcal{L}^*$, $C_P(\mathcal{R}) \neq \emptyset, \mathcal{L}^*$. A universal probabilistic inference operation $\mathbf{C}$ is *founded* iff for each distribution P and for any $\mathcal{R} \subseteq \mathcal{L}^*$, $P \models \mathcal{R}$ implies $C_P(\mathcal{R}) = Th(P)$.

The property of foundedness establishes a close and intuitive relation between a distribution P and its associated inference operation C_P, distinguishing P as its stable starting point. Each C_P is presupposed to be complete, so each element of $Im\, C_P := \{C_P(\mathcal{R}) | \mathcal{R} \subseteq \mathcal{L}^*, C_P(\mathcal{R}) \neq \emptyset, \mathcal{L}^*\}$, corresponds uniquely to a distribution: $C_P(\mathcal{R}) = Th(Q_{P,\mathcal{R}})$, which will be abbreviated by $Q_{P,\mathcal{R}} \equiv C_P(\mathcal{R})$.

DEFINITION 4. Let $\mathbf{C} : P \mapsto C_P$ be a universal inference operation. For each distribution P, define a relation $\leq_P$ on $Im\, C_P$ by setting $P_1 \leq_P P_2$ iff there are sets $\mathcal{R}_1 \subseteq \mathcal{R}_2 \subseteq \mathcal{L}^*$ such that $P_1 \equiv C_P(\mathcal{R}_1)$ and $P_2 \equiv C_P(\mathcal{R}_2)$.

The notion of *strong cumulativity* introduced below describes a cumulative behavior with respect to the distributions underlying the inference operations.

DEFINITION 5. $\mathbf{C}$ is *strongly cumulative* iff for each distribution P and for any distributions $P_1, P_2 \in Im\, C_P$, $P \leq_P P_1 \leq_P P_2$ implies: whenever $\mathcal{R}_1 \subseteq \mathcal{R}_2 \subseteq \mathcal{L}^*$ such that $P_1 \equiv C_P(\mathcal{R}_1)$ and $P_2 \equiv C_P(\mathcal{R}_2)$, we have $P_2 \equiv C_P(\mathcal{R}_2) = C_{P_1}(\mathcal{R}_2)$.

Strong cumulativity states a relationship between inference operations based on different distributions, resp. probabilistic theories, thus linking up the inference operations of $\mathbf{C}$. In fact, it establishes an important coherence property for the universal inference operation: The intermediate knowledge base $C_P(\mathcal{R}_1)$ may be used coherently as a prior for further inferences. The name "strong cumulativity" is justified by the observation that together with foundedness, strong cumulativity implies cumulativity (cf. [Kern-Isberner, 1998b]).

Thus any universal probabilistic inference operation $P \mapsto C_P$ that preserves consistency gives rise to a map $* : \mathcal{BB} \to \mathcal{BS}$, $(P, \mathcal{R}) \mapsto P * \mathcal{R}$, where $P * \mathcal{R}$ is the unique distribution such that $C_P(\mathcal{R}) = Th(P * \mathcal{R})$, i.e. $P * \mathcal{R} \equiv C_P(\mathcal{R})$. We will use a prefix notation as well as an infix notation.

In [Paris, 1994], several probabilistic inference processes are presented and investigated in detail. Among them, inferences based on the principles of maximum entropy resp. of minimum cross-entropy (*ME-inference*) takes an outstanding position as particularly well-behaved inference operations (cf. also [Shore and Johnson, 1980], [Kern-Isberner, 1998a]).

Let $*_e$ denote the *ME-inference operator*, i.e. $*_e$ assigns to each (prior) distribution P and each P-consistent set $\mathcal{R}$ of probabilistic conditionals the (unique) distribution $P_e = P *_e \mathcal{R}$ that has minimum cross-entropy to P among all models of $\mathcal{R}$. That is to say, P_e solves the minimization problem

$$\min_{Q \models \mathcal{R}} R(Q, P) = \sum_{\omega} Q(\omega) \log \frac{Q(\omega)}{P(\omega)}$$

where $R(Q, P)$ is the cross-entropy from Q with respect to P.

For finite P-consistent sets $\mathcal{R} \subseteq \mathcal{L}^*$, $\mathcal{R} = \{\mathrm{A}_1 \leadsto \mathrm{B}_1[x_1], \ldots, \mathrm{A}_n \leadsto \mathrm{B}_n[x_n]\}$, P_e has a representation of the form

$$(1) \quad P_e(\omega) = \alpha_0 P(\omega) \prod_{\substack{1 \leq i \leq n \\ \mathrm{A}_i \mathrm{B}_i(\omega)=1}} \alpha_i^{1-x_i} \prod_{\substack{1 \leq i \leq n \\ \mathrm{A}_i \overline{\mathrm{B}_i}(\omega)=1}} \alpha_i^{-x_i},$$

where the α_i's are suitably chosen so as to make P_e fulfill $\mathcal{R}$ (cf. [Kern-Isberner, 1998a]). In particular, if $\mathcal{R} = \{A[x]\}$ consists of a single probabilistic fact, then we obtain (cf. [Kern-Isberner, 1998c])

$$P *_e \{A[x]\}(\omega) = xP(\omega \mid A) + (1-x)P(\omega \mid \overline{A})$$

which coincides with Jeffrey conditionalization (cf. [Gärdenfors, 1988]). For $x = 1$, we have especially

$$P *_e \{A[1]\} = P(\cdot \mid A)$$

Therefore ME-adaptation generalizes both Bayes and Jeffrey conditioning.

For fixed prior P define the *ME-inference operation* $C_P^e : 2^{\mathcal{L}^*} \to 2^{\mathcal{L}^*}$ by

$$C_P^e(\mathcal{R}) = \begin{cases} Th(P *_e \mathcal{R}) & \text{iff } \mathcal{R}\ P-\text{consistent} \\ \mathcal{L}^* & else \end{cases}$$

Thus C_P^e is a complete inference operation preserving consistency, and $\mathbf{C}^e : P \mapsto C_P^e$ defines a universal inference operation which proves to be reflexive, founded and strongly cumulative (cf. [Kern-Isberner, 1998b]).

In the following, we assume some universal probabilistic inference operation $\mathbf{C}$ preserving consistency to be given.

5 CHANGING PROBABILISTIC BELIEFS

Let us first recapitulate how the terms *revision* and *update* have been used in the literature. In [Gärdenfors, 1988], *revision* is the most general case of belief change, including giving up prior beliefs in establishing new information. Thus it is closely related to the process of *contracting beliefs*, this relationship being expressed by the identities of *Harper* and *Levi* (for more details, cf. e.g. [Gärdenfors, 1988]).

Expansion is revision in the special case that there is no conflict between prior and new information, so contracting of beliefs is not necessary and expansion means mere affiliation of new knowledge. The so-called AGM-postulates for belief revision (cf. [Alchourrón *et al.*, 1985]) constitute an important benchmark for the formal description of revision operations. Katsuno and Mendelzon (cf. [Katsuno and Mendelzon, 1991]), however, claimed that these postulates are only suitable if revision means incorporating new information about a *static world*, but not for modelling changes in belief that are induced by an *evolving world*. They modified the AGM postulates to obtain a new characterization of this latter kind of belief change which they called *updating*.

Most of the work in describing and classifying belief change operations has been done for belief sets based on classical logics (cf. e.g. [Gärdenfors and Rott, 1994]). Gärdenfors [1988] and Dubois and Prade [1994] developed some axioms for probabilistic belief change, being mostly concerned with revising in the sense of establishing facts for certain. While Gärdenfors, however, claimed that conditioning corresponds to expansion (and thus to a certain case of revision) in a probabilistic framework (cf. [Gärdenfors, 1988, pp. 105 ff]), Dubois and Prade emphasize that conditioning is not revising but *focusing*, i.e. applying generic or background knowledge to the reference class describing properly the case under consideration. Paris [1994] and Voorbraak [1996] also consider probabilistic belief revision in the case of uncertain evidences.

For a belief change to be performed in the light of new information, the question whether this new information is contradictory to or consistent with prior knowledge is of great importance, as contradictoriness makes contraction of beliefs necessary (cf. [Gärdenfors and Rott, 1994]). Mostly, in the case of contradictory new information, revision is accomplished by contracting the negation of this information and then simply adding the new knowledge.

In the framework of probabilistic conditionals, however, things are more complicated because negation does not play such a clear role as in propositional two-valued logics. Though many authors agree that the negation of a conditional $\mathrm{A} \rightsquigarrow \mathrm{B}$ should be defined via $\neg(\mathrm{A} \rightsquigarrow \mathrm{B}) := \mathrm{A} \rightsquigarrow \overline{\mathrm{B}}$ (cf. e.g. [Calabrese, 1991]), which might be generalized to $\neg(\mathrm{A} \rightsquigarrow \mathrm{B}[x]) := \mathrm{A} \rightsquigarrow \overline{\mathrm{B}}[x]$, each probabilistic conditional $\mathrm{A} \rightsquigarrow \mathrm{B}[y]$ with $x \neq y$ is definitely different from $\mathrm{A} \rightsquigarrow \mathrm{B}[x]$.

So to get a clear first view on probabilistic belief change, we will exclude the problem of contradictory information here and assume throughout this paper, that all new information is consistent with what is already known. That means that for updating, new information should be consistent with respect to the prior distribution, and for revision, it should be consistent with background as well as with context knowledge. That corresponds to the idea of modeling *evolutions*, not *revolutions* of the world under consideration. Contractions of probabilistic beliefs will be dealt with in a further paper.

We adopt the distinction between revision and updating that was featured by Katsuno and Mendelzon and others: Revision means the procedure of learning new information about a static world, while updating applies to model the changes in an evolving world. But, in properly expanding classical terminology so as to comply with our probabilistic framework, here a *world* may be described by a set of probabilistic conditionals and is completely represented by a distribution. Thus revision requires the separation between background knowledge (i.e. a prior epistemic state) and (explicitly stated, incomplete) contextual knowledge, whereas updating should best start from complete descriptions of worlds, i.e. from distributions, taking into account as much knowledge about the prior world as possible. To realize these notions properly, we take revision (symbol: $\circ$) as an operation on belief bases and update (symbol: $\diamond$) as operating on belief states:

DEFINITION 6. Let $P \in \mathcal{BS}$, $(P, \mathcal{R}) \in \mathcal{BB}$, $\mathcal{R}_1 \subseteq \mathcal{L}^*$ such that $\mathcal{R}_1$ is P-consistent, $\mathcal{R}_2 \subseteq \mathcal{L}^*$ such that $\mathcal{R} \cup \mathcal{R}_2$ is P-consistent.

Then $P \diamond \mathcal{R}_1$ denotes the *update of* P *by* $\mathcal{R}_1$, and $(P, \mathcal{R}) \circ \mathcal{R}_2$ denotes the *revision of* $(P, \mathcal{R})$ *by* $\mathcal{R}_2$.

To satisfy the *principle of categorical matching*, belief change should maintain the level of knowledge (cf. e.g. [Gärdenfors and Rott, 1994]), i.e. $P \diamond \mathcal{R}_1 \in \mathcal{BS}$ and $(P, \mathcal{R}) \circ \mathcal{R}_2 \in \mathcal{BB}$. Note that revision also induces a change of the belief state $P^* = P * \mathcal{R}$, corresponding to $(P, \mathcal{R})$ (cf. section 4), to $(P^*)' = *((P, \mathcal{R}) \circ \mathcal{R}_2) \in \mathcal{BS}$.

6 PROBABILISTIC BELIEF REVISION

To set up axioms for probabilistic belief revision, we follow the ideas of [Gärdenfors, 1988] while observing that in the case of non-contradictory information, revision coincides with expansion. Due to distinguishing background knowledge from context information, we are able to compare the knowledge stored in different belief bases:

DEFINITION 7. A pre-ordering $\sqsubseteq$ on $\mathcal{BB}$ is defined by: $(P_1, \mathcal{R}_1) \sqsubseteq (P_2, \mathcal{R}_2)$ iff $P_1 = P_2$ and $\mathcal{R}_2 \models^{prob} \mathcal{R}_1$. $(P_1, \mathcal{R}_1)$ and $(P_2, \mathcal{R}_2)$ are $\sqsubseteq$*-equivalent*, $(P_1, \mathcal{R}_1) \equiv_{\sqsubseteq} (P_2, \mathcal{R}_2)$, iff $(P_1, \mathcal{R}_1) \sqsubseteq (P_2, \mathcal{R}_2)$ and $(P_2, \mathcal{R}_2) \sqsubseteq (P_1, \mathcal{R}_1)$.

Therefore $(P_1, \mathcal{R}_1) \equiv_{\sqsubseteq} (P_2, \mathcal{R}_2)$ iff $P_1 = P_2$ and $\mathcal{R}_1$ and $\mathcal{R}_2$ are probabilistically equivalent, i.e. iff both belief bases reflect the same probabilistic (background and contextual) knowledge. If the universal inference operation $\mathbf{C}$, resp. $*$, satisfies left logical equivalence, then $(P_1, \mathcal{R}_1) \equiv_{\sqsubseteq} (P_2, \mathcal{R}_2)$ implies $P_1 * \mathcal{R}_1 = P_2 * \mathcal{R}_2$.

The following *postulates* do not make use of the probabilistic inference operation but are to characterize pure base revision:

Let P be a distribution, $\mathcal{R}, \mathcal{R}', \mathcal{S} \subseteq \mathcal{L}^*$, and suppose that all necessary consistency preconditions are satisfied.

(PR1) $(P, \mathcal{R}) \circ \mathcal{S}$ is a belief *base*.

(PR2) If $(P, \mathcal{R}) \circ \mathcal{S} = (P, \mathcal{R}')$ then $\mathcal{R}' \models^{prob} \mathcal{S}$.

(PR3) $(P, \mathcal{R}) \sqsubseteq (P, \mathcal{R}) \circ \mathcal{S}$.

(PR4) $(P, \mathcal{R}) \circ \mathcal{S}$ is a minimal belief base (with respect to $\sqsubseteq$) among all belief bases satisfying (PR1)-(PR3).

(PR1) is the most fundamental axiom and coincides with the demand for categorical matching (see above). (PR2) is generally called *success*: the new context information is now represented (up to probabilistic equivalence). (PR3) states that revision should preserve prior knowledge as long as no conflicts arise (as is assumed here). Thus it is crucial for revision in contrast to update. Finally, (PR4) is in the sense of *informational economy* (cf. [Gärdenfors, 1988]): No unnecessary changes should occur.

The following characterization may be proved easily:

THEOREM 8. *The revision operator $\circ$ satisfies the axioms (PR1)-(PR4) iff*

(2) $(P, \mathcal{R}) \circ \mathcal{S} \equiv_{\sqsubseteq} (P, \mathcal{R} \cup \mathcal{S})$.

So from (PR1)-(PR4), other properties of the revision operator also follow which are usually found among characterizing postulates:

PROPOSITION 9. *Suppose the revision operator $\circ$ satisfies (2). Then it fulfills the following properties:*

(i) If $\mathcal{R} \models^{prob} \mathcal{S}$, *then* $(P, \mathcal{R}) \circ \mathcal{S} \equiv_{\sqsubseteq} (P, \mathcal{R})$;

(ii) If $(P_1, \mathcal{R}_1) \sqsubseteq (P_2, \mathcal{R}_2)$ *then* $(P_1, \mathcal{R}_1) \circ \mathcal{S} \sqsubseteq (P_2, \mathcal{R}_2) \circ \mathcal{S}$;

(iii) $((P, \mathcal{R}) \circ \mathcal{S}_1) \circ \mathcal{S}_2 \equiv_{\sqsubseteq} (P, \mathcal{R}) \circ (\mathcal{S}_1 \cup \mathcal{S}_2)$,

where $(P, \mathcal{R}), (P_1, \mathcal{R}_1), (P_2, \mathcal{R}_2)$ *are belief bases and* $\mathcal{S}, \mathcal{S}_1, \mathcal{S}_2 \subseteq \mathcal{L}^*$.

(i) shows a minimality of change, while (ii) is stated in [Gärdenfors, 1988] as a monotonicity postulate. (iii) deals with the handling of non-conflicting iterated revisions.

In this paper, we investigate revision merely under the assumption that the new information is compatible with what is already known. Belief revision based on classical logics is nothing but expansion in this case, and theorem 8 indeed shows that revision should reasonably mean expanding contextual knowledge. But if we consider the belief states generated by two belief bases $*(P, \mathcal{R}) = P * \mathcal{R}$ and $*(P, \mathcal{R} \cup \mathcal{S}) = P * (\mathcal{R} \cup \mathcal{S})$, we see that the probabilities that $P * \mathcal{R}$ assigns to conditionals occurring in $\mathcal{S}$ will normally differ from those in P as well as from those in $P * (\mathcal{R} \cup \mathcal{S})$ with expanded contextual knowledge. So the probabilistic belief in the conditionals in $\mathcal{S}$ is actually *revised*. Thus we prefer using the more general term here.

According to theorem 8, if the (underlying) universal probabilistic inference operation **C** satisfies left logical equivalence (cf. section 4), then the only reasonable revision operation (as specified by (PR1)-(PR4)) is given on the belief state level by

$$*((P, \mathcal{R}) \circ \mathcal{S}) = P * (\mathcal{R} \cup \mathcal{S}) \equiv C_P(\mathcal{R} \cup \mathcal{S}).$$

This parallels the result for the classical theory, with the probabilistic inference operation C_P taking the part of the classical consequence operation.

7 PROBABILISTIC UPDATING

Updating is to be understood as the process of altering a belief state appropriately when the world described by it *evolves* in the sense that some probabilities may change, but the "structure" of the world is supposed to be maintained as far as possible. Typical situations for updating occur when knowledge about a prior world is to be adapted to more recent information (e.g. a demographic model gained from statistical data of past periods should be brushed up by new data), or when a special context is to be modeled by the use of suitable general knowledge (e.g. when designing a medical diagnostic system by combining theoretical knowledge and actual data obtained in a certain hospital). Semantically, updating a distribution P by a set of conditionals $\mathcal{R}$ should yield a distribution $Q \in Mod(\mathcal{R})$ which is - in a well-defined sense - nearest to the prior P (cf. [Katsuno and Mendelzon, 1991]). This, however, coincides with the intuitive task of the inference operation $\mathbf{C}$, resp. $*$, itself. For reasons of coherence and unambiguity, it appears adequate to realize updating via probabilistic inference:

(3) $\quad P \diamond \mathcal{R} := P * \mathcal{R}$

for a distribution P and a P-consistent set $\mathcal{R} \subseteq \mathcal{L}^*$.

The close connection between belief change on one hand and nonmonotonic logics, i.e. the study of nonmonotonic inference operations, on the other hand, has been known already for a couple of years (cf. e.g. [Makinson and Gärdenfors, 1991], [Gärdenfors and Rott, 1994]) within the framework of classical logics. In the sequel, we will elaborate similar relations between these areas in a probabilistic setting by establishing postulates for belief change and compare them to properties of (universal) nonmonotonic inference operations.

Katsuno and Mendelzon list in [1991] eight axioms (U1)-(U8) that an updating operation should reasonably obey. As the most striking difference to revision, updating is not expected to respect prior knowledge if possible. This is due to the idea of an evolving world that updating is to describe.

In the following, we will translate those *postulates* of [Katsuno and Mendelzon, 1991] which do not make use of classical connectives into a probabilistic framework.

(PU1) $\quad P \diamond \mathcal{R} \models \mathcal{R}.$

(PU2) $\quad$ If $P \models \mathcal{R}$ then $P \diamond \mathcal{R} = P.$

(PU3) If $\mathcal{R}_1$ and $\mathcal{R}_2$ are probabilistically equivalent, then $P \diamond \mathcal{R}_1 = P \diamond \mathcal{R}_2$.

(PU4) If $P \diamond \mathcal{R}_1 \models \mathcal{R}_2$ and $P \diamond \mathcal{R}_2 \models \mathcal{R}_1$ then $P \diamond \mathcal{R}_1 = P \diamond \mathcal{R}_2$.

(PU5) $P \diamond (\mathcal{R}_1 \cup \mathcal{R}_2) = (P \diamond \mathcal{R}_1) \diamond (\mathcal{R}_1 \cup \mathcal{R}_2)$.

Postulates (PU1), (PU2) and (PU3) correspond to (U1), (U2) and (U4), respectively, constituting basic properties of probabilistic belief change. (PU4) states that two updating procedures with respect to sets $\mathcal{R}_1$ and $\mathcal{R}_2$ should result in the same knowledge base if each update represents the new information of the other. This property is called *reciprocity* in the framework of nonmonotonic logics (cf. [Makinson, 1994]).

(PU5) is new insofar as it deals with *iterative updating*. This is generally problematic because updates from different starting points are hardly comparable. (PU5) demands that at least, updating any intermediate world $P \diamond \mathcal{R}_1$ by the full information $\mathcal{R}_1 \cup \mathcal{R}_2$ should lead to the same result as updating P by $\mathcal{R}_1 \cup \mathcal{R}_2$ in one step. The rationale behind this axiom is that if the information about the new world drops in in parts, updating any provisional state of belief by the full information should result unambigously in a final belief state.

Note that in general, the updates $(P \diamond \mathcal{R}_1) \diamond \mathcal{R}_2$ and $(P \diamond \mathcal{R}_1) \diamond (\mathcal{R}_1 \cup \mathcal{R}_2)$ will differ because $(P \diamond \mathcal{R}_1) \diamond \mathcal{R}_2 \not\models \mathcal{R}_1$ – updates do not maintain prior contextual information, in contrast to revision (cf. postulate (PR3)).

(PU5) has proved to be a crucial property for the characterization of ME-inference (cf. [Kern-Isberner, 1998a]) but actually goes back to [Shore and Johnson, 1981]. It is worth noticing that this postulate originally inspired by studying ME-inference is equivalent to a postulate which quite recently was proposed in the context of iterated belief revisions: (PU5) is a probabilistic version of axiom (C1) in [Darwiche and Pearl, 1997].

For representing updating operations satisfying the postulates stated above, we will make use of the relationship between probabilistic updating and probabilistic inference:

PROPOSITION 10. *Suppose updating is being realized via universal probabilistic inference, that means (3) holds.*

(i) $\diamond$ *satisfies (PU1) iff* $*$ *is reflexive.*

(ii) $\diamond$ *satisfies (PU2) iff* $*$ *is founded.*

(iii) $\diamond$ *satisfies (PU3) iff* $*$ *satisfies left logical equivalence.*

(iv) Assuming reflexivity resp. the validity of (PU1), $\diamond$ *satisfies (PU4) iff* $*$ *is cumulative.*

(v) Assuming foundedness resp. the validity of (PU2), $\diamond$ *satisfies (PU5) iff* $*$ *is strongly cumulative.*

From this proposition, a representation result follows in a straightforward manner:

THEOREM 11. *If $\diamond$ is defined by (3), it satisfies all of the postulates (PU1)-(PU5) iff $*$ is reflexive, founded, strongly cumulative and satisfies left logical equivalence.*

EXAMPLE 12. (continued) The psychologist is going to change his job: He will be working in a clinic for people addicted only to alcohol and/or drugs. He is told that the percentage of persons addicted to alcohol, but also addicted to drugs, is higher than usual and may be estimated by 40 %.

So the information the psychologist has about the "new world" is represented by

$$\mathcal{R} = \{A \vee D[1], A \leadsto D[0.4]\}$$

and the distribution P from the end of section 3 represents background or prior knowledge, respectively. Now the psychologist updates P by $\mathcal{R}$ using ME-inference and obtains $P^* = P *_e \mathcal{R}$ as new belief state:

ω	$P^*(\omega)$	ω	$P^*(\omega)$	ω	$P^*(\omega)$	ω	$P^*(\omega)$
ADY	0.099	$\overline{A}DY$	0.425	$AD\overline{Y}$	0.105	$\overline{A}D\overline{Y}$	0.066
$A\overline{D}Y$	0.089	$\overline{A}\,\overline{D}Y$	0.0	$A\overline{D}\,\overline{Y}$	0.216	$\overline{A}\,\overline{D}\,\overline{Y}$	0.0

8 REVISION VS. UPDATING

We have already described in detail the different ideas underlying revision and updating processes. We will now look upon the formal parallels resp. differences. For an adequate comparison, we have to observe the changes of belief *states* that are induced by revision of belief *bases*. Again making use of the universal inference operation $*$, (PR2) and (PR3) translate into

(PR2′) $*((P, \mathcal{R}) \circ \mathcal{S}) \models \mathcal{S}$.

(PR3′) $*((P, \mathcal{R}) \circ \mathcal{S}) \models \mathcal{R}$.

While (PR2′) parallels (PU1), (PR3') establishes the crucial difference between revision and updating: revision preserves prior knowledge, thus it is, in this sense, *monotonic* while updating does not, neither in a classical nor in a probabilistic framework.

The intended effects of revision and updating on a belief state $P * \mathcal{R}$ that is generated by a belief base $(P, \mathcal{R})$ are made obvious by informally writing

(4) $(P * \mathcal{R}) \circ \mathcal{S} = P * (\mathcal{R} \cup \mathcal{S})$,

while

(5) $(P * \mathcal{R}) \diamond \mathcal{S} = (P * \mathcal{R}) * \mathcal{S}$.

This reveals clearly the difference, but also the relationship between revision and updating: Revising $P * \mathcal{R}$ by $\mathcal{S}$ results in the same state of belief as updating P by (the full contextual information) $\mathcal{R} \cup \mathcal{S}$.

Unfortunately, the representation of a probabilistic belief state by a belief base is not unique, different belief bases may generate the same belief state. So we could not use the intelligible formula (4) to define probabilistic revision but had to go back to belief bases in order to separate background and context knowledge unambigously. It is interesting to observe, however, that strong cumulativity, together with foundedness, ensures at least a convenient independence of revision from background knowledge: If two belief bases $(P_1, \mathcal{R}), (P_2, \mathcal{R})$ with different prior distributions but the same context knowledge give rise to the same belief state $P_1 * \mathcal{R} = P_2 * \mathcal{R}$, then – assuming strong cumulativity and foundedness – $P_1 * (\mathcal{R} \cup \mathcal{S}) = (P_1 * \mathcal{R}) * (\mathcal{R} \cup \mathcal{S}) = (P_2 * \mathcal{R}) * (\mathcal{R} \cup \mathcal{S}) = P_2 * (\mathcal{R} \cup \mathcal{S})$.

So strong cumulativity and foundedness guarantee a particular well-behavedness with respect to inference, updating and revision.

9 FOCUSING

According to [Dubois and Prade, 1997], focusing means applying generic knowledge to a reference class appropriate to describe the context of interest. So in a probabilistic setting, focusing is best done by conditioning which, however, is normally used for revision, too. So revision and focusing are supposed to coincide in the framework of Bayesian probabilities though they differ conceptually: Revision is not only *applying knowledge* but means incorporating a new constraint so as to *refine knowledge*.

Making use of ME-inference, it is indeed possible to realize this conceptual difference appropriately. To make this clear, we have to consider belief changes induced by some certain information A[1], that is, we learn proposition A with certainty. The following proposition reveals the connections of both revision and updating to conditioning which is usually considered to be the "classical" belief change operation in probabilistics.

PROPOSITION 13. *Let P be a distribution, $\mathcal{R} \subseteq \mathcal{L}^*$ a P- consistent set of probabilistic conditionals, and suppose $A[1]$ to be a certain probabilistic fact.*

(i) $P \diamond_e \{\mathrm{A}[1]\} = P *_e \{A[1]\} = P(\cdot|\mathrm{A})$.

(ii) $*_e((P, \mathcal{R}) \circ \{\mathrm{A}[1]\}) = P *_e (\mathcal{R} \cup \{\mathrm{A}[1]\}) = P(\cdot|\mathrm{A}) *_e \mathcal{R}$.

Both parts of this proposition may be proved by using the representation (1) of the ME-distribution.

Thus, in the context of ME-inference, updating with a certain fact results in mere conditioning the prior distribution, while revision by a certain fact amounts to conditioning background knowledge which then still has to be adapted to (uncertain) contextual knowledge. So focusing, realized via conditioning, turns out to be a special case of updating: The certain fact $A[1]$ may be considered not only as a proper reference class, but also as representing a new world the prior knowledge has to be adapted to.

The proposition above shows that, in a (generalized) probabilistic framework, a proper distinction between focusing and revision is possible.

EXAMPLE 14. (continued) After having spent a couple of days in the new clinic, the psychologist realized that this clinic was for young people only. So he had to *revise* his knowledge about his new sphere of activity and arrived at the revised belief state $*_e((P,\mathcal{R}) \circ Y[1]) = P *_e (\mathcal{R} \cup Y[1]) =: P_1^*$ shown in the following table:

ω	$P_1^*(\omega)$	ω	$P_1^*(\omega)$	ω	$P_1^*(\omega)$	ω	$P_1^*(\omega)$
ADY	0.120	$\overline{A}DY$	0.700	$AD\overline{Y}$	0.0	$\overline{A}D\overline{Y}$	0.0
$A\overline{D}Y$	0.180	$\overline{A}\,\overline{D}Y$	0.0	$A\overline{D}\,\overline{Y}$	0.0	$\overline{A}\,\overline{D}\,\overline{Y}$	0.0

This distribution is different from that one the psychologist would have obtained by *focusing* his knowledge represented by $P^* = P *_e \mathcal{R}$ on a young patient, given by $P^* \diamond Y[1] = P^*(\cdot \mid Y) =: P_Y^*$:

ω	$P_Y^*(\omega)$	ω	$P_Y^*(\omega)$	ω	$P_Y^*(\omega)$	ω	$P_Y^*(\omega)$
ADY	0.162	$\overline{A}DY$	0.693	$AD\overline{Y}$	0.0	$\overline{A}D\overline{Y}$	0.0
$A\overline{D}Y$	0.145	$\overline{A}\,\overline{D}Y$	0.0	$A\overline{D}\,\overline{Y}$	0.0	$\overline{A}\,\overline{D}\,\overline{Y}$	0.0

10 CONCLUDING REMARKS

The approach to probabilistic belief change presented in this paper uses belief bases and belief states, thus allowing to distinguish between explicitly stated and deduced beliefs. Belief bases represent background knowledge as different from contextual knowledge, and both are combined to yield a distribution by a non-monotonic inference operation. We defined belief revision as a change in contextual knowledge, and belief update as adapting a prior distribution to a new context. Both operations may be realized by virtue of the underlying probabilistic inference operation. It is only the different ways in which it is applied that yield different results in belief change while allowing a convenient homogeneity of methods.

As a particularly well-behaved probabilistic inference operation, we feature reasoning at optimum entropy (ME-inference). One of its characterizing properties, namely (PU5), is stated here as a postulate for handling iterated updates and turned out to be crucial in other frameworks, too (cf. [Darwiche and Pearl, 1997]). Making use of the ME-methods, we show that revision and focusing may be modelled differently in probabilistics, thus obtaining results similar to those of Dubois and Prade in the context of upper and lower probabilities.

Though the concern of this paper is with probabilistic belief change, probabilistic knowledge is actually used only in quite a formal manner. So the approach to realize revision and updating developed here, in particular with respect to the concept of a universal inference operation, may be of interest for other knowledge representation formalisms which are rich enough for distinguishing between background and evidential knowledge, as well as for iterated belief change in general.

FernUniversitaet Hagen, Germany.

REFERENCES

[Alchourrón *et al.*, 1985] C.E. Alchourrón, P. Gärdenfors, and P. Makinson. On the logic of theory change: Partial meet contraction and revision functions. *Journal of Symbolic Logic*, 50(2):510–530, 1985.

[Calabrese, 1991] P.G. Calabrese. Deduction and inference using conditional logic and probability. In I.R. Goodman, M.M. Gupta, H.T. Nguyen, and G.S. Rogers, editors, *Conditional Logic in Expert Systems*, pages 71–100. Elsevier, North Holland, 1991.

[Darwiche and Pearl, 1997] A. Darwiche and J. Pearl. On the logic of iterated belief revision. *Artificial Intelligence*, 89:1–29, 1997.

[Dubois and Prade, 1994] D. Dubois and H. Prade. A survey of belief revision and updating rules in various uncertainty models. *Intern. Journal of intelligent systems*, 9:61–100, 1994.

[Dubois and Prade, 1997] D. Dubois and H. Prade. Focusing vs. belief revision: A fundamental distinction when dealing with generic knowledge. In *Proceedings First International Joint Conference on Qualitative and Quantitative Practical Reasoning, ECSQARU-FAPR'97*, pages 96–107, Berlin Heidelberg New York, 1997. Springer.

[Gärdenfors and Rott, 1994] P. Gärdenfors and H. Rott. Belief revision. In D.M. Gabbay, C.H. Hogger, and J.A. Robinson, editors, *Handbook of Logic in Artificial Intelligence and Logic Programming*, pages 35–132. Oxford University Press, 1994.

[Gärdenfors, 1988] P. Gärdenfors. *Knowledge in Flux: Modeling the Dynamics of Epistemic States*. MIT Press, Cambridge, Mass., 1988.

[Katsuno and Mendelzon, 1991] H. Katsuno and A.O. Mendelzon. On the difference between updating a knowledge base and revising it. In *Proceedings Second International Conference on Principles of Knowledge Representation and Reasoning, KR'91*, pages 387–394, San Mateo, Ca., 1991. Morgan Kaufmann.

[Kern-Isberner, 1998a] G. Kern-Isberner. Characterizing the principle of minimum cross-entropy within a conditional-logical framework. *Artificial Intelligence*, 98:169–208, 1998.

[Kern-Isberner, 1998b] G. Kern-Isberner. Nonmonotonic reasoning in probabilistics. In *Proceedings European Conference on Artificial Intelligence, ECAI'98*, pages 580 – 584, West Sussex, UK, 1998. Wiley & sons.

[Kern-Isberner, 1998c] G. Kern-Isberner. A note on conditional logics and entropy. *International Journal of Approximate Reasoning*, 19:231–246, 1998.

[Makinson and Gärdenfors, 1991] D. Makinson and P. Gärdenfors. Relations between the logic of theory change and nonmonotonic logic. In *Proceedings Workshop The Logic of Theory Change, Konstanz, Germany, 1989*, pages 185–205, Berlin Heidelberg New York, 1991. Springer.

[Makinson, 1994] D. Makinson. General patterns in nonmonotonic reasoning. In D.M. Gabbay, C.H. Hogger, and J.A. Robinson, editors, *Handbook of Logic in Artificial Intelligence and Logic Programming*, volume 3, pages 35–110. Oxford University Press, 1994.

[Paris, 1994] J.B. Paris. *The uncertain reasoner's companion – A mathematical perspective*. Cambridge University Press, 1994.

[Shore and Johnson, 1980] J.E. Shore and R.W. Johnson. Axiomatic derivation of the principle of maximum entropy and the principle of minimum cross-entropy. *IEEE Transactions on Information Theory*, IT-26:26–37, 1980.

[Shore and Johnson, 1981] J.E. Shore and R.W. Johnson. Properties of cross-entropy minimization. *IEEE Transactions on Information Theory*, IT-27:472–482, 1981.

[Voorbraak, 1996] F. Voorbraak. Probabilistic belief expansion and conditioning. Technical Report LP-96-07, Institute for Logic, Language and Computation, University of Amsterdam, 1996.

F. DE ROSIS, E. COVINO, R. FALCONE AND
C. CASTELFRANCHI

BAYESIAN COGNITIVE DIAGNOSIS IN BELIEVABLE MULTIAGENT SYSTEMS

1 INTRODUCTION

Multiagent systems are computational systems in which several agents interact either to solve a common problem or to achieve independent goals, by coordinating with each other. Agents are computational entities aimed at autonomously achieving some goal or assigned task; they can compete, cooperate, communicate and negotiate with each other. A rational agent takes decisions about how to behave in a given circumstance by reasoning on its own mental state, that is on first order beliefs and goals. When it is programmed so as to show a 'socially intelligent' behaviour, it considers, in its reasoning, also the mental state of the agents with which it interacts (second and higher order beliefs). Second order beliefs may be acquired through 'self-introduction' of agents, may be inherited from stereotypes, may be ascribed according to one's own beliefs or may be inferred by observing the other agents' behaviour [Jameson, 1995]. In the absence of any information (for instance, at its entry in the world), the observing agent may start from a default and possibly incomplete model of the other agents: this model will be revised as the interaction proceeds, through a reasoning process that has been named *belief ascription* or *cognitive diagnosis* [Lee and Wilks, 1996], [Self, 1993]. The following problems characterize this reasoning process:

- the behaviour of the observed agent may be 'ambiguous', and subject to different interpretations; in this case, the most likely hypothesis has to be selected, by leaving aside alternatives for future revisions;
- this behaviour may be 'contradictory', for different reasons: because the observed agent may change its mind, because it may lie or just because a previous interpretation was incorrect.

In both cases, a more general knowledge of the observed agent (like the stereotype to which it belongs) may help in selecting the interpretation and in revising it; on the other hand, observing the agent behaviour may help in defining that stereotype. To clarify our idea, let us consider the scenario that Nebel employs to introduce his belief revision algorithm in [Nebel, 1992]:

Assume that a suspect tells you that he went to the beach for swimming and assume that you have observed that the sun was shining. Further, you firmly believe that going to the beach for swimming when the sun is shining implies a sun

M.-A. Williams and H. Rott (eds.), Frontiers in Belief Revision, 409–428.

tan. If you then discover that the suspect is not tanned, there is an inconsistency to resolve.

Nebel resolves the inconsistency by assigning a low priority, in the belief ordering, to the suspect's assertion that he 'went to the beach', and by concluding that he is a liar. However, in more realistic multiagent interactions, this (reasonable) explanation should be contrasted with some alternatives: (i) the 'suspect' might be someone who does not tan easily (in that case, the rule should be retracted); (ii) the sun might be strong for someone coming from Germany, but not enough for someone from southern Italy (in this case, the 'shining sun' belief should be retracted),etc. Every hypothesis about the context (let's say, about the stereotype to which the observed agent may be assigned) involves a different ordering of beliefs, and therefore implies a different selection of the belief to retract. A reasonable belief revision should keep all these alternatives open, even if it will select one of them to take an immediate decision: knowing, in a future step of interaction, that the observed agent was coming from Bari will increase the likelihood of the second explanation. Alternatively, coming to know that he is a German who usually does not lie will increase the likelihood that he is resistant to sun tanning, etc.

In this paper, we investigate how stereotype-based belief ascription and revision can be performed in multiagent systems. We consider particular types of stereotypes, that we call 'personalities', which play a relevant role in believable agent systems [Reilly and Bates, 1995]. We show some examples from an agent factory (named GOLEM), which we designed to test multiagent cooperation theories: in this factory, two personality-rich rational agents interact in a blocks world to try to achieve their own goals by exploiting, when possible, the other agent's help or by helping it [Castelfrachi *et al.*, 1998a]. GOLEM is aimed at modelling multiagent interactions and situations; however, given the cognitive complexity of our agents and the need to first provide refined operational definitions of personalities, we started by modelling only bilateral interactions. We finally approach two topics which are of interest in multiagent interaction: the simulation of deceiving and of suspecting deception and the open world issue.

2 THE PROBLEM

Our rational agents have a mental state which is a conjunction of belief atoms; belief atoms take, as usual, an agent name as a first term and apply to a sentence in a language $\mathcal{L}$. In what follows, without further notice, low-case Latin (resp. Greek) letters denote constants (variables) in $\mathcal{L}$. In particular:

- A and B denote agents' names;
- α denotes a domain action variable;
- $a, a^1, a^2, \ldots$ denote domain action constants;

- ϕ^k denotes variables over sentences in $\mathcal{L}$: the variable α occurs in these sentences;
- f^h denotes variables over ground sentences in $\mathcal{L}$: actions $a, a^1, a^2, \ldots, a^j, \ldots$ occur in these sentences.

EXAMPLE 1.
$f^1 : Cnd\text{-}A(a^1)$, for 'A is able to make the action a^1'
$f^2 : Cnd\text{-}B(a^2)$, for 'B is able to make the action a^2'
$\phi^1 : \neg Cnd\text{-}A(\alpha)$, for '$A$ is not able to make the action α'
$\phi^2 : Cnd\text{-}B(\alpha)$, for 'B is able to make the action α

Let A and B be two *rational agents* living in a *world* W, with A observing the behaviour of B. In what follows, we formally define the *cognitive diagnosis problem*, for A, about B in logical terms. This problem deals with ascribing to B a set of beliefs which are consistent with A's previous beliefs about B and with B's behaviour, and in revising them as far as interaction between A and B proceeds. As we formalize the point of view of A, in all the notations that follow belief formulae should be intended as having a 'B_A' as a prefix, and a 'A believes that' should be premised to their interpretation.

DEFINITION 2. Given $B_B f^h$ a basic belief of agent B about f^h, we call *mental state of* B the conjunction of B's basic beliefs:

$$MS(B) = \bigwedge_{h=1}^{m} B_B f^h.$$

EXAMPLE 3. $MS(B) = B_B Cnd\text{-}A(a^1) \wedge B_B \neg Cnd\text{-}A(a^2) \wedge B_B Cnd\text{-}B(a^1) \wedge B_B Cnd\text{-}B(a^2)$, which stands for: "$B$ believes that A is able to make only a^1, whereas he is able to make a^2, as well".

DEFINITION 4. Given $B_B \phi^k$ a generic belief of agent B about ϕ^k, we call *mental pattern of* B a conjunction of consistent generic beliefs of B:

$$MP^r(B, \Phi) = \bigwedge_{k=1}^{n} B_B \phi^k.$$

with $r = 1, \ldots, w$.

EXAMPLE 5. $MP^2(B, \Phi) = B_B Cnd\text{-}A(\alpha) \wedge B_B \neg Cnd\text{-}B(\alpha)$.

Notice that a possible mental pattern of B differs from a description of B's mental state in that it sets up a condition on the combination of values of a subset of B's beliefs, and that it contains variable names in the second term of all beliefs.

DEFINITION 6. Given $Perf^i(B, \alpha)$ a *generic performance* that B may make concerning α, where $Perf^i$ is an element of a finite set of performance types which include communicative acts or domain transformations ($i = 1, \ldots, p$), we call *behaviour schema of* B a relationship between a possible mental pattern of B and a generic performance that B may make when its mental state matches that mental pattern:

$$BS^{ri}(B, \Phi) = [MP^r(B, \Phi) \overset{?}{\Rightarrow} Perf^i(B, \alpha)],$$

where α occurs in Φ.

EXAMPLE 7. $Perf^1(B, \phi^k) = \textit{Request-to-do}(B, \alpha)$ should be interpreted as: "B requests the other agent to perform action α". $BS^{21}(B, \Phi) = [B_B \textit{Cnd-A}(\alpha) \wedge B_B \neg \textit{Cnd-B}(\alpha) \overset{?}{\Rightarrow} \textit{Request-to-do}(B, \alpha)]$, should be interpreted as: "if B believes that A is able to make the domain action α whereas it has not this ability, it might request A to make it". Notice that the $\overset{?}{\Rightarrow}$ symbol denotes that this relationship may be uncertain.

DEFINITION 8. We call *world model* a finite set of behaviour schemas that represents a theory about the performances that B might 'reasonably' make in correspondence with a set of given mental patterns. The meaning of 'reasonable' depends on the particular application domain, and on agent's A vision of the world.

$$WM(B) = \{BS^{11}(B, \Phi), \ldots, BS^{ri}(B, \Phi), \ldots, BS^{wp}(B, \Phi)\}.$$

DEFINITION 9. Given the observation, from A, of a specific performance $Perf^j(B, a)$ made by B and concerning a, we call *cognitive diagnosis*, for A, the problem of updating its image of B's mental state from $MS(B)$ to $MS^R(B)$ so that:

$$WM(B) \bigcup MS^R(B) \models Perf^j(B, a).$$

This requires selecting the behaviour schema that B likely applied in deciding to make the performance, and enables revising B's mental state so as to insure consistency in that state.

3 BELIEVABLE AGENTS

"Personality" can be defined as a typical behaviour, due to some internal mental state, of a given agent (or a given class of agents) in a given situation (or a given class of situations). As we deal with cognitive agents, we call *personality trait* $T^s(B)$ an aspect of agent B's mental state which influences its behaviour in a 'sufficiently permanent' way, by setting how combinations of values for its beliefs affect its actions. For instance, we defined, in GOLEM, a theory to set up how multiagent cooperation is influenced by the agents' individual and mutually believed abilities [Castelfrachi *et al.*, 1998a]; in this theory, we defined personality traits affecting the delegation and the help behaviour as described in Table 1. A 'believable' agent[1] holds one or more 'personality traits' in addition to a

[1] The adjective 'believable' is usually attached to agents or artificial characters that give 'the illusion of life' [Bates, 1994], by showing emotional behaviours, by using 'realistic language' [Loyall and

set of beliefs: agents in GOLEM hold, for instance, delegation, help and reaction personality traits. Cognitive diagnosis in a believable multiagent‘ world includes personality factors in the abduction process, in at least two ways:

a. revising B's mental state, given a performance made by B and a hypothesis about B's personality traits;

b. revising B's personality traits, given a performance made by B and a hypothesis about B's mental state.

Table 1. Some delegation and help attitudes

Delegation attitudes
a *lazy* agent always delegates tasks if there is another agent which is able to take care of them; it acts by itself only when there is no alternative. a *hanger-on* tends to never act by itself. a *delegating-if-needed* asks for help only if it is not able to do the task by itself. a *never-delegating* considers that tasks should only be achieved if it can perform them.
Help attitudes
a *hyper-cooperative* always helps if it can. a *benevolent* first checks that the request does not conflict with its goal. a *supplier* first checks that the other agent could not do the action by itself. a *selfish* helps only when the requested action achieves its own goals. a *non-helper* does never help, by principle.

An example of relationship between behaviour schemas and delegation personality traits is shown in Figure 1, where behaviour schemas encode the informal description of personality traits that we made in Table 1. For instance: $MP^1 \rightarrow Req$ stands for $B_B Cnd\text{-}A(\alpha) \wedge B_B Cnd\text{-}B(\alpha) \overset{?}{\Rightarrow} Request\text{-}to\text{-}do(B, \alpha)$, which corresponds to a partial description of a *lazy* or a *hanger-on* agent, which "always delegate tasks if there is another agent which is able to take care of them".

The relationship between behaviour schemas and personality traits is such that:

- different mental patterns $MP^r(B, \Phi)$ may lead agents with different personalities to make the same performance $Perf^i(B, \alpha)$. For example: in Figure 1, both $MP^1(B, \Phi)$ and $MP^2(B, \Phi)$ lead to $Request\text{-}to\text{-}do(B, \alpha)$, respectively in agents with the personality traits $T^1(B) = Lazy(B)$ and $T^2(B) = Delegating\text{-}if\text{-}needed(B)$;

Bates, 1997], by displaying an 'artistic personality' [Reilly, 1997], etc. In this paper, we attach this attribute to the mental pattern of agents, to indicate a set of attitudes that include personality traits in addition to beliefs.

- a mental pattern $MP^r(B,\Phi)$ may lead agents with different personalities to make different performances. Again, in Figure 1, MP^1 leads agents with the traits *Lazy* (or *Hanger-on*) and *Delegating-if-needed* (or *Never-delegating*) to make, respectively, the performances: $Request\text{-}to\text{-}do(B,\Phi)$ and $Perform(B,\Phi)$.

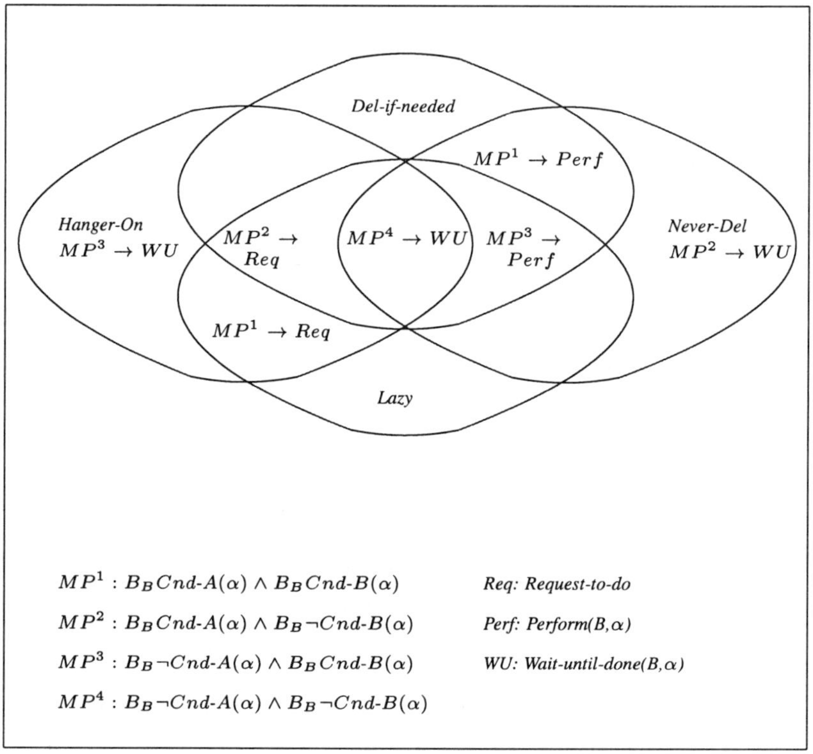

Figure 1. Personality-based behaviour schema in GOLEM

Personality traits define a clustering of behaviour schemas in *WM(B)*; this clustering is such that:

- several schemas are defined for every personality trait. For instance, for $T^1(B) = Lazy(B)$:

$$MP^1(B,\Phi) \overset{?}{\Rightarrow} Request\text{-}to\text{-}do(B,\alpha)$$
$$MP^2(B,\Phi) \overset{?}{\Rightarrow} Request\text{-}to\text{-}do(B,\alpha)$$
$$MP^3(B,\Phi) \overset{?}{\Rightarrow} Perform(B,\alpha)$$
$$MP^4(B,\Phi) \overset{?}{\Rightarrow} Wait\text{-}until\text{-}done(B,\alpha)$$

- a schema can be associated with several personality traits; for instance: $MP^4(B, \Phi) \stackrel{?}{\Rightarrow} Wait\text{-}until\text{-}done(B, \alpha)$ is associated with all the traits.

4 COGNITIVE DIAGNOSIS IN LOGICAL TERMS: AN EXAMPLE

Let us imagine that B makes the performance: $Request\text{-}to\text{-}do(B, a^1)$. Let us suppose that A doesn't know anything about B's personality, whereas he is certain that she is able to make the domain action a^1, for instance because she declared it in her self-introduction. He therefore 'knows' that B's mental state matches the pattern MP^1 and that she applied the behaviour schema $MP^1 \rightarrow Req$. He asks himself whether he can infer something about B's personality, from such a communicative act. He may exclude that B is a *never-delegating* or a *delegating-if-needed*; she is, therefore, a *lazy* or a *hanger-on*. As both hypotheses are plausible, A will have to apply some 'external' criteria to select one of them; for instance, he will select according to his own personality (A may be *trustful* or *suspicious*) and according to how frequently he found the various personalities in previous encounters with other agents. He will update his image of B's mental state after this choice and will adapt his helping behaviour to this ascription of beliefs. After future B's performances, this image will be revised consistently: knowing something about B's personality traits will now enable A to prune out the research space about B's models. For instance, if B subsequently performs some (different) domain action, A will exclude that she is a *hanger-on* as no behaviour schema in this personality cluster has a $Perform$ in its right-side. However, as shown in Figure 1, purely logical reasoning enables a partially efficient pruning, especially when the same performance is repeated in different turns. If, for instance, B makes several *Request-to-do*, A will never have a sufficient evidence to select between the two alternative hypotheses of B being a *lazy* or a *hanger-on*. In addition, if A has no certain knowledge about B's mental state, he will have a limited possibility of revising his second-order beliefs about B. For instance, if A does not know B's abilities, even after a sequence of *Request-to-do* he will remain in a total uncertainty on whether B behaved according to the schemas $MP^1(B, \Phi) \stackrel{?}{\Rightarrow} Request\text{-}to\text{-}do(B, \alpha)$ or $MP^2(B, \Phi) \stackrel{?}{\Rightarrow} Request\text{-}to\text{-}do(B, \alpha)$, and therefore he will have no means for understanding whether B is a *lazy*, a *hanger-on* or a *delegating-if-needed*.

5 PROBABILISTIC COGNITIVE DIAGNOSIS

In what follows, we re-define the cognitive diagnosis problem in probabilistic terms.

DEFINITION 10. We call *believable-mental pattern* of B, $B\text{-}MP^r(B, \Phi)$, a consistent combination of beliefs and personality traits, and *believable-mental state* of

B the conjunction of its basic beliefs and personality traits.

EXAMPLE 11. In our world of cooperating agents, a believable mental pattern is $B\text{-}MP^2(B,\Phi) = Lazy(B) \wedge B_B Cnd\text{-}A(\alpha) \wedge B_B \neg Cnd\text{-}B(\alpha)$.

DEFINITION 12. We call *probabilistic behaviour schema* of B the conditional probability that B makes the generic performance $Perf^i(B,\alpha)$ when its believable mental state matches the mental pattern $B\text{-}MP^r(B,\Phi)$:

$$P\text{-}BS^r(B,\Phi) = P(Perf^i(B,\alpha)|B\text{-}MP^r(B,\Phi))$$

DEFINITION 13. We call *probabilistic world model* of A the table of probabilistic behaviour schemas:

$$P\text{-}WM(B) = P(Perf^i(B,\alpha)|B\text{-}MP^r(B,\Phi)),$$

with $i = 1,\ldots,p$ and $r = 1,\ldots,w$; each row in this table defines the probability that an agent, with a believable mental state that matches the mental pattern $B\text{-}MP^r(B,\Phi)$, performs each of the performances that are 'known' to A.

EXAMPLE 14. A *weakly lazy* agent might have the following probabilistic behaviour schemas $P\text{-}BS^{1i}$ $(i = 1,\ldots,3)$:

$P(Request\text{-}to\text{-}do(B,\alpha)|B\text{-}MP^1(B,\Phi)) = .8$
$P(Perform(B,\alpha)|B\text{-}MP^1(B,\Phi)) = .2$
$P(Wait\text{-}until\text{-}done(B,\alpha)|B\text{-}MP^1(B,\Phi)) = 0$

DEFINITION 15. Given: (i) a specific performance $Perf^j(B,a)$ made by B in a particular phase of interaction and (ii) a probabilistic knowledge, by A, of the individual components of B's mental state and personality traits, respectively denoted with $P(B_B f^h)$ and $P(T^s(B))$ $(h = 1,\ldots,m$ and $s = 1,\ldots,v)$, we call *probabilistic cognitive diagnosis*, for A, the problem of updating A's knowledge of B's personality and mental state components regarding the performed action a after observing the performance:

$$P(T^s(B)|Perf^j(B,a)), s = 1,\ldots,v$$

and

$$P(B_B f^h|Perf^j(B,a)), h = 1,\ldots,m.$$

We introduce the following simplifying assumptions:

HY1 *B's conformism*: the set of behaviour schemas in $P\text{-}WM(B)$ is closed and their probability values are fixed;

HY2 *A's omniscience*: A knows all the behaviour schemas in $P\text{-}WM(B)$, with their probability values;

HY3 *independence of attitudes*: the probability of a given personality trait $T^s(B)$ for B is not influenced by her beliefs and viceversa; B's beliefs are conditionally independent among themselfs, as well:

$P(T^s(B)|B_B\phi^1, B_B\phi^2, \ldots, B_B\phi^n) = P(T^s(B))$, for all $s = 1, \ldots, v$

$P(B_B\phi^k|B_B\phi^1, ..., B_B\phi^{k-1}, \ldots, B_B\phi^{k+1}, \ldots) = P(B_B\phi^k)$,
for all $k = 1, \ldots n$.

Under these hypotheses, A's knowledge of B's believable mental state can be revised by computing the probability that this state matches the pattern $B\text{-}MP^r(B, \Phi)$ after observing the evidence $Perf^j(B, a)$:

$$P(B\text{-}MP^r(B,\Phi)^{\{\alpha/a\}}|Perf^j(B,a)) = \frac{P(Perf^j(B,a)|B\text{-}MP^r(B,\Phi)^{\{\alpha/a\}}) * P(B\text{-}MP^r(B,\Phi)^{\{\alpha/a\}})}{P(Perf^j(B,a))}. \quad (1)$$

In this formula:

a. $P(Perf^j(B,a)|B\text{-}MP^r(B,\Phi)^{\{\alpha/a\}})$ is taken from the probabilistic world model $P\text{-}WM(B)$; we assume that the probability that an agent whose mental state matches the believable pattern $B\text{-}MP^r(B, \Phi)$ makes the performance $Perf^i(B, \alpha)$ is independent of the value assigned to the variable α. For example, the definitions of *lazy*, *hanger-on*, *delegating-if-needed*, *never-delegating* agents in Section 3 may be translated into a believable world model in which the probability of making a *Request-to-do* (or a $Perform$ or a $Wait\text{-}until\text{-}done$), conditional on a combination of the agent's beliefs and personality traits, is independent of the domain action. If, in particular, a combination of beliefs is 'binding', for an agent with a given personality trait, to make a particular performance in a specific context, the mentioned table will be binary. For instance, a *strong lazy* B that is able to do the domain-action α and believes that A is able, as well, to do it will certainly make a *Request-to-do*(B, α). If, on the contrary, an agent with a given personality trait may make, in a given circumstance, different performances, each with a given probability value (like in the example of a *weakly lazy* agent at the beginning of this Section), the $P\text{-}WM(B)$ is not binary .

b. $P(B\text{-}MP^r(B, \Phi))$ is computed from the probabilities of individual components of B's mental state (under assumption HY3) after applying the unification $\{\alpha/a\}$

$$P(B\text{-}MP^r(B,\Phi)^{\{\alpha/a\}}) = \prod_{hs} P(B_B f^h) * P(T^s(B)), \quad (2)$$

the product being extended to all h and s included in $B\text{-}MP^r(B, \Phi)$.

In absence of any information, and by virtue of B's conformism and A's omniscience assumptions, A will assign a uniform probability distribution to the values of individual components of B's mental state.

c. $P(Perf^j(B,a))$ is computed as follows:

$$P(Perf^j(B,a)) = \sum_r P(Perf^j(B,a)|B\text{-}MP^r(B,\Phi)^{\{\alpha/a\}}) * P(B\text{-}MP^r(B,\Phi)^{\{\alpha/a\}}). \quad (3)$$

The posterior probabilities of the individual components of B's mental state and of its personality traits are a function of A's general knowledge $P\text{-}MW(B)$ and of his (prior) knowledge about B's mental state and personality traits, *when he observes the performance* $Perf^j(B,a)$. These posterior probabilities may be computed from (1) by summing up over the $B\text{-}MP^r(B,\Phi)^{\{\alpha/a\}}$ that include $B_B f^h$ or $T^s(B)$ respectively:

$$P(B_B f^h|Perf^j(B,a)) = \frac{\sum_r P(B\text{-}MP^r(B,\Phi)^{\{\alpha/a\}} \wedge Perf^j(B,a))}{P(Perf^j(B,a))}, \quad (4)$$

over all r such that $B_B f^h \in B\text{-}MP^r(B,\Phi)^{\{\alpha/a\}}$.

$$P(T^s(B)|Perf^j(B,a)) = \frac{\sum_r P(B\text{-}MP^r(B,\Phi)^{\{\alpha/a\}} \wedge Perf^j(B,a))}{P(Perf^j(B,a))}, \quad (5)$$

over all r such that $T^s(B) \in B\text{-}MP^r(B,\Phi)^{\{\alpha/a\}}$.

These probabilities are the new values that A will employ to update, in (1), the $P(B\text{-}MP^r(B,\Phi)|Perf^i(B,a^2))$ after B makes a new performance involving a domain action a^2; if a^2 is different from a^1, beliefs regarding a^1 will not be revised at that step. A's knowledge of B's attitudes and personality evolves during interaction as a function of his initial knowledge of these items, of performances made by B and of his general world knowledge $P\text{-}WM(B)$.

We simulated probabilistic cognitive diagnosis in GOLEM with a program in Java, to investigate how different initial states of knowledge and different sequences of performances affect A's knowledge about B's mental state and about her personality traits. To contrast this approach with the purely logical one, let us reconsider the example we introduced in Section 4. We assume that A has initially no knowledge about B's mental state, and therefore equidistributes probabilities among the four delegation personality traits that B might have ($p = .25$ for each of them); he does not know either which are B's abilities ($P(B_A B_B Cnd\text{-}B(\alpha)) = .5$, for all values of α, in particular $\alpha = a^1$ and $\alpha = a^1$) and whether B is informed about A's abilities ($P(B_A B_B Cnd\text{-}A(\alpha)) = .5$, for all values of α): this initial A's image of B's mental state is shown in the second row of Table 2, while the 'real' mental state of B is described in the first row of this Table.

Let us now suppose that B makes a *Request-to-do* about two different domain actions (a^1 and a^2), in two consecutive turns. The third and fourth rows of that

Table 2. An example of updating A's beliefs after B makes some performances

probability values	Cnd B(a^1)	Cnd A(a^1)	Cnd B(a^2)	Cnd A(a^1)	Laz (B)	HaO (B)	DelN (B)	NeDel (B)
B's mental state: B_B	1	1	0	1	1	0	0	0
A's beliefs: $B_A B_B$								
initial beliefs	.5	.5	.5	.5	.25	.25	.25	.25
after $Req(B, a^1)$	.4	.1	.5	.5	.4	.4	.2	0
after $Req(B, a^2)$	.4	.1	.5	.5	.44	.44	.12	0
after $InCnd(B, a^2)$	.4	.1	0	1	.33	.33	.33	0

Req = *Request-to-do*
$InCnd$ = *Inform-not-Cnd*

Laz(B) = *Lazy*(B)
HaO(B) = *Hanger-on*(B)
DelN(B) = *Delegating-if-needed*(B)
NeDel(B) = *Never-delegating*(B)

Table show the results of probabilistic cognitive diagnosis performed by A: after the first *Request-to-do*, A may exclude that B is a *never-delegating* (like in logical cognitive diagnosis); his degree of belief in B being a *lazy* or a *hanger-on* increases and, at the same time, his degree of belief that she is a *delegating-if-needed* decreases; this difference of belief strengths increases after the second performance. Like in the logical case, A hasn't yet enough evidence to select between the hypothesis that B is a *lazy* or a *hanger-on*. However, at least he has some support to privilege these two options against the third one (of B being a *delegating-if-needed*). The advantage of treating this problem probabilistically obviously increases if A has some more background knowledge. For instance, if the prior probabilities of finding (respectively) a lazy, a hanger-on and a delegating-if-needed in the population of agents are, to A, .5, .2 and .1, after the two *Request* these values will become (respectively) .69, .28 and .03. A will then have much more knowledge to take his decision. Another advantage of employing Bayesian methods is that personalities can be defined in a more 'realistic' way, by attaching probabilities to behaviour schemas (as in the case of a 'weakly lazy agent' we did in Example 14): this definition of probabilistic personality-driven behaviours is cognitively more plausible than a purely dichotomic one. Like in the logical case, probabilistic belief updating is nonmonotonic: if, for instance, after the two initial requests, B performs herself some domain action a^3 rather than asking help, the probability attached to the *hanger-on* trait goes to zero.

Logical and probabilistic cognitive diagnosis provide the same results in case of certainty. The advantage of treating the problem probabilistically is that, in case of uncertainty, probability values define an ordering of alternative hypotheses that may be employed in decision-making, either alone or in combination with other types of weights attached to beliefs. The same result is achieved by defining, in general, a belief ordering, like in [Spohn, 1988] and [Gärdenfors, 1992]. In the next Section we will see an example of the advantage of dealing with uncertainty in this type of decision problems.

6 SUSPECTING AND PREVENTING SUSPICION

Personality-based cognitive diagnosis is a kind of stereotypical belief ascription and revision. Like in stereotypical modeling [Rich, 1989], a 'believable' agent inherits the behaviour schemas that are typical of agents with its personality traits: in the example of cooperating agents that we consider in this paper, the behaviour of B results from a consistent integration of a particular *delegation*, a particular *help* and a particular *reaction* trait; she will therefore conform, in her interaction with A, to the *behaviour schemas* which are attached to these traits. The main difference between stereotypical and personality-based modeling is the *social nature* of the latter: in deciding how to behave, personality-based agents take into consideration the characteristics of agents with which they interact. We already said that a *lazy* agent does not perform an action that he believes other agents might do, and therefore tries to delegate it whenever possible; likewise, a *supplier* agent responds positively only to requests of help coming from agents that he presumes would not be able to make the requested action. The consequence of this mechanism of social relationship among agents is to attach *values* to personality traits. As we do not yet represent, in GOLEM, 'exchange personalities' (do-ut-des), delegating always implies an advantage, and helping a cost. It is therefore convenient to be helped, even by profiting, if needed, of erroneous or incomplete beliefs of other agents. In this sense, being considered a *delegating-if-needed* is preferable to being considered a *lazy*, because it gives more chance of receiving help. The same applies to the issue of being considered 'unable to perform the requested action' (though in a different context, and with a different scale of values, this might be considered a negative feature: for instance, in a highly competitive world). Gradual updating of his image of B's mental state implies, for A, attaching different probabilities to attitudes with different 'social values'. This may produce, into A, the onset of a suspicion towards negative characteristics of B.

Let us take again the example in Table 2, to remember that B is, in fact, a *lazy* who is able to make action a^1 and not a^2 (first order beliefs of B, in the first row of the Table). As we said, when B requests A to perform the domain-action a^1, A starts 'suspecting' that she is a *lazy* or a *hanger-on*; this suspicion increases after a second *Request-to-do*, concerning a different action a^2 and becomes a 'reasonable' certainty after a few requests of performing different domain actions. We can therefore assume that the arising of a suspicion, in A, about negative aspects of B's mental state can be modelled by looking at the variation of probabilities attached to A's second order beliefs that concern these aspects. The question is now: can B prevent this arising of suspicion in A by some form of deception? She should decide first *whether* and *when* deception is needed, and then *how* to deceive. To take this decision, B may try to enter into A's mind by applying some form of hypothetical reasoning aimed at *anticipating* the cognitive diagnosis that A will make after her next performance; she will then discover the arising of a suspicion in A and will try to contrast it in some way. Anticipating A's cognitive diagnosis through this identification process means, to B, reproducing in her third-order beliefs the reasoning that A will make after her second $Request\text{-}to\text{-}do$; this produces a copy of A's second-order beliefs (row 4 of Table 2) into B's third order beliefs. By examining these beliefs *before actually making the performance*, B may discover the arising of a suspicion in A and may try to increase the chance of getting help by contrasting A's suspicion through some context-adapted deception strategy.

In [Castelfranchi *et al.*, 1998b], we analyze the different forms of deception that can be made in human-human communication: one of the distinctions we make is between *passive* deception, in which the deceiving agent simply lets the other agent ignore something that is crucial for her or believe something that is wrong, and *active* deception, when the deceiving agent does something to reach the same effect. In our example, B could make a passive deception at the first turn, when she believes that A does not yet suspect that she is *lazy*: she will just ask A to help her without revealing her personality and her abilities. She can shift to an active deception as soon as she imagines that this suspicion becomes too high (for example, at the second or the third $Request\text{-}to\text{-}do$); in this case, she can indirectly deceive about her personality by saying to A that she is not able to make the requested action ($Inform\text{-}not\text{-}Cnd(B, a^2)$). In this way, if A believes her, the probability that she is a *delegating-if-needed* will increase, and B will have a higher opportunity of getting help (row 5 of Table 2). Simulating B's identification into A's mind by reproducing *exactly* A's reasoning into B's mind implies the very strong assumption that B has a precise knowledge of how A will reason, with all uncertainty values he will employ: this entails, of course, the risk, to B, of coming to a wrong conclusion when that knowledge was incorrect.

To generalize the example:

DEFINITION 16. We call *dangerous knowledge* ($\phi^{\neg}$) a sentence in $\mathcal{L}$ that denotes a feature whose social value is negative.

$B_B\phi^{\neg}$ will therefore denote a component of B's mental state about which B has interest to induce wrong beliefs in her interlocutors, because correct knowledge might damage her: her interest will then be to conceal $\phi^{\neg}$ when it is true or to induce the interlocutor to believe in it when it is false.

In our example, $\phi^{\neg}$ might correspond to being a *hanger-on* or a *lazy*, the potential damage being, in this case, of not receiving help. We classify second-order beliefs according to the way that they are acquired: they may be *inferred* through cognitive diagnosis, *communicated* by the other agent or *observed* directly.

a. *Arising of a suspicion*, in A, can be modeled by examining his second-order beliefs about $\phi^{\neg}$: '*do I believe that B is a lazy?*'.

b. *Decision of whether to deceive*, in B, can be modeled by comparing her first-order with her third-order beliefs about $\phi^{\neg}$: '*I know that I'm a lazy: does A believe the same?*'.

c. *Decision of how to deceive*, in B, can be modeled by reasoning on the consequences, on A's beliefs about $\phi^{\neg}$, of deceiving about different components of her mental state (ϕ^1,ϕ^2, ...), to select the ϕ^i that is convenient according to some external criteria. Reasoning is performed, again, on third order beliefs:

'Is it preferable to deceive indirectly, by saying that I'm not able to do the domain-action, or directly, by saying that I'm someone who tends to avoid delegating? In the first case, A will not be sure that I'm a delegating-if-needed ($p = .33$), and therefore I will not be sure of obtaining help; however, I will not lie directly and will only try to induce A to believe the false. In the second case, I will be more sure about the result ($B_A P(Delegating\text{-}if\text{-}needed(B) = 1)$), but with the risk of being discovered, immediately or later on, as a liar'.

d. *Discovering a deception*, in A, can be modeled by comparing second-order communicated, inferred and observed beliefs about ϕ^i. In probabilistic cognitive diagnosis, this comparison does not necessarily discover a *certain contradiction* in the other agent's behaviour but produces, in the majority of cases, only a *suspicion of contradiction*: in our example, after B's performance $Inform\text{-}not\text{-}Cnd(A, a^2)$, A finds out that the probability of his inferred belief about $B_A B_B Cnd\text{-}B(a^2)$ was .4, whereas the communicated probability value is 0; this cannot be interpreted with certainty as an intentional deception unless some *convenience criterion* is applied [Castelfranchi *et al.*, 1998b]. To discover whether B would have any convenience in comunicating the false about ϕ^i, A has to reason on fourth-order beliefs, that is on what he believes might be the consequence, to B, of inducing himself to believe in ϕ^i; consequences entailing a decrease of the probability value attached to A's *beliefs about any dangerous knowledge* $\phi^{\neg}$ will be interpreted as a 'convenience to deceive'. In our example, the reasoning that A might make after suspecting a contradiction, in B, about $Cnd\text{-}B(a^2)$ is the following:

$B_A B_B[P(B_A B_B Cnd\text{-}B(a^2)) = .4 \Rightarrow P(B_A Lazy(B)) = .44]$, while
$B_A B_B[P(B_A B_B Cnd\text{-}B(a^2)) = 0 \Rightarrow P(B_A Lazy(B)) = .33]$.

This difference can be sufficient or not, to A, to conclude that B is deceiving about her abilities, according, again, to A's personality: for instance, as we said in Section 4, according to whether A is *trustful* or *suspicious*.

7 TOWARDS AN 'OPEN WORLD'

The A's omniscience and B's conformism assumptions that we introduced in Section 5 are very strong: they imply that every agent's $P\text{-}WM$ includes a complete knowledge of all performances that can be made in the multiagent world, all behaviour schemas that are logically and cognitively plausible and all the ways that behaviour schemas may cluster into plausible personality traits. This assumption implies a *closed world* framework, which is not realistic: the multiagent world is inherently open and agents should be open to changes that may occur, by revising their world models through a learning process. To this aim, an agent should be able to understand *when* a change occurred in the world, and to *update* its model accordingly. Let us discuss briefly how the two facets of the problem can be handled, by supporting our proposal with some examples from GOLEM.

a. *Discovering changes*: changes are perceived, by agent A, as exceptions in his theory; these exceptions may be *directly observable* or may be *inferred*. Observation of new kinds of performances belongs to the first category.

EXAMPLE 17. Agent B made a $Request$ of help, that A rejected for some reason; A now observes her reaction to this refusal; the only performances that A believes can be made in the reaction phase are a $Perform$, a new $Request$ or a $Wait\text{-}until\text{-}done$; but, B makes an unknown (to A) reaction performance, by suddenly starting to Cry. Inferring inconsistent behaviours, that cannot be explained by the present world model, belongs to the second category; this happens when B makes a performance that cannot be explained in the scope of what A *knows* to be her believable mental state.

Two examples, again in GOLEM:

EXAMPLE 18. A is an *optimistic* agent who believes that only *hyper-cooperative*, *benevolent* or *suppliers* exist in his world; the agent B, that should help him, is able to make the domain action requested by A, this action is not in conflict with her goals and she knows that A would not be able to make the action by himself; in spite of this, B refuses to help A: how can A explain B's behaviour?

EXAMPLE 19. Agent B helped A in the past though A was able to perform the requested action by himself; A could therefore exclude that she is a *supplier* or a *non-helper*, and think that she is a *helper* (the generic category of 'people who help even those who are not in a needing situation' A knows). B now refuses to do what A is asking her, though being able to do it. Let's assume that deceiving attitudes are excluded, in A's world: how can A explain B's behaviour?

b. *Updating the world model*: as we said, A's world model is represented in the table $P(B\text{-}MP^r(B,\Phi)^{\{\alpha/a\}}|P(Perf^j(B,a))$, which provides a probabilistic representation of the behaviour schemas and the way that they cluster into personality traits. Updating the probabilistic world model $P\text{-}WM(B)$ therefore requires updating the set of behaviour schemas and the personality traits, with their probability distributions. Adding a unknown performance requires adding a new column to the table; adding a new behaviour schema or a new personality trait requires adding new rows to the table; adding a new attitude that influences the agents behaviour requires revising the whole table.

- in Example 17, adding the new performance '*Cry*' requires *building the behaviour schemas* that set up when this performance is made, in all personality classes;
- in Example 18, updating the *WM* requires *introducing the new personality trait* of *non-helpers*, and learning all its behaviour schemas;
- in Example 19, updating the *WM* requires *refining the personality trait* of *helpers* by introducing the two new subclasses of *hyper-cooperative* and *benevolent* agents. Any refinement of a personality trait requires *adding new attitudes* to the mental pattern of all its behaviour schemas: in our example, the added attitude is the helping agent's belief that there is no goal conflict with the other agent.

Revision of the world model cannot be contextual to cognitive diagnosis, but should be made separately, after collecting a certain number of exceptions. Analysis of this problem through inductive logic programming techniques is the object of our future work.

8 RELATED WORK

Though we formulated the problem by considering interaction between two agents A and B, our method can be extended to the case of several interacting agents. In this case, A will hold a unique model of the world, that he will apply to revise his image of the mental state of agent B^s after observing the performance $Perf^i(B^s, a)$. In this case, the level of coherence that should be insured in the multiagent system has to be set up. In a *global coherence* view, two or more agents cannot assign a different probability value to a belief of another agent; in a *local coherence* view, the perspective of different agents can be different, if conveniently justified [Mahleiro *et al.*, 1994]; these differences might be due to a different world model or to different initial images of the mental state of the observed agent. Global coherence is justified in centralized multiagent organizations, where information is unique; in decentralized situations (where each agent is really autonomous and therefore holds its own knowledge about other agents and about the domain), local coherence is more reasonable as it reduces the number of interactions and is probably closer to a realistic simulation of multiagent societies.

Research on belief ascription and revision in multiagent systems has focused on plan recognition rather than cognitive diagnosis. Plans may be represented as recipes for achieving certain states of the world or as complex mental attitudes; they concern, in both cases, actions that have to be performed to reach a given goal state. Interest on reasoning about the motivations behind a 'message' in multiagent systems is more recent, probably due to the fact that agents are not programmed, in general, to tailor their forms of cooperation with *other* agents to *their* beliefs, goals and capabilities: the need of keeping and updating a model of other agents' attitudes arises with the increasing interest towards socially intelligent multiagents worlds. The main contributions to cognitive diagnosis are therefore due to those who work on conversational systems. In this case, abduction on the interlocutor is made at several levels: for instance, at the domain level, the problem-solving level, the belief level and the discourse level, in [Carrol and Carberry, 1994]. Logic is employed in most of the belief ascription and revision methods which have been proposed so far (see, for instance, [Mahleiro *et al.*, 1994] and [Rao, 1997]). In fewer cases, the problem has been formulated in probabilistic terms or by Dempster and Shaefer theory [Huber and Durfee, 1996], [Albrecht *et al.*, 1998], while Rich employed an ad hoc theory to treat uncertainty in stereotype-based user modeling in Grundy [Rich, 1989]. The two works with which this paper has more similarities are [Jameson, 1995] and [Gmytrasiewicz, 1998], both based on belief networks. After claiming that any attempt to make inferences about another person's beliefs cannot do without considering uncertainty, Jameson describes how bayesian networks representing these beliefs with links among them can be constructed dynamically and how this network can be employed to interpret an utterance. Gmytrasiewicz represents belief models at several nestings and updates their probability values by a recursive, dynamic programming procedure. The reason why we do not need representing a network of relationships among the observed agent's beliefs and her performances is due to the way we model behaviour schemas: as frame-based structures rather than as chains of rules. Both cited works do not solve the 'open world' problem: Gmytrasiewicz's method does not include the possibility of building or triggering new hypothetical models and the image of the observed agent's mental state structure is built, in Jameson, as a subset of the observing agent's structure. The closed world hypothesis thus seems to be a difficult to overcome obstacle and it is still introduced in very refined simulations, like Sycara's modeling of learning in negotiation in indexmultiagentmultiagent systems: here, the number of players and their identity are assumed to be fixed and known to everyone, and each player set of alternative actions is fixed and known, as well as their risk taking attitudes and utility calculations [Zeng and Sycara, 1998]. Deception is a rather recent research subject which is dealt with, as far as we know, by trying to discover contradictions in the other agent's behaviour through logical reasoning. Some authors investigated how many nesting levels are needed to simulate this kind of reasoning, again in a logical framework [Taylor, 1993], [Taylor *et al.*, 1996]. In our opinion, this is not the best cognitive modeling approach to deception which, in real life, is not discovered 'suddenly', but through an increasing of suspicion; it therefore requires an uncertain reasoning which can be treated conveniently in probabilistic terms. In another paper [Castelfrachi *et al.*, 1998a], we consider several examples of deception and suspicion in medical dialogues, by showing that they need attaching, to beliefs, *degrees of strength* of several types: uncertainty is one of them, and the most important in reasoning about the *plausibility* of a communicated or inferred second-order belief. To separate deception from misunderstanding or misconception [McRoy, 1995] or from conversational implicature [Lee and Wilks, 1997], some form of utility-related strength has to be considered as well [Galliers, 1992], to measure the convenience of a suspected deceptive performance.

Let us say, finally, some words about the interest of uncertainty-based cognitive diagnosis by examining, in particular, two aspects: its relation with the concept of 'trust' in multiagent systems and its potential relevance in classical problems of AI that are usually stated in logical terms. Modelling trust is becoming crucial in agent's theory and in multi agent systems. With the diffusion of Electronic Commerce, virtual organisations and Computer-Supported Cooperative Work and of personal assistants, we will face - beyond problems of security - serious problems of deception and diffidence, of choice among different partners, of credibility of information sources and so on. Four types of trust will become particularly crucial:(i) trust in personal, interface agents; (ii) trust among agents in negotiating, collaborating, exchanging data; (iii) trust in the infrastructure, in the organisation and in third party agents or agencies able to guarantee and control the behavior of partners and agents; (iv) trust in human partners or organisations whose interaction is computer-mediated. In [Castelfranchi and Falcone, 1998], trust is analysed as a typical mental state including a specific set of beliefs and goals, especially concerning evaluations and expectations. This formalisation in terms of beliefs and goals is, however, not really satisfying: trust has degrees, which are crucial for the decision of whether to rely on someonelse; as in game theoretic tradition, it involves a subjective evaluation of the probability of some positive event, a bet on a given alternative, an accepted risk. Trust is closely related to reliance and delegation: on one hand, any decision to delegate is strictly conditioned to a measure of trust and to a threshold of risk acceptance, as the degree of trust represents the basis for a rational decision to delegate; on the other hand, the degree of trust is based on the strength of its component beliefs, that is measured in terms of 'credibility' and 'plausibility': the more uncertain I'm in my evaluation of some situation and of my expectation about a given event, the less I trust in this event, and the less likely will be that I delegate and rely on the event. Logical reasoning seems not sufficient to formalise these topics; or, at least, representing probabilities, degrees, thresholds and rational decision making seems to be more expressive.

Considering uncertainty in cognitive diagnosis might lead to revise the way that classical problems involving interaction have been studied. Our personalities are not conceived only for 'strategic' interactions like in the Prisoner Dilemma (PD): different styles in help and cooperation or in delegation are important also in organisations or in friendly interactions. The personalities we introduced in this paper are of interest, for instance, in building 'believable' or 'life-like' characters, in 'affective computing', in inducing sympathy or hostility towards interface agents and so on. Also the ability to reason about or to recognise the personality or the social attitude of other agents is not necessarily aimed at 'cooperating' or 'defeating' in game-theoretic sense [Castelfranchi and Conte, 1998]. This ability is useful for several purposes that go far beyond the power of the game theoretic approach, not only to decide whether to defeat[2]. For example: it might be useful for understanding how to help someone else, which level of help to provide, whether to spontaneously help or not. Suppose B is a never-delegating: probably A should not spontaneously help her, as she would not like this. Users are not, probably, in strategic interaction with 'personal assistants', that is with agents that help the user in performing a specific class of tasks, since these agents do not usually hold any personal utility or selfish decision making, at least with us; however, they might have a personality in helping us or in relying on us.

To conclude: game theory (and in particular the PD framework) captures only a small part of the social interaction aspects, as it does not consider all social motives and characters; in addition, this part is quite limited and distorted. Of course, our framework is very limited, initial, and rigid as well, as few, quite elementary and fixed personalities have been formalised so far: but, at least it introduces a different perspective as it is not oriented only to rational agents and strategic situations, but to social motives and interactions in general.

Fiorella de Rosis and Emanuele Covino
Department of Informatics, University of Bari, Italy.

Cristiano Castelfranchi and Rino Falcone
Institute of Psychology, National Research Council, Rome, Italy.

REFERENCES

[Albrecht *et al.*, 1998] D. W. Albrecht, I. Zuckerman, A. N. Nicholson. Bayesian models for keyhole plan recognition in an adventure game. To appear in *User Modeling and User Adapted Interaction*.

[Bates, 1994] J. Bates. The role of emotion in believable agents. *Communications of the ACM*, **37**, 7, 1994.

[Castelfrachi *et al.*, 1998a] C. Castelfranchi, F. de Rosis, R. Falcone and S. Pizzutilo. Personality traits and social attitudes in multiagent cooperation. *Applied Artificial Intelligence*, Special Issue on Socially Intelligent Agents, **12**, 7–8, 1998.

[Castelfranchi *et al.*, 1998b] C. Castelfranchi, F. de Rosis and F. Grasso. Deception and suspect in medical interactions: towards a simulation of believable dialogues. In *Human-Computer Conversation*, D. Levy and Y. Wilks, eds. Kluwer, to appear.

[2] A diagnosis of personality or of reputation might be relevant also in one-shot PD, to go beyond pure 'selfish' rationality. Moreover, the diagnosis of personality might be useful also in other kinds of 'game' or in special forms of 'one shot' PD. One might consider, for example, agent' that, even if interacting only once with a given partner, desire to be helpful with pro-social agents and non-cooperative with anti-social personalities; in this example, if the considered agent knows that its partner is, for instance, a hanger-on, which will never 'reciprocate' its help with other partners, it will conclude that it will never have an advantageous collective indirect reciprocation, and will behave consistently with this inferred belief.

[Castelfranchi and Falcone, 1998] C. Castelfranchi and R. Falcone. Principles of trust for MAS: cognitive anatomy, social importance, and quantification. *International Conferences on MAS - ICMAS'98*, Paris, AAAI-MIT Press, 1998.

[Castelfranchi and Conte, 1998] C. Castelfranchi and R. Conte. Limits of economic rationality for agents and MAS. *Robotics and Autonomous Systems*, Special issue on *Multi-Agent Rationality*, Elsevier, 1998.

[Carrol and Carberry, 1994] J. Chu Carrol and S. Carberry. A plan-based model for response generation in collaborative task-oriented dialogues. In *Proceedings of AAAI94*, 1994.

[Gärdenfors, 1992] P. Gärdenfors, ed. *Belief Revision*, Cambridge University Press, 1992.

[Galliers, 1992] J. R. Galliers. Autonomous belief revision and communication. In *Belief Revision*, P. Gärdenfors, ed. Cambridge University Press, 1992.

[Gmytrasiewicz, 1998] P. J. Gmytrasiewicz. Bayesian update of recursive agent models. In *User Modeling and User-Adapted Interaction*, to appear.

[Huber and Durfee, 1996] M. J. Huber and E. H. Durfee. An initial assessment of plan-recognition-based coordination for multi-agent teams. *ICMAS 96*, 1996.

[Jameson, 1995] A. Jameson. Logic is not enough: why reasoning about another person's beliefs is reasoning under uncertainty. In *Knowledge and belief in Phylosophy and Artificial Intelligence*, A. Laux and H. Wansing, eds. Academic Verlag, Berlin, 1995.

[Lee and Wilks, 1996] M. Lee and Y. Wilks. An ascription-based approach to speech acts. *Proceedings of COLING96*, 1996.

[Lee and Wilks, 1997] M. Lee and Y. Wilks. Eliminating deceptions and mistaken beliefs to infer conversational implicature. *IJCAI97 Workshop on Collaboration, Cooperation and Conflict in Dialogue Systems*, 1997.

[Loyall and Bates, 1997] A. B. Loyall and J. Bates. Personality-rich believable agents that use language. In *Autonomous Agents 97*, 1997.

[Mahleiro *et al.*, 1994] B. Mahleiro, N. R. Jennings and E. Oliveira. Belief revision in multi-agent systems. *ECAI 94*, 1994.

[Martins and Shapiro, 1988] J. P. Martins and S. C. Shapiro. A model for belief revision. *Artificial Intelligence*, **35**, 25-79, 1988.

[Nebel, 1992] B. Nebel. Syntax-based approaches to belief revision. In *Belief Revision*, P. Gärdenfors, ed. Cambridge University Press, 1992.

[McRoy, 1995] S. W. McRoy. Misunderstanding and the negotiation of meaning using abduction. *Knowledge-Based Systems*, **8**, 2–3, 1995.

[Rao, 1997] A. S. Rao. A unified view of plans as recipes. *Technical Report of AIIA*, 1997.

[Reilly and Bates, 1995] W. S. Reilly and J. Bates. Natural negotiation for believable agents. School of Computer Science, Carnegie Mellon University, *CMU-CS-95-16*, 1995.

[Reilly, 1997] W. S. N. Reilly. A methodology for building believable social agents. In *Autonomous Agents 97*, 1997.

[Rich, 1989] E. Rich. Stereotypes and user modeling. In *User Models in Dialog Systems*, A. Kobsa and W. Wahlster, eds. Springer Verlag, 1989.

[Self, 1993] J. Self. Model-based cognitive diagnosis. In *User Modeling and User Adapted Interaction*, **3**, 1, 1993.

[Spohn, 1988] W. Spohn. Ordinal conditional functions: a dynamic theory of epistemic states. In *Causation in Decision, Belief Change, and Statistics*, Vol. 2, pp. 105-134, Kluwer Academic Publishers, 1988.

[Taylor, 1993] J. Taylor. An ATMS-based belief model for dialogue simulation. In *CKBS-SIG Proceedings*, Keele. S. M. Deen, ed. pp. 135–159, 1994.

[Taylor *et al.*, 1996] J. Taylor, J. Carletta and C. Mellish. Requirements for belief models in cooperative dialogue. *User Modeling and User-Adapted Interaction*, **6**, 1–21, 1996.

[Zeng and Sycara, 1998] D. Zeng and K. Sycara. Bayesian learning in negotiation. *International Journal of Human-Computer Studies*, **48**, 125–141, 1998.

ALDO FRANCO DRAGONI AND PAOLO GIORGINI

REVISING BELIEFS RECEIVED FROM MULTIPLE SOURCES

1 A BRIEF RETROSPECTIVE

1.1 The AGM paradigm

During the last decade, the logical framework layed down by Alchourrón, Gärdenfors and Makinson [1985] deeply influenced the notion of belief revision. Conceiving both, the *knowledge space* K and incoming information p, as sentences of a propositional language L, they introduced three rational principles for the revision operator (*):

AGM1 *Consistency*: K^*p must be consistent
AGM2 *Minimal Change*: K^*p should alter as little as possible K
AGM3 *Priority to the Incoming Information*: p must belong to K^*p

From these principles they drew eight postulates:

K^*1. For each p and K, K^*p is still a cognitive state
K^*2. $p \in K^*p$
K^*3. $K^*p \subseteq K^+p$
K^*4. If $\neg p \notin K$ then $K^+p \subseteq K^*p$
K^*5. K^*p is inconsistent iff p is inconsistent
K^*6. If p and q are logically equivalent then $K^*p = K^*q$
K^*7. $K^*(p \wedge q) \subseteq (K^*p)^+q$
K^*8. If $\neg q \notin K^*p$ then $(K^*p)^+q \subseteq K^*(p \wedge q)$

These axioms describe the rational properties that revision should obey, but they do not suggest how to perform it. An operative definition came from the Levi's identity:

$$K^*p = Th((K^-\neg p) \cup \{p\})$$

(where "*Th*" represents the deductive closure operator) that suggests to delete $\neg p$ from K (reducing in some way K at a point that $\neg p$ is no longer derivable), add p and "calculate" the deductive closure. The deletion of $\neg p$ from K, $K^-\neg p$, is called *contraction*, and can be defined in terms of "Epistemic Entrenchment" [Gärdenfors, 1988], which is an ordering $\leq$, that envisages the logical dependencies of the formulae in K; it depends on K but it applies to all the formulae of L. $p \leq q$ means that p is less entrenched (more exposed to eventual changes) than q.

M.-A. Williams and H. Rott (eds.), Frontiers in Belief Revision, 429–442.

$\leq$ satisfies the following postulates:

EE1. $\leq$ is transitive
EE2. For all $p, q \in L$, if $p \vdash q$ then $p \leq q$
EE3. For all $p, q \in L$, either $p \leq p \wedge q$ or $q \leq p \wedge q$
EE4. If K is consistent, then $p \notin K$ iff for all $q \in L, p \leq q$
EE5. If for all q of L, it holds $q \leq p$, then p is a tautology

Contraction could be defined from the Epistemic Entrenchment as follows: $q \in K^{-}p$ iff $q \in K$ and, either $p < q \vee p$, or p is a tautology.
There are three problems with such a kind of revision:

1. it deals with infinite sets of sentences

2. $\leq$ depends on K, so it is difficult to iterate the revision because the ordering defined on $K^{*}p$ could be different from the one defined on K

3. the choice of a particular ordering $\leq$ satisfying the postulates EE1$\div$ EE5 is arbitrary; as Gärdenfors wrote: "[the postulates] leave the main problem unsolved: what is a reasonable metric for comparing different epistemic states?".

Mary-Anne Williams [1995] showed how the first two problems "can be solved in theoretically satisfying ways wholely within the AGM paradigm". She pointed out that, belief revision means "epistemic entrenchment revision": incoming information *transmutes* the old epistemic entrenchment into a new one which, in turn, yields a different contraction and, hence, a new revised knowledge space. Given a knowledge space K, let a *base* B be a finite set of sentences of L such that K is the deductive closure of B. She introduced a ranking function on a base B, called *partial entrenchment ranking* (p.e.r), that she proved can be regarded as a specification of a finite epistemic entrenchment on K. AGM revision for finite bases can be iterated by transmuting partial entrenchment rankings. The transmutation is provoked by an incoming, consistent and not-tautological sentence p with a degree of firmness i. A transmuted p.e.r. is one such that p has a degree i and the other beliefs are rearranged in order to respect epistemic entrenchment. She also introduced a particular transmutation, called *adjustment*, that inroduces minimal changes such that p is accepted with degree i.

Partial entrenchment rankings and transmutations respect Dalal's "principle of irrelevance of the syntax" citeDalal88, according to whom syntactically different but logically equivalent formulae represent the same knowledge space. The partisans of *syntax-dependent* belief revision consider knowledge spaces made up of a limited number of sentences. They claim that asserting facts is more important than deriving others from them. Nebel's *epistemic relevance ordering* [Nebel, 1994] stratifies a base B into n priority classes $B_1, ..., B_n$. Epistemic relevance does not respect the logical contents of the sentences as epistemic and partial entrenchment do. A justification seems to rely on the logical paradoxes of the material implication: a rule $q \rightarrow p$ should not necessarily be considered more important than p just because $p \vdash q \rightarrow p$. Let $B{\downarrow}p$ denote the set of the subsets of B that fail to imply p. Nebel defines $B{\Downarrow}p$ as the subset of $B{\downarrow}p$ made of the elements that *contain as many sentences of the highest priority as possible*. The corresponding revision is defined as:

$$B \oplus p = Th\left(\left(\bigcap_{B' \in (B \Downarrow \neg p)} Th(B') \right) \cup \{p\} \right)$$

where $Th(B')$ denotes the deductive closure of B'. There are two problems with this revision:

- it does not satisfy all the AGM postulates
- it is still computationally hard.

We could adopt various criteria to sort and select the elements of $B{\downarrow}p$. Let $B' = B_1^{'} \cup ... \cup B_n^{'}$ and $B'' = B_1^{''} \cup ... \cup B_n^{''}$ two consistent subsets of B where $B_i^{'} = B^{'} \cap B_i$ and $B_i^{''} = B^{''} \cap B_i$. Benferhat *et al.* [1993] suggest (implicitly) three ways to translate the epistemic relevance into a preference relation $\leq$ on $B \downarrow p$.

- *best-out ordering*. $B^{''} \leq B^{'}$ iff the most credible of the sentences in $B \setminus B^{''}$ is less credible than the most credible of the sentences in $B \setminus B^{'}$.
- *inclusion-based ordering*. $B^{''} \leq B^{'}$ iff there exists a stratum i such that $B_i^{'} \supset B_i^{''}$ and for any $j < i$, $B_j^{'} = B_j^{''}$. This preordering is strict but partial; its maximal consistent elements are also maximal for the best-out ordering.
- *lexicographic ordering*. $B^{''} \leq B^{'}$ iff there exists a stratum i such that $|B_i^{'}| > |B_i^{''}|$ and for any $j < i$ $|B_j^{'}| = |B_j^{''}|$, and $B^{''} = B^{'}$ iff for any j, $|B_j^{'}| = |B_j^{''}|$.

$B{\Downarrow}p$ contains the elements of $B{\downarrow}p$ maximal w.r.t. inclusion-based ordering.

1.2 The Truth Maintenance Systems

Even if the AGM paradigm cannot be set aside when speaking of belief revision, and even if Gärdenfors deeply contributed to the development of the field [Gärdenfors, 1988; Gärdenfors, 1992], we must recognize that a parallel conception of belief revision started, even before the AGM framework, from researches on the so called Truth Maintenance Systems [Doyle, 1979] (see, for instance, Martins and Shapiro's modelization [Martins and Shapiro, 1988]). Especially De Kleer's ATMS [De Kleer, 1986], overcoming some limitations of Doyle's TMS, was immediately regarded as a powerful reasoning tool to revise beliefs (and to perform the dual cognitive operation of *diagnosis*). Crucial to the ATMS architecture is the notion of *assumption* which designates a decision to believe something without any commitment as to what is assumed. An *assumed* datum is the problem-solver output that has been assumed to hold after the assumption utilized to derive it. Assumptions are connected to assumed data via justifications and from the foundation to which every datum's support can be ultimately traced. The same assumption may justify multiple data or one datum be justified by multiple assumptions. Taking the notion of logical consequence as justification, the ATMS appears as a mechanism to perform syntax-dependent belief revision for finite bases.

1.3 Numerical approaches

Let us come to the third problem with the AGM approach: "what is a reasonable metric for comparing epistemic states"? We believe that, practically, such computable and reasonable metric can be better provided by numerical approaches, for their natural ability to deal with fine grained values. In particular, when the epistemic states should be ranked according to some degree of certainty (or credibility), then such a metric might be provided by classic uncertainty management techniques. In fact, the knowledge space of a complex knowledge-based system does not suffer only from inconsistency; it can also be affected by uncertainty. Numerical distributions of credibility over the sentences of L or over the set Ω of the models of L, play the same role that "epistemic entrenchment", p.e.r. and epistemic relevance play in the symbolic frameworks. Generally, numerical approaches do not respect logical dependencies among the sentences. Logics of uncertainty often represent a cognitive state K and the incoming information p in terms of their sets of models (also said "possible worlds"), respectively, $[K]$ and $[p]$. A cognitive state is represented not simply by $[K]$, but by an assignment function $d(\omega) : \Omega \to [0,1]$ such that $d(\omega') = 0$ for each $\omega' \notin [K]$. The arrival of p generally means that the real world belongs to $[p]$. This event changes d into a new assignment (new prioritization) d'. Imposing the priority to the incoming information (AGM3) means assigning $d'(\omega) = 0$ to each $\omega \notin [p]$. Minimizing this change (AGM2) means minimizing some kind of distance between d and d'.

In the probabilistic approach [Pearl, 1988] a cognitive state is characterized by a *probability measure* P on 2^{Ω}, whose fundamental property is *additivity*: $\forall A, B \subseteq \Omega, A \cap B \neq \oslash \Rightarrow P(A \cup B) = P(A) + P(B)$. $P(\Omega) = 1$, so if $\bar{A} = \Omega - A$ then $P(A) + P(\bar{A}) = 1$. We might also consider the *probability distribution* $pr(\omega)$ that assignes a probability degree to each world in Ω, where $P(A) = \sum_{\omega \in A} pr(\omega)$. $pr(\omega) = 0$ means that ω is not a possible world. $pr(\omega) = 1$ means that ω is surely the real world. An incoming information p changes the probability measure of any sentence q of L through the very famous Bayes' Conditioning Rule:

$$P(q|p) = \frac{P([q] \cap [p])}{P([p])} = \frac{P([p]|[q]) \cdot P([q])}{P([p])}$$

which can also be expressed in terms of probability distribution:

$$pr(\omega|p) = \begin{cases} \dfrac{pr(\omega)}{P([p])} & \text{if } \omega \in [p] \\ 0 & \text{otherwise} \end{cases}$$

This modification is defined only for $P([p]) > 0$, hence it is not applicable when p is judged impossible by the previously determined probability measure P.

Bayesian conditioning obeys the principle of priority to incoming information (AGM3); it increases the probability of the not-impossible worlds belonging to $[p]$ to the prejudice of those external to $[p]$ which become all impossible.

In the probabilistic framework the probability of a sentence p is simply the probability measure $P([p])$. Thus, probability measures order the sentences of L, but, unfortunately, they do not generate epistemic entrenchments. In effect, probability measures satisfy EE1 since they are, obviously, transitive (if $P([p]) \leq P([q])$ and $P([q]) \leq P([r])$ then $P([p]) \leq P([r])$. EE2 too is verified since $p \vdash q$ means $[p] \subseteq [q]$ hence $P([p]) \leq P([q])$ (it is always easier to retract p than q). Even EE4 is verified; in fact, $p \notin K$ means $P([p]) = 0$, and if K is consistent then there are sentences q such that $P([q]) = 0$, hence $P([p]) = 0$ iff $\forall q \in L$ $(P([p]) \leq P([q]))$. Finally, EE5 is verified since if $\forall q \in L$ $P([q]) \leq P([p])$ then $[p] = \Omega$ which means that p is a tautology. Unfortunately, EE3 is generally unsatisfied since $[p \wedge q] \subseteq [p]$ and $[p \wedge q] \subseteq [q]$ so that $P([p \wedge q]) \leq P([p])$ and $P([p \wedge q]) \leq P([q])$; normally it is easier to retract a conjunction than any of its conjuncts.

Also the belief function framework [Shafer, 1990; Shafer and Srivastava, 1990] assignes a probability P to the subsets of Ω, with the constraints $P(\oslash) = 0$ and $\sum_{A \subseteq \Omega} P(A) = 1$. If $P(A) > 0$ then A is said to be a *focal element*. The *belief function* on the subsets of Ω is defined as

$$Bel(A) = \sum_{X \subseteq A} P(X)$$

$Bel(A)$ measures the persuasion that the real world is inside A; maybe that there is no evidence that directly support A but it cannot be excluded because there is evidence that supports some of its subsets. This function is not additive: $Bel(A) + Bel(\bar{A}) \leq 1$. The knowledge is:

- *certain* and *precise* if there exists a $\omega \in \Omega$ such that $P(\{\omega\}) = 1$
- *certain* and *imprecise* as if there exists a $A \subset \Omega$ such that $P(A) = 1$ but A is not singleton
- *consistent* if all the focal elements are nested
- *inconsistent* if all the focal elements are disjoint

- *void* if $P(\Omega) = 1$ and for all $A \subseteq \Omega$, $P(A) = 0$.

This framework deals also with uncertain inputs. They are treated as new probability assignments on 2^{Ω}. The change consists of merging the two evidences (the prior P_1 and the new P_2) through the Dempster's Rule of Combination:

$$P(A) = \frac{\sum_{X_1 \cap X_2 = A} P_1(X_1) \cdot P_2(X_2)}{\sum_{X_1 \cap X_2 = \emptyset} P_1(X_1) \cdot P_2(X_2)}$$

for all $A \subset \Omega$. This rule, easily extensible to combine n probability assignments, reinforces concordant evidence and weakens conflicting ones. It can be applied only if evidences are independent and referred to the same Ω. Because of the commutativity of the product, the rule is independent from the sequence $P_1...P_n$ so *it violates the principle of priority to the incoming information*! From a knowledge engineering point of view, the worst problem with the Dempster's Rule of Combination is its computational complexity. One should generate a frame of $2^{|\Omega|}$ elements to calculate it! However, much work has been spent in reducing the complexity of that rule. Such methods range from "efficient implementations" [Kennes, 1992] to "qualitative approaches" [Parsons, 1994] through "approximate techniques" with statistical methods as the Montecarlo sampling algorithm [Wilson, 1991; Moral and Wilson, 1996].

2 REQUIREMENTS FOR A BELIEF REVISION FRAMEWORK IN A MULTI SOURCE ENVIRONMENT

We think that to revise beliefs in a Multi-Agent scenario, where many sources give information about a same static situation, the framework should satisfy some requisites.

- Ability to reject incoming information

A belief revision system for multi source environments should drop the rationality principle of "priority to the incoming information" which is not acceptable since there is no strict correlation between the chronology of the informative acts and the credibility of their contents [Dragoni *et al.*, 1995]; it seems more reasonable to treat all the available pieces of information as they had been collected at the same time.

- Ability to recover previously discarded beliefs

Cognitive agents should be able to recover previously discarded pieces of knowledge after that new evidence redeems them. The point is that this should be done not only when the new information directly "supports" a previously rejected belief, but also when the incoming information indirectly supports it, by disclaiming the beliefs that contradicted it, causing its ostracism. More formally, for each cognitive state K, and sentences p and q such that $K \vdash p$ and $K^*q \not\vdash p$, there can always be another piece of information r such that $(K^*q)^*r \vdash p$, even if $r \not\vdash p$. An obvious case should be $r = \neg q$. We elsewhere called this rule *principle of recoverability*: "any previously held piece of knowledge must belong to the current knowledge space if consistent with it" [Dragoni *et al.*, 1995; Dragoni, 1997; Dragoni and Giorgini, 1997a]. The rationale for this principle is that, if someone gave us a piece of information (sometime in the past) and currently there is no reason to reject it, then we should accept it! This is stronger than the traditional "coherence" spirit of belief revision, since the piece of knowledge to accept is not a *generic* sentence of the language but a *generated* piece of information; somewhere there is an utilitarian intelligent information source that guarantees for it. Of course, this principle does not hold for updating, where changes may be irrevocable. This feature could also be subtitled: "revocable treatment of consistency". We remember of Minsky's lection: "I do not believe that consistency is necessary or even desirable in a developing intelligent system ... What is important is how one handles paradoxes or conflicts ... *Enforcing consistency produces limitations*. As we will see in a moment, we overcome this problem by defining a single global, never forgetting, eventually inconsistent *Knowledge Background*, upon which act multiple specific, competitive, ever changing, *consistent* cognitive states.

- Ability to *combine* contradictory and concomitant evidences

The notion of *beliefs integration* should blend that of revision [Dragoni and Giorgini, 1997b]. Every incoming information changes the cognitive state. Rejecting the incoming information does not mean leaving beliefs unchanged since, in general, incoming information alters the distribution of the weights. Surely the last incoming information decreased the credibility of the beliefs with whom it got in contradiction, even in the case that it has been rejected. The same when receiving a piece of information which we were already aware of; it is not the case that nothing happened (as AGM K^*4 states) since we are now, in general, more sure about that belief. More generally, there is no reason to limit the changes introduced by the new information to an insertion into a pre-established relative order with consequent rearrangement of the ranking to accomplish the logical relations between beliefs (as Williams' transmutation does). If it is true that new incoming information affects the old one, it is likewise true that the latter affects the former. In fact, an autonomous agent (where "autonomous" means that his cognitive state is not *determined* by other agents) judges the credibility of new information on the basis of its previous cognitive state. "Revising beliefs" should simple mean "dealing with a new broader set of pieces of information".

- Ability to deal with couples <source,information> rather than with information alone

The way the credibility ordering is generated and revised must reflect the fact that beliefs come from different sources of information, since the reliability and the number of independent informants affect the credibility of the information and vice-versa [Dragoni, 1992].

- Ability to maintain and compare multiple candidate *cognitive states*

This ability is part of humans intelligence which does not limit its action to comparing single pieces of information but goes on trying to reconstruct alternative cognitive scenarios as far as it is possible.

- Sensibility of the syntax

Despite Dalal's mentioned principle, syntax plays an important role in everyday life. The way we pack (and unpack) pieces of information reflects the way we organize thinking and judge credibility, importance, relevance and even truthfulness. A testimony of the form $\alpha \wedge \delta \wedge ... \wedge \zeta \wedge \neg\alpha$ from a defendant A in a trial has the same semantic truth value than the testimony $\beta \wedge \neg\beta$ from defendant B, but we remember many cases in which B has been condemned while A has been absolved, being regarded his/her testimony "partially true", contrasting with the B's one regarded as "absolutely contradictory". A set of sentences seems not to be logically equivalent to their conjunction and we could change a cognitive state by simply clustering the same beliefs in a different way.

3 OUR BELIEF REVISION FRAMEWORK FOR A MULTI SOURCE ENVIRONMENT

From this discussion it should be evident that we cannot rely on the AGM framework to build a method for revising belief in a multi source environment. We better repose on the ATMS abstract conception. Our sentence-based approach for belief revision [Dragoni, 1997] conceives two knowledge repositories:

1. the *knowledge background* KB, which is the set of all the propositional sentences available to the reasoning agent (as assumptions); since it can be inconsistent, it cannot be used as a whole to support reasoning and decision processes

2. the *knowledge base* $B \subseteq KB$, which is the maximally consistent, currently preferred piece of knowledge that should be used for reasoning and decision supporting; since it is determined by imposing the maximal consistency, it may contain pieces of knowledge with low degrees of credibility.

The reason why we pick *maximally* consistent subsets of KB is that this is the perfect implementation of the "Principle of Recoverability": everything were known in the past should be believed again now (or still believed) if nothing prevents that. Computationally, our way to belief revision consists of four steps (figure 1) [Dragoni and Giorgini, 1997a; Dragoni and Giorgini, 1997b]:
S1. Detection of the minimally inconsistent subsets of $KB \cup \{p\}$ (*nogoods*)

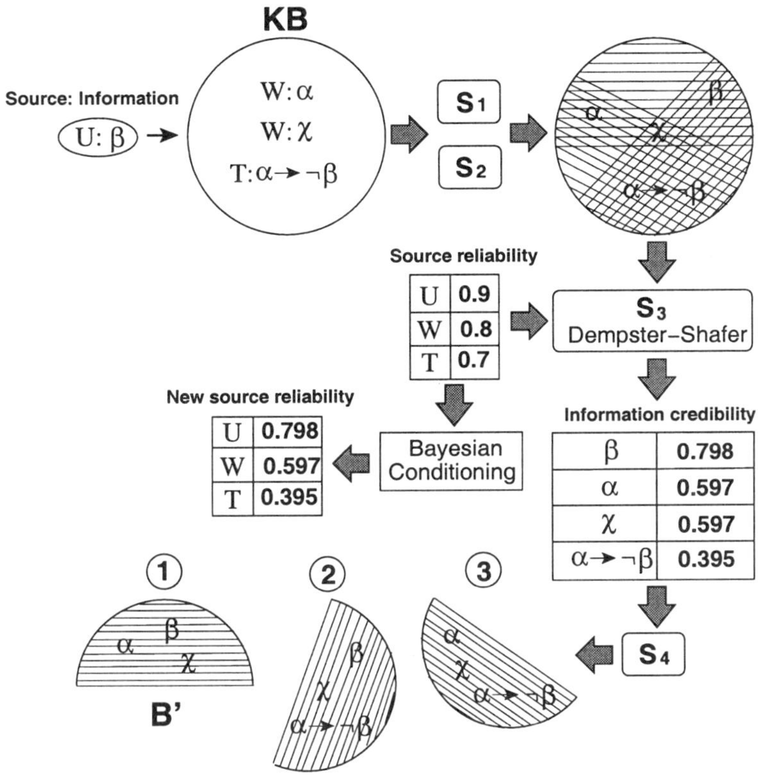

Figure 1. Dempster's and Bayes rules at work

S2. Generation of the maximally consistent subsets of $KB \cup \{p\}$ (*goods*)
S3. Revision of the credibility weights of the sentences in $KB \cup \{p\}$
S4. Choice of a preferred *good* as the new revised base B'

The incoming information p, with its weight of evidence, is evaluated not just within the current base B, but within the overall knowledge background KB. Doing so, the degrees of credibility of the sentences in $KB \cup \{p\}$ are reviewed on a broader and less prejudicial basis (S3). As already explained, the main advantage is that we can rescue sentences from KB by virtue of the maximal consistency of B'. If we'd revise only B by p, we could not recover information from KB. For instance, Nebel's revision would select some $B' \in B \Downarrow \neg p$, but it will be always possible to find out some $B'' \in KB \Downarrow \neg p$ such that $B' \subseteq B''$. S4 might choose a new base B' syntactically equal to the previous B (meaning that p has been rejected) but, in general, B' will have a different credibility distribution than B. p might be rejected even if S4 chooses a base B' different from B, but that still containing sentences incompatible with p.

When p is consistent with B, not necessarily $B'=B\cup\{p\}$, since S3 may yield a totally different choice at S4. Previously rejected pieces of knowledge $R\subset KB$ can be rescued simply by determining some upsetting between the credibility of a set $S\subset B$ and the credibility of R, this may happen if p *supports* R against S. The rejection of the priority to the incoming information principle implies that K^*4 and and K^*5 hold no longer (if p is inconsistent it will be part of none of the goods produced at S2, so it will never be part of a base).

S1 and S2 deal with consistency and derivation, and act on the symbolic part of the information. Operations are in ATMS style; to find out nogoods and goods, we adopt (and adapt) the most efficient set-covering algorithm that we are aware of [Reiter, 1987]. Notwithstanding this, even in the propositional case, determining all the minimal inconsistencies can be very hard. However, such condition can be relaxed (the consequence is that some of the goods are not really consistent) and in practical applications dealing with commonsense knowledge (for instance [Dragoni and Di Manzo, 1995]), such minimal inconsistencies could be provided interactively by the external user.

S3 and S4 deal with uncertainty and work with the numerical weight of the information. Both contribute to the choice of the revised knowledge space so their reasonableness should be evaluated as a couple. Numerical formalisms are able to perform both of them since the credibility of a single sentence p is determined in the same way as the credibility of a set of sentences B by the weights attached to $[p]$ and $[B]$, respectively. Flexibility is an advantage in separating the two steps; for instance, depending on the characteristics of the knowledge domain under consideration and the kind of task and/or decision that should be taken on the basis of the revision outcome, the selection function could consider also one (or a combination) of the methods described in [Benferhat *et al.*, 1993].

Probabilistic methods with uncertain inputs seem inadequate for the strong dependence that they impose on the credibility of a sentence and that of its negation. The "drowning problem" is a limit of the possibilistic approach (see [Benferhat *et al.*, 1993]). We see that the belief-function formalism, in the special guise in which Shafer and Srivastava apply it to auditing [Shafer and Srivastava, 1990], could work well because it treats all the pieces of information as they had been provided at the same time.

The method has the following I/O:

INPUT: list of pairs <source,piece of information>
list of pairs <source,reliability>
OUTPUT: list of pairs <piece of information,credibility>
list of pairs <source,reliability>

Let S=$\{s_1, ..., s_n\}$ be the set of the sources, and let kb_i be the subset of KB received from s_i. Each source s_i is associated with a *reliability* $R(s_i)$, that is regarded as the *probability* that the source is faithful. The main idea with this multi-source version of the belief function framework is that a reliable source cannot give false information, while an unreliable source can give correct information;

the hypothesis that s_i is reliable is compatible only with the models of kb_i, while the hypothesis that s_i is unreliable is compatible with the overall Ω. Each source s_i is an evidence for KB and generates the following *bpa* $m_i(\cdot)$ on 2^Ω:

$$m_i(X) = \begin{cases} R(s_i) & \text{if } X = [kb_i] \\ 1 - R(s_i) & \text{if } X = \Omega \\ 0 & \text{otherwise} \end{cases}$$

All these *bpas* will be then combined through the Dempster Rule of Combination. From the combined *bpa* $m(\cdot)$, the credibility of a sentence p of L is given, as usual, by:

$$Bel(p) = \sum_{X \subseteq [p]} m(X)$$

From this mechanism we obtained an easy way to calculate the new reliabilities of the sources. Let Φ be an element of 2^S. If the sources are independent, the reliability of Φ is

$$R(\Phi) = \prod_{S \in \Phi} R(s) \cdot \prod_{S \in \Phi} (1 - R(s))$$

It holds that

$$\sum_{\Phi \in 2^S} R(\Phi) = 1$$

It maybe that some source fall in contradiction, so that some elements of 2^S are impossible. The remaining elements are subjected to bayesian conditioning so that their reliabilities sum up again to 1. The revised reliability $R^*(s)$ of a source s is the sum of the new reliabilities of the surviving elements of 2^S that contain s. If a source has been involved in some contradictions, then $R^*(s) \leq R(s)$, otherwise $R^*(s) = R(s)$.

The main problem with this formalism is its computational complexity. Contradictions help us because they reduce the size of Ω. However, to cancel an impossible world, we must first generate it. This imposes severe limits on the number of sentences acceptable in input (about 30) even for "off-line" applications.

Yet, from an input-output analysis of the mechanism we realized that two properties hold.

1. Sentences not involved in contradictions and received from a single source s, do not contribute to the mechanism, in the sense that the degrees of credibility of the other sentences do not depend on their presence. Their own credibility is $R^*(s)$.

2. Multiple contradictions involving sentences received exclusively from exactly the same sources are redundant; all the sentences from the same source receive the same degree of credibility, independently of the number and the cardinality of the contradictions.

Property (1) implies that we can temporarily leave out of the process those sentences received from a single source, and that are not involved in contradictions. In many cases, this dramatically reduces the size of Ω. Property (2) says that, what is important is that a set of sources was contradictory, not how many times nor about what or about how many sentences they did. This allows us to temporarily leave out of the process also some sentences involved in contradictions; this is significant in situations like that of two sources systematically in contradiction only with each others.

S4 translates such ordering on the *sentences* in $KB \cup \{p\}$ into an ordering on the *goods* of $KB \cup \{p\}$. The best classified good is selected as the preferred revised knowledge base. If the ordering on $KB \cup \{p\}$ is not strict, then there can be multiple preferred goods. In this case we could take their intersection as revised knowledge base ([Benferhat *et al.*, 1993]); however, the intersection is not maximally consistent and this means that all the conflicting pieces of knowledge with the same credibility will be rejected.

Another question is: S4 should consider only the *qualitative* ordering of the sentences in $KB \cup \{p\}$ (relative classification without the numerical weights) or could it take advantage of the *explicit* ordering (numerical weights). The first approach seems closer to the human cognitive behavior (which normally refrains from numerical calculus). The second one seems more informative (it takes into account not only relative positions but also the gaps between the items). In our model we do not use the "best-out" ordering for its "drowning effect" [Benferhat *et al.*, 1993]. The lexicographic one could be justified in some particular application domains (e.g. diagnosys). The inclusion-based method seems the most reasonable since it eliminates always the least credible one among conflicting pieces of knowledge.

As an example of a numerical way to perform S4, ordering the goods according to their average credibility seems reasonable and easy to calculate. With this method the preferred good may not contain the most credible sentence.

In the belief function framework, a "good" g is an element of Ω, precisely the one in which all the sentences in g are considered "true" and all the sentences out of g are considered "false". This implies that the belief-function formalism is able to attach directly a degree of credibility to g, bypassing S4 in our framework. Unfortunately, when a good contains only part of the information supplied by a source, the belief-function formalism puts at zero its degree of credibility. This is unreasonable and, unluckily, the event is all but infrequent, so that often the credibility of all the goods is null.

A final step in our revision mechanism is the selection of the derived sentences which are still derivable from B' since the assumptions on which they rely are all contained in B'. Theoretically, it simply consists in applying classical entailment on the preferred good to deduce plausible conclusion from it. We adopted an ATMS and we stored each sentence derived by the Theorem Prover with an *origin set* [Martins and Shapiro, 1988], i.e., a set of basic assumptions which are all *necessary* to derive it. Practically, this step (not represented in figure 1) consists in selecting from the derived sentences, all those whose origin set is subset of the preferred good. We could relax the definition of origin set to that of a set of basic assumptions used to derive the sentence. This is easier to compute and does not have harmful consequences; the worst it can happen is that, being this relaxed origin set a superset of the real one, it is not certain that it will be a subset of the preferred good as the real one is, and so some derived logical consequences of the preferred good may be not recognized (at first).

Besides recoverability, this computational model for belief revision overcomes various limitations of other classic approaches, in particular:

- the revision can be iterated
- inconsistent incoming information does not yield inconsistent revised knowledge spaces
- the numerical revision is performed on a broader base (the overall KB)
- the revision is more flexible;
- the complete numerical ordering renders the revision as least drastic as possible
- the splitting between the symbolic treatment of the inconsistencies and the numerical revision of the credibility weights, provides a clear understanding of what is going on and lucid explanations for the choices.

We are currently applying this conception of belief revision in a distributed monitoring system [Dragoni and Giorgini, 1998] and in the police inquiry domain [Dragoni *et al.*, 1996].

University of Ancona, Italy.

REFERENCES

[Alchourrón *et al.*, 1985] C. E. Alchourrón, P. Gärdenfors and D. Makinson. On the logic of theory change: Partial meet contraction and revision functions. *The Journal of Symbolic Logic*, **50**, 510–530, 1985.

[Benferhat *et al.*, 1993] S. Benferhat, C. Cayrol, D. Dubois D., J. Lang and H. Prade. Inconsistency management and prioritized syntax-based entailment. In *Proceedings of the 13th International Joint Conference on Artificial Intelligence*, pp. 640–645, 1993.

[Dalal, 1988] M. Dalal. Investigations into a theory of knowledge base revision. In *Proceedings of the 7th National Conference on Artificial Intelligence*, pp. 475–479, 1988.

[Doyle, 1979] J. Doyle. A truth maintenance system. *Artificial Intelligence*, **12**, 231–272, 1979.

[Dragoni, 1992] A. F. Dragoni. A model for belief revision in a multi-agent environment. In *Decentralized A.I. 3*, E. Werner and Y. Demazeau, eds. North Holland Elsevier Science, 1992.

[Dragoni, 1997] A. F. Dragoni. Belief revision: from theory to practice. *The Knowledge Engineering Review*, **12**, 1997.

[Dragoni *et al.*, 1996] A. F. Dragoni, C. Ceresi and V. Pasquali. A system to support complex detective inquiries. In *Proceedings of the V Iberoamerican Conference on Computer Science and Law*, La Habana, 1996.

[Dragoni and Giorgini, 1997a] A. F. Dragoni and P. Giorgini. Belief revision through the belief function formalism in a multi-agent environment. In *Intelligent Agents III*, M. Wooldridge, N. R. Jennings and J. Muller, eds. Volume 1193 LNCS. Springer-Verlag, 1997.

[Dragoni and Giorgini, 1997b] A. F. Dragoni and P. Giorgini. Distributed knowledge revision-integration. In *Proceedings of the Sixth ACM International Conference on Information Technlogy and Management*. ACM Press, 1997.

[Dragoni and Giorgini, 1998] A. F. Dragoni and P. Giorgini. Sensor data validation for nuclear power plants through bayesian conditioning and dempster's rule of combination. *Computers and Artificial Intelligence*, **17**, 151–168, 1998.

[Dragoni and Di Manzo, 1995] A. F. Dragoni and M. Di Manzo. Supporting complex inquiries. *International Journal of Intelligent Systems*, **10**, 959–986, 1995.

[Dragoni *et al.*, 1995] A. F. Dragoni, F. Mascaretti and P. Puliti. A generalized approach to consistency-based belief revision. In *Proceedings of the Conference of the Italian Association for Artificial Intelligence*, M. Gori and G. Soda, eds. Volume 992, LNAI. Springer Verlag, 1995.

[Dubois and Prade, 1992] D. Dubois and H. Prade. Belief change and possibility theory. In *Belief Revision*, P. Gärdenfors, ed. Cambridge University Press.

[Gärdenfors, 1988] P. Gärdenfors. *Knowledge in Flux: Modeling the Dynamics of Epistemic States*. MIT Press, Cambridge, MA, 1988.

[Gärdenfors, 1992] P. Gärdenfors. *Belief Revision: An Introduction*. Cambridge University Press., 1992.

[Kennes, 1992] R. Kennes. Computational aspects of the möbius transform of a graph. *IEEE Transactions in Systems, Man and Cybernetics*, **22**,201–223, 1992.

[De Kleer, 1986] J. De Kleer. An assumption based truth maintenance system. *Artificial Intelligence*, **28**, 127–162, 1986.

[Martins and Shapiro, 1988] J. P. Martins and S. C. Shapiro. A model for belief revision. *Artificial Intelligence*, **35**,25–97, 1988.

[Moral and Wilson, 1996] S. Moral and N. Wilson. Importance sampling monte-carlo algorithms for calculation of Dempster–Shafer belief. In *Proceedings of IPMU'96*, Granada, 1996.

[Nebel, 1994] B. Nebel. Base revision operations and schemes: Semantics, representation, and complexity. In *Proceedings of the 11th European Conference on Artificial Intelligence*, A. G. Cohn, editor, John Wiley & Sons, 1994.

[Parsons, 1994] S. Parsons. Some qualitative approaches to applying the dempster-shafer theory. *Information and Decision Technologies*, **19**, 321–337, 1994.

[Pearl, 1988] J. Pearl. *Probabilistic Reasoning for Intelligent Systems*. Morgan Kaufmann, 1988.

[Reiter, 1987] R. Reiter. A theory of diagnosis from first principles. *Artificial Intelligence*, **53**, 1987.

[Shafer, 1990] G. Shafer. Belief functions. In *Readings in Uncertain Reasoning*. G. Shafer and J. Pearl, eds. Morgan Kaufmann, 1990.

[Shafer and Srivastava, 1990] G. Shafer and R. Srivastava. The Bayesian and belief-function formalisms a general perspective for auditing. In *Readings in Uncertain Reasoning*. G. Shafer and J. Pearl, eds. Morgan Kaufmann, 1990.

[Williams, 1995] M. A. Williams. Iterated theory base change: A computational model. In *Proceedings of the 14th International Joint Conference on Artificial Intelligence*, pp. 1541–1547, 1995.

[Wilson, 1991] N. Wilson. A monte-carlo algorithm for dempster-shafer belief. In *Proceedings of the Seventh Conference*, P. Smets, B. D. D'Ambrosio and P. Bonissone, eds. pp. 414–417, 1991.

INDEX

APPLIED LOGIC SERIES

1. D. Walton: *Fallacies Arising from Ambiguity.* 1996 ISBN 0-7923-4100-7
2. H. Wansing (ed.): *Proof Theory of Modal Logic.* 1996 ISBN 0-7923-4120-1
3. F. Baader and K.U. Schulz (eds.): *Frontiers of Combining Systems.* First International Workshop, Munich, March 1996. 1996 ISBN 0-7923-4271-2
4. M. Marx and Y. Venema: *Multi-Dimensional Modal Logic.* 1996 ISBN 0-7923-4345-X
5. S. Akama (ed.): *Logic, Language and Computation.* 1997 ISBN 0-7923-4376-X
6. J. Goubault-Larrecq and I. Mackie: *Proof Theory and Automated Deduction.* 1997 ISBN 0-7923-4593-2
7. M. de Rijke (ed.): *Advances in Intensional Logic.* 1997 ISBN 0-7923-4711-0
8. W. Bibel and P.H. Schmitt (eds.): *Automated Deduction - A Basis for Applications.* Volume I. Foundations - Calculi and Methods. 1998 ISBN 0-7923-5129-0
9. W. Bibel and P.H. Schmitt (eds.): *Automated Deduction - A Basis for Applications.* Volume II. Systems and Implementation Techniques. 1998 ISBN 0-7923-5130-4
10. W. Bibel and P.H. Schmitt (eds.): *Automated Deduction - A Basis for Applications.* Volume III. Applications. 1998 ISBN 0-7923-5131-2
    (Set vols. I-III: ISBN 0-7923-5132-0)
11. S.O. Hansson: *A Textbook of Belief Dynamics.* Theory Change and Database Updating. 1999 Hb: ISBN 0-7923-5324-2; Pb: ISBN 0-7923-5327-7
    Solutions to exercises. 1999. Pb: ISBN 0-7923-5328-5
    Set: (Hb): ISBN 0-7923-5326-9
    Set: (Pb): ISBN 0-7923-5329-3
12. R. Pareschi and B. Fronhöfer (eds.): *Dynamic Worlds from the Frame Problem to Knowledge Management.* 1999 ISBN 0-7923-5535-0
13. D.M. Gabbay and H. Wansing (eds.): *What is Negation?* 1999 ISBN 0-7923-5569-5
14. M. Wooldridge and A. Rao (eds.): *Foundations of Rational Agency.* 1999 ISBN 0-7923-5601-2
15. D. Dubois, H. Prade and E.P. Klement (eds.): *Fuzzy Sets, Logics and Reasoning about Knowledge.* 1999 ISBN 0-7923-5911-1
16. H. Barringer, M. Fisher, D. Gabbay and G. Gough (eds.): *Advances in Temporal Logic.* 2000 ISBN 0-7923-6149-0
17. D. Basin, M.D. Agostino, D.M. Gabbay, S. Matthews and L. Viganò (eds.): *Labelled Deduction.* 2000 ISBN 0-7923-6237-3
18. P.A. Flach and A.C. Kakas (eds.): *Abduction and Induction.* Essays on their Relation and Integration. 2000 ISBN 0-7923-6250-0

19. S. Hölldobler (ed.): *Intellectics and Computational Logic.* Papers in Honor of Wolfgang Bibel. 2000 ISBN 0-7923-6261-6
20. P. Bonzon, M. Cavalcanti and Rolf Nossum (eds.): *Formal Aspects of Context.* 2000 ISBN 0-7923-6350-7
21. D.M. Gabbay and N. Olivetti: *Goal-Directed Proof Theory.* 2000 ISBN 0-7923-6473-2
22. M.-A. Williams and H. Rott (eds.): *Frontiers in Belief Revision.* 2001 ISBN 0-7923-7021-X

KLUWER ACADEMIC PUBLISHERS – DORDRECHT / BOSTON / LONDON